World Record Breakers in Track & Field Athletics

Gerald Lawson, MD

Human Kinetics

Library of Congress Cataloging-in-Publication Data

Lawson, Gerald, 1948-
    World record breakers in track & field athletics / Gerald Lawson.
      p.   cm.
    Includes index.
    ISBN 0-88011-679-X (pbk.)
    1. Track-athletics--Records.   2. Track and field athletes.
  I. Title.
  GV1060.67.L39   1997
  796.42'06--dc21
                                      96-54043
                                        CIP

ISBN: 0-88011-679-X

Developmental Editor: Kristine Enderle; **Assistant Editor:** Coree Schutter; **Editorial Assistant:** Laura Ward Majersky; **Copyeditor:** Karen Bojda; **Proofreader:** Jim Burns; **Graphic Designer:** Judy Henderson; **Graphic Artist:** Judy Henderson, Denise Lowry; **Cover Designer:** Jack Davis; **Photographer (cover):** Dave Black; **Printer:** Braun-Brumfield

Printed in the United States of America   10   9   8   7   6   5   4   3   2   1

Human Kinetics
Web site: http://www.humankinetics.com/

United States: Human Kinetics, P.O. Box 5076, Champaign, IL 61825-5076
1-800-747-4457
e-mail: humank@hkusa.com

Canada: Human Kinetics, Box 24040, Windsor, ON N8Y 4Y9
1-800-465-7301 (in Canada only)
e-mail: humank@hkcanada.com

Europe: Human Kinetics, P.O. Box IW14, Leeds LS16 6TR, United Kingdom
(44) 1132 781708
e-mail: humank@hkeurope.com

Australia: Human Kinetics, 57 Price Avenue, Lower Mitcham, South Australia 5062
(08) 277 1555
e-mail: humank@hkaustralia.com

New Zealand: Human Kinetics, P.O. Box 105-231, Auckland 1
(09) 523 3462
e-mail: humank@hknewz.com

DEDICATION

This book is dedicated to my wife, Lynne Maree,
and to my daughters, Claudia Kelly and Edwina Frances.

Contents

Preface

For those interested in athletic records, sports personalities, or sports history, *World Record Breakers in Track & Field Athletics* is a complete and comprehensive guide. The accomplishments of the early stars of track and field put the achievements of modern athletes into context and offer a perspective that will enrich the understanding of track and field fans as they observe the long tradition of record breaking. The glimpses into the lives and times of past record holders can help modern fans and athletes appreciate the way culture, politics, and personalities have shaped the sport over time.

The book concentrates on the athletic events at the Olympic Games. Accordingly, the old "English" distances such as 100 yards, 220 yards, etc. are not included. The one exception is the one-mile run, which still generates great public interest. Indoor records also are not included, nor are annual "rankings." In addition, the walks, which deserve a knowledgeable enthusiast to do them justice, are not found in this book, except as listed records in chapter 40.

Although all current records must seem close to their limit, advances in training, equipment, diet, and track surfaces should allow even further improvement. Nonetheless, champions still occasionally emerge from nowhere, without the benefit of all these modern aids, and break records. In addition, if one athlete can turn in a record performance, there seems no reason why one day another athlete will not come along to challenge it.

World Record Breakers in Track & Field Athletics is divided into two sections for men's and women's track and field athletics. A chapter is dedicated to each event. Within each chapter is a brief history and description of the event, followed by a table of all the athletes who have held a world record in that event, including their record and where and when the record was achieved. A short biography of the record holders offers other notable highlights of their athletic careers as well as putting their achievements in historical perspective. Each chapter concludes with a list of the current top five athletes, who may not necessarily have broken records in that event, my personal prediction of the world record in the year 2015, and choice of the top three outstanding athletes to date for that event.

Predictions in this area are hazardous indeed. They are notoriously unreliable, and I would be pleased if my suggestions turn out to be conservative. The choice of the top three athletes is complicated by the fact that major figures in athletics may not have set a world record in their event, for example Carl Lewis (long jump) and Harrison Dillard (110m hurdles). Readers should feel quite free to disagree, as I am sure they will. My own choice was dictated by the longevity of a record, an athlete's achievement of multiple records, a significant improvement on the existing world record, an athlete's career longevity, other major honors obtained, a strong competitive record, and the breaking of a significant barrier.

Each of these biographies provide a glimpse of their character as well as the athletic ability of these talented men and women. *World Record Breakers in Track & Field Athletics* is a tribute to those world record holders. Indeed, some world record holders lived and died with very little recognition. I hope this book corrects that inequity.

Gerald Lawson

Acknowledgments

This book was possible only through the goodwill of a vast number of people. I would first like to thank a number of recognized athletic experts who lent to me their time and expertise: *United States:* Ed Fox and Jon Hendershott of *Track and Field News,* Hal Bateman of USA Track & Field, Don Potts, Frank Zarnowski, Bill Mallon, David Martin; *Great Britain:* Peter Matthews, Richard Hymans, Ian Buchanon, Peter Lovesey; *Australia:* David Tarbotton, Malcolm Harrison, Paul Jenes; *Holland:* Ruud Paauw; *South Africa:* Gert Le Roux; *Japan:* Yoshimasa Naguchi.

Those who contributed in a variety of ways to this project include Martha Parsons, Maryanne Knox, Dr. Helmut Brunner, Dr. Alan Hewson, NIB Health Funds, Evelyn Kepreotis, Eeva-Liisa Langille, Danial McCormack, Jan Benton, Mrs. Inge Burke, Dr. Stephen Don, Lic. Ricardo Contreras Hernandez, and Barry Nancarrow. There are many others, too numerous to list, to whom I would like to express my gratitude.

Early in this project, I was very fortunate to have the assistance of England's leading sports photographer, George Herringshaw, of Associated Sports Photography, Leicester. Horst Muller of Düsseldorf, Germany, was also most helpful.

I am also deeply indebted to the late Mstislav Botashev of Moscow. From 1948 until his death in 1992, he was the longest serving sports photographer in the Soviet Union, covering Olympic Games, World Championships, and a host of sporting events both in and outside the Soviet Union. He supplied almost all the photos of athletes from the former Soviet Union and Eastern Europe. His collection and his work have not been lost with his death but are being carried on by his son Nikolai, now resident in Sydney, Australia. It is one of my regrets that, although I corresponded often with the elder Mr. Botashev, I never met him.

A large number of museums and libraries around the world graciously provided me with photographic material. I must mention the generosity of dozens of U.S. colleges and universities who supplied me with materials and photographs of champion athletes who had attended these institutions as students. In addition, there were three U.S. bodies who were particularly helpful: the United States National Archives in Maryland (through its Assistant Chief for Reference Mr. Fred Pernell), the United States Library of Congress in Washington, DC, and the Amateur Athletic Association of Los Angeles.

Further illustrations were sent to me by a number of individuals. It is not possible to list them all, but I must particularly thank Basilio Fuentes (Cuba), Ottavio Castellini (Italy), Ove Karlsson (Sweden), and Robert Maximov (Soviet Union). In addition, a great number of athletes kindly made available to me photographs from their own private collections. Bruce Turnbull and his staff at the Medical Communications Units, Royal Newcastle Hospital, Newcastle, helped to collate and prepare these photos.

Although it is perhaps perfunctory for an author to thank his or her publisher, I owe an immense debt to Ted Miller, director of trade books at Human Kinetics and to developmental editor, Kristine Enderle. They nursed the manuscript through many stages with their professional expertise, all from 10,000 miles distance.

Photo Credits

Page numbers are listed in parentheses.

Photos courtesy of U.S. National Archives Percy Williams 306-NT-38637 (14), Eulace Peacock 306-NT-105680 (15), William Carr 306-NT-172666C (49), Cornelius Johnson 208-PU-103L-15 (177), Charles Dumas 306-PS-56-14360 (180), John Thomas 306-PSA-60-7107 (181), Charles Hoff 306-NT-16701 (194), Jesse Owens 306-NT-111998 (216), John Lyman 306-NT-95248 (235), Jim Fuchs 306-PS-51-186 (237), Clarence Houser 306-NT-6521B (249).

Photos courtesy of U.S. Library of Congress Glenn Cunningham and Jack Lovelock LC-USZ62-468475 (73), F. Morgan Taylor LC-USZ62-094110 (157), James Duncan LC-USZ62-110638 (247), Fanny Blankers-Koen LC-USZ62-084232 (447).

Reproduced with the permission of the Keeper of Public Records
200m medalists (Thane Baker, Bobby Morrow, Andy Stanfield) PROV VPRS 10742 B926 (38), Manfred Germar PROV VPRS 10742 A121 (39), Ron Clarke PROV VPRS 10742 A78 (105), Vladimir Kuts PROV VPRS 10742 A245 (116), 110m-hurdle medalists (Lee Calhoun, Martin Lauer, Jack Davis) PROV VPRS 10742 B1036 (146), Glenn Davis PROV VPRS 10742 A392 (159), Adhemar da Silva PROV VPRS 10742 A400 (224), Parry O'Brien PROV VPRS 10742 A616 (238), Harold Connolly PROV VPRS 10742 B889 (267), Egil Danielsen PROV VPRS 10742 B1067 (280), Women's 80m hurdles (Norma Thrower, Shirley Strickland, Gisela Birkemeyer) PROV VPRS 10742 B994 (374), Mildred McDaniel PROV VPRS 10742 C1647 (395).

Photo courtesy of the National Archives of Sweden, the Åhlén and Åkerlund Collection
Lennart Strand (75)

Photos by Kurt Eriksson, courtesy of the Swedish Sports Confederation
Arne Andersson and Gundar Hägg (89), Sten Pettersson (140), Erik Lemming (275)

Photos by Horst Müller
Heinz Fütterer (19), Zhu Jian Hua (187), Alessandro Andrei (244), Rickard Bruch (257), Wolfgang Schmidt (260), Karl Hans Riehm (270), Carlo Lievore (281), Kurt Bendlin (297), Bill Toomey (298), Jürgen Hingsen (301), Paola Pigni (343), Ulrike Meyfarth (397), Hildrun Claus (405), Margitta Gummel (420).

Photos by George Herringshaw, courtesy of Associated Sports Photography
Jackson Scholz (11), Calvin Smith (33), Carl Lewis (34), Leroy Burrell (34), Donovan Bailey (35), Peter Radford (40), Pietro Mennea (43), Michael Johnson (44), Harry Reynolds (57), Roger Moens (63), David Wottle (66), Sidney Maree (82), Britain's trio of golden milers (Sebastian Coe, Steve Cram, Steve Ovett) (95), Noureddine Morceli (97), Gordon Pirie (105), Henry Rono (108), David Moorcroft (109), Said Aouita (109), Haile Gebrselassie (110), Lasse Viren (118), John Hayes (125), Sohn Kee Chung (128), Robert de Castella (134), Steve Jones (135), Carlos Lopes (136), Willie Davenport (148), Rod Milburn (149), Roger Kingdom (152), Colin Jackson (153), David Hemery (161), John Akii-Bua (162), Edwin Moses (163), Gaston Roelants (169), Anders Gärderud (171), Moses Kiptanui (173), Dwight Stones (184), Dietmar Mogenburg (186), Patrik Sjöberg (189), Javier Sotomayor (190), Frank Foss (194), Bob Seagren (203), Pierre Quinon (209), Jonathan Edwards (230), Randy Barnes (244), Ludvik Danek (256), John Powell (258), Mac Wilkins (259), Sergey Litvinov (272), Tom Petranoff (285), Jan Zelezny (287), Steve Backley (288), Dan O'Brien (301), Annegret Richter (313), Florence Griffith Joyner (315), Nadezhda Olizarenko (340), Jarmila Kratochvilova (340), Tatyana Kazankina and Mary Decker (345), Qu Junxia (346), Wang Junxia (350), Olga Bondarenko (355), Grete Waitz (366), Joan Benoit (367),

Ingrid Kristiansen (367), Sally Gunnell (387), Kim Batten (387), Jean Shiley and Mildred Didriksen (390), Rosemarie Ackermann (398), Sara Simeoni (399), Tamara Bykova (399), Stefka Kostadinova (400), Valeria Ionescu (410), Galina Chistyakova (412), Natalya Lisovskaya (422), Fatima Whitbread (443).

Photos by George Herringshaw, courtesy of Provincial Sports Photography
Wladyslaw Kozakiewicz (207), Daley Thompson (300), Marlies Gohr (314).

Photos by E.D. Lacey, courtesy of Associated Sports Photography
James Hines (26), Enrique Figuerola (26), Eddie Hart (29), Steve Williams (30), Henry Carr (42), Filbert Bayi (80), Michel Jazy (93), Kip Keino (106), David Bedford (119), Leonard Edelen (132), Basil Heatley (133), Ben Jipcho (171), Bob Beamon (218), Josef Schmidt (226), Allan Feuerbach (240), Klaus Wolfermann (283), Bruce Jenner (299), Nicole Duclos and Colette Besson (327), Vera Nikolic (338), Hildegard Falck (338), Lyudmila Bragina (344), Karin Balzer (377), Annelie Ehrhardt (380), Mary Rand (406), Liesel Westermann (427), Mary Peters (451).

Photos by Stuart D. Franklin, courtesy of Associated Sports Photography Yobes Ondieki (122), Renaldo Nehemiah (151), Kevin Young (163), Sergey Bubka (210); **Photo by Andy Maw, courtesy of Associated Sports Photography** Arturo Barrios (121).

Photos by Mstislav Botashev, courtesy of Nikolai Botashev
Don Quarrie (32), Livio Berruti (41), Otis Davis (53), Sándor Iharos (77), Pyotr Bolotnikov (117), Sergey Popov (130), Abebe Bikila (131), Semyon Rzhishchin (167), Yuriy Stepanov (181), Valeriy Brumel (182), Volodomir Yashchenko (184), Gerd Wessig (187), Wolfgang Nordwig (205), Thierry Vigneron (208), Ralph Boston (217), Pedro Perez (228), João de Oliveira (229), Dallas Long (239), Aleksandr Baryshnikov (241), Udo Beyer (242), Ulf Timmermann (243), Jay Silvester (255), Al Oerter (255), Gyula Zsivótzky (267), Anatoliy Bondarchuk (268), Juri Tamm (272), Janusz Sidlo (280), Janis Lusis (282), Uwe Hohn (286), Rafer Johnson and Vasiliy Kuznetsov (295), Renate Stecher (312), Marita Koch (321), Polina Lazareva (325), Sin Kim Dan (326), Nina Otkalenko and Shirley Strickland (334), Lyudmila Shevtsova (335), Yordanka Donkova (381), Tatyana Zelentsova (384), Margarita Ponomaryeva (385), Sabine Busch (386), Iolanda Balas (394), Chen Feng-Jung (396), Elzbieta Krzensinska (405), Heide Rosendahl (407), Angela Voigt (408), Anisoara Cusmir (409), Tatyana Sevryukova (417), Galina Zybina (418), Nadezhda Chizhova (419), Helena Fibingerova (421), Nina Dumbadze (425), Nina Ponomaryeva (426), Tamara Press (427), Faina Melnik (428), Evelin Jahl (430), Gabriele Reinsch (431), Natalya Smirnitskaya (435), Dana Zátopková (436), Elvira Ozolina (437), Yelena Gorchakova (438), Ewa Gryziecka (438), Ruth Fuchs (439), Kate Schmidt and Svetlana Koroleva (440), Sofia Sakorafa (442), Petra Felke (442), Aleksandra Chudina (448), Nina Martynenko and Galina Bystrova (448), Irina Press (450), Ramona Neubert (454), Jackie Joyner-Kersee (455).

Photos by: Ron Linstead Marilyn Neufville (328); **Franz Leo Mai** Liane Winter, Chantal Langlace, Christa Vahlensieck, Manuela Preuss-Augenvoorth, Jackie Hansen, Dr. Joan Ullyot (364); **Herbert Sundhofer, Foto Sundhofer** Liese Prokop (450); **Don Chadez** Jim Ryun (80), Irena Szewinska (329); **Andy Bernstein, Andy Bernstein and Associates** Mike Powell (219).

Photographs from: The Olympic collection of Dr. Stephen Don, Sydney, Australia Ralph Metcalfe and Eddie Tolan (13), caricature of Luigi Beccali (72), Johannes Kolehmainen (100), George Saling (143), Chuhei Nambu (215), Emil Hirschfeld and John Kuck (234), Stanislawa Walasiewicz (306), Lina Radke-Batschauer (333); **The Australian Archives** Herb Elliott (79).

Photos courtesy of: Australian Department of Foreign Affairs and Trade John Landy (91), Derek Clayton (134), Betty Cuthbert (318); **National Library of Australia** Anthony Winter (222); **Marks collection, State Library of New South Wales** Harold Osborn (176), Marc Wright (193), Ralph Rose (233); **The Herald and Weekly Times, Melbourne, Australia** Herb McKenley (51); **The West Australian** Dixie Willis (336); **Japan Track and Field Magazine** Bob Hayes (25), Mike Larrabee (55), Peter Snell (64), Yasuo Ikenaka (128), Naoto Tajima (224), Ann Packer (336); **Track and Field News/Jeff Kroot** Tommie Smith (55); **Track and Field News** Roger

Bannister (90), Emil Zatopek (102), Cornelius Warmerdam (198), Don Bragg (199), John Uelses (200), Dave Tork (200), Earl Bell (207), Jack Torrance (236), Terry Albritton (241), Richard Babka (254), Al Cantello (281); **Dagbreek and the South African Amateur Athletic Union** Paul Nash (27); **Die Burger and the South African Amateur Athletic Union** John van Reenen (257); **GJJ Le Roux, Former Secretary of the South African Amateur Athletic Union** George Weightman-Smith (141); **Amateur Athletic Foundation of Los Angeles** Maxey Long (47), Forrest Smithson (139), Bill Graber (197), Daniel Ahearn (222), Bob Mathias (294), Chi Cheng (379); **Archives nationales du Québec** Guy Drut (150), Miklós Németh (284), Sigrun Siegl (408), **FIDAL** Adolfo Consolini (252), Ondina Valla (371).

Photos courtesy of: Auburn University Harvey Glance (31), Percy Beard (142); **Dartmouth College Library** Earl Thomson (140); **Georgia Tech Alumni Association** Edward Hamm (214); **Grambling State Sports Information** Stone Johnson (40); **Indiana State University Audio/ Visual Department** Cheryl Bridges (362); **Indiana University** Archie Harris (251); **Louisiana State University Office of Sports Information** Glenn Hardin (158); **Manhattan College/Albert Guida** Louis Jones (52); **Morgan State University** George Rhoden (52); **National Track and Field Hall of Fame, Irwin Library, Butler University** Fred Wolcott (145); **Northeast Louisiana University** John Pennel (202); **Occidental College** Bob Gutowski (198); **Ohio State University** Jack Keller (143); **Penn State University** Barney Ewell (18); **Rice University/Lou Witt** Fred Hansen (203); **San Jose State University** Ray Norton (22), Christos Papanikolaou (205); **Texas A&M Athletic Department** Randy Matson (240); **University of California** Harold Davis (17), Archie Williams (50); **University of California at Los Angeles (UCLA)** Yang Chuan-Kwang (296), Willie Banks (229); **University of Georgia Athletic Association** Forrest Towns (145); **University of Kansas** Wes Santee (76); **University of Minnesota** Fortune Gordien (253); **University of Nebraska Sports Information Department** Charles Greene (28); **University of Notre Dame Sports Information Department** Thomas Lieb (248); **University of Oregon Archives** Lester Steers (179); **University of Southern California** Charles Paddock (12); **University of Southwest Louisiana** John Morriss (144); **University of Washington** Brian Sternberg (201); **University of Wisconsin** Patrick Matzdorf (183).

Photos courtesy of: Professor Hajo Bernett Rudolf Harbig (63); **Fionnbarr Callanan** Jacek Wszola (185); **Syd Kronenthal** Michiko Gorman (363); **Armando Libotte** Christiaan Berger (15), Sera Martin and Otto Peltzer (60), Ville Ritola and Paavo Nurmi (113), Sabin Carr (195), Jonni Myyrä (276), Lisa Gelius (372), Claudia Testoni (372), Kinue Hitomi (403), Gisela Mauermayer (446); **Peter Lovesey** Peter O'Connor (213), Harald Andersson (250); **Robert Maximov** Yuriy Sedykh (271), Nikolay Avilov (298); **McDonald Bailey** E. McDonald Bailey (19); **Mexican National Olympic Committee** Ralph Doubell (65), Viktor Saneyev, Nelson Prudencio, Giuseppe Gentile (226); **Professor Peter Nagy** Argentina Menis (429); **Robert Pariente** Jules Ladoumègue (87); **Pentti and Tuula Pekkala** Paavo Yrjölä (292); **Don Potts** Ira Murchison (21); **Jesus Rocamora, through Basilio Fuentes** Alberto Juantorena (67), Alejandro Casanas **(by S. Amaya)** (150), Evelyn Ashford (314), Heike Drechsler **(by Lozaro Rodes)** (321); **Ed Temple** Wilma Rudolph (309), Wyomia Tyus (309); **David Terry** Sydney Wooderson (89), Matti Järvinen (278); **Dr. Frank Zarnowski** Glenn Morris (294).

Unless otherwise noted, all remaining photos were supplied by the athletes, their families, or from the personal collections of the author and his colleagues. Every reasonable attempt was made to locate and contact the owners of all photos.

Abbreviations

Times in this book are expressed as follows: 2 hr 23:11.15 notes a performance in 2 hours, 23 minutes and 11.15 seconds. In the list of current top five athletes at the end of each chapter tailwinds have been marked with a + and headwinds have been marked with a –. Both have been measured in meters per second.

Miscellaneous Abbreviations

m	meters	HJ	High jump	S/C	Steeplechase
m/s	meters per second	J	Javelin	SP	Shot put
A	Altitude	LJ	Long jump	TJ	Triple jump
H	Hurdles	PV	Pole vault		

National Abbreviations

ALG	Algeria	GDR	East Germany	POR	Portugal
AUST	Australia	GER	Germany	ROM	Romania
AUT	Austria	GRE	Greece	RUS	Russia
BEL	Belgium	HAI	Haiti	S.AF	South Africa
BLR	Belarus	HOL	Netherlands	SEN	Senegal
BRA	Brazil	HUN	Hungary	S.KOR	South Korea
BUL	Bulgaria	ITA	Italy	SPA	Spain
CAN	Canada	IRE	Ireland	SWE	Sweden
CHN	China	JAM	Jamaica	SWI	Switzerland
CZH	Czechoslovakia	JPN	Japan	SYR	Syria
	or Czech Republic	KEN	Kenya	TAI	Taiwan
DEN	Denmark	MEX	Mexico	TAN	Tanzania
DJI	Djibouti	MOR	Morocco	UGA	Uganda
EST	Estonia	NAM	Namibia	UKR	Ukraine
ETH	Ethiopia	N.KOR	North Korea	USA	United States
FIN	Finland	NOR	Norway	USSR	Soviet Union
FRA	France	NZ	New Zealand	VEN	Venezuela
FRG	West Germany	PAN	Panama	YUG	Yugoslavia
GBR	Great Britain	POL	Poland	ZAM	Zambia

Organizations

AAA	Amateur Athletic Association (Britain)
AAU	Amateur Athletic Union (United States)
IAAF	International Amateur Athletic Federation
ICAAAA	Inter Collegiate Amateur Athletic Association of America
ITA	International Track Association
NAIA	National Association of Intercollegiate Athletics (United States)
NCAA	National Collegiate Athletic Association (United States)
RSFSR	Russian Soviet Federative Socialist Republic
USTFF	United States Track & Field Federation
WAAA	Women's Amateur Athletic Association (Britain)

Introduction: A Short History of Track and Field Athletics

The history of track and field has had three distinct phases. In the beginning it was closely linked to ancient Greece, and in particular to the ancient Olympic Games. These were held at Olympia in Greece every four years, at least from 776 B.C. until abolished in A.D. 393 by the Roman Emperor Theodosius I. During the duration of the Games all military activity ceased. The victors were celebrated in music and poem and became national heroes. Theodosius, a Christian, apparently objected to pagan rituals associated with the Games.

After 1100 years of continuous celebration, the Imperial decree banning the Olympic Games led to a "dark age," a span of some 1500 years before organized athletics began to slowly reemerge. There were reports of very early Celtic Games in Ireland and Scotland. Perhaps there were local competitions among military units from time to time over this vast span of time. Nonetheless, there were effectively no athletic competitions on a regional, national, or international basis during this 15-century gap.

Rebirth of Modern Athletics

Finally, after a millennium and a half, isolated athletic activities in Great Britain heralded a slow rebirth of the sport. There were rural games in Scotland and England from the early 1800s. Professional running matches developed, on racecourses or turnpike roads, usually involving betting.

The next major development in the rebirth of modern athletics was the adoption in the mid-1800s of the concept of *amateur athletics* by the British public schools and universities, which meant competing without any financial reward. The middle and upper classes in England made a very clear distinction between this approach to athletics (the "gentleman amateur") and the approach of those connected to the professional athletic world. The latter drew its athletes from the lower classes, who usually needed the money and had no qualms about accepting it.

The officials of amateur athletics gradually established almost total control of the entire athletic world. Their amateur code was enforced ruthlessly, with a passion that bordered on fanaticism. Some of the great champions over the years who were expelled from the amateur ranks for allegedly breaking the rules were Jules Ladoumègue (1929), Paavo Nurmi (1932), Gunder Hägg and Arne Andersson (1946), and Wes Santee (1955).

Revival of the Olympic Games

After an interval of 1500 years, the Olympics were reestablished by the tireless efforts of the French nobleman Baron Pierre de Coubertin. The first of the modern Olympics duly

1

took place in Athens in April 1896. Thirteen countries were represented by the athletes, and of course, no professionals were permitted. These Games were a mixed success in pure sporting terms. Nonetheless, whatever the shortcomings in terms of athletic results, the important point was that the Games had been reestablished and would continue.

The second Games in Paris in 1900 were a very disorganized affair, submerged amid a World Exhibition. The next in St. Louis, Missouri, were not much better, held as part of a world's fair and running from July to November. However, from 1908 onward the Olympics were well run and both an administrative and a sporting success.

The Creation of the International Amateur Athletic Federation

A post-Olympic event in Stockholm after the 1912 Games was possibly just as significant as the Games themselves. After the conclusion of the athletic events, representatives of 17 countries met to establish a worldwide governing body for athletics. The International Amateur Athletic Federation (IAAF) was born. A committee of six was set up to decide a formal world record list. Their brief was to establish which events were to be accorded official world record status and which athletes were to be recognized as official world record holders. This committee also laid down guidelines for conditions and circumstances under which world records would be recognized. This inaugural list contained running records in both the "English" distances, such as 100 yards, and the European distances over meters, for example, 100 meters. However, in 1976 almost all the English distances were abolished for world record purposes. The only exception to this major change was the mile, kept because of its long tradition and popularity.

It is worth noting that the IAAF also recognizes a number of athletic events for world record purposes that are not on the athletic program of the Olympic Games, such as the 1000m. In addition, the IAAF list of world records has slowly expanded in recent years, mainly to permit the women's program of events to match the men's.

Athletics Around the Globe

Athletics developed different structures in different countries. Although Oxford and Cambridge Universities supplied a disproportionately high percentage of England's elite athletes, there was also a strong nationwide club system that allowed promising talent to mature. Across the Atlantic, the United States easily dominated athletics for the first 60 years of the 20th century. However, this domination was almost entirely achieved through its universities and colleges, which had strong, competitive athletic programs. A club system outside the university circuit simply did not exist. This U.S. domination of world athletics started to fade somewhat after the 1960s as a number of European and African countries actively challenged U.S. supremacy. At the same time, the status of track and field has diminished considerably in the United States in recent years and many U.S. universities simply dropped it altogether from their sports programs. Despite the fall-off in interest in track and field in the United States, the United States remains a major powerhouse of world athletics.

Another important aspect of the pre-World War II athletic scene was the absence of the Soviet Union. Tsarist Russia had competed at the early Olympics. That changed after the Russian Revolution in 1917 and the new Soviet Union withdrew from all international athletics for 30 years. Finally, in 1946, a Soviet team arrived at the European Championships in Oslo, Norway, and the Soviets returned to the Olympic Games in 1952. The main impact of Soviet athletes upon their return to international athletics was in the women's throwing events and middle distances.

There still remain many parts of the world where track and field athletics simply does not flourish. In South America soccer (football) is king, and few elite athletes have emerged from that continent, except from Brazil and Cuba. India has had little international success. China, despite its vast population, has only recently made an impact with the astonishing success of its female middle-distance runners in 1993.

From 1960 onward a new force in athletics emerged. Africa had largely been a blank spot in world athletics up to that time. But at the 1960 Rome Olympics, unheralded Ethiopian Abebe Bikila won the marathon. That triumph released a steady flow of athletes, generally distance runners, from North and East Africa. Most prominent among these were the distance runners from Kenya, who above all else dominated the 3000m steeplechase.

Another national success story during this era was that of East Germany, or the German Democratic Republic (GDR). This communist state saw a way to international respectability through sporting success. East Germany made a conscious decision to pour vast resources into sport, reputedly two percent of its entire budget. Whether one philosophically agrees with the channeling of so much of the nation's wealth in this direction, results ultimately came through in both world records and Olympic success. There were 20 years of athletic triumphs through the 1970s and 1980s. All this came to an end with the collapse of the GDR in 1989.

In the 1970s, athletics prospered as television arrived, and television money and sponsorship deals crept in. In such circumstances, money inevitably passed between athlete and promoter, whether above or under the table. In fact, this was nothing new, except the sums of money became substantial. The code of amateurism has long since died, but the formal burial has not yet taken place. The word "amateur" is still the second name of the IAAF, even though that body reigns over a multi-million-dollar industry.

What Is a World Record?

A world athletic record is a performance that equals or improves on an existing record in an event recognized by the IAAF as having world record status. For instance, 5000 meters is recognized, but 3 miles (which is 4828.04 meters) is not.

At the Olympic Games hand-timed results were officially used until 1960, following which results were electronically timed. Analysis of photos taken at the 1952, 1956, and 1960 Olympics meant that electronically-timed results were also available for those years. Where both results are available electronic times have been used in this book.

All the events up to 400m must be timed by fully electronic timing devices with photo finish facilities that allow measurement to 0.01 second. Distances of 800m and above can be read to 0.1 second. For the 100m, 200m, and 110m hurdles, long jump, and triple jump, a wind reading from behind the competitor in excess of 2.0 meters per second invalidates the record.

There appears to be compelling logic in invalidating performances in these short, "explosive" events if they take place more than 2000 meters (6562 feet) above sea level because of the recognized benefit in performing at high altitude, but this is not current IAAF policy. In contrast, the times achieved in the long distance events at high altitude are much worse than those achieved at low altitude.

The race must be in a genuine competition. Pacemaking is technically illegal in the middle- and long-distance events, but this rule is routinely ignored at all levels. Pacemaking is openly planned, and the pacemaker is usually financially rewarded for his or her contribution.

Drug taking is banned, and the IAAF may later decertify a record if the athlete subsequently admits to the use of banned substances. This took place in the celebrated case of

Canadian sprinter Ben Johnson, found to have a positive drug test at the 1988 Olympics. His 1987 100m world record was subsequently removed.

The competition must take place outdoors, to distinguish it from the separate indoor world records. Mixed competition between male and female athletes is not allowed, except in the marathon.

Official IAAF world records as of February 1997 are as follows:

Men's

100m	9.84	Donovan Bailey (USA)	Atlanta	27 Jul 1996
200m	19.32	Michael Johnson (USA)	Atlanta	1 Aug 1996
400m	43.29	Butch Reynolds (USA)	Zurich	17 Aug 1988
800m	1:41.73	Sebastian Coe (GBR)	Florence	10 Jun 1981
1500m	3:27.37	Noureddine Morceli (ALG)	Nice	12 Jul 1995
1 mile	3:44.39	Noureddine Morceli (ALG)	Rieti	5 Sep 1993
5000m	12:44.39	Haile Gebrselassie (ETH)	Zurich	16 Aug 1995
10,000m	26:38:08	Salah Hissou (MOR)	Brussels	23 Aug 1996
Marathon	2 hr 6:50	Belayneh Densimo (ETH)	Rotterdam	17 Apr 1988
110m H	12.91	Colin Jackson (GBR)	Stuttgart	20 Aug 1993
400m H	46.78	Kevin Young (USA)	Barcelona	6 Aug 1992
3000m S/C	7:59.18	Moses Kiptanui (KEN)	Zurich	16 Aug 1995
High jump	2.45m	Javier Sotomayor (CUBA)	Salamanca	27 Jul 1993
Pole vault	6.14m	Sergey Bubka (UKR)	Sestriere	31 Jul 1994
Long jump	8.95m	Mike Powell (USA)	Tokyo	30 Aug 1991
Triple jump	18.29m	Jonathan Edwards (GBR)	Gothenburg	7 Aug 1995
Shot put	23.12m	Randy Barnes (USA)	Los Angeles	20 May 1990
Discus	74.08m	Jurgen Schult (GDR)	Neubrandenburg	6 Jun 1986
Hammer	86.74m	Yuriy Sedykh (USSR)	Stuttgart	30 Aug 1986
Javelin	98.48m	Ján Zelezny (CZH)	Jena	25 May 1996
Decathlon	8891	Dan O'Brien (USA)	Talence	4-5 Sep 1992

Women's

100m	10.49	F. Griffith Joyner (USA)	Indianapolis	16 Jul 1988
200m	21.34	F. Griffith Joyner (USA)	Seoul	29 Sep 1988
400m	47.60	Marita Koch (GDR)	Canberra	6 Oct 1985
800m	1:53.28	Jarmila Kratochvilova (CZH)	Munich	26 Jul 1983
1500m	3:50.46	Qu Junxia (CHN)	Beijing	11 Sep 1993
3000m	8:06.11	Wang Junxia (CHN)	Beijing	13 Sep 1993
5000m	14:36.45	Fernanda Ribeiro (POR)	Hechtel	22 Jul 1995
10,000m	29:31.78	Wang Junxia (CHN)	Beijing	8 Sep 1993
Marathon	2 hr 21:06	Ingrid Kristiansen (NOR)	London	21 Apr 1985
100m H	12.21	Yordanka Donkova (BUL)	Stara Zagora	20 Aug 1988
400m H	52.61	Kim Batten (USA)	Gothenburg	11 Aug 1995
High jump	2.09m	Stefka Kostadinova (BUL)	Rome	30 Aug 1987
Pole vault	4.55m	Emma George (AUST)	Melbourne	20 Feb 1997
Long jump	7.52m	Galina Chistyakova (RUS)	Leningrad	11 Jun 1988

Triple jump	15.50m	Inessa Kravets (UKR)	Gothenburg	10 Aug 1995
Shot put	22.63m	Natalya Lisovskaya (RUS)	Moscow	7 Jun 1987
Discus	76.80m	Gabriele Reinsch (GDR)	Neubrandenburg	9 Jul 1988
Hammer	69.42m	Mihaela Melinte (ROM)	Cluj	12 May 1996
Javelin	80.00m	Petra Felke (GDR)	Potsdam	9 Sep 1988
Heptathlon	7291	Jackie Joyner-Kersee (USA)	Seoul	23-24 Sep 1988

Why Have World Records Improved?

This may seem a simplistic question. Everyone accepts that performances set at the start of the 20th century are far inferior to those established as the century draws to a close. To fully explore this topic would require a book in itself. The following tables highlight the improvement in world records over the years.

Improvement in Records

Event	First record (year)	Current record (year)	% Improvement
Men's			
100m	10.6 (1912)	9.84 (1996)	7.17%
1 mile	4:14.4 (1913)	3:44.39 (1993)	11.80%
Marathon	2 hr 55:18 (1908)	2 hr 6:50 (1988)	27.65%
High jump	2.00m (1912)	2.45m (1993)	22.5%
Shot put	15.54m (1909)	23.12m (1990)	48.78%
Women's			
100m	11.7 (1934)	10.49 (1988)	10.34%
1500m	4:17.3 (1967)	3:50.46 (1993)	10.43%
Marathon	3 hr 27:45 (1964)	2 hr 21:06 (1985)	32.08%
High jump	1.65m (1932)	2.09m (1987)	26.67%
Shot put	14.38m (1934)	22.63m (1987)	57.37%

The comparative improvements in the above tables should be treated with some caution. Some events achieved world record status early in the century, when the event was not challenged as seriously as events introduced more recently. Nonetheless, whether rapidly or slowly, smoothly or erratically, there has been improvement in all events over the years. Common sense indicates that such improvement cannot be endless and should eventually plateau.

Factors contributing to improvements in world records:

- Global competition. The expansion of athletics to countries all around the globe.
- Nutrition and stature. The general increase in stature and nutrition during the 20th century.
- Track surfaces. The improvement in track surfaces with the widespread use of polyurethane tracks, which are weatherproof and have a high degree of compliance.
- Track design. Ovals with very sharp bends require the runner to use more centripetal force to follow the curve, which leads to slower times, than tracks with more gentle curves.
- Landing surfaces. The improvement in landing surfaces for high jumpers and pole vaulters, now composed of foam bags, which remove the fear of sustaining a major injury.

- Coaching. The quality of coaching in the early years of the sport varied greatly and still does to a degree. Obviously, there are a multitude of factors affecting any coaching situation, not the least being the financial resources available. However, coaching advances are now rapidly disseminated worldwide, and there are many structured coaching courses so that the general standard is improving.
- Money. The open introduction of prize money and sponsorship money means that an elite athlete can make a comfortable living from the sport. This in turn means that the longevity of an athlete's career can be much extended.
- Altitude. The benefits of high altitude were clearly demonstrated at the 1968 Mexico City Olympics. The reduced atmospheric pressure meant that athletes in the short, explosive events greatly benefited.
- Clothes and footwear design. Even minimal changes can reduce air resistance.
- Drug use. Many athletes are pathologically competitive to the degree that they would turn to any aid to success, legal or illegal. The most publicized are anabolic steroids, especially since the very public disqualification of Canada's Ben Johnson after winning the 1988 Olympic 100m gold medal. The collapse of Eastern Europe has led to many revelations: It seems almost every athlete was taking steroids except the champions, who furiously protested their innocence. Another technique banned by the IAAF is blood doping. New illicit substances in this area are growth hormone and erythropoietin. The IAAF is taking an increasingly hard line on these various practices, but it may be impossible to detect and eliminate all these abuses. The idea that an athlete is successful due to pharmacology is offensive to most of the athletic world. Just because it is difficult to detect these abuses does not mean that attempts to do so should be abandoned.
- Nonstandard track lengths. One little recognized problem is the assumption that a 400m track is 400 meters long. This assumption was questioned in a 1993 study in the United States of over 35 tracks. These were measured precisely and varied from 398.6 meters to 411.3 meters.

Men's Track and Field Athletics

The men's track and field program includes the following events: track events (sprints, middle distance, long distance); hurdles and steeplechase; jumps (high jump, long jump, pole vault, triple jump); throws (shot put, discus, hammer, javelin); decathlon; and walks.

These events were introduced at the turn of the century and little has changed in the program since. If anything, it is somewhat surprising that there has been so little innovation in this area over the last 100 years. Perhaps some energetic soul will apply some lateral thinking and come up with a new athletic event in the 21st century. If each athletic discipline on the existing program had to justify its existence, perhaps the hammer throw and the walks would have to try the hardest.

The major international events in track and field athletics have expanded over the last 100 years. The commencement date of the key ones are:

1896 Modern Olympic Games

1930 British Empire (later Commonwealth Games)

1934 European Athletic Championships

1951 Asian Games

1951 Pan-American Games

1965 African Games

1983 World Athletic Championships

1985 IAAF Athletics Grand Prix

S printing is perhaps the oldest and simplest of all sports, and the 100m sprint remains one of the glamour events of track and field. It is also the shortest sporting competition in existence. Usually, a sprint is all over in 10 seconds, whereas a Wimbledon tennis final can take five hours. Nonetheless, that 10-second sprint might have been a decade in preparation. The successful elite champions in this event can justifiably call themselves the "fastest men on earth." There is a lifetime of prestige from being the 100m Olympic champion that is probably not matched by success in any other event.

Sprinters have had two major advances in the last 100 years: the adoption of starting blocks in the 1930s and the introduction of all weather synthetic tracks in the 1960s. The timekeeping procedures for this event have also changed over the years, from handheld stopwatches to extremely accurate, electronic, automatic timing devices. However, the new accurate devices have, if anything, shown that the old hand-timed stopwatches usually flattered the athletes with faster times than they deserved. As of 1 January 1977 handheld watches were abandoned when electronic timing devices were introduced that could record times to $1/100$ (0.01) of a second. Technology already exists to time races to $1/1000$ (0.001) of a second, and this may be the next development in recording 100m sprinting.

An additional factor that favors fast times is high altitude, where reduced atmospheric pressure offers less resistance to sprinters. This was spectacularly demonstrated at the 1968 Mexico City Olympics, sited 2248 meters (7375 feet) above sea level. A string of world records were achieved at these Games in the "explosive" events.

Sprinters are not actually getting all that much faster. The introductory chapter noted that the improvement in the world record for 100m since 1912 was 7.17 percent. To run the 100m under 10 seconds is still a rare event. It was first achieved (timed electronically) in 1968 at the altitude-aided Mexico City Olympics by Jim Hines, who ran 9.95 seconds. Almost 30 years later, only 19 men have broken 10 seconds for 100m, three of which were at high altitude. The list is dominated by black athletes from the United States, along with others from Africa or the Caribbean.

Altogether, 41 athletes have set or equaled the 100m world record 59 times. Ten of them have also been Olympic champions: Paddock, Williams, Tolan, Owens, Morrow, Hary, Hayes, Hines, Lewis, and Bailey.

Men's World Records for 100m

Record time	Record holder	Location	Date
10.6	Donald Lippincott (USA)	Stockholm, Sweden	6 Jul 1912
10.6	Jackson Scholz (USA)	Stockholm, Sweden	16 Sep 1920
10.4	Charles Paddock (USA)	Redlands, USA	23 Apr 1921
10.4	Eddie Tolan (USA)	Stockholm, Sweden	8 Aug 1929
10.4	Eddie Tolan (USA)	Copenhagen, Denmark	25 Aug 1929
10.3	Percy Williams (CAN)	Toronto, Canada	9 Aug 1930
10.3	Eddie Tolan (USA)	Los Angeles, USA	1 Aug 1932
10.3	Ralph Metcalfe (USA)	Budapest, Hungary	12 Aug 1933
10.3	Eulace Peacock (USA)	Oslo, Norway	6 Aug 1934
10.3	Christiaan Berger (HOL)	Amsterdam, Netherlands	26 Aug 1934
10.3	Ralph Metcalfe (USA)	Osaka, Japan	15 Sep 1934
10.3	Ralph Metcalfe (USA)	Dairen, China	23 Sep 1934
10.3	Takayoshi Yoshioka (JPN)	Tokyo, Japan	15 Jun 1935

10.2	Jesse Owens (USA)	Chicago, USA	20 Jun 1936
10.2	Harold Davis (USA)	Compton, USA	6 Jun 1941
10.2	Lloyd La Beach (PAN)	Fresno, USA	15 May 1948
10.2	Barney Ewell (USA)	Evanston, USA	9 Jul 1948
10.2	E. McDonald Bailey (GBR)	Belgrade, Yugoslavia	25 Aug 1951
10.2	Heinz Fütterer (FRG)	Yokohama, Japan	31 Oct 1954
10.2	Bobby Morrow (USA)	Houston, USA	19 May 1956
10.2	Ira Murchison (USA)	Compton, USA	1 Jun 1956
10.2	Bobby Morrow (USA)	Bakersfield, USA	22 Jun 1956
10.2	Ira Murchison (USA)	Los Angeles, USA	29 Jun 1956
10.2	Bobby Morrow (USA)	Los Angeles, USA	29 Jun 1956
10.1	Willie Williams (USA)	Berlin, West Germany	3 Aug 1956
10.1	Ira Murchison (USA)	Berlin, West Germany	4 Aug 1956
10.1	Leamon King (USA)	Ontario, USA	20 Oct 1956
10.1	Leamon King (USA)	Santa Ana, USA	27 Oct 1956
10.1	Ray Norton (USA)	San Jose, USA	18 Apr 1959
10.0	Armin Hary (FRG)	Zürich, Switzerland	21 Jun 1960
10.0	Harry Jerome (CAN)	Saskatoon, Canada	15 Jul 1960
10.0	Horacio Esteves (VEN)	Caracas, Venezuela	15 Aug 1964
10.0	Bob Hayes (USA)	Tokyo, Japan	15 Oct 1964
10.0	James Hines (USA)	Modesto, USA	27 May 1967
10.0	Enrique Figuerola (CUBA)	Budapest, Hungary	17 Jun 1967
10.0	Paul Nash (S.AF)	Krugersdorp, S. Africa	2 Apr 1968
10.0	Oliver Ford (USA)	Albuquerque, USA	31 May 1968
10.0	Charles Greene (USA)	Sacramento, USA	20 Jun 1968
10.0	Roger Bambuck (FRA)	Sacramento, USA	20 Jun 1968
9.9	James Hines (USA)	Sacramento, USA	20 Jun 1968
9.9	Ronnie Ray Smith (USA)	Sacramento, USA	20 Jun 1968
9.9	Charles Greene (USA)	Sacramento, USA	20 Jun 1968
9.9*	James Hines (USA)	Mexico City, Mexico	14 Oct 1968
9.9	Eddie Hart (USA)	Eugene, USA	1 Jul 1972
9.9	Reynaud Robinson (USA)	Eugene, USA	1 Jul 1972
9.9	Steve Williams (USA)	Los Angeles, USA	21 Jun 1974
9.9	Silvio Leonard (CUBA)	Ostrava, Czechoslovakia	5 Jun 1975
9.9	Steve Williams (USA)	Siena, Italy	16 Jul 1975
9.9	Steve Williams (USA)	Berlin, West Germany	22 Aug 1975
9.9	Steve Williams (USA)	Gainesville, USA	27 Mar 1976
9.9	Harvey Glance (USA)	Columbia, USA	3 Apr 1976
9.9	Harvey Glance (USA)	Baton Rouge, USA	1 May 1976
9.9	Don Quarrie (JAM)	Modesto, USA	22 May 1976

Electronic Timing:

9.95*	James Hines (USA)	Mexico City, Mexico	14 Oct 1968
9.93	Calvin Smith (USA)	Colorado Springs, USA	3 Jul 1983
9.92	Carl Lewis (USA)	Seoul, South Korea	24 Sep 1988

9.90	Leroy Burrell (USA)	New York, USA	14 Jun 1991
9.86	Carl Lewis (USA)	Tokyo, Japan	25 Aug 1991
9.85	Leroy Burrell (USA)	Lausanne, Switzerland	6 Jul 1994
9.84	Donovan Bailey (CAN)	Atlanta, USA	27 Jul 1996

*Jim Hines's 14 Oct 1968 race was timed manually at 9.9 seconds and electronically at 9.95 seconds.

Donald Lippincott (United States, 1893–1962)

10.6   **Stockholm, Sweden**   **6 Jul 1912**

Donald Lippincott was the first officially recognized 100m world record holder. A graduate of the University of Pennsylvania, he set this record of 10.6 in winning the semifinal at the 1912 Olympics in Stockholm. There were six "semifinals" altogether, and Ralph Craig (USA) was the next fastest winner in 10.7.

At the final there were no less than seven false starts. During one of these false starts, both Craig and Lippincott ran the entire distance. At the eighth attempt Lippincott could not reproduce his form from the previous round and finished third to Ralph Craig, who won in 10.8. Second was Alvah Meyer (USA) who recorded 10.9, as did Lippincott.

Lippincott ran second in the 200m in 21.8. Craig once again was the winner in 21.7.

Lippincott later graduated with a BS in Economics in 1915. During World War I he served in the U.S. Navy and after the war became an investment banker.

Jackson Scholz (United States, 1897–1986)

10.6   **Stockholm, Sweden**   **16 Sep 1920**

Jackson Scholz was one of the top U.S. sprinters throughout the 1920s. He participated in three Olympics: 1920, 1924, and 1928. In 1920 he was fourth in the 100m and was a member of the 4 × 100m relay team that won the gold medal. At the Paris 1924 Games he won the gold medal in the 200m and was second in the 100m. In 1928 he was fourth in the 200m.

Scholz competed against Charley Paddock 10 times, winning 5 and tying 1. Surprisingly, however, he won only one U.S. AAU title: the 220 yards in 1925. He equaled the world record at an international meet in Stockholm in 1920, after the Antwerp Olympics.

Jackson Scholz, United States (100m), 1924 Olympic 200m champion.

Scholz was a graduate of the University of Missouri, earning a degree in journalism. A coach for many years, he was also a prolific author of pulp fiction, churning out no less than 31 novels.

Toward the end of his life, he was brought back into public awareness by the 1980 film *Chariots of Fire* in which his character had a supporting role. The scriptwriters chose to portray him as a man of religious conviction. This resulted in letters to him requesting religious counsel from some who had seen the film, which surprised and amused him.

Charles Paddock   (United States, 1900-1943)

10.4   **Redlands, USA**   **23 Apr 1921**

Charles Paddock, United States (100m), 1920 Olympic 100m champion, with his famous "jump" finish.

Charles "Charley" Paddock was the first great showman/entertainer/superstar of modern track and field. He first came to public attention when he won the 100m at the Inter Allied Military Games in Paris in 1919. Like Jackson Scholz, he also competed in the three Olympics of the 1920s. In 1920 he won the gold medal in the 100m, was second in the 200m, and was a member of the winning 4 × 100m relay. At the 1924 Olympics in Paris he was fifth in the 100m and second in the 200m. In 1928, when past his prime, he could not get beyond the semifinals of the 200m.

He spent much of the 1920s touring the United States, showing off his athletic prowess. He set a string of records in a variety of unofficial events, such as 110 yards, 135 yards, and 250 meters. A compulsive self-publicist, he wore colorful outfits and had a special "jump-finish" to the tape. Many coaches thought this jump actually slowed him down, but the crowds lapped it up. His memoirs were characteristically titled *The Fastest Human.*

Paddock went on to a brief foray as an actor in Hollywood (*Campus Flirt, Thief of Baghdad*) and later to a career as a newspaper manager. He joined the Marines in World War II, serving as an aide to Major General Upshur. On a flight to the Pacific in July 1943 with General Upshur, the plane crashed over Alaska, and all on board perished.

Eddie Tolan   (United States, 1908–1967)

10.4	Stockholm, Sweden	8 Aug 1929
10.4	Copenhagen, Denmark	25 Aug 1929
10.3	Los Angeles, USA	1 Aug 1932

Eddie Tolan was the first black man to hold the 100m world record and the first black Olympic champion over 100m. His father was a hotel cook, and his mother was a washerwoman. He was born in Denver, Colorado, but the family moved to Detroit in 1924. In 1928 he won a sporting scholarship to the University of Michigan. A knee injury ended any hope of a football career, so he decided to concentrate on track athletics. His athletic career flourished, and he equaled the world record twice during a trip to Europe in 1929.

The highlight of his career was his Olympic success in 1932, winning both the 100m and the 200m in front of an American crowd. To this day, the outcome of the 100m final remains controversial. The other great U.S. sprinter of the time, Ralph Metcalfe, crossed the finish line with Tolan in a desperately close finish. Photos taken at the time were inconclusive. Tolan was awarded first place, though Metcalfe felt he had won. In the 200m Tolan had an easy victory, by 5 to 6 meters.

After the year of Olympic glory, Tolan had to face the Depression. He worked as a filing clerk from 1933 until 1942, except for a short visit to Australia in 1935, where he ran in the

Ralph Metcalfe, United States (100m), *left*, with Eddie Tolan, United States (100m) at the 1932 Los Angeles Olympics.

professional running circuit and was described as a great hit with the women. He later worked as a stock control officer for the Packard car firm and subsequently as a physical education teacher in Detroit. Tolan died at age 58 from kidney and heart failure.

Percy Williams   (Canada, 1908–1982)

| 10.3 | Toronto, Canada | 9 Aug 1930 |

Percy Williams became a national hero in Canada when he won both the 100m and 200m at the 1928 Amsterdam Olympic Games. He was only 19 at the time.

He was born in Vancouver and was brought up by his mother when his parents separated. His athletic talent was developed by coach Bob Granger, who recognized his talents early and in many ways was a father figure to him.

Williams was a slight figure of 5' 7" (170 centimeters) weighing 125 pounds (56 kilograms). He was given a rousing reception upon his return from the Olympics, as Canadians outdid themselves to welcome him and shower praise upon him. His sprint career continued into 1929, when he won 21 out of 22 races in a U.S. tour. In 1930 he reduced the world record to 10.3 at the Canadian championships in Toronto. At the inaugural

Commonwealth Games the same year he won the 100-yards title, but in doing so he tore a hamstring muscle and was never the same sprinter again. He traveled to Los Angeles for the 1932 Olympics but failed to make the finals in the 100m and 200m.

During his athletic career, Williams felt much bitterness toward Canadian athletic officials, who he felt lived well while he and his coach struggled to raise money to get to various meets. After his athletic career was over he obtained a commercial pilot's license and also sold insurance. A shy man, he was a loner with few friends. He lived with his mother until she died, when he was in his fifties, and then he lived alone. Toward the end of his life he was plagued by painful arthritis and, after suffering two strokes, committed suicide at age 74.

Percy Williams, Canada (100m), upset winner of the 100m and 200m at the 1928 Olympics.

Ralph Metcalfe   (United States, 1910–1978)

10.3	Budapest, Hungary	12 Aug 1933
10.3	Osaka, Japan	15 Sep 1934
10.3	Dairen, China	23 Sep 1934

Ralph Metcalfe was second to Eddie Tolan in the controversial 100m final in 1932. Metcalfe remained convinced until the day he died that he himself had won. He was also third in the 200m in the same Olympics.

In the 1936 Berlin Olympics he was second, well beaten by the new star, Jesse Owens. At these Olympics Metcalfe ran in the 4 × 100m relay and finally gained an Olympic gold medal.

Perhaps his best year was 1934, when he equaled the world record twice and represented the United States in a tour to Asia. He was NCAA champion over both 100 and 220 yards three times (1932-34) and AAU champion over 100 yards (1932-34) and 220 yards (1932-36).

Metcalfe was born in Atlanta and grew up in Chicago. From 1954 until 1970 he served as an alderman for the city of Chicago. In 1970 he was elected to the U.S. Congress as a Democrat and served there until 1978, the year he died.

The American AAU Convention after the Olympics voted to declare the 1932 100m result a tie, but this determination was never accepted by the Olympic officials.

Eulace Peacock   (United States, 1914–1996)

| 10.3 | Oslo, Norway | 6 Aug 1934 |

Eulace Peacock and Jesse Owens were the two great sprinters/long jumpers of the 1930s. Jesse Owens went on to fame (if not fortune), whereas Peacock disappeared into obscurity.

Peacock was, in fact, the only athlete to have a win-loss record superior to Jesse Owens's. In 1935 he competed against Owens in long jumps and sprints 10 times and won 7. He also became the second athlete to leap 8 meters. Charley Paddock backed him as the Olympic 100m gold medalist, but it was not to be. Peacock suffered a severe hamstring injury at the Penn Relays in early 1936 and never recaptured his earlier form, although he competed on and off until 1948.

As an all-around athlete he won the AAU pentathlon championship in 1933-34, 1937, and 1943-45. He later became president of the Allstar Trading Company, a meat packing firm in New York.

Eulace Peacock, United States (100m).

Christiaan Berger   (Netherlands, 1911-1965)

10.3   **Amsterdam, Netherlands**   **26 Aug 1934**

Christiaan Berger, Netherlands (100m), 1934 European 100m and 200m champion.

Christiaan Berger was the first European athlete to officially hold the world record in the 100m. He won both the 100m and the 200m at the first European Championships, held in Turin, Italy in 1934, with times of 10.6 and 21.5. In 1935 he had a notable win over Eulace Peacock during the American's otherwise triumphal tour of Europe.

Berger was Dutch champion over both 100m and 200m in 1930, 1931, 1933, and 1934. At the 1932 Olympics he got through to the second round of both the 100m and the 200m but advanced no further. At the 1936 Berlin Olympics he was also eliminated in the second round of the 100m.

Takayoshi Yoshioka   (Japan, 1909–1984)

| 10.3 | Tokyo, Japan | 15 Jun 1935 |

Takayoshi Yoshioka was the first (and only) Asian athlete to be a world record holder in the 100m. He achieved this record at an international match between Japan and the Philippines in Tokyo in 1935. He also achieved the first and only victory by a Japanese athlete over a top U.S. sprinter when he defeated Ralph Metcalfe during a 1934 tour of Japan by an American team.

He competed at both the 1932 and 1936 Olympics. He was sixth in the 100m at the Los Angeles Games. In Berlin he went out in the early rounds.

Jesse Owens   (United States, 1913–1980)

| 10.2 | Chicago, USA | 20 Jun 1936 |

Jesse Owens is one of the very few athletes who routinely have the adjective *immortal* attached to their name. The two special highlights of his career are his one-day, six–world record haul in Ann Arbor in 1935 and his four gold medals at the 1936 Berlin Olympics.

He was born in Alabama, the son of a sharecropper and the grandson of a slave. When he was nine years old, his family moved to Cleveland, Ohio. He earned the nickname "Jesse" when he informed a teacher that his name was J.C. Owens. The teacher misheard and registered him as Jesse Owens. The name stuck.

The six world records that he achieved in one day in 1935 were for 100 yards, long jump, 220 yards, 200m, and 220-yard and 200m hurdles.

His four gold medals (100m, 200m, long jump, 4 × 100m relay) at the Berlin Olympics established him as one of the all-time Olympic greats. Even in the atmosphere of the Nazi era, he nonetheless became a favorite of the German crowds. Yet almost as soon as the Olympics were over, so was his athletic career. He fell foul of U.S. athletic officials who wanted him to go on a post-Olympic tour to Scandinavia. When he declined the tour, he was suspended by U.S. officials. In those days their power was such that there was nothing an athlete could do to reverse such an edict. After the Olympics Owens found that celebrity as an athlete did not translate into wealth or even job security, although accounts differ as to his exact financial situation. He competed in exhibition races against horses, dogs, and motorcycles. During World War II he was largely forgotten, but in the 1950s he was "rediscovered" and established a career as a public speaker. His critics felt that he was little more than a "professional good example," but that era seems to have passed. Owens is today seen as a black pioneer of success in sport and as an inspiration to athletic excellence.

Harold Davis   (United States, b. 1921)

| 10.2 | Compton, USA | 6 Jun 1941 |

Harold Davis was seen as something of a "Great White Hope" after the domination of the U.S. sprint scene by African Americans in the 1930s. But World War II meant that Davis and many others of his generation never had the chance to shine at an international level, as the Olympic Games of 1940 and 1944 were canceled.

Born in Salinas, California, Davis was noted for his "abysmal" starts and his remarkable finishes. Nicknamed the California Comet, he dominated the U.S. sprint world from

1940-43 in both the 100m and the 200m. He was AAU 100m champion in 1940, 1942, and 1943 and the AAU 200m champion for four years in a row (1940-43).

In 1946 he sustained a severe hamstring injury and never again achieved his previous form.

Harold Davis, United States (100m) and Grover Klemmer, United States (400m).

Lloyd La Beach   (Panama, b. 1923)

| 10.2 | Fresno, USA | 15 May 1948 |

Lloyd La Beach is the only athlete from Panama both to set a world record and to be an Olympic medalist. Born in Panama, he was educated in Jamaica and initially ran for that country. But after a dispute with Jamaican athletic officials, he chose to run for Panama. He later was awarded a sports scholarship to the University of California, Los Angeles, and moved to the United States.

His best year was 1948, when he had a series of wins against the top U.S. sprinters, such as Mel Patton (later to be the 1948 200m Olympic champion). In Fresno, California, on 15 May 1948 in his second race for the day he equaled the world record for the 100m with 10.2.

At the London Olympics 100m in August, all the top names were beaten that day by a rank outsider, hurdler Harrison Dillard. Second was Barney Ewell (USA), and La Beach was third. La Beach was also third in the 200m.

Barney Ewell   (United States, 1918–1996)

| 10.2 | Evanston, USA | 9 Jul 1948 |

Barney Ewell was AAU champion over 100m in 1941, 1945, and 1948 and 200m champion in 1946 and 1947. At age 30 he won the 1948 U.S. Olympic trials, equaling the world record in the process.

In the Olympic 100m final he ran in lane 1 and actually thought he'd won, so he did a little victory jig. But photos clearly showed that Harrison Dillard in lane 6 had won the race. In the 200m Ewell was again second.

Ewell had one more chance for an Olympic gold medal in the 4 × 100m relay. The U.S. team won by 6 meters but was then disqualified because a track official alleged that the change-over between Barney Ewell and Lorenzo Wright took place outside the ex-change zone. The U.S. team protested this decision. Three days later the Jury of Appeal reviewed a film of this change-over and found no fault with it. So the disquali-fication was rescinded, and the U.S. team was declared the winner.

Later in life Ewell worked for an electric company in Lancaster, Pennsylvania. He was declared a professional athlete by U.S. athletic offi-cials in the early 1950s.

Barney Ewell, United States (100m).

E. McDonald Bailey   (Great Britain, b. 1920)

10.2   **Belgrade, Yugoslavia**   **25 Aug 1951**

McDonald Bailey was born in Trinidad but moved to England in 1942. He represented Britain in the 1948 and 1952 Olympics. From 1946 to 1953, he won the British sprint double (100 and 220 yards) seven times, a record that will probably never be equaled. Together with Jamaican quarter-miler Arthur Wint, he helped attract vast crowds to English track and field in those postwar years.

In 1948 he went into the London Olympics as one of the favorites but was troubled by a hamstring injury and finished sixth in the 100m. Harrison Dillard (USA) won in 10.3; Bailey recorded 10.6.

In the 1952 Games at Helsinki the 100m final result was the tightest in Olympic history. Only inches separated the first six places. McDonald Bailey ran in lane 5, which was soaked from water coming off the stadium roof. He finished third in 10.83, a few centimeters behind Lindy Remigino (USA) and Herb McKenley (Jamaica), both in 10.79. In the 200m he finished fourth in 21.14, with winner Andy Stanfield (USA) recording 20.81.

As his sprinting career wound down, he had little to show financially for his years at the top. He briefly tried rugby without success and then endorsed a new brand of starting blocks. This earned him the wrath of the British amateur athletic officials, who readily forgot his many years of dedication to his sport. He was later active for many years in coaching and sport administration in Guyana, England, Ireland, and Trinidad.

E. McDonald Bailey, Great Britain (100m).

Heinz Fütterer   (West Germany, b. 1931)

10.2   **Yokohama, Japan**   **31 Oct 1954**

Heinz Fütterer was born in Illingen-am-Rhein in 1931. A former soccer player, he turned to track and field in the early 1950s. He was West German champion over 100m in 1951, 1953, 1954, and 1955 and was also 200m champion in 1953 and 1954.

In 1954 he duplicated the feat of another world record holder (Christiaan Berger) by winning both the 100m and 200m at the European Championships in Bern, Switzerland, in times of 10.5 and 20.9, respectively. On a tour of Japan he recorded 10.2, equaling the world record for the 100m.

By the time of the 1956 Olympic Games in Melbourne his form appeared to have

Heinz Fütterer, West Germany (100m).

slipped a little. He came in fifth in the second round of the 100m and did not advance to the next round. However, he did win a bronze medal in the 4 × 100m relay when the West German team came in third.

Bobby Morrow   (United States, b. 1935)

10.2	Houston, USA	19 May 1956
10.2	Bakersfield, USA	22 Jun 1956
10.2	Los Angeles, USA	29 Jun 1956

Bobby Morrow is the last white U.S. athlete to hold the world record in the 100m. Born in Texas, he attended Abilene Christian College and showed early talent as a sprinter in the mid-1950s. He was NCAA champion of both sprints in 1956 and 1957 and also became AAU champion in the 100m in 1955, 1956, and 1958 and in the 200m in 1958.

In 1956 he was untouchable, equaling the world record for the 100m three times that season. In November at the Melbourne Olympics he powered to easy victories in the 100m and 200m. The U.S. team of which he was a member won the 4 × 100m relay in world record time, so he won three gold medals.

Forty years later, it is hard to convey the publicity and praise that fell upon Morrow after his Olympic victories. It didn't hurt that he was clean-cut, wholesome, just 21, good looking, and articulate. He was trumpeted and feted like a Roman general returning from great victories. The U.S. State Department persuaded him to go on a series of overseas goodwill missions, and he was promoted as a role model for American youth. But the relentless tours and the relentless publicity started to take their toll. His family life suffered, and eventually his marriage ended in divorce. He competed for a few more years but just missed out on selection to the U.S. team for the Rome Olympics.

Morrow moved on through a series of business ventures. In some of these, fast-talking entrepreneurs used his name for their own purposes and then left Morrow to face the consequences when they did not succeed. Like Jesse Owens 20 years earlier, he found that Olympic success did not lend itself to long-term career prospects. He eventually remarried and established the Bobby Morrow Clothing Store in Harlingen, Texas.

Ira Murchison   (United States, 1933–1994)

10.2	Compton, USA	1 Jun 1956
10.2	Los Angeles, USA	29 Jun 1956
10.1	Berlin, West Germany	4 Aug 1956

Born in Chicago, Ira Murchison served in the U.S. Army. He was only 5′ 2″ tall (157 centimeters) and was the smallest sprinter to hold a world record. In his day he raced against Bobby Morrow, who stood 6′ 2″ tall (188 centimeters). Murchison equaled the 100m world record twice in June 1956.

He competed at the International Military Championships in Berlin in August 1956, where he became the second man to run 10.1 seconds for the 100m. (On the previous day Willie Williams became the first man to do this.)

At the Melbourne Olympics three months later Murchison won a semifinal in 10.5. Morrow won the other semifinal in 10.3. In the final Murchison could not stay with the taller man and finished fourth (10.8) as Morrow cruised to victory (10.5). However, Murchison did earn a gold medal in the 4 × 100m relay; the U.S. team won easily, break-

ing the world record set back in 1936 by the team led by Jesse Owens at the Berlin Olympics.

Murchison died in 1994 of bone cancer.

Ira Murchison, United States (100m).

Willie Williams   (United States, b. 1931)

10.1   **Berlin, West Germany**   **3 Aug 1956**

Willie Williams achieved his world record at the same venue as Ira Murchison, the International Military Championships in Berlin. He was the first man to run 10.1 seconds for the 100m, 20 years after Jesse Owens first ran 10.2. Williams achieved his record in one of the heats. Unfortunately, Williams had already missed out on selection to the U.S. team for the 1956 Olympics by the time he set his world record.

His earlier successes included winning the NCAA title in 100 yards in 1953 and 1954. He went on to a long career in coaching at a high school in Gary, Indiana and later at his alma mater, the University of Illinois. He coached the Saudi Arabian team in 1988 at the Seoul Olympics.

Leamon King   (United States, b. 1936)

10.1   **Ontario, USA**   **20 Oct 1956**
10.1   **Santa Ana, USA**   **27 Oct 1956**

Leamon King had a short athletic career in the mid-1950s. He missed out on the 100m at the 1956 Olympics but made the U.S. 4 × 100m relay squad. Just before the Games he equaled the 100m world record twice. The U.S. team easily won the 4 ×100m gold medal in 39.5, a new world record.

Ray Norton (United States, b. 1937)

10.1 **San Jose, USA** **18 Apr 1959**

Ray Norton, United States (100m, 200m).

Ray Norton was the top U.S. sprinter in the late 1950s and the early part of 1960. He was AAU champion in both 100m and 200m in 1959 and 1960.

He was perhaps unfortunate in that he peaked in the weeks just before the 1960 Olympics took place in September. In 1959 he had been supreme and held world records in that year in both the 100m and the 200m. He was also the 1959 Pan-American champion at both sprints. However, in a bleak Olympics for U.S. sprinters, West Germany's Armin Hary won the 100m and Italy's Livio Berruti won the 200m. To make an Olympic final is an achievement for any athlete. Norton made both sprint finals, but he had the unusual misfortune to come in last in both events. In an ironic twist, his girlfriend at the time, Wilma Rudolph, won both the 100m and the 200m and was part of the winning 4 × 100m relay.

Norton had a chance to win a gold medal in the 4 × 100m relay. The U.S. team crossed the line first but was disqualified because Frank Budd and Norton exchanged the baton outside the correct zone.

After the Olympics, Norton played football with the San Francisco 49ers for two seasons.

Armin Hary (West Germany, b. 1937)

10.0 **Zürich, Switzerland** **21 Jun 1960**

Armin Hary achieved two landmarks during his athletic career. He was the first man to run the 100m in 10.0 seconds. And he won the Olympic 100m final in Rome against the Americans, the first non-U.S. athlete to do so since Percy Williams of Canada in 1928.

He came to international attention, however, with his win in the 1958 European Championships over 100m (10.3). The main feature of his running was his lightning-fast start. Some observers thought his start was too fast, but he appeared to have the ability to anticipate exactly when the starter would fire. In Zürich in June 1960 he achieved history's first 10.0-second run over 100m.

Armin Hary, West Germany, 1960 Olympic 100m champion and first man to run 10 seconds for 100m.

In the September 1960 Olympic final he initially had a false start recorded against him, so one more false start and he would have been disqualified. Nonetheless, he kept his poise, and at the next attempt the field got away to a fair start. Hary was already 1 meter ahead at the 5-meter mark. Dave Sime of the United States stormed through in the second half of the race, but Hary held on to win 10.32 to 10.35. This triumph caused immense publicity in Germany: A German athlete had beaten the American sprinters at the Olympics.

Hary sustained a knee injury in a car accident in 1961 and retired. Never very popular with his fellow athletes, he also fell foul of the German press, who perhaps preferred more modest champions.

Hary later married and went into the real estate business. However, his name resurfaced in the papers in 1981, when he and his partner were charged by the police for embezzling from the Roman Catholic church in a real estate deal. Both were convicted and Hary went to jail for five months, which attracted major publicity in West Germany. After his release he resumed a private life with his wife, who remained steadfast behind him despite his troubles.

Harry Jerome   (Canada, 1940–1982)

| 10.0 | Saskatoon, Canada | 15 Jul 1960 |

Harry Jerome was the son of a black railway porter, and his family settled in Vancouver in 1950. He attended the University of Oregon and obtained a master's degree in physical education.

A promising sprinter, he staggered observers at the Canadian Olympic trials in 1960 by equaling the world record while only 19 years of age. But at Rome he had the misfortune to pull a hamstring while in the lead in the semifinals of the 100m and collapsed onto the track.

When he finished last in the 100 yards at the 1962 Commonwealth Games, much of the Canadian press called him a "choker" at high-pressure athletic meets. However, most of the press did not realize that during the event he suffered a complete separation of the quadriceps muscle, one of the most serious injuries an athlete can sustain. He was flown home to Vancouver and underwent surgery to repair the torn edges of the muscle. The injury is generally regarded as career crippling, yet Jerome underwent a year of rehabilitation and with remarkable determination became once again a world-class competitor.

Jerome finally earned an Olympic medal when he finished third in the 100m at the 1964 Tokyo Olympics, won by the invincible Bob Hayes. He was also fourth in the 200m. He became the first Canadian sprinter to reach either final since Percy Williams in 1928. Jerome went on to win the 1966 Commonwealth 100 yards title and the 1967 Pan-American 100m. In his third Olympics in 1968 at Mexico City he was seventh in the 100m in the first all-black final.

At age 42, while riding in a friend's car, he suffered an epileptic seizure and died.

Horacio Esteves   (Venezuela, b. 1940)

10.0   **Caracas, Venezuela**   **15 Aug 1964**

Horacio Esteves is the only athlete from Venezuela to have held a world record. At age 19 he had run at the 1960 Rome Olympics, finishing fifth in the semifinal of the 100m. In the 4 × 100m relay the Venezuelan team came in fifth. Esteves ran his world record shortly before the 1964 Olympics, becoming the third man to run it in 10.0 seconds. However, injury kept him from competing at the Games. At the 1968 Mexico City Olympics he was eliminated in the heats of the 100m.

His other major success was winning the 200m at the South American championships in 1961.

Horacio Esteves, Venezuela (100m).

Bob Hayes   (United States, b. 1942)

10.0   **Tokyo, Japan**   **15 Oct 1964**

Bob Hayes's first love was football; sprinting came second. He grew up in poverty after his father returned from World War II in a wheelchair. However his muscular build and sporting talents led to a sporting scholarship at Florida A & M University. He squeezed in track around his football commitments and was AAU champion from 1962-64 in 100 yards/ 100m (1962-1963, 100 yards; 1964, 100m).

Bob Hayes had an aggressive, muscular style of sprinting, more like a heavyweight boxer than a classic sprinter. He dominated the 1964 Olympic 100m final, winning easily in 10.0 seconds on a lane cut up by the distance runners. In the 4 × 100m relay he was awesome, storming home to turn a 3-meter deficit into a 3-meter lead.

Hayes immediately retired from track and field to pursue a football career. He joined the Dallas Cowboys in the NFL and played with them for nine years, setting many records in the process. In his debut year he had 46 pass receptions for 1003 yards, with an average of 21.8 yards per catch. In 1972 the Dallas Cowboys won the Super Bowl against the Miami Dolphins.

In 1974 at the age of 34 he was traded to the San Francisco 49ers but only stayed six months. His marriage broke up, he drifted into alcoholism, and he finally hit rock bottom when he was arrested for cocaine dealing. He served 10 months in prison.

A second marriage broke up as well, but he bounced back from all these setbacks. Described as a "fun-loving, ebullient" character, he has since been involved in community and anti-drug programs.

Bob Hayes, United States (100m), 1964 Olympic 100m champion.

James Hines   (United States, b. 1946)

10.0	Modesto, USA	27 May 1967
9.9	Sacramento, USA	20 Jun 1968
9.9 (9.95 on electronic timing)	Mexico City, Mexico	14 Oct 1968

Born in Arkansas, Hines was one of ten children of an Oakland construction worker and his sprinting prowess led to a scholarship at Texas Southern University. He burst into sporting prominence in 1967 with wins over Charlie Greene, who appeared to be Bob Hayes's heir. Greene and Hines exchanged wins in a series of duels leading up to the 1968 Mexico City Olympics. Hines ran 10.0 seconds for the 100m to equal the world record at the California relays in 1967.

The classic sprint confrontation between Hines and Greene was perhaps not the Olympic final, but the AAU races in Sacramento earlier in the year. Hines set the stadium alight in the first semifinal with history's first ever 9.9 seconds. In second place Ronnie Ray Smith was given the same time. Greene responded by equaling 9.9 seconds in his semifinal five minutes later. In the much-anticipated final Greene just won from Hines; both men recorded 10.0 seconds.

In the first all-black Olympic 100m final, Hines took the lead at 70 meters and just held on to win in 9.95 seconds (electronically). Greene was narrowly defeated for second place by Jamaican Lennox Miller.

Like Bob Hayes four years earlier, Hines signed on for football with the Miami Dolphins. Although Hayes had been an established football player, Hines had not really played since his high school days, and the move was not a great success. He went on to work for various sporting and local government organizations as an administrator.

Jim Hines, United States (100m),
1968 Olympic 100m champion.

Enrique Figuerola   (Cuba, b. 1938)

10.0   **Budapest, Hungary**   **17 Jun 1967**

Figuerola was Cuban 100m champion for most of the 1960s. At the 1963 Pan-American Games in São Paulo, Brazil, he won the 100m in 10.46. Four years later in Budapest he became the sixth man to run 10.0 seconds for the 100m.

He attended three Olympics. He was fourth in the 1960 Rome Olympics in 100m at 10.3. He was second at the 1964 Tokyo Olympics to the invincible Bob Hayes, 10.0 to 10.2. At his third Olympics in 1968 he was fifth in his 100m semifinal (10.23) and did not progress to the final. But the Cuban team made the final of the 4 × 100m relay and came in a close second to the United States (38.2 to 38.3), so he earned a silver medal.

Enrique Figuerola, Cuba (100m).

Paul Nash   (South Africa, b. 1947)

10.0   **Krugersdorp, South Africa**   **2 Apr 1968**

Paul Nash was born in South Africa, and accordingly, his athletic career was plagued by political problems because of the apartheid system active at the time. South Africa was banned from the Olympics from 1964 until reform arrived in 1992. South African athletes still competed abroad, but they were stopped by an IAAF decision in 1976 to expel South Africa from international athletics. That decision was reversed in 1991.

In April 1968 Nash equaled the world record at the Krugersdorp Wanderers Ground. His performance was somewhat helped by being 1740 meters (5709 feet) above sea level.

Nash experimented with the idea of using starting blocks while still in a standing position, which he felt allowed a faster getaway than the traditional start on one's knees.

He had his last race in 1969. A week later he got married and, on his wedding night, hit his foot against a cupboard, which seemed to initiate the symptoms of arthritis. Now in middle age, he is severely plagued by rheumatoid arthritis, so that he can no longer work for a full day and at times has to use a wheelchair.

Paul Nash, South Africa (100m).

Oliver Ford   (United States, b. 1947)

10.0   **Albuquerque, USA**   **31 May 1968**

Oliver Ford was a student at Southern University in New Orleans. He equaled the world record while running for Southern University in a meet in Albuquerque, New Mexico, at the NAIA Championships. This took place at Bernalillo County Stadium, situated 1507 meters (4944 feet) above sea level.

The very next day he suffered a severe leg injury while running the 200m, and that was more or less the end of his effective sprinting career. He currently resides in Orlando, Florida.

Charles Greene   (United States, b. 1945)

10.0   **Sacramento, USA**   **20 Jun 1968 (Heat)**
9.9   **Sacramento, USA**   **20 Jun 1968 (Semifinal)**

Charlie Greene was a student at the University of Nebraska and the only U.S. athlete to get close to Bob Hayes in the 1964 season. But he blew his chances for the 1964 Olympics

Charles Greene, United States (100m).

when he came in only sixth at the 1964 U.S. trials. With Hayes's retirement, Greene established himself as the world's top sprinter in the next two seasons. He developed his image as Mr. Cool, complete with sunglasses and a fast-talking, unsmiling attitude toward his competitors. In 1967 his dominance was challenged by Jim Hines. Their most absorbing encounter was at the AAU titles in Sacramento, four months before the Olympic Games. Hines ran 9.9 seconds in one of the semifinals. Five minutes later Greene ran 9.9 seconds in the other semifinal. In the final later that evening the electronic timer recorded Greene at 10.11 and Hines at 10.13.

Unfortunately for Greene, he could not maintain that edge at the Mexico City Olympics: Hines won in an electronically timed 9.95 seconds, and Greene was beaten into third place at 10.07 by Jamaica's Lennox Miller at 10.04.

Greene was NCAA champion in 100 yards in 1965-67 and AAU champion in 1966 and 1968. He made a career in the U.S. Army, achieving the rank of major.

Roger Bambuck   (France, b. 1945)

10.0   **Sacramento, USA**   **20 Jun 1968**

Roger Bambuck was born in the French Caribbean island of Guadeloupe. In 1966, representing France, he became the first black athlete to win a gold medal at the European Championships when he won the 200m in 20.9.

He participated in the famous AAU Championships in Sacramento in 1968. In heat 4 Bambuck equaled the existing world record, despite coming in second to Charlie Greene; both men were given a time of 10.0 seconds. The 10-second barrier was beaten two hours later in the first semifinal by Jim Hines with 9.9 seconds and in the second semifinal by Charlie Greene. In the final, all athletes were marginally slower. The results were Greene, 10.11; Hines, 10.13; Miller (Jamaica), 10.18; and Bambuck, 10.19.

At the 1968 Mexico City Olympics Bambuck came in fifth in the 100m (10.15) and fifth in the 200m (20.51). In the 4 × 100m relay he earned a bronze medal when the French team came in third.

Later in life he entered politics and served as France's Minister for Sport in the 1980s.

Ronnie Ray Smith   (United States, b. 1949)

9.9   **Sacramento, USA**   **20 Jun 1968**

Ronnie Ray Smith was yet another of the sprinters who achieved world record status at the famous AAU Championships in Sacramento in 1968. In the first semifinal he came in second to Jim Hines when Hines ran history's first 9.9 seconds for the 100m. Although in second place, Smith was also given a time of 9.9 seconds as all three stopwatches on him recorded 9.9, and so he became a joint world record holder. In the final later that night he was fifth in 10.1.

A graduate of San Jose State University, he was picked as part of the U.S. 4 × 100m relay team for the Mexico City Games, which went on to win the gold medal in a world record time of 38.2.

Eddie Hart (United States, b. 1948)

9.9   **Eugene, USA**   **1 Jul 1972**

Eddie Hart, United States (100m).

Eddie Hart established himself as a favorite for the Olympics at the U.S. Olympic trials in Eugene in July 1972 by equaling the world record with a time of 9.9. His main opponent for that title was the Soviet athlete Valeriy Borzov, who had beaten the best U.S. athletes in the preceding season. Alas, Hart's career is forever marked by a monumental Olympic debacle, and 20 years later how it came to pass is still not certain.

Hart and Borzov cruised through the preliminary rounds. Later that afternoon Hart and his teammates were relaxing in the Olympic village, watching on television what they thought were reruns of the morning's heats. To their horror, they were informed that these were not televised heats, but a direct, live broadcast of the quarterfinals, which should have included the three of them.

A frantic dash to the stadium ensued, but for Hart and his teammate Reynaud Robinson, it was too late—they missed their races. The other U.S. sprinter, Robert Taylor, arrived just in time to be included in his race and duly qualified through to the final. The 1972 Olympic 100m final on 1 September 1972 was won by Borzov in 10.14 seconds. Second, in 10.24, was Taylor.

One theory is that the U.S. team was using an old schedule, prepared well before the Games. Another is that the time of the race was expressed as 1715, using the 24-hour system widely used in Europe but not widely used in the United States, which indicates 5:15 P.M. It was suggested that the Americans thought the first digit *1* was a spelling mistake and that the race actually was scheduled for 7:15 P.M. However, it must be said that Borzov looked very strong and that he went on to win the 200m against a full field of U.S. athletes. Hart had some consolation by winning a 4 × 100m relay gold medal. He went on to be a physical education teacher in California, and the lost opportunity has become part of athletic and Olympic folklore.

Reynaud Robinson   (United States, b. 1952)

| 9.9 | Eugene, USA | 1 Jul 1972 |

Reynaud Robinson's story is very similar to that of Eddie Hart. A student at Florida A & M University, he had run second to Eddie Hart at the 1972 U.S. Olympic trials but was given the same time as Hart: 9.9 seconds. This made him the sixth man to run 9.9 seconds for the 100m.

At the Munich Olympics he also cruised through the preliminary rounds; he won his heat in 10.56. He later joined teammate Eddie Hart back at the U.S. team quarters, watching on television what they thought were highlights of the previous round. They were horrified to realize that it was a live broadcast and that their races were about to start. Robinson joined the mad dash back to the stadium but arrived too late to participate. Despite protests, he was out of the Olympic 100m.

Steve Williams   (United States, b. 1953)

9.9	Los Angeles, USA	21 Jun 1974
9.9	Siena, Italy	16 Jul 1975
9.9	Berlin, West Germany	22 Aug 1975
9.9	Gainesville, USA	27 Mar 1976

Steve Williams was the world's top sprinter in the mid-1970s. He was AAU champion in 1973 and 1974 in the 100m and in the 200m in 1973. He missed the 1972 Olympics because of an injury.

At that time, apart from the Olympics, there were not many major international events for U.S. athletes. The only major international event he won in those years was the 1977 World Cup in Düsseldorf, West Germany. Nonetheless, from 1974 to 1976 he equaled the world record four times, something no other sprinter has achieved. So it was a bitter pill for him when he pulled a hamstring muscle during the 1976 season, which put him out of the Montreal Olympics.

Steve Williams, United States (100m), with 1924 Olympic 100m champion Harold Abrahams.

Silvio Leonard   (Cuba, b. 1955)

9.9   **Ostrava, Czechoslovakia**   **5 Jun 1975**

Silvio Leonard was the son of a carpenter, one of 18 children, born in Sierra Adelaides in the south of Cuba. He was the second Cuban to hold the world record for 100m; Enrique Figuerola was the first.

He was the Pan-American champion in the 100m in 1975 and 1979 and in the 200m in 1979. He competed at the top level of international track and field for many years, often with intermittent disputes with the Cuban athletic federation.

His world record came at an international meet in Czechoslovakia in 1975, when he ran 9.9. He stepped on a bottle 10 days before the 1976 Montreal Olympics began and badly cut his foot. He ran anyway and was eliminated in the second round. At the 1980 Olympics, boycotted by the United States, he was one of the favorites but was just outleaned at the finish by Alan Wells of Great Britain. Both were timed at 10.25 seconds.

Harvey Glance   (United States, b. 1957)

9.9   **Columbia, USA**   **3 Apr 1976**
9.9   **Baton Rouge, USA**   **1 May 1976**

Harvey Glance, United States (100m).

Harvey Glance came to sprinting success early. A precocious talent, he had equaled the world record twice at age 19, just before the 1976 Montreal Olympics.

He was one of two U.S. sprinters in the final, but perhaps his lack of international experience at this stage handicapped him. In the waiting room prior to the 100m final, all eight finalists were gathered. In that hothouse atmosphere, experienced veteran Hasely Crawford of Trinidad and Tobago boldly announced to the assembled athletes that he was certain to win. In the process he possibly outpsyched some of the other finalists. Crawford won in 10.06, while Glance finished fourth in 10.19.

To finish fourth in the Olympic Games at age 19 is no mean achievement, but it was the first Olympic Games since 1928 in which no U.S. sprinter had won a medal in the 100m final. The U.S. team compensated somewhat by winning the 4 × 100m relay.

He continued sprinting after the Montreal Games, but any chance of Olympic success at the Moscow Games was dashed by the U.S. boycott of those Olympics.

Glance continued competing for a number of years without quite reaching his 1976 form. In 1986, 10 years after his first great season, he had a notable victory over Carl Lewis. He has since become coach of track and field athletics at Auburn University in Alabama, his alma mater.

Don Quarrie   (Jamaica, b. 1951)

9.9   **Modesto, USA**   **22 May 1976**

The island of Jamaica has produced a remarkable number of top sprinters, the most successful being Don Quarrie. He was the third of six children; his father was a police officer in Jamaica. Don Quarrie had an international career extending over 16 years.

Don Quarrie, Jamaica (100m, 200m), 1972 Olympic 200m champion.

1968	Selected for the Mexico City Olympics at age 17 but injured in training
1970	First in the 100m and 200m at the Edinburgh Commonwealth Games
1971	First in the 100m and 200m at the Pan-American Games
1972	Pulled a hamstring in the 200m semifinal at the Munich Olympics; retired hurt
1974	First in the 100m and 200m at the Commonwealth Games, Auckland
1976	Second in the 100m and first in the 200m at the Montreal Olympics
1978	First in the 100m at the Commonwealth Games, Edmonton, Canada
1980	Third in the 200m at the Moscow Olympics
1984	Eliminated in the second round of the 200m at Los Angeles Olympics; however, won a silver medal as Jamaica came in second in the 4 × 100m relay

He set his 100m world record of 9.9 at Modesto at the California Relays. A statue honors his achievements in Kingston, Jamaica. He has since coached at the University of Southern California and runs sprint clinics in that state and around the world.

Calvin Smith   (United States, b. 1961)

9.93   **Colorado Springs, USA**   **3 Jul 1983**

Calvin Smith was a top athlete through the 1980s and into the early 1990s. He achieved a number of triumphs, but for almost his entire career he was overshadowed by Carl Lewis.

Born in Bolton, Mississippi, he attended the University of Alabama. He did not chase the limelight, but his record over the years is substantial.

1983	Gold medal, 200m, Helsinki World Championships
	World record, 100m (9.93) at 2194 meters (7198 feet) above sea level
1984	Member of Olympic gold medal 4 × 100m relay team
1987	Gold medal, 200m, Rome World Championships
1988	Third in the 100m final at the Seoul Olympics

He is one of the few athletes to have achieved the rare feat of beating 10.00 seconds for the 100m and 20.00 seconds for the 200m in one day, which he did in 1983 at an international meet in Zurich, Switzerland, when he ran 9.97 and 19.99.

Known as the gentleman among the top sprinters, he offered support to Andre Cason in 1992, when the latter suffered a serious hamstring injury that put him out of the Barcelona Olympics. Cason later made the point that no other athlete, apart from Smith, showed any sympathy.

Calvin Smith, United States (100m).

Carl Lewis   (United States, b. 1961)

| 9.92 | Seoul, South Korea | 24 Sep 1988 |
| 9.86 | Tokyo, Japan | 25 Aug 1991 |

Carl Lewis was born in Birmingham, Alabama, the third son of two track coaches. At age 16 he had a major growth spurt and started to show remarkable athletic abilities in the sprints and long jump that he previously had not demonstrated. His international career began just after his 18th birthday when he came in third at the Pan-American Games in 1979 in the long jump.

He remained for so long at the very top of the sprints and the long jump that, in the words of one writer, "we are in danger of taking him for granted." He went 10 years in the long jump without a defeat, winning this event in four successive Olympics.

In the sprints he captured world imagination when he duplicated Jesse Owens's feat of winning four Olympic gold medals at the 1984 Los Angeles Games: the 100m, 200m, long jump, and 4 × 100m relay. He went on to capture nine Olympic gold medals altogether, with further gold medals in 1988 (100m, long jump), 1992 (long jump, 4 × 100m relay), and 1996 (long jump).

Lewis had been given the world record (9.92) for his time in the Seoul Olympics. He finished second to Canada's Ben Johnson, but Johnson was disqualified for a positive drug test. But it was at the Tokyo World Championships three years later that he finally achieved a world record on his own terms; he recorded his fastest time ever, 9.86, as he overtook fellow countryman Leroy Burrell in the last 10 meters of a classic race.

The U.S. pulic never quite warmed to Carl Lewis. This ambivalence was highlighted at the 1996 Olympics. He won the long jump, his ninth gold medal, the high point of his career. Then followed probably his low point, days of messy speculation that he should be included in the relay team. (He wasn't.) This was despite the fact that he had come in eighth at the U.S. 100m trials and had chosen not to attend the compulsory relay training camp. Nonetheless, excellence in any profession over a long period of time is to be admired. More than that, he has long campaigned against drugs in sport and has refused to go to high altitude to chase records. He remains an enduring champion.

Carl Lewis, United States (100m), multiple Olympic gold medalist over 12 years.

Leroy Burrell   (United States, b. 1967)

| 9.90 | New York, USA | 14 Jun 1991 |
| 9.85 | Lausanne, Switzerland | 6 Jul 1994 |

The name "Leroy" comes from the French for "the king," and for two or three years in the early 1990s Leroy Burrell was the king of the sprinters. Like Carl Lewis, he went to the University of Houston and joined the Santa Monica Track Club. The first five times they raced against each other, Lewis won. But finally, at the 1990 Goodwill Games, Burrell broke through with his first win over Lewis. He seemed to have the edge over Lewis from then on, highlighted by a new world record at the 1991 U.S. trials for the World Championships. However, Lewis turned the tables on Burrell at the World Championships in Tokyo two months later, winning in a new world record of 9.86 seconds. Burrell had led all the way to be beaten in the last 10 meters.

Leroy Burrell, United States (100m).

This surprise upset seemed to erode Burrell's confidence for some years. He made the U.S. team for the 1992 Olympics but in the final of the 100m was warned for a false start. Video recordings later indicated that, in fact, he had not moved. Perhaps unnerved by the warning (one more such warning and he would have been disqualified), he didn't do himself justice and finished fifth.

He finally bounced back in 1994 in Switzerland, taking 0.01 second off Carl Lewis's record with 9.85. Unfortunately, in 1996 he was troubled by injury. He came in sixth in the 100m at the U.S. Olympic trials and missed out on the Atlanta Games.

Donovan Bailey (Canada, b. 1967)

9.84   **Atlanta, USA**   **27 Jul 1996**

Donovan Bailey's journey to become the world's fastest man somewhat paralleled that of Ben Johnson. Both were born in Jamaica and moved to Canada as youngsters with their families. Both went on to set 100m world records at the Olympics. But there the similarities end: Johnson tested positive for anabolic steroids and later admitted to long-term drug use; no such charge has ever been entertained against Bailey.

Bailey was born in Manchester, Jamaica, and moved to Oakville, Ontario, in 1981 at the age of 13. Although some athletes have gone on to a business career after their athletic days are over, Bailey did it the other way around. In his early 20s he became a successful marketing consultant and manager of investment portfolios. He turned to track and field only at the ripe age of 23, relatively old for a newcomer to sprinting. He was selected as a reserve for the Canadian 4 × 100m squad in the 1993 World Championships but, to his irritation, did not get to run. Determined to improve, he spent 1994 training in Baton Rouge. However, he was not selected for the 100m at the 1994 Commonwealth Games because he did not return for the Canadian trials. He finally broke 10 seconds in April 1995 with 9.99. A month later he had to undergo knee surgery on a torn knee ligament but

Donovan Bailey, Canada (100m).

made a remarkable recovery to win the 100m in 9.97 at the World Championships three months later.

For the Atlanta Olympics, the favorites were Namibia's Frank Fredericks and Trinidad's Ato Boldon, who won their semifinals in 9.94 and 9.93, respectively. The final was plagued by three false starts, two of which led to the disqualification of defending champion Linford Christie. At the fourth attempt Fredericks and Boldon were in the lead at 60 meters, but Bailey accelerated past them both to win in 9.84 seconds.

Bailey got as much if not more delight from the Canadian victory over the U.S. in the 4 × 100m relay seven days later. The U.S. camp was distracted by an argument over whether to include Carl Lewis on the team. The idea that Canada might win anyway was not considered.

Conclusions

The men's 100m world record has improved only 7.17 percent since 1912, the smallest improvement of any of the athletic disciplines. This suggests that human beings can't get much faster over the sprints. However, there yet may be further refinements in track surfaces or footwear technology. Improvements in the sprint records may also come about if electronic timing down to 0.001 second is introduced. This more precise timing already takes place in swimming and has been used at some athletic meets.

Five All-Time Fastest: Men's 100m			(Wind)
Donovan Bailey (CAN)	9.84	1996	+0.7
Leroy Burrell (USA)	9.85	1994	+1.2
Carl Lewis (USA)	9.86	1991	+1.2
Frank Fredericks (NAM)	9.86	1996	-0.4
Linford Christie (GBR)	9.87	1993	+0.3
Prediction	*9.79*	*2015*	

Top Three: Men's 100m

GOLD MEDAL:	**Carl Lewis (USA)**
SILVER MEDAL:	**Bob Hayes (USA)**
BRONZE MEDAL:	**Jesse Owens (USA)**

For the first half of this century the 200m race (and the 220 yards, which measures 201.17 meters) was run over both curved and straight courses. In 1951 the IAAF decided only to recognize world records set on a curved track as part of a 400m circuit. This means that times run in the first half of the century are no longer recognized for world record purposes. So athletes such as Jesse Owens, who ran 20.7 at the Berlin Olympics, are no longer in the record books for the 200m.

Only 17 athletes have run 200m in under 20 seconds. The first was Tommie Smith (USA), who ran 19.83 measured by electronic timing at the Mexico City Olympics in 1968. As with the top 100m sprinters, the list is dominated by black athletes from the United States, Africa, and Jamaica.

Altogether, 14 athletes have set or equaled the world record 22 times. There have been seven Olympic champions among them: Stanfield, Morrow, Berruti, Carr, Smith, Mennea, and Johnson.

Men's World Records for 200m

Record time	Record holder	Location	Date
20.6	Andy Stanfield (USA)	Philadelphia, USA	26 May 1951
20.6	Andy Stanfield (USA)	Los Angeles, USA	28 Jun 1952
20.6	Thane Baker (USA)	Bakersfield, USA	23 Jun 1956
20.6	Bobby Morrow (USA)	Melbourne, Australia	27 Nov 1956
20.6	Manfred Germar (FRG)	Wuppertal, West Germany	1 Oct 1958
20.6	Ray Norton (USA)	Berkeley, USA	19 Mar 1960
20.6	Ray Norton (USA)	Philadelphia, USA	30 Apr 1960
20.5	Peter Radford (GBR)	Wolverhampton, England	28 May 1960
20.5	Stonewall Johnson (USA)	Stanford, USA	2 Jul 1960
20.5	Ray Norton (USA)	Stanford, USA	2 Jul 1960
20.5	Livio Berruti (ITA)	Rome, Italy	3 Sep 1960
20.5	Livio Berruti (ITA)	Rome, Italy	3 Sep 1960
20.5	Otis Drayton (USA)	Walnut, USA	23 Jun 1962
20.3	Henry Carr (USA)	Tempe, USA	23 Mar 1963
20.2	Henry Carr (USA)	Tempe, USA	4 Apr 1964
20.0	Tommie Smith (USA)	Sacramento, USA	11 Jun 1966
19.83	Tommie Smith (USA)	Mexico City, Mexico	16 Oct 1968
19.8	Don Quarrie (JAM)	Cali, Colombia	3 Aug 1971
19.8	Don Quarrie (JAM)	Eugene, USA	7 Jun 1975
19.72	Pietro Mennea (ITA)	Mexico City, Mexico	12 Sep 1979
19.66	Michael Johnson (USA)	Atlanta, USA	23 Jun 1996
19.32	Michael Johnson (USA)	Atlanta, USA	1 Aug 1996

Andy Stanfield (United States, 1927–1985)

| 20.6 | Philadelphia, USA | 26 May 1951 |
| 20.6 | Los Angeles, USA | 28 Jun 1952 |

Andy Stanfield was recognized as the first official world record holder over 200m on a curved track. He set the record twice, first at the ICAAAA championships in 1951 and once again at the U.S. Olympic trials in 1952. Nicknamed "Handy Andy," he came from Jersey City, New Jersey. He studied at Lincoln High School, then had a stretch in the army, and finally graduated from Seton Hall University. Stanfield was AAU 100m champion in 1949 and 200m champion in 1949, 1952, and 1953.

At the 1952 Olympics he was simply too good and won in 20.7 from two other U.S. sprinters, Thane Baker and James Gathers (both 20.8). He was also part of the winning 4 × 100m relay. He returned to the Olympics in 1956, hoping to be the first man to win the Olympic 200m title twice. It wasn't to be: Bobby Morrow won in 20.6, with Stanfield second in 20.7 and Thane Baker third in 20.9.

Stanfield died at age 57 after a long illness.

The three medalists in the 1956 Olympic 200m, all from the United States, all 200m world record holders: Thane Baker, *left*, bronze; Bobby Morrow (100m and 200m world record holder), *center*, gold; and Andy Stanfield, silver.

Thane Baker   (United States, b. 1931)

20.6   **Bakersfield, USA**   **23 Jun 1956**

Thane Baker was second in the 200m at the 1952 Helsinki Olympics, running in lane 6. Four years later he was still in top form, and at the AAU Championships he ran 20.6 to equal the world record. He was picked for his second Olympics in Melbourne.

A graduate of Kansas State University, he had hopes of improving on his Helsinki placing. Unfortunately, when the lane allocations were given out for the 200m final, he once again drew lane 6. He was so upset that he put his starting blocks in back-to-front, causing a delay.

Bobby Morrow was in such fine form at this stage, it seems unlikely Baker could have denied him victory even in a favorable lane. In the end, Baker came in third. However, he also ran in the 100m at the Melbourne Olympics and came in a surprise second to Bobby Morrow—a surprise because Ira Murchison was considered the number two U.S. sprinter over 100m. Baker finally got his gold medal as part of the winning U.S. 4 × 100m relay team.

After retirement from track and field Baker became a purchasing agent for Mobil Oil in Dallas, Texas.

Bobby Morrow   (United States, b. 1935)

20.6   **Melbourne, Australia**   **27 Nov 1956**

Bobby Morrow has been described in more detail in the 100m chapter. In 1956 everything went right for him; he won the Olympic 100m and 200m events and was part of the 4 × 100m relay team that won the gold medal. In the 200m final he equaled the world record.

Manfred Germar   (West Germany, b. 1935)

20.6   **Wuppertal, West Germany**   **1 Oct 1958**

Manfred Germar was one of the top European sprinters for much of the 1950s. He was German 100m champion from 1956-59 and again in 1961 and 200m champion from 1956-59 and 1961-62. In 1958 he equaled the world record in Wuppertal with 20.6.

Germar attended the 1956 Melbourne Olympics and came in fifth in the final of the 100m. In the 4 × 100m relay the German team came in third. He was undefeated in the 200m from 1956 until July 1960, but that record is not as impressive as it looks, as he rarely competed against top U.S. sprinters during that time. At the Rome Olympics he was fifth in his heat of the 100m and third in his heat of the 200m, and he did not progress to further rounds.

Manfred Germar, West Germany (200m).

Ray Norton   (United States, b. 1937)

20.6	**Berkeley, USA**	**19 Mar 1960**
20.6	**Philadelphia, USA**	**30 Apr 1960**
20.5	**Stanford, USA**	**2 Jul 1960**

Norton has been described in the chapter on the 100m champions. He had won the Pan-American 100m and 200m in 1959 and showed top form in the first half of 1960. He set three world record times between March and July 1960: two at 20.6 and one at 20.5.

The Rome Olympics were held at the end of August. Perhaps it was the summer heat that year in Rome, said to be the worst in 50 years, that prevented many athletes from reproducing their real form. Whatever the reason, he finished sixth in both the 100m and 200m finals.

Peter Radford   (Great Britain, b. 1939)

20.5   **Wolverhampton, England**   **28 May 1960**

Peter Radford's career as an athlete is remarkable in that he spent two years as a child in a wheelchair because of a kidney disease. Nonetheless, he emerged as a highly promising sprinting talent. He sported a beard while running as a schoolboy. In the Olympic year of 1960 he astonished the spectators by breaking the 200m world record in an obscure meet in England.

A restriction English athletes faced in gaining international experience was the rigid policy adopted by their aging athletic officials. Radford had hoped to travel to the United

Peter Radford, Great Britain (200m).

States to race the top U.S. sprinters, but officials vetoed the trip on the ground that he had a commitment to his local club.

At the Olympics Radford did not get past the semifinal stage of the 200m but was a finalist in the 100m. He finished strongly to cross the finish line in third place, behind Armin Hary and Dave Sime (USA). The electronic times were 10.32, 10.35, and 10.42.

Later in life he became a professor of physical education at the University of Glasgow. In 1993, unhappy with the performance of officials at the British Athletic Federation, he led a successful revolt and took the position of chairman.

Stone Johnson   (United States, 1940-1963)

20.5   **Stanford, USA**   **2 Jul 1960**

"Stone" Johnson was a graduate of Grambling State University, Louisiana. At the 1960 U.S. Olympic trials he ran a brilliant 20.5 in a heat, defeating Ray Norton and Bobby Morrow in the process. This time equaled the world record. In the final, 50 minutes later, Norton won, also equaling the world record. Johnson was second in 20.8. At the Rome Olympics he couldn't quite reproduce his world record form and finished fifth in 20.8, one position ahead of Norton.

In 1963, while playing football for Kansas City, he died after breaking his neck in a freak accident during a preseason game.

Stone Johnson, United States (200m).

Livio Berruti   (Italy, b. 1930)

| 20.5 | Rome, Italy | 3 Sep 1960 (Semifinal) |
| 20.5 | Rome, Italy | 3 Sep 1960 (Final) |

Livio Berruti achieved the ultimate triumph in track and field: winning an Olympic gold medal in front of his own people and running a world record time twice in the process. He was a graduate in chemistry from the University of Padua. He was nearsighted and al-

Livio Berruti, Italy (200m), Olympic 200m champion, Rome 1960.

ways ran in dark glasses. He won the Italian 100m and 200m titles from 1957-62. By 1960 he was beating the top U.S. sprinters.

He reached his peak of condition at the Rome Olympics. Both semifinal and final of the 200m were held on the same afternoon, less than three hours apart. In his semifinal he beat a top field that included Ray Norton, Stone Johnson, and Peter Radford, recording 20.5 seconds to equal the world record.

A wildly enthusiastic Italian crowd watched the final, held at 6 P.M. (1800 hours). Berruti was always strong on the curve, and he led into the straight by 1 meter. There was a fast finish by Lester Carney (USA) but Berruti kept his form all the way to the tape, despite a last desperate lunge by Carney. Berruti recorded another 20.5; Carney was second in 20.6. The Italian crowd went berserk, cheering nonstop for five minutes. They set newspapers alight and held them up like flaming torches. At the medal ceremony the young girl carrying his gold medal burst into tears. Livio Berruti was the first non-North American to win the Olympic 200m.

After such a triumph the rest of his career was inevitably something of an anticlimax. At the 1964 Olympics he finished fifth in the 200m. He now has a career in advertising and public relations.

Otis Drayton   (United States, b. 1939)

| 20.5 | Walnut, USA | 23 Jun 1962 |

Otis Drayton was a graduate of Villanova University in Pennsylvania. He and Henry Carr dominated 200m running in the early 1960s. Drayton won the U.S. AAU 200m title in 1961 and 1962 and dead-heated in 1963 with Carr. He achieved his world record at the 1962 AAU Championships in the Mount San Antonio College Stadium in Walnut, California.

By 1964 Henry Carr was in the ascendancy, but Drayton won the U.S. Olympic trials. However, at the Tokyo Olympics Carr was able to reverse the result, winning in 20.3 to Drayton's 20.5.

Drayton was selected for the 4 × 100m relay, while Carr was picked for the 4 × 400m relay. Both relays resulted in U.S. victories in world record times.

Later in life Drayton went on to a career as assistant counsel to the governor of New Jersey.

Henry Carr   (United States, b. 1942)

| 20.3 | Tempe, USA | 23 Mar 1963 |
| 20.2 | Tempe, USA | 4 Apr 1964 |

Henry Carr created a lasting impression of supremacy at the Tokyo Olympics in the 200m, much as Bob Hayes had in the 100m. Carr was born in Alabama and attended Arizona

State University. His two world records, both at university meets in Tempe, Arizona, ultimately brought the world record down by 0.3 second, a huge reduction in a sprint.

His career as a sprinter peaked to perfection for the 1964 Olympics. Carr dead-heated the 1963 AAU 200m title with Otis Drayton and won it out-right in 1964. He was beaten by Drayton in the 1964 U.S. Olympic trials, but he paced himself effectively through the preliminary rounds at the Olympics at Tokyo. In the final he overtook Drayton early and won 20.3 to 20.5. He ran in the 4 × 400m relay at these Games and led the U.S. team to victory in a new world record to earn his second gold medal.

After the 1964 Olympics, he played football be-tween 1965-67 with the New York Giants and later the Detroit Lions with moderate success.

Henry Carr, United States (200m),
Olympic 200m champion, Tokyo 1964.

Tommie Smith (United States, b. 1944)

| 20.0 | Sacramento, USA | 11 Jun 1966 |
| 19.83 | Mexico City, Mexico | 16 Oct 1968 |

Tommie Smith is well known for his highly politicized demonstration on the victory stand at the Mexico City Olympics after the 200m final, when he and countryman John Carlos gave a closed fist Black Power salute. That remains one of the enduring images of the 1968 Olympics.

A student at San Jose State University in California (along with 400m champion Lee Evans), Smith was much influenced by the civil rights movement in the United States in the 1960s. He rejected the idea that he was merely the "fastest nigger on campus," as he put it. In a 1967 interview for *Track and Field News* he said that he would give up track and field in a minute to "die for my people." He and Evans contemplated a boycott of the Mexico City Olympics by black athletes as a way of highlighting their agenda. In the end, both men attended the Games, though it was Smith who made the most striking gesture, which effectively ended his career.

Smith was brilliant over 100m, 200m, and 400m and had set a 200m world record in 1966. The 1968 Olympic 200m final was widely believed to be a contest between Smith and John Carlos, also from San Jose State. In the final, Smith turned on his "Tommie-jets," his ability to accelerate even faster while running at speed. Carlos was narrowly defeated for second place by Australia's Peter Norman.

The demonstration on the victory stand brought him the cold, hard fury of the athletic establishment. Carlos and Smith were suspended from the Olympics and ordered to leave the Olympic village.

Both men endured difficulties back in the United States, and the marriages of both broke up. Tommie Smith played three seasons of football with the Cincinnati Bengals. He became an athletic director at Oberlin College, Ohio and later in Los Angeles.

Don Quarrie   (Jamaica, b. 1951)

| 19.8 | Cali, Colombia | 3 Aug 1971 |
| 19.8 | Eugene, USA | 7 Jun 1975 |

Don Quarrie's career has been outlined in the chapter on 100m champions. To a degree, he was more successful over 200m, and that is where he won his Olympic gold medal (Montreal 1976). His first world record over 200m took place at the 1971 Pan-American Games in Cali, Colombia, situated 1046 meters (3432 feet) above sea level, which is helpful for fast times over short distances. The second world record took place four years later in Eugene, Oregon, at the Prefontaine Classic. In an extremely tight finish Quarrie just passed Steve Williams (USA) to record another 19.8.

Pietro Mennea   (Italy, b. 1952)

| 19.72 | Mexico City, Mexico | 12 Sep 1979 |

Pietro Mennea ran for more than a decade at the top levels of international track and field. This was partly because he chose to race sparingly each season. He competed as an international from 1971-84, and was Italian 200m champion 10 times and 100m champion 3 times. He competed in the 200m at five Olympics: 1972 (where he came in third), 1976 (fourth), 1980 (first), 1984 (seventh), and 1988 (went out in the heats). Mennea was also European 200m champion in 1974 and 1978.

His victory in the 1980 Olympics showed exquisite timing. Alan Wells of Scotland, already the winner of the 100m, took an early lead. Mennea did not lose his nerve, but chased him down the final straight. He caught him in the last 20 meters to win 20.19 to 20.21.

In 1979 he set himself the target of the world record. For the attempt, Mennea chose to make use of the high altitude at the World University Games in Mexico City. In the final he won in a record 19.72 (with the help

Pietro Mennea, Italy (200m), Olympic 200m champion, Moscow 1980.

of a 1.8 meter per second wind behind him). That proved to be a most durable record, even allowing for the altitude factor: It lasted almost 17 years.

Mennea in his long career had his share of disputes with other athletes and with the Italian athletic authorities. His decision to run only a few meets a year possibly upset some promoters, but no doubt contributed to his longevity. He currently runs his family's sportswear company.

Michael Johnson (United States, b. 1967)

| 19.66 | Atlanta, USA | 23 Jun 1996 |
| 19.32 | Atlanta, USA | 1 Aug 1996 |

Michael Johnson, United States (200m).

It is now perhaps surprising to reflect that at the beginning of 1996 Michael Johnson, aged 28, had not won any Olympic medal at either 200m or 400m, nor had he set a world record at either event. Yet such was his stature in both events that he single-handedly pushed the International Olympic Committee and the International Amateur Athletic Federation to change the Olympic program merely to give him an easier run at both events. In the original schedule, the heats, quarterfinals, semifinals, and finals of the 200m and 400m were intermingled. After his lobbying the timetable was changed. All 400m races were run first, then after a rest day all 200m races were run.

A student of marketing at Baylor University in Texas, he had run at the 1988 U.S. Olympic trials and finished seventh in a heat, plagued by a stress fracture to his calf bone. From that time on he became the master of both events, a rare and difficult double. He rarely lost at 200m, and he has not lost a final in the 400m since 1989. He was world champion of the 200m (1991), the 400m (1993), and both in 1995. However, at the 1992 Olympics he was plagued by stomach illness and went out in the semifinals of the 200m. (He was not contesting the 400m at the time.)

At the 1996 Olympic trials Johnson finally did what he had been threatening to do for some years. He removed Pietro Mennea's 17-year-old 200m record from the books with

19.66 seconds. One of the features of his running style that has captured public imagination is his upright stance and his minimal knee lift, not textbook form, but obviously effective.

Having personally influenced the change in the Olympic program to aim for the 200m-400m double, he was under enormous public pressure to achieve victories in both. At the Olympics, watched by his parents and running in specially prepared gold shoes, he duly won the 400m in 43.49, an Olympic record. Four days later Johnson exceeded even his own most optimistic prediction when he demolished his six-week-old 200m record in an awesome, almost brutal display of speed. The time of 19.32 seconds left statisticians gasping in disbelief. It is so much faster than anything previously dreamed of that it should last at least a generation. Michael Johnson's two crushing victories made him the star of the 1996 Olympics.

Conclusions

Many of the points made about the 100m world record seemed to apply to the 200m: Sprinters aren't getting that much faster. That statement seemed fairly noncontroversial until Michael Johnson's mind-boggling time of 19:32 at the Atlanta Olympics. It is hard to believe that this record will be approached within a generation.

Six All-Time Fastest: Men's 200m			(Wind)
Michael Johnson (USA)	19.32	1996	+0.4
Frank Fredericks (NAM)	19.68	1996	+0.4
Pietro Mennea (ITA)	19.72 A	1979	+1.8
Michael Marsh (USA)	19.73	1992	−0.2
Carl Lewis (USA)	19.75	1983	+1.5
Joe DeLuach (USA)	19.75	1988	+1.7
Prediction	*19.32*	*2015*	

Top Three: Men's 200m

GOLD MEDAL:	Michael Johnson (USA)
SILVER MEDAL:	Tommie Smith (USA)
BRONZE MEDAL:	Henry Carr (USA)

Many records set in this event in the early part of this century actually took place over the English distance of 440 yards. This is marginally longer than 400 meters—402.34 meters—which is worth about an extra 0.26 second. From 1976 only electronic timing for this event was recognized, in $\frac{1}{100}$ (0.01) second. The distance is one circuit of a modern stadium.

The 400m is too far a distance to allow a straight sprint. Accordingly, pace judgment in this event is critical, especially the avoidance of starting out either too fast or too slow. The end effort required makes it a particularly punishing event.

White athletes feature in the 400m records, but only in the first 65 years of the 20th century. The top 400m times for the last 30 years have been dominated by African Americans. Only seven athletes have ever run under 44 seconds for 400m, and all are African Americans.

Nineteen athletes have set or equaled the 400m world record. Seven of them were also Olympic 400m champions: Long, Carr, Williams, Rhoden, Davis, Larrabee, and Evans.

Men's World Records for 400m

Record time	Record holder	Location	Date
47.8	Maxey Long (USA)	New York, USA	29 Sep 1900
47.4	Edward "Ted" Meredith (USA)	Cambridge, USA	27 May 1916
47.0	Emerson "Bud" Spencer (USA)	Stanford, USA	12 May 1928
46.4	Ben Eastman (USA)	Stanford, USA	26 Mar 1932
46.2	William Carr (USA)	Los Angeles, USA	5 Aug 1932
46.1	Archie Williams (USA)	Chicago, USA	19 Jun 1936
46.0	Rudolf Harbig (GER)	Frankfurt am Main, Germany	12 Aug 1939
46.0	Grover Klemmer (USA)	Philadelphia, USA	29 Jun 1941
46.0	Herb McKenley (JAM)	Berkeley, USA	5 Jun 1948
45.9	Herb McKenley (JAM)	Milwaukee, USA	2 Jul 1948
45.8	George Rhoden (JAM)	Eskilstuna, Sweden	22 Aug 1950
45.4	Louis Jones (USA)	Mexico City, Mexico	18 Mar 1955
45.2	Louis Jones (USA)	Los Angeles, USA	30 Jun 1956
44.9	Otis Davis (USA)	Rome, Italy	6 Sep 1960
44.9	Carl Kaufmann (FRG)	Rome, Italy	6 Sep 1960
44.9	Adolph Plummer (USA)	Tempe, USA	25 May 1963
44.9	Mike Larrabee (USA)	Los Angeles, USA	12 Sep 1964
44.5	Tommie Smith (USA)	San Jose, USA	20 May 1967
44.1	Larry James (USA)	Echo Summit, USA	14 Sep 1968
43.86	Lee Evans (USA)	Mexico City, Mexico	18 Oct 1968
43.29	Harry "Butch" Reynolds (USA)	Zürich, Switzerland	17 Aug 1988

Maxey Long (United States, 1878–1959)

47.8   **New York, USA**   **29 Sep 1900**

Maxey Long was a student at Columbia University in New York. He was the U.S. AAU champion in the 440 yards from 1898-1900 and the first official world record holder in the 400m.

At the 1900 Paris Olympics the final of the 400m was held on a Sunday, and three finalists refused to run on religious grounds. Only three competitors lined up for the final: Long, William Holland (USA), and Ernest Schultz (Denmark). Long raced in the colors of Columbia University: blue and white. In those days it was not necessary to race in national colors. The colors were similar to those of the Racing Club of France, so many of the French spectators thought a French athlete was leading and cheered Long all the way home. He won in 49.4 seconds.

Two months later he ran the distance in New York over a 440-yard course on a track 352 yards in circumference. In a handicap race Long's time of 47.8 seconds was the first 400m record.

Maxey Long, United States (400m),
1900 Olympic 400m champion.

Edward "Ted" Meredith (United States, 1891–1957)

47.4   **Cambridge, USA**   **27 May 1916**

Ted Meredith, United States (400m, 800m), 1912 Olympic 800m champion.

Ted Meredith was a graduate of the University of Pennsylvania in Philadelphia. He was successful at both 400m and 800m. At the 1912 Olympics in Stockholm he finished fourth in the 400m. In the 800m he upset the defending champion Mel Sheppard, winning in a new world record time of 1:51.9. He was also part of the 4 × 400m relay team that won the gold medal.

Four years later he beat Maxey Long's long-standing 400m record: In a race at the Harvard University Stadium, on a course with one turn, he took 0.4 second off Long's record.

In 1916 he graduated with a BS in economics from the University of Pennsylvania. During World War I he became a captain in the U.S. Aviation Corps. He returned to the Olympics in 1920 with less success. In the 400m he was fourth in the semifinal; the United States 4 × 400m relay team, of which he was a member, came in fourth.

He later coached at his old university and also coached the Olympic teams of Cuba and Czechoslovakia in the 1930s. He went on to a career as an investment broker and held a position with the Internal Revenue Service in his later years.

Emerson "Bud" Spencer   (United States, 1906–1985)

47.0   **Stanford, USA**   **12 May 1928**

A graduate of Stanford University, Bud Spencer usually ran in sunglasses, like Charlie Greene and Livio Berruti years later. He was the NCAA champion over 440 yards in 1928.

At a meet in Stanford, California in May 1928 he took 0.4 second off the record when he ran the full 440 yards distance (402.34 meters). However, when the U.S. Olympic trials came around, he could not reproduce this form and was selected only for the 4 × 400m relay. In Amsterdam the U.S. team duly won the gold medal in this event.

Spencer coached for 2 years, then had 30 years as a sportswriter. He coauthored one of the classic books on coaching, *Champions in the Making* (1968), with Payton Jordan.

Ben Eastman   (United States, b. 1911)

46.4   **Stanford, USA**   **26 Mar 1932**

Ben Eastman was a student at Stanford University and was coached by one of the doyens of U.S. coaches, Richard "Dink" Templeton. Eastman was advised by Templeton that the 400m record was one of the "softest" in the books, so he made an attempt on the record in a competition between the Los Angeles Athletic Club and Stanford University. Templeton was hospitalized at the time and gave his athlete last minute instructions by telephone from his sick bed.

The 440 yards/400m race had been generally regarded as an event in which an athlete cruised during the middle part of the race to save energy for the final sprint. Templeton urged a more sustained effort throughout. The tactics worked, and Eastman reduced the record by 0.6 second with 46.4.

This was early in 1932, an Olympic year. Unfortunately for Eastman, a faster athlete was just about to emerge, William Carr of Pennsylvania, who went on to win the gold medal at the Los Angeles Games in 46.2, a new world record. Eastman came in second with 46.4.

After the Olympics Eastman turned to running the 800m and in 1934 set a world record in this event. In 1936, however, he finished fifth at the U.S. Olympic trials.

William Carr   (United States, 1909–1966)

46.2   **Los Angeles, USA**   **5 Aug 1932**

William Carr, United States (400m), *left,* defeating Ben Eastman, United States (400m, 800m).

William Carr emerged from nowhere in 1932 to achieve Olympic success and set a world record. The rivalry between Carr (a student at the University of Pennsylvania) and Eastman had as much to do with the rivalry between their respective coaches, Lawson Robertson and Dink Templeton. Eastman had set a world record for the event in March 1932. Nonetheless, in their three head-to-head clashes, Carr won all three:

The ICAAAA championships	47.0 to 47.2
The U.S. Olympic trials	46.9 to 47.1
The Los Angeles Olympics	46.2 to 46.4

On each occasion, Eastman led out, but Carr came from behind to win. Carr's Los Angeles Olympic win was a new world record, taking 0.2 second off the record Eastman set five months earlier.

In 1933 Carr graduated with a BS in economics. But in the same year he was badly injured in a motor vehicle accident and sustained a broken pelvis and fractured ankles. He recovered but never ran again. At his peak he was nicknamed the "Fastest Carr in America."

During World War II he served as a commander in naval intelligence. After the war he held positions with Pan American Airways and later was a vice president of a company that manufactured highway safety equipment. He died in Tokyo in 1966.

Archie Williams   (United States, 1915–1993)

46.1   **Chicago, USA**   **19 Jun 1936**

Archie Williams was the first great black 400m runner. He emerged from nowhere in an Olympic year to achieve the highest honors in the sport, a world record, and an Olympic gold medal.

Totally unfavored, he ran his world record (46.1) in a heat of the NCAA championships in Chicago. He had no idea he was going that fast; his only objective was to qualify for the next round.

At the Berlin Olympics he won the 400m final in 46.5. Neither Williams nor the 400m bronze medalist, Jimmy Lu Valle, were selected for the U.S. 4 × 400m relay team. The end result was that the U.S. team came in second to Great Britain.

After his athletic days Williams had a number of distinguished careers. He obtained degrees in mechanical engineering from the University of California (Berkeley) and in aeronautical engineering from the Air Force Engineering School. During World War II he was a flying instructor for the Air Force, and during the Korean War he flew missions in B-29 bombers. Later in life he was active in teaching computer studies. Interviewed in 1984, when he was 68, he said he thought he was good for another 10 years. Archie Williams died in 1993.

Archie Williams, United States (400m), 1936 Olympic 400m champion.

Rudolf Harbig   (Germany, 1913–1944)

46.0   **Frankfurt am Main, Germany**   **12 Aug 1939**

Rudolf Harbig was the first European to hold the world record over 400m. He was part of the German team at the 1936 Berlin Olympics, but he had not yet hit his peak and was sixth in a heat of the 800m. He was also part of the German 4 × 400m relay team, which came in third.

By 1938 he had reached his full powers as an athlete. He won the 1938 800m title at the European Championships in Vienna by 1.2 seconds, winning in 1:50.6.

In the summer of 1939, as World War II approached, he set two classic world records. In Milan he set a world record for the 800m that was to last 16 years. Four weeks later in Frankfurt he attacked the 400m world record and ran 46.0. This record lasted just under 10 years.

Three weeks after this race World War II commenced. Harbig ran occasionally in the early years of the war, then served in the German army. In 1944, under obscure circumstances, he died on the Eastern Front fighting Soviet forces.

Grover Klemmer   (United States, b. 1921)

46.0   **Philadelphia, USA**   **29 Jun 1941**

Grover Klemmer was a graduate of the University of California and won the U.S. 400m AAU title in 1940 and 1941. It was in the 1941 championships that he set his world record. It was a highly competitive race, with the first three men all home within 0.1 second of each other. In those days the 440-yard/400m race was not run in lanes. In this particular race the first three who placed—Klemmer, Hubert Kerns, and Clifford Bourland—all drifted away from the inside lane and finished the race on the outside lane, next to the brick wall of the grandstand. They obviously ran considerably farther than was required. The result was Klemmer (46.0), Kerns (46.1), and Bourland (46.1).

Klemmer went on to a career as head of physical education at the City College in San Francisco. He was a leading football referee in the NFL (1962-82) and the USFL (1983-85). He later described his greatest achievement in his life as being married to the same woman since 1944.

Herb McKenley   (Jamaica, b. 1922)

| 46.0 | Berkeley, USA | 5 Jun 1948 |
| 45.9 | Milwaukee, USA | 2 Jul 1948 |

Herb McKenley was the first of a great trio of Jamaican quarter-milers who emerged in the post-war era, the others being Arthur Wint and George Rhoden. McKenley studied at Boston College and later at the University of Illinois. He won both the 220- and 440-yards NCAA titles in 1946-1947. The main feature of his running was his "suicidal" fast starts. He usually ran the first 200m in 21 seconds and the second in 25. With this technique he established two world records in mid-1948. He won three AAU titles over 400m (1945, 1947, 1948) and in his third became the first man to run 400m under 46 seconds.

At the 1948 London Olympics, perhaps overconfident, he went out like a bullet on a slow, wet track. He passed the 200m in 21.4 but started to fade in the last 30 meters. He was caught by the long-legged Wint just before the tape, 46.2 to 46.4. At these Games McKenley finished fourth in the 200m. He was also part of the Jamaican 4 × 400m relay team, which failed to finish when Arthur Wint pulled up with a hamstring injury.

Herb McKenley, Jamaica (400m).

Four years later, at the Helsinki Olympics, he ran in the 100m and finished second to Lindy Remigino (USA). Both were electronically timed at 10.79. In the 400m he was determined not to repeat the mistake of going out too hard. Perhaps this time he was too cautious: The new Jamaican star George Rhoden stole the race, with McKenley second for another silver medal. Both men were timed at 45.9.

His final chance for an Olympic gold medal came in the 4 × 400m relay, as the Jamaicans took on the United States. It was David versus Goliath, but in a famous victory the Jamaican team won by 0.1 second, which caused wild celebrations back in Jamaica.

George Rhoden   (Jamaica, b. 1926)

| 45.8 | Eskilstuna, Sweden | 22 Aug 1950 |

Jamaican George Rhoden initially lived under the shadow of his countrymen Arthur Wint and Herb McKenley. In the 1948 Olympics he went out in the semifinals of the 400m, while Wint went on to become the gold medalist in the event, with McKenley second. McKenley and Rhoden lived in the United States, while Wint resided in England.

Herb McKenley was the U.S. AAU quarter-mile champion in 1945, 1947, and 1948, while Rhoden won in the years 1949-51. His world record came in an international meet in Sweden in 1950, and he was the next man after McKenley to run under 46 seconds for the distance. From then on, he and McKenley exchanged victories. At the 1952 Helsinki Olympics Rhoden saved himself for the 400m, whereas McKenley warmed up by entering the 100m and finished a close second.

Remarkably, at the 1952 Olympics Wint and McKenley both reversed their 400m tactics of 1948: Wint, who had held back in 1948, sprinted away at the start, while McKenley held back. After 200m Wint ran out of steam, and Rhoden moved past him. McKenley gained at the finish, but too late—Rhoden won by half a stride. Both men were timed at 45.9. Rhoden was also part of the famous Jamaican 4 × 400m victory over the U.S. team.

George Rhoden, Jamaica (400m), 1952 Olympic 400m champion.

Louis Jones   (United States, b. 1932)

| 45.4 | Mexico City, Mexico | 18 Mar 1955 |
| 45.2 | Los Angeles, USA | 30 Jun 1956 |

Louis Jones was the first athlete to demonstrate the positive effect of high altitude on performance in explosive events (such as sprints and horizontal jumps). He competed at the 1955 Pan-American Games at Mexico City, which is 2248 meters (7375 feet) above sea level. The rarefied air helped him to storm home in a new world record of 45.4 seconds, 0.4 second under the old record. Jones was exhausted by his effort and lay on the track for some minutes, a victim of the thin atmosphere.

Jones proved it was no fluke by improving on the record in June 1956 at the U.S. Olympic trials in Los Angeles. He took another 0.2 second off the record. But somewhere between the U.S. Olympic trials in June and the Olympics in Melbourne in November he lost his form. He finished fifth in the 400m final, 1.4

Louis Jones, United States (400m).

seconds behind winner Charlie Jenkins, also of the United States. However, he had the consolation of being part of the U.S. 4 × 400m relay team that won the gold medal.

Otis Davis (United States, b. 1932)

44.9 **Rome, Italy** **6 Sep 1960**

Otis Davis, United States (400m), *left,* just defeats Carl Kaufmann, West Germany, in the 1960 Olympic 400m at Rome. Both men were timed at 44.9, the first race for the distance under 45 seconds.

Otis Davis was a student at the University of Oregon and initially showed promise as a basketball player. Davis was persuaded to try the high jump but then moved on to the quarter-mile at the relatively advanced age of 26. Showing remarkable improvement, he scraped onto the U.S. team for the 1960 Olympics when he came in third at the U.S. trials.

Davis improved further and won the semifinal in 45.5 seconds. The West German Carl Kaufmann won the other semifinal in 45.7. In the final the South African Mal Spence took off in a suicidal sprint over the first 200m, with Davis and Kaufmann about 6 meters behind. At this point Davis made a sustained burst over the next 100m and entered the finishing straight some 7 meters ahead of Kaufmann, who had passed the struggling Spence. In a dramatic last 100m, Kaufmann clawed back the gap, with Davis hanging on grimly for the tape. They went over the line together, inseparable, and were both given the same time: 44.9 seconds. However, a photo finish revealed that Davis had been ahead by a few centimeters. This race was the first in which the 400m had been run under 45 seconds.

Davis collected a second gold medal when the U.S. team won the 4 × 400m relay; Kaufmann once again had to be content with the silver medal.

Carl Kaufmann (West Germany, b. 1936)

44.9 **Rome, Italy** **6 Sep 1960**

As just described in Davis's biography, Otis Davis and Carl Kaufmann both broke the existing world record in their epic race at the 1960 Rome Olympics. Both men were given the time of 44.9 seconds. Photos showed that Davis finished first by a few centimeters. In the 4 × 400m relay, in which the U.S. team defeated West Germany, Kaufmann won another silver medal.

Kaufmann won the German 200m championship at age 19 in 1955 and the 400m title in the years 1958-1960. He had been fourth at the 1958 European Championships in the 400m.

Apart from his athletic career, Kaufmann is a man of many talents. Born in New York, he was very heavily involved with the theater. Before the Rome Olympics he had already released two records as a tenor. He went on to a long career as a general manager and artistic director of Die Kauze (The Owl), a theater in Karlsruhe, Germany, and has been involved in opera, film, and television productions for many years, both in Germany and abroad.

Adolph Plummer   (United States, b. 1938)

44.9   Tempe, USA   25 May 1963

Adolph Plummer was a top athlete at both 200m and 400m. In the shorter distance he was AAU champion in 1965. He was a student at the University of New Mexico, where he graduated with a degree in physical education. The special day in his racing career was in 1963, when in a race at Tempe, Arizona, over the slightly longer distance of 440 yards (402.34 meters) he went through the tape at 44.9 seconds. Plummer had hopes for the Tokyo Olympics, but injuries hindered his selection chances and he missed making the team. He went on to a career in education, with 22 years at the Denver public schools before returning to the University of New Mexico as a director of Academic and Student Affairs.

Adolph Plummer, United States (400m).

Mike Larrabee   (United States, b. 1933)

44.9   Los Angeles, USA   12 Sep 1964

Mike Larrabee had been racing since 1956, with good years and bad. He won the AAU title only once, in 1964, when everything fell into place for him.

In his first attempt at the Olympics in 1956 he finished last in the final of the U.S. trials. In 1960 he didn't even make the final of the U.S. trials, finishing fifth in his heat. At the age of 30, in his third attempt to make the Olympic team, he won the U.S. trials in a time equaling the world record. He kept his nerve in the Olympic final when the others went off in a mad rush. In the last 100m he moved from fifth to first to take the gold medal.

Later in life Larrabee attributed his success in 1964 to a much lighter training program than in earlier years. This reduced training came about by an accident: A high school student performing judo accidentally stomach-chopped him, bruising his abdominal muscles. Forced to reduce his training, he found to his astonishment that he was running better than ever. He also realized that he could "kick and win" from the 200m mark. That is what allowed him to win in Tokyo, even though he had been last at the 200m point.

Larrabee went on to a career as a regional distributor for Coors Brewing in California.

Mike Larrabee, United States (400m).

Tommie Smith   (United States, b. 1944)

44.5   **San Jose, USA**   **20 May 1967**

Tommie Smith has been described in the chapter on 200m world record holders. He ran the 400m race on very few occasions, preferring the 200m. He and his friend Lee Evans both attended San Jose State University. They were both world class over 200m and 400m, so their first clash over 400m was awaited with much interest.

Running in sunglasses, Smith allowed Evans to set the pace for the first half of the race. From the halfway point Smith accelerated and inflicted a rare defeat on his colleague. He won by 0.5 second and with his time of 44.5 seconds took 0.4 second off the 400m world record in the process. Despite this success, he didn't race the 400m again but stayed with the 200m.

Tommie Smith, United States (200m, 400m) inflicts a rare defeat on Lee Evans, United States (400m) at San Jose, 1967, in the 400m. In 1968 Evans set a 400m world record that was to last almost 20 years.

Larry James   (United States, b. 1947)

44.1	Echo Summit, USA	14 Sep 1968

Larry James competed at the U.S. Olympic trials at Echo Summit for a place on the 400m team. The race was actually won by Lee Evans, but he was wearing new experimental shoes with brush spikes. These shoes were ruled illegal for record purposes, so Evans's time of 44.0 was not accepted as a new world record. James came in second with 44.1, and his time was recognized as a new world record. The times were helped by the altitude of Echo Summit, 2250 meters (7382 feet) above sea level.

At the Mexico City Olympics, James lined up in the final against Lee Evans and another American, Ron Freeman. Evans was once again triumphant in a close race, with the first two under the 44-second barrier: Evans ran in 43.86, and James in 43.97. Freeman was third in 44.41.

Larry James's major title win was the AAU 400m championship in 1970.

Lee Evans   (United States, b. 1947)

43.86	Mexico City, Mexico	18 Oct 1968

Lee Evans was a student at San Jose State University, California, in the mid-1960s. Apart from a defeat by Tommie Smith at San Jose in 1967, Evans had been supreme over the distance for several years. He was AAU champion in the years 1966-69 and again in 1972. Described by fellow athlete Larry King as knowing "when to party and when to concentrate on training," Evans went into the Mexico City Games as a firm favorite for the 400m title. At the high altitude of Mexico City (2248 meters, or 7375 feet, above sea level) he became the first man to run the 400m in under 44 seconds, recording 43.86, followed by Larry James's 43.97. This record was to last almost 20 years. Evans also won a gold medal in the 4 × 400m relay; the world record time for this event lasted for 24 years.

Although a Black Power advocate, Evans was not as demonstrative as Smith during the victory ceremonies. In fact, this lack of a distinctive protest was viewed with scorn by some black radicals, who felt he had chickened out at this critical moment when millions around the world were watching on television. Because his protest wasn't as high profile as Tommie Smith's, he did not suffer the establishment fury that Smith experienced. He kept running for a few more years and won the 1972 AAU title. He missed out on selection for the individual 400m race at the 1972 Munich Olympics, although he did earn a place on the 4 × 400m relay team. At the Munich Games, however, two U.S. athletes (Vincent Matthews and Wayne Collett) were suspended for showing contempt during the playing of the U.S. national anthem in the 400m victory ceremony. The United States could no longer field a full relay squad, so Evans never got a chance to run.

Evans later spent many years coaching in Africa, mainly in Nigeria.

Harry "Butch" Reynolds   (United States, b. 1964)

43.29	Zürich, Switzerland	17 Aug 1988

Harry "Butch" Reynolds attended Ohio State University, which includes Jesse Owens among its alumni. Reynolds ran in the 1984 U.S. Olympic trials and made it to the semifinals before being eliminated. His next few years were plagued by injuries, but in 1987 he was problem-free and started running some serious times. He was a favorite for the 1987 World Championships but was struck down by diarrhea before the final and finished third.

By mid-1988 he was running times just over 44 seconds. In Zürich, Reynolds finally decided that whatever happened, he would push on through the pain barrier in an attempt to break the 19-year-old record. The result was a startling 43.29, which was more than 0.5 second off the long-standing record. This race was six weeks before the Olympics in Seoul. Perhaps he became overconfident. At the Olympics he allowed Steve Lewis (no relation to Carl) to steal too big a lead. Despite a furious finish, Reynolds could not make up the distance: Lewis came in first (43.87), and Reynolds second (43.93).

Despite these near misses at gold medals, Reynolds was still regarded as the world's premier 400m runner. However, his athletic career changed forever in August 1990 in Monaco, when he was accused of a positive test for anabolic steroids. Reynolds vehemently denied the charges and began a long series of exhaustive appeals all the way to the U.S. Supreme Court to have the verdict overturned because of alleged irregularities in the testing procedure. However, the two-year ban on his career by

Harry "Butch" Reynolds, United States (400m).

the IAAF stood, which meant that he missed out on the 1992 Barcelona Olympics. He subsequently sued the IAAF, and an Ohio judge found in his favor, awarding him $27.3 million. The IAAF, based in Europe, refused to recognize this judgment but eventually appealed, and the original decision in Reynolds's favor was overturned in 1994. Unfortunately for Reynolds, a new generation of top 400m runners, such as Michael Johnson and Quincy Watts, had arrived on the U.S. scene by the time the legal process was exhausted.

In the 1996 Olympics he was unable to finish a 400m semifinal because of leg cramps at midrace.

Conclusions

Lee Evans's 1968 record lasted almost 20 years, and Butch Reynolds's current record (1988), which sliced off a massive 0.57 second, seemed destined for similar longevity. However, the current world record has been approached recently by other athletes, whereas Evans's record seemed quite untouchable for many years. This suggests that the current 400m world record faces further reduction in the not too distant future.

Five All-Time Fastest: Men's 400m		
Butch Reynolds (USA)	43.29	1988
Michael Johnson (USA)	43.39	1995
Quincy Watts (USA)	43.50	1992
Danny Everett (USA)	43.81	1992
Lee Evans (USA)	43.86 A	1968
Prediction	*43.20*	*2015*

Top Three: Men's 400m

GOLD MEDAL:	Lee Evans (USA)
SILVER MEDAL:	Butch Reynolds (USA)
BRONZE MEDAL:	Herb McKenley (JAM)

The 800m is the first of the middle-distance events and is two laps of a modern track circuit. The jump from 400m to the 800m is a clear transition from a near sprint to a run. Pace judgment and tactics become critical. The men's 800m world record has had the fewest improvements of any track event over the years. On four occasions the world record has lasted over a decade. The current record by Sebastian Coe has lasted over 15 years.

The record has been held by 16 men, who have set or equaled the world record 18 times. Only five of the world record holders were also Olympic gold medalists in the event: Meredith, Hampson, Snell, Doubell, and Wottle.

Men's World Records for 800m

Record time	Record holder	Location	Date
1:51.9	Edward "Ted" Meredith (USA)	Stockholm, Sweden	8 Jul 1912
1:51.6	Otto Peltzer (GER)	London, England	3 Jul 1926
1:50.6	Seraphin Martin (FRA)	Paris, France	14 Jul 1928
1:49.8	Thomas Hampson (GBR)	Los Angeles, USA	2 Aug 1932
1:49.8	Ben Eastman (USA)	Princeton, USA	16 Jun 1934
1:49.7	Glenn Cunningham (USA)	Stockholm, Sweden	20 Aug 1936
1:49.6	Elroy Robinson (USA)	New York, USA	11 Jul 1937
1:48.4	Sydney Wooderson (GBR)	London, England	20 Aug 1938
1:46.6	Rudolf Harbig (GER)	Milan, Italy	15 Jul 1939
1:45.7	Roger Moens (BEL)	Oslo, Norway	3 Aug 1955
1:44.3	Peter Snell (NZ)	Christchurch, New Zealand	3 Feb 1962
1:44.3	Ralph Doubell (AUST)	Mexico City, Mexico	15 Oct 1968
1:44.3	David Wottle (USA)	Eugene, USA	1 Jul 1972
1:43.7	Marcello Fiasconaro (ITA)	Milan, Italy	27 Jun 1973
1:43.5	Alberto Juantorena (CUBA)	Montreal, Canada	25 Jul 1976
1:43.4	Alberto Juantorena (CUBA)	Sofia, Bulgaria	21 Aug 1977
1:42.33	Sebastian Coe (GBR)	Oslo, Norway	5 Jul 1979
1:41.73	Sebastian Coe (GBR)	Florence, Italy	10 Jun 1981

Edward "Ted" Meredith (United States, 1892–1957)

1:51.9   Stockholm, Sweden   8 Jul 1912

Ted Meredith has been described in the chapter on the 400m; he was the second athlete to hold the world record in that event. At the 1912 Olympics, at the age of 19, he competed in both the 800m and 400m and placed fourth in the 400m.

In the 800m the favorite was Mel Sheppard, who had been 800m Olympic champion in 1908. In the 1912 final Sheppard set off with an extremely fast pace for those days, 52.4 seconds for the first lap, which is still a respectable pace today. He led all the way, but Meredith made a great finishing burst to catch him in the last 10 meters, winning in world record time. Meredith's winning time of 1:51.9 was accepted as the inaugural world record.

Otto Peltzer   (Germany, 1900-1970)

1:51.6   **London, England**   **3 Jul 1926**

Sera Martin, France (800m) leading Otto Peltzer, Germany (800m, 1500m).

Otto Peltzer was a doctor by profession and was Germany's top middle-distance runner of the 1920s. He won the 800m national title six times between 1923 and 1934, and the 1500m title five years in a row (1922-26). However, injury prevented Peltzer from running in the 1924 Olympics.

In 1926 he was invited to England to compete in the British AAA Championships against Douglas Lowe, the 1924 800m Olympic champion. He followed Lowe through the first lap (54.6), then unleashed a devastating kick in the last 100m to win by 0.4 second in front of Lowe. His time of 1:51.6 took 0.3 second off the world record.

Peltzer also claimed the 1500m world record in 1926, defeating the great Paavo Nurmi in the process. However, in the 1928 Olympics he could not reproduce his world record form, and he went out in the semifinals of the 800m. At the 1932 Olympics he was ninth in the 800m.

Life became more serious when the Nazis came to power in Germany in 1933. Peltzer was a fierce critic of their policies and was arrested three times. Peltzer had infuriated the Nazis by supporting changes to the laws on homosexuality, to which they were deeply opposed. He moved to Norway in 1937 but foolishly returned in 1941 after World War II commenced. On his return he was promptly arrested and spent the next four years in a concentration camp. He was extremely lucky to survive and was finally freed in 1945.

In his later years Peltzer was an inveterate traveler. He spent many years as a coach in India, until his death at age 70. He traveled to China in 1929 and met with Eric Liddell, the 400m gold medalist at the 1924 Olympics and the subject of the film *Chariots of Fire*. At this time Liddell was working as a missionary. In November 1929 in this unlikely setting Liddell and Peltzer had a race over 400m in Tientsin. Liddell is recorded as the winner in 49.1

Séraphin Martin   (France, 1906-1993)

1:50.6   **Paris, France**   **14 Jul 1928**

Séra Martin set his world record on Bastille Day, 1928, and took a second off Peltzer's record. He traveled to the Olympics in Amsterdam a few weeks later with the hopes of all France on his shoulders. Perhaps it was too much of a burden. Douglas Lowe, the defending champion from Great Britain, ran away with the race in 1:51.8. Martin finished well back in sixth place, and French commentators were aghast. It later was revealed that he had severe tonsillitis at the time.

Martin never again repeated his world record performance, though he still dominated the French 800m scene for the next few years. Martin competed at one more Olympics, at Los Angeles in 1932. He made the final but finished well down in eighth place in 1:53.6. Great Britain's Thomas Hampson won with a new world record of 1:49.8. The only person Martin did defeat that day was former world record holder Otto Peltzer. He died in 1993, aged 86.

Thomas Hampson   (Great Britain, 1907–1965)

1:49.8   **Los Angeles, USA**   **2 Aug 1932**

Great Britain had a remarkable run of success in the 800m in the Olympics between the World Wars. The 1920 race was won by Albert Hill, and the 1924 and 1928 gold medals were won by Douglas Lowe. Tom Hampson won in 1932. A student at Oxford, he initially was only a moderate athletic performer. However, a tour of the United States and Canada with a group of athletes from Oxford and Cambridge Universities saw him improve greatly. He went on to become the first champion in the inaugural Empire Games (later the Commonwealth Games) over the 880-yard distance in Hamilton, Canada, winning in 1:52.4.

At the 1932 Los Angeles Olympics he ran a tactical race and refused to be drawn into the hot pace set by Canada's Phil Edwards. At the end of the first lap he was 20 meters behind, in fifth place. But in the second lap he moved up rapidly, passing runner after runner, until he finally hit the lead in the last few moments of the race, winning in 1:49.8, a new world record. He had also broken the 1:50 barrier.

Incidentally, no other world record holder could have been more hopelessly in love than Tommie Hampson. His diary at the time of the Olympics is full of emotion and anguish over how much he was missing his fiancée, Winnie. When the Olympics were over he commented that a "world beater must, like a great artist, be inspired—and what greater inspiration can anyone have than the love of such a beautiful, kind, gentle, sweet, good creature." Fortunately, *amor vincit omnia*, and after the Olympics he returned home to marry his beloved. His first career was as a schoolteacher. During the war, he served as an education officer in the Royal Air Force. Later in life he worked in social welfare for various institutions, before dying at the early age of 57 in 1965.

Ben Eastman   (United States, b. 1911)

1:49.8   **Princeton, USA**   **16 Jun 1934**

Ben Eastman achieved world records over both 400m and 800m, an achievement matched only by Ted Meredith and Rudolf Harbig. His 400m record took place in March 1932. Unfortunately, at the Olympics in August he came up against new 400m star William Carr from the University of Pennsylvania, who beat him and took away his world record in the process.

Eastman kept running for the next few years and in 1934 equaled Hampson's record when he ran 1:49.8 over 880 yards at the Princeton Invitational. The 800m time was also taken and was registered as 1:49.1, but as there was only one stopwatch recording this time (and not the mandatory three), it could not be submitted as an official record. So Eastman's time over the 880-yard distance was submitted as an 800m world record, even though it was over a distance of 804.67 meters.

Glenn Cunningham   (United States, 1909-1988)

1:49.7   **Stockholm, Sweden**   **20 Aug 1936**

Glenn Cunningham was a top U.S. miler for most of the 1930s and was a 1500m finalist in two Olympics: fourth in 1932 and second in 1936. He also set the world mile record in 1934, and his career is covered in more detail in chapter 6.

Cunningham had his heart set on winning the 1500m gold medal in Berlin, and it took a world record performance by Jack Lovelock of New Zealand to beat him, 3:47.8 to 3:48.4. Cunningham was deeply disappointed and was said to have wept after leaving the stadium.

He had some consolation two weeks later. In a race in Stockholm after the Games, he took 0.1 second off the old 800m record, running 1:49.7.

Elroy Robinson   (United States, 1913-1989)

1:49.6   **New York, USA**   **11 Jul 1937**

Elroy Robinson had a short-lived career as an international athlete. He seemed to perform well in the odd-numbered years (1935 and 1937) and not so well in the even years. He won the AAU 800m Championships in 1935 and the NCAA title the same year, representing Fresno State University in California. But he missed the 1936 Olympic Games due to injury. In 1937 he had some classic duels with John Woodruff, the 1936 Olympic 800m champion, but Woodruff won most of them.

However, at the World Labor Athletic Carnival in New York on 11 July 1937 Robinson ran the 880 yards without serious competition, because Woodruff decided to run the mile instead. Robinson led from start to finish and took 0.1 second off Cunningham's record with 1:49.6.

Sydney Wooderson   (Great Britain, b. 1914)

1:48.4   **London, England**   **20 Aug 1938**

Sydney Wooderson was short in stature, with defective eyesight that precluded war service. He was nonetheless a dominating force in middle-distance running in England for over a decade in a range of events from 800m to cross-country. In 1937 he broke the world record for the mile; further career details are given in chapter 6. His 800m world record took place in 1938 in a specially staged attempt on Elroy Robinson's time of 1:49.6. Six other runners were given various handicap starts to help Wooderson to the record. The "race" was actually over 880 yards, with timekeepers at the 800m mark as well. One of the handicap runners was his brother Stanley, who actually finished first. Sydney's time for the 800m distance was a new world record of 1:48.4.

Rudolf Harbig   (Germany, 1913-1944)

1:46.6   **Milan, Italy**   **15 Jul 1939**

Rudolf Harbig has been described in the chapter on 400m world record holders. His 1939 world record at 800m was not just another world record but a massive quantum jump to a higher level of performance. It took place in an international meet, Italy vs. Germany, seven weeks before World War II commenced.

Harbig had competed at the 1932 Olympics in Los Angeles but did not advance beyond the first round. In 1936 he did a little better, finishing sixth in a heat of the 800m, but did win a bronze medal in the 4 × 400m relay. By 1938 he had reached his full maturity as an athlete and won the European Championships over 800m in 1:50.6, a German record.

In the 800m at Milan the following year, Harbig's main rival was Mario Lanzi of Italy, who had finished second in the 800m at the 1936 Olympics. Lanzi took the lead, and the first lap was completed in 52.5. Lanzi continued to lead up to the 700m mark, at which stage Harbig simply exploded past him and went on to win by 40 meters. The time—1:46.6—took a massive 1.8 seconds off the world record. His new record was destined to stand for 16 years.

Harbig was German 800m champion from 1936 to 1941. In World War II he was killed on the Russian Front in 1944.

Rudolf Harbig, Germany (400m, 800m), whose 800m record lasted 16 years.

Roger Moens   (Belgium, b. 1930)

1:45.7   **Oslo, Norway**   **3 Aug 1955**

Roger Moens, a police inspector by profession, achieved athletic fame by breaking Rudolf Harbig's venerable world record at the Bislett Games in Oslo. A pacesetter led the field through the first lap in 52.0 seconds, with Moens on his shoulder and Norwegian Audun Boysen just behind. When he heard the time for the first lap, Moens made a decision to push on in pursuit of a great performance. Although Boysen challenged him, Moens never wavered and held on steadfast to the finish, just winning by 0.2 second. Both men were well under the record, but Moens had won in 1:45.7, 0.9 second under Harbig's great record.

Moens missed the 1956 Olympics because of injury in an accident two months before the Games. While training on a tennis court at night, he ran into a spike in the ground. After his missed opportunity in 1956 he patiently awaited four long years until the 1960 Olympics. In the

Roger Moens, Belgium (800m), who broke Harbig's long-standing 800m record.

Rome 800m final he was headed down the straight for victory, when unknown Peter Snell of New Zealand came steaming through on the inside to win in the last few strides, 1:46.3 to 1:46.5.

Peter Snell   (New Zealand, b. 1938)

1:44.3   **Christchurch, New Zealand**   **3 Feb 1962**

New Zealand's Peter Snell came out of nowhere to win the 800m title at the Rome Olympics in 1960. Snell was coached with a different philosophy. Many of the previous world record holders were 400m/800m types, strong on speed. Snell's coach, Arthur Lydiard, concentrated on stamina. He advised long training runs, near-marathons, to build up a large stamina base. At Rome Lydiard told Snell: "Only you have the stamina to run four hard 800m races in three days." So it proved—Snell improved by a massive 2.9 seconds on his pre-Rome personal best over the distance to snatch the race from Roger Moens in the last stride in 1:46.3.

His world record over 800m (1:44.3), recorded during an 880-yard race, was set on a grass track in New Zealand in 1962. He also claimed the mile record that year, again on a grass track. Two years later he went on to win both the 800m and the

Peter Snell, New Zealand (800m, mile) wins the 1964 Olympic 800m title in Tokyo.

1500m at the 1964 Olympics. His main weapon was his ability to sprint away from the rest of the field, usually with about 250 meters to go, while already running at high speed. His world record was not broken for 11 years.

Snell moved into the field of exercise physiology, eventually becoming a professor in this discipline at the University of California at Davis.

Ralph Doubell   (Australia, b. 1945)

1:44.3   **Mexico City, Mexico**   **15 Oct 1968**

Ralph Doubell was a graduate in zoology and psychology at the University of Melbourne. At the university he was coached by Franz Stampfl, the advisor to Roger Bannister at the time of his assault on the four-minute mile.

Ralph Doubell, Australia (800m), 1968 Olympic 800m champion.

Ralph Doubell had a relatively short international career but peaked when it mattered. He won the 800m at the World University Games in 1967, defeating European record holder Franz-Joseph Kemper. Doubell also proved remarkably successful on the indoor circuit on boards in the United States. Despite these credentials, he was not regarded as the gold medal favorite in the 800m in Mexico. Most experts picked Wilson Kiprugut from Kenya, who had won the bronze medal in the event four years earlier. The Australian was also plagued by Achilles tendon injuries during the early season runs. He was beaten in his own national titles for the first time in four years.

In the end the Olympic 800m final went exactly to plan for Doubell. Wilson Kiprugut took the pace out very early, aiming to lead from start to finish, and went through the first lap in 51.0 seconds. However, Doubell kept within contact, although 6 to 8 meters behind, and swept past in the last 40 meters of the race to win in 1:44.3. His time equaled Snell's world record.

Doubell had hoped to compete at the 1972 Munich Olympics, but calf injuries made him abandon the idea shortly before the Games. He was accepted into business administration at Harvard University and from there went on to a career in commerce. His current position is with the firm Deutsche Bank in Sydney.

David Wottle   (United States, b. 1950)

1:44.3   **Eugene, USA**   **1 Jul 1972**

David Wottle was a graduate of Bowling Green University in Ohio and had run for several years without conspicuous success. He surprised observers by winning the 800m at the U.S. Olympic trials in 1:44.3, equaling Peter Snell's and Ralph Doubell's world record in the process.

In the 800m final at the Munich Games he ran a remarkably even race. To observers he seemed not just last, but hopelessly last, as the rest of the field took off at high speed. At

David Wottle, United States (800m), 1972 Olympic 800m champion, who always raced in a cap.

the 600m mark he was still in eighth and last position. Showing impeccable timing, he started to move rapidly through the field. In a frenzied sprint to the line, he beat front-runner Yevgeniy Arzhanov of the Soviet Union by 0.03 second. The winning time was 1:45.86. It is interesting to look at each of the 200m times in Wottle's race—26.4, 26.9, 26.4, 26.2—which reflect his remarkable judgment of pace.

That day should have been a time of undiluted joy for Wottle, but the rest of the day ended in misunderstanding. He had always run, trained, and raced in an old golf hat and did so in the Olympic final and for the victory ceremony. During the playing of the U.S. national anthem he put his hand on his heart, inadvertently covering up the USA emblem on his tracksuit. Some reporters assumed that the wearing of a hat and the covering up of his country's emblem was a deliberate protest. When this was put to Wottle at the subsequent press conference, he dissolved into tears and later made an emotional apology to the American people if they had misconstrued his actions. It was universally accepted as an honest oversight. Spiro Agnew, vice-president of the United States at the time, sent him a telegram: "Hat on or hat off, you're my kind of American."

Marcello Fiasconaro   (South Africa/Italy, b. 1949)

1:43.7   **Milan, Italy**   **27 Jun 1973**

Marcello Fiasconaro was a South African athlete with an Italian heritage. His father, an Italian airman, had been a prisoner of war during World War II and was sent to South Africa. After the war he chose to settle there.

Fiasconaro had to face the reality that South Africa was banned from Olympic participation at the time. He made a decision to move to Italy and run for that country.

He arrived, not speaking a word of Italian, and 10 days later was granted permission to run for Italy. Antiapartheid feeling was not strong in Italy in the 1970s, and Fiasconaro experienced no problems with this change of colors. His initial performances in Italian colors were not without incident. In a European Cup 800m race in 1973, he false-started twice, which meant he was disqualified from the race. This led to an invasion of the track by angry Italian supporters. Most of the Italian team later boycotted the official banquet.

He finally justified those who had faith in him by beating Peter Snell's long standing

800m record. In a match between Italy and Czechoslovakia in Milan, held at the same arena where Rudolf Harbig had set his record 34 years earlier, he raced through the first lap in 51.2. His second lap of 52.5 meant that his time of 1:43.7 took 0.6 off Snell's 11-year-old record.

Injuries prevented him from running in both the 1972 Munich and 1976 Montreal Olympics. He later settled back in South Africa.

Alberto Juantorena   (Cuba, b. 1950)

| 1:43.5 | Montreal, Canada | 25 Jul 1976 |
| 1:43.4 | Sofia, Bulgaria | 21 Aug 1977 |

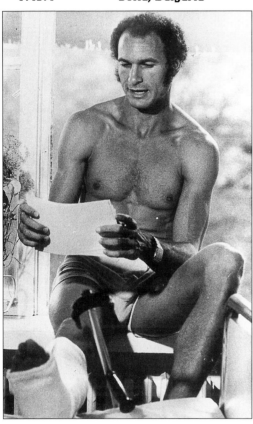

Alberto Juantorena, Cuba, Olympic 400m and 800m champion in 1976, a rare double.

Alberto Juantorena took the 1976 Montreal Olympics by storm when he achieved a unique and grueling double—he won both the 400m and the 800m gold medals. A tall athlete (188 centimeters, 6' 2"), he was initially a basketball player but turned to track and field in 1971 and made rapid progress, reaching the 400m semifinals in the 1972 Olympics.

Juantorena had limited experience over 800m, but over 400m he was the World Student Games champion in 1973 and was second at the Pan-American Games in 1975. When he arrived in Montreal, he was one of the favorites for the 400m but was not regarded as such for the 800m.

In the 800m final the first 300 meters were run in separate lanes. Juantorena went through the first lap in 50.85. In the second lap he simply stormed home with his long stride to beat Ivo van Damme (Belgium) and Rick Wohlhuter (USA) in a world record time of 1:43.5. In the 400m final he beat Fred Newhouse (USA) in 44.26. This unique double victory involved seven punishing races in six days.

Juantorena's tall physique and huge long strides led to the nickname "El Caballo" (the horse). His two stunning performances at the Olympics made him the center of attention, and according to 400m bronze medalist Herman Frazier, "the women went wild over him." All of Cuba went wild over him too; on his return home he was personally greeted by Fidel Castro at the airport.

Juantorena had another top year in 1977, with two classic races against Kenya's Mike Boit, who had been forced to miss the Olympics because of an African boycott. In August 1977 in Bulgaria he took another 0.1 second off the record. From then on he was plagued by injuries but managed a fourth place in Moscow in the Olympic 400m final. He sustained a final injury at the 1983 World Championships when he fell heavily during an 800m heat, and that finished off his career. He is now president of the Cuban Athletic Federation.

Sebastian Coe   (Great Britain, b. 1956)

1:42.33	Oslo, Norway	5 Jul 1979
1:41.73	Florence, Italy	10 Jun 1981

Sebastian Coe, together with Steve Ovett and Steve Cram, was part of a golden era of British middle-distance running in the late 1970s and 1980s. Slight in stature and only weighing 58 kilograms (128 pounds), he first came to prominence in the 1978 European 800m Championship, when he tried to front-run the entire race but finished third. A year later, at the age of 22, he had a 41-day saga that remains unique in track and field history: the 800m world record on 5 July, the mile world record on 17 July, and the 1500m world record on 15 August. His 800m record was somewhat startling in that it improved Juantorena's record time by 1.07 seconds.

At the 1980 Olympics, to everyone's astonishment, he froze in the 800m final before finally getting a second place behind Steve Ovett. He made up for it six days later by winning the 1500m with Ovett trailing in third behind East Germany's Jurgen Straub.

In 1981 he improved the 800m world record by another 0.6 second. However, in 1982 he again came in second in the European Championships when in a position to win. It turned out that he had a chronic viral infection, and his future looked bleak. But he bounced back at the 1984 Los Angeles Olympics. He finished second in the 800m to young Joaquim Cruz of Brazil, but again made up for it a few days later with a win in the 1500m. Finally, in 1986, he won his third try at the European 800m Championships.

An economics graduate of Loughborough University, he later went into politics and became the Conservative member of Parliament for Falmouth and Camborne.

Conclusions

Coe's 1981 world record has resisted challenges for 15 years. His lap times were 49.7 and 52.0. This suggests that a slightly slower first lap may lead to an overall improvement by a supremely gifted athlete.

Five All-Time Fastest: Men's 800m

Sebastian Coe (GBR)	1:41.73	1981
Joaquim Cruz (BRA)	1:41.77	1984
Wilson Kipketer (DEN)	1:41.83	1996
Sammy Koskei (KEN)	1:42.28	1984
Vebjorn Rodal (NOR)	1:42.58	1996
Prediction	*1:40.20*	*2015*

Top Three: Men's 800m

GOLD MEDAL:	Sebastian Coe (GBR)
SILVER MEDAL:	Peter Snell (NZ)
BRONZE MEDAL:	Rudolf Harbig (GER)

The 1500m race is the metric equivalent of the mile and is generally regarded as the "European mile." It is actually less than a mile by 109.36 meters, or 119 yards 21.6 inches. It is in some ways an anomaly—three and three-quarters laps of a standard 400m oval. The mile seems much more symmetrical, exactly four laps of the old 440-yard circuits. There have been calls to replace the 1500m with the 1600m, but the 1500m event has a long tradition in Europe, and change seems unlikely.

The 1500m, possibly because of those three and three-quarters laps, has never quite had the same appeal as the mile. The breaking of the 3:30 barrier in 1985 by Cram and Aouita, a major track and field event, never generated quite the same public interest as the breaking of the first four-minute mile.

The record has been set or equaled 37 times by 30 athletes. Thirteen of them have held both the 1500m and the mile record. Only six have been Olympic gold medalists in the 1500m: Nurmi, Beccali, Lovelock, Elliott, Coe, and Morceli. Only two have set their world records at their Olympic triumphs: Lovelock in 1936, Elliott in 1960.

Men's World Records for 1500m

Record time	Record holder	Location	Date
3:55.8	Abel Kiviat (USA)	Cambridge, USA	8 Jun 1912
3:54.7	John Zander (SWE)	Stockholm, Sweden	5 Aug 1917
3:52.6	Paavo Nurmi (FIN)	Helsinki, Finland	19 Jun 1924
3:51.0	Otto Peltzer (GER)	Berlin, Germany	11 Sep 1926
3:49.2	Jules Ladoumègue (FRA)	Paris, France	5 Oct 1930
3:49.2	Luigi Beccali (ITA)	Turin, Italy	9 Sep 1933
3:49.0	Luigi Beccali (ITA)	Milan, Italy	17 Sep 1933
3:48.8	Bill Bonthron (USA)	Milwaukee, USA	30 Jun 1934
3:47.8	Jack Lovelock (NZ)	Berlin, Germany	6 Aug 1936
3:47.6	Gunder Hägg (SWE)	Stockholm, Sweden	10 Aug 1941
3:45.8	Gunder Hägg (SWE)	Stockholm, Sweden	17 Jul 1942
3:45.0	Arne Andersson (SWE)	Gothenburg, Sweden	17 Aug 1943
3:43.0	Gunder Hägg (SWE)	Gothenburg, Sweden	7 Jul 1944
3:43.0	Lennart Strand (SWE)	Malmö, Sweden	15 Jul 1947
3:43.0	Werner Lueg (FRG)	Berlin, West Germany	29 Jun 1952
3:42.8	Wes Santee (USA)	Compton, USA	4 Jun 1954
3:41.8	John Landy (AUST)	Turku, Finland	21 Jun 1954
3:40.8	Sándor Iharos (HUN)	Helsinki, Finland	28 Jul 1955
3:40.8	László Tábori (HUN)	Oslo, Norway	6 Sep 1955
3:40.8	Gunnar Nielsen (DEN)	Oslo, Norway	6 Sep 1955
3:40.6	Istvan Rózsavölgyi (HUN)	Tata, Hungary	3 Aug 1956
3:40.2	Olavi Salsola (FIN)	Turku, Finland	11 Jul 1957
3:40.2	Olavi Salonen (FIN)	Turku, Finland	11 Jul 1957
3:38.1	Stanislav Jungwirth (CZH)	Stara Boleslav, Czechoslovakia	12 Jul 1957
3:36.0	Herb Elliott (AUST)	Gothenburg, Sweden	28 Aug 1958
3:35.6	Herb Elliott (AUST)	Rome, Italy	6 Sep 1960
3:33.1	Jim Ryun (USA)	Los Angeles, USA	8 Jul 1967
3:32.2	Filbert Bayi (TAN)	Christchurch, New Zealand	2 Feb 1974
3:32.1	Sebastian Coe (GBR)	Zürich, Switzerland	15 Aug 1979

3:32.1	Steve Ovett (GBR)	Oslo, Norway	15 Jul 1980
3:31.36	Steve Ovett (GBR)	Koblenz, West Germany	27 Aug 1980
3:31.24	Sydney Maree (USA)	Cologne, West Germany	28 Aug 1983
3:30.77	Steve Ovett (GBR)	Rieti, Italy	4 Sep 1983
3:29.67	Steve Cram (GBR)	Nice, France	16 Jul 1985
3:29.46	Said Aouita (MOR)	Berlin, West Germany	23 Aug 1985
3:28.86	Noureddine Morceli (ALG)	Rieti, Italy	6 Sep 1992
3:27.37	Noureddine Morceli (ALG)	Nice, France	12 Jul 1995

Abel Kiviat   (United States, 1892–1991)

3:55.8   **Cambridge, USA**   **8 Jun 1912**

Abel Kiviat's parents had come to the United States to avoid the pogroms in Russia. Kiviat won the Canadian mile championship in 1909 when he was just 17 years old, and in 1911 won the U.S. AAU mile title in 4:19.

His world 1500m record came in the U.S. trials for the Stockholm Olympics. He led from the 500m mark all the way to the tape in a time of 3:55.8, the inaugural world record.

In the 1912 Olympic 1500m final Kiviat lined up with 6 other U.S. runners in a field of 14. (The restriction of three athletes per national team didn't apply in those days). Kiviat took the lead at the beginning of the last lap, but Britain's Arnold Jackson timed a perfect sprint finish to win by two meters in 3:56.8. However, Kiviat did win a gold medal in the 3000m team race.

He served at the front line in the army in France in World War I. He was rediscovered 70 years later when the United States hosted the 1984 Olympic Games in Los Angeles. At the age of 92, Kiviat was found to be the oldest surviving U.S. gold medalist at the time. He described his Olympic experiences in the book *Tales of Gold* by Carlson and Fogarty.

He continued to attend athletic events in his mid-90s and died at age 99.

John Zander   (Sweden, 1890–1967)

3:54.7   **Stockholm, Sweden**   **5 Aug 1917**

Zander was seventh in the 1912 Olympic 1500m final, but another Swede, Edwin Wide, was fourth. For a long time, Wide was regarded as the premier Swedish athlete over 1500m.

In World War I, Sweden was neutral, and Zander kept up his training. In top condition in 1917, he made an attempt on the world record in the Stockholm championships. He had no serious rivals in the race and ran it almost as a solo time trial. On a 385-meter track, in front of a huge crowd, he finished in 3:54.7, taking 1.1 seconds off the old record. This was achieved without competition or the aid of handicap runners or pacesetters.

Paavo Nurmi   (Finland, 1893–1973)

3:52.6   **Helsinki, Finland**   **19 Jun 1924**

Paavo Nurmi was the undisputed superstar of track and field in the 1920s. Some would say his achievements make him the athlete of the century. He held world records from

1500m up to 20,000m. In addition, he won nine gold medals over three Olympics, four in events still held (1500m, 5000m, and 10,000m twice) and five in events now discontinued.

Paavo Nurmi's personality was solemn, serious, and studious. His father had died when Paavo was 12, and the family of six struggled in poverty. As the eldest child, Nurmi had to pursue work and toiled at various menial jobs to help the family survive. It may be that the grind of poverty brought a seriousness to his personality. He found himself inspired by the victories of Finland's first long-distance hero, Johannes Kolehmainen, who had won the 5000m and 10,000m at the 1912 Stockholm Olympics. Nurmi set out to emulate Kolehmainen, and Nurmi's feats eventually outstripped those of his boyhood hero. He concentrated on carefully timed laps and adopted the practice of running with a stopwatch in his hands.

For the 1924 Olympics, at the height of his fame, he set himself a special challenge: to win both the 1500m and 5000m at the Olympics in July, a feat never accomplished before or since. To mimic the timing of the two races, scheduled only 55 minutes apart, he contrived a practice run. At Helsinki in June he scheduled a 1500m race and a 5000m race within an hour as an Olympic test. His 1500m time of 3:52.6 removed 2.1 seconds off the old record. Then, 50 minutes later, he raced the 5000m and broke that world record too. His subsequent wins in the Paris Olympics in these two events were almost an anticlimax, such was his stature. Those 1500m and 5000m achievements will never be repeated.

Otto Peltzer   (Germany, 1900–1970)

3:51.0   **Berlin, Germany**   **11 Sep 1926**

Otto Peltzer has been described in the chapter on 800m world record holders. His 800m world record made him a national hero, and a special challenge race was set up three months later in Berlin. Four runners were invited to race: Peltzer, Nurmi, Edwin Wide of Sweden, and Herbert Bocher of Germany. Nurmi's reputation at this time was at its peak.

The stadium on the Avus was sold out. The seemingly invincible Nurmi took the lead and led through 400m, 800m, and 1200m. Suddenly Wide raced to the front and led all the way to the finishing straight until Peltzer launched a meteoric drive, which carried him past Nurmi and Wide in the last few meters of the race. His winning time of 3:51.0 took 1.6 seconds off Nurmi's world record, and the jubilant crowd's ecstatic ovation went on for 15 minutes. It was the highlight of Peltzer's career. Nurmi, for the first time in his career, had finished third.

Jules Ladoumègue   (France, 1906–1973)

3:49.2   **Paris, France**   **5 Oct 1930**

Jules Ladoumègue rose in 12 months from a promising talent to Olympic favorite for the 1928 Olympic 1500m. But at the Olympics he lost to Harry Larva (Finland), who was having his day of glory. Larva won the race in the last 40 meters with 3:53.2; Ladoumègue was second in 3:53.8.

Over the next two to three years the Frenchman dominated the 1500m, and in October 1930 he chose to make an attack on the world record. On that day he noticed his mother pouring fluid onto the track. Later he discovered it was holy water from Lourdes. It must have helped. He took almost 2 seconds off Peltzer's record, breaking the 3:50 barrier by 0.8 second. The thought that most impressed him was that he was now faster than Nurmi.

The following year he claimed the mile record. His next objective was the 1932 Olympic gold medal over 1500m. It was not to be. French athletic authorities, zealous in their preservation of the concept of amateurism, took exception to a number of under-the-table payments Ladoumègue was supposed to have received. He was disqualified for life. Widespread indignation throughout France did not reverse this ban, and it was the end of his athletic career.

Luigi Beccali   (Italy, 1907–1990)

| 3:49.2 | Turin, Italy | 9 Sep 1933 |
| 3:49.0 | Milan, Italy | 17 Sep 1933 |

Born in Milan, Luigi Beccali turned to running in 1925 after spending three years trying to become a top cyclist. After army service in 1927, he qualified for the 1928 Olympics in the 1500m but went out in the semifinals. Over the next four years he showed steady improvement and fortunately reached his peak form in Olympic year 1932. In the Los Angeles Coliseum he started the last lap 20 meters behind but judged the race perfectly and won by 1.2 seconds in 3:51.2. He was perhaps the first miler to perfect the last-lap sprint finish.

In 1933 in Turin, racing New Zealand's Jack Lovelock, he equaled Ladoumègue's world record of 3:49.2. Eight days later he broke it by 0.2 second in a competition between Great Britain and Italy. In 1934 he won the inaugural European Championship 1500m in 3:54.6.

At the 1936 Olympics in Berlin, Lovelock's time had come, and Beccali had to settle for the bronze medal. He won one last bronze medal at the 1938 European Championships.

Caricature of Luigi Beccali, Italy, 1932 Olympic 1500m champion.

Bill Bonthron   (United States, 1912–1983)

| 3:48.8 | Milwaukee, USA | 30 Jun 1934 |

Bill Bonthron, a graduate of Princeton University, was one of the top U.S. milers in the 1930s. Like Glenn Cunningham he had suffered burns to his leg as a child, and a doctor suggested running to strengthen the tissues.

Bonthron competed in the Princeton Invitational race in 1933 at which Lovelock set a record for the mile. In the second Princeton Invitational in 1934 Cunningham won in yet another new world mile record. Once again, Bonthron was second. However, two weeks later he raced Cunningham in the 1500m at the AAU championships. Bonthron was determined that this time he would not be the "bridesmaid." He made a determined sprint in the last 100 meters and passed Cunningham to win by 0.1 second in a new world record time of 3:48.8.

Possibly Bonthron raced too often, as members of the U.S. university track and field teams were expected to in those days. By the time the 1936 U.S. Olympic trials came around, he could not reproduce his world-class times. He finished fourth and missed out on the Berlin Olympics.

Jack Lovelock   (New Zealand, 1910-1949)

3:47.8   **Berlin, Germany**   **6 Aug 1936**

Jack Lovelock, New Zealand, (1500m, mile) with Glenn Cunningham,United States (800m, mile) at the Berlin Olympics.

Jack Lovelock was the great New Zealand miler who achieved every possible athletic honor in the 1930s: 1500m world record holder and 1936 Olympic champion, world record holder at the mile (1933), 1934 Empire Games mile champion, and 1934 British AAA champion.

Born in the South Island of New Zealand, he was a brilliant student and athlete and won a Rhodes scholarship to study medicine at Oxford University in 1930. He was selected to run for New Zealand in the 1500m in the 1932 Los Angeles Olympics and finished seventh.

Despite his apparently happy-go-lucky personality, he was described by his contemporaries as very difficult to get to know. He was, however, singularly determined to win the 1936 Olympic 1500m gold medal, and didn't mind losing a few races along the way, such as the defeats by the rising young star Sydney Wooderson in the British AAA mile title in 1935 and 1936.

Lovelock made a calculated decision before the Olympic 1500m final that he would sprint from 300 meters out, no matter what. This plan came off beautifully, and although Glenn Cunningham chased him all the way to the tape, Lovelock won in a new world record of 3:47.8.

Lovelock retired from the sport after the Olympics. After graduation he practiced medicine in New York and married an American. Gold medalists at the Berlin Olympics were given seedlings of an oak tree; Lovelock's is now a towering oak tree at Timaru High School in New Zealand.

Gunder Hägg   (Sweden, b. 1918)

3:47.6	Stockholm, Sweden	10 Aug 1941
3:45.8	Stockholm, Sweden	17 Jul 1942
3:43.0	Gothenburg, Sweden	7 Jul 1944

From 1939 to 1945 the world was consumed by World War II, but Sweden was neutral. Two Swedish distance runners emerged who together rewrote a whole series of world records. They are little known outside their own country, yet they made major improvements in records that would take the rest of the world almost a decade to match. The two Swedes were Gunder Hägg and Arne Andersson. Hägg set world records over distances from 1500m up to 5000m and from 1941 to 1944 reduced Lovelock's 1500m record three times, overall by 4.8 seconds.

The duels between Hägg and Andersson caught the imagination of all Sweden. Unfortunately, by the end of the war, Hägg's best years were behind him. His career was terminated in 1946, when the Swedish athletic authorities charged him with accepting under-the-table payments from promoters and banned him from athletics for life.

Arne Andersson   (Sweden, b. 1917)

3:45.0	Gothenburg, Sweden	17 Aug 1943

As described in the previous section on Gunder Hägg, Arne Andersson and Hägg were a remarkable Swedish athletic duo; they challenged each other 26 times in all. Of their races Andersson won 11, and Hägg won 15. Professionally, Hägg was a firefighter and Andersson a teacher.

Andersson first came to notice when he won the 1500m in the 1939 Sweden vs. Finland match. He held the 1500m world record once and the mile record three times between the years 1942 to 1944. His 1500m world record took place in August 1943, while Hägg was on a U.S. tour.

Supporters of Hägg had a grievance against Andersson. Hägg usually led, and Andersson followed, attempting to beat Hägg with a sprint finish. Hägg's fans felt that Andersson should do more of the hard work of leading.

After the war Andersson had two highly publicized mile races against the pre–World War II mile record holder, Sydney Wooderson of England. Andersson won both, though that was more or less his last hurrah. In September 1945 the new Swedish champion Lennart Strand beat both Andersson and Hägg convincingly. In 1946 both Hägg and Andersson were banned for life from athletics for receiving secret payments.

Lennart Strand   (Sweden, b. 1921)

3:43.0	Malmö, Sweden	15 Jul 1947

Toward the end of the era of Hägg and Andersson, a third Swede emerged to end their careers. On 21 September 1945 a crowd of 19,000 turned up at Stockholm to see yet another of the famed Hägg-Andersson duels over a mile. Instead, there was a major upset: Lennart Strand won in 4:04.8. Andersson was well beaten into second place with 4:07.2. Hägg came in fourth with 4:12.2. Strand went on to become the 1946 European champion in the 1500m, defeating Henry Eriksson, also of Sweden, 3:48.0 to 3:48.8. He had a little trick that he felt helped his running action. He would carry small stones and switch them from hand to hand while running.

Strand and Eriksson had another major battle in Malmö in 1947. Once again, Strand proved too strong and equaled Hägg's world record in the process with 3:43.0; Eriksson ran 3:44.4.

Strand was a strong favorite for the 1948 Olympic 1500m in London. Eriksson had never beaten him, but in pouring rain, he finally did it. With only 50 meters to go, Eriksson pulled away, and Strand could not respond. Eriksson was first in 3:49.8, Strand second in 3:50.4.

Lennart Strand, Sweden (1500m), silver medalist in the 1948 Olympics. For the first time in his career he was beaten by countryman Henry Eriksson.

Werner Lueg   (West Germany, b. 1931)

3:43.0   **Berlin, West Germany**   **29 Jun 1952**

Werner Lueg surprised himself and many observers in May 1952, when he ran a mile in 4:06.4, the fastest mile of the season. He consolidated this newfound status in the German 1500m championships by equaling the world record with 3:43.0.

At the Olympics in July, Lueg won his heat and cruised in second in his semifinal. The final, with 12 finalists, was a crowded race. Lueg moved up into the lead after the 800m mark, with the pack right behind him. With 300 meters to run, Lueg made a sprint for home. He almost made it. He kept the lead all the way round the bend and entered the home straight apparently victorious. However, with 50 meters to go, his legs began to tie up on him, and he could not prevent Joseph Barthel of Luxembourg and then Bob McMillen of the United States from sweeping past him. The final result was Barthel 3:45.1, McMillen 3:45.2, and Lueg 3:45.4.

Lueg ran for a few more years and was West German champion at 1500m for four years in a row, from 1952 to 1955. He finished fifth in the 1954 European Championships over 1500m in 3:46.4; England's Roger Bannister won in 3:43.8.

Wes Santee   (United States, b. 1932)

3:42.8   **Compton, USA**   **4 Jun 1954**

Wes Santee competed in the 1952 Olympics in the 5000m but was eliminated in the early rounds. He won the AAU mile championship in 1952, 1953, and 1955. A graduate of the

Wes Santee, United States (1500m).

University of Kansas, he surprised himself with a very fast mile in 1953 (4:02.4), the fourth fastest mile ever. The magic figure of four minutes for the mile beckoned, and it would bring fame, if not fortune, to the athlete who could first better it. Santee came from a farm background in Kansas. After his university days he joined the U.S. Marines but was allowed to maintain his training. Although he made numerous attempts on the four-minute mile, it always eluded him; Roger Bannister finally got there first on 6 May 1954 in Oxford.

Santee made another determined attempt on 4 June 1954 with stopwatches at both the 1500m point and the mile. At the three-quarter-mile mark he was actually faster than Bannister, and he went through the 1500m mark in 3:42.8, a new world record for the distance. However, from then on his legs tied up, and he fell behind Bannister's pace to finish in 4:00.6. That was to be his fastest mile.

He had hoped to go to the Melbourne Olympics, but he fell foul of U.S. officials, who charged him with receiving payments for some of his races. The missionary, almost fanatical, zeal to preserve the amateurism of the sport was alive and well in the United States in 1955, especially under Olympic President Avery Brundage. Santee was banned from competing abroad for two years and thus was denied a trip to the Melbourne Olympics.

John Landy (Australia, b. 1930)

3:41.8   **Turku, Finland**   **21 Jun 1954**

John Landy, Roger Bannister, and Wes Santee were the three athletes who chased the four-minute mile. Britain's Roger Bannister achieved it first in May 1954. Six weeks later Landy ran in Finland, with stopwatches at both the 1500m and the mile marks. He achieved world records at both distances: 1.4 seconds off the mile record and 1.0 second off the 1500m record en route. (More details about Landy are given in the chapter on the mile.)

In later years his many positions in Australia have included chairman of the Wool Research and Development Council, consultant to the Dairy Research and Development Corporation, and a foundation member of the Land Conservation Council. He has written two books, *Close to Nature* and *A Coastal Diary*.

Sándor Iharos (Hungary, 1930–1996)

3:40.8   **Helsinki, Finland**   **28 Jul 1955**

Hungary in the mid-1950s produced three world-class middle-distance athletes: Sándor Iharos, László Tábori, and Istvan Rózsavölgyi. All three went on to produce world records in the 1500m.

Iharos had run for Hungary at the 1952 Olympics in the 1500m but was eliminated in the heats. He became a physical education instructor in the army, with the rank of captain. He burst into international prominence in July 1954 with a win in Oslo in 3:42.4, a new European record. However, at the European Championships in August he was sixth.

A year later he and Rózsavölgyi lined up for the Hungary vs. Finland match in Helsinki. The two Finnish runners were left far behind as the two Hungarians pushed themselves to the limit. It was Iharos who held on to win in 3:40.8, 1 second under Landy's record.

That same year Iharos went on to achieve further world records in the 5000m and the 10,000m, a rare triple that only the great Paavo Nurmi has also accomplished. But Nurmi also enjoyed multiple Olympic triumphs, whereas this was not the case for Iharos. The Soviet invasion of Hungary just before the 1956 Melbourne Olympics knocked the spirit out of Iharos. He was also troubled by sore ankles and a difficult romance. In the end he did not compete in Melbourne.

Sándor Iharos, Hungary (1500m, 5000m, 10,000m).

László Tábori   (Hungary, b. 1931)

3:40.8   **Oslo, Norway**   **6 Sep 1955**

See the biography below.

Gunnar Nielsen   (Denmark, b. 1928)

3:40.8   **Oslo, Norway**   **6 Sep 1955**

Five weeks after Iharos's 1500m record (3:40.8) an attack on it was planned in Oslo by László Tábori and Gunnar Nielsen. Tábori's previous best was 3:41.6 run one month earlier, and Nielsen's was 3:43.0.

The 800m point was reached in 1:58. Both Tábori and Nielsen charged to the front with 250 meters to go. It was neck and neck to the finish, with Tábori just ahead. The three watches on Tábori read 3:40.8, 3:40.8, and 3:40.7. All three watches on Nielsen read 3:40.8. In the end, both men were given the official time of 3:40.8. So now there were three men with the record of 3:40.8.

Nielsen traveled to Melbourne for the 1956 Olympics but was plagued by a foot injury and could not start in the semifinal of the 800m. In the 1500m he was tenth.

At the same Olympics, Tábori decided to run, despite the recent Soviet invasion of Hungary. He finished fourth in the 1500m and sixth in the 5000m. After these Games he made a decision not to return to Hungary, but moved to the United States. He won the 1960 British AAA mile, but without a nationality at that time he could not compete at the Rome Olympics. He currently runs a sports store in Los Angeles.

Istvan Rózsavölgyi   (Hungary, b. 1929)

3:40.6   **Tata, Hungary**   **3 Aug 1956**

Rózsavölgyi, by occupation an army captain, was the third of the Hungarian trio who held the world record for the 1500m in the mid-1950s. He had been second to Iharos in the latter's world record 1500m in July 1955. He was able to reverse that earlier result in a trial for the Olympics three months before the Games. Although Iharos and Rózsavölgyi were together at the 1200m mark, Rózsavölgyi simply ran away with the race and set a new world record of 3:40.6.

Rózsavölgyi traveled to Melbourne for the Olympics but, no doubt troubled by the recent Soviet invasion, never reproduced his best. He went out in the heats of the 1500m. He was fourth in the 1958 European 1500m Championships. At the 1960 Olympics he won a bronze medal with his personal best time of 3:39.2, behind Herb Elliott (Australia) and Michel Jazy (France).

Olavi Salsola   (Finland, 1933–1995)

3:40.2   **Turku, Finland**   **11 Jul 1957**

See the biography below.

Olavi Salonen   (Finland, b. 1933)

3:40.2   **Turku, Finland**   **11 Jul 1957**

In Finland on 11 July 1957 a dead heat took place in a 1500m race, with two athletes sharing the world record. Remarkably both these athletes and the third place-getter, Olavi Vuorisalo, had the same first name. All three were born in the same year.

In this unheralded race in Turku there were 13 runners, all Finns except Sweden's Dan Waern. The Swede took them through a very fast 1200m, and then the Olavis fought all the way to the finish, astonishing the crowd with a new world record of 3:40.2. Ninth man in the race was Matti Nurmi, son of the great Paavo.

Olavi Salsola was an engineer and later became a sports shoe manufacturer. He had run in the Melbourne Olympics but went out in the heats of the 1500m. He never improved on that 1957 performance. At the 1958 European Championships he came in twelfth and last.

Olavi Salonen was six days Salsola's senior and had a longer career, winning 15 Finnish titles through 1965. He did not make it through to the finals of the 1958 European Championships nor to the 1960 or 1964 Olympics, but did come in fourth in the 1962 European 800m Championships, although many Finns swear he actually finished second.

Stanislav Jungwirth   (Czechoslovakia, 1930–1986)

3:38.1   **Stara Boleslav, Czechoslovakia**   **12 Jul 1957**

Alas for Finland, the world record of Olavi Salsola and Olavi Salonen lasted just 24 hours. Stanislav Jungwirth already had quite a respectable career by 1957. He had run third in the 1954 European Championships, behind Roger Bannister and Gunnar Nielsen. Originally a race walker, he had been inspired by the feats of Emil Zatopek and changed to middle-distance running. He was sixth in the final of the 1500m at the Melbourne Olympics in 1956.

Jungwirth had been running excellent times in the summer of 1957, and he seriously believed he could break the elusive 3:40 barrier. In the Czech town of Stara Boleslav, in front of a tiny crowd of 421 spectators, on a track 364 meters in circumference and with only four other runners, Jungwirth ran 3:38.1. He was jubilant—he had smashed the world record by over two seconds and had done it entirely through his own efforts.

However, the rest of his career proved to be anticlimactic. What he couldn't have foreseen was the arrival of a new athlete who would rapidly eclipse his times. In 1957 Herb Elliott of Australia began his unbeaten career. The two finally met on 28 August 1958 in Gothenburg, and the Australian won by three seconds. The world record was once again reduced by a further 2.1 seconds to 3:36.0, with Jungwirth second in 3:39.0.

Perhaps that defeat diminished his enthusiasm. He was unable to run faster than 3:42 in future races and retired in 1961. Jungwirth died at age 56 of kidney cancer.

Herb Elliott   (Australia, b. 1938)

| 3:36.0 | Gothenburg, Sweden | 28 Aug 1958 |
| 3:35.6 | Rome, Italy | 6 Sep 1960 |

Herb Elliott had a brief international career—really only two full seasons: 1958 and 1960—and retired at the ripe old age of 22. His career is detailed in chapter 6 on the mile. He went undefeated through a very long 1958 season, becoming the new mile record holder on 6 August. Twenty-two days later he lined up against the best 1500m runners in Gothenburg. In this race he took off after the 800m mark, his usual tactic, and just kept going, demolishing Jungwirth's record by 2.1 seconds. He won the race by three seconds, and the performance was so impressive that many well-known milers did not contest the 1500m at the 1960 Rome Olympics.

In Rome the 1500m final followed a similar pattern: Elliott broke away at the 900m mark, and that was it. None of the other runners could stay with him. He took another 0.4 second off the world record with 3:35.6.

He eventually went into a career in business. He is currently general manager of the North American operations of a sport shoe company.

Herb Elliott, Australia (1500m, mile), undefeated over these distances in his career.

Jim Ryun   (United States, b. 1947)

| 3:33.1 | Los Angeles, USA | 8 Jul 1967 |

Jim Ryun held world records in both the 1500m and the mile. His career is covered in more detail in chapter 6 on the mile. He broke the 1500m world record at age 20 in a match between the United States and the British Commonwealth in Los Angeles. With a last lap of 53.3 seconds, he demolished Kenya's Kip Keino in 3:33.1 to take 2.5 seconds off Herb

Elliott's respected world record. He seemed to have a brilliant career stretching out in front of him.

Ironically, his best years were already behind him, although this was partly caused by factors outside his control. The 1968 Mexico City Olympics at high altitude suited the African distance runners, many of whom were born and trained at high altitude. Kip Keino took advantage of this factor to run a calculated front race in the 1500m and established a lead that Ryun could not overcome.

At the 1972 Munich Olympics Ryun was suddenly bumped or pushed in his 1500m heat and fell heavily onto the track. By the time he regained his feet, he was way behind and out of the running. Ryun always believed that the push was deliberate and that he had been targeted before the race. It took him a long time to come to terms with the incident, though ultimately he overcame his resentment.

Jim Ryun, United States (1500m, mile).

Filbert Bayi   (Tanzania, b. 1953)

3:32.2   **Christchurch, New Zealand**   **2 Feb 1974**

Filbert Bayi was Tanzania's one and only world record holder. He is chiefly remembered for his "suicidal" tactics in the first half of a race, where he set an extremely fast pace. These tactics were generally more successful in the early part of his career.

He was born in a grass house, 130 kilometers (81 miles) from Kilimanjaro in Tanganyika (now Tanzania). At age 17 he joined the air force to train as a mechanic. He earned a trip to the 1972 Munich Olympics but went out in the heats of the 1500m and the steeplechase.

Filbert Bayi, Tanzania (1500m, mile), wins the 1974 Commonwealth Games 1500m in world record time from John Walker, New Zealand.

However, in 1973 he inflicted an unexpected defeat on the great Kip Keino and developed his technique of "catch me if you can." This led to his world record run in the 1974 Commonwealth Games 1500m in Christchurch, New Zealand. His first lap was timed at 54.4 seconds, the 800m time was 1:51.8, and the 1200m time was 2:50.3. Bayi held his form to the tape, even though John Walker of New Zealand closed within two meters at the end. Bayi's time was 3:32.2.

In many ways, that race was the highlight of his career, even though he became world mile record holder in 1975. He missed the 1976 Olympics because of the African boycott, a great personal disappointment. Bayi had to wait until 1980 to earn an Olympic silver medal in the 3000m steeplechase. He graduated in physical education and sports administration from the University of Texas, El Paso, and is currently head coach of the Tanzanian army athletic team.

Sebastian Coe (Great Britain, b. 1956)

3:32.1	Zürich, Switzerland	15 Aug 1979

Bayi's record lasted five years, until Britain's Sebastian Coe had his magic record breaking spree in 1979. On 5 July 1979 Coe set a new 800m record. Twelve days later he set a new mile record in Oslo. Accordingly, the pressure on him to take the 1500m world record was immense. His attempt was made in Zürich on 15 August in front of a packed stadium of 26,000 enthusiasts. So great was the craving for a world record that anything less would have been seen as a flop. After a pacesetter led the first lap, Coe took off from the 700m mark. Running the second half of the race entirely on his own, he went through the tape in 3:32.03. Under the rules of the day, this was rounded up to 3:32.1, just under Bayi's record.

Coe ran his personal best over this distance seven years later, when he ran 3:29.77 in 1986. The chapters on the 800m and the mile present more information about his career.

Steve Ovett (Great Britain, b. 1955)

3:32.1	Oslo, Norway	15 Jul 1980
3:31.36	Koblenz, West Germany	27 Aug 1980
3:30.77	Rieti, Italy	4 Sep 1983

Steve Ovett's family were market traders in Brighton. His international career started some four years before Coe's, when he came in second in the 1974 European 800m Championships at age 18. At the Montreal Olympics he was fifth in the 800m in 1:45.4. From that time on, he was largely invincible in the 1500m and mile, with impressive wins in the 1977 World Cup and the 1978 European Championships. He had a streak of 45 consecutive wins over 1500m or the mile and became the focus of the media by refusing to talk to them. Few athletes have generated such massive media interest in the sport. He also patented a "wave to the crowd" gesture as he came down the finishing straight, almost invariably in front. The crowd (most of them) loved it, although his opponents were less enthusiastic.

When Sebastian Coe arrived on the scene and set three world records in 1979, Ovett turned his attention to world records. He equaled Coe's 1500m mark one week before the 1980 Moscow Olympics. At the Olympics Ovett easily won the 800m. In the 1500m, perhaps overconfident and disturbed by a family row about his girlfriend, he couldn't match Coe's sprint finish and drifted back to third.

Three weeks after the Games Ovett set a new 1500m record of 3:31.36. After missing most of 1982 because of a spiked leg, he brought the record down to 3:30.77 in 1983.

In many ways that was the high-water mark of his career. He ran a disappointing 1983 World Championship 1500m to finish fourth and was ill at the 1984 Olympics, although he bounced back two years later to win the Commonwealth 5000m title. Along with Coe, Ovett missed selection to the 1988 Seoul Olympics. He now lives in Scotland.

Sydney Maree   (South Africa/United States, b. 1956)

3:31.24   Cologne, West Germany   28 Aug 1983

Sydney Maree was born in South Africa but had to emigrate to have any chance of an international career. He was restricted by the ban on South African athletes because of the apartheid policy and found it necessary to take on a new nationality. His father had served time as a political prisoner on Robbin Island, where Nelson Mandela was long imprisoned.

Whereas other South Africans such as Zola Budd and Marcello Fiasconaro were given instant citizenship in their new countries, Maree had to sit out several frustrating years before he could eventually compete for the United States. He enrolled at Villanova University in 1979 and showed his talent in 1981 by winning the AAU 1500m title and later by inflicting a significant defeat on the apparently invincible Steve Ovett. He acquired full U.S. citizenship in 1984; his wife, Lisa, is an American.

Maree achieved a 1500m world record in 1983, when he stormed home in Cologne in 3:31.24. He was injured during the 1984

Sydney Maree, South Africa/United States (1500m).

Olympics and later moved up to the 5000m. In 1985 in Oslo he chased Said Aouita home, pushing the Moroccan to a new world 5000m record and setting an American record himself that lasted 10 years (13:01.15). Maree won the 1987 AAU 5000m title and was fifth at the 1988 Olympics in Seoul.

Steve Cram   (Great Britain, b. 1960)

3:29.67   Nice, France   16 Jul 1985

Steve Cram was the third Englishman to dominate the 1500m and mile distances in the late 1970s and early 1980s. For many years he lived under the shadow of Coe and Ovett. He broke the four-minute mile at age 17, ran at the 1978 Commonwealth Games, and was eighth in the 1980 Olympic 1500m final. Both Coe and Ovett missed much of the 1982 season from illness and injury, so when Cram won both the European and Commonwealth 1500m titles that year, it was thought that he really only did so by default. He finally put that right in 1983, when he beat Ovett twice, first at the World Championships and later in a memorable duel in London. However, at the 1984 Olympics, he couldn't match a rejuvenated Coe in the 1500m and came home second.

In 1985 he had a dream year and took both 1500m and mile world records. The 1500m was an epic duel between Cram and the new Moroccan star, Said Aouita. Cram made a calculated sprint with 350 meters of the race to go. It opened a critical gap, which Aouita could not quite close: Cram timed 3:29.67, and Aouita 3:29.71. Both men had broken the 3:30 barrier.

Cram also set the mile record that season and in 1986 achieved the European and Commonwealth Games 1500m double again. He slipped ever so slightly from then on and could not quite recapture his glory days of 1985-86. In 1988 he finished fourth in the 1500m at the Seoul Olympics; at the 1990 European Championships he was fifth.

After Cram's departure from the scene, it was realized that a golden era in British middle-distance running had come to an end.

Said Aouita   (Morocco, b. 1959)

3:29.46   **Berlin, West Germany**   **23 Aug 1985**

Said Aouita was the first great distance runner to come out of Morocco. He was initially more interested in the national sport, soccer, but took up track and field seriously in 1978. By 1983 he went to the World Championships as a likely favorite for the 1500m. However, Cram and American Steve Scott moved past him in a tactical race.

He made no mistakes at the Olympics in 1984. He could have chosen either the 1500m or the 5000m, as he was now brilliant at both events. He chose the longer distance and did not disappoint, winning Morocco's first men's Olympic gold medal. Aouita did not let modesty interfere with his public pronouncements. He claimed he would have won the Olympic 1500m if he had chosen to enter. Indeed, he became much irritated when later races against Coe didn't materialize. His dream to become the first man to break 3:30 for the 1500m was shattered when Cram just beat him to it in Nice in 1985. Determined to make up for this, he went to Berlin six weeks later and duly took 0.21 second off Cram's new record with 3:29.46.

The 1988 Olympics were not kind to him: He suffered a hamstring injury in finishing third in the 800m. He set one more world record in 1989 in the 3000m. This meant that he simultaneously held world records for 1500m, 2000m, 3000m, and 5000m, a remarkable achievement. But in the 1990s his star started to fade as another North African emerged, Noureddine Morceli. Despite his public bravado, Aouita is said to be very courteous in private.

Noureddine Morceli   (Algeria, b. 1970)

3:28.86   **Rieti, Italy**   **6 Sep 1992**
3:27.37   **Nice, France**   **12 Jul 1995**

Algeria has had a few champions in distance running. Under French Colonial rule, Boughèra El Ouafi won the Olympic marathon in 1928, and Alain Mimoun won it in 1956. Both these runners ran in French colors. But after Algerian independence in 1959 no further champions emerged until Noureddine Morceli burst on to the middle-distance scene in 1990. His career is detailed more fully in chapter 6 on the mile. Essentially, from 1990 he became the world's premier 1500m and mile runner and has remained as such through to

1996. He has won the World Championships 1500m title three times in a row in 1991, 1993, and 1995.

Not particularly tall, he weighs only 62 kilograms (137 pounds) but is deceptively fast, especially over the last lap. However, Morceli disappointed his fans in the 1992 Olympics when he came in seventh in the 1500m, possibly because of leg injuries before the Olympics that caused him to miss seven weeks of training.

Much disappointed by his Olympic showing, he determined to make amends. He had been knocking on the door of a world record for two or three seasons, and he finally achieved this in Rieti, Italy, where he sliced 0.6 second off Aouita's 1500m record.

Three years later in Nice, he took almost 1½ seconds off his own 1500m record. His younger brother Ali acted as pacemaker for the first 600 meters. Noureddine himself hit the front with 600 meters left to run and ran a 54-second last lap to record 3:27.37. In the interim he had broken the mile record in 1994.

In 1996 he finally obtained his Olympic gold medal. The 1500m went uneventfully for him, helped by the fall of the impressive young Moroccan Hicham El Guerroudj.

A modest teetotaler remarkably unchanged by his years of success, Morceli held world records in 1995 in the 1500m, mile, 2000m, and 3000m.

Conclusions

The 1500m has been dominated by Noureddine Morceli in recent years and no other athlete currently seems capable of challenging his times. That will change. The record perhaps may be further reduced by Morceli himself, who is still in his mid-20s, unless a hitherto unknown talent emerges to challenge it.

Six All-Time Fastest: Men's 1500m		
Noureddine Morceli (ALG)	3:27.37	1995
Hicham El Guerroudj (MOR)	3:29.05	1996
Said Aouita (MOR)	3:29.46	1985
Steve Cram (GBR)	3:29.67	1985
Sebastian Coe (GBR)	3:29.77	1986
Sydney Maree (USA)	3:29.77	1985
Prediction	*3:25.0*	*2015*

Top Three: Men's 1500m

GOLD MEDAL: Noureddine Morceli (ALG)
SILVER MEDAL: Herb Elliott (AUST)
BRONZE MEDAL: Jim Ryun (USA)

The mile run has a mystique unlike any other track and field event and is the only nonmetric distance still officially recognized for world records. The mystique arises from the mathematical simplicity of a hypothetical race consisting of four laps of one-minute duration, resulting in a four-minute mile. There have been 22 men who have broken or equaled the world mile record 31 times since records were officially recognized in 1912: six Britons; four Americans; three New Zealanders; two each from Sweden, France, and Australia; and one athlete each from Finland, Tanzania, and Algeria. Of these athletes, seven have won Olympic 1500m gold medals: Nurmi, Lovelock, Elliott, Snell, Walker, Coe, and Morceli.

No track and field event before or since has captured the imagination of the sporting public as did the assault on the four-minute barrier in the 1950s. The mathematical equation of running four laps in exactly four minutes generated enormous interest, especially as there were attempts on it by athletes from three continents. When it was finally broken, people realized that the barrier—like most athletic barriers—was purely psychological. The four-minute mile has an enduring appeal and 40 years on still represents a useful landmark for the up-and-coming miler.

Men's World Records for One Mile

Record time	Record holder	Location	Date
4:14.4	John Paul Jones (USA)	Cambridge, USA	31 May 1913
4:12.6	Norman Taber (USA)	Cambridge, USA	16 Jul 1915
4:10.4	Paavo Nurmi (FIN)	Stockholm, Sweden	23 Aug 1923
4:09.2	Jules Ladoumègue (FRA)	Paris, France	4 Oct 1931
4:07.6	Jack Lovelock (NZ)	Princeton, USA	15 Jul 1933
4:06.8	Glenn Cunningham (USA)	Princeton, USA	16 Jun 1934
4:06.4	Sydney Wooderson (GBR)	London, England	28 Aug 1937
4:06.2	Gunder Hägg (SWE)	Gothenburg, Sweden	1 Jul 1942
4:06.2	Arne Andersson (SWE)	Stockholm, Sweden	10 Jul 1942
4:04.6	Gunder Hägg (SWE)	Stockholm, Sweden	4 Sep 1942
4:02.6	Arne Andersson (SWE)	Gothenburg, Sweden	1 Jul 1943
4:01.6	Arne Andersson (SWE)	Malmö, Sweden	18 Jul 1944
4:01.4	Gunder Hägg (SWE)	Malmö, Sweden	17 Jul 1945
3:59.4	Roger Bannister (GBR)	Oxford, England	6 May 1954
3:58.0	John Landy (AUST)	Turku, Finland	21 Jun 1954
3:57.2	Derek Ibbotson (GBR)	London, England	19 Jul 1957
3:54.5	Herb Elliott (AUST)	Dublin, Ireland	6 Aug 1958
3:54.4	Peter Snell (NZ)	Wanganui, New Zealand	27 Jan 1962
3:54.1	Peter Snell (NZ)	Auckland, New Zealand	17 Nov 1964
3:53.6	Michel Jazy (FRA)	Rennes, France	9 Jun 1965
3:51.3	Jim Ryun (USA)	Berkeley, USA	17 Jul 1966
3:51.1	Jim Ryun (USA)	Bakersfield, USA	23 Jun 1967
3:51.0	Filbert Bayi (TAN)	Kingston, Jamaica	17 May 1975
3:49.4	John Walker (NZ)	Gothenburg, Sweden	12 Aug 1975
3:49.0	Sebastian Coe (GBR)	Oslo, Norway	17 Jul 1979
3:48.8	Steve Ovett (GBR)	Oslo, Norway	1 Jul 1980
3:48.53	Sebastian Coe (GBR)	Zürich, Switzerland	19 Aug 1981

3:48.40	Steve Ovett (GBR)	Koblenz, West Germany	26 Aug 1981
3:47.33	Sebastian Coe (GBR)	Brussels, Belgium	28 Aug 1981
3:46.32	Steve Cram (GBR)	Oslo, Norway	27 Jul 1985
3:44.39	Noureddine Morceli (ALG)	Rieti, Italy	12 Sep 1993

John Paul Jones   (United States, 1890–1970)

4:14.4   **Cambridge, USA**   **31 May 1913**

John Paul Jones's mile time in 1913 was recognized as the first official one-mile world record by the newly formed IAAF. His father died when John was young, so when he became a student of engineering at Cornell University, he worked in a laundry to pay his way. At Cornell he won the intercollegiate cross-country championship three years in a row (1910-12). He traveled to the 1912 Stockholm Olympics as one of the favorites for the 1500m. Perhaps the rough sea voyage put him out of condition. He and the other highly fancied Americans were outkicked by the British runner Arnold Jackson (3:56.8). In a tight finish Jones finished fourth.

In 1913 he raced a mile at the Harvard Stadium against Norman Taber of Brown University. Taber led the way to the three-quarter-mile mark in 3:16.1. But Jones ran away in the last lap to finish in 4:14.4. The mile record by professional athletes was held by Britain's Walter George, who ran 4:12.75 in 1886, but Jones's time was the first official mile record by an amateur.

Jones later became a successful engineer. His firm was based in Cleveland and built the Anabel Taylor Hall at Cornell University.

Norman Taber   (United States, 1891–1952)

4:12.6   **Cambridge, USA**   **16 Jul 1915**

Norman Taber was one of the six Americans in the 1500m final at the 1912 Stockholm Olympics, where he finished third. The next year he finished second by two seconds to John Paul Jones in the mile record at the Harvard Stadium as described in the previous section on Jones.

In 1914 Taber traveled to England, having won a Rhodes scholarship. On his return to the United States, he made up his mind to train hard, something that wasn't common in those days, and make a determined effort on the one-mile record. In addition to the amateur record, he wanted to beat the long-standing professional record of 4:12.75, set by England's Walter George in 1886.

The attempt was made in the same Harvard Stadium that Jones had set his record, but this time three men were given handicap starts. The farthest away from the start, J.M. Burke, was given a 355-yard start. Taber had the encouragement of his fiancée, who was one of the spectators. Taber's time for each lap was 58, 67, 68, and finally 59.6 seconds, for a final time of 4:12.6

Taber apparently had a letdown after this victory because he was defeated a month later at the AAU titles in San Francisco. He was outkicked by Joie Ray of Illinois in a 4:23.2 mile. Taber won the AAU title once, in 1913, with a time of 4:26.0.

Paavo Nurmi (Finland, 1897–1973)

4:10.4   **Stockholm, Sweden**   **23 Aug 1923**

The great Paavo Nurmi, megastar of running in the 1920s, ran the mile rarely, mainly on his U.S. tour in 1925. However, in 1923 he took part in a two-man race, a rare phenomenon in track and field. Sweden's Edwin Wide had been running impressive times and challenged Nurmi to a duel at a race of the Finn's choosing. Nurmi could have chosen the 5000m, his forte, but chose a distance at which Wide was strong, the mile. The race took place at the Olympic stadium in Stockholm in front of a crowd of 18,000. Wide led at the ¼-mile stage with 60.1, but Nurmi took over to lead narrowly at the ½-mile mark in 2:03.2. In those days most athletes cruised the third lap in preparation for the last-lap sprint. But Nurmi pushed the third lap hard, in 63.5, to reach the ¾-mile mark in 3:06.7, with Wide 0.6 second behind. But when Nurmi continued this pressure in the last lap, Wide was unable to respond. Nurmi went on to win in 4:10.4, with Wide 18 yards behind (4:13.1).

More information about Nurmi can be found in the chapters on 1500m, 5000m, and 10,000m.

Jules Ladoumègue (France, 1906–1973)

4:09.2   **Paris, France**   **4 Oct 1931**

Jules Ladoumègue was the first athlete to break 4:10 for the mile. He was born in Bordeaux in 1906. His father, working on the wharves, was killed by a collapse of timber before Jules was born. His mother died in a house fire shortly after his birth. These events left him with a sensitive nature, although he was subsequently raised in an affectionate household.

From 1929 to 1931 he was invincible. Yet throughout his career he suffered from extreme prerace nerves, often vomiting before the race began. Once the race started, he was fine—until the next race.

In 1930 Ladoumègue had broken Peltzer's world 1500m record by 1.8 seconds. Accordingly, in 1931 in Paris he made a deliberate attempt on Nurmi's mile record. In a race with seven Frenchmen, with two false starts,

Jules Ladoumègue, France (1500m, mile), the first man to run the mile under 4:10.

he took 1.2 seconds off Nurmi's record. He was actually 1.3 seconds down at the ¾-mile mark but had a much faster finish than Nurmi. Ladoumègue ran the last lap in 61.2 seconds, whereas Nurmi had run his last lap in 63.7. Ladoumègue's winning time was 4:09.2.

Ladoumègue was now the toast of France and was expected to win the 1932 Olympic 1500m title. But to the dismay of all France, he was charged by the French athletic federation for receiving illegal payments for his races. The penalty was disqualification for life.

Jack Lovelock   (New Zealand, 1910–1949)

4:07.6   **Princeton, USA**   **15 Jul 1933**

One of the major meets in the 1930s was that between the Oxford-Cambridge and the Princeton-Cornell Universities. Lovelock was selected to run the mile in the 1933 race in Princeton. The main challenge was 20-year-old Bill Bonthron, who in 1934 broke the world 1500m record.

Bonthron took the lead after two laps (2:03.5) and went through the ¾-mile mark in 3:08.6, with Lovelock one pace behind. Bonthron put on a sprint with 300m to go, but Lovelock always stayed with him. Entering the home straight, Lovelock made a last surge and went on to win in 4:07.6, a new world record. Bonthron recorded 4:08.7, also under the old record.

Lovelock had other triumphs as 1934 Empire Games mile champion and 1936 Olympic 1500m champion in a new world record time. He eventually practiced medicine in New York. At age 39 he fell under an oncoming train while waiting at a New York subway. His accident was said to be caused by an epileptic seizure, although some of his contemporaries said he actually committed suicide.

Glenn Cunningham   (United States, 1909–1988)

4:06.8   **Princeton, USA**   **16 Jun 1934**

In the 1930s, the director of athletics at Princeton University had the idea of an Invitational Games, staged after the Yale-Princeton baseball game. For the 1934 mile, three men were invited: Bill Bonthron, Glenn Cunningham, and Gene Venzke. They were watched by a crowd of 25,000.

Cunningham had been burnt as a child in a kerosene fire, suffering extensive leg burns, and spent six months in the hospital. He started running to strengthen his legs. Despite this major trauma he went on to become one of America's great milers in the 1930s. He was fourth in the 1932 Los Angeles Olympic 1500m and won the AAU title five times.

In the 1934 Invitational mile Venzke led at the ¼-mile mark in 61.7 seconds, but Cunningham forced himself into the lead at the ½-mile mark with 2:05.8. He held the lead at the 3/4-mile mark in 3:07.6 and went on to win by 20 yards in 4:06.8, taking 0.8 second off the world record.

Cunningham had high hopes of being the Olympic 1500m champion in Berlin in 1936. However, he was caught napping by Jack Lovelock of New Zealand, who sprinted with 300 meters to go. Lovelock won in world record time, 3:47.8; Cunningham was second in 3:48.4.

In World War II Cunningham served in the U.S. Navy. After the war he ran a ranch in Kansas, where he and his wife raised twelve children of their own and also took in underprivileged children. He appeared at the 1988 USA Indoor Championships at age 78; he died a few weeks later.

Sydney Wooderson   (Great Britain, b. 1914)

4:06.4   **London, England**   **28 Aug 1937**

Sydney Wooderson won the Public School Mile in 1933 and then became an articled clerk to study law. He represented England at the 1934 Commonwealth Games, finishing second to Jack Lovelock in the mile. But he did achieve some significant victories over Lovelock at both the 1935 and 1936 AAA mile championships. However, shortly after his 1936 win Wooderson stumbled into a rabbit hole. The resulting ankle injury ruined his Olympic chances, and he did not finish his 1500m heat.

In 1937 at his local club ground Wooderson made a successful attempt on the mile record, helped by handicap runners. His lap times were 58.6, 2:02.6, 3:07.2, and finally 4:06.4.

His poor eyesight meant that he was not in a combat role in World War II, and he served in the National Fire Service during the worst days of the Blitz. In 1946 he was European 5000m champion, but by this time new milers (Hägg and Andersson) had emerged from Sweden. Wooderson had two epic races with Andersson just after the war, but the Swede won both. He finished a distinguished career by winning the 1948 British Cross Country Championships.

Sydney Wooderson, Great Britain (800m, mile), defeating Jack Lovelock, New Zealand (1500m, mile), in 1935.

Gunder Hägg   (Sweden, b. 1918)

4:06.2	Gothenburg, Sweden	1 Jul 1942
4:04.6	Stockholm, Sweden	4 Sep 1942
4:01.4	Malmö, Sweden	17 Jul 1945

Sweden's magic milers, Gundar Hägg (1500m, mile, 5000m), *left*, and Arne Andersson (1500m, mile).

Gunder Hägg was born in Jamtland, Sweden's forest country, where his father was a forest worker. His career has been covered in the chapter on 1500m. Hägg's first mile record came in July 1942 when he ran 4:06.1, with Arne Andersson second in 4:06.4. Under the rules then in effect the record was rounded up to 4:06.2. Andersson equaled this record nine days later in Stockholm, but Hägg reduced it to 4:04.6 in September.

In July 1943 Andersson took a further two seconds off the record (4:02.6) and in 1944 one further second off (4:01.6), when he beat Hägg by 0.4 second.

However, in 1945 it was Hägg's turn. In July he led all the way to a record 4:01.4, with Andersson second in 4:02.2. That was their last world record race; the record was to survive nine years.

Arne Andersson   (Sweden, b. 1917)

4:06.2	Stockholm, Sweden	10 Jul 1942
4:02.6	Gothenburg, Sweden	1 Jul 1943
4:01.6	Malmö, Sweden	18 Jul 1944

Arne Andersson was the other half of the great Swedish duo and, with Gunder Hägg, reduced the mile record by five seconds during the war years. Details of their clashes are given in the preceding section on Hägg. Andersson's best year was 1944, and he beat Hägg six times out of seven in that season. The two Swedish milers were years ahead of their contemporaries. But as the war ended, a new generation of Swedish milers emerged, led by Lennart Strand. Strand beat both Andersson and Hägg in September 1945, the first time both men had been beaten comprehensively by another runner. It was the end of a golden era in Swedish distance running.

Roger Bannister   (Great Britain, b. 1929)

| 3:59.4 | Oxford, England | 6 May 1954 |

Roger Bannister entered Oxford University to study medicine. He showed remarkable maturity in declining a chance to run in the 1948 Olympics in London on the grounds that he was not yet fully ready. He preferred to wait until the 1952 Olympics. In the fullness of time he did run in the 1500m final at the Helsinki Olympics in 1952 but finished fourth.

In fact, 1954 was to be his year of athletic glory. He had run the mile in 4:02.0 in 1953, but the pacesetting was so blatant that the British officials would not accept it. However, he now knew that a four-minute mile was within his capabilities. A new attempt was made at Oxford in 1954. His friend Chris

Roger Bannister, Great Britain, the world's first four-minute miler.

Brasher ran the first two laps in 1:58. Then Chris Chataway took over in the third lap to reach the ¾-mile mark in 3:00.7. This was prearranged so that Bannister could then challenge for the record in the last lap. He stormed home in 58.7 seconds to record 3:59.4. The four-minute mile barrier had been broken. No other track and field milestone has so captured public imagination.

Bannister went on to complete a vintage season. John Landy reduced the world record six weeks later, so the world's first two four-minute-milers met in August 1954 at the Commonwealth Games in Vancouver, Canada. Bannister proved too strong at the finish and won in 3:58.8, 0.8 second ahead of Landy. Three weeks later he won the European 1500m championship.

After this remarkable year Bannister retired and in due course became a consultant neurologist in London. He edited a textbook, *Brain's Clinical Neurology,* in 1969, which was later retitled *Brain and Bannister's Clinical Neurology* in 1990. He was knighted in 1975 and has been master of Pembroke College, Oxford, since 1985.

John Landy   (Australia, b. 1930)

3:58.0   **Turku, Finland**   **21 Jun 1954**

John Landy, Australia (1500m, mile), the second man to break the four-minute mile.

John Landy was an agricultural student competent at both Australian rules football and running. At age 22 he was selected for the 1952 Olympics in both the 1500m and the 5000m but was eliminated in the early rounds. On his return home he broke with his coach, Percy Cerutty, to try new training methods he had learned overseas. By the end of 1952 he had improved nine seconds in the mile to record 4:02.1. The four-minute mile seemed to be his for the taking.

It was not to be. There were no other quality milers in Australia at that time, so most of his runs were almost solo time trials. Time and again, he made attempts on the record but couldn't drop below 4:02 in Australia. In 1954 he accepted an invitation to travel to Finland, where the better tracks and competition might allow him to challenge the record. But while there, he learned that Bannister had crossed the four-minute barrier first.

However, six weeks later Chris Chataway, who had helped Bannister to the new record, came over to Finland to race against Landy. Under perfect conditions, Landy improved his personal best by 3.7 seconds to record 3:57.9, rounded up under the rules of the day to 3:58.0.

In many ways, that was to be the highlight of his career. He lost to Roger Bannister in the clash between the two at the Empire Games in August 1954, 3:58.8 to 3:59.4, and came in third at the 1956 Melbourne Olympic 1500m.

Perhaps his most remarkable performance came in the 1956 Australian Mile Championships. In the middle of the race, young Ron Clarke tripped and fell. Landy actually stopped running and went back to Clarke to check that he was not hurt. Then he turned back to the race; the field was by this time some 40 yards ahead, yet he still managed to win.

Derek Ibbotson   (Great Britain, b. 1932)

3:57.2   **London, England**   **19 Jul 1957**

Derek Ibbotson came from Yorkshire, where he began life as a coal miner. His promise as an athlete developed rapidly after joining the Royal Air Force in 1954. He entered the Emsley Carr Mile in 1956, largely because his fiancée wanted an extra ticket for the subsequent banquet. Without exhaustion, he won in 3:59.4 to equal Bannister's British record. He was selected for the 5000m at the 1956 Melbourne Olympic Games, although his preference had been for the 1500m. In the end, he achieved a bronze medal behind the all-conquering Vladimir Kuts (USSR) and Gordon Pirie (Great Britain).

Ibbotson broke Landy's record with 3:57.2 in a highly competitive race at the White City Stadium in London in 1957. The first four men home all came in under four minutes.

After this brilliant success Ibbotson probably harmed his athletic career by racing too frequently. That year he raced over 70 times. A cheerful, carefree type, he took on perhaps too many racing commitments and never reproduced his 1957 season.

Herb Elliott   (Australia, b. 1938)

3:54.5   **Dublin, Ireland**   **6 Aug 1958**

Herb Elliott holds a record that will probably never be beaten: He won every mile or 1500m race that he contested as a senior athlete. From 1957 to 1961 he raced over these distances 42 times and came in first 42 times. Born in 1938 in Perth, Western Australia, he showed schoolboy promise but gave up athletics in 1955 after an injury to his foot while moving a piano. However, a trip to Melbourne to watch the 1956 Olympic Games reawakened his enthusiasm, and he remained in Melbourne to train under the eccentric coach Percy Cerutty. As his career unfolded his winning streak simply continued. In a very long season in 1958 he continued his unbeaten record, despite challenges from the best American and European milers in tours across the Northern Hemisphere. At the Commonwealth Games in Cardiff he won both the 880 yards and the mile. He finally broke the world record in Dublin, running against Olympic 1500m gold medalist Ron Delaney. Elliott took a massive 2.7 seconds off Ibbotson's time, running 3:54.5. Later that season Elliott took the 1500m world record as well (3:36.0).

Elliott drifted away from athletics after that exhausting season. In May 1959 he married and then began studying for entrance exams to Cambridge University. However, as the Olympic year came around, he started training seriously again. He was duly rewarded with a gold medal in Rome, with another 1500m world record (3:35.6) to conclude an impeccable career.

Peter Snell   (New Zealand, b. 1938)

3:54.4   **Wanganui, New Zealand**   **27 Jan 1962**
3:54.1   **Auckland, New Zealand**   **17 Nov 1964**

Peter Snell was the unknown athlete who won the 1960 Olympic 800m title in the last strides of the race. From this meteoric beginning, Snell dominated the world's middle distance runners for the next four years. In 1962 he duplicated Herb Elliott's feat of winning both the 880 yards and the mile at the Commonwealth Games. Although he occasionally lost unimportant races, he won both the 800m and the 1500m at the 1964 Tokyo Olympics.

Snell had first reduced Elliott's mile record in 1962 on a grass track in Wanganui, New Zealand. His time of 3:54.4 took 0.1 second off Elliott's record. It was a unique race in that all of his lap times increased in speed: 60.7, 59.9, 59.0, and 54.8 seconds. In 1964, after his Olympic victories, he again attacked the world mile record, this time with the tactic of leading all the way. He raced to a ¾-mile time of 2:54.3, well ahead of world record pace. But his legs tied up in the last 300m, and he removed "only" 0.3 second off the world record.

Snell's remarkable career includes world records in the 800m and the mile and three Olympic gold medals.

Michel Jazy   (France, b. 1936)

3:53.6   **Rennes, France**   **9 Jun 1965**

Michel Jazy, France (mile).

Michel Jazy had competed in the 1956 Melbourne Olympic Games in the 1500m but had gone out in the heats. In 1960 he was a surprise silver medalist in the 1500m behind Herb Elliott, finishing 0.1 second off the European record with 3:38.4.

Jazy was born in Oignies on 13 June 1936. His father died while Michel was young. Jazy went to work as a printer on *L'Equipe,* the famous French sports paper.

In many ways 1962 was his best year. He set world record times in the 2000m and 3000m and won the French 800m championship. Then he won the European 1500m championship to cap a great season.

For the 1964 Tokyo Olympics he chose the 5000m. He dashed to the front with 400m to run but faded in the last 50m and finished fourth. A disappointed Jazy talked of retiring, but thousands of his supporters met him at the airport on his return and persuaded him to continue his career. The following year he surprised himself with a European record for the mile in early June, so he decided to make an attack on the world record. In a field of nine runners, all Frenchmen, Jazy had lap times of 57.5, 59.0, 60.9, and 56.2 for a final total 3:53.6. He took 0.5 second off Peter Snell's record. For the second time, this most English of records was held by a Frenchman.

Jazy won the 1966 European 5000m Championships and was second in the 1500m. Later that season he also set a world record over 2000m. This remains a French record, 30 years later.

Jim Ryun   (United States, b. 1947)

| 3:51.3 | Berkeley, USA | 17 Jul 1966 |
| 3:51.1 | Bakersfield, USA | 23 Jun 1967 |

Jim Ryun achieved such great heights as a teenage athlete that it was not surprising that his later career was one of mixed fortunes. Born in Wichita, Kansas, he took up track and field seriously at age 15 by doing 10- to 15-mile runs, remarkable workouts for a schoolboy. By age 17 he had beaten four minutes for the mile, something rarely achieved even by today's young athletes. This generated enormous media interest. He qualified as the third runner on the U.S. 1500m team for the 1964 Tokyo Olympics. Plagued by flu, however, he went out in the semifinals.

He achieved a notable victory over Peter Snell in 1965, toward the end of the latter's career, at the AAU Championships in San Diego. He had, in fact, developed a "Snell-like" burst of pace in the last lap that few could match. In 1966 he took a massive 2.3 seconds off the mile record with 3:51.3. A year later he took the 1500m world record and also reduced the mile record further, by another 0.2 second.

His Olympic hopes in 1968 were dashed by the high altitude of Mexico City, which favored African runners born and trained at high altitude. Kip Keino raced away with the 1500m title, while Ryun finished second 15 meters behind, 3:37.89 to 3:34.91.

At age 25 at the Olympic Games in Munich in 1972, Ryun fell, apparently pushed, in one of the 1500m heats and was not able to make up the distance. He subsequently ran for a short while with the professional group ITA. Ryun still holds the U.S. high school records for the 1500m and mile. In 1996 he was elected to the U.S. House of Representatives as a republican, representing a district in Kansas.

Filbert Bayi   (Tanzania, b. 1953)

| 3:51.0 | Kingston, Jamaica | 17 May 1975 |

Filbert Bayi was the first African to hold the world mile record. His father died young, and Filbert was raised by his mother and stepfather on a corn farm. His race tactic was to run the first two laps extremely fast. With this approach Bayi won the 1974 Commonwealth Games 1500m title, setting a world record in the 1500m of 3:32.2.

The next year he set his sights on the mile record. Using his usual front-running tactics, in Jamaica he took 0.1 second off Jim Ryun's eight-year-old record of 3:51.1.

Unfortunately for Bayi, politics prevented him from taking part in the 1976 Montreal Olympics. Black African countries boycotted the Games as a protest against a New Zealand rugby tour of South Africa. Malaria had weakened him, however, so he would have been less than fit anyway.

He finished second in the 1500m at the 1978 Commonwealth Games. He also went to the 1980 Moscow Olympics and came in second in the 3000m steeplechase.

John Walker   (New Zealand, b. 1952)

| 3:49.4 | Gothenburg, Sweden | 12 Aug 1975 |

New Zealand's John Walker improved his personal best over 1500m by four seconds when he finished second to Filbert Bayi's world record 3:32.2 at the 1974 Commonwealth Games. That brilliant second place (3:32.5) launched Walker as an international athlete. They ran again later that year at Helsinki. Bayi again started fast, but Walker caught him in the last lap. He finally set a mile record of his own in 1975 at Gothenburg. Walker led all the way from the halfway point, winning in 3:49.4. This took 1.6 seconds off Bayi's time and allowed Walker to become the first man to run the mile under 3:50.

At the 1976 Montreal Olympics the 1500m was a slow, tactical race, which he won narrowly in 3:39.17. Having conquered the twin peaks of track and field—a world record and an Olympic gold medal—he felt his career was complete. But he continued to run for many years and in fact improved on his world record time seven years later, running 3:49.08 in 1982. He could still break four minutes for the mile at age 38 and passed another milestone in February 1985 by becoming the first man to run 100 four-minute miles. He subsequently bred horses in New Zealand. In 1996 John Walker revealed that he was plagued by Parkinson's disease.

Sebastian Coe   (Great Britain, b. 1956)

3:49.0	Oslo, Norway	17 Jul 1979
3:48.53	Zürich, Switzerland	19 Aug 1981
3:47.33	Brussels, Belgium	28 Aug 1981

Britain's three golden milers in the 1984 Los Angeles 1500m final: Sebastian Coe (800m, 1500m, mile) leads over Steve Cram (1500m, mile) and Steve Ovett (1500m, mile). Ovett collapsed shortly after this picture was taken. Coe went on to win, with Cram second.

In July 1979 Coe astonished the athletic world by setting an 800m world record in Oslo, taking more than a second off the record with 1:42.33. On the strength of that performance, he was invited back to Oslo 12 days later to run in the "Golden Mile." Coe took over the race with 400 meters to go and took 0.4 second off John Walker's record.

Steve Ovett reduced the world record by 0.2 second in 1980. Coe reduced it again in Zürich on 19 August 1981 to 3:48.53. However, seven days later Ovett reduced it yet again by another 0.13 second, only to have Coe break the record two days after that by the huge margin of 1.07 seconds, down to 3:47.33.

Coe's other career highlights are covered in the 800m and 1500m chapters. To an observer, the one blemish in the careers of Sebastian Coe and Steve Ovett was their tactic of avoiding competing with each other at their career heights. None of the other champion milers had conspicuously done this. Coe also never raced against the new star, Said Aouita. Coe and Ovett raced against each other only in events such as the Olympic Games, where they could not avoid each other.

Steve Ovett   (Great Britain, b. 1955)

| 3:48.8 | Oslo, Norway | 1 Jul 1980 |
| 3:48.40 | Koblenz, West Germany | 26 Aug 1981 |

Steve Ovett competed as a top international athlete for four years before Sebastian Coe emerged. But 1979 saw Sebastian Coe break multiple world records, and Ovett now focused on them, something he had previously disdained. One year later he lowered Coe's mile record by 0.2 second. This was just prior to the 1980 Moscow Olympics, where he went as favorite for the 1500m. He won the 800m easily, but finished third in the 1500m to a reinvigorated Coe.

In 1981 the two Britons exchanged the mile record, though without racing against each other. A training run for Ovett in 1982 went wrong when he spiked himself against a fence, and he lost most of the season. He bounced back in 1983 with a world 1500m record but had a disappointing Olympics in 1984, when he was struck down by a virus. Ovett finished eighth in the 800m, clearly unwell, and was hospitalized briefly. He contested the 1500m but collapsed after three laps. His last major success was the 5000m at the 1986 Commonwealth Games.

Ovett never remained far from controversy with many feuds with the press. At the end of his career he was involved in a public, emotional, tearful denunciation of his former agent, Andy Norman, for allegedly not offering appearance money to Sebastian Coe. He has a unique record with wins at 800m (1980 Olympics), 1500m (1985 European Championships), and 5000m (1986 Commonwealth Games).

Steve Cram   (Great Britain, b. 1960)

| 3:46.32 | Oslo, Norway | 27 Jul 1985 |

Steve Cram was overshadowed by Coe and Ovett in the early part of his career. By 1982 he had moved up a level and started winning major championships. That year he won both the European and the Commonwealth 1500m titles, a rare achievement that he duplicated in 1986. In 1983 he beat Steve Ovett for the first time in winning the World Championships 1500m, in which Ovett finished fourth, and repeated the victory four weeks later in London. However, in 1984 he was outsprinted by Sebastian Coe in the 1500m final at the Los Angeles Olympics.

In many ways his best year was 1985, when he set world records at three distances: 1500m, 1 mile, and 2000m. His world mile record occurred at the famed Bislett Games in Oslo. Cram raced around the last lap in 54.2 seconds to finish with 3:46.32.

Although he won gold medals at the European, Commonwealth, and World Championships, Olympic gold medals have eluded him. Running in three Olympics in the 1500m, he finished eighth in 1980, second in 1984, and fourth in 1988.

Noureddine Morceli   (Algeria, b. 1970)

3:44.39   **Rieti, Italy**   **5 Sep 1993**

Noureddine Morceli was the first world record holder to emerge from Algeria. He was one of a family of nine and has a twin sister. Young Noureddine enrolled at the Riverside Junior College in California (1989-90). His coach there, Ted Banks, appreciated his special talent but found it hard to accept Morceli's confident predictions. In a 1990 interview with the British magazine *Athletics Today*, Banks was quoted: "He is very naive. He has said that he is capable of running a 3 minute 44 second mile." But in 1993 this happened. Morceli ran 3:44.39 in Rieti, Italy, to remove almost two seconds from Steve Cram's eight-year-old record, something he had been threatening to do for several seasons.

Prior to this world record he had effortlessly won the 1991 1500m World Championships in Tokyo, showing a capacity to run a very fast last lap of 51.5. However, the next year he finished a disappointing seventh in the 1500m at

Noureddine Morceli, Algeria (1500m, mile), 1996 Olympic 1500m champion.

the 1992 Barcelona Olympics. He ran uncharacteristically in a slow, boring, tactical final, in which the winning time (3:40.12) was the slowest performance since the 1956 Olympics. His seventh place was perhaps partly due to a right hip injury, which meant that he missed 45 days of training before the Games. Perhaps to atone for his Olympic failure, he attacked the world 1500m record later that season and reduced it by 0.64 second. A year later he aimed for the mile record and took 1.93 seconds off Cram's world record, averaging 56.10 seconds per lap with a time of 3:44.39.

His brother Abderahmane, fourth in the 1977 World Cup 1500m, acts as his coach, and his younger brother Ali is now acting as his pacesetter. In 1995 Noureddine won the 1500m at the World Championships to add to his previous 1991 and 1993 wins at the same competition. Finally, in 1996, he won the only athletic honor that had eluded him by comfortably winning the 1500m at the Atlanta Olympics.

Conclusions

Morceli's domination over the mile is similar to his domination over the 1500m; he remains a quantum leap above all other current milers. But the parade of milers is ever changing and new faces will surely emerge.

Five All-Time Fastest: Men's Mile

Noureddine Morceli (ALG)	3:44.39	1993
Steve Cram (GBR)	3:46.32	1985
Said Aouita (MOR)	3:46.76	1987
Sebastian Coe (GBR)	3:47.33	1981
Steve Scott (USA)	3:47.69	1982
Prediction	*3:42.00*	*2015*

Top Three: Men's Mile

GOLD MEDAL:	Noureddine Morceli (ALG)
SILVER MEDAL:	Sebastian Coe (GBR)
BRONZE MEDAL:	Roger Bannister (GBR)

The distance of 5000m is 12½ laps of the standard 400m oval. In much of the English-speaking world, three miles (4828.05 meters) was run as the standard distance for the first 75 years of the 20th century, until 1976, when only metric distances were accepted as world records.

The 15-minute barrier for the distance was first beaten in the 1912 Olympics, when Johannes Kolehmainen (Finland) just beat Jean Bouin (France) in 14:36.6. That time was recognized as the first official world record. Fourteen minutes was beaten for the first time with 13:58.2 by Gunder Hägg (Sweden) 30 years later in September 1942. The 13-minute barrier was achieved 45 years on by Said Aouita (Morocco), when he ran 12:58.39 in Rome in July 1987.

Twenty athletes have set the world record 31 times. Six have also been Olympic gold medalists in the event: Kolehmainen, Nurmi, Lehtinen, Zatopek, Kuts, and Viren. Only one, Kolehmainen back in 1912, actually set his world record at the Olympics.

Men's World Records for 5000m

Record time	Record holder	Location	Date
14:36.6	Johannes Kolehmainen (FIN)	Stockholm, Sweden	10 Jul 1912
14:35.4	Paavo Nurmi (FIN)	Stockholm, Sweden	12 Sep 1922
14:28.2	Paavo Nurmi (FIN)	Helsinki, Finland	19 Jun 1924
14:17.0	Lauri Lehtinen (FIN)	Helsinki, Finland	19 Jun 1932
14:08.8	Taisto Mäki (FIN)	Helsinki, Finland	16 Jun 1939
13:58.2	Gunder Hägg (SWE)	Gothenburg, Sweden	20 Sep 1942
13:57.2	Emil Zatopek (CZH)	Paris, France	30 May 1954
13:56.6	Vladimir Kuts (USSR)	Bern, Switzerland	29 Aug 1954
13:51.6	Christopher Chataway (GBR)	London, England	13 Oct 1954
13:51.2	Vladimir Kuts (USSR)	Prague, Czechoslovakia	23 Oct 1954
13:50.8	Sándor Iharos (HUN)	Budapest, Hungary	10 Sep 1955
13:46.8	Vladimir Kuts (USSR)	Belgrade, Yugoslavia	18 Sep 1955
13:40.6	Sándor Iharos (HUN)	Budapest, Hungary	23 Oct 1955
13:36.8	Gordon Pirie (GBR)	Bergen, Norway	19 Jun 1956
13:35.0	Vladimir Kuts (USSR)	Rome, Italy	13 Oct 1957
13:34.8	Ron Clarke (AUST)	Hobart, Australia	16 Jan 1965
13:33.6	Ron Clarke (AUST)	Auckland, New Zealand	1 Feb 1965
13:25.8	Ron Clarke (AUST)	Los Angeles, USA	4 Jun 1965
13:24.2	Kip Keino (KEN)	Auckland, New Zealand	30 Nov 1965
13:16.6	Ron Clarke (AUST)	Stockholm, Sweden	5 Jul 1966
13:16.4	Lasse Viren (FIN)	Helsinki, Finland	14 Sep 1972
13:13.0	Emiel Puttemans (BEL)	Brussels, Belgium	20 Sep 1972
13:12.9	Dick Quax (NZ)	Stockholm, Sweden	5 Jul 1977
13:08.4	Henry Rono (KEN)	Berkeley, USA	8 Apr 1978
13:06.2	Henry Rono (KEN)	Knarvik, Norway	13 Sep 1981
13:00.41	David Moorcroft (GBR)	Oslo, Norway	7 Jul 1982
13:00.40	Said Aouita (MOR)	Oslo, Norway	27 Jul 1985
12:58.39	Said Aouita (MOR)	Rome, Italy	22 Jul 1987
12:56.96	Haile Gebrselassie (ETH)	Hengelo, Netherlands	4 Jun 1994

| 12:55.30 | Moses Kiptanui (KEN) | Rome, Italy | 8 Jun 1995 |
| 12:44.39 | Haile Gebrselassie (ETH) | Zürich, Switzerland | 16 Aug 1995 |

Johannes Kolehmainen   (Finland, 1889-1966)

14:36.6   **Stockholm, Sweden**   **10 Jul 1912**

Johannes Kolehmainen was the first of a line of great Finnish long-distance runners who made their mark in the first half of the 20th century. At his first Olympics in 1912 he had to run in Russian colors, as Finland was then part of the Russian Tsarist empire. His triumphs were considered very important to Finnish national pride and helped develop their faith in independence. Kolehmainen won the 10,000m easily and two days later ran in the 5000m final. This race developed into a classic duel with Jean Bouin of France. Bouin led, and Kolehmainen followed. In the last lap Kolehmainen fought for the lead several times, but each time Bouin was able to deny him. Finally, in the last 20

Johannes Kolehmainen, Finland (5000m, marathon), just beats France's Jean Bouin (10,000m) in the 1912 Olympic 5000m final.

meters of the race, Kolehmainen hit the front to win by half a stride, and his winning time of 14:36.6 was recognized as the first world record at this distance.

After the Olympics he moved to New York and was fourth in the Boston Marathon in 1917. He returned to the Olympics in 1920 and won the marathon, this time in Finnish colors, as Finland had become independent of Russia following the 1917 Russian Revolution.

Later in life Kolehmainen moved back to Finland. At the 1952 Olympics in Helsinki he took the Olympic torch from Paavo Nurmi and carried it up the stairs to the top of the Olympic tower.

Paavo Nurmi   (Finland, 1897-1973)

14:35.4   **Stockholm, Sweden**   **12 Sep 1922**
14:28.2   **Helsinki, Finland**   **19 Jun 1924**

Paavo Nurmi is a symbol of Finnish supremacy in distance running that endures more than half a century after he raced. He captured Olympic gold medals at the 1920, 1924, and 1928 Olympics, set 22 world records at a range of distances, and remains a national hero. A great admirer of Johannes Kolehmainen, he was determined to become the best distance runner in the world, a title that few would deny him.

His first 5000m world record was set in 1922, when he broke his hero's 10-year-old record by 1.2 seconds. The second world record was a more serious affair. As detailed in the chapter on 1500m, he set 1500m and 5000m world records within an hour at a pre-Olympic test, an achievement that will never be duplicated. He reduced the 5000m time by another 7.2 seconds. In a way, the subsequent 1500m and 5000m Olympic triumphs in Paris were almost an anticlimax.

Nurmi won the 10,000m at the 1928 Olympics and had hopes of winning the marathon at the 1932 Olympics in Los Angeles. But he had fallen foul of the Finnish athletic officials who charged him with professionalism, and he was banned from competing. However, he was later allowed to run as a Finnish national and won the 1500m at the 1933 Finnish championships.

He went on to a career as a draftsman, a builder, and a businessman. In private life, he was said to be lonely, shy, reclusive, and at times bitter—an enigmatic champion whose reputation as the greatest track and field athlete of the 20th century endures, despite the passing of the years.

Lauri Lehtinen   (Finland, 1908–1973)

14:17.0   **Helsinki, Finland**   **19 Jun 1932**

At the early age of four Lauri Lehtinen, like Nurmi, lost his father. There were eight children when his father died, so he also experienced childhood poverty but apparently without becoming as serious and studious as Nurmi. Later in life Lehtinen became a police officer.

Lehtinen ran against Nurmi several times toward the end of the latter's career. Lehtinen was second in Nurmi's last world record race over two miles in 1931. Lehtinen set his own world record in the 5000m six weeks before the Los Angeles Olympics.

Lehtinen went on to win the gold medal in the 5000m at Los Angeles, but in a manner that earned him some controversy. Lehtinen and U.S. runner Ralph Hill contested the finish. Down the finishing straight, Hill moved twice to overtake Lehtinen, but the Finn swerved out each time to block his path, and then hung on to win by a few inches. The crowd responded by a round of booing at Lehtinen's tactics.

Lehtinen also won the silver medal at the 1936 Berlin Olympics in the 5000m.

Taisto Mäki   (Finland, b. 1910)

14:08.8   **Helsinki, Finland**   **16 Jun 1939**

Taisto Mäki was probably the least-celebrated Finnish distance champion. At age 21 he was working at a warehouse for the government alcohol company and considered himself lucky to have a job in the middle of the Depression. He rose at 4 A.M., ran 10 to 15 kilometers, then went to work by train. After work he would run the 23 kilometers home.

Mäki won the Finnish 5000m title in 1934 but was still not able to force his way into the Finnish 5000m team for the 1936 Berlin Olympics. At the Games, Finnish runners came in first and second. His international breakthrough came in 1938, when he won the European 5000m Championship in Paris. Later that year he set a world record over 10,000m.

In June 1939 he achieved a world record over 5000m, thus becoming one of only nine men to have held the world record at both the 5000m and 10,000m distances. (The others were Nurmi, Zatopek, Kuts, Clarke, Iharos, Viren, Rono, and Gebrselassie.) But his running career and Finland's isolation from World War II came to an end when the Russo-Finnish war broke out in November 1939.

Gunder Hägg   (Sweden, b. 1918)

13:58.2   **Gothenburg, Sweden**   **20 Sep 1942**

Gunder Hägg's career has been described in the chapters on 1500m and the mile. He also tackled longer distances and in 1942 made an attempt on the world 5000m record. One of the attractions was the 14-minute barrier. In a field of 11, he was over 40 seconds ahead of the second runner at the finish but still managed to sprint the last 200 meters in 29 seconds. It was enough. He had beaten the 14-minute barrier by 1.8 seconds. This record was to last almost 12 years.

Emil Zatopek   (Czechoslovakia, b. 1922)

13:57.2   **Paris, France**   **30 May 1954**

Emil Zatopek, Czechoslovakia (5000m, 10,000m), sprints to victory in the 1952 Olympic 5000m, one of three gold medals he won at that Olympics.

Emil Zatopek dominated long-distance running in the postwar era. He broke the 10,000m record four times and the 5000m record once, right at the end of his career. Nonetheless, it is his feat of winning the 5000m, 10,000m, and marathon at one Olympics that forever captured the imagination of track and field enthusiasts. Zatopek was working as an apprentice at a shoe factory in Zlin and was inspired by a short visit to Czechoslovakia by the great Swedish runner Arne Andersson. Zatopek came in fifth in the 5000m at the 1946 European Championships. At the 1948 London Olympics he won the 10,000m and almost won the 5000m, making up 40 meters on the winner, Gaston Reiff, in the last lap and losing by 0.2 second.

His style was characterized by a rolling of the shoulders and a wobbling of the head, so that he appeared to be in the stages of exhaustion. He also adopted unconventional training methods such as running in boots. The highlight of his career was his triple gold medal performance at the 1952 Helsinki Olympics. His wife, Dana, won the javelin gold medal to complete the fairy tale.

His 5000m world record took place in May 1954. He became the second man under 14 minutes when he ran 13:57.2 at the Colombes Stadium in Paris. This suggested that the 1954 European 5000m Championships would be another Zatopek triumph, especially after he won the 10,000m. But the unexpected happened. Vladimir Kuts (USSR) simply ran away from the rest of the field, breaking Zatopek's world record in the process. Zatopek was third. No one realized it at the time, but Zatopek's days of glory were over. Zatopek's later years of treatment as a "non-person" by the communist government of Czechoslovakia are described in the chapter on the 10,000m.

Vladimir Kuts   (Soviet Union, 1927–1975)

13:56.6	Bern, Switzerland	29 Aug 1954
13:51.2	Prague, Czechoslovakia	23 Oct 1954
13:46.8	Belgrade, Yugoslavia	18 Sep 1955
13:35.0	Rome, Italy	13 Oct 1957

Vladimir Kuts took up running quite late for an athlete, at age 22. He had served in the Soviet navy as a gunner in the Baltic fleet and had a previous sporting career as a boxer. He was a determined front-runner, and he usually ran the first half of the race faster than the second. In 1953 he won both the 5000m and the 10,000m at the Soviet championships. However, when he first came up against Zatopek, the Czech was able to pass him in the last lap.

Their second meeting was at the European 5000m Championships in 1954. Kuts decided to race so far ahead that no one could catch him. He put on a suicidal pace, while Zatopek and the others bided their time. Too late they realized that Kuts was not going to slow down, and he won by 12 seconds in a new world record, his first of four at the distance.

He lost two significant 5000m races in his career, and each time the victor had to run a new world record to beat him—Chataway in 1955 and Pirie in 1956. But he did not alter his tactics; he only knew one way to run, so he would try to run faster the next time. His tactics proved supreme in the 1956 Melbourne Olympics. He first won the 10,000m after an epic struggle with Gordon Pirie, when both men were at the point of exhaustion, but the Englishman cracked first. Kuts then faced the 5000m with renewed confidence and won again.

Kuts set his fourth 5000m world record in 1957 and then retired. The athletic world was astonished to hear of his death in 1975 at the age of 48. After his retirement from athletics his weight had ballooned from 72 kilograms (159 pounds) to 120 kilograms (265 pounds).

Christopher Chataway   (Great Britain, b. 1931)

| 13:51.6 | London, England | 13 Oct 1954 |

Christopher Chataway's preferred distance was three miles or 5000m, though he showed himself to be a world-class miler. He paced Bannister to his first four-minute mile and was second when Landy did the same thing six weeks later in Finland. Chataway himself broke four minutes in 1955.

Chataway ran in the 5000m at the 1952 Olympics and was coming in third with 150 meters to go when he tripped and fell. He managed to finish fifth. Two years later he won the Empire Games three-mile title in Vancouver, Canada. He had visions of winning the European 5000m title three weeks later by beating Emil Zatopek. In fact, he did finish ahead of Zatopek, but the two of them were outpaced by Vladimir Kuts who won by 12 seconds in world record time of 13:56.6.

Chataway and Kuts were rematched in 1954 in a Moscow vs. London meet in England. Kuts stormed away as usual, but Chataway hung on grimly. In a televised race watched by millions, the seemingly invincible Kuts led into the last lap. In the last moments of the race Chataway passed Kuts with 10 meters to go, to win by 0.2 second and break the world record in the process with 13:51.6. Chataway was the toast of Britain.

However, Kuts retook his world record in Prague 10 days later. At the 1956 Olympics the Soviet won both the 5000m and the 10,000m. Chataway ran in the 5000m but, troubled by stomach cramps, faded to 11th position.

After his athletic days he was the first broadcaster for Independent Television in Britain and was a member of parliament with ministerial positions from 1959 to 1966 and 1969 to 1974. He is currently chairman of the Civil Aviation Authority and was recently knighted.

Sándor Iharos   (Hungary, 1930–1996)

| 13:50.8 | Budapest, Hungary | 10 Sep 1955 |
| 13:40.6 | Budapest, Hungary | 23 Oct 1955 |

Sándor Iharos set world records at 1500m, 5000m (twice), and 10,000m. The only other athlete to hold records at these three distances was Paavo Nurmi. Yet unlike Nurmi, he never enjoyed Olympic success. In 1952 he ran in the 1500m but was eliminated in the heats. His 5000m and 10,000m records were set in the Nepstadium in Budapest in front of his own people. His first 5000m record was in a Hungary vs. Poland match, in which he took 0.4 second off Kuts's second world record with 13:50.8. However, Kuts promptly reclaimed the record eight days later, reducing it by four seconds (13:46.8). But five weeks later Iharos lowered the record by a further six seconds with 13:40.6 at the Hungarian Championships in Budapest.

The Soviet invasion of Hungary four weeks before the Olympics meant that the Hungarian athletes were demoralized. Iharos was also troubled by a bad ankle and a bad romance and did not go to Melbourne. From then on his glory days were behind him. At the 1958 European Championships he was sixth in the 5000m, while at the Rome Olympics he was tenth.

Gordon Pirie   (Great Britain, 1931–1991)

| 13:36.8 | Bergen, Norway | 19 Jun 1956 |

Gordon Pirie was a great admirer of Emil Zatopek and was determined to emulate him. In the process, he managed to inspire or irritate those around him, and his clashes with British athletic officials in the 1950s were ferocious. His father Alick had been an international cross-country runner for Scotland. Gordon put in a prodigious amount of training; later in life he wondered if perhaps he'd put in too much. At the 1952 Helsinki Olympics he ran against his hero, who won his unique 5000m, 10,000m, and marathon victories. Pirie finished fourth in the 5000m and seventh in the 10,000m.

Gordon Pirie, Great Britain (5000m).

Pirie missed most of the 1954 season with injury, but for the rest of the 1950s he ran at the top and achieved remarkable results at distances from the mile (at which he broke four minutes) to cross-country running (at which he was three times British champion). Pirie set world records at 3000m, 5000m, and six miles. His best year was 1956, when he defeated Vladimir Kuts over 5000m in world record time and broke the 3000m world record twice.

At the Melbourne Olympics Kuts and Pirie drove each other to exhaustion in the 10,000m before Pirie finally dropped back. The Soviet took the 5000m gold medal as well, with Pirie second.

Pirie had one more Olympics, in Rome in 1960, but in the fiercely high temperatures he could not get through his heat. He spent most of the rest of his life coaching, for a long time in New Zealand. At 60 he was struck down by cancer. His old hero, Emil Zatopek, sent flowers to the funeral service.

Ron Clarke   (Australia, b. 1937)

13:34.8	Hobart, Australia	16 Jan 1965
13:33.6	Auckland, New Zealand	1 Feb 1965
13:25.8	Los Angeles, USA	4 Jun 1965
13:16.6	Stockholm, Sweden	5 Jul 1966

Ron Clarke was a giant among distance runners and set 18 world records at various distances from two miles up to 20,000m. The one thing he didn't do was win an Olympic gold medal. Young Ron set a junior world mile record and had the honor of carrying the torch into the stadium at the Melbourne Olympics, suffering burns to his arm in the process.

The young Ron Clarke, Australia (5000m, 10,000m), carries the torch into the Olympic stadium at the 1956 Melbourne Games.

After the Olympics Clarke's career faded as he trained as an accountant, so he retired. But in 1962 he made a comeback and was delighted to come in second in the three-mile event at the Commonwealth Games that year in Perth. In 1963 he made the big breakthrough by claiming the world 10,000m record, but at the Tokyo Olympics he was surprised in the 10,000m by two unknowns, Billy Mills (USA) and Mohamed Gammoudi (Tunisia). In the 5000m he finished sixth.

His golden year was 1965. He set four world records at 5000m, something only he and Vladimir Kuts have achieved, and a memorable 10,000m record. Alas, the one thing wrong with 1965 was that it wasn't an Olympic year. When 1968 came around, it was a high-altitude Olympics at Mexico City, and the Africans who were born and trained at that altitude took most of the distance-running medals. Clarke collapsed in total exhaustion, close to death, after the 10,000m.

Perhaps the one gap in his armor was lack of a sprint finish—he never quite broke four minutes for the mile. Nonetheless, he was an extremely "honest" runner, making sure that every race he was in was run hard. One of his peers paid him an appropriate tribute: Emil Zatopek gave him one of his Olympic gold medals. Ron Clarke is now an executive developing fitness clinics.

Kip Keino (Kenya, b. 1940)

13:24.2　　　　**Auckland, New Zealand**　　　　**30 Nov 1965**

Kip Keino, Kenya (5000m), the first great Kenyan distance runner.

Kip Keino was the great pioneer of distance running in Kenya. He was born in the Rift Valley in 1940 and was initially a physical education instructor in the police force. He ran in the 1962 Perth Commonwealth Games without success and then at the 1964 Tokyo Olympics was fifth in the 5000m, one place ahead of Ron Clarke. His strong races were over 1500m and 5000m, while Clarke preferred 5000m and 10,000m. That meant that Keino usually had a sprinter's edge over Clarke.

Keino's 5000m world record was achieved in New Zealand in 1965, when he took 1.6 seconds off Clarke's record.

Helped by his background of altitude training, he ran away from Jim Ryun in the 1500m at the Mexico City Olympics. He finished a close second in the 5000m to Tunisia's Mohamed Gammoudi.

Keino cheerfully maintained an exhausting racing schedule and was a popular character in his orange cap, which he usually threw away as the race neared its climax. At the 1972 Olympics he won the 3000m steeplechase but was outsprinted in the 1500m by Finland's Pekka Vasala.

Keino returned to running in 1994 for the 40th anniversary of Bannister's first four-minute mile and won the handicap mile at age 54. He and his wife, Eldoret, run an orphanage in Kenya.

Lasse Viren   (Finland, b. 1949)

13:16.4   **Helsinki, Finland**   **14 Sep 1972**

Lasse Viren became a national hero in Finland when he won both the 5000m and the 10,000m at the 1972 Munich Olympics and revived memories of Finland's prewar victories. To the outside world, Viren appeared to come from nowhere. But just prior to the Games, he had soundly thrashed all the other top Olympic contenders over a two-mile race. In his first Olympic final, the 10,000m, he clipped one second off the world record. In the 5000m, he won by a second from Mohamed Gammoudi of Tunisia. This gold medal double set off national rejoicing in Finland, and his mother received enough flowers "to fill a battleship."

After the Games he returned to Helsinki to make an attempt on Ron Clarke's 5000m record. Before a delirious home crowd, he took 0.2 second off the record. Finland ran out of superlatives. At Paavo Nurmi's funeral in 1973, Viren was one of the pallbearers. Viren's career is covered in more detail in chapter 8 on the 10,000m.

Emiel Puttemans   (Belgium, b. 1947)

13:13.0   **Brussels, Belgium**   **20 Sep 1972**

Emiel Puttemans, a gardener from Louvain, set two Olympic records at the 1972 Munich Olympics. He had reached the final of the 5000m at the 1968 Mexico City Olympics, finishing 12th. At the 1972 Olympics, he made the possible mistake of pushing himself too hard in the heats. In the 10,000m heat he and Britain's David Bedford ran a punishing race. Puttemans came in first in a new Olympic record, 27:53.4. Viren, in his heat, qualified with 28:04.4 without pushing himself. In the final Viren won in 27:38.4, a new world record for the 10,000m, with Puttemans 1.2 seconds behind.

In the 5000m heats, Puttemans did it again. He won the heat in 13:31.8, another Olympic record, while Viren ran 13:38.4. Viren won the final in 13:26.4, while Puttemans finished fifth.

Back in Finland Viren broke the 5000m world record by 0.2 second one week after the Games. Puttemans made his own attempt on the new record six days later. Helped by Britain's David Bedford, Puttemans was able to slice a sizable 3.4 seconds off the record.

That was perhaps the highlight of his career. He ran in the 1976 Montreal Olympics but went out in the heats of the 5000m and did not finish in the final of the 10,000m. He ran in the 1980 Moscow Games but went out in the semifinals of the 5000m.

Dick Quax   (New Zealand, b. 1948)

13:12.9   **Stockholm, Sweden**   **5 Jul 1977**

Dick Quax's family originally came from the Netherlands, where Quax was born. His initial interest was rugby football before he changed to track and field. At the 1970 Commonwealth Games he was second in the 1500m to Kip Keino and seventh in the 5000m. He ran at the Munich Olympics in 1972 but went out in the heats of the 5000m.

Quax attempted the 5000m/10,000m double at the 1976 Montreal Olympics. He was kept up most of the night before the 10,000m heat with diarrhea. Not surprisingly, he did not get through to the final. After regaining his health he fronted up for the final of the 5000m. In a very close race, Viren won (13:24.76), and Quax came in second (13:25.16).

A year later Quax made an attempt on the world 5000m record. With pacesetters through to 4000m, he came home fast, to take 0.1 second off the record.

Quax later turned to marathon running and won the Auckland marathon in 1980 in 2 hr 13:12.

Henry Rono   (Kenya, b. 1952)

| 13:08.4 | Berkeley, USA | 8 Apr 1978 |
| 13:06.2 | Knarvik, Norway | 13 Sep 1981 |

Henry Rono, Kenya (3000m steeplechase, 5000m, 10,000m).

Henry Rono was inspired to take up track and field following a visit by Kip Keino to his village in 1971. He showed great promise and won an athletic scholarship to attend Washington State University in 1977. In 1978 he achieved something even the great Paavo Nurmi never quite managed by setting world records in four separate events in one year: 3000m, 3000m steeplechase, 5000m, and 10,000m.

Rono's first world record (5000m) in Berkeley, California, made him very much in demand. He ran a remarkable 82 times that season before his body protested and he finished the season in exhaustion. Ironically, after that brilliant season, he suffered major disappointments in his athletic career through factors outside his control. The Kenyan government boycotted both the 1976 and 1980 Olympics, so he never competed at the Olympic Games. However, he did run in the 1978 Commonwealth Games, winning both the 3000m steeplechase and the 5000m.

In the next few years he had other problems: His weight blew up, he had injuries, he had fights with the Kenyan athletic federation, and he experienced an increasing alcohol problem. Nonetheless, in 1981 he bounced back to something like his 1978 form and set a new 5000m record in Norway. This was set with no less than three pacesetters, who all took turns and did so again after they were lapped, a farcical situation. But the record was recognized. However, Rono's problems surfaced again, especially his alcoholism, and his form fell away. After numerous incidents, promoters became wary of him, and he never regained his career.

David Moorcroft   (Great Britain, b. 1953)

| 13:00.41 | Oslo, Norway | 7 Jul 1982 |

David Moorcroft's career was largely overshadowed by the success of Britain's other distance talents: Ovett, Coe, and Cram. He was also much plagued by injuries. However, Moorcroft had a substantial record of his own. He had been the 1978 Commonwealth 1500m champion and the 1982 Commonwealth 5000m champion. At the 1980 Moscow Olympics he suffered from stomach cramps and did not make it to the final.

David Moorcroft, Great Britain (5000m).

His status changed overnight on 7 July 1982 at the Bislett Games in Oslo. It was not a planned world record attempt, and there were no well-paid pacesetters, just an old-fashioned race. But after 800 meters it was clear that no one wanted to push the pace, so Moorcroft decided to take off. No one followed, and some of the others thought he was a pacesetter who had become confused. As he headed into the last lap and saw the time clock, Moorcroft realized that he was about to break the world record. He won in 13:00.41, taking almost six seconds off Rono's record (who finished fourth) and finishing extremely close to the 13-minute barrier.

That success meant he was now a target for other runners. At the European 5000m Championships he was watched very closely and beaten by Thomas Wessinghage (West Germany) and Werner Schildhauer (East Germany). At the Los Angeles Olympics in 1984 he was troubled by a hip injury. He made the final of the 5000m but, running in pain, he settled for merely finishing the race, which he did almost a lap behind the winner, Said Aouita of Morocco.

Moorcroft's 1982 time remains a European record. Regarded as "Mr. Nice Guy" of track and field and possessed of a remarkable memory, he has since gone on to a career in community service.

Said Aouita   (Morocco, b. 1959)

| 13:00.40 | Oslo, Norway | 27 Jul 1985 |
| 12:58.39 | Rome, Italy | 22 Jul 1987 |

Said Aouita, Morocco (1500m, 5000m).

Said Aouita was the king of the 5000m in the 1980s. He was the first Moroccan to become a world record holder and the first Moroccan man to win an Olympic gold medal. He was undefeated for 10 years in the 5000m and justifiably earned the nickname the "Moroccan Express."

Equally brilliant over 1500m, he chose to enter the 5000m at the Los Angeles Olympics and won in a fast time of 13:05.59, still an Olympic record. His first world record at 5000m came in Oslo in 1985, where he took a mere 0.01 second off David Moorcroft's record time. But his second record in 1987 was the significant one: He broke the 13-minute barrier with 12:58.39.

Aouita chose to contest the 800m at the 1988 Seoul Olympics as a new challenge. Despite a hamstring injury, he came in a creditable third. However, this race aggravated the hamstring injury even further, and he could not contest any other races at this Olympics.

He broke the 3000m world record in 1989 but then had to give way to the new star from North Africa, Noureddine Morceli.

Haile Gebrselassie   (Ethiopia, b. 1973)

| 12:56.96 | Hengelo, Netherlands | 4 Jun 1994 |
| 12:44.39 | Zürich, Switzerland | 16 Aug 1995 |

Haile Gebrselassie, Ethiopia (5000m, 10,000m).

Haile Gebrselassie was the next man to beat the 13-minute barrier for the 5000m after Said Aouita. Despite Ethiopia's long tradition of world-class marathon runners, he was the first Ethiopian to hold a world record on the track and had a meteoric rise to success. He was first in the World Junior Championships in 1992 over 5000m and 10,000m. A year later at the senior World Championships in Stuttgart he was first in the 10,000m and second in the 5000m.

A police officer by profession, Gebrselassie is small in stature, only 5' 3" (160 centimeters) tall. His world record day in the Netherlands was wet and cold, not exactly ideal world record conditions. The conditions appeared to irritate the Ethiopian, who channeled his irritation into the race, taking 1.43 seconds off Said Aouita's seven-year-old record.

In June 1995 the record had passed to Kenya's Moses Kiptanui with 12:55.30. Two months later Gebrselassie ran the 5000m an astonishing almost 11 seconds faster. Running on his own after three kilometers, his time of 12:44.39 was an improvement of almost one second per lap, a truly amazing performance that ranks with the best of all time.

Moses Kiptanui   (Kenya, b. 1971)

12:55.30   **Rome, Italy**   **8 Jun 1995**

Moses Kiptanui is another Kenyan athlete who came out of nowhere to become world class. His career is described in chapter 12 on the 3000m steeplechase, which has been his main event. However, he showed his potential over straight distance events when he set a 3000m world record in 1992. In 1995 he became the third man to run 5000m in under 13 minutes. In a competitive race he was actually behind the latest Kenyan distance find, Daniel Komen, with half a lap to run, but a determined sprint saw him win 12:55.30 to 12:56.12.

Conclusions

Haile Gebrselassie's 1995 5000m world record seemed to be the sort of record that would last a lifetime. Yet within a year several other runners were already approaching it. The next reduction is not far off.

Five All-Time Fastest: Men's 5000m

Haile Gebrselassie (ETH)	12:44.39	1995
Daniel Komen (KEN)	12:45.09	1996
Salah Hissou (MOR)	12:50.80	1996
Phillip Mosima (KEN)	12:53.72	1996
Paul Tergat (KEN)	12:54.72	1996
Prediction	*12:25.00*	*2015*

Top Three: Men's 5000m

GOLD MEDAL:	**Haile Gebrselassie (ETH)**
SILVER MEDAL:	**Vladimir Kuts (USSR)**
BRONZE MEDAL:	**Said Aouita (MOR)**

The 10,000m race is 25 laps around a standard 400m track and is 6 miles, 376 yards, 4 inches in length. Nine of the athletes who held the 5000m world record have also held the world record for 10,000m: Nurmi, Mäki, Zatopek, Kuts, Iharos, Clarke, Viren, Rono, and Gebrselassie.

The 30-minute barrier was broken by Taisto Mäki (Finland) in 1939, the 29-minute barrier by Emil Zatopek (Czechoslovakia) in 1954, the 28-minute barrier by Ron Clarke (Australia) in 1965, and the 27-minute barrier by Yobes Ondieki (Kenya) in 1993. The first world record holder, Jean Bouin of France, averaged 74.4 seconds per lap in 1911. The current world record holder, Salah Hissou, averaged 63.9 in 1996.

Altogether 22 athletes have set the world record 32 times to date since 1911. The greatest single improvement took place in 1965, when Ron Clarke removed 36.2 seconds off the record, an improvement of approximately 1.4 seconds per lap. Eight world record holders were also Olympic champions: Nurmi, Ritola, Salminen, Zatopek, Kuts, Bolotnikov, Viren, and Gebrselassie.

Men's World Records for 10,000m

Record time	Record holder	Location	Date
30:58.8	Jean Bouin (FRA)	Paris, France	16 Nov 1911
30:40.2	Paavo Nurmi (FIN)	Stockholm, Sweden	22 Jun 1921
30:35.4	Ville Ritola (FIN)	Helsinki, Finland	25 May 1924
30:23.2	Ville Ritola (FIN)	Paris, France	6 Jul 1924
30:06.2	Paavo Nurmi (FIN)	Kuopio, Finland	31 Aug 1924
30:05.6	Ilmari Salminen (FIN)	Kuovola, Finland	18 Jul 1937
30:02.0	Taisto Mäki (FIN)	Tampere, Finland	29 Sep 1938
29:52.6	Taisto Mäki (FIN)	Helsinki, Finland	17 Sep 1939
29:35.4	Viljo Heino (FIN)	Helsinki, Finland	25 Aug 1944
29:28.2	Emil Zatopek (CZH)	Ostrava, Czechoslovakia	11 Jun 1949
29:27.2	Viljo Heino (FIN)	Kuovola, Finland	1 Sep 1949
29:21.2	Emil Zatopek (CZH)	Ostrava, Czechoslovakia	22 Oct 1949
29:02.6	Emil Zatopek (CZH)	Turku, Finland	4 Aug 1950
29:01.6	Emil Zatopek (CZH)	Stara Boleslav, Czechoslovakia	1 Nov 1953
28:54.2	Emil Zatopek (CZH)	Brussels, Belgium	1 Jun 1954
28:42.8	Sándor Iharos (HUN)	Budapest, Hungary	15 Jul 1956
28:30.4	Vladimir Kuts (USSR)	Moscow, USSR	11 Sep 1956
28:18.8	Pyotr Bolotnikov (USSR)	Kiev, USSR	5 Oct 1960
28:18.2	Pyotr Bolotnikov (USSR)	Moscow, USSR	11 Aug 1962
28:15.6	Ron Clarke (AUST)	Melbourne, Australia	18 Dec 1963
27:39.4	Ron Clarke (AUST)	Oslo, Norway	14 Jul 1965
27:38.4	Lasse Viren (FIN)	Munich, Germany	3 Sep 1972
27:30.8	David Bedford (GBR)	London, England	13 Jul 1973
27:30.5	Samson Kimobwa (KEN)	Helsinki, Finland	30 Jun 1977
27:22.4	Henry Rono (KEN)	Vienna, Austria	11 Jun 1978
27:13.81	Fernando Mamede (POR)	Stockholm, Sweden	2 Jul 1984
27:08.23	Arturo Barrios (MEX)	Berlin, Germany	18 Aug 1989
27:07.91	Richard Chelimo (KEN)	Stockholm, Sweden	5 Jul 1993
26:58.38	Yobes Ondieki (KEN)	Oslo, Norway	10 Jul 1993

26:52.23	William Sigei (KEN)	Oslo, Norway	22 Jul 1994
26:43.53	Haile Gebrselassie (ETH)	Hengelo, Netherlands	5 Jun 1995
26:38.08	Salah Hissou (MOR)	Brussels, Belgium	23 Aug 1996

Jean Bouin   (France, 1888–1914)

30:58.8   Paris, France   16 Nov 1911

Jean Bouin was born in Marseilles and, superstitious by nature, always ran with a toothpick in his mouth. His world record took place at the Colombes Stadium near Paris, and he was the first athlete to run the distance under 31 minutes. At the 1912 Olympics he did not run in the 10,000m but contested the 5000m and had an epic duel with Johannes Kolehmainen of Finland. After an exhausting last lap the Finn inched ahead to win in 14:36.6 to Bouin's 14:36.7. This time was regarded as the inaugural world record for 5000m.

Bouin was tragically killed by friendly fire (French artillery) in the early days of World War I. The athletic stadium in Paris is named after him.

Paavo Nurmi   (Finland, 1897–1973)

30:40.2   Stockholm, Sweden   22 Jun 1921
30:06.2   Kuopio, Finland   31 Aug 1924

The immortal Paavo Nurmi dominated this event in the 1920s. He set his first 10,000m world record in 1921 and won Olympic gold medals at this distance in 1920 and 1928. He may well have been able to win three in a row, but Finnish officials chose not to include him in the 1924 10,000m team, apparently on the grounds that he had already won enough gold medals at that Olympics (1500m and 5000m). It is said that Nurmi was so angered by the decision that he ran the 10,000m race outside the stadium in a time allegedly superior to the winner, Ville Ritola, who set a new world record of 30:23.2. Whatever the truth of

Finland's two megastars of the 1920s: Ville Ritola (10,000m) leads Paavo Nurmi (1500m, mile, 5000m, 10,000m) in the 1928 Amsterdam Olympic 10,000m, which Nurmi eventually won by 0.6 second.

that story, Nurmi chose to officially reclaim the record after the Games. This he did one month later, taking 17 seconds off Ritola's time with 30:06.2.

The two great Finnish 10,000m men finally met for the first time over 10,000m at the 1928 Olympics. Ritola now resided in the United States. At the end, there was only 0.6 second between them: Nurmi 30:18.8, Ritola 30:19.4.

Ville Ritola (Finland, 1896-1982)

| 30:35.4 | Helsinki, Finland | 25 May 1924 |
| 30:23.2 | Paris, France | 6 Jul 1924 |

Ville Ritola was the other great Finnish distance superstar of the 1920s. The Olympic medal tally of these two athletes is nine gold and three silver medals for Nurmi and five gold and three silver for Ritola. Some of these medals were won in events, such as cross-country, that have since been discontinued.

Ritola was the 14th child of a family of 20 and was raised in poverty. At age 17 he was packed off to the United States to make a living there and became a carpenter. In 1919 he joined the Finnish-American Athletic Club and was second in the Boston Marathon in 1922. He returned to Finland in 1924 to be selected for the Paris Olympics, and he broke Nurmi's 10,000m record by 4.8 seconds in an Olympic trial. (Nurmi did not compete that day.)

In Paris Ritola showed his class by winning the 10,000m and taking another 12.2 seconds off his six-week-old world record. Ritola also won the 3000m steeplechase, a rare double.

After the Games Ritola returned to his life in the United States, but he returned once more to Europe for the 1928 Olympics in Amsterdam. The two great Finnish athletes were at last to run against each other. There was some support among Finns for Nurmi because he lived in Finland. The 10,000m proved to be a worthy duel. At the end, Nurmi managed a spurt and won by 0.6 second. However, in the 5000m Ritola had his revenge and won by 2 seconds.

That was to be the end of their clashes. Ritola returned to the United States and did not come back to Finland until he was in his 70s.

Ilmari Salminen (Finland, 1902-1986)

| 30:05.6 | Kuovola, Finland | 18 Jul 1937 |

Ilmari Salminen, like wine, improved with age. He set his world record and won European and Olympic gold medals while in his 30s. He actually won the Olympic trials in 1928 for the 10,000m but was not selected. The exact reason is not clear, but perhaps the reputations of Nurmi and Ritola were so high that the trial victory was not enough. In 1932 he once more ran in the Olympic trials and finished seventh in the 5000m. At age 30, it seemed his best years were behind him. Yet over the next five years he was European 10,000m champion (1934), Olympic champion (1936), world record holder (1937), and European champion again (1938).

Salminen broke Nurmi's 13-year-old record by the small margin of 0.6 second in front of 6000 people in the small town of Kuovola. He was able to win the Finnish 10,000m championship in 1942, a few days short of his 40th birthday. An army officer by profession, after his 1936 Olympic victory he was known as the "Golden Sergeant."

Taisto Mäki   (Finland, b. 1910)

| 30:02.0 | Tampere, Finland | 29 Sep 1938 |
| 29:52.6 | Helsinki, Finland | 17 Sep 1939 |

Taisto Mäki is one of the least-known distance champions, even though he was world record holder at 5000m and twice at 10,000m, 1938 European 5000m champion, and the first man to run 10,000m under 30 minutes. This was because his performances took place in the shadow of World War II. When he broke the 30-minute barrier in his second world record, Germany was invading Poland. Finland was neutral at this stage but had troubles of its own when the Russian-Finnish conflict broke out in November 1939. After heroic resistance, Finland was forced to cede. All these events meant that Mäki's achievements were buried under more important issues.

Viljo Heino   (Finland, b. 1914)

| 29:35.4 | Helsinki, Finland | 25 Aug 1944 |
| 29:27.2 | Kuovola, Finland | 1 Sep 1949 |

Viljo Heino saw active war service in the Russian-Finnish conflict. He started the war as an infantryman and finished as a sergeant, winning first- and second-class freedom medals in the process. Despite World War II, there was still athletic activity in Finland. In 1944 Heino had become the second man to break the 30-minute barrier for 10,000m. In a special world record attempt in August 1944 Heino took over 17 seconds off Mäki's previous record.

Heino's career had one hiccup when he was suspended for two months in early 1946 for accepting payments to run. Nonetheless, he duly won the European 10,000m Championships later that season by 39 seconds. However, a new track and field star was emerging, Emil Zatopek of Czechoslovakia. Zatopek's decisive burst at the 15th lap in the 1948 London Olympic 10,000m seemed to demoralize Heino, who did not finish. However, he was 11th in the marathon.

After these Olympics Heino had a personal tragedy: His wife died in childbirth and Heino had to raise four children alone. But remarkably, he reclaimed the world record in 1949 at age 35.

Emil Zatopek   (Czechoslovakia, b. 1922)

29:28.2	Ostrava, Czechoslovakia	11 Jun 1949
29:21.2	Ostrava, Czechoslovakia	22 Oct 1949
29:02.6	Turku, Finland	4 Aug 1950
29:01.6	Stara Boleslav, Czechoslovakia	1 Nov 1953
28:54.2	Brussels, Belgium	1 Jun 1954

Emil Zatopek's main claim to fame is that he achieved the legendary feat of winning Olympic gold medals at 5000m, 10,000m, and the marathon at the 1952 Helsinki Games. He first attracted attention when, as a private in the Czech army, he rode on a bicycle from Prague to Berlin to enter the 5000m in the Allied Occupation Forces Meet, which he won. After a fifth place in the 1946 5000m European Championships, he entered an eight-year period of domination over the 10,000m. He won the 1948 and 1952 Olympic 10,000m gold medals and the 1950 and 1954 European 10,000m Championships, set five 10,000m world records, and was the first man to break the 29-minute barrier. He seemed so indomitable that it was a shock when his triumphs came suddenly to an end at the 1954 5000m European Championships, in which he finished third.

His command of many languages and his personal charm have won him legions of admirers over the years. However, his support for the reformists in the 1968 "Czech Spring" made him suspect to the hard-line communists who ruled Czechoslovakia after the Soviet invasion in August 1968. In 1969 the government deprived him of his rank of colonel and imposed multiple restrictions on him. He and his wife, Dana (the 1952 Olympic javelin champion), suffered many humiliations over 20 years until the final collapse of communism in Eastern Europe in the late 1980s.

Sándor Iharos   (Hungary, 1930-1996)

28:42.8   **Budapest, Hungary**   **15 Jul 1956**

After the long years of domination by Zatopek, it was the Hungarian Sándor Iharos who improved the 10,000m record. He ran some wonderful times in 1955-56, with world records at 1500m, 5000m, and 10,000m, but could not reproduce the same form in major international competitions. His 10,000m record was set at the Hungarian national championships in front of a rapturous crowd. He took 11.4 seconds off Zatopek's record.

As mentioned in the 1500m and 5000m chapters, he missed the Melbourne Olympics, which took place one month after the Soviet invasion of Hungary, and never managed to recapture his previous form. At the 1960 Rome Olympics, he came in 11th in the 10,000m.

Vladimir Kuts   (Soviet Union, 1927-1975)

28:30.4   **Moscow, USSR**   **11 Sep 1956**

In four seasons (1954-57) Vladimir Kuts achieved world records and Olympic gold medals at both 5000m and 10,000m. He was as much admired for his relentless front-running tactics as for his victories. No pacesetters or "rabbits" were required—Kuts did it all on his own.

His greatest 10,000m race was at the Melbourne Olympics. He took on Gordon Pirie of England in a memorable duel. Kuts began with a first lap of 61 seconds, unheard of in those days. In the second half of the race he played cat and mouse with Pirie until, four laps from home, the Englishman had to drop back. Kuts later admitted that he too was close to exhaustion.

Vladimir Kuts, Soviet Union (5000m, 10,000m) at the 1956 Melbourne Olympics, where he won both events.

Kuts showed another side to his personality on the way home. The Soviet team had flown out to Melbourne, but for the journey home they took a boat back to the far eastern Soviet Union. However the boat lacked many basic supplies, including toilet paper, and the voyage was a disaster. Kuts and many other athletes deeply resented the conditions; as a protest, Kuts went on a three-day drinking binge. He was hauled before a committee to explain himself, but he could not stand up because he was too drunk, and the attempt to reprimand him was abandoned. Back in Moscow he was given a hero's reception and was awarded the Order of Lenin.

Pyotr Bolotnikov   (Soviet Union, b. 1930)

| 28:18.8 | Kiev, USSR | 5 Oct 1960 |
| 28:18.2 | Moscow, USSR | 11 Aug 1962 |

Pyotr Bolotnikov had run at the 1956 Melbourne Olympics, finishing 16th, but went on to displace Vladimir Kuts as the next 10,000m champion. Bolotnikov established himself by inflicting a rare defeat on Kuts toward the end of the latter's career, winning the 1957 Soviet 10,000m championships by 0.2 second. He went on to win this particular title seven times between 1957 and 1964 and set the world record twice, winning by over 45 seconds in both races.

Bolotnikov was Olympic 10,000m champion (1960), European 10,000m champion (1962), and five times the Soviet 5000m champion. His last Soviet 10,000m title was in 1964, and he was picked for his third Olympics. But in Tokyo he was never a contender and finished 25th.

Pyotr Bolotnikov, Soviet Union (10,000m), leads in a United States vs. Soviet Union match.

Ron Clarke   (Australia, b. 1937)

| 28:15.6 | Melbourne, Australia | 18 Dec 1963 |
| 27:39.4 | Oslo, Norway | 14 Jul 1965 |

Ron Clarke caused a quantum leap in standards in long distance running in the mid-1960s, but was unfortunate never to win a major title. At the 1964 Tokyo Olympics 10,000m final he was outsprinted by unknowns Billy Mills (USA) and Mohamed Gammoudi (Tunisia). At the 1966 Commonwealth Games in Jamaica he wilted under the extreme heat. In Mexico City in 1968 he collapsed because of the rarefied atmosphere.

During his career he set two world 10,000m records. The first was at a low-key meet in 1963 in Melbourne, where he reduced Bolotnikov's record by 2.6 seconds. The second came in his super year, 1965, when he revolutionized a whole range of world records. In London he set a dazzling three-mile world record in July and then traveled to Oslo for a 10,000m race four days later. This race, with only two other runners, was one of the great performances of all time. Running on an old cinder track and without any sort of competition, he took 36 seconds off the record. It remained an Australian record for 31 years.

Lasse Viren   (Finland, b. 1949)

27:38.4   **Munich, Germany**   **3 Sep 1972**

Lasse Viren, Finland (5000m, 10,000m), won both events at the 1972 and 1976 Olympics.

As mentioned in chapter 7 on the 5000m, Viren became Finland's national hero after winning the 5000m and 10,000m at the 1972 Munich Olympic Games. These were the first distance gold medals for Finland since the 1936 Berlin Olympics. Born and bred in Myrskyla, a country village near Helsinki, Viren had run in the 1971 European Championships, where he finished 7th in the 5000m and 17th in the 10,000m. However, before the 1972 Olympics he set an impressive world record for two miles. At the Olympics his 10,000m victory was a world record, despite a fall at the 4-kilometer mark, which cost him a few seconds. His main tactic was a major surge four laps from home, described as "applied acceleration," turning those last laps into a sprint. Between the Olympic Games he had less success. He was third in the 1974 European 5000m and seventh in the 10,000m. However, in 1976 he bounced back to win both the 5000m and 10,000m at the Montreal Olympics. He then came in fifth at his first marathon at these Games. Viren's brilliant Olympic career, compared to his undistinguished results in non-Olympic years, causes some people to suggest, fairly or unfairly, that he used blood doping. Viren strongly denies this. However, Finnish runner Kaarlo Maaninka (second in the Moscow 10,000m and third in the 5000m) admitted to blood doping in 1981. Perhaps the advisers who looked after Maaninka may one day reveal further details. Despite these allegations, Viren's Olympic victories cause him to remain a national sporting hero in Finland.

David Bedford   (Great Britain, b. 1949)

27:30.8   **London, England**   **13 Jul 1973**

David Bedford achieved notoriety by winning the Southern Junior Cross Country title in 1970; he lined up 20 minutes later for the senior event and won that too. These victories were accompanied by streams of youthful bravado about future triumphs. The press loved it, and Bedford rapidly became a media celebrity. One of Bedford's classic performances was at a press conference in London. "Come and see me break the world 5000m record," he told assembled reporters. (He didn't.) But the crowds came along anyway. His long hair and Zapata moustache gave extra flair to his image, and to add color, he sometimes ran in shocking red socks. His main tactic was to be a front-runner, like Vladimir Kuts. It worked brilliantly early in his career, but experienced international runners rapidly adapted to such a strategy.

At the 1971 European 10,000m Championships Bedford led but couldn't shake off the following pack. Juha Vaatainen of Finland sprinted past him with a last lap of 53.8 seconds, and Bedford dropped back to sixth. He tried the same tac-

David Bedford, Great Britain (10,000m).

tics in the 10,000m at the 1972 Munich Olympics, but the pack moved past him at six kilometers. He came in sixth and went off the track in tears.

In 1973, however, he was back to his brilliant best. At the British AAA Championships in London he removed 7.6 seconds from Viren's 10,000m world record. In his last major race he was fourth in the 10,000m at the Commonwealth Games in Christchurch. A teacher by profession, he went on to become secretary of the AAA.

Samson Kimobwa   (Kenya, b. 1955)

27:30.5   **Helsinki, Finland**   **30 Jun 1977**

Samson Kimobwa became Kenya's first world record holder at the 10,000m distance while a student at Washington State University, where he studied agriculture and economics. Another Kenyan athlete at WSU was Henry Rono. Kimobwa surprised the crowd with a 27:30.5 at the World Games in Helsinki that took 0.3 second off David Bedford's record. Three days after his record he ran another 10,000m in 27:37 to prove it was no fluke.

His world record led to a flood of invitations from race promoters all over Europe, and he accepted most of them. Perhaps the relentless racing from then on led to an overdose of hard racing. He seemed to lose his form and never went on to other athletic achievements.

In 1980 Kenya followed the United States in boycotting the Moscow Olympics following the Soviet invasion of Afghanistan. Kimobwa was thus never seen on the Olympic stage. He went on to a career in Kenya in agriculture.

Henry Rono   (Kenya, b. 1952)

27:22.4   **Vienna, Austria**   **11 Jun 1978**

Henry Rono was a student at Washington State University, alongside fellow Kenyan Samson Kimobwa. As a Kenyan racing in the United States college circuit, Rono received hostility from some U.S. athletes who felt that foreigners should not be part of the U.S. college sporting scene. In 1978 he achieved the unprecedented feat of setting world records at four separate distances in the one year: 5000m (8 April), 3000m steeplechase (13 May), 10,000m (11 June), and 3000m (27 June).

However, like Ron Clarke's magic year in 1965, Rono's 1978 season was not an Olympic year. He missed out on the Olympics altogether because Kenya decided to boycott the 1980 Moscow Games. Furthermore, being a celebrity athlete proved to be a major personal strain for Henry Rono, and he turned to drink. He did enjoy one more top season in 1981, when he further reduced his 5000m record and graduated from WSU in psychology. However, he began to have bouts of alcoholism and had trouble controlling his weight. Henry Rono hit rock bottom in 1988, living in desperation in a shelter for homeless men in New York. He attempted various rehabilitation programs for his problem. In the mid 1990s he was working in Portland, Oregon as a car park attendant.

Fernando Mamede   (Portugal, b. 1951)

27:13.81   **Stockholm, Sweden**   **2 Jul 1984**

Fernando Mamede was an example of an athlete who could run brilliant times but was not able to do himself justice at major track and field championships. He had been an international runner since running in the 1971 European 800m Championships. Mamede started running world-class times 10 years later, when he set the European 10,000m record twice in 1981.

It was in 1984 that he achieved the high point of his career with a world record of 27:13.81 in the 10,000m at Stockholm on 2 July 1984. He was chased home by his countryman Carlos Lopes, and both men finished under the old record. This record, just before the Los Angeles Olympics, naturally led all Portugal to think Mamede was a hot favorite for the 10,000m gold medal. But he was a nervous runner at these big meetings and rarely reproduced his best form. The night before the Los Angeles 10,000m final he hardly slept at all. His coach literally had to push him to the starting line. After 13 laps, well behind in the race, he simply ran off the track and out of the stadium. Back home in Portugal his fans expressed their disappointment by tossing paint over his house.

Arturo Barrios   (Mexico/USA, b. 1963)

27:08.23   **Berlin, Germany**   **18 Aug 1989**

Arturo Barrios came from a large family, with five sisters and three brothers. He started running at age 15 and was regarded as something of an eccentric in soccer-mad Mexico. He moved to Texas A & M University to study mechanical engineering and became very successful on the road-running scene. He won the Bay-to-Breakers race in San Francisco four years in a row (1987-90). In track racing, he was Pan-American champion over 5000m (1987, 1991) and came in fifth in the 10,000m at both the 1988 and 1992 Olympics.

In 1989 he broke the world record for the 10,000m in Berlin. Helped by two pacesetters, he pounded his way to the finish in 27:08.23, taking 5.58 seconds off Mamede's five-year-old record.

Barrios never had a top sprint finish, which probably accounted for his lack of success at the big meets. He married an American woman and lives in the United States. After years of dispute with the Mexican athletic federation, he chose to change his nationality. He finished his career as a U.S. citizen.

Arturo Barrios, Mexico (10,000m).

Richard Chelimo   (Kenya, b. 1973)

27:07.91   Stockholm, Sweden   5 Jul 1993

Richard Chelimo was born in Chesubet and is a civil servant with the Kenyan army. His international breakthrough came when he won the World Junior Cross Country title in 1990. He confirmed his talent when he finished second in the 10,000m at the 1991 World Championships in Tokyo. He received worldwide attention during the 1992 Olympics in the closing stages of the 10,000m. The race was down to him and Khalid Skah of Morocco. However, Hammou Boutayeb, also of Morocco, about to be lapped by these two athletes, chose to speed up and run alongside them. It appeared to the crowd that he was helping his countryman Skah by obstructing Chelimo. At the end, although Skah sprinted away to win, officials took the view that Boutayeb had unfairly assisted Skah, who was disqualified. Chelimo was thus declared the winner, but upon appeal by the Moroccans, the decision was reversed. Accordingly, Skah won the gold medal and Chelimo the silver. The crowd's sympathies were entirely with Chelimo.

The following year Chelimo took 0.32 second off the world record in Stockholm.

Yobes Ondieki   (Kenya, b. 1961)

26:58.38   Oslo, Norway   10 Jul 1993

Yobes Ondieki became the first man to break through the 27-minute barrier for 10,000m. Born in Kisii, he attended Iowa State University and later studied business administration in Albuquerque, New Mexico. Ondieki had long been regarded as a 5000m runner and in 1989 became the first man in 10 years to beat Said Aouita over that distance. At the Olympics Ondieki had finished 12th in 1988 and 5th in 1992. His major international 5000m victory was at the 1991 World Championships in Tokyo. He made a major break after four laps and held on to victory despite the extreme humidity on the day.

With his long background at 5000m, he was not really regarded as a 10,000m runner. But he surprised everyone at the 1993 Bislett Games in Oslo by taking nine seconds off the world record and breaking the 27-minute barrier in the process. He was married to Lisa Martin of Australia, who was second in the marathon at the 1988 Olympics.

Yobes Ondieki, Kenya (10,000m), the first man to run the distance under 27 minutes.

William Sigei (Kenya, b. 1969)

26:52.23 **Oslo, Norway** **22 Jul 1994**

William Sigei is a civil servant in the Kenyan army. He initially established himself as a cross-country runner by winning the International Cross Country Championships in 1993 and 1994. When Yobes Ondieki broke the 27-minute barrier in July 1993, Sigei was 18 seconds behind in second place. At the same venue a year later he became the second man to run 10,000m in under 27 minutes, taking over six seconds off Ondieki's time. A man of few words, he attributes his success to hard training. But presumably altitude helps, as he lives at 1675 meters (5495 feet) above sea level.

In the Kenyan army his duties include long-distance truck driving. He plows his earnings from his success into a cattle farm, which is run in his absence by his three brothers and two sisters.

Haile Gebrselassie (Ethiopia, b. 1973)

26:43.53 **Hengelo, Netherlands** **5 Jun 1995**

Haile Gebrselassie's career is detailed in the chapter on the 5000m. A brilliant junior athlete, he won the World Junior Championships over 5000m and 10,000m in 1992. A year later he moved effortlessly into the top ranks of senior athletes. At the 1993 World Championships in Stuttgart he won the 10,000m in somewhat controversial circumstances from Moses Tanui, after clipping off Tanui's shoe in the last lap. He also came in second in the 5000m. In 1994 he added to his reputation by setting a new 5000m world record (12:56.96), becoming the second man to break the 13-minute barrier for this distance (Said Aouita was the first).

A year later Gebrselassie became the ninth man to hold both 5000m and 10,000m world records when he took eight seconds off the world 10,000m mark at Hengelo, Netherlands, the site of his 5000m world record one year earlier.

However, his status as double world record holder only lasted three days; on 8 June 1995 Moses Kiptanui broke his 5000m world record. However, two months later Gebrselassie reclaimed his 5000m in Zurich, so he once again held both records.

A police officer by profession, he resides in the Netherlands during the summer track and field season. His brother Tekeye is a respected marathon runner. Haile Gebrselassie added to his laurels in 1996 when he won the 10,000m with an Olympic record (27:7.34).

Salah Hissou   (Morocco, b. 1972)

26:38.08	Brussels, Belgium	23 Aug 1996

Salah Hissou was a promising junior athlete in the early 1990s. He made a major international breakthrough with several strong times in 1994 at 5000m and 10,000m. In 1995 he set a Moroccan record for the 10,000m (27:09.30) and finished fourth in the same event at the World Championships in Gothenberg. At the age of 21, he seemed poised to break through the 27-minute barrier in the near future.

At the Atlanta Olympics, Hissou couldn't keep up with the leading pair, Heile Gebrselassie and Paul Tergat (Kenya). Although Hissou won the bronze medal, he was more than twenty seconds behind Gebrselassie's winning time (27:07.34).

However, three weeks after the Games, Hissou revealed his potential. Running in Brussels, he removed 5.45 seconds from Gebrselassie's world record with a time of 26:38.08.

The 27-minute barrier was beaten for the first time in 1993. Now three years later the 22-year-old Moroccan is already 20 seconds faster than that breakthrough performance.

Conclusions

The longer distances depend on especially favorable conditions for a world record: good track, good weather, good competition, and—in this day and age—good pacesetting. Nonetheless, the 10,000m world record seems capable of much further reduction. An average improvement of only 0.1 second per lap would result in an overall improvement of 2.5 seconds off the world record.

Five All-Time Fastest: Men's 10,000m

Salah Hissou (MOR)	26:38.08	1996
Haile Gebrselassie (ETH)	26:43.53	1995
William Sigei (KEN)	26:52.23	1994
Paul Tergat (KEN)	26:54.41	1996
Paul Koech (KEN)	26:56.78	1996
Prediction	*26:10.00*	*2015*

Top Three: Men's 10,000m

GOLD MEDAL:	Paavo Nurmi (FIN)
SILVER MEDAL:	Emil Zatopek (CZH)
BRONZE MEDAL:	Ron Clarke (AUST)

The commonly believed story about the origin of the marathon race is that in 490 B.C. an Athenian soldier named Pheidippides ran from Marathon to Athens to announce the victory over the invading Persians. Having made his announcement ("Rejoice, we conquer"), he died. However, historical confirmation of this event is lacking. It is important to note that no such long-distance event was ever held at the ancient Olympic Games. However, when the modern Olympic Games were revived, the Frenchman Michel Breal suggested that a distance event be included in the 1896 Olympics, to be called the marathon. This suggestion was accepted, and the first Olympic marathon was run from Marathon Bridge to Athens, a distance of approximately 40,000 meters (24.9 miles). The event was fittingly won by the Greek Spiridon Louis, an event that generated scenes of great emotion in the stadium.

Many of the early marathon champions were obscure figures, and details about their date of birth or death are lacking.

The distance varied considerably over the next few years but was fixed at 42,195 meters (26 miles, 385 yards) after the 1908 London Olympics. This was the distance from Windsor Castle, where Queen Alexandra gave the starting signal, to the stadium in Shepherds Bush. This was the famous marathon in which Dorando Pietri collapsed in the stadium several times and was helped across the line, leading to his disqualification. However, the marathon did not have a particularly high profile until the running boom from the 1970s onward. With the running boom came sponsors, television exposure, and large monetary prizes, so that elite marathon running is now a serious and lucrative business.

Although marathons have been run in stadiums, it is generally accepted that the event is run outside a track. The marathon course can have several configurations: one or more loops, out and back from the starting point, or a point-to-point course. Naturally, the topography on marathon courses can vary a great deal, as can the weather conditions. Accordingly, marathon records cannot be interpreted in the same way as track records. The IAAF does not recognize official world records for the marathon, instead it uses the phrase *world's best*.

The elite marathon runner today has come to enjoy prestige and handsome remuneration. Twenty-four athletes have set the world "record" 29 times. Only five of them have also been Olympic champions: Hayes, Kolehmainen, Son, Bikila, and Lopes.

Men's World Records for the Marathon

Record time	Record holder	Location	Date
2 hr 55:18.4	John Hayes (USA)	London, England	24 Jul 1908
2 hr 52:45.4	Robert Fowler (USA)	New York, USA	1 Jan 1909
2 hr 46:52.8	James Clark (USA)	New York, USA	12 Feb 1909
2 hr 46:04.6	Albert Raines (USA)	New York, USA	8 May 1909
2 hr 42:31.0	Harry "Fred" Barrett (GBR)	London, England	26 May 1909
2 hr 36:06.6	Alexis Ahlgren (SWE)	London, England	31 May 1913
2 hr 32:35.8	Johannes Kolehmainen (FIN)	Antwerp, Belgium	22 Aug 1920
2 hr 29:01.8	Albert Michelsen (USA)	Port Chester, USA	12 Oct 1925
2 hr 27:49.0	Fusashige Suzuki (JPN)	Tokyo, Japan	31 Mar 1935
2 hr 26:44.0	Yasuo Ikenaka (JPN)	Tokyo, Japan	3 Apr 1935
2 hr 26:42.0	Sohn Kee Chung (Kitei Son) (JPN/S.KOR)	Tokyo, Japan	3 Nov 1935
2 hr 25:39.0	Yun Bok Suh (S.KOR)	Boston, USA	19 Apr 1947
2 hr 20:42.2	Jim Peters (GBR)	London, England	14 Jun 1952
2 hr 18:40.2	Jim Peters (GBR)	London, England	13 Jun 1953

2 hr 18:34.8	Jim Peters (GBR)	Turku, Finland	4 Oct 1953
2 hr 17:39.4	Jim Peters (GBR)	London, England	26 Jun 1954
2 hr 15:17.0	Sergey Popov (USSR)	Stockholm, Sweden	24 Aug 1958
2 hr 15:16.2	Abebe Bikila (ETH)	Rome, Italy	10 Sep 1960
2 hr 15:15.8	Toru Terasawa (JPN)	Beppu, Japan	17 Feb 1963
2 hr 14:28.0	Leonard "Buddy" Edelen (USA)	London, England	15 Jun 1963
2 hr 13:55.0	Basil Heatley (GBR)	London, England	13 Jun 1964
2 hr 12:11.2	Abebe Bikila (ETH)	Tokyo, Japan	21 Oct 1964
2 hr 12:00.0	Morio Shigematsu (JPN)	London, England	12 Jun 1965
2 hr 9:36.4	Derek Clayton (AUST)	Fukuoka, Japan	3 Dec 1967
2 hr 8:33.6	Derek Clayton (AUST)	Antwerp, Belgium	30 May 1969
2 hr 8:18.0	Robert de Castella (AUST)	Fukuoka, Japan	6 Dec 1981
2 hr 8:05.0	Steve Jones (GBR)	Chicago, USA	21 Oct 1984
2 hr 7:12.0	Carlos Lopes (POR)	Rotterdam, Netherlands	20 Apr 1985
2 hr 6:50.0	Belayneh Densimo (ETH)	Rotterdam, Netherlands	17 Apr 1988

John Hayes (United States, 1886–1965)

2 hr 55:18.4   London, England   **24 Jul 1908**

John Hayes was the man who came in second in the 1908 London Olympic marathon. This was the celebrated affair at which Italy's Dorando Pietri staggered into the stadium first, in a state of total exhaustion. He collapsed several times, was helped up several times, and finally was assisted across the line in 2 hr 54:46. The rules strictly state that no assistance shall be given to an athlete. After Hayes entered the stadium and trotted across the line, the American team quickly appealed against the aid given to Pietri, and athletic officials had no option but to disqualify him. Pietri, often known later merely as Dorando, was awarded a special trophy by Queen Alexandra.

Hayes was a 22-year-old clerk from Bloomingdale's department store in New York. He was promoted to manager of the sports department after his gold medal performance, but he decided to cash in on his new celebrity status. He and Pietri both turned professional and staged a series of races in America, which Pietri usually won. Pietri enjoyed enduring fame from the London marathon and Hayes hardly any.

John Hayes, United States (marathon), 1908 Olympic marathon champion after the disqualification of Dorando Pietri.

Robert Fowler   (United States)

2 hr 52:45.4   New York, USA   **1 Jan 1909**

The drama of Dorando Pietri's finish in the 1908 London Olympic marathon set off a wave of enthusiasm for the marathon in the United States. On New Year's Day 1909, in freezing conditions, 59 runners set off on a marathon race in New York. The first three miles were on the road, and the rest of the race was run on the Empire City horse race-track. The crowd of spectators became unruly so that the meet director, James Sullivan, stopped the race after only seven athletes had crossed the line. Robert Fowler of Cambridge, Massachusetts, won in 2 hr 52:45.4. Second was John Daly of the Irish American Athletic Club in 2 hr 55:44.8.

James Clark   (United States)

2 hr 46:52.8   New York, USA   **12 Feb 1909**

Six weeks after Fowler's run, yet another marathon was held in New York, this time from the National Guard Armory in Brooklyn to Coney Island and back. There were 164 runners in the race. The favorite was James Crowley, who had won a marathon just six days earlier, but he dropped back after 14 miles, and James Clark took the lead. Clark finished almost six minutes faster than the previous record. Crowley finished in second place, two and a half minutes later. According to the newspaper report in *The World,* Clark ran "without a falter in his stride to a clear cut victory." The paper described the enthusiastic crowd as numbering more than 100,000. "It seemed as though Brooklyn's entire population and most of Manhattan had turned out."

Albert Raines   (United States)

2 hr 46:04.6   New York, USA   **8 May 1909**

The 1909 Bronx Marathon was run by the Northwestern Athletic Club, with the start and the finish at the Bronx oval. Albert Raines took the lead at the 17th mile and went on to win by over 11 minutes from Gustav Wass of Sweden. His time took 48 seconds off Clark's three-month-old world record. Little information is available about Albert Raines.

Harry "Fred" Barrett   (Great Britain, 1879–1927)

2 hr 42:31.0   London, England   **26 May 1909**

This marathon was organized by the newspaper *Sporting Life.* The British had not had any success in the 1908 London Marathon, and to correct this the newspaper offered a handsome silver trophy to the winner of an annual marathon. This marathon was organized by the Polytechnic Harriers and came to be known as the "Poly" marathon. Barrett was a member of the club. He had run in the 1908 Olympic marathon but had failed to finish.

At this inaugural Poly, Barrett ran a cautious race, placed ninth at 15 miles, but moved up to third at 22 miles. He took the lead at the 25-mile mark. His win was greeted rapturously by the crowd of 25,000. His time of 2 hr 42:31 took over three and a half minutes off the record.

Alexis Ahlgren   (Sweden, 1887–?)

2 hr 36:06.6   London, England   **31 May 1913**

The next marathon record also took place at the Poly marathon, in 1913. The Swede Alexis Ahlgren, who had a substantial reputation in his own country, finished over six minutes faster than Barrett had in 1909. Ahlgren completed the course in 2 hr 36:06. At the finish Ahlgren was greeted by the Swedish crown prince. Second was Tatu Kolehmainen of Finland, brother of Johannes (the 1912 Olympic 5000m and 10,000m champion and 1920 Olympic marathon champion). An unskilled laborer, he later moved to the United States and worked in the car industry in Detroit.

Johannes Kolehmainen   (Finland, 1889–1966)

2 hr 32:35.8   Antwerp, Belgium   **22 Aug 1920**

Johannes Kolehmainen was the great pioneer of Finnish distance running. His father died in 1895 when Johannes was five years old, and his mother Sofia, a washerwoman, was the sole breadwinner for many years. Three Kolehmainen brothers became marathon runners. Tatu Kolehmainen ran in the 1920 Olympics and finished 10th. Wiljani Kolehmainen became a professional runner in Scotland and the United States. Young Johannes ran his first marathon in 1907 at the age of 17 and in 1909 ran three marathons on consecutive Sundays.

After his 1912 Olympic victories at 5000m and 10,000m Kolehmainen settled in the United States and came in fourth at the Boston Marathon in 1917. In the 1920 Olympic marathon, in steady rain, Johannes and the South African Christian Gitsham shared the lead from the halfway mark. However, the South African faded badly at the finish, and Johannes took three and a half minutes off the world record. He thus achieved Olympic gold medals at 5000m, 10,000m, and the marathon. A symbol of Finnish independence, he was also a symbol of reconciliation after Finland's bitter civil war in 1919 in which 30,000 people died. In 1920 Kolehmainen joined both the right-wing SVUL and the left-wing TUL sporting associations. This gesture helped the nation to see that the wounds of the civil war could be healed.

Albert Michelsen   (United States, 1893–1993)

2 hr 29:01.8   Port Chester, USA   **12 Oct 1925**

Al Michelsen was a marathon runner during the 1920s and 1930s who often finished in the minor places. He didn't have the celebrity status of Clarence DeMar, who won the Boston Marathon seven times. Michelsen usually finished second or third in DeMar's big wins.

However, in a race that didn't attract much attention, Michelsen beat de Mar at the inaugural marathon at Port Chester, north of New York City. His time of 2 hr 29:01.8 made him the first man to beat the 2 hr 30 barrier; it was first broken by a woman, Grete Waitz, in 1979.

Fusashige Suzuki   (Japan, b. 1914)

2 hr 27:49.0   Tokyo, Japan   **31 Mar 1935**

Fusashige Suzuki was the first of a series of top Japanese marathon runners who emerged as world-class athletes in the 1930s. Suzuki's big race took place in Tokyo, from Jingu

Stadium to Rokugo and back. Suzuki was 22 years old at the time and was only 162 centimeters tall (5' 3"). He had already run another marathon 10 days earlier, finishing second to the Korean Sohn Kee Chung (Kitei Son), who was destined to become the Olympic gold medalist at the marathon in 1936.

On this occasion Suzuki won in 2 hr 27:49, which took 1:12.8 off Michelsen's 10-year-old record. Suzuki ran in the 10,000m at the Berlin Olympics but finished well behind.

Yasuo Ikenaka   (Japan, 1914–1992)

2 hr 26:44.0   Tokyo, Japan   **3 Apr 1935**

Suzuki's record lasted only three days. Suzuki and Sohn Kee Chung (Kitei Son) were regarded as the two leading Asian marathon runners. They both entered a marathon on 3 April 1935, the third marathon in 15 days for both men. However, a young Toyo University student, Yasuo Ikenaka, surprised both of them by winning in a new world record time: 2 hr 26:44, which took over a minute off Suzuki's recent record. Perhaps fatigue had caught up with the favorites. Suzuki came in second in 2 hr 33:05, and Sohn was third in 2 hr 39:24.

Yasuo Ikenaka, Japan (marathon).

Sohn Kee Chung (Kitei Son)   (Japan/South Korea, b. 1914)

2 hr 26:42.0   Tokyo, Japan   **3 Nov 1935**

Sohn Kee Chung was a native of Korea, born four years after occupation by Japanese forces. He began running in 1933 and was second in the Tokyo Marathon on 31 March 1935, in which Suzuki set a world's best time. Three days later Sohn was third in another marathon, at which Ikenaka set a world best. Finally, on 3 November 1935 Sohn established a world record at a marathon in Tokyo, when he took two seconds off Ikenaka's record with 2 hr 26:42.

Sohn Kee Chung was selected for the Berlin Olympics, but he had to run us-

Sohn Kee Chung, South Korea (marathon), at the 1936 Berlin marathon, forced to run as Kitei Son in Japanese colors.

ing the Japanese name of Kitei Son. Sohn and the Englishman Ernest Harper took over the lead at the 28-kilometer point. At 31 kilometers the Korean moved ahead and drew away to win in 2 hr 29:19.2. At the victory ceremony the Japanese flag was raised and the Japanese national anthem was played.

After the war, Korea became independent again, only to become divided into north and south. Sohn reverted back to his original name and lived in South Korea. Fifty-two years after his Berlin victory, in 1988, the Olympics came to Seoul. At the age of 74, Sohn was given the honor of carrying the Olympic torch into the stadium, wearing South Korean colors.

Yun Bok Suh   (South Korea, b. 1923)

2 hr 25:39.0   Boston, USA   **19 Apr 1947**

Yun Bok Suh came from South Korea and, at 5' 1" (155 centimeters) tall, was the shortest athlete to set a world record at the distance. He had impressed U.S. soldiers stationed in South Korea, and they helped finance his trip to the United States in 1947 for the Boston Marathon. Also in the party was Sohn Kee Chung, the winner of the 1936 Olympic marathon. It is thought that Yun would never have tried to defeat his mentor, if Sohn had chosen to run, such was the respect he felt for the veteran. However, in the end Sohn did not compete and Yun ran to win. In a completely unheralded showing, he shared the lead with the Finn Mikko Hietanen. At the notorious Heartbreak Hill he was attacked by a fox terrier, which knocked him to the ground. Nonetheless, he resumed the race and went on to win by four minutes from Hietanen. His time took over a minute off his mentor's record.

Yun Bok Suh, South Korea (marathon).

Jim Peters   (Great Britain, b. 1918)

2 hr 20:42.2	London, England	14 Jun 1952
2 hr 18:40.2	London, England	13 Jun 1953
2 hr 18:34.8	Turku, Finland	4 Oct 1953
2 hr 17:39.4	London, England	26 Jun 1954

Jim Peters's marathon career is similar to that of Dorando Pietri back in 1908 in that both achieved enormous publicity in races where they collapsed at the point of victory. Peters had run at the 1948 London Olympics, finishing ninth in the 10,000m. He made the decision to move up to the marathon after his career appeared static. His first marathon in 1951 resulted in a British record of 2 hr 29:24. A year later he set his first of four world records. Three of these came in the London Polytechnic Marathon (the "Poly").

Jim Peters, Great Britain (marathon), collapsing at the end of the 1954 Empire Games marathon, Vancouver.

He naturally hoped to win at the 1952 Helsinki Olympics, but Emil Zatopek, in his debut marathon, was not to be denied. The two men shared the lead when Zatopek asked Peters, "Is this pace too slow?" Peters thought they were already going quite fast enough. Whatever the truth of that anecdote, Zatopek pulled away, and Peters dropped back, later to pull out with leg cramps.

Peters's most publicized moment came at the 1954 Empire Games in Vancouver, Canada. The marathon took place on an extremely hot day. Peters took a commanding lead but at the conclusion of the race began to suffer sunstroke and entered the stadium disoriented. Staggering all over the track, he came very close to death. Finally, discus thrower John Savidge could not stand it anymore and carried him off the track to be raced away to the hospital. When Peters finally regained consciousness, he asked the nurse, "Did I win?" She replied, "You did very well." He made a full recovery but never ran the marathon again.

Sergey Popov   (Soviet Union, b. 1930)

2 hr 15:17.0   Stockholm, Sweden   24 Aug 1958

Sergey Popov came from central Russia, about 180 kilometers (112 miles) from Mongolia. He had become the first Soviet athlete to break the 2 hr 20 barrier for the marathon when he won the Soviet title in 1957 in 2 hr 19:50. Popov set his world record at the 1958 European Championships in Stockholm, on a hilly course in wet weather. A runner of small stature (5' 3" or 160 centimeters tall), he pushed the pace with

Sergey Popov, Soviet Union (marathon), the only Soviet athlete to hold the record for the marathon.

Alain Mimoun, the French-Algerian winner of the 1956 Olympic marathon. But at 25 kilometers Popov surged and was never headed. Popov's time (2 hr 15:17.0) was a world record and a Soviet record for the next 12 years.

Popov ran at the 1960 Rome Olympics, finishing fifth, as the winner, Abebe Bikila, set a new world record (2 hr 15:16.2). Popov also won the Soviet marathon title from 1957 to 1959.

Abebe Bikila   (Ethiopia, 1932–1973)

| 2 hr 15:16.2 | Rome, Italy | 10 Sep 1960 |
| 2 hr 12:11.2 | Tokyo, Japan | 21 Oct 1964 |

Abebe Bikila is one of the enduring, almost mythical figures of the marathon. A soldier in the guard of Emperor Haile Selassie, he seemed to come out of nowhere in 1960 to win the Olympic marathon in a world record time. He had run only two marathons prior to this, both in Ethiopia. His run in Rome was done in bare feet and sliced 0.8 second off the record. His gaunt figure and stoic and spartan demeanor evoked an image of the "Marathon Man."

Over the next few years he won a number of marathons, 12 out of the 15 he entered. One of the big ones he didn't win was Boston in 1963, where he came in fifth. He was next seen by the general public at the 1964 Tokyo Olympics, where he simply ran away with the race, taking three minutes off his previous world record. This time, he ran in shoes. After finishing the race, he lay on his back and mimicked riding a bicycle to amuse the crowd before the next runner entered the stadium.

Abebe Bikila, Ethiopia (marathon), winning his second Olympic marathon in Tokyo, 1964.

He ran at the 1968 Mexico City Olympics, but injuries made him withdraw at the 17-kilometer mark. Tragedy struck in 1969 when a motor vehicle accident left him with a broken neck and spinal injuries. He was confined to a wheelchair and died of a stroke four years later at the age of 41.

Toru Terasawa   (Japan, b. 1935)

| 2 hr 15:15.8 | Beppu, Japan | 17 Feb 1963 |

Toru Terasawa broke the 2 hr 20 barrier, when he ran 2 hr 16:18.4 in 1962 while winning the famed Fukuoka Marathon on the southern Japanese island of Kyushu. A few months later he ran in the Beppu Marathon, also in Kyushu. His time took a mere 0.4 second off Bikila's record.

Toru Terasawa won the Fukuoka Marathon again in 1964 (2hr 14:48.2) and naturally had high hopes for success at the Tokyo Olympics in 1964. It was not to be, and he came in 15th, much disappointed with the result. The first Japanese runner home, Kokichi Tsuburaya, was even more disappointed. He entered the stadium in second place but was passed in the last lap by Britain's Basil Heatley. Despite his bronze medal, Tsuburaya was depressed by "failing" in front of his own people. Later, plagued by injuries, he took his life.

Leonard "Buddy" Edelen　(United States, 1937–1997)

2 hr 14:28.0　London, England　　　　　　　　　　15 Jun 1963

Buddy Edelen, United States (marathon).

Born in Kentucky, Buddy Edelen spent five years in England teaching in Essex. He ran to and from school each day, a distance of about 3 miles (4.8 kilometers). He was very conscious that U.S. distance runners were not highly regarded by European athletes and was determined to change that. He ran 13 marathons between 1962 and 1966, winning 7 of them and beating just about every significant marathon runner in the process. In 1963 he won the London Polytechnic Marathon in a new world record time, taking 47.8 seconds off Terasawa's time.

He returned to the United States to secure his place on the 1964 U.S. Olympic team and won the U.S. trial easily. But at Tokyo Abebe Bikila was unbeatable, and Edelen, plagued with a sciatic injury, came home in sixth place, running 2 hr 18:12.4.

Despite his pioneering efforts, Edelen never got much recognition in the United States for his marathon achievements—the running boom would not take off until the 1970s. Nor was there any money or sponsorship around in those days. Edelen returned to live in the United States and was married and divorced twice. He spent 15 years as a professor of psychology in Colorado.

Basil Heatley　(Great Britain, b. 1933)

2 hr 13:55.0　London, England　　　　　　　　　　13 Jun 1964

Basil Heatley was the British Midlands marathon champion in 1956 and 1957, winning in 2 hr 36:55 and 2 hr 32:01, respectively. He then turned to cross-country running and was the winner of the International Cross Country Championship in 1961. However, in 1962 he failed to win selection to the English team for the Commonwealth Games, so he turned once again to the marathon. In his comeback race in 1963 he ran a very encouraging 2 hr 19:56. He entered the London Polytechnic Marathon in June 1964 and won in a new world record of 2 hr 13:55.

The Tokyo Olympics took place four months later, and Heatley was one of the favorites, if there is such a thing in an Olympic marathon. But Abebe Bikila was back in town and back in form, despite an appendix operation six weeks earlier. The Ethiopian won clearly by over four minutes in 2 hr 12:11.2. Heatley entered the stadium in third position but managed to overtake Japan's Kokichi Tsuburaya to win the silver medal in 2 hr 16:19.2.

Basil Heatley, Great Britain (marathon).

Morio Shigematsu   (Japan, b. 1940)

2 hr 12:00.0	London, England	12 Jun 1965

Morio Shigematsu was a graduate in business studies of Fukuoka University on the southern Japanese island of Kyushu. He was a surprise winner of the Boston Marathon in April 1965 in 2 hr 16:33. He then traveled to London to contest the Polytechnic Marathon two months later. Toru Terasawa also entered and, because of his 1963 world record, was generally regarded as the favorite. Terasawa actually ran faster than his 1963 time but still finished second. Shigematsu, running in white gloves, ran exactly 2 hr 12:00, taking 11.2 seconds off Bikila's 1964 record.

For the third consecutive year (1963-65), a world record had been set at the Poly marathon, something almost certain never to happen again.

Derek Clayton   (Australia, b. 1942)

2 hr 9:36.4	Fukuoka, Japan	3 Dec 1967
2 hr 8:33.6	Antwerp, Belgium	30 May 1969

Derek Clayton was born in Lancashire, England, and his family moved to Northern Ireland when he was eight. They next migrated to Australia when he was 21, and he made his life there. He was a tall man for a marathon runner (188 centimeters, 6' 2"), and he believed in punishing training schedules—perhaps too punishing, because much of his career was plagued by injuries. At his peak he ran 200 miles (300 kilometers) a week, almost a marathon a day.

He had won marathons in Australia but had no international recognition. All that changed when he traveled to Japan in 1967 to run the Fukuoka Marathon. Running with Japan's Seiichiro Sasaki, he broke away toward the end to smash the 2 hr 10 barrier, recording 2 hr 9:36.4.

Clayton ran in the Mexico City Olympics but struggled at the high altitude and finished seventh. He was determined to prove his Japanese run was no fluke, so he competed at the Antwerp Marathon in 1969. He deliberately pushed himself very hard and recorded 2 hr 8:33.6. This record lasted 12 years. In his last major marathon, he was 13th at the 1972 Olympics.

Derek Clayton, Australia (marathon), the first man to run the marathon under 2 hr 10.

Robert de Castella   (Australia, b. 1957)

2 hr 8:18.0   Fukuoka, Japan   6 Dec 1981

Robert de Castella was one of seven children. His father took up marathon running late in life and, at age 56, ran 2 hr 58:48. Much like Derek Clayton 14 years earlier, the junior de Castella had not quite established himself in the marathon elite when he traveled to Japan in 1981. However, in Japan he outdid himself and came home in 2 hr 8:18, over 15 seconds under Clayton's record.

Over the next few years de Castella had a series of brilliant wins. He won the 1982 Brisbane Commonwealth Games marathon in a come-from-behind victory. He defeated U.S. champion Alberto Salazar at the Rotterdam Marathon in 1983 and later that year

Robert de Castella, Australia (marathon).

won the inaugural World Championships marathon in Helsinki. In 1986 he won both the Boston Marathon and the Commonwealth marathon in Edinburgh. His Boston time of 2 hr 7:51 was to remain his personal best. He became a role model to a generation of Australian runners.

The Olympics were not so kind to him. After he came in tenth in 1980, he was fifth in 1984 and eighth in 1988. His participation in his fourth Olympics was not without controversy. No one had ever run four Olympic marathons before. De Castella was "preselected" on the basis of his win at the Rotterdam Marathon in 1991, more than a year before the Olympics began. But his form just before the 1992 Olympics was nothing special, and there was public questioning of the policy of preselecting any athlete, however eminent, so far before the Games actually began. However, de Castella chose to take his place on the Australian team. At Barcelona, at the age of 35, he finished the marathon in 26th place. In London a year later, in his last marathon, he finished 33rd.

From 1990 to 1995 he was the director of the Australian Institute of Sport.

Steve Jones   (Great Britain, b. 1955)

2 hr 8:05.0   **Chicago, USA**   **21 Oct 1984**

Steve Jones, Great Britain (marathon).

Welsh-born Steve Jones ran as an international distance runner for some years without quite obtaining any major victories. He then turned to marathon running with instant and remarkable success. Prior to his marathon debut he had reached a number of finals: 1978 Commonwealth Games 5000m (11th), 1982 European Championships 10,000m (7th), 1983 World Championships 10,000m (12th), and 1984 Olympic Games 10,000m (8th).

After the Los Angeles Games he ran in the 1984 Chicago Marathon. The big names in the race were Robert de Castella and Carlos Lopes. There were still six athletes in the leading pack with 10 kilometers (6 miles) to go. Jones just took off at this stage, and no one else could respond. He finished in a time of 2 hr 8:05, 13 seconds under the old record.

That race rocketed Jones to marathon celebrity status. A mechanic in the Royal Air Force, he won the 1985 London Marathon and the Chicago Marathon again in 1985. In the interim, however, Carlos Lopes had lowered the record even further to 2 hr 7:12 in Rotterdam. In his 1985 Chicago win Jones ran just one second slower than this time on a course generally regarded as far more arduous than the flat terrain of Rotterdam.

In some ways, after such a brilliant start, his subsequent marathon career never quite recaptured those glory days of 1984-85. In 1986 he had a two-minute lead in the European Championships, but became dehydrated, and staggered in 20th. He left the Air Force in 1988 and won the New York City Marathon that year. However it was seven years before he represented Great Britain again, at the 1993 World Championships, where at age 38 he finished 13th.

Carlos Lopes   (Portugal, b. 1947)

2 hr 7:12.0   Rotterdam, Netherlands   20 Apr 1985

Carlos Lopes, Portugal (marathon), 1984 Olympic marathon champion.

Carlos Lopes was another established distance runner who turned to the marathon late in his career with remarkable success. He had run in the 10,000m back in 1976 at the Montreal Olympics and finished second to Lasse Viren. He was also a highly successful cross-country runner, winning the International Cross Country Championships three times (1976, 1984, and 1985). He ran his first marathon in 1982 in New York, dropping out at 34 kilometers with leg cramps. His second in 1983 at Rotterdam proved much more successful and ended up with a sprint finish between Lopes and Robert de Castella. The Australian won by a mere two seconds.

At the 1984 Los Angeles Olympics he was 37 years old and the least experienced of the marathon entrants. However, he stayed with the leading pack in the humid conditions and pushed ahead at the 35-kilometer mark. The others could not respond, and he went on to win by 35 seconds in 2 hr 9:21. After this Olympic victory, all Portugal was determined to give him an "Olympic" reception, which they did.

Three months after the Olympics Lopes was surprised by newcomer Steve Jones in the Chicago Marathon, who won in a new world record (2 hr 8:05). However, six months later Lopes made a determined effort to better this time in a planned attempt at the flat marathon course in Rotterdam. At age 38, he astonished even possibly himself by taking almost a minute off the record (2 hr 7:12) in windy conditions. Lopes remains one of Portugal's great sporting heroes: the oldest man to win an Olympic marathon, the oldest man to set a world's best for the marathon, and the oldest man to win the International Cross Country Championships.

Belayneh Densimo   (Ethiopia, b. 1957)

2 hr 6:50.0   Rotterdam, Netherlands   17 Apr 1988

Rotterdam provided another marathon world record when Ethiopia's Belayneh Densimo ran under the 2 hr 7 barrier in 1988. In a competitive race, he was pushed all the way by

Ahmed Salah of the African nation of Djibouti, who finished only 17 seconds behind. Both men ran under the time set by Carlos Lopes on the same course three years earlier. Their times were 2 hr 6:50 (Densimo) and 2 hr 7:07 (Salah).

Densimo was not exactly an unknown when he set the new world record. His marathon debut had been in 1985 in Ethiopia at the Abebe Bikila Memorial Marathon, where he came in 13th. In a marathon in Tokyo in 1986 he was second to Tanzania's Juma Ikangaa in an Ethiopian record. He won the marathon at the Goodwill Games in Moscow later that year, and the Rotterdam marathon for the first time in 1987.

Densimo might well have been a force at the 1988 Seoul Olympics, but the Ethiopian government chose to boycott the Games to protest North Korea's noninvolvement in the Games.

He won the Rotterdam Marathon for the third time in 1989 and the Japanese Fukuoka Marathon in 1990. A police officer by profession, he decided to stay away from the 1992 Barcelona Olympics after his house was ransacked by bandits shortly before the Games began. He is so far the only athlete to run the marathon under 2 hr 7.

Conclusions

The marathon is a formidable event and cannot be readily categorized alongside other long-distance track events such as the 10,000m. Nonetheless, it is curious that the 10,000m world record has steadily improved over the last few years, while the marathon world best time has remained relatively static. However, it is accepted that a fast marathon time depends on a flat course, gentle weather conditions, good competition, and good pacing.

Only a few athletes have approached the world best time of 2 hr 6:50, but a reduction in the 1988 record seems overdue. That was a competitive race, which suggests that competition is as important in marathon times as in any other running event.

Five All-Time Fastest: Men's Marathon

Belayneh Densimo (ETH)	2 hr 6:50	1988
Sammy Lelei (KEN)	2 hr 7:03	1995
Ahmed Salah (DJI)	2 hr 7:07	1988
Carlos Lopes (POR)	2 hr 7:12	1985
Steve Jones (GBR)	2 hr 7:13	1985
Prediction	*2 hr 5:55*	*2015*

Top Three: Men's Marathon

GOLD MEDAL:	**Abebe Bikila (ETH)**
SILVER MEDAL:	**Jim Peters (GBR)**
BRONZE MEDAL:	**Derek Clayton (AUST)**

Competitors in this event have to clear 10 hurdles, each of which is 3' 6" high (1.067 meters). The original rules did not allow a world record if any of the hurdles were displaced, but this rule eventually lapsed. As of 1 January 1977, records had to be achieved with electronic timing to $\frac{1}{100}$ (0.01) of a second.

The original hurdles were solid sheep hurdles. At the turn of the century, modern hurdles in the shape of an inverted T were introduced. In 1935 the U.S. coach Harry Hillman designed the L shaped hurdles, which will topple over if struck with significant force. This allows speed hurdling without fear of injury. The postwar hurdlers have since combined top speed and good hurdling technique. The 110m hurdle event was dominated by U.S. hurdlers for the first 75 years of the 20th century, and they also dominated Olympic gold medals. Of the 25 world record holders, 16 have come from the United States. Nine world record holders have also been Olympic champions, of whom seven were U.S. athletes. The nine are Smithson, Thomson, Saling, Towns, Calhoun, Davenport, Milburn, Drut, and Kingdom.

The major barrier in the 110m hurdles was the 13-second mark, first broken by Renaldo Nehemiah in 1981. Even today only five athletes have beaten this barrier.

Men's World Records for 110m Hurdles

Record time	Record holder	Location	Date
15.0	Forrest Smithson (USA)	London, England	25 Jul 1908
14.8	Earl Thomson (CAN)	Antwerp, Belgium	18 Aug 1920
14.8	Sten Pettersson (SWE)	Stockholm, Sweden	18 Sep 1927
14.6	George Weightman-Smith (S.AF)	Amsterdam, Netherlands	31 Jul 1928
14.4	Eric Wennström (SWE)	Stockholm, Sweden	25 Aug 1929
14.4	Bengt Sjöstedt (FIN)	Helsinki, Finland	5 Sep 1931
14.4	Percy Beard (USA)	Cambridge, USA	18 Jun 1932
14.4	Jack Keller (USA)	Stanford, USA	16 Jul 1932
14.4	George Saling (USA)	Los Angeles, USA	2 Aug 1932
14.4	John Morriss (USA)	Budapest, Hungary	12 Aug 1933
14.4	John Morriss (USA)	Turin, Italy	8 Sep 1933
14.3	Percy Beard (USA)	Stockholm, Sweden	26 Jul 1934
14.2	Percy Beard (USA)	Oslo, Norway	6 Aug 1934
14.2	Alvin Moreau (USA)	Oslo, Norway	2 Aug 1935
14.1	Forrest Towns (USA)	Chicago, USA	19 Jun 1936
14.1	Forrest Towns (USA)	Berlin, Germany	6 Aug 1936
13.7	Forrest Towns (USA)	Oslo, Norway	27 Aug 1936
13.7	Fred Wolcott (USA)	Philadelphia, USA	29 Jun 1941
13.6	Dick Attlesey (USA)	College Park, USA	24 Jun 1950
13.5	Dick Attlesey (USA)	Helsinki, Finland	10 Jul 1950
13.4	Jack Davis (USA)	Bakersfield, USA	22 Jun 1956
13.2	Martin Lauer (FRG)	Zürich, Switzerland	7 Jul 1959
13.2	Lee Calhoun (USA)	Bern, Switzerland	21 Aug 1960
13.2	Earl McCullouch (USA)	Minneapolis, USA	16 Jul 1967
13.2	Willie Davenport (USA)	Zürich, Switzerland	4 Jul 1969
13.2*	Rod Milburn (USA)	Munich, West Germany	7 Sep 1972
13.1	Rod Milburn (USA)	Zürich, Switzerland	6 Jul 1973

13.1	Rod Milburn (USA)	Siena, Italy	22 Jul 1973
13.1	Guy Drut (FRA)	St. Maur, France	23 Jul 1975
13.0	Guy Drut (FRA)	Berlin, Germany	22 Aug 1975

Electronic timing:

13.24*	Rod Milburn (USA)	Munich, West Germany	7 Sep 1972
13.21	Alejandro Casanas (CUBA)	Sofia, Bulgaria	21 Aug 1977
13.16	Renaldo Nehemiah (USA)	San Jose, USA	14 Apr 1979
13.00	Renaldo Nehemiah (USA)	Los Angeles, USA	6 May 1979
12.93	Renaldo Nehemiah (USA)	Zürich, Switzerland	19 Aug 1981
12.92	Roger Kingdom (USA)	Zürich, Switzerland	16 Aug 1989
12.91	Colin Jackson (GBR)	Stuttgart, Germany	20 Aug 1993

*Rod Milburn's 7 Sep 1972 race was timed manually at 13.2 seconds and electronically at 13.24 seconds.

Forrest Smithson   (United States, 1881-1962)

15.0   **London, England**   **25 Jul 1908**

Forrest Smithson attended the University of Oregon and competed at the 1908 Olympics. He won the 110m hurdles and his time (15.0) was accepted as the first official record over the distance. He led a clean sweep: All four finalists were from the United States.

A much-reproduced photo shows Smithson hurdling with a Bible in his hand, apparently as a protest against the race being held on a Sunday. However, Olympic historian David Wallechinsky questioned this version. He found that none of Smithson's races took place on a Sunday, nor did any of the contemporary newspapers make any mention of it. He felt that the photo was staged.

In later life Smithson went on to become a Baptist minister and a sports broadcaster.

Forrest Smithson, United States (110m hurdles), at the 1908 London Olympics with Bible in hand.

Earl Thomson   (Canada, 1895-1971)

14.8   **Antwerp, Belgium**   **18 Aug 1920**

Earl Thomson was born in Saskatchewan, Canada, but his parents moved to southern California when he was eight. He represented Canada at the 1920 Olympics, even though he lived in the United States for 17 of his 25 years. He was somewhat superstitious and before a major race would tie his foot to the end of the bed, so that it would not curl up and cramp during the night.

The United States had won every Olympic 110m hurdle race up to that time. However, Thomson had set a world record over the English distance of 120 yards just prior to the Games and was the hot favorite. He did not disappoint and went on to win by 0.3 second in a new world record time of 14.8. The United States took the silver and bronze medals.

Thomson went on to be a track coach at the U.S. Naval Academy at Annapolis for 37 years.

Earl Thomson, Canada (110m hurdles), 1920 Olympic 110m hurdles champion.

Sten Pettersson   (Sweden, 1902–1984)

14.8   **Stockholm, Sweden**   **18 Sep 1927**

Sten Pettersson of Sweden is the only athlete who has held world records at both 110m and 400m hurdles. He had competed at the 1924 Paris Olympics and came in third in the 110m hurdles (15.4). In the 1928 Amsterdam Olympics, he was fourth in the 400m hurdles, was third in his semifinal of the 110m hurdles, and was part of the 4 × 400m relay team that came in fourth.

His world record, which equaled Thomson's seven-year-old record, was set in Stockholm in 1927 at an international meet.

Pettersson also competed at the 1932 Olympics (400m and 400m hurdles) but did not progress beyond the early rounds.

Sten Pettersson, Sweden (110m and 400m hurdles), on his 50th birthday.

George Weightman-Smith   (South Africa, 1905-1972)

14.6   **Amsterdam, Netherlands**   **31 Jul 1928**

George Weightman-Smith (290), South Africa (110m hurdles), with countryman Syd Atkinson (287) at the 110m hurdles at the 1928 Olympics. Weightman-Smith set the world record in the semifinals, but Atkinson won the final.

Weightman-Smith was one of two South Africans in the finals of the 110m hurdles at the 1928 Amsterdam Olympics. The other was his close friend, Syd Atkinson, who had come in second at the 1924 Olympics in the same event. Timing in those days was in fifths of a second (0.2). In his heat Weightman-Smith had been timed at 14.8 seconds, which equaled the world record. In his semifinal he was timed at 14.6 seconds, which set a new world record.

The semifinal took place two hours after the heat. In the final, his countryman Syd Atkinson was allocated the inside lane, which was severely chewed up by the distance runners. Atkinson was deeply upset, as he thought he would once again lose an Olympic final. Weightman-Smith, in a remarkable gesture, offered to swap lanes to give his friend a better chance at a gold medal. The offer was accepted. In the final Atkinson raced to victory in 14.8. Weightman-Smith paid for his good sportsmanship by finishing fifth in 15.0, in a close finish.

Weightman-Smith had studied at Cambridge University in 1925. Later in life he became a journalist and for many years was the chief subeditor of *The Star* in Johannesburg.

Eric Wennström   (Sweden, 1909-1970)

14.4   **Stockholm, Sweden**   **25 Aug 1929**

Eric Wennström was second to Sten Pettersson in 1927, when the latter ran his world record of 14.8; Wennström ran 14.9. At the Amsterdam Olympics in 1928 he was third in the semifinal of the 110m hurdles and did not progress to the final.

Wennström set his world record in 1929 in a match between Norway and Sweden in Stockholm. Wennström won in 14.4 seconds. All three timekeepers recorded the same time. There was some skepticism that he had actually run that fast, but he ran 14.6 later in the season to prove it was no fluke.

Bengt Sjöstedt   (Finland, 1906-1981)

14.4   **Helsinki, Finland**   **5 Sep 1931**

A contemporaneous account of Bengt Sjöstedt's described his style as "lacking finish. . . . [H]e flattens out at the hurdle a shade too early, so he has difficulty in bringing the rearward leg over the hurdle without touching it." He competed at the 1928 Olympics in the 110m hurdles and came in fourth in his semifinal.

His world record came in 1931 at an international meet in Helsinki, when he equaled Wennström's 14.4. Second was former world record holder Sten Pettersson in 14.8. This race was part of a trio of races between Sjöstedt and Pettersson. Pettersson won the other two races set over three successive nights. At the 1932 Olympics Sjöstedt was fifth in his semifinal.

Percy Beard   (United States, 1908–1990)

14.4	Cambridge, USA	18 Jun 1932
14.3	Stockholm, Sweden	26 Jul 1934
14.2	Oslo, Norway	6 Aug 1934

Percy Beard, United States (110m hurdles).

Percy Beard, a student at the University of Florida, at 6' 4" (193 centimeters) was tall for a hurdler. He became one of the favorites for the Olympic gold medal at Los Angeles by equaling the world record in the U.S. Olympic trials. He ran 14.4 in one of the semifinals. At the Olympics he was one of three U.S. athletes with Jack Keller and George Saling. Beard took the lead at the fifth hurdle but then hit the sixth. This allowed George Saling to come through and win in 14.6. Beard was second in 14.7.

Beard made a successful tour of Europe in 1934. He set a new world record in Stockholm of 14.3. Eleven days later, in Oslo, he reduced it to 14.2.

Percy Beard later graduated as a civil engineer and used his background in engineering to become a pioneer in the development of all-weather tracks. The athletic track at the University of Florida was named after him in 1974.

Jack Keller   (United States, 1911–1978)

| 14.4 | Stanford, USA | 16 Jul 1932 |

Jack Keller, a student at Ohio State University, won the 1932 U.S. Olympic trials, equaling the world record in the process with 14.4. This was the first world record in which there was an official wind-speed reading (–0.2 meters per second).

At the Olympics Keller took the lead early and was in front until he hit the fifth hurdle. This allowed Beard, then Saling, to go past him. Keller was given third place and awarded the bronze medal in the official ceremony. But a viewing of a film of the final revealed that Keller had been fourth to Britain's Donald Finlay. When the revised results came through, Keller located Finlay in the Olympic village and gave him the medal.

Jack Keller, United States (110m hurdles).

George Saling   (United States, 1909–1933)

14.4   **Los Angeles, USA**   **2 Aug 1932**

George Saling was a student at the University of Iowa. He exhibited prowess at 110m hurdles and also had run the 400m hurdles in 52.1. The world record at the time was 52.0

At the U.S. Olympic trials Saling came in second to Jack Keller. However, at the Games he won his semifinal in 14.4, to equal the world record. In the final Keller led till the fifth hurdle, which he hit. Then Beard led but hit the sixth hurdle. This allowed Saling to take the lead, which he held to the finish. His winning time was 14.6; Beard was second in 14.7. The Englishman Donald Finlay took third with 14.8; Keller also managed 14.8 in fourth place.

Sadly, in April 1933 Saling was killed in a car crash.

George Saling, United States (110m hurdles), gold medalist at the 1932 Los Angeles Olympics.

John Morriss   (United States, 1908–1993)

| 14.4 | Budapest, Hungary | 12 Aug 1933 |
| 14.4 | Turin, Italy | 8 Sep 1933 |

John Morriss, United States (110m hurdles).

John Morriss attended Southwestern Louisiana University and lettered in football, basketball, track and field, and golf. At the 1932 Olympic trials he came in fourth behind world record holders Keller, Beard, and Saling and missed the Olympics.

Morriss had a very successful tour of Europe in 1933. He equaled the world record twice, once in Budapest and again in Turin at the World Student Games.

He missed out again in 1936 for the U.S. Olympic team and spent the rest of his life as a track and field coach at the University of North Carolina (1936-42), U.S. Navy (1942-45), University of Southern Louisiana (1947-49), University of Arkansas (1950-52), University of Houston (1955-76), and finally Houston Baptist University (1976-83). He died in 1993 of Alzheimer's disease at the age of 84.

His main recreation was golf, and he achieved a hole-in-one six times.

Alvin Moreau   (United States, 1910–1990)

| 14.2 | Oslo, Norway | 2 Aug 1935 |

In an era when U.S. hurdling had enormous depth, Moreau never won a significant title. He had no Olympic, AAU, or NCAA victories. Moreau attended Louisiana State University and was second in the 1933 NCAA title, which was won by August Meier of Stanford.

He had a good year in 1935 and on a tour to Europe equaled the world record in Oslo at the Bislett Games. After the race (perhaps because of his relative lack of successful results in the past) he was described as "so happy that he had tears in his eyes."

He became a long-term track and field coach at Louisiana State and died at age 80 of cancer.

Forrest Towns   (United States, 1914–1991)

14.1	Chicago, USA	19 Jun 1936
14.1	Berlin, Germany	6 Aug 1936
13.7	Oslo, Norway	27 Aug 1936

Forrest Towns was nicknamed "Spec" early in life because of his freckles. The fifth of six children, he was raised in Fitzgerald, a town in south Georgia that was settled by Yankee soldiers after the Civil War. He won a sports scholarship at the University of Georgia, where he played football and track. At hurdles he was AAU champion in 1936 and NCAA champion in 1936-37. He ran 14.1 at the 1936 NCAA championships, his first world record at the distance.

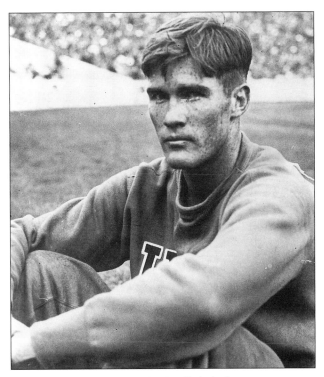

Forrest Towns, United States (110m hurdles), the first man to run under 14 seconds.

At the Berlin Olympics he was simply too good. He ran another 14.1 in the semifinals and won the final in 14.2 by a comfortable two yards. It was after the Olympics that he set off shock waves. In a meet in Oslo, three weeks after the Games, the timekeepers refused to believe that their watches were functioning correctly. He had recorded 13.7, an improvement over the existing record of 0.4 second, unheard of before or since. He later reflected that he got off to an unusually fast start that day: "When I broke the tape, the nearest guy was just then clearing the last hurdle."

Describing himself as a loner, he served as an officer in World War II. He had a 37-year career as a football and track coach at the University of Georgia. The athletic track at the University of Georgia was named after him in 1990.

Fred Wolcott   (United States, 1915–1972)

13.7   **Philadelphia, USA**   **29 Jun 1941**

It took only five years until Forrest Towns's amazing record was matched by Fred Wolcott of Texas. He earlier had become the second man to run under 14 seconds, recording 13.9 in 1938. Wolcott had a strong competitive record and was AAU champion in 1938, 1940, and 1941 and NCAA champion in 1938 and 1939.

A student at Rice University in Texas, he equaled Towns's record in 1941 at the AAU championships in Franklin Field, Philadelphia.

Fred Wolcott, United States (110m hurdles).

Dick Attlesey   (United States, 1929–1984)

| 13.6 | College Park, USA | 24 Jun 1950 |
| 13.5 | Helsinki, Finland | 10 Jul 1950 |

Dick Attlesey reduced Forrest Towns's esteemed record not once, but twice. But his best form was in non-Olympic years, and few have heard of him. A big man (6' 3", or 192 centimeters), he was AAU champion 1950-51 and NCAA champion in 1950. He was Pan-American champion in the first Pan-Am Games in Buenos Aires in 1951.

However, Attlesey was injured in 1952 and was last in his heat at the U.S. Olympic trials.

Attlesey died of leukemia at age 55. His daughter Kim competed in the long jump at the 1972 Olympics but did not get through to the finals.

Jack Davis   (United States, b. 1930)

| 13.4 | Bakersfield, USA | 22 Jun 1956 |

Three 110m hurdle world record holders at the 1956 Melbourne Olympics: Lee Calhoun, United States, *left* (first); Martin Lauer, West Germany (fourth); and Jack Davis, United States (second).

Jack Davis had the misfortune to come in second in two Olympic finals by minuscule margins. Davis was a student at the University of Southern California and came on the track and field scene toward the end of Harrison Dillard's career. Dillard won every honor except the world record over 110m hurdles. He had achieved the world record over 120-yard hurdles and had been Olympic champion at 100m in 1948 and at 110m hurdles in 1952. Davis came very close to denying him the 1952 Olympic gold medal. Both men were credited with 13.7

Davis went on to become AAU champion in 1953-54. At the 1956 AAU championships he reduced Attlesey's world record by 0.1, when he ran 13.4 in his heat. The final was actually won by rising new star Lee Calhoun from North Carolina. That star, unfortunately for Davis, continued to rise. At the Melbourne Olympics in November Calhoun squeaked home just ahead of Davis: 13.70 to 13.73 on electronic timing.

Martin Lauer   (West Germany, b. 1937)

13.2   **Zürich, Switzerland**   **7 Jul 1959**

Martin Lauer was the first European to run under 14 seconds for 110m hurdles and came in fourth in two Olympics (1956 and 1960). An accomplished all-round athlete, at age 19 he was fifth in the decathlon as well as fourth in the 110m hurdles at the Melbourne Olympics.

Lauer was West German 110m hurdles champion five years in a row (1956-60) and in 1958 won the 110m hurdles at the European Championships. In 1959 he really set the track and field world alight by taking 0.2 second off the world record in Zurich with 13.2.

Alas, at the Olympics the United States had a clean sweep in both 1956 and 1960. Lauer had one consolation by winning a gold medal in the 1960 4 × 100m relay. The U.S. team finished ahead of the West Germans but were disqualified for a baton change outside the regulation zone.

Lee Calhoun   (United States, 1933–1989)

13.2   **Bern, Switzerland**   **21 Aug 1960**

Lee Calhoun won Olympic gold medals in 1956 and 1960, both by very narrow margins. He first came to attention when he inflicted a surprise defeat on hurdle supremo Jack Davis at the 1956 AAU titles. Davis reestablished his supremacy in pre-Olympic meets, but Calhoun was able to win at the Melbourne Olympics in November. He won 13.70 to 13.73.

Calhoun retained his AAU title in 1957 and 1959 and was NCAA champion in 1956-57. However, he had a hiccup in his career: In 1957 he chose to marry on the television show "Bride and Groom" and received some gifts from the television company in the process. This was deemed professionalism by the ever-vigilant athletic authorities of the day, and he was suspended for the rest of the season.

The 110m hurdles at the 1960 Rome Olympics had an even closer final than at Melbourne. Calhoun won in 13.98; Willie May was second in 13.99.

Later in life Calhoun became a coach, first at Grambling University, then at Yale, and finally at Western Illinois University. He died at the age of 55.

Earl McCullouch   (United States, b. 1946)

13.2   **Minneapolis, USA**   **16 Jul 1967**

Earl McCullouch was a supremely talented hurdler who preferred American football. A student at the University of Southern California, his world record came when he won the U.S. trials for the 1967 Pan-American Games. He ran 13.2 to equal the world record of Lauer and Calhoun. McCullouch duly went on to win the Pan-Am title in Winnipeg. His other wins include NCAA titles in 1967-68 and the AAU championship in 1968. But at this point in his career he chose football and decided not to go to the Mexico City Olympics.

In American football he was drafted by the Detroit Lions and named NFL Rookie of the Year in 1968. His career record was 124 catches, 2319 yards, 18.7 average, and 19 touchdowns.

Willie Davenport   (United States, b. 1943)

| 13.2 | Zürich, Switzerland | 4 Jul 1969 |

Willie Davenport,
United States, 1968
Olympic 110m
hurdles champion.

Willie Davenport was a graduate of Southern University, New Orleans, and surprised observers by winning the U.S. Olympic trials in 1964. But an injury prevented him from progressing beyond the semifinals in Tokyo. Over the next few years he won three AAU titles (1965-67). At the Mexico City Olympics, although nervous at being the favorite, he took control of the race to win in 13.3.

His world record came in 1969. He was competing at an international meet in Zürich on American Independence Day when he equaled the record of Lauer, Calhoun, and McCullouch (13.2).

By 1972, there was a new U.S. star, Rod Milburn, and at the Munich Olympics Davenport finished fourth. It seemed his career was winding down, especially after he tore a tendon in his left knee in 1975. He spent much of that summer in the hospital. However, he came back from this handicap to make his fourth Olympics in 1976. At the Montreal Olympics in a tight finish Davenport, aged 33, claimed the bronze medal, behind gold medalist Guy Drut (France) and silver medalist Alejandro Casanas (Cuba). The times were 13.30, 13.33, and 13.38.

His Olympic days were not over yet. In 1980 he was part of the U.S. team in the Winter Olympics and competed in the four-man bobsled event.

Rod Milburn   (United States, b. 1950)

13.2	Munich, West Germany	7 Sep 1972 (13.24 timed electronically)
13.1	Zürich, Switzerland	6 Jul 1973
13.1	Siena, Italy	22 Jul 1973

"Hot" Rod Milburn, like Willie Davenport, was another top hurdler from Southern University in Baton Rouge. During 1971 and much of 1972 he won 27 races in a row, including

"Hot" Rod Milburn, United States, 1972 Olympic 110m hurdles champion.

the 1971 Pan-American Games. His winning streak came to an end under almost disastrous circumstances at the U.S. trials for the Munich Olympics. He hit the seventh and tenth hurdles heavily, and just squeaked into the U.S. team by coming in third. After this scare he made no mistakes in Munich and won in 13.2 seconds to equal the world record. With electronic timing he was recorded at 13.24, which was accepted as the inaugural electronic world record for the 110m hurdles.

A year later he ran 13.1 at Zurich and repeated this 16 days later in Italy. By this stage Rod Milburn had nothing left to prove in the world of amateur track and field and chose to join the newly formed professional group ITA. However, this group only lasted a few years before it collapsed. Unfortunately, he had forfeited his amateur status in the process, so he watched the 1976 Montreal Olympics on television with some frustration at not being able to compete.

He was able to resume his amateur status in time for a comeback at the 1980 Olympics, but President Carter imposed a boycott of the Moscow Olympics. Milburn finally retired after the 1984 season.

Guy Drut   (France, b. 1950)

| 13.1 | St. Maur, France | 23 Jul 1975 |
| 13.0 | Berlin, Germany | 22 Aug 1975 |

Guy Drut was the first European to successfully challenge and defeat the U.S. hurdlers. He was also the first man to run 13 seconds (hand-timed) for the 110m hurdles. Drut was born in the town of Oignies. His mother was English, his father French. Drut became French 110m hurdle champion eight times between 1970 and 1980. In the 1971 European championships he fell in the first heat. But from then on, he was largely unchallenged by any other European. At the 1972 Munich Olympics he was a close second to the new world record holder, Rod Milburn, 13.24 to 13.34. He equaled Milburn's world record of 13.1 in France in July 1975. One month later in Berlin he went one better and recorded 13.0, the last hand-timed world record in the 110m hurdles.

At the 1976 Montreal Olympics he got off to a fast start, took the lead by the third hurdle, and won narrowly from Cuba's Alejandro Casanas, 13.30 to 13.33.

After his Olympic win Drut publicly attacked the "shamateurism" of amateur athletics, whereby under-the-table payments to athletes (including himself) were widespread. These charges sent the French Athletic Federation into a rage: He was banned, but, fairly predictably, was reinstated as an amateur a few years later.

Guy Drut, France (110m hurdles), celebrates his gold medal at the 1976 Montreal Olympics.

Alejandro Casanas   (Cuba, b. 1954)

| 13.21 | Sofia, Bulgaria | 21 Aug 1977 |

Alejandro Casanas, Cuba (110m hurdles).

After 1976, Rod Milburn's 13.24 run at the Munich Olympics was accepted as the first electronically timed world record for the distance.

Alejandro Casanas, at age 18, was selected for the 110m hurdles at the Munich Olympics but fell in his heat and failed to qualify. Three years later, he won the hurdles at the Pan-American Games in Cali, Colombia, the first non-U.S. athlete to win this event. At the Montreal Olympics he once again beat the U.S. athletes but couldn't quite catch Guy Drut, who won 13.30 to 13.33. In 1977, competing at the World Student Games, he reduced Rod Milburn's record to 13.21.

The United States boycotted the 1980 Moscow Olympics because of the Soviet 1979 invasion of Afghanistan. This left Casanas as one of the favorites. In the final he hit the first two hurdles heavily and was just beaten by Thomas Munkelt of East Germany, 13.39 to 13.40. Thus, Casanas had the same fate as Jack Davis, second in two Olympics.

Renaldo Nehemiah (United States, b. 1959)

13.16	San Jose, USA	14 Apr 1979
13.00	Los Angeles, USA	6 May 1979
12.93	Zürich, Switzerland	19 Aug 1981

Renaldo Nehemiah had an impeccable career but missed out on the Olympics. As a junior athlete in high school, he commented that one day he would run under 13 seconds for the hurdles. That was an outrageous comment at the time, but it eventually came true. He was one of the first U.S. athletes to break free of the college system. He left the University of Maryland after two years and made a contract with Puma. This generated some controversy, but he justified the move by setting three world records between 1979 and 1981.

In 1980 President Carter's boycott of the Moscow Games denied him a chance of an Olympic gold medal. He kept winning races and in 1981 brought his record down to 12.93 to become the first man to break the 13-second barrier. With few mountains left to climb, he turned to football and signed with the San Francisco 49ers. That made him ineligible for amateur athletics, but his football career was not a success. After one injury too many, he was let go. He fought to be reinstated as an amateur, and this was granted in 1986. However, there was now a new generation of hurdlers, including in particular Roger Kingdom. At the 1988 U.S. Olympic trials Nehemiah failed to finish the final.

In 1991 he achieved his fastest time (13.19) since his return. He was actually

Renaldo Nehemiah, United States, the first man to run 110m hurdles under 13 seconds.

selected for the U.S. team for the 1991 Tokyo World Championships, his first U.S. representation in 10 years. However, he was injured and could not compete.

The ultimate irony occurred in 1989, when he withdrew from the Zürich track and field meet because he and the promoter could not agree on financial terms. He sat in the stands and watched Roger Kingdom take 0.01 second off his old record in the same stadium in which he had set it eight years earlier.

He retired a few years later and became an investment manager. He also runs a radio program and coaches at George Mason University in Fairfax, Virginia.

Roger Kingdom   (United States, b. 1962)

12.92   **Zürich, Switzerland**   **16 Aug 1989**

Roger Kingdom, United States (110m hurdles), two-time Olympic gold medalist, 1984 and 1988.

Roger Kingdom achieved almost every honor in his career: Olympic champion twice (1984 and 1988), world record holder (1989), Pan-American champion (1983 and 1995), NCAA champion (1983), and AAU champion (1985, 1988-90, 1995). The only honor he missed was world champion.

Although Kingdom was obviously a top hurdler when he made the final of the 1984 Olympics, the favorite was his countryman Greg Foster. But Foster got away to a slow start in the final, and Kingdom seized the opportunity. He won in 13.20, with Foster second in 13.23.

Kingdom was injured and inactive during much of 1986-87, but in 1988 he was back better than ever. He went through the entire 1988 season undefeated and won the Olympic final in 12.98. One of the features of his running in those days was the strength with which he attacked each hurdle, often knocking them down. He once joked that if hitting hurdles was a crime, he should be in jail. But these collisions with the hurdles didn't seem to slow him down.

The day came in 1989 in Zurich when he ran a superb race without hitting any hurdles. The result was a time of 12.92, which broke Nehemiah's eight-year-old record by 0.1 second.

Injuries slowed him down, and he didn't make it through the 1992 U.S. Olympic trials.

He underwent reconstructive knee surgery in September 1992. In his thirties at that time, he was plagued by further injuries for several years, and no one took him seriously when he said he was still aiming for the Atlanta Games. But in 1995, his first year free of injury in almost five years, he won the Pan-American Games and later the AAU title. Until that time he had won only gold medals at the major championships. However, in Sweden at the 1995 World Championships he walked away without a gold medal for the first time in his career when he finished third at age 32. The next year he finished fifth at the U.S. Olympic trials.

Colin Jackson   (Great Britain, b. 1967)

12.91   Stuttgart, Germany   20 Aug 1993

Colin Jackson was born in Cardiff, Wales. Early in his career he hovered near the top of international hurdling without quite being number one. It was not until 1993 that he finally established his supremacy. For many years he was just behind Roger Kingdom. His record wasn't helped by last-minute injuries at some of the big competitions, such as at the 1991 World Championships and at the 1992 Barcelona Olympics. In the latter event he was plagued by a painful rib injury in the final and finished seventh.

Finally in Stuttgart, at the 1993 World Championships, everything came together. With impeccable technique, he recorded 12.91 to take 0.1 second off Roger Kingdom's record.

Originally an electrical apprentice before he hit the big-time in track and field, he lists his interests as listening to music and most other sports. Here is his record to date:

Colin Jackson, Great Britain (110m hurdles).

1986 Commonwealth Games, second
1987 World Championships, third
1988 Seoul Olympics, second
1990 European Championships, first
1990 Commonwealth Games, first
1992 Barcelona Olympics, seventh
1993 World Championships, first (world record)
1994 European Championships, first
1994 Commonwealth Games, first

At his third Olympics at Atlanta he missed out on a medal when he finished fourth in 13.19.

Conclusions

Much improvement in the 110m hurdles world record took place in the early years. The world record reached 12.93 in 1981. Since then progress has been modest, down only to 12.91. Much like the sprints, the capacity for significant further improvement seems unlikely unless an athlete shows both world-class sprinting form and impeccable hurdling technique.

Five All-Time Fastest: Men's 110m Hurdles			(Wind)
Colin Jackson (GBR)	12.91	1993	+0.5
Roger Kingdom (USA)	12.92	1989	−0.1
Allen Johnson (USA)	12.92	1996	+0.9
Renaldo Nehemiah (USA)	12.93	1981	−0.2
Jack Pierce (USA)	12.94	1996	+1.6
Prediction	*12.86*	*2015*	

Top Three: Men's 110m Hurdles

GOLD MEDAL:	Renaldo Nehemiah (USA)
SILVER MEDAL:	Roger Kingdom (USA)
BRONZE MEDAL:	Forrest Towns (USA)

This race is possibly more punishing than the 400m flat race in that the athletes have to maintain hurdling technique to the finish as well as combating fatigue and lactic acid buildup. Each competitor must clear 10 hurdles, 3 feet (0.914 m) high and 35 meters apart. There is a distance of 45 meters to the first hurdle and 40 meters from the final hurdle to the finish.

There have been 16 athletes who have held this world record on 22 occasions. All but four have been from the United States. A high proportion have won Olympic gold medals: 10 out of 16. Six of these 10 set their world records in the Olympic final: Bacon, Loomis, Hardin, Hemery, Akii-Bua, and Moses.

Glenn Davis became the first man to break the 50-second barrier in 1956. The 49-second barrier was broken by Geoff Vanderstock (1968), the 48-second barrier by John Akii-Bua (1972), and the 47-second barrier by Kevin Young (1992). However, few athletes have dominated an event for as long as Edwin Moses did the 400m hurdles between 1976 and 1988.

There is considerable variation in the number of steps taken between each hurdle by different athletes. Early coaching manuals suggested 15 steps between each hurdle. Most athletes try to start with 13 steps between some of the hurdles, dropping back to 15 for the latter part of the race. Edwin Moses first mastered the art of taking 13 steps between every hurdle in the 1970s. Kevin Young learned to take 12 steps between certain hurdles and 13 for the rest.

Men's World Records for 400m Hurdles

Record time	Record holder	Location	Date
55.0	Charles Bacon (USA)	London, England	22 Jul 1908
54.2	John Norton (USA)	Pasadena, USA	26 Jun 1920
54.0	Frank Loomis (USA)	Antwerp, Belgium	16 Aug 1920
53.8	Sten Pettersson (SWE)	Paris, France	4 Oct 1925
52.6	John Gibson (USA)	Lincoln, USA	2 Jul 1927
52.0	F. Morgan Taylor (USA)	Philadelphia, USA	4 Jul 1928
52.0	Glenn Hardin (USA)	Los Angeles, USA	1 Aug 1932
51.8	Glenn Hardin (USA)	Milwaukee, USA	30 Jun 1934
50.6	Glenn Hardin (USA)	Stockholm, Sweden	26 Jul 1934
50.4	Yuriy Lituyev (USSR)	Budapest, Hungary	20 Sep 1953
49.5	Glenn Davis (USA)	Los Angeles, USA	29 Jun 1956
49.2	Glenn Davis (USA)	Budapest, Hungary	6 Aug 1958
49.2	Salvatore Morale (ITA)	Belgrade, Yugoslavia	14 Sep 1962
49.1	Warren "Rex" Cawley (USA)	Los Angeles, USA	13 Sep 1964
48.8	Geoffrey Vanderstock (USA)	Echo Summit, USA	11 Sep 1968
48.12	David Hemery (GBR)	Mexico City, Mexico	15 Oct 1968
47.82	John Akii-Bua (UGA)	Munich, West Germany	2 Sep 1972
47.64	Edwin Moses (USA)	Montreal, Canada	25 Jul 1976
47.45	Edwin Moses (USA)	Los Angeles, USA	11 Jun 1977
47.13	Edwin Moses (USA)	Milan, Italy	3 Jul 1980
47.02	Edwin Moses (USA)	Koblenz, West Germany	31 Aug 1983
46.78	Kevin Young (USA)	Barcelona, Spain	6 Aug 1992

Charles Bacon   (United States, 1885–1968)

55.0   **London, England**   **22 Jul 1908**

Charles Bacon was the Olympic champion at the 400m hurdles at the 1908 London Olympics. His time (55.0) was taken as the first official world record at this distance.

In this race he veered over to a lane outside of his own and actually jumped a hurdle in the wrong lane midway through the race. But the judges decided that he had incurred extra distance in so doing and that he had not interfered with any other athlete, so he was not disqualified.

Charles Bacon had also competed at the 1904 Olympics in the 1500m, coming in ninth. He had also competed at the 1906 Interim Games in Athens and came in fifth in the 400m and sixth in the 800m. Despite his world record, Bacon never won a senior AAU title.

John Norton   (United States, 1893–1979)

54.2   **Pasadena, USA**   **26 Jun 1920**

John Norton set a world record for the 400m hurdles of 54.2 a few weeks before the 1920 U.S. Olympic trials. A student at Stanford University, he had not had previous success at this distance. (The event was not run at the NCAA championships until 1932.)

The AAU winner in 1920 was Frank Loomis in 55.0. It was Loomis who continued to dominate the rest of the season. He won the U.S. Olympic trials, with Norton second. He won again at the Antwerp Olympics in 54.0 to break Norton's record. Norton was second in 54.3.

Frank Loomis   (United States, 1896–1962)

54.0   **Antwerp, Belgium**   **16 Aug 1920**

Frank Loomis was AAU champion over 200m hurdles in 1917 and 1918 as a member of the Chicago Athletic Association. In 1920 he turned to the 400m hurdles and won the AAU title. He also comfortably beat the new world record holder for 400m hurdles, John Norton, at the U.S. Olympic trials.

He continued his domination at the 1920 Games in Antwerp and took 0.2 second off Norton's record with an easy win in 54.0, a new world record. Norton was second in 54.3.

Loomis's brother Jo also made the 1920 Olympic team as a reserve in the 4 × 100m relay.

Sten Pettersson   (Sweden, 1902–1984)

53.8   **Paris, France**   **4 Oct 1925**

As mentioned in the chapter on 110m hurdlers, Sten Pettersson was the only athlete to hold the world record at both 110m (1927) and 400m hurdles (1925).

Pettersson won the bronze medal in the 100m hurdles at the 1924 Paris Olympics. At the 1928 Olympics he finished third in his semifinal of the 110m hurdles, finished fourth in the final of the 400m hurdles, and was in the Swedish team that finished fourth in the 4 × 400m relay. At the 1932 Los Angeles Olympics he was fourth in the heat of the 400m flat and fifth in the semifinals of the 400m hurdles.

He had a long career, winning 22 Swedish titles altogether. His 400m world record took place at the Colombes track in Paris, which was actually 500m in circumference, requiring fewer sharp turns and allowing for a faster time.

John Gibson   (United States, 1905–1971)

52.6   **Lincoln, USA**   **2 Jul 1927**

John Gibson won the AAU title in 1927 and set a world record in the process. His time of 52.6 took a massive 1.2 seconds off the world record. In this race he defeated Morgan Taylor, who dominated the 440-yard/400m hurdles in the United States for much of the 1920s. In a close race, Gibson was timed at 52.6, while Taylor's estimated time was 52.7.

Gibson ran in the 1928 Olympics in Amsterdam. He was fourth with 54.4 in the semifinals of the 400m hurdles.

F. Morgan Taylor   (United States, 1903–1975)

52.0   **Philadelphia, USA**   **4 Jul 1928**

F. Morgan Taylor, United States (400m hurdles), 1924 Olympic champion.

Morgan Taylor was the premier 440-yard/400m hurdler in the United States for much of the 1920s. A graduate of Grinnell College in Iowa, he won the gold medal at 400m hurdles at the Paris Olympics in 1924. His winning time that day, 52.6, was not accepted as a world record because he had knocked down a hurdle, which at the time invalidated a record.

Taylor was the U.S. AAU champion in 1924 through 1926 and again in 1928. Late in his career he finally achieved a world record at the 1928 U.S. Olympic trials in Philadelphia. Taylor won in a tight finish from Frank Cuhel, 52.0 to 52.1 (estimated). However, at the Games in Amsterdam the event was won by Britain's Lord Burghley in 53.4, with Taylor third in 53.6. At his last Olympics in 1932 at Los Angeles Taylor won another bronze medal with 52.0.

Taylor was also a long jumper of note, and achieved 25' 2" (7.67 meters). This was a "family" record until his son Buzz, who long-jumped for Princeton, exceeded it in 1952.

Morgan Taylor later worked as a salesman for the *Chicago Tribune* and then as a sales executive and divisional manager of Edwards Company, a department store in New York.

Glenn Hardin   (United States, 1910–1975)

52.0	Los Angeles, USA	1 Aug 1932
51.8	Milwaukee, USA	30 Jun 1934
50.6	Stockholm, Sweden	26 Jul 1934

Glenn Hardin, United States (400m hurdles), 1936 Olympic champion.

Glenn Hardin of Louisiana State University competed at the 1932 Los Angeles Olympics. The race was dominated by Irishman Robert Tisdall, who won in a world record time of 51.7. However, during the race Tisdall knocked a hurdle over and invalidated the record. Hardin, who finished second, was also under the old record. As he had not knocked down any hurdles, he was declared the new world record holder under the rules of the time.

After that second place to Tisdall in 1932, Hardin never lost another 400m hurdle race in his career. He went on to be AAU champion in 1933, 1934, and 1936. At the 1934 AAU championships he achieved the world record in his own right, running 51.8. Later that season, on a trip to Europe, he diminished the record by an additional 1.2 seconds in Stockholm. It was a record that would last 19 years, one of the longest-enduring track and field records.

Hardin won the gold medal at the 1936 Berlin Olympics and then retired. His son Billy competed in the 400m hurdles at the 1964 Tokyo Olympics; he had already beaten the family record at the U.S. Olympic trials with 49.8. In Tokyo he went out in the semifinals.

Yuriy Lituyev   (Soviet Union, b. 1925)

| 50.4 | Budapest, Hungary | 20 Sep 1953 |

Yuriy Lituyev was the Soviet Union's one and only world record holder over 400m hurdles. He had been second at the 1950 European Championships and second at the 1952 Olympics. Lituyev achieved his world record in a Soviet Union vs. Hungary meet in Budapest in 1953. He proved it was no fluke in London in 1954 by running a world record of 51.3 over the slightly longer 440-yard hurdle distance (402.34 meters). However, he was to miss out again on major honors when he was second in the 1954 European Championships to his countryman Anatoliy Yulin.

By the time the 1956 Olympics came around there was a new breed of U.S. 400m hurdlers. The U.S. team members finished first, second, and third; Glenn Davis won in 50.1, and Lituyev came in fourth in 51.7.

Finally, at the end of his career at age 33, he won a gold medal at the 1958 European Championships in Stockholm, winning in 51.1. In his own national championships he won the 400m hurdles title eight times (1950-55, 1957-58).

Glenn Davis   (United States, b. 1934)

| 49.5 | Los Angeles, USA | 29 Jun 1956 |
| 49.2 | Budapest, Hungary | 6 Aug 1958 |

Glenn Davis, United States (400m hurdles), *center*, after winning the 1956 Olympic gold medal, being congratulated by teammates Eddie Southern (279), second, and Josh Culbreath (277), third.

Glenn Davis won back-to-back Olympic 400m hurdle victories in 1956 and 1960. He was also part of the 4 × 400m U.S. team that won a gold medal at the Rome Olympics. He broke the world record over both the 440-yard flat (45.7) and the 400m hurdles. This achievement in setting world records over both the hurdles and the flat race is unique.

One of 10 children, he later described his childhood as "very, very poor"; both his parents died on the same day. A highly talented athlete, he excelled at both track and field and football. He took up the 400m hurdles only in the Olympic year of 1956 and had a truly meteoric rise to success. First, he eclipsed established star Josh Culbreath by winning the AAU title. Then, at the U.S. Olympic trials he became the first athlete to break the 50-second barrier when he ran 49.5.

At the Melbourne Olympics Davis won comfortably in 50.1, with U.S. athletes Eddie Southern and Josh Culbreath in second and third places. He won AAU titles in 1957, 1958, and 1960. In 1958 he took an additional 0.3 second off his 400m hurdle record. At the Rome Olympics he drew the difficult outside lane in the final, in which he was unable to see the other runners. Nonetheless, he kept his nerve and won in 49.3 for two successive Olympic wins.

Later in life he had a brief football career, playing two seasons with the Detroit Lions and the Los Angeles Rams. At 73 kilograms (161 pounds), Davis was one of the lightest football players at that time. After his football days were over he opened a series of restaurants. He said his main regret was that he and Edwin Moses never had a chance to run against each other in their prime.

Salvatore Morale   (Italy, b. 1938)

| 49.2 | Belgrade, Yugoslavia | 14 Sep 1962 |

Morale had competed at the 1960 Rome Olympics, coming in fourth in a semifinal of the 400m hurdles. He was the first European to run under 50 seconds when he ran 49.7 in 1961.

At the 1962 European Championships in Belgrade everything fell into place: He ran the first 200m in 23.9 and the second in 25.3, to equal Davis's world record. Both Davis in 1958 and Morale in 1962 used 15 steps between each hurdle.

Morale had hopes of an Olympic gold medal in Tokyo, but a new star emerged, Rex Cawley, who set a new world record (49.1) at the U.S. Olympic trials. In the Olympic final Morale drew the outside lane, never easy. He led for the first five hurdles, but then Cawley swept past him to win the gold medal. Britain's John Cooper just beat Morale for the silver medal. The times were 49.6, 50.1, and 50.1.

Warren "Rex" Cawley   (United States, b. 1940)

49.1   **Los Angeles, USA**   **13 Sep 1964**

In 1959 Rex Cawley was a finalist at all three hurdles events at the U.S. AAU championships: fifth in the 120-yard hurdles, third in the 220 low hurdles, and sixth in the 440-yard hurdles.

He missed out on the 1960 Rome Olympics when he finished seventh at the U.S. Olympic trials. Cawley went on to study at the University of Southern California and was AAU champion over 440-yard hurdles in 1963 and 1965 and NCAA champion in 1963.

In 1964, at the U.S. Olympic trials in California, he took 0.1 second off Glenn Davis's and Salvatore Morale's world record. At the Tokyo Games he ran a controlled race, sweeping into the lead after the sixth hurdle. He won in 49.6 from John Cooper (England) and Salvatore Morale (Italy).

After winning the AAU title in 1965 he retired because of increasing problems from injuries.

Geoffrey Vanderstock   (United States, b. 1946)

48.8   **Echo Summit, USA**   **11 Sep 1968**

The 1968 U.S. Olympic trials were held at Echo Summit, near South Lake Tahoe in California, which is 2248 meters (7375 feet) above sea level, an altitude similar to Mexico City. Under these high-altitude conditions, Geoffrey Vanderstock ran 48.8. A student at the University of Southern California, he had won neither the AAU nor the NCAA championships. Nonetheless, he went to Mexico with high hopes for an Olympic gold medal. However, he ran into Britain's David Hemery, who ran the race of his life to take nearly 0.7 second off Vanderstock's five-week-old record. Vanderstock was not able to reproduce his world record-breaking form and finished fourth, running 49.06.

Vanderstock was plagued by an allergic skin rash every time he undertook physical activity.

David Hemery   (Great Britain, b. 1944)

48.12   **Mexico City, Mexico**   **15 Oct 1968**

David Hemery was born in England, but when he was 12, his family moved to the United States. As a hurdler he had two coaches on different continents. At Boston University he was coached by Billy Smith. During his visits to England he was coached by Fred Housden.

He started out as a 120-yard/110m hurdler. He won the 1966 and 1970 Commonwealth

David Hemery, Great Britain (400m hurdles), 1968 Olympic champion.

Games title, set six British records at this distance, and was silver medalist at the 1969 European Championships. However, after the 1966 season he made a decision to contest the 400m hurdles at the 1968 Olympics. In fact, he won the NCAA title that year, but Geoff Vanderstock (USA) set a new world record five weeks before the Games and was the obvious favorite.

Hemery ran the heats and semifinals at Mexico in a restrained manner. The night before the final, he carefully visualized the race in the manner he intended it to take place. The race went exactly to plan. He took an immediate lead with a very fast first 200m. Instead of falling back, Hemery just went further ahead and crossed the line in a world record time of 48.12

He chose not to run the distance again until 1972, concentrating on the 110m hurdles and on competing in the decathlon. However, a new star had risen, Uganda's John Akii-Bua, who won at the Munich Games with a new world record of 47.82, while Hemery finished third (48.52).

After the Olympics, Hemery produced a plan to revitalize track and field in England, which brought him into conflict with the "old guard," such as Harold Abrahams. He authored a number of books dealing with sport (including *Another Hurdle, Winning Without Drugs,* and *The Pursuit of Sporting Excellence*).

John Akii-Bua   (Uganda, b. 1949)

47.82   **Munich, West Germany**   **2 Sep 1972**

John Akii-Bua's father had eight wives and forty-three children. Young Akii-Bua took up hurdling in 1967 and came in fourth at the 1970 Commonwealth Games. Just before the

1972 Munich Olympics he was beaten in the British AAA titles by defending Olympic champion David Hemery. Nonetheless, at the Munich final Akii-Bua outdid himself. Hemery went off at extreme pace, even faster than at Mexico, but Akii-Bua kept his nerve and took the lead at the eighth hurdle. He finished strongly to take 0.3 second off Hemery's record with 47.82 and became Uganda's one and only Olympic gold medalist. He ran a victory lap with delight etched all over his body, and none could deny him his moment of triumph.

Things were not so happy back in Uganda, where the country was in the iron grip of the erratic dictator Idi Amin. The country slowly disintegrated into chaos. Akii-Bua's

John Akii-Bua, Uganda (400m hurdles), 1972 Olympic champion.

hopes of competing at the 1976 Montreal Olympics were dashed by the African boycott of those Games. In 1979, after Ugandan military incursions on its territory, neighboring Tanzania decided to invade and remove Idi Amin from power for good. Akii-Bua escaped to Kenya, where he was initially imprisoned before he could establish his identity.

Akii-Bua attempted a comeback and at the 1980 Olympics came in seventh in a semifinal.

Edwin Moses   (United States, b. 1955)

47.64	Montreal, Canada	25 Jul 1976
47.45	Los Angeles, USA	11 Jun 1977
47.13	Milan, Italy	3 Jul 1980
47.02	Koblenz, West Germany	31 Aug 1983

Edwin Moses won everything that mattered: He was Olympic champion twice (1976 and 1984), set four world records, was twice world champion (1983 and 1987), and asserted a decade-long domination of the sport. In those years he won 122 races without defeat. He would almost certainly have won another Olympic gold medal except for the U.S. boycott of the 1980 Moscow Olympics.

A popular and enduring champion, he was the first athlete to master the difficult technique of taking only 13 steps between each hurdle for the whole race. He was a student at Morehouse College in Atlanta, Georgia, studying physics and mechanical engineering, when he turned to the 400m hurdles in 1976 with meteoric results. Improving weekly, he became American record holder and then Olympic gold medalist with a new world record at the Montreal Games (47.64).

After that dream start he lost a race in 1977 to West Germany's Harald Schmid but then went almost a decade before his next defeat, to fellow American Danny Harris in Spain.

In the meantime he reduced the record another three times.

In 1985 he turned 30, but his domination continued until the 1987 defeat by Danny Harris. But he bounced back from that defeat to just barely win the world championship later that season. He went to the Seoul Olympics, aiming for his third Olympic gold medal. It was not to be. Andre Phillips had never beaten Moses, but that changed in the most crucial of moments, the 1988 Olympic 400m hurdles final. Moses's 33-year-old legs couldn't respond to the younger man's challenge. Phillips won in 47.19, and Moses dropped back to third.

That loss marked the end of his track and field career. He spent 1990 and 1991 bobsledding with the U.S. World Cup team. His career record remains one of the very best in any field of athletics.

Edwin Moses, United States (400m hurdles), four-time world record holder and twice Olympic champion, 1976 and 1984.

Kevin Young   (United States, b. 1966)

46.78   **Barcelona, Spain**   **6 Aug 1992**

For many years Kevin Young, 6' 4" (194 centimeters) tall, was another hurdler in the long shadow of Edwin Moses. Young studied sociology at UCLA. He made the breakthrough to international class in his early 20s but could not quite make the next step to win the big meets. He was second in the 1987 Pan-American Games and fourth at the 1988 Olympics. At the 1991 World Championships in Tokyo he was once again fourth.

Young began experimenting with his stride. He could run 13 strides between hurdles but managed to drop to 12 steps between some, changing his lead leg as he did so. The experiments with different stride techniques took time to master, but

Kevin Young, United States (400m hurdles), 1992 Olympic Champion.

finally in 1992 it all came together. He didn't lose a race all season, and just before the Barcelona Olympics he told *Track and Field News* that he would break the 47-second barrier, despite his personal best at the start of the season being 47.72.

In the Barcelona final Young took control of the race after the fifth hurdle and relentlessly moved to a huge lead. He hit the last hurdle heavily but was still far enough ahead to raise his arms in triumph several meters before the finish. Despite the mishap and the gesture, he went through the finish in a breathtaking 46.78 seconds and smashed the 47-second barrier.

Young proved his Barcelona victory was no fluke with a comfortable win in 47.18 at the 1993 World Championships in Stuttgart. He remains the only man to have run under 47 seconds to date. By 1996 time had moved on and he was fifth in a semifinal at the U.S. Olympic trials.

Conclusions

The 1992 world record by Kevin Young of 46.78 has not been seriously challenged in the last few years. However, even Young's remarkable record run was not impeccable as he hit the last hurdle during this race and slowed down for a victory gesture over the last 10 meters. Perhaps the development of new stride techniques by talented athletes may reduce the existing record.

Five All-Time Fastest: Men's 400m Hurdles		
Kevin Young (USA)	46.78	1992
Edwin Moses (USA)	47.02	1983
Samuel Matete (ZAM)	47.10	1991
Andre Phillips (USA)	47.19	1988
Amadou Dia Ba (SEN)	47.23	1988
Prediction	*46.78*	*2015*

Top Three: Men's 400m Hurdles

GOLD MEDAL: Edwin Moses (USA)
SILVER MEDAL: Glenn Davis (USA)
BRONZE MEDAL: Glenn Hardin (USA)

The steeplechase has been run in circumstances that have varied enormously. Varying factors include the length of the course, the number and type of hurdles, and the presence or absence of a water jump. It was not until 1954 that the event was standardized to allow official world records. The 3000m steeplechase at the 1954 European Championships was designated as the first official world record (8:49.6). Currently, runners must negotiate 28 solid hurdles and seven water jumps in the 7 ½-lap race. The lead runner has a clear approach to the hurdles, while those behind have a somewhat restricted approach.

The record has been held by 16 athletes a total of 28 times. Three of these athletes have been Olympic gold medalists since 1956 (Krzyszkowiak, Roelants, and Gärderud). The most striking feature of the steeplechase in recent times is Kenyan athletes' absolute domination of the event, which shows no sign of abating. The top ten fastest athletes in this event to date are all Kenyans. This may partly be due to Kenya's high altitude. In addition, their success has produced a tradition that younger Kenyan athletes aim to join.

Men's World Records for 3000m Steeplechase

Record time	Record holder	Location	Date
8:49.6	Sándor Rozsnyói (HUN)	Bern, Switzerland	28 Aug 1954
8:47.8	Pentti Karvonen (FIN)	Helsinki, Finland	1 Jul 1955
8:45.4	Pentti Karvonen (FIN)	Oslo, Norway	15 Jul 1955
8:45.4	Vasiliy Vlasenko (USSR)	Moscow, USSR	18 Aug 1955
8:41.2	Jerzy Chromik (POL)	Brno, Czechoslovakia	31 Aug 1955
8:40.2	Jerzy Chromik (POL)	Budapest, Hungary	11 Sep 1955
8:39.8	Semyon Rzhishchin (USSR)	Moscow, USSR	14 Aug 1956
8:35.6	Sándor Rozsnyói (HUN)	Budapest, Hungary	16 Sep 1956
8:35.6	Semyon Rzhishchin (USSR)	Tallinn, USSR	21 Jul 1958
8:32.0	Jerzy Chromik (POL)	Warsaw, Poland	2 Aug 1958
8:31.4	Zdzislaw Krzyszkowiak (POL)	Tula, USSR	26 Jun 1960
8:31.2	Grigoriy Taran (USSR)	Kiev, USSR	28 May 1961
8:30.4	Zdzislaw Krzyszkowiak (POL)	Walcz, Poland	10 Aug 1961
8:29.6	Gaston Roelants (BEL)	Leuven, Belgium	7 Sep 1963
8:26.4	Gaston Roelants (BEL)	Brussels, Belgium	7 Aug 1965
8:24.2	Jouko Kuha (FIN)	Stockholm, Sweden	17 Jul 1968
8:22.2	Vladimir Dudin (USSR)	Kiev, USSR	19 Aug 1969
8:22.0	Kerry O'Brien (AUST)	Berlin, West Germany	4 Jul 1970
8:20.8	Anders Gärderud (SWE)	Helsinki, Finland	14 Sep 1972
8:19.8	Ben Jipcho (KEN)	Helsinki, Finland	19 Jun 1973
8:14.0	Ben Jipcho (KEN)	Helsinki, Finland	27 Jun 1973
8:10.4	Anders Gärderud (SWE)	Oslo, Norway	25 Jun 1975
8:09.8	Anders Gärderud (SWE)	Stockholm, Sweden	1 Jul 1975
8:08.0	Anders Gärderud (SWE)	Montreal, Canada	28 Jul 1976
8:05.4	Henry Rono (KEN)	Seattle, USA	13 May 1978
8:05.35	Peter Koech (KEN)	Stockholm, Sweden	3 Jul 1989
8:02.08	Moses Kiptanui (KEN)	Zürich, Switzerland	19 Aug 1992
7:59.18	Moses Kiptanui (KEN)	Zürich, Switzerland	16 Aug 1995

Sándor Rozsnyói   (Hungary, b. 1930)

| 8:49.6 | Bern, Switzerland | 28 Aug 1954 |
| 8:35.6 | Budapest, Hungary | 16 Sep 1956 |

The 3000m steeplechase at the 1954 European Championships was taken as the first modern official world record, although faster runs had actually been recorded. Rozsnyói won that race easily in 8:49.6, nearly three seconds ahead of the Finn Olavi Rinteenpää. The record was then beaten several times in the next few years—five times in 1955 alone.

Rozsnyói was able to reclaim the record with 8:35.6 in 1956, two months before the Olympics. However, at the Melbourne Games Britain's Christopher Brasher, who had been one of the pacesetters in Bannister's first four-minute mile, came into peak condition. In the final, Brasher made a decisive break with 200 meters to go and won in 8:41.2. Rozsnyói was second in 8:43.6. However, Australian officials had the idea that Brasher had fouled Ernst Larsen (Norway) during his move forward, and he was initially disqualified. Rozsnyói, who was second, was then declared the winner. All the athletes involved said no foul took place, and upon appeal, the disqualification was reversed. Accordingly, Brasher claimed the gold medal, Rozsnyói the silver, and Larsen the bronze.

Pentti Karvonen   (Finland, b. 1931)

| 8:47.8 | Helsinki, Finland | 1 Jul 1955 |
| 8:45.4 | Oslo, Norway | 15 Jul 1955 |

A year after Rozsnyói's record, Pentti Karvonen of Finland ran 8:47.8 in an international meet in Helsinki. Because a Finnish runner had actually run faster than this (Olavi Rinteenpää, 8:44.4, July 1953), the Finnish authorities did not accept this new world record as a Finnish national record. Two weeks later Karvonen improved his time again to 8:45.4—still slower than Rinteenpää's 1953 time. So once again Karvonen had set a new world record but not a Finnish record.

After his 1955 season Karvonen was plagued by stomach ulcers and underwent major surgery. Remarkably, he made a comeback in 1960 and ran in the 1960 Olympics in Rome, although he did not progress past the heats. His younger brother Reino was also a competent steeplechaser with a best time of 8:54.0. Since 1981 Karvonen has been vice president of the Finnish Athletic Federation. By profession he is a clocksmith.

Vasiliy Vlasenko   (Soviet Union, b. 1928)

| 8:45.4 | Moscow, USSR | 18 Aug 1955 |

Pentti Karvonen's second record was equaled five weeks after he had set it by Vasiliy Vlasenko at the Soviet Spartakiade in Moscow. Vlasenko won by over 20 seconds.

Vlasenko ran in the 1956 Melbourne Olympics but came in seventh in his heat. He did not enjoy great success in the Soviet championships, coming in third in 1956 and fourth in 1954, 1957, and 1958.

Jerzy Chromik   (Poland, 1931–1987)

8:41.2	Brno, Czechoslovakia	31 Aug 1955
8:40.2	Budapest, Hungary	11 Sep 1955
8:32.0	Warsaw, Poland	2 Aug 1958

Jerzy Chromik set the world record twice in 1955 and regained it in 1958 after it had been reduced three more times in the interim. Record number one was set in an international match between Poland and Czechoslovakia, in which he took 4.2 seconds off the record. Eleven days later, he set his second world record in another international match, this time between Poland and Hungary. In this race he was chased home by former (and future) world record holder Sándor Rozsnyói.

Unfortunately, he was ill in 1956 and did not compete in the Melbourne Olympics. But he won the 1958 European Championships by 0.6 second from Semyon Rzhishchin (USSR), 8:38.2 to 8:38.8.

His third world record came in another international match, this time between Poland and the United States in front of his own people. He ran 8:32.0, and in second place was another future world record holder, Zdzislaw Krzyszkowiak, 1.6 seconds behind. Chromik finished his career by coming in seventh in his heats of both the 1960 Olympics and the 1962 European Championships.

Semyon Rzhishchin   (Soviet Union, b. 1933)

| 8:39.8 | Moscow, USSR | 14 Aug 1956 |
| 8:35.6 | Tallinn, USSR | 21 Jul 1958 |

Semyon Rzhishchin broke through the 8:40 barrier with 8:39.8 at the Lenin Stadium in Moscow at the 1956 Spartakiade. Rzhishchin had a long career as a steeplechaser: He was the Soviet champion from 1955 to 1959 and was second in 1960. His second world record was at the 1958 Soviet championships.

At the Olympics he was fifth in 1956 (8:44.6) and third in 1960 (8:42.2). He almost won the 1958 European Championships, finishing just behind Poland's Jerzy Chromik, 8:38.2 to 8:38.8.

Semyon Rzhishchin, Soviet Union (3000m steeplechase).

Zdzislaw Krzyszkowiak   (Poland, b. 1929)

8:31.4	Tula, USSR	26 Jun 1960
8:30.4	Walcz, Poland	10 Aug 1961

Zdzislaw Krzyszkowiak had an impressive athletic record: world record holder twice at the 3000m steeplechase, Olympic champion over the same distance at Rome in 1960, and European champion over both 5000m and 10,000m in 1958. He had run in the 1956 Melbourne Olympics, finishing fourth in the 10,000m (29:05.0). In the steeplechase he was fifth in his heat and did not progress. In 1958 he achieved the difficult double of winning both the 5000m (13:53.4) and the 10,000m (28:56.0) at the European Championships.

In the 1960 Olympic year he broke Chromik's world record for the steeplechase by 0.6 second (8:31.4) in a Soviet Union vs. Poland match 10 weeks before the Games. At Rome he sat with the leading pack for most of the race, while the Soviets ran a team race, trying to outwit him. The tactics didn't work, and he broke away with 250 meters to go to win comfortably in 8:34.2.

The world record was improved by 0.2 second the following year by Grigoriy Taran (USSR) in May. Krzyszkowiak took it back again in August by slicing another 0.8 second off this new record. He returned to the European Championships in 1962, but he came in fifth in his heat and did not progress.

Grigoriy Taran   (Soviet Union, b. 1937)

8:31.2	Kiev, USSR	28 May 1961

Grigoriy Taran was one of the more obscure world record holders. Apart from his world record, he had a modest career as a steeplechaser, placing fifth in the 1958 Soviet titles and seventh in 1960.

In 1961 he was part of a four-team race between Moscow, Leningrad, the RSFSR, and the Ukraine. Without any close competition, he ran 8:31.2 to take 0.2 second off the world record. Before this world record his personal best had been 8:45.0. After this world record performance his subsequent best was 8:43.6. He did not compete at the Rome Olympics or the European Championships.

Gaston Roelants   (Belgium, b. 1937)

8:29.6	Leuven, Belgium	7 Sep 1963
8:26.4	Brussels, Belgium	7 Aug 1965

Gaston Roelants showed himself to be master of three events: the 3000m steeplechase, the marathon, and international cross-country running. He had a number of steeplechase triumphs: world record holder twice (1963 and 1965), the first man to run under 8:30, and Olympic champion in Tokyo in 1964. Apart from steeplechasing, he won the International Cross Country Championships four times (1962, 1967, 1969, and 1972). In addition, he had a highly respectable marathon career. At the European Championships he was second in 1969, fifth in 1971, and third in 1974. He also ran in the marathon at the 1968 Mexico City Olympics and, at high altitude, finished a creditable eleventh. His other Olympic placings were fourth in the 1960 3000m steeplechase, seventh in the same event at Mexico City in 1968, and a marathon that he did not finish at the 1972 Games.

His steeplechase tactic was usually to go out hard and establish a lead. He used this tactic in the 1964 Tokyo Olympics and had a 50-meter lead by the start of the last lap. At the finish Britain's Maurice Herriott was only 10 meters down, but Roelants won in 8:30.8.

Roelants had won the 1962 European Championships, and in 1966 he tried his usual tactic of building up a significant lead. This time, the chasing pack allowed him to get only 15 meters ahead, and he was caught in the last lap and dropped back to third.

An expressive and charming man, he also held world records for 20km and the one-hour run.

Gaston Roelants, Belgium (3000m steeplechase), the first man under 8:30.

Jouko Kuha   (Finland, b. 1939)

| 8:24.2 | Stockholm, Sweden | 17 Jul 1968 |

Jouko Kuha provided Finland with its first world record in 20 years, and the country was delighted. Kuha was one of the first Finns to leave the long Finnish winters to train overseas rather than plow through the snow. He spent most of the European winter months in Spain. He returned each year to improve the Finish national steeplechase record. Finally, in 1968 in Stockholm he reduced Roelants's record by 2.2 seconds with 8:24.2.

This was an Olympic year, and Jouko was immediately hailed as a possible gold medalist. But he had traveled to Mexico in 1967 and realized that he could never run that fast at high altitude. He had the wit to stay away. At age 50 he could still run the 10,000m in 32 minutes. He has gone on to a career in the import and wholesale of textiles.

Jouko Kuha, Finland (3000m steeplechase).

Vladimir Dudin   (Soviet Union, b. 1941)

8:22.2   **Kiev, USSR**   **19 Aug 1969**

Vladimir Dudin had his record-breaking day at the 1969 Soviet championships, when he trimmed two seconds off Kuha's world record. He ran a very even race, the first half in 4:10.5 and the second in 4:11.7. That 1969 Soviet championship victory was his only Soviet success at the steeplechase. He was third in 1971, fifth in 1968 and 1970, and seventh in 1973.

His other major victory was the European Cup in 1970. Dudin was also third in the European Championships in 1969 and ninth in 1971.

Kerry O'Brien   (Australia, b. 1946)

8:22.0   **Berlin, West Germany**   **4 Jul 1970**

Kerry O'Brien had his own style of hurdling, which involved standing on the top of each hurdle and pushing off with his right leg rather than clearing the hurdle. He first represented Australia in the 1966 Commonwealth Games, finishing second in the steeplechase (8:32.58). He traveled to Mexico in 1968 for the Olympics and, considering that he was a low-altitude runner, did well to finish fourth (8:52.0), only one second behind the winner, Amos Biwott of Kenya (8:51.0).

In 1970 O'Brien had his best season ever and won 16 straight races, including a world record in Berlin. He ran 8:22.0 to take 0.2 second off Vladimir Dudin's record and was the favorite to win at the Commonwealth Games that year. Unfortunately, he was persuaded to try a new set of running shoes for the final. The heel and back portion of the shoe were made of rubber and expanded every time he went through the water jump, until they finally came completely loose as he went over the second-to-last water jump. He lost his footing, crashed heavily into the water, and did not finish the race.

In the 1972 Olympics he again hit a hurdle and did not finish, but he was having major ankle problems at this time and probably would not have been a contender in the final. He currently resides in South Australia, where he runs a horse stud service and the Kerry O'Brien Fitness Centre.

Anders Gärderud   (Sweden, b. 1946)

8:20.8	**Helsinki, Finland**	**14 Sep 1972**
8:10.4	**Oslo, Norway**	**25 Jun 1975**
8:09.8	**Stockholm, Sweden**	**1 Jul 1975**
8:08.0	**Montreal, Canada**	**28 Jul 1976**

Anders Gärderud broke the world record four times and was the Olympic gold medalist in 1976. He ran at the 1968 Mexico City Olympics, going out in the heats of the 800m and 1500m. In the 1972 Munich Olympics he was fifth in his heat of the 3000m steeplechase.

In 1974 he had his best result in the European Championships, when he came in second in the 3000m steeplechase, beaten by 0.4 second by Poland's Bronislaw Malinowski.

His first world record in 1972 was in a very competitive race, which he won by a mere 0.2 second from fellow countryman Tapio Kantanen. Ben Jipcho (Kenya) reduced the record twice before Gärderud set his next world record of 8:10.4 in a 1975 match between Norway,

Sweden, and East Germany. A week later he reduced it to 8:09.8, with his old rival Malinowski second.

As Gärderud, then 30, lined up for the 1976 Olympic final, he had never won a gold medal. However, the race went well for him. He raced to the front with 300 meters to go. East Germany's Frank Baumgartl was right beside him but hit the last hurdle and fell. Gärderud won in 8:08.0, his fourth world record. Baumgartl's fall allowed Malinowski to take the silver medal.

Anders Gärderud, Sweden (3000m steeplechase), 1976 Olympic champion.

Ben Jipcho   (Kenya, b. 1943)

| 8:19.8 | Helsinki, Finland | 19 Jun 1973 |
| 8:14.0 | Helsinki, Finland | 27 Jun 1973 |

Ben Jipcho, Kenya (3000m steeplechase).

The first 12 steeplechase record holders had been Europeans, with the exception of Australian Kerry O'Brien. Then the Kenyans arrived and more or less took over the event. The first was Ben Jipcho. Originally a prison guard in Nairobi, he was selected for the 1968 Mexico City Olympics. In the 1500m final he set up a fast pace for fellow Kenyan Kip Keino, at the cost of his own prospects, by running the first lap in 56.0 seconds. Jipcho faded after this fast start to finish tenth.

At the 1972 Munich Olympics he had a genuine race with Kip Keino over the 3000m steeplechase, but Keino was too fast for him on the last lap, winning 8:23.6 to 8:24.6.

In 1973 Jipcho had a great season and reduced the world record twice. He ran 8:19.8 at an international match in Helsinki. Eight days later at the World Games, also in Helsinki, he took almost six seconds off the record with 8:14.0.

The next year he had a brilliant performance at the Commonwealth Games in Christchurch, winning both the 5000m and the 3000m steeplechase and coming in third in Filbert Bayi's 1500m world record race. However, Jipcho was then persuaded to abandon amateur athletics and join the newly formed professional circuit, ITA. In fact, Jipcho was the leading money winner on the circuit for 1974 and 1975. But the concept had only limited success in the 1970s, and the professional circuit eventually folded in 1976.

Henry Rono   (Kenya, b. 1952)

8:05.4	Seattle, USA	13 May 1978

Much of Henry Rono's career has been detailed in the chapters on the 5000m and 10,000m. But he was a steeplechaser from his early days and during his "golden year" in 1978 attempted the world record in Seattle at the Northwest Relays. He had no serious competition and won by over 30 seconds. At the finish, he had taken 2.6 seconds off Gärderud's world record with 8:05.4.

Although he had another brilliant season in 1981, with another world record in the 5000m, he never really attacked the steeplechase record again.

Because of Kenyan boycotts at the 1976 and 1980 Olympics, the 1978 Commonwealth Games were his only major international meet. He won the same double as Ben Jipcho in 1974—5000m and 3000m steeplechase—in times of 13:23.04 and 8:26.54. In the steeplechase Kenyans were first, second, and third.

Peter Koech   (Kenya, b. 1958)

8:05.35	Stockholm, Sweden	3 Jul 1989

Henry Rono's steeplechase record lasted 11 years, the first prolonged interval in which there was no improvement in the record. Then along came another Kenyan to break it, Peter Koech.

Koech was a student at Washington State University but did not take up the steeplechase until his last two years there. He was the 1985 NCAA champion at the distance (8:19.84), while his younger brother Jonah was the NCAA cross-country champion in 1990 for Iowa State University.

At the 1988 Seoul Olympics Peter Koech came in a close second in the steeplechase to fellow Kenyan Julius Kariuki, who sprinted past with 600 meters to go. Kariuki held on to win, 8:05.51 to 8:06.79.

Koech finally reduced the decade-old world record by 0.05 second at an international meet in Stockholm. Unlike Rono, who ran the race more or less solo, Koech was chased home by another Kenyan, Patrick Sang, who finished 0.68 second behind him, 8:05.35 to 8:06.03.

Moses Kiptanui   (Kenya, b. 1971)

8:02.08	Zürich, Switzerland	19 Aug 1992
7:59.18	Zürich, Switzerland	16 Aug 1995

Kenya's domination of the 3000m steeplechase continued with the arrival of Moses Kiptanui. A member of the Marakwet tribe, he is a cousin of Richard Chelimo, former 10,000m world record holder. Initially a soccer fan, Kiptanui was persuaded to try track and field and had great success, even by Kenyan standards. By age 19, he was the 1991 world champion in the 3000m steeplechase.

In 1992 Kiptanui was unfortunately injured during the Kenyan Olympic trials and finished fourth. He watched the Olympics on television. The Kenyan team still placed first,

Moses Kiptanui, Kenya (3000m steeplechase, 5000m), first man under eight minutes for the steeplechase.

second, and third in the steeplechase, and the commentator's remark, "and to think they could do this without Moses Kiptanui," brought tears to Kiptanui's eyes.

When the Olympics were over, Kiptanui showed the world what they had missed. He set new world records at both 3000m and 3000m steeplechase. His 3000m time was 7:28.96 and his 3000m steeplechase time was 8:02.08, a difference between the two events of 33.12 seconds.

Further steeplechase successes were his victory in the 1993 and 1995 World Championships and a new 5000m world record in 1995 (12:55.30). He rounded off the 1995 season with a major steeplechase world record—the long-awaited breaking of the eight-minute barrier. He achieved this without any pacesetters, claiming that they would have just got in the way. His time of 7:59.18 won him $50,000 and a one-kilogram gold ingot.

Alas, an Olympic gold medal escaped him in 1996 as well. He made the Kenyan team, but in Atlanta he was outsprinted down the final straight by his teammate Joseph Keter, 8:07.12 to 8:08.33.

Conclusions

Since 1954 the world record has been reduced by 50 seconds. Nonetheless, improvements in the last few years have been modest. It has taken 20 years to move the world record from 8:10 (1975) to under 8:00 (1995), an average improvement of 0.5 second per year. Perhaps the record will be reduced further by an elite distance runner with impeccable hurdling technique.

Five All-Time Fastest: Men's 3000m Steeplechase

Moses Kiptanui (KEN)	7:59.18	1995
Eliud Barngetuny (KEN)	8:05.01	1995
Peter Koech (KEN)	8:05.35	1989
Philip Barkutwo (KEN)	8:05.37	1992
Henry Rono (KEN)	8:05.4	1978
Prediction	*7:53.00*	*2015*

Top Three: Men's 3000m Steeplechase

GOLD MEDAL: Moses Kiptanui (KEN)

SILVER MEDAL: Anders Gärderud (SWE)

BRONZE MEDAL: Henry Rono (KEN)

T he high jump is very basic—the athlete obviously clears the bar or doesn't. A competitor may pass at any height. However, three successive misses, even at different heights, result in elimination.

High jumping is a relatively modern sport; the only jumping event in the ancient Olympics was the long jump. The first six-foot (1.83-meter) jump was achieved using the scissors style by Marshall J. Brooks in 1876 at the Oxford University Sports Day. Seven feet (2.13 meters) was achieved in 1956 by Charles Dumas (USA) using the straddle, and 8 feet (2.44 meters) by Javier Sotomayor (Cuba) with the flop in 1989.

World records in the high jump (and all the field events) run into difficulty when an athlete sets a new record measured imperially (feet and inches). This is because the IAAF only accepts metric measurements for world records. Therefore, the new record must first be converted to a metric measurement. This can lead to much confusion. For instance, the majority of world record holders in the high jump are U.S. athletes who usually jump over heights measured imperially (e.g., 6' 11"). This height was cleared by Lester Steers in 1941 and converts to 2.1082m. However, the IAAF chose to accept the height as 2.11m, which became the new record. This official record was marginally more than Steers actually jumped.

High-jump records have evolved over more than a century with a series of different styles: the scissors, the eastern cutoff, the western roll, the straddle, and the Fosbury flop. The western roll became the established technique between the world wars, but after World War II the straddle emerged. In the late 1960s the Fosbury flop took over, executed with the athlete's back to the bar as he or she goes over, allowing for a more efficient weight distribution. It was invented by Dick Fosbury (USA) who used the innovative technique to win the 1968 Olympic gold medal in Mexico, and it is now used by all elite high jumpers. One factor that made these higher jumps possible, and safer, was the introduction of foam bags in the landing pits.

If two or more athletes have cleared the same height at the end of the competition the "count-back" rule is used to separate them. The highest place goes to the competitor with the fewest misses at the highest height cleared. If the tie remains it goes to the one with the fewest total misses in the overall competition. For first place if a tie still remains, there is a jump-off. If the tie is for another place, the tie stands.

Twenty-four men have held the world high-jump record since the IAAF officially recognized records in 1912; they have set or equaled the world record 40 times. Eight of these athletes have also been Olympic champions—Osborn, Johnson, Dumas, Brumel, Wszola, Mogenburg, Wessig, and Sotomayor—but only Wessig (1980) achieved his world record in Olympic competition.

Men's World Records for the High Jump

Record height	Record holder	Location	Date
2.00m (6' 7")	George Horine (USA)	Palo Alto, USA	18 May 1912
2.01m (6' 7 ¼")	Edward Beeson (USA)	Berkeley, USA	2 May 1914
2.03m (6' 8")	Harold Osborn (USA)	Urbana, USA	27 May 1924
2.04m (6' 8 ¼")	Walter Marty (USA)	Fresno, USA	13 May 1933
2.06m (6' 9")	Walter Marty (USA)	Palo Alto, USA	28 Apr 1934
2.07m (6' 9 ¾")	Cornelius Johnson (USA)	New York, USA	12 Jul 1936
2.07m (6' 9 ¾")	Dave Albritton (USA)	New York, USA	12 Jul 1936
2.09m (6' 10 ¼")	Mel Walker (USA)	Malmö, Sweden	12 Aug 1937
2.11m (6' 11")	Lester Steers (USA)	Los Angeles, USA	17 Jun 1941
2.12m (6' 11 ½")	Walter "Buddy" Davis (USA)	Dayton, USA	27 Jun 1953
2.15m (7' 0 ½")	Charles Dumas (USA)	Los Angeles, USA	29 Jun 1956

2.16m (7' 1")	Yuriy Stepanov (USSR)	Leningrad, USSR	13 Jul 1957
2.17m (7' 1 ½")	John Thomas (USA)	Philadelphia, USA	30 Apr 1960
2.17m (7' 1 ½")	John Thomas (USA)	Cambridge, USA	21 May 1960
2.18m (7' 2")	John Thomas (USA)	Bakersfield, USA	24 Jun 1960
2.22m (7' 3 ½")	John Thomas (USA)	Palo Alto, USA	1 Jul 1960
2.23m (7' 3 ¾")	Valeriy Brumel (USSR)	Moscow, USSR	18 Jun 1961
2.24m (7' 4 ¼")	Valeriy Brumel (USSR)	Moscow, USSR	16 Jul 1961
2.25m (7' 4 ½")	Valeriy Brumel (USSR)	Sofia, Bulgaria	31 Aug 1961
2.26m (7' 5")	Valeriy Brumel (USSR)	Palo Alto, USA	22 Jul 1962
2.27m (7' 5 ¼")	Valeriy Brumel (USSR)	Moscow, USSR	29 Sep 1962
2.28m (7' 5 ¾")	Valeriy Brumel (USSR)	Moscow, USSR	21 Jul 1963
2.29m (7' 6 ¼")	Patrick Matzdorf (USA)	Berkeley, USA	3 Jul 1971
2.30m (7' 6 ½")	Dwight Stones (USA)	Munich, West Germany	11 Jul 1973
2.31m (7' 7")	Dwight Stones (USA)	Philadelphia, USA	5 Jun 1976
2.32m (7' 7 ¼")	Dwight Stones (USA)	Philadelphia, USA	4 Aug 1976
2.33m (7' 7 ¾")	Volodomir Yashchenko (USSR)	Richmond, USA	3 Jul 1977
2.34m (7' 8")	Volodomir Yashchenko (USSR)	Tbilisi, USSR	16 Jun 1978
2.35m (7' 8 ½")	Jacek Wszola (POL)	Eberstadt, West Germany	25 May 1980
2.35m (7' 8 ½")	Dietmar Mogenburg (FRG)	Rehlingen, West Germany	26 May 1980
2.36m (7' 8 ¾")	Gerd Wessig (GDR)	Moscow, USSR	1 Aug 1980
2.37m (7' 9 ¼")	Zhu Jian Hua (CHN)	Beijing, China	11 Jun 1983
2.38m (7' 9 ¾")	Zhu Jian Hua (CHN)	Shanghai, China	22 Sep 1983
2.39m (7' 10")	Zhu Jian Hua (CHN)	Eberstadt, West Germany	10 Jun 1984
2.40m (7' 10 ½")	Rudolf Povarnitsyn (USSR)	Donetsk, USSR	11 Aug 1985
2.41m (7' 10 ¾")	Igor Paklin (USSR)	Kobe, Japan	4 Sep 1985
2.42m (7' 11 ¼")	Patrik Sjöberg (SWE)	Stockholm, Sweden	30 Jun 1987
2.43m (7' 11 ½")	Javier Sotomayor (CUBA)	Salamanca, Spain	8 Sep 1988
2.44m (8' 0")	Javier Sotomayor (CUBA)	San Juan, Puerto Rico	29 Jul 1989
2.45m (8' 0 ½")	Javier Sotomayor (CUBA)	Salamanca, Spain	27 Jul 1993

George Horine (United States, 1890-1948)

2.00m (6' 7")   **Palo Alto, USA**   **18 May 1912**

George Horine is credited with the first official world high-jump record. He is also credited with introducing the western roll, which replaced the traditional scissors style of jumping. A graduate of Stanford University, he began with the scissors technique and jumped 5' 1" with this method, approaching from the right side. When his family moved to Palo Alto, their new backyard was so laid out as to force him to jump from the left. He therefore learned to jump off his left foot and, in the process, to roll over the bar. A new technique was born. Horine now jumped more than a foot higher than with the scissors. He jumped 6' 1 ½" (1.87 meters) in 1910 and 6' 4" (1.93 meters) in 1911. Finally, in a trial for the 1912 Olympics he cleared 6' 7" (2.00 meters), which was later accepted as the first world record. However, at the Olympics Horine came in third with 6' 2 ¼" (1.89 meters). The winner was Alma Richards (USA) with 6' 4" (1.93 meters). Horine's only major high-jump win was the 1915 AAU Championship.

Edward Beeson   (United States, 1890–1972)

2.01m (6' 7 ¼")   **Berkeley, USA**   **2 May 1914**

Edward Beeson was also a student at Stanford University and another pioneer of the western roll. Originally a hurdler, his talent as a high jumper emerged, and he had a series of duels with George Horine. He had been second during Horine's 1912 record.

On 2 May 1914 an invitational high-jump meet took place. Only two athletes were invited, Horine and Beeson. It was not a long competition. The initial height was 6' 0 ½" (1.84 meters). Both jumpers went over on their first try. The bar then went directly to a new world record height of 6' 7 ¼" (2.01 meters). Horine failed at all three attempts, but Beeson went over on his second try.

In World War I Beeson served as first lieutenant in the U.S. Army Dental Corps and went on to a career in dentistry. He was also active in coaching and served as a high-jump official in 1960, when John Thomas set his fourth world record of 7' 3 ½" (2.22 meters), 46 years after Beeson's record.

Edward Beeson, United States (high jump).

Harold Osborn   (United States, 1899–1975)

2.03m (6' 8")   **Urbana, USA**   **27 May 1924**

Harold Osborn was the only male athlete to hold a track and field world record in both an individual event and the decathlon and the only athlete to win Olympic gold medals for both an individual event and the decathlon. He modified the western roll technique and also used his hand to press the bar back

Harold Osborn, United States (high jump, decathlon), double gold medalist at the 1924 Olympics.

against the uprights to prevent its falling off. This trick led the IAAF to introduce a new rule, so that in the future the bar could fall off on either side of the uprights.

He achieved his world record in a pre-Olympic meet in Urbana, Illinois, jumping 6' 8" (2.03 meters).

At the 1924 Paris Olympics he cleared all heights on his first attempt, winning at 1.98 meters (6' 6"). He then failed to clear at 2.02 meters (6' 7 ½"). He also won the decathlon title with a world record.

Osborn returned to the Olympics in 1928 in Amsterdam, where he finished fifth with 1.91 meters (6' 3 ¼"). He went on to a career as a teacher (1922-33) and then a long career as an osteopath. He was an elder of the First Presbyterian Church and a president of the Illinois Osteopathic Association.

Walter Marty   (United States, b. 1910)

2.04m (6' 8 ¼")	**Fresno, USA**	**13 May 1933**
2.06m (6' 9")	**Palo Alto, USA**	**28 Apr 1934**

Walter Marty was a graduate of Fresno State University. He shared the 1934 NCAA title with George Spitz of New York University and the 1934 AAU title with Cornelius Johnson.

He set his first world record at the West Coast Relays in Fresno, jumping 6' 8 1/4" (2.04 meters). A year later he set his second world record at a track and field meet between Fresno and Stanford University, where he jumped 6' 9" (2.06 meters) on his third attempt.

At the 1936 U.S. Olympic trials he finished tied for fourth (1.93 meters) and missed out on selection for the Games. The winners that day were Cornelius Johnson and Dave Albritton, who both cleared 2.07 meters (6' 9 ¾"), a new world record.

Cornelius Johnson   (United States, 1913–1946)

2.07m (6' 9 ¾")	**New York, USA**	**12 Jul 1936**

Cornelius Johnson was the first black to achieve a world record in the high jump and to win an Olympic gold medal in this event. He was only a high school student when he competed in the 1932 Los Angeles Olympics, where he finished fourth in a jump-off.

From 1932 to 1936 he won the AAU title five times, either outright or shared with another athlete.

Cornelius Johnson, United States (high jump), 1936 Olympic high-jump champion.

In 1936 he set a new world record at the Olympic trials, a height he shared with Dave Albritton. Both men cleared 6' 9 ¾" (2.07 meters) on their second attempt. Johnson went on to win the Olympic gold medal, with Albritton second. In fact, Johnson jumped in his tracksuit until the bar reached 2.00 meters (6' 6 ¾"). He won the event at 2.03 meters (6' 8"), clearing every height at his first attempt.

The enduring myth of the 1936 Berlin Olympics is that Adolf Hitler snubbed Jesse Owens. In fact, if anybody was snubbed by Hitler, it was Cornelius Johnson. On the first day of Olympic competition, Hitler had already congratulated the winners of the men's shot put (Hans Wolke, Germany) and the 10,000m (Ilmari Salminen, Finland). But as the high jump was concluding, it was obvious that the two African Americans, Johnson and Albritton, would fight out first and second place. It was at this point that Hitler departed the stadium; it is generally accepted that Hitler did not wish to congratulate a black. The International Olympic Committee then asked that Hitler congratulate all winners or none. Hitler decided not to congratulate any further winners. This took place before any of Owens's victories.

Dave Albritton   (United States, 1913–1994)

2.07m (6' 9 ¾")   New York, USA   12 Jul 1936

Dave Albritton was an African American athlete from Alabama. He and Jesse Owens were life-long friends. Albritton was the first of the straddlers, rolling his abdomen over the bar. A student at Ohio State University, he won the NCAA title three times from 1934 to 1936, each time shared with another athlete. He also won or shared the AAU title seven times from 1936 through 1950. His world record was achieved when he and Cornelius Johnson both went over 2.07 meters (6' 9 ¾") on their second attempt at the U.S. Olympic trials. At the Olympics in Berlin Albritton was second to Johnson, 2.00 meters to 2.03 meters.

Albritton became a coach in football, basketball, and track and field. Then he had a four-year tour for the U.S. State Department as a track coach in Iran and Pakistan. He later opened an insurance agency in Dayton, Ohio, and served for 12 years as a state legislator in Ohio.

Mel Walker   (United States, b. 1914)

2.09m (6' 10 ¼")   Malmö, Sweden   12 Aug 1937

Mel Walker was a student at Ohio State University. He was deeply disappointed at missing the U.S. team for the 1936 Olympics, as he had jumped 6' 8" (2.03 meters) earlier in the season at Princeton. At the U.S. Olympic trials the high jump approach was not wide enough for his particular style. He had to run on rough grass except for the last two strides before takeoff, and he went out at 6' 5" (1.96 meters).

In 1937 he compensated by setting the world record twice, more or less. In his first "record," in Stockholm, he jumped 2.08 meters (6' 9 ¾"). But this jump wasn't recognized, as it was claimed that the bar fell off some minutes after the jump. Nonetheless, it was accepted as an American record. In Malmö six days later he jumped 2.09 meters (6' 10 ¼") on his third attempt.

On the U.S. domestic scene he shared both the 1936 NCAA title and the 1938 AAU title with Dave Albritton.

Lester Steers   (United States, b. 1917)

2.11m (6' 11")   Los Angeles, USA   17 Jun 1941

Lester Steers was another early straddle jumper and pushed the record ever closer to the seven-foot barrier. He had won the U.S. AAU title in 1939 and 1940 and the NCAA title in 1941, representing the University of Oregon. Early in 1941 he set two "records" that were

superior to the official world record, but these were not accepted by the IAAF as official world records. Nonetheless, they were accepted by U.S. officials as American records, so the American record was higher than the world record. Finally, he established an official world record when he jumped 6' 11" (2.11 meters) at the P.C.C.-Big 10 track and field meet in Los Angeles in June 1941.

In an exhibition jump in Boston in February 1941 he is said to have jumped over seven feet in a meet that was never recognized as an official competition.

Lester Steers, United States (high jump).

Walter "Buddy" Davis   (United States, b. 1931)

2.12m (6' 11 ½")   Dayton, USA   **27 Jun 1953**

Walter Davis is the tallest athlete to hold the world record for the high jump. He is 6' 8" (203 centimeters) tall. Davis was an All-American basketball player, and high jumping was a secondary interest. In fact, his basketball coach thought that high jumping might help his basketball performance. He used the western roll and was the last athlete to set a world record using this technique.

As a child he had a three-year battle with polio, which affected both legs and his right arm. He eventually overcame these disabilities by installing a cycling pedestal in his home. A graduate of Texas A & M University, he won the NCAA title in 1952 and the AAU title in 1952 and 1953.

At the 1952 Helsinki Olympics he won with 2.04 meters. The following year, he set a world record at the AAU championships, jumping 6' 11 ½" (2.12 meters) on his third jump. He retired shortly thereafter and went on to an active basketball career, playing for six years with the Philadelphia Warriors and backing up superstar Wilt Chamberlain.

Charles Dumas   (United States, b. 1937)

2.15m (7' 0 ½")   Los Angeles, USA   **29 Jun 1956**

Charles Dumas was the man who finally officially cracked the seven-foot barrier. He was a straddler with a very smooth technique. His special moment came at the U.S. trials for the 1956 Olympics. He had won at 2.08 meters, and he then had the bar raised to 2.15 meters, half an inch over the magic seven-foot barrier. On his first attempt he was up and over. As a reward, his coach slipped him $10.

Charles Dumas, United States (high jump), the first man to jump over seven feet.

He traveled to Melbourne four months later for the 1956 Olympics. There he had a surprising struggle with unknown local jumper Charles "Chilla" Porter, who improved his personal best by seven centimeters that day. In the end, late at night, with all other competitions long since ended, Dumas went over 2.12 meters (6' 11 ½") on his third try, and Porter took the silver medal.

Dumas was AAU champion from 1956 to 1959 and Pan-American champion in 1959. But at the Rome Olympics a new generation of jumpers had arrived: John Thomas (USA) and the Soviet duo of Robert Shavlakadze and Valeriy Brumel. Dumas finished fifth with 2.03 meters.

Dumas retired after these Games but made a comeback four years later, when he was still only 27, and managed to clear 2.14 meters.

Yuriy Stepanov   (Soviet Union, 1932–1965)

2.16m (7' 1")   **Leningrad, USSR**   **13 Jul 1957**

Yuriy Stepanov had placed fifth in the 1954 European Championships using the eastern cutoff technique. But he changed to the straddle in 1956 with much improved results and reached 2.04 meters (6' 8 ¼"), though he was not part of the Soviet team for the 1956 Olympics.

In July 1957 he participated in a Leningrad vs. Helsinki track and field meet. He went over 2.11 meters on his second attempt and then cleared 2.16 meters on his first attempt, a new world record.

Although this was credited as a world record, it was soon appreciated that he jumped with a specially built-up shoe on his takeoff leg. It had a sole some three to five centimeters thick. This was banned the following year by the IAAF. A maximum thickness of 13 millimeters (0.5") was then

Yuriy Stepanov, Soviet Union (high jump). Note the thickened sole on his left shoe. This was later banned.

permitted for future world records, but Stepanov's record was allowed to stand.

Stepanov developed severe emotional and psychiatric problems and committed suicide at age 33.

John Thomas   (United States, b. 1941)

2.17m (7' 1 ½")	Philadelphia, USA	30 Apr 1960
2.17m (7' 1 ½")	Cambridge, USA	21 May 1960
2.18m (7' 2")	Bakersfield, USA	24 Jun 1960
2.22m (7' 3 ½")	Palo Alto, USA	1 Jul 1960

John Thomas, United States (high jump).

John Thomas had shown early promise in 1957 and 1958, but in 1959 he caught his foot in an elevator shaft and lost most of the season. As the 1960 track and field season opened, however, John Thomas could do no wrong. Now a student at Boston University, he won the NCAA and AAU titles and then set world records in April, May, June, and July. His last record was a massive four centimeters (1 ½") above the previous record, an improvement unheard of in high jumping. No man traveled to the Rome Olympics a hotter favorite than John Thomas.

But the Olympics can play tricks on hot favorites. Thomas had little international experience. In addition, it was a particularly fierce Roman summer, and a number of athletes underperformed. Two Soviet athletes coped better than Thomas. The gold medal went to Robert Shavlakadze, the silver to teenager Valeriy Brumel; both men cleared 2.16 meters (7' 1"). Thomas managed 2.14 meters for bronze.

Although barely 20, Thomas never regained the world record momentum that he established in 1960. Brumel set six records between 1961 and

1963. However, at the 1964 Tokyo Olympics Thomas came very close to winning the gold medal. He and Brumel both jumped 2.18 meters (7' 1 ¾") and could go no further. Brumel won the gold medal only on the count-back rule.

Thomas retired after the 1964 Olympics and worked as a sales manager for Bell Telephone Company.

Valeriy Brumel   (Soviet Union, b. 1942)

2.23m (7' 3 ¾")	Moscow, USSR	18 Jun 1961
2.24m (7' 4 ¼")	Moscow, USSR	16 Jul 1961
2.25m (7' 4 ½")	Sofia, Bulgaria	31 Aug 1961
2.26m (7' 5")	Palo Alto, USA	22 Jul 1962
2.27m (7' 5 ¼")	Moscow, USSR	29 Sep 1962
2.28m (7' 5 ¾")	Moscow, USSR	21 Jul 1963

Valeriy Brumel, Soviet Union (high jump), being congratulated after his sixth world record in 1963.

Valeriy Brumel was only 18 when he was a late inclusion in the Soviet team for the 1960 Rome Olympics. He surprised the spectators by finishing second to his countryman Robert Shavlakadze; both beat the highly fancied American John Thomas. Brumel missed out on the gold medal by count-back.

He was not particularly tall for a high jumper (185 centimeters, 6' 0 ¾") but had very powerful legs and a superb straddle technique. After his Olympic debut he set a series of world records over the next few years: three in 1961, two in 1962, and one in 1963. These performances made him a national hero in the Soviet Union. His sixth and last world record jump was watched by Soviet Premier Nikita Khrushchev, who hugged U.S. diplomat Averell Harriman with delight.

Brumel went on to win the 1962 European Championships and the gold medal at the 1964 Tokyo Olympics, but only just. He and John Thomas jumped the same height, 2.18 meters (7' 1 ¾"), but Brumel had fewer misses and won on the count-back.

Brumel's world came crumbling down in October 1965, when he was involved in a serious motorcycle accident in which he sustained a compound fracture of his right foot. He endured a series of operations between 1965 and 1968.

Remarkably, he made a comeback in 1970 and managed to reach 2.06 meters. He has become an established writer and has written four plays, a film script, and a novel.

Patrick Matzdorf   (United States, b. 1949)

2.29m (7' 6 ¼")   Berkeley, USA   3 Jul 1971

Patrick Matzdorf was a student of mathematics at the University of Wisconsin and had broken a string of schoolboy records. He was a straddler, but with a bent-knee approach on his lead leg over the bar, and brought the world record back to the United States at a meet between the United States, Soviet Union, and World All-Stars in Berkeley, California. He jumped 2.29 meters (7' 6 ¼") on his third try.

Patrick Matzdorf, United States (high jump).

His previous best jump was 7' 2" (2.18 meters), although he had jumped 7' 3" (2.21 meters) indoors. Nonetheless, he proved he was no overnight success by winning the Pan-American Games title later that year. Matzdorf also tried the new Fosbury flop and achieved 2.24 meters (7' 4 ¼").

Unfortunately, he was injured during much of 1972 and came in only fifth at the U.S. Olympic trials. In 1974 he attempted a comeback as a flopper and came in sixth at the AAU titles. That year he jumped 7' 2 ¾" (2.20 meters) but did not achieve further success. He went on to a career developing computer software for cellular phone systems.

Dwight Stones   (United States, b. 1953)

2.30m (7' 6 ½")	**Munich, West Germany**	**11 Jul 1973**
2.31m (7' 7")	**Philadelphia, USA**	**5 Jun 1976**
2.32m (7' 7 ¼")	**Philadelphia, USA**	**4 Aug 1976**

A tall athlete (6' 5", 196 centimeters) of Swedish extraction, at age 10 Dwight Stones had watched Brumel's last world record on television. This inspired him to build a high-jump pit in his own backyard. He mastered the flop early in his career and at age 19 won the U.S. Olympic trials. At the Munich Games he was a surprise bronze medalist, only two centimeters below the winning height (2.23 meters). He returned to Munich in 1973 and achieved the first of his world records in a United States vs. West Germany vs. Switzerland track and field meet. This was the first world record using the Fosbury flop.

Stones spent the next few years relentlessly promoting the high jump. With his loquacious personality and talent for showmanship, he generated enormous interest in the event. Six weeks before the Montreal Olympics he set his second world record (2.31

meters, 7' 7"). However, rain inhibited his performance more than most, and at the high jump final in Montreal it poured. Jacek Wszola of Poland coped best with the rain and won with 2.25 meters (7' 4 ½"). Canada's Greg Joy was second with 2.23 meters (7' 3 ¾"), and Stones was third with 2.21 meters (7' 3"). Four days later, back in Philadelphia, Stones upped his world record to 2.32 meters (7' 7 ¼").

Dwight Stones, United States (high jump).

Stones's career had a major hiccup in 1978, when he entered and won the television show "SuperStars." He gave the money to his local club. U.S. athletic officials argued that the money should be passed on to the AAU and banned Stones from competition for 18 months; eventually Stones returned the money.

The U.S. boycott of the Moscow Olympics prevented him from competing, but he won the 1984 U.S. Olympic trials with an American record of 2.34 meters (7' 8"). At the Los Angeles Games, Stones finished fourth with 2.31 meters (7' 7"), four centimeters behind the winning height. A graduate of Cal State, Long Beach, he now commentates for television, especially for the high jump at major games.

Volodomir Yashchenko   (Soviet Union, b. 1959)

2.33m (7' 7 ¾")	Richmond, USA	3 Jul 1977
2.34m (7' 8")	Tbilisi, USSR	16 Jun 1978

Volodomir Yashchenko, Soviet Union (high jump), the last of the straddlers.

With the flop established, it was something of a shock when a young Soviet athlete in 1977 set a new world record with the straddle. It took place in a United States vs. Soviet Union junior athlete meet in Richmond, Virginia. Yashchenko, a Ukrainian, is the son of a steelworker. When he jumped a world record of 2.33 meters, the Soviet team went berserk, rushing on to the field, tossing him in the air, and carrying him around on their shoulders in celebration. In June of the next year Yashchenko set another world record (2.34 meters) and won the 1978 European Championships. He was still only 19.

Sadly, injuries then brought his career to a premature end. He had the first of a series of operations to remove excess cartilage on his takeoff knee in September 1979. In fact, that year was the last in which he had an official competition. More operations were to follow, including one in Austria by famed orthopedic surgeon Dr. Edgar Baumgartz, but none of them allowed him to capture his form of those brilliant 1977 and 1978 seasons, and he retired while in his early 20s.

Jacek Wszola   (Poland, b. 1956)

2.35m (7' 8 ½")   **Eberstadt, West Germany**   **25 May 1980**

Jacek Wszola, Poland (high jump), 1976 Olympic champion.

Jacek Wszola's father, Roam, was a school sports teacher, and his mother trained gymnasts. Much of Wszola's vacations were at sport camps that his father ran in the school holidays. At age 18, Jacek was fifth in the 1974 European Championships.

He continued to improve but was not considered a special prospect for the gold medal at the 1976 Olympics. On the way to Montreal he read the predictions in *Track and Field News* concerning the Olympic high jump. The magazine favored Stones, and the article irritated him. He became determined to prove it wrong. In the rain, Stones managed 2.21 meters, Canada's Greg Joy 2.23 meters, and Wszola 2.25 meters (7' 4 ½"), an Olympic record. Later the three of them wrote a textbook on high jumping.

Stones set a new world record four days after the 1976 Olympics, and the feeling was that Wszola had been lucky on the day of the Olympic competition. He came in only sixth at the 1978 European Championships in Prague. Two years later he proved himself to his critics with a world record jump of 2.35 meters at Eberstadt in Germany.

Wszola had the prospect of winning the Olympic gold medal in the high jump twice, something that had never been done before or since. But out of nowhere came East Germany's Gerd Wessig, who won the title with 2.36 meters (7' 8 ¾"). Wszola was second with 2.31 meters.

A dispute with his national federation meant he was sent home from the 1982 European Championships. He had hopes of doing well at the 1984 Los Angeles Olympics, but Poland followed the Soviet boycott of these Games, much to his disgust. After 10 years as a top high jumper, he decided to retire and study law.

Dietmar Mogenburg   (West Germany, b. 1961)

2.35m (7' 8 ½")   **Rehlingen, West Germany**   **26 May 1980**

Dietmar Mogenburg, West Germany (high jump), 1984 Olympic champion.

Dietmar Mogenburg is tall (201 centimeters, 6' 7") and achieved early success as a teenager. He dramatically burst onto the track and field scene in 1979, when he won the European Cup at age 17 and was the world's leading high jumper that year with 2.32 meters (7' 7 ¼").

On 25 May 1980 Jacek Wszola raised the world record to 2.35 meters. The very next day Mogenburg equaled this record at a meet in Rehlingen on his third try. Unfortunately for Mogenburg, West Germany followed the United States' lead in boycotting the Moscow Olympics.

Mogenburg was European champion in 1982 and won the German championship a record 10 times between 1980 and 1990. He made his Olympic debut in 1984 and had a flawless competition. He went over every jump at his first attempt: 2.27, 2.31, 2.33, and 2.35 meters. With only four jumps he won the gold medal. That was perhaps the highlight of his career.

The last half of Mogenburg's career wasn't quite as successful. He was fourth at the 1986 European Championships, sixth at the 1988 Seoul Olympics, and tied for fourth in the 1990 European Championships. His best outdoor jump was 2.36 meters in 1984; his best indoor jump was 2.39 meters in 1985.

Gerd Wessig   (East Germany, b. 1959)

2.36m (7' 8 ¾")   **Moscow, USSR**   **1 Aug 1980**

Gerd Wessig was a 21-year-old cook who went to instant stardom at the 1980 Moscow Olympics with an unexpected victory that gave him the gold medal and a world record. In a fairy-tale performance, he went to the Games with a personal best of 2.30 meters (7' 6 ¼"). The favorite was Jacek Wszola of Poland, who had set a new world record of 2.35 meters two months earlier.

In a dream performance, Wessig climbed over 2.31 meters at his first attempt, a personal best. Wszola failed at 2.33 meters. When Wessig went over that height on his second attempt, he won the competition and set another personal best. He had the bar set at 2.36 meters, a new world record height. On his second attempt he was over, the first time anyone had won an Olympic high jump gold medal with a world record.

He seemed to be a young man with a golden future. It was not to be. Wessig did not compete much after the Moscow Olympics and never jumped that high again. In 1986 he was seventh in the European Championships. He was plagued by injuries and apparently had ongoing disputes with the notoriously dictatorial East German athletic authorities, who resented his celebrity status. He had had his one moment of glory, and that was all.

Gerd Wessig, East Germany (high jump), ecstatic after his world record at the 1980 Moscow Olympics.

Zhu Jian Hua   (China, b. 1963)

2.37m (7' 9 ¼")	Beijing, China	11 Jun 1983
2.38m (7' 9 ¾")	Shanghai, China	22 Sep 1983
2.39m (7' 10")	Eberstadt, West Germany	10 Jun 1984

Zhu Jian Hua, the youngest of five children, was born in Shanghai and became a student at the Shanghai Physical Culture Institute. He was tall (193 centimeters, 6' 4") and lightweight (70 kilograms, 154 pounds) for a high jumper.

Zhu came in second at the World Student Games in 1981 and first in the Asian Games in 1982. Then in June 1983 he added one centimeter to the world record in Beijing, clearing 2.37 meters on his first attempt. In August he traveled to Helsinki for the 1983 World Championships to show some of the skeptics that he was indeed world class. But he finished third, a major disappointment for him.

He returned to China to make amends by adding another centimeter to the world record one month later, jumping 2.38 meters. A year later he traveled to Germany for the invitational high jump at Eberstadt. With just about every top high jumper in the world present, he added one more centimeter to the record with 2.39 meters (7' 10").

Two months later, the same group of high jumpers all competed again at the Los Angeles

Zhu Jian Hua, China (high jump), ecstatic after his 1984 world record.

Olympics. Four men cleared 2.31 meters: Mogenburg, Sjöberg, Zhu, and Stones. Zhu missed 2.33 meters once and on his second attempt was unsettled by the collapse of 1500m runner Steve Ovett at the edge of the high-jump apron. He decided not to try again at 2.33 meters, but to attempt 2.35 meters. It was a gamble that didn't pay off—he couldn't clear it, but Mogenburg did. The results were Mogenburg first, Sjöberg second, and Zhu third. Despite Zhu's disappointment, it was still China's first ever Olympic medal in track and field.

Zhu later became a physical education student at Cal State University in 1991.

Rudolf Povarnitsyn   (Soviet Union, b. 1962)

2.40m (7' 10 ½")   **Donetsk, USSR**   **11 Aug 1985**

Rudolf Povarnitsyn, a virtual unknown, was the first man to break the 2.40-meter barrier, which he did while competing in Donetsk in the Ukraine. His previous best before that meet was 2.26 meters. In a long day's jumping, he cleared 2.13, 2.16, 2.19, 2.22, 2.25, 2.29, and 2.32 meters. He was already six centimeters above his previous best and hadn't missed a jump. He then jumped 2.35 meters on his third attempt. He had the bar moved up to 2.40 meters. He made it on his third attempt. Perhaps no one else in history has improved 14 centimeters in one meet.

Povarnitsyn was Soviet champion in 1989 and won a bronze medal at the 1988 Olympic Games.

Igor Paklin   (Soviet Union, b. 1963)

2.41m (7' 10 ¾")   **Kobe, Japan**   **4 Sep 1985**

Igor Paklin won the 1983 and 1985 World Student Games. At the 1985 Games, after jumping 2.35 meters on his first attempt, he cleared 2.41 meters on his third attempt, a new world record.

Paklin added to his laurels by winning the 1986 European Championships and coming in second at the 1987 World Championships. But he was disappointed with his seventh place at the 1988 Olympics. He blamed it on a cold he picked up from a prolonged sauna just before the Olympics.

His seventh place also disappointed Soviet athletic officials. In 1989 he was expelled from the Soviet track and field team for his "extreme independence." His alleged "impossible temper" hadn't helped matters, although he defended it as part of the makeup of a world champion. There was a dispute over shoes: He preferred Japanese Tiger shoes, but the Soviets had an arrangement with the German company Adidas. He disappeared for several years but resurfaced at the 1993 World Championships, jumping for Kazakhstan.

Patrik Sjöberg   (Sweden, b. 1965)

2.42m (7' 11 ¼")   **Stockholm, Sweden**   **30 Jun 1987**

Patrik Sjöberg made his debut at age 17 at the 1982 European Championships, when he finished tied for tenth. At the 1984 Olympics he came in second to Dietmar Mogenburg, 2.33 meters to 2.35 meters.

Sjöberg became a regular in the small band of six to eight elite international high jumpers who travel the world to the top meets. With his long blonde hair and athletic prowess, he developed the image of the playboy athlete, complete with fast cars and other trimmings.

He was finally rewarded with a world record at the ripe old age of 22, in front of his own people in Stockholm. Sjöberg cleared 2.32 meters and 2.35 meters on his first tries. The bar was then moved to 2.42 meters (7' 11 ¼"). On his third try, to the delight of the crowd, he made it.

That year he also won the World Championships in Rome with 2.38 meters. However, at the 1988 Olympics he was tied for third with 2.36 meters; Gennadiy Avdeyenko (USSR) won with 2.38 meters.

In 1989 in New York he came very close to being the first man to clear eight feet. But Cuban Javier Sotomayor achieved the magic barrier one week later.

At the Barcelona Olympics in 1992 Sjöberg finished second with 2.34 meters, the same height as Sotomayor, but the Cuban won on a count-back rule. Sjöberg became the first man to win a medal in the high jump at three Olympics. He was injured in 1996 and missed the Atlanta Games.

Patrik Sjöberg, Sweden (high jump).

Javier Sotomayor   (Cuba, b. 1967)

2.43m (7' 11 ½")	Salamanca, Spain	8 Sep 1988
2.44m (8' 0")	San Juan, Puerto Rico	29 Jul 1989
2.45m (8' 0 ½")	Salamanca, Spain	27 Jul 1993

Javier Sotomayor is the first man to jump over eight feet. In addition, he won the gold medal at the Barcelona Games and has broken the world record three times using the flop.

Sotomayor was a talented prospect as a teenager and in 1984, at age 16, jumped 2.33 meters. He had every reason to be considered a medal favorite for the 1988 Olympics, especially since he broke the world record two weeks before the Games began. But Fidel Castro decided that Cuba should boycott the Seoul Games.

His first world record took place in Salamanca, Spain, in September 1988; he cleared 2.43 meters on his second attempt. He went over the eight-foot barrier (2.44 meters converts to 8' 0 ⅛") the following year at the Caribbean Championships. Captured on amateur video, he made this record on his second attempt after leaving the opposition behind at 2.26 meters. The Puerto Rican crowd went wild over the first world record ever set in that country.

His Barcelona Olympic triumph was not a clear-cut victory. Five men went over 2.34 meters, and Sotomayor won on a count-back, as he had cleared that height on his first attempt.

In 1993, he achieved 2.45 meters (8' 0 ½"), world record number three, once again in Salamanca. Sotomayor was also Pan-Am Games champion in 1987, 1991, and 1995. However, the Atlanta Olympics proved to be a disappointment as ankle injuries plagued him during the Games and he finished 11th. Sotomayor is married to Maria del Carmen Garcia, who has high jumped 1.88m.

Javier Sotomayor, Cuba (high jump), the first man to jump eight feet.

Conclusions

If any track and field event has an absolute limit, that event would appear to be the high jump. Although there have been periods in the past when the record improved fairly rapidly, such as in the early 1960s and mid-1980s, those days seem to be over. The record has been somewhat static in recent years and has been advanced solely by one man, Javier Sotomayor. It is also hard to conceive of any new high-jump style replacing the flop. All these facts suggest that the world high-jump record won't go much higher. However, advances such as new jumping surfaces may give more compliance and spring to the athlete.

The view that the limit has been reached has been proved to be naive many times in the past. Perhaps in 50 years' time, a 2.45-meter jump will seem ordinary, much like the four-minute mile.

Six All-Time Highest: Men's High Jump

Javier Sotomayor (CUBA)	2.45m (8' 0 ½")	1993
Patrik Sjöberg (SWE)	2.42m (7' 11 ¼")	1987
Igor Paklin (USSR)	2.41m (7' 10 ¾")	1985
Rudolf Povarnitsyn (USSR)	2.40m (7' 10 ½")	1985
Sorin Matei (ROM)	2.40m (7' 10 ½")	1990
Charles Austin (USA)	2.40m (7' 10 ½")	1991
Prediction	*2.48m (8' 1 ½")*	*2015*

Top Three: Men's High Jump

GOLD MEDAL:	**Javier Sotomayor (CUBA)**
SILVER MEDAL:	**Valeriy Brumel (USSR)**
BRONZE MEDAL:	**Dwight Stones (USA)**

T here have been two major areas of technical advance in pole vaulting that make comparisons among different eras more difficult than usual. One of these, of course, has been the material used in the making of the pole, which over the years has included wood, bamboo, steel, aluminum, and fiberglass. The fiberglass poles require special strength and gymnastic ability to master.

In addition, vaulters through to the 1950s were landing in pits that were essentially level sand and sawdust. That more injuries didn't occur as athletes dropped from 15 feet onto these surfaces is remarkable. Foam rubber landing bags eventually allowed greater heights to be surmounted safely.

Because of the many changes in pole technology, no other track and field event has had more world record holders. Thirty-two athletes have set or equaled the world record 70 times.

Eleven of the 32 world record holders have been Olympic champions as well. Two of them (Foss, 1920; Kozakiewicz, 1980) achieved world records during the Olympics.

Performance can easily be affected by wind conditions, and most vaulters generally wait until wind has settled before beginning their run. The rules of competition are the same as for the high jump: Three successive misses, even at different heights, and the athlete is out of the competition. Most major competitions are very long affairs, often 8 to 10 hours. Many of the top athletes carefully select their vault heights, passing at certain stages so as to conserve their strength and to try to achieve a tactical advantage over their competitors. This can sometimes result in an athlete's entering the competition too high and fouling three times at the opening height. This results in a *no height* and was the fate of the overwhelming favorite, Sergey Bubka, at the 1992 Olympics.

Men's World Records for the Pole Vault

Record height	Record holder	Location	Date
4.02m (13' 2 ¼")	Marc Wright (USA)	Cambridge, USA	8 Jun 1912
4.09m (13' 5")	Frank Foss (USA)	Antwerp, Belgium	20 Aug 1920
4.12m (13' 6 ¼")	Charles Hoff (NOR)	Copenhagen, Denmark	3 Sep 1922
4.21m (13' 9 ¾")	Charles Hoff (NOR)	Copenhagen, Denmark	22 Jul 1923
4.23m (13' 10 ½")	Charles Hoff (NOR)	Oslo, Norway	13 Aug 1925
4.25m (13' 11 ¼")	Charles Hoff (NOR)	Turku, Finland	27 Sep 1925
4.27m (14' 0")	Sabin Carr (USA)	Philadelphia, USA	28 May 1927
4.30m (14' 1 ½")	Lee Barnes (USA)	Fresno, USA	28 Apr 1928
4.37m (14' 4 ¼")	Bill Graber (USA)	Palo Alto, USA	16 Jul 1932
4.39m (14' 5")	Keith Brown (USA)	Cambridge, USA	1 Jun 1935
4.43m (14' 6 ½")	George Varoff (USA)	Princeton, USA	4 Jul 1936
4.54m (14' 11")	William Sefton (USA)	Los Angeles, USA	29 May 1937
4.54m (14' 11")	Earle Meadows (USA)	Los Angeles, USA	29 May 1937
4.60m (15' 1")	Cornelius "Dutch" Warmerdam (USA)	Fresno, USA	29 Jun 1940
4.72m (15' 5 ¾")	Cornelius "Dutch" Warmerdam (USA)	Compton, USA	6 Jun 1941
4.77m (15' 7 ¾")	Cornelius "Dutch" Warmerdam (USA)	Modesto, USA	23 May 1942
4.78m (15' 8 ¼")	Bob Gutowski (USA)	Palo Alto, USA	27 Apr 1957
4.80m (15' 9 ¼")	Don Bragg (USA)	Stanford, USA	2 Jul 1960
4.83m (15' 10 ¼")	George Davies (USA)	Boulder, USA	20 May 1961
4.89m (16' 0 ½")	John Uelses (USA)	Santa Barbara, USA	31 Mar 1962

4.93m (16' 2")	Dave Tork (USA)	Walnut, USA	28 Apr 1962
4.94m (16' 2 ½")	Pentti Nikula (FIN)	Kauhava, Finland	22 Jun 1962
5.00m (16' 5")	Brian Sternberg (USA)	Philadelphia, USA	27 Apr 1963
5.08m (16' 8")	Brian Sternberg (USA)	Compton, USA	7 Jun 1963
5.13m (16' 10 ¼")	John Pennel (USA)	London, England	5 Aug 1963
5.20m (17' 0 ¾")	John Pennel (USA)	Coral Gables, USA	24 Aug 1963
5.23m (17' 2")	Fred Hansen (USA)	San Diego, USA	13 Jun 1964
5.28m (17' 4")	Fred Hansen (USA)	Los Angeles, USA	25 Jul 1964
5.32m (17' 5 ½")	Bob Seagren (USA)	Fresno, USA	14 May 1966
5.34m (17' 6 ¼")	John Pennel (USA)	Los Angeles, USA	23 Jul 1966
5.36m (17' 7")	Bob Seagren (USA)	San Diego, USA	10 Jun 1967
5.38m (17' 7 ¾")	Paul Wilson (USA)	Bakersfield, USA	23 Jun 1967
5.41m (17' 9")	Bob Seagren (USA)	South Lake Tahoe, USA	12 Sep 1968
5.44m (17' 10 ¼")	John Pennel (USA)	Sacramento, USA	21 Jun 1969
5.45m (17' 10 ½")	Wolfgang Nordwig (GDR)	Berlin, East Germany	17 Jun 1970
5.46m (17' 11")	Wolfgang Nordwig (GDR)	Turin, Italy	3 Sep 1970
5.49m (18' 0 ¼")	Christos Papanikolaou (GRE)	Athens, Greece	24 Oct 1970
5.51m (18' 1")	Kjell Isaksson (SWE)	Austin, USA	8 Apr 1972
5.54m (18' 2")	Kjell Isaksson (SWE)	Los Angeles, USA	15 Apr 1972
5.55m (18' 2 ½")	Kjell Isaksson (SWE)	Helsingborg, Sweden	12 Jun 1972
5.63m (18' 5 ¾")	Bob Seagren (USA)	Eugene, USA	2 Jul 1972
5.65m (18' 6 ½")	Dave Roberts (USA)	Gainesville, USA	28 Mar 1975
5.67m (18' 7 ¼")	Earl Bell (USA)	Wichita, USA	29 May 1976
5.70m (18' 8 ¼")	Dave Roberts (USA)	Eugene, USA	22 Jun 1976
5.72m (18' 9 ¼")	Wladyslaw Kozakiewicz (POL)	Milan, Italy	11 May 1980
5.75m (18' 10 ½")	Thierry Vigneron (FRA)	Paris, France	1 Jun 1980
5.75m (18' 10 ½")	Thierry Vigneron (FRA)	Lille, France	29 Jun 1980
5.78m (18' 11 ¾")	Wladyslaw Kozakiewicz (POL)	Moscow, USSR	30 Jul 1980
5.80m (19' 0 ½")	Thierry Vigneron (FRA)	Macon, France	20 Jun 1981
5.81m (19' 0 ¾")	Vladimir Polyakov (USSR)	Tbilisi, USSR	26 Jun 1981
5.82m (19' 1 ¼")	Pierre Quinon (FRA)	Cologne, West Germany	28 Aug 1983
5.83m (19' 1 ½")	Thierry Vigneron (FRA)	Rome, Italy	1 Sep 1983
5.85m (19' 2 ½")	Sergey Bubka (USSR)	Bratislava, Czechoslovakia	26 May 1984
5.88m (19' 3 ½")	Sergey Bubka (USSR)	Paris, France	2 Jun 1984
5.90m (19' 4 ¼")	Sergey Bubka (USSR)	London, England	13 Jul 1984
5.91m (19' 4 ¾")	Thierry Vigneron (FRA)	Rome, Italy	31 Aug 1984
5.94m (19' 5 ¾")	Sergey Bubka (USSR)	Rome, Italy	31 Aug 1984
6.00m (19' 8 ¼")	Sergey Bubka (USSR)	Paris, France	13 Jul 1985
6.01m (19' 8 ¾")	Sergey Bubka (USSR)	Moscow, USSR	8 Jul 1986
6.03m (19' 9 ½")	Sergey Bubka (USSR)	Prague, Czechoslovakia	23 Jun 1987
6.05m (19' 10 ¼")	Sergey Bubka (USSR)	Bratislava, Czechoslovakia	9 Jun 1988
6.06m (19' 10 ½")	Sergey Bubka (USSR)	Nice, France	10 Jul 1988
6.07m (19' 11")	Sergey Bubka (USSR)	Shizuoka, Japan	6 May 1991
6.08m (19' 11 ½")	Sergey Bubka (USSR)	Moscow, USSR	9 Jun 1991

6.09m (19' 11 ¾")	Sergey Bubka (USSR)	Formia, Italy	8 Jul 1991
6.10m (20' 0 ¼")	Sergey Bubka (USSR)	Malmö, Sweden	5 Aug 1991
6.11m (20' 0 ½")	Sergey Bubka (UKR)	Dijon, France	13 Jun 1992
6.12m (20' 1")	Sergey Bubka (UKR)	Padua, Italy	30 Aug 1992
6.13m (20' 1 ½")	Sergey Bubka (UKR)	Tokyo, Japan	19 Sep 1992
6.14m (20' 1 ¾")	Sergey Bubka (UKR)	Sestriere, Italy	31 Jul 1994

Marc Wright   (United States, 1890-1975)

4.02m (13' 2 ¼")   **Cambridge, USA**   **8 Jun 1912**

Marc Wright, United States (pole vault).

The pole vault was dominated by U.S. athletes for the first 70 years of the 20th century. The first official world record was set by Marc Wright at the U.S. (Eastern) Olympic trials in 1912 for selection to the Stockholm Olympics.

Wright's jump was the first over four meters, but he could not reproduce his form at the Olympic Games. The winner was Harry Babcock (USA) with 3.95 meters (12' 11 ½"). Wright and Frank Nelson (USA) were tied for second with 3.85 meters (12' 7 ½").

Frank Foss   (United States, 1895-1989)

4.09m (13' 5")   **Antwerp, Belgium**   **20 Aug 1920**

Frank Foss was a graduate of Cornell University and was AAU champion in 1919 and 1920. He traveled to Antwerp for the 1920 Olympics and was the only one to clear 3.80

meters (12' 5 ½"). He had the bar raised to 4.10 meters, a world record height, and went over it on his first attempt. Upon rechecking the height, it was found to be only 4.09 meters (13' 5").

Foss's margin of victory was a huge 39 centimeters (15"), the largest in Olympic history.

Frank Foss, United States (pole vault), 1920 Olympic champion.

Charles Hoff   (Norway, 1902–1985)

4.12m (13' 6 ¼")	Copenhagen, Denmark	3 Sep 1922
4.21m (13' 9 ¾")	Copenhagen, Denmark	22 Jul 1923
4.23m (13' 10 ½")	Oslo, Norway	13 Aug 1925
4.25m (13' 11 ¼")	Turku, Finland	27 Sep 1925

The U.S. domination of the pole vault was interrupted by Norwegian Charles Hoff. He set the record four times between 1922 and 1925, all four in Scandinavia. He had been the first European over four meters, and his final record remained a European record until 1937.

He would have been the heavy favorite for the event at the 1924 Olympics but, because of injury, decided not to contest it. Instead, he felt he was fit to run the 400m and 800m and managed to come in eighth in the 800m final. In the 400m he reached the semifinals.

In 1926 he went on an extensive and successful tour of the United States. While he was on this tour, Norwegian

Charles Hoff, Norway (pole vault).

athletic authorities decided that he had breached amateur rules by accepting money, and he was banned from the sport. Hoff continued to compete as a professional, achieving better results than the official world record. He was quite a showman in these professional exhibitions, and introduced "jumping with music." He was eventually requalified as a national amateur and won the 1933 Norwegian title.

Sabin Carr   (United States, 1904–1983)

4.27m (14' 0")   **Philadelphia, USA**   **28 May 1927**

Sabin Carr, United States (pole vault).

While a student at Yale University, Sabin Carr was the first to break the 14-foot barrier. His record was achieved at the 1927 ICAAAA championships in Philadelphia. The bar was set at 14 feet (4.267 meters). Second, at 4.20 meters, was Lee Barnes, who broke Carr's world record with 4.30 meters (14' 1 ¼") 11 months later. However, Carr got his revenge by winning at the Amsterdam Olympics with 4.20 meters (13' 9 ¼") , while Barnes only managed fifth.

Carr never won an AAU title; he never finished higher than third. He later went into the timber business, becoming president of the Sterling Lumber Company in California.

Lee Barnes   (United States, 1906–1970)

4.30m (14' 1 ½")   **Fresno, USA**   **28 Apr 1928**

Lee Barnes achieved fame as the high school boy who became an Olympic gold medalist. He was 17 and a student at Hollywood High School in California at the time that he won the pole vault at the 1924 Paris Olympics. In the absence of the injured Charles Hoff, Lee Barnes continued the unbroken string of U.S. Olympic victories in the pole vault. He and fellow American Glenn Graham both jumped 3.95 meters (12' 11 ½"), but Barnes won on a jump-off.

Barnes went on to study at the University of Southern California under famous coach Dean Cromwell and was AAU champion in 1927 and 1928. On the day in 1927 when Sabin Carr became the world record holder with the first ever clearance of 14 feet, Barnes was second. Eleven months later, in April 1928, Barnes finally became the world record holder with 4.30 meters (14' 1 ½") at the West Coast Relays. A few months later at the Amsterdam Olympics Carr was able to reverse fortunes by winning the gold medal (4.20 meters, 13' 9 ¼") with Barnes in fifth place.

Barnes came in seventh at the 1932 U.S Olympic trials when he was still only 25. He went on to a career as a manufacturing executive in California.

Bill Graber   (United States, 1911–1996)

4.37m (14' 4 ¼")   **Palo Alto, USA**   **16 Jul 1932**

Bill Graber shot to athletic prominence in the 1932 U.S. Olympic trials, where he won with a new world record of 4.37 meters (14' 4 ¼").

At the Los Angeles Olympics he took a risky gamble. Having jumped 4.15 meters (13' 7 ¼"), he made a decision not to attempt 4.20 meters (13' 9 ¼"). Three other athletes were successful at this height. When Graber reentered the competition at 4.25 meters (13' 11 ¼"), he couldn't make it. So he was stuck in fourth place, out of the medals. The event was finally won by Bill Miller (USA) at 4.31 meters (14' 1 ¾").

Graber won the AAU title in 1932 and was tied for first in 1934. He was NCAA champion in 1931 and 1933 for the University of Southern California.

Graber returned to the Olympics in 1936 but was once again out of luck. He finished fifth with 4.15 meters. The winning height was 4.35 meters (14' 3 ¼") by Earle Meadows (USA).

Bill Graber, United States (pole vault), with bamboo pole.

Keith Brown   (United States, 1913–1991)

4.39m (14' 5")   **Cambridge, USA**   **1 Jun 1935**

Keith Brown added two centimeters (¾") to the world record at the ICAAAA championships at Harvard University in 1935, jumping 4.39 meters (14' 5"). Future top U.S. jumpers Earle Meadows and Bill Sefton shared second spot that day with 4.20 meters (13' 9 ¼").

Brown had been tied for first in the AAU titles in 1933 and 1934 with 14' 0" (4.27 meters) and 13' 11" (4.24 meters), respectively. A graduate of Yale, he toured Britain after his world record and won the British AAA title that season. In 1936 he missed out on selection to the Berlin Olympics and retired.

George Varoff   (United States, b. 1914)

4.43m (14' 6 ½")   **Princeton, USA**   **4 Jul 1936**

George Varoff was born to a poor family of immigrants from the Ukraine and studied music at the University of Oregon, majoring in the violin. He achieved athletic fame in 1936 by winning the AAU title in Princeton, New Jersey, with a new world record of 14' 6 ½" (4.43 meters). Second and third that day were Earle Meadows and Bill Sefton, both of whom became world record holders in 1937.

Alas, at the Olympic trials a week later Varoff could only manage 14' 3" (4.35 meters), not good enough to qualify for the U.S. team , which was overloaded with talent. The three spots went to Bill Graber (1932 world record holder), Sefton, and Meadows. In Berlin it was Meadows who won the gold medal with 14' 3" (4.35 meters).

William Sefton   (United States, 1915–1982)

4.54m (14' 11")   **Los Angeles, USA**   **29 May 1937**

George Varoff had jumped 14' 6 ½" in 1936, so the 15-foot barrier still seemed some way off. But at the Los Angeles Coliseum on 29 May 1937 two athletes shared a new world record just one inch short of 15 feet. The only reason they didn't try for the magic 15-foot barrier was that the uprights wouldn't go any higher. The two were Bill Sefton and Earle Meadows, both students at the University of Southern California and inveterate rivals. In achieving the world record, Sefton went over it on his second try, Meadows on his third.

At the NCAA titles Sefton was tied for first in 1935 and 1936 (sharing the title both years with Earle Meadows) and won it outright in 1937. He shared the AAU title in 1935, again with Earle Meadows, and won it outright in 1937. All these shared titles with Earle Meadows led to their nickname, the "Heavenly Twins."

At the Berlin Olympics it was Earle Meadows who won with 4.35 meters (14' 3 ¼"). Sefton was plagued by painful shinsplints from landing on the hard European jump pits prior to the Games and could only manage fourth that day, with 4.25 meters (13' 7 ½").

Bill Sefton went on to a career as a sales manager for a manufacturer of oil field and mining products in Texas.

Earle Meadows   (United States, 1913–1992)

4.54m (14' 11")   **Los Angeles, USA**   **29 May 1937**

As mentioned in the previous section on William Sefton, Earle Meadows was the other half of the pole vault duo known as the "Heavenly Twins." Both were students at the University of Southern California. They tied for the 1935 and 1936 NCAA pole vault titles. They also tied for the 1935 AAU title and shared the world record together at their famous duel at the Los Angeles Coliseum on 29 May 1937. On that occasion Sefton went over the new record on his second attempt, Meadows at his third.

Meadows, however, was the one who had success in the Olympic year 1936. He won the U.S. trials. And in Berlin he won the gold medal, withstanding a serious Japanese challenge from Shuhei Nishida and Sueo Oe, who finished tied for second. Meadows's winning height was 4.35 meters (14' 3 ¼"). Meadows competed in the 1948 U.S. Olympic trials at age 35 but finished sixth.

Later in life he ran a musical instrument shop in Fort Worth, Texas, with his brother Clyde.

Cornelius "Dutch" Warmerdam   (United States, b. 1915)

4.60m (15' 1")	**Fresno, USA**	**29 Jun 1940**
4.72m (15' 5 ¾")	**Compton, USA**	**6 Jun 1941**
4.77m (15' 7 ¾")	**Modesto, USA**	**23 May 1942**

"Dutch" Warmerdam was the supreme pole vaulter of his generation. However, his years of domination were in the early 1940s, and his achievements were obscured by World War II. He was born to Dutch immigrants, hence his nickname. A student at Fresno State

Cornelius "Dutch" Warmerdam, United States (pole vault), the first man over 15 feet.

University, he continued his sport after graduation, not a common practice among U.S. athletes in those days.

In 1940 he became the first athlete to exceed the 15-foot barrier. Warmerdam jumped this height again and again and again. By the end of his career he had jumped it 43 times; no other athlete managed it before 1951. He pushed the record first to 15' 1" (4.60 meters), then to 15' 5 ¾" (4.72 meters), and finally to 15' 7 ¾" (4.77 meters). Warmerdam was AAU champion in 1938 and from 1940 to 1944.

He went on to be a coach at his old university for 33 years. He was the last athlete to use the bamboo pole to set a world record, a record that lasted 15 years. In the mid-1950s an aluminum pole was developed, which was in common use until 1960. Modest about his accomplishments, he nevertheless believed that with the fiberglass poles of the 1980s he would have vaulted 18 or more feet. But he also acknowledged that modern vaulters had progressed in technique, strength, and gymnastic ability.

Bob Gutowski (United States, 1935–1960)

4.78m (15' 8 ¼")   **Palo Alto, USA**   **27 Apr 1957**

Bob Gutowski was a graduate of Occidental University in California and had been tied for NCAA champion in 1956 and outright champion in 1957. He had competed at the Melbourne Olympics in 1956, partly by luck. He had placed fourth in the U.S. Olympic trials and was omitted. But Jim Graham, who came in second, suffered an ankle injury and graciously gave up his spot on the team to Gutowski. At the Olympics Gutowski won the silver medal behind the "Vaulting Vicar," Reverend Bob Richards. The pole vault runway at these Games, incidentally, was thought to be one of the worst ever for the Olympic Games.

Gutowski's world record took place at a university match in 1957 between Occidental and Stanford Universities, where he cleared 4.78 meters (15' 8 ¼") on his first attempt.

Bob Gutowski, United States (pole vault).

Gutowski was seventh at the 1960 U.S. Olympic trials. He was killed in a car crash later that season.

Don Bragg   (United States, b. 1935)

4.80m (15' 9 ¼")   **Stanford, USA**   **2 Jul 1960**

Don Bragg, United States (pole vault), 1960 Olympic champion and Tarzan fan.

Don Bragg set his new world record at the 1960 U.S. Olympic trials using a steel pole. This type of pole had a very short life and was replaced by fiberglass. Bragg jumped 4.80 meters (15' 9 ¼") on his first attempt, adding two centimeters to the record.

Bragg was nicknamed "Tarzan" because of his lifetime enthusiasm for the jungle hero. A graduate of Villanova University, he was the 1955 NCAA champion and won the 1959 AAU title. After his 1960 world record he traveled to Rome. He won at 4.70 meters (15' 5") without a miss. On the victory stand he startled officials by giving out a Tarzan cry. He was actually selected for the role of Tarzan in the film *Tarzan Goes to India,* but the movie got caught up in litigation and was never released.

He graduated with a bachelor of science degree in finance and was a member of the Villanova Singers for three years. He later released a book of poetry. Later in life he opened a series of summer camps for boys, bought a lot of land, and then fell foul of environmental officials and entered a three-year period of bankruptcy. He currently rents kayaks in New Jersey.

George Davies   (United States, b. 1940)

4.83m (15' 10 ¼")   **Boulder, USA**   **20 May 1961**

George Davies was the first athlete to set a world record with the new fiberglass pole. He was born in Missouri, became a student at Oklahoma State University, and shared the NCAA title in 1961.

Davies jumped his record at the "Big 8" championship in Boulder, Colorado. Having cleared 4.69 meters (15' 4 ½") on his first attempt, he had the bar raised to 4.83 meters (15' 10 ¼"), an inch above Don Bragg's record. He made it on his third try.

The fiberglass pole set off an explosion of world records. At the 1960 Rome Olympics the world record was 4.80 meters, whereas at the 1964 Tokyo Olympics it was 5.28 meters, an improvement of 48 centimeters (18 ¾"). By contrast, from the 1956 Melbourne to the 1960 Rome Games, the record moved just 3 centimeters (about 1 ½").

John Uelses   (United States, b. 1937)

4.89m (16' 0 ½")   **Santa Barbara, USA**   **31 Mar 1962**

John Uelses was the first man to break the 16-foot barrier. He was born in Berlin as John Feigenbaum, and his father was killed in World War II while fighting on the Russian front. In 1949, at age 11, John entered the United States through the help of his mother's aunt, Mrs. Uelses of Miami, Florida. She adopted him and legally changed his name to Uelses. In 1952 Uelses became a U.S. citizen. He graduated from Miami High School in 1956 and entered the Marines in 1958.

He achieved his world record at the 1962 Easter Relays in Santa Barbara, California. He had cleared 4.78 meters (15' 8 ¼") and asked the bar to be put up to 4.89 meters, which was just marginally above the 16-foot barrier (16' 0 ½"), a world record height. On his second effort he cleared it.

Uelses was AAU champion in 1964, jumping exactly 16 feet (4.88 meters).

John Uelses, United States (pole vault), the first man to vault 16 feet.

Dave Tork   (United States, b. 1939)

4.93m (16' 2")   **Walnut, USA**   **28 Apr 1962**

Dave Tork had been in second place when John Uelses made history's first 16-foot vault in March 1962. Four weeks later Tork became the new world record holder at the Mount San Antonio College Relays in California. He became world record holder with just four jumps: one at 15 feet (4.57 meters), one at 15' 7" (4.75 meters), and then two at the world record height of 16' 2" (4.93 meters). Tork was the Pan-American champion in 1963 but unfortunately "no-heighted" at the 1964 U.S. Olympic trials.

Dave Tork, United States (pole vault).

Pentti Nikula   (Finland, b. 1939)

| 4.94m (16' 2 ½") | Kauhava, Finland | 22 Jun 1962 |

The United States domination of the pole vault had an interruption when Pentti Nikula of Finland broke the world record two months after Tork's record. This was the first time in 35 years that a non-U.S. athlete had held the record since Charles Hoff of Norway in the 1920s.

Nikula jumped one centimeter above the record at the Johannis Games in Finland. He achieved his world record with just three jumps: one at 4.50 meters, one at 4.70 meters, and one at 4.94 meters.

He won the European Championships in Belgrade in 1962, jumping 4.80 meters (15' 9"). At the 1964 Tokyo Olympics he was seventh.

Brian Sternberg   (United States, b. 1943)

| 5.00m (16' 5") | Philadelphia, USA | 27 Apr 1963 |
| 5.08m (16' 8") | Compton, USA | 7 Jun 1963 |

Brian Sternberg, United States (pole vault), paralyzed after a trampoline accident.

The first five-meter pole vault record was claimed by Brian Sternberg of Seattle, who was a student at the University of Washington. Sternberg had a brilliant year in 1963. He won both the AAU and the NCAA titles and set two world records when only 19.

His first world record took place at the Penn Relays in Philadelphia. He went over five meters on his first attempt. His second world record was six weeks later in competition with John Pennel. After Sternberg won, the bar was raised to 5.08 meters (16' 8"). On his second attempt he was over.

On 2 July 1963 Sternberg's career came to a tragic end. While working on a trampoline, he came down with a horrific crack on his neck on the metallic side frame. He suffered major damage to the vertebrae of his neck and to his spinal cord. This left him a paraplegic. With minimal recovery he is largely confined to bed and a wheelchair.

He has continued to be active as far as his limitations allow in the Fellowship of Christian Athletes. Another of his long-term interests is radio communication.

John Pennel (United States, 1940-1993)

5.13m (16' 10 ¼")	London, England	5 Aug 1963
5.20m (17' 0 ¾")	Coral Gables, USA	24 Aug 1963
5.34m (17' 6 ¼")	Los Angeles, USA	23 Jul 1966
5.44m (17' 10 ¼")	Sacramento, USA	21 Jun 1969

John Pennel, United States (pole vault), first man over 17 feet.

John Pennel was born in Memphis, Tennessee, and was a student at Northeast Louisiana University. He set four official world records over a six-year period and was the first man to vault 17 feet. He had a lack of fortune at the Olympics. In 1964 he was plagued by back pain during the final. He took a risk and passed on the 4.80 meters (15' 9"). When he was unable to clear the next height, he was left in 11th place.

At Mexico City in 1968 he broke his pole during a warm-up session. He was upset when his best friend and roommate Bob Seagren (USA) refused to lend him his spare pole. Pennel eventually obtained another pole and jumped 5.40 meters (17' 8 ½") , which equaled the winning height. However, his pole passed under the bar, and this was deemed illegal at that time. He therefore finished fifth on 5.35 meters (17' 6 ¾"), with Seagren taking the gold medal at 5.40 meters. This incident permanently soured his relationship with Seagren.

Pennel died of stomach cancer in September 1993, at the age of 53.

Fred Hansen (United States, b. 1940)

5.23m (17' 2")	San Diego, USA	13 Jun 1964
5.28m (17' 4")	Los Angeles, USA	25 Jul 1964

Fred Hansen was the second man to jump 17 feet. He was a graduate of Rice University in Texas. His grandfather came from Denmark, and his father ran a large cattle and turkey ranch.

Everything went right for Hansen in 1964. His first world record was at the San Diego Invitational meet, where he cleared 5.23 meters. (17' 2"). Six weeks later Hansen added another two inches to the record at the United States vs. Soviet Union meet in Los Angeles, clearing 17' 4" (5.28 meters).

In October he traveled to Tokyo to defend the unbroken string of Olympic successes by U.S. athletes in the pole vault. After clearing 5.00 meters, Hansen took the risk of passing on 5.05 meters. Only West Germany's Wolfgang Reinhardt cleared it. Reinhardt and Hansen both attempted 5.10 meters and both missed on their first two tries. Hansen had to face an extremely high-pressure last jump. If he missed, not only would he lose the competition, but it would bring to an end the unbroken string of U.S. Olympic victories dating back to

1896. To the delight of U.S. supporters, he made it. Reinhardt missed his last jump, and it was all over—Hansen had won.

Hansen subsequently became a dentist in Dallas. As well as being a top track and field athlete, he is a competent golfer and played in the match-play section of the 1980 U.S. Amateurs.

Fred Hansen, United States (pole vault), 1964 Olympic champion.

Bob Seagren (United States, b. 1946)

5.32m (17' 5 ½")	Fresno, USA	14 May 1966
5.36m (17' 7")	San Diego, USA	10 Jun 1967
5.41m (17' 9")	South Lake Tahoe, USA	12 Sep 1968
5.63m (18' 5 ¾")	Eugene, USA	2 Jul 1972

Bob Seagren set four world records in his career, from 5.32 meters to 5.63 meters. His last world record (1972) was one foot higher than his first (1966). A graduate of the University of Southern California, he was one of the new generation of fiberglass vaulters who knew more about the technique and technology of the new poles than the coaches. As the 1968 Olympics approached, he won the U.S. trial at Los Angeles, only to be told there was to be a "final" trial two weeks later. Just prior to this new trial, he badly

Bob Seagren, United States (pole vault), last U.S. Olympic champion (1968).

strained a disk in his spine and was hospitalized in traction. To his astonishment, a week later not only was he able to jump at the trial, but he set his third world record, 17' 9" (5.41 meters).

At the Mexico City Olympics he won with 5.40 meters (17' 8 ½") on a count-back from Claus Schiprowski (West Germany) and Wolfgang Nordwig (East Germany). Early in the competition he had a heated clash with official Adriaan Paulen about the type of poles that could be used.

Four years later he went to Munich to defend his title. However, on the eve of the Olympics the IAAF announced that the latest poles, which had become available that season, were now to be banned from Olympic competition. Fourteen of the 21 vaulters were forced to jump on unfamiliar poles, including Bob Seagren. This led to much bitterness, which still lingers, because nothing in the rules justified this decision. The ruling was pushed by Adriaan Paulen, who later became IAAF president.

In the end, Seagren came in second with 5.40 meters (17' 8 ½"). Wolfgang Nordwig, who had chosen earlier in the season not to use the new poles, jumped a lifetime best to win with 5.50 meters (18' 0 ½"), an Olympic record. This brought to an end the unbroken string of U.S. Olympic victories since 1896.

Paulen is regarded as a benign figure in track and field history, but his handling of the pole vault situation is a permanent stain on his career.

Seagren went on to win the television contest "U.S. Superstars" in 1973 and the World Superstars competition in 1977. He subsequently worked as an executive for Puma for 18 years.

Paul Wilson   (United States, b. 1947)

5.38m (17' 7 ¾")   **Bakersfield, USA**   **23 Jun 1967**

Paul Wilson grew up in the same area of Los Angeles as Bob Seagren. He beat Bob Seagren when they were both schoolboy vaulters, a shock to the previously unbeaten Seagren. Both went on to the University of Southern California and made meteoric progress to become world-class vaulters. They both set the world record in June 1967.

On 10 June 1967 at the San Diego Invitational meet Seagren jumped 17' 7" (5.36 meters), with Wilson second. Thirteen days later at the AAU Championships the order was reversed. Wilson jumped 17' 7 ¾" (5.38 meters), and Seagren was second with 17' 3 ¾" (5.28 meters).

Wilson's career was hampered by a major sciatic nerve injury. It has been suggested that he never got effective treatment for this. There were not many sports medicine doctors in the United States familiar with the types of injuries that pole vaulters are prone to, and his career came to an end.

Wolfgang Nordwig   (East Germany, b. 1943)

5.45m (17' 10 ½")   **Berlin, East Germany**   **17 Jun 1970**
5.46m (17' 11")   **Turin, Italy**   **3 Sep 1970**

Wolfgang Nordwig was the athlete who broke the American stranglehold on Olympic victories in the pole vault. He also set the world record twice and was European champion in 1966, 1969, and 1971.

An engineer by profession with a special interest in cybernetics and photography, he had first become East German pole vault champion in 1965 and won this title eight times (1965-72).

His two world records came in 1970. The first was at an "Olympic Day" athletic meet in East Berlin, when he added one centimeter to the existing record. Ten weeks later he added another centimeter to the record at the World Student Games in Turin.

In his first Olympics in 1968 he equaled the winning height of Bob Seagren (5.40 meters, 17' 8 ½"), but had more misses, and ended up third, behind Seagren and Claus Schiprowski (West Germany).

At the 1972 Olympics his victory was somewhat overshadowed by the bitter controversy of the suspension of the new poles. He was relatively unaffected by this, as he had chosen not to use them earlier in the season. Nordwig won at 5.45 meters and then cleared 5.50 meters (18' 0 ½"), a personal best, an Olympic record, and an historic win. Despite the pole controversy, he was a worthy Olympic champion.

Wolfgang Nordwig, East Germany (pole vault), the man who ended the U.S. Olympic pole vault supremacy.

Christos Papanikolaou   (Greece, b. 1941)

5.49m (18' 0 ¼")   Athens, Greece   24 Oct 1970

Christos Papanikolaou was Greece's first world record holder, the first man over 18 feet, and the first left-handed vaulter to set a world record. He was born in Trikalla in central Greece. A promising athlete, he went across to San Jose State University in California to further his pole vaulting career.

In 1970 he was second when Wolfgang Nordwig set a world record of 5.46 meters (17' 11"). Seven weeks later Papanikolaou competed in Athens in an athletic meet between Athens and Belgrade. He entered the competition only after all the other athletes had failed. He cleared 5.00 meters, 5.20 meters, and then 5.49 meters, a new world record. With only three jumps, he had become the new world record holder and broken the 18-foot barrier. The Greek crowd went berserk: Pandemonium broke out, and Papanikolaou himself was reduced to tears.

He had only mixed fortunes in the various important competitions. In the European Championships he was second in 1966, fourth in 1969 (in Athens), and failed to qualify in 1971.

Christos Papanikolaou, Greece (pole vault), the first man over 18 feet.

At the Olympic Games he was 18th at Tokyo (1964), 4th in Mexico (1968), and 11th at Munich (1972).

Kjell Isaksson (Sweden, b. 1948)

5.51m (18' 1")	**Austin, USA**	**8 Apr 1972**
5.54m (18' 2")	**Los Angeles, USA**	**15 Apr 1972**
5.55m (18' 2 ½")	**Helsingborg, Sweden**	**12 Jun 1972**

Kjell Isaksson had a long background in gymnastics, before he turned to track and field in 1964. He came in tenth at the Mexico City Olympics and in 1969 was second at the European Championships to Wolfgang Nordwig. He was second to Nordwig again at the 1971 European Championships.

Isaksson briefly enrolled at the University of Southern California and used California as a training base for his 1972 season. The first half of the year was magic for him. He traveled all round the country and had a series of classic duels with Bob Seagren. He officially broke the world record twice in these matches and achieved other unofficial records that were not accepted.

Isaksson set one more world record in Sweden, where he not only added one centimeter to the record, but also defeated Wolfgang Nordwig. That was a good omen for the Olympics. But the Swede was one of the unfortunate casualties of the IAAF's ban on the new poles just prior to the 1972 Munich Olympics. Isaksson jumped with an unfamiliar pole and did not qualify for the final.

Isaksson was sixth at the 1974 European Championships. At the 1976 Olympics he had a dreaded "no-height" when he failed at his opening height of 5.20 meters (17' 0 ¾").

Dave Roberts (United States, b. 1951)

5.65m (18' 6 ½")	**Gainesville, USA**	**28 Mar 1975**
5.70m (18' 8 ¼")	**Eugene, USA**	**22 Jun 1976**

Dave Roberts was a graduate in zoology and a left-handed vaulter. He had missed selection to the 1972 U.S. Olympic team by finishing fourth at the selection trials. Representing Rice University in Texas, he was the NCAA champion three times (1971-73) and twice AAU champion (1972 and 1974). In 1975 at the Florida Relays he added two centimeters to Bob Seagren's record. He set another world record at the 1976 U.S. Olympic trials with 5.70 meters (18' 8 ¼") and hoped to return the gold medal to the United States.

On the day of the Montreal Olympic final, three athletes all cleared 5.50 meters (18' 0 ½"). This final was much hampered by wind and rain. Roberts had had a crucial miss at an earlier height, which put him behind on the count-back rule. He made a calculated decision to pass at 5.55 meters, which was attempted by Tadeusz Slusarski (Poland) and Antti Kalliomaki (Finland). However, both these athletes failed at this height. Roberts came back in to attempt 5.60 meters, but this was beyond him—his gamble had failed. Once again the gold medal went to a European—Slusarski.

Earl Bell (United States, b. 1955)

5.67m (18' 7 ¼")	**Wichita, USA**	**29 May 1976**

Earl Bell was the twenty-second and last of the U.S. world record holders. He was actually born in Panama, where his father was stationed as a pathologist. He won the NCAA title in the years 1975 through 1977 for Arkansas State University. Bell was also AAU champion in 1976, 1984, and 1990, the first athlete to achieve AAU wins in three separate decades and the first American to break the 19-foot barrier (1984).

His world record took place two months before the Montreal Olympics. At the USTFF Championships in Wichita, Kansas, he cleared 18' 7 ¼" (5.67 meters) on his first attempt. However, one month later, at the U.S. Olympic trials, Dave Roberts added another three centimeters to the record.

At the Montreal Olympics Bell struggled at 5.45 meters (17' 10 ¾") and got over only on his third try. This put him behind on the count-back rule, so he gambled by passing on 5.50 meters (18' 0 ½"). He then attempted 5.55 meters (18' 2 ½") but was unsuccessful. This left him in sixth place.

He missed the 1980 Moscow Olympics because of the U.S. boycott but competed at the 1984 Los Angeles Games. Bell and Frenchman Thierry Vigneron tied for third place with 5.60 meters (18' 4 ½"). In 1986 Bell earned a degree as an accountant. He came in fourth in the 1988 Seoul Olympics with 5.70 meters. In 1992 he tried out for the U.S. team but did not qualify.

Earl Bell, United States (pole vault).

Wladyslaw Kozakiewicz   (Poland, b. 1953)

| 5.72m (18' 9 ¼") | Milan, Italy | 11 May 1980 |
| 5.78m (18' 11 ¾") | Moscow, USSr | 30 Jul 1980 |

Wladyslaw Kozakiewicz, Poland (pole vault), 1980 Olympic champion.

Wladyslaw Kozakiewicz achieved the ultimate double at the 1980 Moscow Olympics: a gold medal and a new world record. His older brother Edward was Poland's decathlon champion and introduced him to pole vaulting. Wladyslaw competed at the Montreal Olympics in 1976, but an ankle injury left him in 11th position. He compensated somewhat in 1977 with two European records but was fourth at the 1978 European Championships.

Kozakiewicz went to Italy in early 1980 to prepare himself for the Moscow Olympics and avoided the indoor circuit. In May he added two centimeters to the record, clearing 5.72 meters (18' 9 ¼").

In Moscow the competition was between him, defending champion Slusarski (Poland), and Russian favorite Konstantin Volkov. The Polish athletes faced hostile jeering from the Soviet crowd whenever it was their turn to jump. Nonetheless, Kozakiewicz won without missing a jump. Finally, he had the bar put up to a world record 5.78 meters (18' 11 ¾") and, on his second attempt, went over.

Despite his gold medal, life in Poland had its problems, as the Communist regime was in terminal decline. In 1982 Kozakiewicz defected to West Germany. He won the West German title in 1986 and 1987, and his 5.70-meter win (18' 8 ¼") in 1986 remains a German record.

Thierry Vigneron   (France, b. 1960)

5.75m (18' 10 ½")	Paris, France	1 Jun 1980
5.75m (18' 10 ½")	Lille, France	29 Jun 1980
5.80m (19' 0 ½")	Macon, France	20 Jun 1981
5.83m (19' 1 ½")	Rome, Italy	1 Sep 1983
5.91m (19' 4 ¾")	Rome, Italy	31 Aug 1984

Thierry Vigneron, France (pole vault).

Thierry Vigneron led a French revival in the pole vault in which two Frenchmen were world record holders in the early 1980s. Born at Gennevilliers, Vigneron's early interests were gymnastics and cross-country running before he turned to the pole vault. He was the first man over the 19-foot barrier with his 5.80-meter jump in 1981. His first two world records in 1980 made him a favorite for the Moscow Olympics, but he never had good fortune at the Olympics. In 1980 he was seventh, in 1984 he was tied for third, and in 1988 he was tied for fifth.

In the European Championships success also eluded him. He was tied for fifth in 1982 in Athens and unfortunately "no-heighted" in 1986 in Stuttgart.

His last world record in Rome in 1984 was in a fabulous competition with the new Soviet star, Sergey Bubka. Both men had gone over 5.84 meters (19' 2"). The bar was then raised to the new world record height of 5.91 meters (19' 4 ¾"). Bubka missed and then made the remarkable decision to pass to the next height. Vigneron, however, went over at his second attempt. Ten minutes later, with the bar now at 5.94 meters (19' 5 ¾"), Bubka went over the first time to erase Vigneron's record. Two new world records were set within 10 minutes. Vigneron's 10-minute world record in 1984 remained a French record for almost 10 years.

Vladimir Polyakov   (Soviet Union, b. 1960)

| 5.81m (19' 0 ¾") | Tbilisi, USSR | 26 Jun 1981 |

Vladimir Polyakov was born in Aleksin in the Tula region. At age 16, he had a bad landing after clearing 5.00 meters (16' 5") and had a serious dislocation of vertebral disks. He was bedridden for two months. Yet he slowly came back to the sport and in 1979 won the European junior title.

His was an unheralded world record. In a Soviet Union vs. East Germany meet in Tbilisi, Georgia, he surprised the track and field world by adding one centimeter to Thierry Vigneron's world record. Needing three attempts to get over 5.20 meters (17' 0 ¾"), he then had first-time clearances over 5.40, 5.60, 5.72, and finally 5.81 meters. Suddenly, he was the new world record holder.

After a second place at the 1982 European Championships and a win at the 1983 Soviet titles, he missed the 1984 Los Angeles Olympics because of the Soviet boycott.

Pierre Quinon   (France, b. 1962)

5.82m (19' 1 ¼")   **Cologne, West Germany**   **28 Aug 1983**

Pierre Quinon was part of the French resurgence in this event in the early 1980s. At the 1982 European Championships he finished 12th. However, a year later, at an international meet in Cologne in August 1983, he added one centimeter to Polyakov's 1981 record with 5.82 meters. After that triumph the season finished on a low note when he "no-heighted" at the World Championships.

In 1984, with the boycott by the Soviet bloc, the Los Angeles Olympics came down to a duel between France and the United States: Earl Bell and Mike Tully (USA) vs. Thierry Vigneron and Pierre Quinon (France). It was a very tactical final, with much "cat and mouse" passing of heights. Tully alone cleared 5.65 meters, which the others passed on. Tully then passed on 5.70 meters, while the other three attempted it. Quinon cleared it at his first attempt, while both Bell and Vigneron missed on

Pierre Quinon, France (pole vault).

all three tries and were out. The bar was raised to 5.75 meters, and Quinon once again went over the first time. Tully made a decision to pass on this height and to try for 5.80 meters, but he was now tiring and couldn't make it. So Pierre Quinon became the first Frenchman to win an Olympic gold medal in the pole vault.

Sergey Bubka   (Soviet Union/Ukraine, b. 1963)

5.85m (19' 2 ½")	**Bratislava, Czechoslovakia**	**26 May 1984**
5.88m (19' 3 ½")	**Paris, France**	**2 Jun 1984**
5.90m (19' 4 ¼")	**London, England**	**13 Jul 1984**
5.94m (19' 5 ¾")	**Rome, Italy**	**31 Aug 1984**
6.00m (19' 8 ¼")	**Paris, France**	**13 Jul 1985**

6.01m (19' 8 3/4")	Moscow, USSR	8 Jul 1986
6.03m (19' 9 ½")	Prague, Czechoslovakia	23 Jun 1987
6.05m (19' 10 ¼")	Bratislava, Czechoslovakia	9 Jun 1988
6.06m (19' 10 ½")	Nice, France	10 Jul 1988
6.07m (19' 11")	Shizuoka, Japan	6 May 1991
6.08m (19' 11 ½")	Moscow, USSR	9 Jun 1991
6.09m (19' 11 ¾")	Formia, Italy	8 Jul 1991
6.10m (20' 0 ¼")	Malmö, Sweden	5 Aug 1991
6.11m (20' 0 ½")	Dijon, France	13 Jun 1992
6.12m (20' 1")	Padua, Italy	30 Aug 1992
6.13m (20' 1 ½")	Tokyo, Japan	19 Sep 1992
6.14m (20' 1 ¾")	Sestriere, Italy	31 Jul 1994

Sergey Bubka, Soviet Union/Ukraine (pole vault), the master, first man over both six meters and 20 feet.

Sergey Bubka was born in the Ukraine and grew up in Voroshilovgrad. His father is a noncommissioned officer, his mother a nurse. His older brother Vasiliy is also an international pole vaulter, who was second in the 1986 European Championships to his younger brother.

Sergey arrived as a late inclusion in the 1983 World Championships. He had a perfect score to 5.50 meters, needed three jumps at 5.60 meters, and was the only one over 5.70 meters. Suddenly, the unknown athlete was world champion. It was the beginning of a long and illustrious career. Over the next 12 years he achieved 17 world records, five World Championships, the 1986 European Championship, and the 1988 Olympic gold medal. (He had missed the 1984 Olympics because of the Soviet boycott.) One major hiccup took place in 1992: He "no-heighted" the Barcelona Olympics. He was the first man over both six meters and 20 feet and was world champion in 1983, 1987, 1991, and 1993. At his Olympic debut in 1988 he came from behind, winning with a last-gasp jump, as he also did in the 1991 World Championships in Tokyo. He had performed a similar magic act in 1984 when competing against Thierry Vigneron: The Frenchman set a world record of 5.91 meters (19' 4 ¾"), only to see Bubka go higher 10 minutes later with 5.94 meters (19' 5 ¾").

His flop at the Barcelona Olympics showed that he is not invincible. Perhaps one reason for his seeming invincibility was that he enjoyed such reverential status that obliging officials often gave him several minutes to prepare for his jump. At the Olympics only two minutes are allowed, and the other athletes insisted that this rule be enforced for everybody. Perhaps the unexpected pressure flustered him.

Apart from his Olympic hiccup in 1992, how has he been so good for so long? He appears to combine great strength with gymnastic ability, along with all the other attributes of a great vaulter, including immaculate technique and a capacity to hold the pole at the very end.

He reads a lot and has an interest in poetry. His favorite poets are Omar Khayyam and Rasal Gamzatov. His wife, Liliya, is a master of sport in modern gymnastics. Since the breakup of the Soviet Union, he now represents Ukraine but competes for the OSC Berlin club while residing in Paris and Donetsk. However, a rare event took place in 1995: He was seriously challenged, and occasionally beaten, by a newcomer from South Africa, Okkert Brits, 10 years his junior. Three months before the Atlanta Olympics he suffered an ankle injury which refused to improve. He traveled to Atlanta but chose not to jump because of the ongoing pain.

Conclusions

Although it is a temptation to think that vaulters cannot go much higher, they continually surprise observers with their capacity to reach greater and greater heights. The various barriers, from 16 to 20 feet, have remorselessly been broken over the last four decades.

Of course, no other track and field event has been as influenced by technological changes, such as those described in the introduction to this chapter. It is not easy to predict the possible future changes in pole technology that may lead to yet another quantum leap in performance.

Five All-Time Highest: Men's Pole Vault

Sergey Bubka (UKR)	6.14m (20' 1 ¾")	1994
Okkert Brits (S.AF)	6.03m (19' 9 ½")	1995
Igor Trandenkov (RUS)	6.01m (19' 8 ¾")	1996
Radion Gataulin (RUS)	6.00m (19' 8 ¼")	1993
Lawrence Johnson (USA)	5.98m (19' 7 ½")	1996
Prediction	*6.20m (20' 4 ¼")*	*2015*

Top Three: Men's Pole Vault

GOLD MEDAL:	**Sergey Bubka (UKR)**
SILVER MEDAL:	**Cornelius Warmerdam (USA)**
BRONZE MEDAL:	**Bob Seagren (USA)**

Long Jump

The long jump—sometimes known in the United States as the broad jump—is one of the more basic of track and field endeavors and was the only jumping event that was held at the ancient Olympics. Of the field events, the long-jump world record has shown the smallest improvement over the years. There have been two occasions when the record lasted over 20 years: Jesse Owens's 1935 record (25 years 79 days) and Bob Beamon's 1968 jump (22 years 316 days).

A valid jump must take place from behind the takeoff board. Jumps are measured to the nearest mark in the sandpit made by any part of the jumper's body. The records have largely improved through greater sprinting speed and better long-jump surfaces in the runway.

Bob Beamon's 1968 world record of 8.90 meters (29' 2 ½") was set at high altitude in Mexico City with wind assistance of 2.0 meters per second. This was an improvement of 6.5 percent at one stroke. That jump led to debate about having separate high-altitude and low-altitude world records, an idea that was not accepted by the IAAF.

Only 12 men have been world record holders in this event, the smallest number in any men's track and field discipline. The record has been set or equaled 18 times. Five record holders have also won Olympic gold medals: DeHart Hubbard, Hamm, Owens, Boston, and Beamon. Only Beamon set his world record during the Olympics. One all-time great, but a man who never set a world record, was Carl Lewis (USA), who won four Olympic gold medals in the long jump (1984-96).

Men's World Records for the Long Jump

Record distance	Record holder	Location	Date
7.61m (24' 11 ¾")	Peter O'Connor (GBR/IRE)	Dublin, Ireland	5 Aug 1901
7.69m (25' 3")	Edward Gourdin (USA)	Cambridge, USA	23 Jul 1921
7.76m (25' 5 ¼")	Robert LeGendre (USA)	Paris, France	7 Jul 1924
7.89m (25' 10 ¾")	William DeHart Hubbard (USA)	Chicago, USA	13 Jun 1925
7.90m (25' 11")	Edward Hamm (USA)	Cambridge, USA	7 Jul 1928
7.93m (26' 0 ¼")	Silvio Cator (HAI)	Paris, France	9 Sep 1928
7.98m (26' 2 ¼")	Chuhei Nambu (JPN)	Tokyo, Japan	27 Oct 1931
8.13m (26' 8 ¼")	Jesse Owens (USA)	Ann Arbor, USA	25 May 1935
8.21m (26' 11 ¼")	Ralph Boston (USA)	Walnut, USA	12 Aug 1960
8.24m (27' 0 ½")	Ralph Boston (USA)	Modesto, USA	27 May 1961
8.28m (27' 2")	Ralph Boston (USA)	Moscow, USSR	16 Jul 1961
8.31m (27' 3 ¼")	Igor Ter-Ovanesyan (USSR)	Yerevan, USSR	10 Jun 1962
8.31m (27' 3 ¼")	Ralph Boston (USA)	Kingston, Jamaica	15 Aug 1964
8.34m (27' 4 ¼")	Ralph Boston (USA)	Los Angeles, USA	12 Sep 1964
8.35m (27' 5")	Ralph Boston (USA)	Modesto, USA	29 May 1965
8.35m (27' 5")	Igor Ter-Ovanesyan (USSR)	Mexico City, Mexico	19 Oct 1967
8.90m (29' 2 ½")	Bob Beamon (USA)	Mexico City, Mexico	18 Oct 1968
8.95m (29' 4 ½")	Mike Powell (USA)	Tokyo, Japan	30 Aug 1991

Peter O'Connor (Great Britain/Ireland, 1872–1957)

7.61m (24' 11 ¾")   **Dublin, Ireland**   **5 Aug 1901**

Peter O'Connor was born in Wicklow, Ireland, at a time when all Ireland was under British rule. Between 1901 and 1906 he won the British AAA high-jump title twice and the

Peter O'Connor, Great Britain/Ireland (long jump).

long-jump title six times. It was in 1901 that he set a world record for the long jump in Dublin, at the Royal Irish Constabulary (Depot) Sports Day. Using a wooden runway, his leap of 24' 2 ¾" (7.61 meters) was a world record for almost 20 years and an Irish record until 1990.

He did not compete in the 1904 Olympics for reasons that are not clear. Perhaps the cost of the trip to St. Louis, Missouri, was too much for a man without adequate financial support. However, he traveled to Athens in 1906 for the Interim Games to celebrate the 10th year of the modern Olympics. He placed second in the long jump and won the triple jump with 14.08 meters (46' 2 ¼"). He did not attend the 1908 London Olympics; this may have been because, as an Irishman, he felt unhappy to continue competing in Great Britain's colors.

A solicitor by profession, he attended all the Olympics from 1924 to 1948. O'Connor acted as a long-jump official at the 1932 Los Angeles Games.

Edward Gourdin   (United States, 1897–1966)

7.69m (25' 3")   **Cambridge, USA**   **23 Jul 1921**

Edward Gourdin was the first of a long line of black athletes to hold the world long-jump record. He was a graduate of Harvard University and, at the Harvard-Yale vs. Oxford-Cambridge track and field meet in 1921, he set a world record of 25' 3" (7.69 meters). This remains to this day a Harvard University record.

He traveled to the 1924 Olympics and finished second to his U.S. teammate DeHart Hubbard. They were the first two blacks to win medals in an Olympic long jump. DeHart Hubbard jumped 7.44 meters (24' 5"), and Gourdin 7.27 meters (23' 10 ¼").

Robert LeGendre   (United States, 1898–1931)

7.76m (25' 5 ¼")   **Paris, France**   **7 Jul 1924**

Robert LeGendre was born to French parents and did not speak English fluently until he was a teenager. He contested the pentathlon event—not the modern pentathlon (horse riding, shooting, fencing, swimming, and running), but rather a type of mini-decathlon, which included long jump, javelin, 200m, discus, and 1500m. He contested this event in the 1919 Inter-Allied Military Games in Paris, a great military sports festival. LeGendre won the pentathlon but was denied entry into the long-jump competition by team management, a decision that long irritated him. In 1920 he was selected for the Antwerp Olympics but suffered a broken leg and did not compete.

In 1924 he returned to Paris, this time with the U.S. Olympic team. Once again he was selected for the pentathlon but not for the long jump. However, the incident five years previous made him highly motivated to excel in the long-jump section of the pentathlon, whatever the winner of the individual long jump achieved. It was DeHart Hubbard who won the long jump at these Olympics with 7.44 meters (24' 5"). In the pentathlon LeGendre jumped all the way to 7.76 meters (25' 5 ¼") on his third jump. This not only exceeded DeHart Hubbard's winning mark in the individual long jump event, but was a new world record in the bargain.

LeGendre did not have such good results in the other events of the pentathlon and finished third overall. He graduated with a PhD from Georgetown and went on to become a company dentist for Hecht & Company in Washington. He died at the age of 33 of bronchial pneumonia.

William DeHart Hubbard   (United States, 1903–1976)

7.89m (25' 10 ¾")   Chicago, USA   13 Jun 1925

William DeHart Hubbard was the first black to win an Olympic track and field gold medal when he won the long jump at the 1924 Paris Games. He studied at the University of Michigan and for six years in a row (1922-27) won the AAU long-jump title. He also won the AAU triple jump in 1922 and 1923. In his long jumping he believed in only a short run-up of about 30 meters, with very rapid acceleration. In his Olympic win he defeated the existing world record holder Edward Gourdin, 7.44 meters (24' 5") to 7.27 meters (23' 10 ¼").

His world record came at the 1925 NCAA championships when he added 13 centimeters to the record. DeHart Hubbard competed at the 1928 Olympics and finished tied for 11th in the long jump.

Edward Hamm   (United States, 1906–1982)

7.90m (25' 11")   Cambridge, USA   7 Jul 1928

Edward Hamm was a student at Georgia Tech and won the 1927 NCAA long-jump title. In 1928 he did everything right. First he won the NCAA title again. Then, at the U.S. Olympic trials, he won with a new world record of 25' 11" (7.90 meters). Finally, three weeks later, he won the gold medal at Amsterdam with a leap of 7.73 meters (25' 4 ½").

In 1930 he joined the Coca Cola Company and eventually became vice president of its West Coast division.

Edward Hamm, United States (long jump), 1928 Olympic champion.

Silvio Cator   (Haiti, 1900–1953)

7.93m (26' 0 ¼")   **Paris, France**   **9 Sep 1928**

Silvio Cator was an all-round natural athlete from the island of Haiti and was captain of the Haitian soccer team. In the 1924 Paris Olympics he competed in the high jump and long jump. In the long jump he was 12th, and in the high jump he did not qualify for the final.

At the 1928 Olympics he was second to Edward Hamm (USA) in the long jump. Hamm won with 7.73 meters (25' 4 ¼"), and Cator jumped 7.58 meters (24' 10 ½").

Six weeks later he achieved a new world record in Paris: 7.93 meters. This was one quarter of an inch over the 26-foot barrier and was achieved on his last jump.

Chuhei Nambu   (Japan, b. 1904)

7.98m (26' 2 ¼")   **Tokyo, Japan**   **27 Oct 1931**

Chuhei Nambu was part of an unexpected string of successes in the jumps by Japanese athletes in the 1930s, which resulted in world records and Olympic gold medals. He had competed at the 1928 Amsterdam Olympics, coming in ninth in the long jump and fourth in the triple jump.

In October 1931 in a match between Japan and Japanese students at the Meiji Jingu Stadium, Chuhei Nambu recorded 7.98 meters (26' 2 ¼") on his first jump. On the same day he ran a creditable 10.6 seconds for the 100m.

Nambu showed that his success was no fluke when he traveled to Los Angeles for the 1932 Olympics and defeated the Americans. In fact, he won a gold medal, not in the long jump, but in the triple jump, with a world record of 15.72 meters (51' 7"). In the long jump he finished third with 7.45 meters (24' 5 ¼").

Chuhei Nambu, Japan (long jump, triple jump),
the only man to hold world records in both
the long jump and the triple jump.

Jesse Owens   (United States, 1913–1980)

8.13m (26' 8 ¼")   **Ann Arbor, USA**   **25 May 1935**

The late, great Jesse Owens was a supreme athlete who set six world records in one day (1935) and won four Olympic gold medals (1936). Married at age 16, he was a student at Ohio State University. He won the AAU long-jump title in 1933, 1934, and 1936. One of his six world records, set at Ann Arbor in 1935 in the long jump, was to last for 25 years.

At the Berlin Olympics the long jump was no walkover. Owens had a long, drawn-out duel with the German Luz Long before Owens finally won.

Owens's post-Olympic career and his postwar efforts as a role model and a public speaker have been described in the chapter on the 100m. However, he had his critics: The radical blacks of the 1960s disowned him, and even some of the elite athletes were critical. Discus thrower Mac Wilkins felt he was out of date: "Every time he opens his mouth, the sport goes backwards."

However the majority of Americans continue to see him as a positive symbol of athletic excellence. Throughout his ups and downs in life, he remained a courteous and gentle man.

The immortal Jesse Owens, United States (long jump), at the 1936 Olympics.

Ralph Boston   (United States, b. 1939)

8.21m (26' 11 ¼")	Walnut, USA	12 Aug 1960
8.24m (27' 0 ½")	Modesto, USA	27 May 1961
8.28m (27' 2")	Moscow, USSR	16 Jul 1961
8.31m (27' 3 ¼")	Kingston, Jamaica	15 Aug 1964
8.34m (27' 4 ¼")	Los Angeles, USA	12 Sep 1964
8.35m (27' 5")	Modesto, USA	29 May 1965

Jesse Owens's 25-year-old record fell in 1960 to Ralph Boston, who was the first man to exceed 27 feet. Born in Mississippi, Boston was known as "Hawkeye" and had two brothers who were All-American football players. He went to Tennessee State University where he majored in biochemistry. Boston won the AAU title six years in a row, from 1961 to 1966.

In a meet two weeks before the Olympics began, he broke the world record on his fifth jump with 26' 11 ¼". In the emotion of the occasion he passed the final jump.

In Rome, far from having a walkover, he had an extremely close contest, because four men went over eight meters: Boston jumped 8.12 meters, Bo Roberson (USA) 8.11 meters, Igor Ter-Ovanesyan (USSR) 8.04 meters, and Manfred Steinbach (West Germany) 8.00 meters.

He won other events, including the AAU indoor hurdles title in 1965, placed fourth in

the 1963 Pan-Am Games high jump, and was the leading triple jumper in the United States in 1963.

He set world records twice in 1961, twice in 1964, and once in 1965. During much of this time he was in perpetual rivalry with Soviet star Igor Ter-Ovanesyan. Boston was also Pan-American champion in 1963 and 1967. Prior to the Tokyo Olympics he had set a world record at the U.S. Olympic trials. However, at the Games the event took place in pouring rain, and he slipped back to second spot, as Welshman Lynne Davies won, 8.07 meters to 8.03 meters. At the Mexico City Olympics, Boston came in third with 8.16 meters (26' 9 ½"), after Bob Beamon had sailed out to 8.90 meters (29' 2 ½").

Boston retired after these Olympics to join the administrative staff at the University of Tennessee.

Ralph Boston, United States, and Igor Ter-Ovanesyan, Soviet Union, long jump rivals in the 1960s.

Igor Ter-Ovanesyan (Soviet Union, b. 1938)

| 8.31m (27' 3 ¼") | Yerevan, USSR | 10 Jun 1962 |
| 8.35m (27' 5") | Mexico City, Mexico | 19 Oct 1967 |

Igor Ter-Ovanesyan's father, Aram, had been the Soviet discus champion in 1933. His mother died during World War II. Young Igor won 12 Soviet long-jump titles and went to four Olympics. At age 18, he competed at the 1956 Melbourne Games but fouled three times in the final. At the Rome Olympics he was a bronze medalist with 8.04 meters, a new European record.

Over the next eight years he and Boston extended the world record out to 8.35 meters. The Soviet athlete had his greatest successes at the European Championships, winning in 1958, 1962, and 1969 and coming in second in 1964 and 1971. At the 1964 Olympics, in pouring rain, he came in third again (7.99 meters). Four years later at the Mexico City Olympics the new star Bob Beamon destroyed the competition with 8.90 meters; Ter-Ovanesyan finished fourth with 8.12 meters.

After Mexico, Ter-Ovanesyan became the long-time head coach of the Soviet athletic team and later became head of the Russian Track and Field Association.

Bob Beamon (United States, b. 1946)

| 8.90m (29' 2 ½") | Mexico City, Mexico | 18 Oct 1968 |

Bob Beamon was the man who owned the world record for almost 23 years. Born in Jamaica, New York, he was a track and field talent at Jamaica High School and later at the University of Texas, El Paso, and came in second in the long jump at the 1967 Pan-American Games. The next year he won all but one of his long-jump contests, including the AAU title.

At the Olympics in Mexico City, on his first jump, he exploded into sports history. He jumped a staggering 8.90 meters (29' 2 ½"). He had jumped past both the 28-foot and 29-foot barrier at one leap. It took a few moments for the impact of what he had done to sink in. He fell to his knees almost in a trance.

Beamon never did anything remotely like "The Jump" again. He was unable to jump over even 27 feet (8.23 meters). A serious hamstring injury in 1969 ended his career.

Track and field statisticians were not really comfortable with Beamon's world record. Apart from the high altitude (2248 meters [7375 feet] above sea level), the supporting wind was 2.0 meters per second, the exact upper

Bob Beamon, United States (long jump). The Jump.

limit allowed for world records. That figure was the exact same figure registered for four other world record performances at these Olympics. This does not take away from the fact that it was a massive jump, fully deserving of the gold medal.

After his athletic career, Beamon became a community and social worker.

Mike Powell　(United States, b. 1963)

8.95m (29' 4 ½")　　　**Tokyo, Japan**　　　　　　　**30 Aug 1991**

Mike Powell was the man who finally broke Bob Beamon's legendary world record. This was at sea level and without a 2.0-meter-per-second wind behind him. He did it in an enthralling contest with the long-time heir apparent to Beamon's record, Carl Lewis.

For 10 long years, the long jump had belonged to Lewis. Lewis, in addition to his sprinting talent, had regularly jumped over 28 feet (8.53 meters), which only a handful of other athletes have ever achieved. He had won long-jump gold medals at both the 1984 and 1988 Olympics and had not lost a long-jump contest since March 1981.

Mike Powell was born in Philadelphia and attended the University of California, Irvine, and later UCLA, where he obtained a sociology degree. He teamed up with team coach Randy Huntington in 1987, who helped correct his tendency to foul, a problem Powell never completely eliminated. In 1988 he made it onto the U.S. Olympic team on his very last jump at the U.S. selection trials. At the Games he managed a respectable silver behind Lewis, 8.72 meters to 8.49 meters.

From that point on, he started to get nearer and nearer to King Carl. He came in second to Lewis in the 1990 Goodwill Games by only four centimeters. Lewis perhaps made a mistake in jumping very rarely at this stage of his career, while Powell was jumping everywhere, in any conditions. Powell came within one centimeter of Lewis in the selection trials for the 1991 Tokyo World Championships. On the flight over, he confidently told a reporter, "Twenty-nine feet, six inches."

The finals in Tokyo saw Lewis jump past Beamon's record, 8.91 meters, but with too much wind assistance. But then Powell made his extraordinary jump. When he landed, he knew instantly that he had done it. The wind reading was legal, so he did a dance of joy while awaiting the official result. Finally it was flashed on a screen: 8.95 meters (29' 4 ½"). Powell met Bob Beamon on his return to the United States and the two men embraced.

Mike Powell, United States (long jump), the man who broke Bob Beamon's 23-year-old record.

However, Lewis bounced back at the Barcelona Olympics the next year by winning his third gold medal in the long jump on his first leap (8.67 meters). Powell got within three centimeters with 8.64 meters. Lewis triumphed yet again in 1996 and Powell, slowed down by a groin injury, finished fifth.

Conclusions

The long jump, like the high jump, is an event in which the world record appears to be reaching its ultimate limit. No radical changes in jumping style or equipment that could significantly improve long-jump performances seem possible. As Soviet athlete Igor Ter-Ovanesyan commented, "The long jump is difficult to improve on. What can you do after you've learned your technique and are reaching top speed?"

Mike Powell's 1991 world record (8.95 meters) was exceeded in 1995 by Ivan Pedroso of Cuba (8.96 meters) only to be disallowed on technical grounds. This suggests that if one elite athlete can achieve a record, there is no real reason why another athlete should not emerge sooner or later to duplicate or exceed it. The next target for long jumpers is the nine-meter barrier.

Six All-Time Best: Men's Long Jump			(Wind)
Mike Powell (USA)	8.95m (29' 4 ½")	1991	+0.3
Bob Beamon (USA)	8.90m (29' 2 ½") A	1968	+2.0
Carl Lewis (USA)	8.87m (29' 1 ¼")	1991	−0.2
Robert Emmiyan (USSR)	8.86m (29' 1") A	1987	+1.9
Larry Myricks (USA)	8.74m (28' 8 ¼")	1988	+1.4
Erick Walder (USA)	8.74m (28' 8 ¼") A	1994	+2.0
Prediction	*9.00m (29' 6 ½")*	*2015*	

Top Three: Men's Long Jump

GOLD MEDAL: Jesse Owens (USA)

SILVER MEDAL: Ralph Boston (USA)

BRONZE MEDAL: Bob Beamon (USA)

However, a non-world record holder must be recognized as being the all-time great: *Carl Lewis.*

T his event used to be known as the hop, step, and jump, which more accurately describes it. The athlete must first take off and land on the same foot, step on to the other foot, and then leap into the sandpit. Like the long jump, records are permissible only if the wind speed behind the athlete is less than 2.0 meters per second. Eight of the 27 world records have been set at high-altitude games, which has diminished their credibility somewhat.

The triple jump has suffered a bit of an image problem, being regarded as artificial, as something from a music hall routine. The event has endured, despite its somewhat unfashionable status. It has been in every modern Olympics since 1896, unlike the 200m, 3000m steeplechase, 5000m, 10,000m, 400m hurdles, hammer throw, javelin, both walks, and the relays.

No single country has dominated this event. The 18 world record holders come from nine different countries. A curiosity in triple-jump history is the domination of the event by the Japanese between the world wars: they won three Olympic gold medals in a row, from 1928 to 1936.

Men's World Record Holders for Triple Jump

Record distance	Record holder	Location	Date
15.52m (50' 11")	Daniel Ahearn (USA)	New York, USA	30 May 1911
15.52m (50' 11")	Anthony Winter (AUST)	Paris, France	12 Jul 1924
15.58m (51' 1 ½")	Mikio Oda (JPN)	Tokyo, Japan	27 Oct 1931
15.72m (51' 7")	Chuhei Nambu (JPN)	Los Angeles, USA	4 Aug 1932
15.78m (51' 9 ¼")	Jack Metcalfe (AUST)	Sydney, Australia	14 Dec 1935
16.00m (52' 6")	Naoto Tajima (JPN)	Berlin, Germany	6 Aug 1936
16.00m (52' 6")	Adhemar da Silva (BRA)	São Paulo, Brazil	3 Dec 1950
16.01m (52' 6 ¼")	Adhemar da Silva (BRA)	Rio de Janeiro, Brazil	30 Sep 1951
16.12m (52' 10 ¼")	Adhemar da Silva (BRA)	Helsinki, Finland	23 Jul 1952
16.22m (53' 2 ½")	Adhemar da Silva (BRA)	Helsinki, Finland	23 Jul 1952
16.23m (53' 3")	Leonid Shcherbakov (USSR)	Moscow, USSR	19 Jul 1953
16.56m (54' 4")	Adhemar da Silva (BRA)	Mexico City, Mexico	16 Mar 1955
16.59m (54' 5 ¼")	Oleg Ryakhovskiy (USSR)	Moscow, USSR	28 Jul 1958
16.70m (54' 9 ½")	Oleg Fedoseyev (USSR)	Nalchik, USSR	3 May 1959
17.03m (55' 10 ½")	Josef Schmidt (POL)	Olsztyn, Poland	5 Aug 1960
17.10m (56' 1 ¼")	Giuseppe Gentile (ITA)	Mexico City, Mexico	16 Oct 1968
17.22m (56' 6")	Giuseppe Gentile (ITA)	Mexico City, Mexico	17 Oct 1968
17.23m (56' 6 ¼")	Viktor Saneyev (USSR)	Mexico City, Mexico	17 Oct 1968
17.27m (56' 8")	Nelson Prudencio (BRA)	Mexico City, Mexico	17 Oct 1968
17.39m (57' 0 ¾")	Viktor Saneyev (USSR)	Mexico City, Mexico	17 Oct 1968
17.40m (57' 1")	Pedro Perez (CUBA)	Cali, Colombia	5 Aug 1971
17.44m (57' 2 ¾")	Viktor Saneyev (USSR)	Sukhumi, USSR	17 Oct 1972
17.89m (58' 8 ½")	João de Oliveira (BRA)	Mexico City, Mexico	15 Oct 1975
17.97m (58' 11 ½")	Willie Banks (USA)	Indianapolis, USA	16 Jun 1985
17.98m (59' 0")	Jonathan Edwards (GBR)	Salamanca, Spain	18 Jul 1995
18.16m (59' 7")	Jonathan Edwards (GBR)	Gothenburg, Sweden	7 Aug 1995
18.29m (60' 0 ¼")	Jonathan Edwards (GBR)	Gothenburg, Sweden	7 Aug 1995

Daniel Ahearn   (United States, 1888–?)

15.52m (50' 11")   **New York, USA**   **30 May 1911**

Daniel Ahearne was born in County Limerick, Ireland, in 1888. His older brother Timothy won the triple jump at the 1908 London Olympics, wearing British colors. (All of Ireland was under British rule at that time.) Young Daniel emigrated to the United Stated in 1908 and dropped the "e" off the end of his name. He won the U.S. AAU triple jump eight times (1910-11, 1913-18) and in 1911 set the first officially recognized world record in Celtic Park, New York.

Being Irish, he was not eligible to represent the United States at the 1912 Olympics, although his world record is attributed to him as a U.S. citizen. By 1920 he qualified for the U.S. team for that year's Olympics, but at age 32, he was past his peak and came in sixth with 14.08 meters (46' 2 ¼").

Daniel Ahearn, United States (triple jump).

Anthony Winter   (Australia, 1894–1955)

15.52m (50' 11")   **Paris, France**   **12 Jul 1924**

Winter's father ran a number of snooker saloons, and young "Nick" Winter became a highly competent player himself. A triple jumper, by profession he was a fireman in the Sydney suburb of Manly. Winter was one of nine Australian track and field athletes sent to the 1924 Olympics.

At the Games in Paris the initial leader was Luis Brunetto of Argentina, with 15.42 meters (50' 7 ¼"). On his last jump, Winter sailed out to 15.52 meters (50' 11"), 14 inches more than his previous best. On his return to Australia he was given a hero's welcome by 200 members of the Manly Fire Brigade.

Winter returned to the Olympics in 1928, placing 12th in the triple jump with 14.14 meters (46' 4 ¾"). He died in 1955 in tragic circumstances. His wife was in the hospital, dying of cancer. At home, Winter apparently stumbled in the bathroom; his head hit and broke open a gas pipe. He was found dead the next day in a gas-filled house.

Anthony Winter, Australia (triple jump), 1924 Olympic champion.

Mikio Oda   (Japan, b. 1905)

15.58m (51' 1 ½")   **Tokyo, Japan**   **27 Oct 1931**

Mikio Oda was the first male Asian athlete to set a world record (1931) and the first Asian track and field athlete to win an Olympic gold medal when he won the triple jump in 1928.

Oda was born in Hiroshima and competed at the Paris Olympics in 1924, where he came in sixth in the triple jump and tied for 10th in the long jump. At the 1928 Amsterdam Olympics, he won the triple jump with 15.21 meters (49' 10 ¾") from Levi Casey (USA), who managed 15.17 meters (49' 9 ¼"). Oda also competed in the long jump, tying for 11th.

It was in Tokyo in 1931 that Oda set his world record. In a contest between Japanese Students and Japan, he jumped 15.58 meters. At the same meet, his countryman Chuhei Nambu set a new world record for the long jump of 7.98 meters (26' 2 ¼"). It was an historic day for Japanese track and field.

Oda was injured in 1932 and came in 12th in the triple jump at the Los Angeles Olympics. As Japan's first Olympic gold medallist he is revered in that country as a "god of athletics."

Chuhei Nambu   (Japan, b. 1904)

15.72m (51' 7")   **Los Angeles, USA**   **4 Aug 1932**

Chuhei Nambu was the second of the three great Japanese triple jumpers between the wars, alongside Oda and Tajima. Nambu is the only athlete to have held the world record in both the long jump (1931) and the triple jump (1932). He was also the first athlete to win Olympic medals in both events, a feat duplicated by his countryman Naoto Tajima in 1936.

At the 1928 Olympics Nambu was fourth in the triple jump (15.01 meters), which was won by his countryman Mikio Oda (15.21 meters). Nambu was also ninth in the long jump. Nambu's long-jump world record of 7.98 meters (26' 2 ¼") was set at the same meet in Tokyo in 1931 as Oda's triple-jump world record.

At the Los Angeles Olympics Nambu came in third in the long jump. In the triple jump it was only on his fifth jump that Nambu took the lead with a new world record of 15.72 meters (51' 7").

Jack Metcalfe   (Australia, 1912–1994)

15.78m (51' 9 ¼")   **Sydney, Australia**   **14 Dec 1935**

Jack Metcalfe was an all-round athlete who held Australian records for high jump, long jump, and triple jump and was Australian javelin champion in 1936. A graduate of the University of Sydney, he won the triple jump at the British Empire Games in 1934 and 1938.

Metcalfe added six centimeters to Nambu's world record at the Sydney Cricket Ground in 1935. At the 1936 Berlin Olympics Metcalfe jumped 15.50 meters (50' 10 ¼") for a bronze medal. A Japanese athlete, Naoto Tajima, won with a world record performance of 16.00 meters (52' 6").

Metcalfe was later manager of the Australian track and field team at the 1948 Olympics and a referee at the 1956 Melbourne Olympics. He later admitted that despite being a "crank" on health matters, he was also an inveterate smoker since his 20s. He finally gave cigarettes up on 16 July 1969 at the age of 57. It was too late: He was plagued with emphysema for the rest of his days. Nonetheless, he lived on to the age of 81 in retirement on the east coast of Australia.

Naoto Tajima   (Japan, 1912–1990)

16.00m (52' 6")   **Berlin, Germany**   **6 Aug 1936**

Naoto Tajima was the first athlete to reach the 16-meter barrier. A graduate of the University of Kyoto, he had competed at the 1932 Olympics, finishing sixth in the long jump with 7.15 meters (23' 5 ½"). At the Berlin Olympics he won a bronze medal in the long jump with 7.74 meters (25' 4 ¾").

Before the 1936 Olympics, Tajima's best triple jump was 15.40 meters (50' 6 ¼"). In the triple-jump final he opened with a strong leap of 15.76 meters (51' 8 ½"), only two centimeters less than Metcalfe's world record. On his fourth jump he went all the way to 16.00 meters (52' 6").

Tajima and fellow Japanese athlete Chuhei Nambu are the only two athletes who have won Olympic medals in both long jump and triple jump. Tajima later became director of the Japan Amateur Sports Association.

Naoto Tajima, Japan (triple jump), 1936 Olympic champion and first man to jump 16 meters.

Adhemar da Silva   (Brazil, b. 1927)

16.00m (52' 6")	**São Paulo, Brazil**	**3 Dec 1950**
16.01m (52' 6 ¼")	**Rio de Janeiro, Brazil**	**30 Sep 1951**
16.12m (52' 10 ¼")	**Helsinki, Finland**	**23 Jul 1952**
16.22m (53' 2 ½")	**Helsinki, Finland**	**23 Jul 1952**
16.56m (54' 4")	**Mexico City, Mexico**	**16 Mar 1955**

Adhemar da Silva became Brazil's first world record holder in track and field and first track and field gold medalist at the Olympics. He was born in São Paulo and attended four Olympic Games: 1948 (where he came 11th), 1952 (1st), 1956 (1st), and 1960 (14th). He was also triple-jump champion at the Pan-American Games in 1951, 1955, and 1959.

In 1950 he equaled Tajima's record with 16 meters exactly. Ten months later he added one centimeter to the record. But it was at the Helsinki Olympics in 1952 that he really extended the record. He set new world records in his second (16.12 meters, 52' 10 ¼") and fifth jumps (16.22 meters, 53' 2 ½").

The silver medalist at these Games, Leonid Shcherbakov, took over the world record one

Adhemar da Silva, Brazil (triple jump), 1952 and 1956 Olympic champion.

year later by adding one centimeter to it. But the Brazilian bounced back at the 1955 Pan-American Games. These were the first major games set at the high altitude of Mexico City, and da Silva bounced all the way out to 16.56 meters (54' 4"), a massive improvement of 34 centimeters over his previous record.

Always sporting a guitar at his athletic meets, he had a brief movie career in 1958, when he played the leading role in the film *Black Orpheus*.

Leonid Shcherbakov   (Soviet Union, b. 1927)

16.23m (53' 3")   **Moscow, USSR**   **19 Jul 1953**

Leonid Shcherbakov was the top European triple jumper for many years but was somewhat overshadowed by the achievements of da Silva. He was Soviet champion seven times and was European champion in 1950 (15.39 meters, 50' 6") and again in 1954 (15.90 meters, 52' 2").

In 1952 at the Helsinki Olympics he was second to da Silva. His best jump of 15.98 meters (52' 5 ¼") was a European record at that time. Da Silva's winning leap was 16.22 meters (53' 2 ½").

Shcherbakov set his world record at the Dynamo Stadium in Moscow a year after these Olympics. On his fifth jump he managed one more centimeter than da Silva's record. In Melbourne at the 1956 Olympics Shcherbakov came in sixth (15.80 meters, 51' 10").

He had his own training methods and jumped with weights tied around his waist.

Oleg Ryakhovskiy   (Soviet Union, b. 1933)

16.59m (54' 5 ¼")   **Moscow, USSR**   **28 Jul 1958**

Ryakhovskiy was born in Tashkent in the Asiatic part of the Soviet Union. At the Soviet championships, he was first in 1957 and 1958, second in 1959, and third in 1960. He competed at the Universiades in 1957, 1959, and 1961 with two firsts and a second.

Oleg Ryakhovskiy set his world record at the inaugural United States vs. Soviet Union meet in Moscow in 1958. He jumped 16.59 meters (54' 5 ¼") to add three centimeters to da Silva's 1955 record. That year he was second to Poland's Josef Schmidt at the European Championships in Stockholm, jumping 16.02 meters (52' 6 ¾") to Schmidt's 16.43 meters (53' 10 ¾").

Oleg Fedoseyev   (Soviet Union, b. 1936)

16.70m (54' 9 ½")   **Nalchik, USSR**   **3 May 1959**

Oleg Fedoseyev added 11 centimeters (4 ¼") to Ryakovskiy's record when he jumped 16.70 meters (54' 9 ½") at a spring competition at Nalchik, in southwestern Russia. After this leap he was too overcome with emotion to take any more jumps.

He was Soviet champion in 1959, second in 1964, and third in 1962 and 1965. He competed at the 1964 Tokyo Olympics, where Schmidt of Poland was way ahead of the rest of the field. Schmidt won with 16.85 meters (55' 3 ½"). Fedoseyev took the silver medal on his fifth jump with 16.58 meters (54' 4 ¾"), one centimeter ahead of his countryman Viktor Kravchenko. He had previously won the Soviet long-jump championship in 1956 and 1958 and competed in the long jump at the Melbourne Olympics, where he came in eighth.

Josef Schmidt   (Poland, b. 1935)

17.03m (55' 10 ½")   Olsztyn, Poland   5 Aug 1960

Josef Schmidt, Poland (triple jump), the first man over 17 meters and Olympic champion in 1960 and 1964.

Josef Schmidt was one of the great triple jumpers. He won the Olympic gold medal twice (1960 and 1964), was European champion twice (1958 and 1962), and was the first man to break the 17-meter barrier.

His world record was achieved at the 1960 Polish championships. He achieved 17.03 meters (55' 10 ½") on his first jump, an improvement of 33 centimeters (13") on the old record. He went on to win 10 Polish championships between 1958 and 1971.

His major wins were by big margins: 41 centimeters (European Championships, 1958), 18 centimeters (Rome Olympics, 1960), 16 centimeters (European Championships, 1962), and 27 centimeters (Tokyo Olympics, 1964). He underwent a knee operation two months before the 1964 Olympics. At the Olympics he needed injections of local anesthetic to get through the competition. But he came through on the day and broke his own Olympic record with 16.85 meters (55' 3 ½") on his sixth jump.

He continued to compete, though without the same triumphant results. He was fifth in the 1966 European Championships and seventh in the 1968 Mexico City Olympics.

Giuseppe Gentile   (Italy, b. 1943)

17.10m (56' 1 ¼")   Mexico City, Mexico   16 Oct 1968
17.22m (56' 6")   Mexico City, Mexico   17 Oct 1968

Giuseppe Gentile was one of three triple jumpers who broke the world record a total of five times at the high-altitude 1968 Mexico City Olympics. In addition, the wind reading at three of these world records was at the exact upper limit for world records: 2.0 meters per second.

Triple jump, 1968 Mexico City Olympics. Three medalists, three world record holders: Nelson Prudencio, Brazil, *left*, second; Viktor Saneyev, Soviet Union, first; Giuseppe Gentile, Italy, third.

The first world record holder in this bonanza was Italy's Giuseppe Gentile. Prior to the Games his best jump was 16.74 meters (54' 11 ½"). In 1966 he had been ninth at the European Championships. In the qualifying rounds at Mexico City he jumped 17.10 meters (56' 1 ¼"), a new world record. The wind speed was 0.0 meters per second.

The next day, in the final, his first jump was even further: 17.22 meters (56' 6"), again with a wind reading of 0.0 meters per second. However, he finished up with the bronze medal as Saneyev (USSR) and Prudencio (Brazil) went even further with their jumps.

After the Games the best he could achieve was 16.72 meters (54' 10"). He had a short movie career and played Jason in the film *Medea* with Maria Callas as Medea.

Viktor Saneyev   (Soviet Union, b. 1945)

17.23m (56' 6 ¼")	**Mexico City, Mexico**	**17 Oct 1968**
17.39m (57' 0 ¾")	**Mexico City, Mexico**	**17 Oct 1968**
17.44m (57' 2 ¾)	**Sukhumi, USSR**	**17 Oct 1972**

Viktor Saneyev from Georgia was Olympic champion three times, Soviet champion eight times, European champion twice, and world record holder three times—an impressive record.

Two of his world records occurred at the Mexico City Olympics. The Italian Giuseppe Gentile had set a world record in the qualifying round (17.10 meters, 56' 1 ¼") and another in the first round of the final (17.22 meters, 56' 6"). But on his third jump, Saneyev improved the world record by an extra centimeter with 17.23 meters (56' 6 ¼", wind speed 2.0 meters per second). However, the Brazilian Nelson Prudencio jumped 17.27 meters (56' 8", wind speed 2.0 meters per second), another world record, to take the lead on his fifth jump. Saneyev had only one jump left. He soared to 17.39 meters (57' 0 ¾", wind speed 2.0 meters per second) for yet another world record.

Unlike the other world record holders that day, Saneyev proved he was no flash in the pan. He improved the world record one more time, at low altitude in Sukhumi with 17.44 meters.

Four years later, his first jump of 17.35 meters (56' 11") proved good enough to win at the Munich Olympics. At the 1976 Montreal Games he hit the lead only on his fifth jump (17.29 meters, 56' 8 ¾"). He had achieved the rare feat of winning gold medals at three successive Olympics.

At age 34, he had one more Olympics: Moscow in 1980. He was troubled by leg injuries, but his last jump (17.24 meters, 56' 6 ¾") earned him the silver medal.

Ten years later, with the Soviet Union disintegrating, he moved to Australia to work as a sports teacher in north Sydney.

Nelson Prudencio   (Brazil, b. 1944)

17.27m (56' 8")	**Mexico City, Mexico**	**17 Oct 1968**

Nelson Prudencio was one of the three athletes to break the world record in the triple jump final at the Mexico City Olympics on 17th Oct. 1968. The exact sequence of events was as follows:

			Wind
3:15 P.M. (1515 hours)	Giuseppe Gentile (Italy)	17.22m (56' 6")	0.0
4:05 P.M. (1605 hours)	Viktor Saneyev (USSR)	17.23m (56' 6 ¼")	2.0
5:00 P.M. (1700 hours)	Nelson Prudencio (Brazil)	17.27m (56' 8")	2.0
5:05 P.M. (1705 hours)	Viktor Saneyev (USSR)	17.39m (57' 0 ¾")	2.0

Prudencio was thus a world record holder for five minutes. That left him with the silver medal.

At the 1972 Munich Olympics he jumped 17.05 meters (55' 11 ¼") for a bronze medal. He returned to the Olympics in 1976 but could not get past the qualifying rounds.

Pedro Perez   (Cuba, b. 1952)

17.40m (57' 1")   Cali, Colombia   5 Aug 1971

At age 19, Pedro Perez Duenas came out of nowhere to win the 1971 Pan-Am Games at Cali, Colombia. There was help from high altitude: Cali is 1046 meters (3433 feet) above sea level.

Perez jumped 17.40 meters (57' 1") on his second leap to add one centimeter to Saneyev's world record. This performance made him a national hero in Cuba. Upon his return, 30,000 people turned up at the airport to greet him. Fidel Castro made a speech that lasted for an hour.

Apart from this special day, he never came close to this record again, partly because injuries plagued his athletic career. In 1972, suffering from injuries, he withdrew from the Munich Olympics after only two jumps in the qualifying rounds. At the 1976 Montreal Olympics he actually led at the beginning of the final with 16.81 meters (55' 1 ¾) but couldn't improve and finished fourth.

He went on to graduate as a doctor. In 1993 he was involved in the treatment of Cuban 800m star Anna Quirot when she suffered massive burns in a domestic fire while pregnant.

Pedro Perez, Cuba (triple jump).

João de Oliveira   (Brazil, b. 1954)

17.89m (58' 8 ½")   Mexico City, Mexico   15 Oct 1975

João de Oliveira made a sensational debut in international track and field at the 1975 Pan-American Games in Mexico. He won both the long jump and the triple jump, a rare double. In the latter he leaped to 17.89 meters (58' 8 ½"), an amazing 45-centimeter (17 ¾") improvement on Saneyev's existing mark.

A great career seemed in the offing. But at the 1976 Montreal Olympics he was plagued by sciatica and finished third with 16.90 meters (55' 5 ½") the day after finishing fifth in the long jump.

In the 1980 Moscow Olympics he appeared to be a victim of cheating by the Soviet athletic officials. Four of his jumps were declared fouls by the referees. Track and field historian Roberto Quercetani wrote diplomatically about this incident ten years later: "Strange things happened that day." De Oliveira was once more third.

In January 1982 de Oliveira suffered extensive trauma in a motor vehicle accident in Brazil when his car was hit head on by a drunken driver, who died instantly. De Oliveira suffered a fractured skull, a broken pelvis, and a right leg fractured in two places. After a nine-month battle to save his right leg, it was amputated below the knee.

João de Oliveira, Brazil (triple jump).

Willie Banks   (United States, b. 1956)

17.97m (58' 11 ½")   **Indianapolis, USA**   **16 Jun 1985**

Willie Banks was born at the Travis Air Force Base in California in 1956. In the triple jump he was fourth at the 1976 U.S. Olympic trials and so just missed the team. He went on to become a four-time AAU champion in the event (1980, 1981, 1983, and 1985). In 1980 the United States boycotted the Moscow Games. In the interim Banks went to UCLA as a law student.

Known as the bouncing barrister, he personally popularized the event with his audience-participation techniques. In particular, he encouraged the crowd to clap as he prepared to begin his run-up. He would also bring his Walkman radio on to the field, wander around, talk to the crowds, and in general make his presence felt.

At last, in 1984, the Olympics came to his home state of California. He traveled to Los Angeles as favorite for the event. On the day it all went wrong. He wasn't allowed to walk around chatting to the crowds, and he later described some of the officials as "Gestapo." The restrictions appeared to affect Banks more than the others. Two other U.S. athletes fought out the gold medal (Al Joyner and Mike Conley), and Banks slipped back to sixth.

Willie Banks, United States (triple jump).

That night he wept in his hotel room. Trying to work out what he could next do to compensate for this disappointment, he looked for a new goal and decided to go for the world record. This he achieved 10 months later. At the 1985 U.S. championships, he bounced to 17.97 meters (58' 11 ½") on his second jump. This world record survived a decade.

He had one more Olympic experience when he competed in 1988 at Seoul, where he finished sixth with 17.03 meters (55' 10 ½"). He then retired from athletics.

Jonathan Edwards   (Great Britain, b. 1966)

17.98m (59' 0")	Salamanca, Spain	18 Jul 1995
18.16m (59' 7")	Gothenburg, Sweden	7 Aug 1995
18.29m (60' 0 ¼")	Gothenburg, Sweden	7 Aug 1995

Jonathan Edwards, Great Britain (triple jump), the first man over 18 meters.

In the results of the 1988 Seoul Olympics and of the 1992 Barcelona Olympics, buried in the list of those who didn't qualify for the triple jump final, one comes across the name "J. Edwards (GBR)."

Jonathan Edwards's curriculum vitae prior to 1995 suggested an athlete at the international level who hadn't quite broken through to the very top rank. However, his Olympic results didn't tell the whole story. He had been second at the Commonwealth Games in 1990 and 1994, sixth at the European Championships in 1994, and third at the 1993 World Championships. The son of a vicar, he had refused to compete on Sundays for many years because of his religious convictions. Having refused to compete at the 1991 World Championships for this reason, he changed his position on this issue in 1993.

In 1995 his low public profile in the world of track and field changed forever. Having developed what he described as "speed on the ground" and "speed through the jump," he revolutionized not just the records but conventional thinking about the triple jump. His style seemed not so much a triple jump as a triple skip, keeping much lower to the ground than previous champions. Whatever his exact technique, he improved the world record three times and broke the 59-foot, the 60-foot, and the 18-meter barriers.

His first world record was in Salamanca, where he added one centimeter to the record of Willie Banks, which had lasted a decade. He had some extraordinary jumps early in that season, but they had been wind assisted. However, at the fifth World Championships in Gothenburg he produced two world record jumps without wind assistance. The first broke through the 18-meter barrier, a leap of 18.16 meters (59' 7"). The next went all the way out to 18.29 meters (60' 0 ¼"). Sport journalists present that day struggled to find the right words to describe this quantum jump in the event. Edwards, ever modest, also struggled to find words that properly articulated his new elite status and merely described himself as a "skinny, ordinary-looking guy." Alas, Edwards could not reproduce his 1995 form at the Atlanta Olympics. Kenny Harrison (USA) won with 18.09 meters while Edwards was second with 17.88 meters.

A graduate with a university degree in physics, Edwards works as a geneticist in the field of chromosome analysis.

Conclusions

Before 1995 the triple-jump world record had been static for a decade. It was nevertheless thought that the 18-meter barrier would be broken sooner or later, especially as it had already been beaten with wind-assisted jumps. However, Jonathan Edwards's 1995 world records have caused a major reappraisal of what is ultimately possible in this event.

The relative simplicity of the event suggests there won't be radical improvements to the record. There have been long gaps between world records in the triple jump in the past. Unless Edwards can improve on his startling 1995 record, it seems destined to remain unchanged for years. Perhaps Edwards, much like Beamon in the long jump, has "destroyed" the record for a generation.

Five All-Time Best: Men's Triple Jump			(Wind)
Jonathan Edwards (GBR)	18.29m (60' 0 ¼")	1995	+1.3
Kenny Harrison (USA)	18.09m (59' 4 ¼")	1996	-0.4
Willie Banks (USA)	17.97m (58' 11 ½")	1985	+1.5
Khristo Markov (BUL)	17.92m (58' 9 ½")	1987	+1.6
James Beckford (JAM)	17.92m (58' 9 ½")	1995	+1.9
Prediction	*18.29m (60' 0 ¼")*	*2015*	

Top Three: Men's Triple Jump

GOLD MEDAL:	Viktor Saneyev (USSR)
SILVER MEDAL:	Jonathan Edwards (GBR)
BRONZE MEDAL:	Adhemar da Silva (BRA)

T he shot put is thought to have originated from the ancient Celtic games in Scotland and Ireland and subsequently to have spread across to the East Coast of the United States, where there were large Irish and Scottish communities.

The shot is an iron or brass ball weighing 16 pounds (7.26 kilograms), thrown from the shoulder from within a circle 7 feet (2.13 meters) in diameter. In competition each athlete has six throws.

This throwing event has been dominated by the United States, especially in the first 65 years of the 20th century. Then, much like the discus, that domination was challenged by East Europeans and slipped away. Of the first 16 world record holders, 13 were U.S. athletes. Since then, only one of the subsequent five have been Americans.

There has been a gain in bulk by the elite shot putters. The average weight of the first 10 world record holders is 105 kilograms (231 pounds), while the average of the last 10 is 119 kilograms (262 pounds).

Twenty-one athletes have set or equaled the world record 51 times. Eleven have also won Olympic gold medals: Rose, Kuck, Sexton, O'Brien, Nieder, Long, Matson, Beyer, Andrei, Timmermann, and Barnes. Only Kuck (1928) has achieved a world record in Olympic competition.

Men's World Records for Shot Put

Record distance	Record holder	Location	Date
15.54m (51' 0")	Ralph Rose (USA)	San Francisco, USA	21 Aug 1909
15.79m (51' 9 ¾")	Emil Hirschfeld (GER)	Breslau, Germany	6 May 1928
15.87m (52' 0 ¾")	John Kuck (USA)	Amsterdam, Netherlands	29 Jul 1928
16.04m (52' 7 ½")	Emil Hirschfeld (GER)	Bochum, Germany	26 Aug 1928
16.04m (52' 7 ½")	Frantisek Douda (CZH)	Brno, Czechoslovakia	4 Oct 1931
16.05m (52' 8")	Zygmunt Heljasz (POL)	Poznan, Poland	29 Jun 1932
16.16m (53' 0 ½")	Leo Sexton (USA)	Freeport, USA	27 Aug 1932
16.20m (53' 1 ¾")	Frantisek Douda (CZH)	Prague, Czechoslovakia	24 Sep 1932
16.48m (54' 1")	John Lyman (USA)	Palo Alto, USA	21 Apr 1934
16.80m (55' 1 ½")	Jack Torrance (USA)	Des Moines, USA	27 Apr 1934
16.89m (55' 5")	Jack Torrance (USA)	Milwaukee, USA	30 Jun 1934
17.40m (57' 1")	Jack Torrance (USA)	Oslo, Norway	5 Aug 1934
17.68m (58' 0 ¼")	Charles Fonville (USA)	Lawrence, USA	17 Apr 1948
17.79m (58' 4 ½")	Jim Fuchs (USA)	Oslo, Norway	28 Jul 1949
17.82m (58' 5 ½")	Jim Fuchs (USA)	Los Angeles, USA	29 Apr 1950
17.90m (58' 8 ¾")	Jim Fuchs (USA)	Visby, Sweden	20 Aug 1950
17.95m (58' 10 ¾")	Jim Fuchs (USA)	Eskilstuna, Sweden	22 Aug 1950
18.00m (59' 0 ¾")	Parry O'Brien (USA)	Fresno, USA	9 May 1953
18.04m (59' 2 ¾")	Parry O'Brien (USA)	Compton, USA	5 Jun 1953
18.42m (60' 5 ¼")	Parry O'Brien (USA)	Los Angeles, USA	8 May 1954
18.43m (60' 5 ¾")	Parry O'Brien (USA)	Los Angeles, USA	21 May 1954
18.54m (60' 10")	Parry O'Brien (USA)	Los Angeles, USA	11 Jun 1954
18.62m (61' 1")	Parry O'Brien (USA)	Salt Lake City, USA	5 May 1956
18.69m (61' 4")	Parry O'Brien (USA)	Los Angeles, USA	15 Jun 1956
19.06m (62' 6 ¼")	Parry O'Brien (USA)	Eugene, USA	3 Sep 1956
19.25m (63' 2")	Parry O'Brien (USA)	Los Angeles, USA	1 Nov 1956
19.25m (63' 2")	Dallas Long (USA)	Santa Barbara, USA	28 Mar 1959
19.30m (63' 4")	Parry O'Brien (USA)	Albuquerque, USA	1 Aug 1959
19.38m (63' 7")	Dallas Long (USA)	Los Angeles, USA	5 Mar 1960

19.45m (63' 10")	Bill Nieder (USA)	Palo Alto, USA	19 Mar 1960
19.99m (65' 7")	Bill Nieder (USA)	Austin, USA	2 Apr 1960
20.06m (65' 10")	Bill Nieder (USA)	Walnut, USA	12 Aug 1960
20.08m (65' 10 ½")	Dallas Long (USA)	Los Angeles, USA	18 May 1962
20.10m (65' 11 ½")	Dallas Long (USA)	Los Angeles, USA	4 Apr 1964
20.20m (66' 3 ¼")	Dallas Long (USA)	Los Angeles, USA	29 May 1964
20.68m (67' 10")	Dallas Long (USA)	Los Angeles, USA	25 Jul 1964
21.52m (70' 7 ¼")	Randy Matson (USA)	College Station, USA	8 May 1965
21.78m (71' 5 ½")	Randy Matson (USA)	College Station, USA	22 Apr 1967
21.82m (71' 7")	Allan Feuerbach (USA)	San Jose, USA	5 May 1973
21.85m (71' 8 ½")	Terry Albritton (USA)	Honolulu, USA	21 Feb 1976
22.00m (72' 2 ¼")	Aleksandr Baryshnikov (USSR)	Paris, France	10 Jul 1976
22.15m (72' 8")	Udo Beyer (GDR)	Gothenburg, Sweden	6 Jul 1978
22.22m (72' 10 ¾")	Udo Beyer (GDR)	Los Angeles, USA	25 Jun 1983
22.62m (74' 2 ½")	Ulf Timmermann (GDR)	Berlin, East Germany	22 Sep 1985
22.64m (74' 3 ½")	Udo Beyer (GDR)	Berlin, East Germany	20 Aug 1986
22.72m (74' 6 ½")	Alessandro Andrei (ITA)	Viareggio, Italy	12 Aug 1987
22.84m (74' 11 ¼")	Alessandro Andrei (ITA)	Viareggio, Italy	12 Aug 1987
22.91m (75' 2")	Alessandro Andrei (ITA)	Viareggio, Italy	12 Aug 1987
23.06m (75' 8")	Ulf Timmermann (GDR)	Khania, Crete	22 May 1988
23.12m (75' 10 ¼")	Randy Barnes (USA)	Los Angeles, USA	20 May 1990

Ralph Rose   (United States, 1885-1913)

15.54m (51' 0")   **San Francisco, USA**   **21 Aug 1909**

Ralph Rose was a giant of a man for his day, 6' 6" tall (198 centimeters) and weighing in at 253 pounds (115 kilograms). He was the first official holder of the shot put world record. Born in California, he attended the University of Michigan and studied law in Chicago. He excelled at a number of the throwing events and represented the United States at three Olympics:

1904 St. Louis: Shot put (first); discus (second); hammer (third)
1908 London: Shot put (first)
1912 Stockholm: Shot put (second); hammer (ninth); two-handed shot put (first)

He was the first U.S. flag bearer who refused to dip the U.S. flag at the 1908 Olympic opening ceremonies, unlike those of all other countries. This tradition survives.

Ralph Rose, United States, Olympic shot put champion, 1904 and 1908.

Emil Hirschfeld   (Germany, 1903–1968)

| 15.79m (51' 9 ¾") | Breslau, Germany | 6 May 1928 |
| 16.04m (52' 7 ½") | Bochum, Germany | 26 Aug 1928 |

John Kuck, United States (shot put), *left*, with Emil Hirschfeld, Germany (shot put), at the 1928 Amsterdam Olympics. Kuck won gold, Hirschfeld bronze.

In May 1928 Emil Hirschfeld broke Ralph Rose's 19-year-old record in a meet between Southeast Germany and East Prussia. He added 25 centimeters (9 ¾") to Rose's record.

At the Amsterdam Olympics eight weeks later, he threw 15.72 meters (51' 7") but had to be content with a bronze medal as John Kuck (USA) threw 15.87 meters (52' 0 ¾"), a new world record.

A month after the Games Hirschfeld regained the record with 16.04 meters (52' 7 ½"), the first throw over 16 meters. Hirschfeld threw exactly 16 meters on his first throw and then moved on to 16.04 meters on his third attempt.

He finished fourth at the 1932 Los Angeles Olympics with 15.56 meters (51' 0 ½"). He was German shot put champion in 1928, 1929, 1931, and 1932 and was also the German discus champion in 1929 and 1932.

John Kuck   (United States, 1905–1986)

| 15.87m (52' 0 ¾") | Amsterdam, Netherlands | 29 Jul 1928 |

John Kuck was a graduate of Emporia State University in Kansas. He won the NCAA shot put title in 1926 and the AAU title in 1927. He was also highly competent at the javelin, winning the 1926 AAU title and setting an American record in the event later in the year.

At the 1928 Olympics it was his countryman Herman Brix who led the field with 15.75 meters (51' 8"), ahead of world record holder Emil Hirschfeld with 15.72 meters (51' 7") and Kuck with 15.03 meters (49' 3 ¾"). However, Kuck improved to 15.87 meters (52' 0 ¾"), a new world record. Brix took the silver medal.

Frantisek Douda   (Czechoslovakia, 1908–1990)

| 16.04m (52' 7 ½") | Brno, Czechoslovakia | 4 Oct 1931 |
| 16.20m (53' 1 ¾") | Prague, Czechoslovakia | 24 Sep 1932 |

Frantisek Douda equaled Hirschfeld's three-year-old record in a national meet in Brno, Czechoslovakia in 1931.

Douda competed at the Los Angeles Olympics in August 1932 but there was a strong U.S. challenge. Leo Sexton (USA) won with 16.00 meters (52' 6"), with another U.S. athlete, Harlow Rothert, second with 15.67 meters (51' 5"). Douda finished third with 15.61 meters (51' 2 ½"). Heljasz finished ninth.

Sexton raised the world record to 16.16 meters (53' 0 ½") one month after the Games. Douda responded four weeks later with another world record. In a match between Czechoslovakia and Poland, Douda threw 16.20 meters (53' 1 ¾").

This was the highlight of his career. He was third at the 1934 European Championships and seventh at the 1936 Berlin Olympics.

Zygmunt Heljasz   (Poland, 1908–1963)

16.05m (52' 8")   **Poznan, Poland**   **29 Jun 1932**

Zygmunt Heljasz added one centimeter to the record at a meet between the cities of Poznan, Poland, and Vienna in June 1932. That throw was to be the highlight of Heljasz's career.

At the Olympics five weeks later he performed below his best and finished ninth with 14.49 meters (47' 6 ½"). At the 1934 European Championships he finished seventh with 14.78 meters (48' 6").

Leo Sexton   (United States, 1909–1968)

16.16m (53' 0 ½")   **Freeport, USA**   **27 Aug 1932**

There were three world record holders in the shot put in 1932: Heljasz, Douda, and Sexton. Of the three, it was Leo Sexton who won the Olympic gold medal, with a new Olympic record.

A big man, weighing 240 pounds (109 kilograms) and 6' 4" (193 centimeters) tall, he was a student at Georgetown University. In 1932 he was throwing around 52 feet (15.8 meters) all season and won the AAU title. At the Olympics in Los Angeles he led after three rounds and threw 16.00 meters (52' 6") on his sixth throw to win by 33 centimeters.

A month after the Olympics, at the Nassau Fireman's Games, Sexton threw a world record of 16.16 meters (53' 0 ½"). He went on to become an insurance broker, later becoming vice president of an insurance corporation in Oklahoma.

John Lyman   (United States, 1912–1989)

16.48m (54' 1")   **Palo Alto, USA**   **21 Apr 1934**

John Lyman was a student at Stanford University in California. He set his world record in a Stanford University vs. University of Southern California meet at Stanford in 1934. On his first throw, he achieved 54' 1" (16.48 meters), the first throw over 54 feet.

He is one of the few U.S. shot put champions never to win an NCAA or AAU title. He was rapidly overtaken by the next champion, Jack Torrance, who six days later threw over 55 feet.

Two months later at the 1934 AAU titles Lyman improved to 54' 9 ½" (16.70 meters), but Torrance threw another record, 55' 5"

John Lyman, United States (shot put).

(16.89 meters). The two U.S. athletes toured Europe later that season, but by then Torrance was the greater star and achieved a third world record in Oslo.

Lyman earned a master's degree in chemistry and missed the Berlin Olympics because of his studies.

Jack Torrance   (United States, 1912–1970)

16.80m (55' 1 ½")	Des Moines, USA	27 Apr 1934
16.89m (55' 5")	Milwaukee, USA	30 Jun 1934
17.40m (57' 1")	Oslo, Norway	5 Aug 1934

Jack Torrance was the heaviest man to hold the shot put world record, weighing 304 pounds (138 kilograms); he was nicknamed "Elephant Baby." As a student at Louisiana State University, Torrance achieved his first world record six days after John Lyman first broke 54 feet. He surpassed the 55-foot barrier by 1 ½" with his victory in the Drake Relays in Des Moines, Iowa. Two months later he won the AAU title with a further 9-centimeter (3 ½") improvement to the record.

On a tour to Europe Torrance broke through the 56- and 57-foot barriers in one heave in Oslo. With the same throw he also broke through the 17-meter barrier with 17.40 meters (57' 1"). The crowd literally screamed with delight, and Torrance had to run a lap of honor.

Torrance never reached the heights of his 1934 season again, although he was AAU champion from 1933 to 1935. At the 1936 Olympics he finished fifth with a throw of 15.38 meters (50' 5 ½").

Jack Torrance, United States (shot put).

Charles Fonville   (United States, 1927–1994)

17.68m (58' 0 ¼")	Lawrence, USA	17 Apr 1948

Jack Torrance's record lasted 14 years and was finally broken by Charles Fonville, the only black athlete to hold the world record in the shot put. He was a student at the University of Michigan and won the NCAA title in 1947 and 1948. He was 6' 2" tall (188 centimeters) and weighed 194 pounds (88 kilograms), relatively lightweight by the standards of some modern shot put champions. A competent sprinter, he had been improving his shot put performances all through the 1947 season and finally broke the record early in 1948 at the Kansas Relays.

Unfortunately, he aggravated a rib injury prior to the U.S. Olympic trials and finished fourth, missing selection for the U.S. team. The United States managed to take the first three places at the London Olympics anyway. After his athletic days Fonville became a tax lawyer in Detroit.

Jim Fuchs   (United States, b. 1927)

17.79m (58' 4 ½")	Oslo, Norway	28 Jul 1949
17.82m (58' 5 ½")	Los Angeles, USA	29 Apr 1950
17.90m (58' 8 ¾")	Visby, Sweden	20 Aug 1950
17.95m (58' 10 ¾)	Eskilstuna, Sweden	22 Aug 1950

Jim Fuchs, United States (shot put).

Jim Fuchs of Yale University finished third at the 1948 U.S. Olympic trials and finished third at the Olympics as well. From then on, he rapidly became the world's leading shot putter. He won the NCAA and AAU titles in 1949 and 1950. In those years he also set four world records and, strangely for an American, set most of them abroad.

He set the first of his world records in Oslo at the Bislett Games, adding 11 centimeters (4 ¼") to the record on his second throw. He began a wild dance of joy when the record was confirmed beyond doubt. Then followed a lap of honor.

In 1950 he raised the record three more times and went on a winning streak of 88 competitions without loss. However, this came to a halt in 1951, when he was beaten by rising star Parry O'Brien, who was to begin an even longer domination of the world shot putting scene.

Accordingly, at his second Olympics Fuchs had to be content with another bronze medal as O'Brien and another U.S. athlete, Darrow Hooper, took the first two places.

Parry O'Brien   (United States, b. 1932)

18.00m (59' 0 ¾")	Fresno, USA	9 May 1953
18.04m (59' 2 ¾")	Compton, USA	5 Jun 1953
18.42m (60' 5 ¼")	Los Angeles, USA	8 May 1954
18.43m (60' 5 ¾")	Los Angeles, USA	21 May 1954
18.54m (60' 10")	Los Angeles, USA	11 Jun 1954
18.62m (61' 1")	Salt Lake City, USA	5 May 1956
18.69m (61' 4")	Los Angeles, USA	15 Jun 1956
19.06m (62' 6 ¼")	Eugene, USA	3 Sep 1956
19.25m (63' 2")	Los Angeles, USA	1 Nov 1956
19.30m (63' 4")	Albuquerque, USA	1 Aug 1959

Parry O'Brien revolutionized the shot put with a new technique. Previously, all athletes had shuffled across the ring, facing the direction in which they were going to throw the shot. During a trip to Europe in 1951 O'Brien was injured and had to modify his technique. He found it easier to throw by starting with his back initially to the direction in which he had to throw and rotating 180 degrees before completing his throw. This new rotational technique allowed him to completely dominate the event for the rest of the decade. He won two Olympic gold medals (1952 and 1956), two Pan-American titles (1955 and 1959), and set ten world records.

He first came to notice when he won the 1951 AAU title, a victory that ended Jim Fuchs's winning streak of 88 consecutive victories. O'Brien went on to his own winning streak of 116 victories. By the end of the 1950s, a new generation of U.S. throwers had finally caught up with him. He made the U.S. team for the 1960 Olympics and led for the first four rounds. However, Bill Nieder took over in the fifth round with 19.68 meters (64' 6 ½"). O'Brien took the silver medal with 19.11 meters (62' 8 ½").

O'Brien went to the 1964 Olympics and threw the furthest of all his Olympic throws: 19.20 meters (63' 0"). But this secured him only fourth place. He kept training and set the longest throw of his career in 1966, at the age of 34, when he threw 19.70 meters (64' 7 ½").

Parry O'Brien, United States (shot put), double Olympic champion and 10-time world record holder, whose technique revolutionized the shot put.

Dallas Long   (United States, b. 1940)

19.25m (63' 2")	Santa Barbara, USA	28 Mar 1959
19.38m (63' 7")	Los Angeles, USA	5 Mar 1960
20.08m (65' 10 ½")	Los Angeles, USA	18 May 1962
20.10m (65' 11 ½")	Los Angeles, USA	4 Apr 1964
20.20m (66' 3 ¼")	Los Angeles, USA	29 May 1964
20.68m (67' 10")	Los Angeles, USA	25 Jul 1964

Dallas Long was one of two athletes who finally matched Parry O'Brien; the other was Bill Nieder. Long was born in Arkansas and became a student at the University of Southern California. In 1959, at age 18, he burst into prominence by equaling the 9th of Parry O'Brien's 10 world records. O'Brien competed that day and finished third. An era was coming to an end.

In those days, U.S. shot putters ruled the world. O'Brien set ten world records, Long six, and Nieder three. All Long's world records were set in California.

Dallas Long, United States (shot put), 1964 Olympic champion.

At the 1960 Rome Olympics it was Nieder first, O'Brien second, and Long third. Nieder then retired, and four years later Long was favored to be Olympic champion. However, in the Tokyo final he was almost upstaged by 19-year-old Randy Matson. Long led with 19.61 meters (64' 4"), but Matson threw 19.88 meters (65' 2 ¾") in the third round and 20.20 meters (66' 3 ¼") in the fourth. Long kept his nerve and then threw 20.33 meters (66' 8 ½"), which was to remain the winning throw.

Long retired after these Olympics and is a practicing medical doctor in Arizona and Southern California.

Bill Nieder   (United States, b. 1933)

19.45m (63' 10")	Palo Alto, USA	19 Mar 1960
19.99m (65' 7")	Austin, USA	2 Apr 1960
20.06m (65' 10")	Walnut, USA	12 Aug 1960

Bill Nieder had been a promising football player at school, but a knee injury restricted his potential in that sport. As a shot putter, he was for a long time in the shadow of Parry O'Brien. He won the AAU title once (1957); O'Brien won it eight times. At the 1956 Melbourne Olympics it was O'Brien first (18.57 meters, 60' 11 ¼") and Nieder second (18.18 meters, 59' 7 ¾").

A graduate of the University of Kansas, Nieder persevered, and in March 1960 he set his first world record. However, at the 1960 U.S. Olympic trials Nieder hurt his wrist and finished only fourth. That left him out of the team. However, one of those selected, Dave Davis, later suffered an injury of his own and graciously withdrew from the team, so that Nieder could have his spot.

Nieder seized the opportunity by winning the gold medal in Rome. It wasn't all that easy—he took the lead only in the fifth round. Nieder won with 19.68 meters (64' 6 ¾"), O'Brien was second with 19.11 meters (62' 8 ½"), and Long third with 19.01 meters (62' 4 ½").

His third world record (20.06 meters) in August 1960 made him the first athlete to surpass the 20-meter barrier. Nieder retired after his Olympic victory and had ambitions to become a professional boxer. In his first fight, he was knocked out in the first round. He then tried to regain his amateur status, but this was denied him. Subsequently, he worked for Tartan, a division of the 3M company, which later developed synthetic athletic tracks.

Randy Matson   (United States, b. 1945)

21.52m (70' 7 ¼")	College Station, USA	8 May 1965
21.78m (71' 5 ½")	College Station, USA	22 Apr 1967

Randy Matson was born in Kilgore, Texas, and showed extraordinary athletic talent as a school-age shot putter. He was overwhelmed with scholarship offers from a host of U.S.

universities and chose to go to Texas Agricultural and Mechanical University. He grew into a 265-pound (120-kilogram), 6' 6" (200-centimeter) giant and at age 19 made the 1964 U.S. Olympic team.

He nearly won at the Olympics. He took the lead from favorite Dallas Long and led until the fourth round, when Long snatched the lead back: Long 20.33 meters (66' 8 ½"), Matson 20.20 meters (66' 3 ¼").

Matson's special day arrived in 1965, when he added almost three feet to the world record, to crash through the 70-foot barrier with 70' 7 ¼" (21.52 meters).

Matson added almost another foot to the record in 1967. At the 1968 Mexico City Olympics he won comfortably with 20.54 meters (67' 4 ¾"). He was also AAU champion six times.

Matson was also a highly competent discus thrower and in 1967 came within six centimeters of the world record. However, by 1972 a new generation of U.S. shot putters had arrived, and to general dismay, he finished fourth in the U.S. Olympic trials. He promptly retired but made a limited comeback when the professional athletic group ITA was formed. He has subsequently worked for his alma mater as director of the Association of Former Students.

Randy Matson, United States (shot put), 1968 Olympic champion and first man over 70 feet.

Allan Feuerbach   (United States, b. 1948)

21.82m (71' 7")   **San Jose, USA**   **5 May 1973**

Allan Feuerbach is the son of a veterinarian from Preston, Iowa, and was a student at Emporia State University, Kansas. His dedication to shot putting was a source of amusement to his friends. "Only" 6' 0 ¾" (185 centimeters) tall, at his peak he weighed 265 pounds (120 kilograms). He first defeated Randy Matson in 1971 and at the Munich Olympics came in fifth with 21.01 meters (68' 11 ¼").

The next year he had a great season, winning 38 out of 39 competitions, and added four centimeters (1 ½") to the world record. He had a series of memorable duels with Brian Oldfield, who later joined the short-lived professional circuit, a move that Feuerbach resisted.

Allan Feuerbach, United States (shot put).

At the Montreal Olympics, Feuerbach was the leading American but finished fourth. He kept performing until 1980 but retired after President Carter imposed a U.S. boycott of the Moscow Olympics.

Terry Albritton   (United States, b. 1955)

21.85m (71' 8 ½")   **Honolulu, USA**   **21 Feb 1976**

Terry Albritton set the only world record ever achieved in Honolulu. He won All-American football honors while a student at Newport Harbor, California. He was also a champion school shot putter and had scholarship offers from 150 colleges. He had one year at Stanford and then decided to withdraw "from the energy of the collegiate scene." He later moved to Hawaii but eventually returned to Stanford, where he studied communications and film-making.

In 1976 at Cooke Field in Honolulu he posted a new world record on his sixth and last throw. Two days later he suffered a major injury while doing a 525-pound reverse bench press; the weight came down on his chest, bruising a chest muscle. He still hoped to make the U.S. Olympic team but came in fourth at the U.S. trials. He was AAU champion in 1976 and 1977 and NCAA champion in 1977.

Terry Albritton, United States (shot put).

Aleksandr Baryshnikov   (Soviet Union, b. 1948)

22.00m (72' 2 ¼")   **Paris, France**   **10 Jul 1976**

Aleksandr Baryshnikov spent his childhood in the far east of the Soviet Union and became a physical education teacher in Khaborovsk. After moving to Leningrad, he introduced a new rotational style of throwing, not unlike the discus throw. However, at the 1972 Munich Olympics he did not get past the qualifying rounds. Four years later, just before the Olympics, Baryshnikov broke the world record in Paris, at a France vs. Soviet Union meet. He reached 22.00 meters.

Aleksandr Baryshnikov, Soviet Union (shot put), pioneer of the rotational method.

At the Olympic Games at Montreal he threw 21.32 meters (69' 11 ½") in the qualifying rounds, a new Olympic record. But in the final neither he nor anyone else could get near this figure. In a tight finish, Udo Beyer of East Germany won with 21.05 meters (69' 0 ¾"), Yevgeniy Mironov (USSR) won silver with 21.03 meters (69' 0"), and Baryshnikov won the bronze medal with 21.00 meters (68' 10 ¾").

Four years later in Moscow he came in second with 21.08 meters (69' 2"), behind fellow countryman Vladimir Kiselyov, who threw 21.35 meters (70' 0 ½").

Baryshnikov's rotational technique has been adopted by some athletes—such as Randy Barnes (USA), the current world record holder—but the majority stayed with the O'Brien method.

Udo Beyer   (East Germany, b. 1955)

22.15m (72' 8")	Gothenburg, Sweden	6 Jul 1978
22.22m (72' 10 ¾")	Los Angeles, USA	25 Jun 1983
22.64m (74' 3 ½")	Berlin, East Germany	20 Aug 1986

Udo Beyer, East Germany (shot put), surprise 1976 Olympic shot put champion.

Udo Beyer was a last-minute inclusion to the East German team for the 1976 Olympics in Montreal. At the Montreal Olympics the favorites were Baryshnikov (USSR) and Feuerbach (USA), both world record holders. Baryshnikov actually set an Olympic record of 21.32 meters (69' 11 ½") in the qualifying rounds. However, in the final Beyer unexpectedly took the lead in the fifth round with a throw of 21.05 meters (69' 0 ¾"), and suddenly he was the gold medalist.

Beyer went on to dominate the event for years to come. He won the 1978 European Championships and set the first of his three world records that year. In addition, he won 11 East German championships in a row (1977-87). He went to the 1980 Moscow Olympics as overwhelming favorite, having won 34 competitions in a row since 1978. Nonetheless, he was never in the lead and ended up with a bronze medal. What went wrong? A knee injury seemed to slow him down, and he underwent surgery later that year.

He kept competing for many years more and was European champion once again in 1982. He set his second world record the next year at a USA vs. East Germany match in Los Angeles. However, by this time a new East German star had arrived to threaten his supremacy: Ulf Timmermann. Both men missed the 1984 Olympics because of the Soviet boycott, but the following year Timmermann added a massive 40 centimeters (1' 3 ¾") to the world record with 22.62 meters (74' 2 ½"). Beyer responded in 1986 by adding two centimeters to Timmermann's throw. However, at the 1988 Seoul Olympics Beyer dropped to fourth with 21.40 meters (70' 2 ½"). The event was won by Timmermann with 22.47 meters (73' 8 ¾").

At the age of 36 Beyer took part in one more Olympics, at Barcelona in 1992, but did not get through to the final. His sister, Gisela, was fourth in the discus at the Moscow Olympics.

Ulf Timmermann   (East Germany, b. 1962)

22.62m (74' 2 ½")	**Berlin, East Germany**	**22 Sep 1985**
23.06m (75' 8")	**Khania, Crete**	**22 May 1988**

Ulf Timmermann, East Germany (shot put), 1988 Olympic shot put champion.

Ulf Timmermann came to international attention with a second place at the 1983 World Championships, while Beyer, the European champion, only finished fifth. Both Beyer and Timmermann missed the 1984 Olympics because of the communist boycott. The next year Timmermann threw a massive 40 centimeters (1' 3 ¾") beyond Beyer's 1983 record with 22.62 meters (74' 2 ½"). However, at the 1986 European Championships Timmermann came in second to the Swiss Werner Gunthor, and Beyer reclaimed his world record with 22.64 meters (74' 3 ½").

Just before the 1987 World Championships Timmermann developed mumps and finished fifth. So by the time the 1988 Olympics came around, he had been a top international athlete for five years but had never won a gold medal. The season started well for him when he set his second world record in Crete, 23.06 meters (75' 8").

In the 1988 Olympic final Timmermann led, but Randy Barnes (USA) hit the front on his very last throw. After Timmermann concentrated intensely, his final throw exceeded Barnes's by eight centimeters, 22.47 meters (73' 8 ¾") to 22.39 meters (73' 5 ½"). "Now I have gray hair," he concluded emotionally after his last-gasp victory.

Timmermann won the 1990 European Championships and was fifth at the 1992 Olympics.

Alessandro Andrei   (Italy, b. 1959)

22.72m (74' 6 ½")	**Viareggio, Italy**	**12 Aug 1987**
22.84m (74' 11 ¼")	**Viareggio, Italy**	**12 Aug 1987**
22.91m (75' 2")	**Viareggio, Italy**	**12 Aug 1987**

Alessandro Andrei is a policeman, born in Florence, who set 16 Italian shot put records between 1982 and 1985. He had been 10th at the 1982 European Championships, 7th at the 1983 World Championships, and then gold medalist at the 1984 Los Angeles Olympics. This last event was somewhat devalued by the absence of the boycotting East Germans, but he defeated the best America could produce at that time by throwing 21.26 meters (69' 9").

He set three world records in one day in 1987 in the central Italian city of Viareggio. At that evening meet he threw world records on his third, fourth, and fifth throws. These achievements aroused some skepticism but the throws were found to be authentic.

That was the high-water mark of his career. His next-best career performance was 74 centimeters (2' 5") less than his Viareggio throws. Later that season at the World Championships in Rome, despite the home crowd support, he finished second. At the 1988 Olympics Games he was 7th, and four years later in Barcelona he was 11th.

Alessandro Andrei, Italy (shot put), 1984 Olympic champion.

Randy Barnes　(United States, b. 1966)

23.12m (75' 10 ¼")　Los Angeles, USA　20 May 1990

Randy Barnes was born in West Virginia and attended Texas A and M University (the same school Randy Matson attended in the early 1960s), where he broke most of Matson's college records. At the 1988 Olympics he came very close to winning. Ulf Timmermann had led all through the final, with Barnes in fourth place. "I decided to get reckless," the American explained later, feeling that he had been afraid of fouling in the early throws. His final throw reached 22.39 meters (73' 5 ½"), and suddenly he was in the gold medal position. But Timmermann somehow responded and on his very last throw managed 22.47 meters (73' 8 ¾") to snatch victory.

Barnes is one of the few shot putters to prefer the rotational method. He proved his point when he set a new world record in 1990 in California. He added six centimeters (2 ¼") to Timmermann's world record. As an extra bonus, the promoters had offered $50,000 for a world record.

Randy Barnes, United States (shot put), 1996 Olympic shot put champion.

Later that season Barnes tested positive for drugs during a competition in Malmö, Sweden, and was given a two-year suspension from athletics. This occurred at the same time that 400m runner Butch Reynolds was also suspended for drug use. While Reynolds made a highly publicized series of appeals against his suspension, Barnes made a much more low-key appeal as the 1992 Olympics approached, seeking damages, but the case was dismissed.

After his suspension expired, Barnes was second at the World Championships in Stuttgart in 1993 and third at the same event in Gothenburg in 1995. Finally, in 1996, he had a fairy-tale win at the Atlanta Games. Barnes won on his last throw (21.62 meters, 70' 11 ¼"), a reversal of his experience at the Seoul Olympics.

Conclusions

The shot put world record has remained static for the last few years. Perhaps the world record will be improved in the near future and is merely going through a quiet phase. However, it will probably be impossible to judge to what extent anabolic steroids helped in the elevation of the world record over the last few decades.

Barnes threw 23.12 meters in 1990, and Ulf Timmermann 23.06 meters in 1988. No athlete has thrown farther than 22 meters since 1990 other than Barnes (22.40m).

Improvements or modifications in style to elevate the record remain possible, but little immediate change is likely.

Five All-Time Best: Men's Shot Put

Randy Barnes (USA)	23.12m (75' 10 ¼")	1990
Ulf Timmermann (GDR)	23.06m (75' 8")	1988
Alessandro Andrei (ITA)	22.91m (75' 2")	1987
Brian Oldfield (USA)	22.86m (75' 0")	1975
Werner Gunthor (SWI)	22.75m (74' 7 ¾")	1988
Prediction	*23.30m (76' 5 ½") 2015*	

Top Three: Men's Shot Put

GOLD MEDAL:	Parry O'Brien (USA)
SILVER MEDAL:	Randy Matson (USA)
BRONZE MEDAL:	Ulf Timmermann (GDR)

DISCUS

The discus is one of the classic events that can be traced back to the ancient Olympic Games. The famous statue *Discobolus* by Myron captures the athlete about to release the discus. The event was naturally included in the first modern Olympic Games in 1896 but caused much dismay to the Greeks when the event was won by a foreigner, Robert Garrett (USA).

The men's discus weighs two kilograms (4 pounds 7 ounces), and is thrown from a circle 2.50 meters (8' 2 ½") in diameter. The main characteristic of the event is the use of rotational force to release the implement. Minor variations in technique over the years have evolved, but the basics of the throw remain. What has altered massively is the distance thrown: An improvement of 55.7% has occurred since the first world record in 1912 (47.58 meters) to the current record set in 1986 (74.08 meters). This current record has been static, and no one has remotely approached it for a decade.

The first 70 years of the 20th century saw U.S. domination in the event. That domination has since slipped, mainly due to challenges by athletes from Eastern Europe. Overall, 26 athletes have set or equaled 42 world records. Seven of these athletes have also been Olympic champions: Houser, Consolini, Iness, Oerter, Danek, Wilkins, and Schult. However, no world record has ever been set at the Olympic Games.

Men's World Records for Discus

Record distance	Record holder	Location	Date
47.58m (156' 1")	James Duncan (USA)	New York, USA	27 May 1912
47.61m (156' 2")	Thomas Lieb (USA)	Chicago, USA	14 Sep 1924
47.89m (157' 1 ½")	Glenn Hartranft (USA)	San Francisco, USA	2 May 1925
48.20m (158' 2")	Clarence Houser (USA)	Palo Alto, USA	3 Apr 1926
49.90m (163' 8")	Eric Krenz (USA)	Palo Alto, USA	9 Mar 1929
51.03m (167' 5")	Eric Krenz (USA)	Palo Alto, USA	17 May 1930
51.73m (169' 9")	Paul Jessup (USA)	Pittsburgh, USA	23 Aug 1930
52.42m (172' 0")	Harald Andersson (SWE)	Oslo, Norway	25 Aug 1934
53.10m (174' 2")	Willi Schroder (GER)	Magdeburg, Germany	28 Apr 1935
53.26m (174' 9")	Archie Harris (USA)	Palo Alto, USA	20 Jun 1941
53.34m (175' 0")	Adolfo Consolini (ITA)	Milan, Italy	26 Oct 1941
54.23m (177' 11")	Adolfo Consolini (ITA)	Milan, Italy	14 Apr 1946
54.93m (180' 3")	Robert Fitch (USA)	Minneapolis, USA	8 Jun 1946
55.33m (181' 6")	Adolfo Consolini (ITA)	Milan, Italy	10 Oct 1948
56.46m (185' 3")	Fortune Gordien (USA)	Lisbon, Portugal	9 Jul 1949
56.97m (186' 11")	Fortune Gordien (USA)	Hameenlinna, Finland	14 Aug 1949
57.93m (190' 0")	Simeon Iness (USA)	Lincoln, USA	20 Jun 1953
58.10m (190' 7")	Fortune Gordien (USA)	Pasadena, USA	11 Jul 1953
59.28m (194' 6")	Fortune Gordien (USA)	Pasadena, USA	22 Aug 1953
59.91m (196' 6")	Edmund Piatkowski (POL)	Warsaw, Poland	14 Jun 1959
59.91m (196' 6")	Richard "Rink" Babka (USA)	Walnut, USA	12 Aug 1960
60.56m (198' 8")	Jay Silvester (USA)	Frankfurt am Main, West Germany	11 Aug 1961
60.72m (199' 2")	Jay Silvester (USA)	Brussels, Belgium	20 Aug 1961
61.10m (200' 5")	Al Oerter (USA)	Los Angeles, USA	18 May 1962
61.64m (202' 3")	Vladimir Trusenyev (USSR)	Leningrad, USSR	4 Jun 1962
62.45m (204' 10")	Al Oerter (USA)	Chicago, USA	1 Jul 1962
62.62m (205' 5")	Al Oerter (USA)	Walnut, USA	27 Apr 1963
62.94m (206' 6")	Al Oerter (USA)	Walnut, USA	25 Apr 1964
64.55m (211' 9")	Ludvik Danek (CZH)	Turnov, Czechoslovakia	2 Aug 1964
65.22m (213' 11")	Ludvik Danek (CZH)	Sokolov, Czechoslovakia	12 Oct 1965

66.54m (218' 4")	Jay Silvester (USA)	Modesto, USA	25 May 1968
68.40m (224' 5")	Jay Silvester (USA)	Reno, USA	18 Sep 1968
68.40m (224' 5")	Rickard Bruch (SWE)	Stockholm, Sweden	5 Jul 1972
68.48m (224' 8")	John van Reenen (S.AF)	Stellenbosch, South Africa	14 Mar 1975
69.08m (226' 8")	John Powell (USA)	Long Beach, USA	4 May 1975
69.18m (226' 11")	Mac Wilkins (USA)	Walnut, USA	24 Apr 1976
69.80m (229' 0")	Mac Wilkins (USA)	San Jose, USA	1 May 1976
70.24m (230' 5")	Mac Wilkins (USA)	San Jose, USA	1 May 1976
70.86m (232' 6")	Mac Wilkins (USA)	San Jose, USA	1 May 1976
71.16m (233' 5")	Wolfgang Schmidt (GDR)	Berlin, East Germany	9 Aug 1978
71.86m (235' 9")	Yuriy Dumchev (USSR)	Moscow, USSR	29 May 1983
74.08m (243' 0")	Jurgen Schult (GDR)	Neubrandenburg, East Germany	6 Jun 1986

James Duncan   (United States, 1887–?)

47.58m (156' 1")   **New York, USA**   **27 May 1912**

James Duncan, United States (discus), *center,* en route to the 1912 Stockholm Olympics.

James Duncan was the first official world record holder in the discus. He achieved this record at the Post Office Clerk's Association Games in 1912 at Travers Island, New York, in a two-hands competition. With his right hand he threw 47.58 meters (156' 1"). With his left hand he threw 29.75 meters (97' 8"). His right-handed throw was recognized as the first world record.

He was selected for the Olympics that year in Stockholm. Another athlete on the ship to Sweden was 1500m runner Abel Kiviat. Seventy years later Kiviat recalled that Duncan was "ugly looking" and started "calling me names." Hammer throwers Matt McGrath and Pat McDonald grabbed hold of Duncan and threatened to throw him through a porthole if he troubled Kiviat again. At the Olympics Duncan was third with a throw of 42.28 meters (138' 8").

Thomas Lieb   (United States, 1899–1962)

47.61m (156' 2")   **Chicago, USA**   **14 Sep 1924**

Thomas Lieb was a student at Notre Dame University in Indiana, a celebrated halfback on the football team, and an All-American tackle. He was a star tackle in Knute Rockne's Notre Dame teams in 1920, 1921, and 1922.

In the discus he was NCAA champion in 1922 and 1923 and AAU champion in 1923 and 1924. He threw his world record in 1924 at Stagg Field in Chicago.

At the 1924 Paris Olympics he finished third with 44.82 meters (147 feet). The event was won by Clarence Houser (USA). Lieb was generally regarded as a stronger thrower than Houser, but Lieb appeared to freeze in the heat of the Olympic competition. Later in life Houser, a dentist, looked after Lieb's teeth.

Lieb went on to become a mathematics teacher and football coach. He coached at Notre Dame, Loyola University, and the Universities of Florida and Alabama.

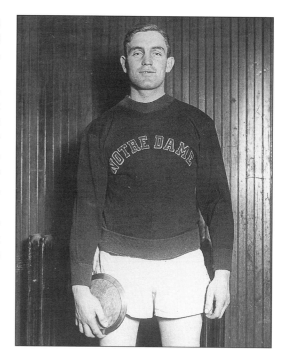

Thomas Lieb, United States (discus).

Glenn "Tiny" Hartranft   (United States, 1901–1970)

47.89m (157' 1 ½")   San Francisco, USA   2 May 1925

Glenn Hartranft was 6' 3" tall (190 centimeters), weighed 250 pounds (115 kilograms), and was nicknamed "Tiny." Hartranft was a student at Stanford University, California and was NCAA shot put champion in 1925. He was selected for both the shot put and the discus at the 1924 Paris Olympics. In the discus he was sixth, while in the shot put he won the silver medal. Hartranft apparently suffered from nerves during the Olympic finals and didn't do himself justice.

A year later he broke the world record at the Pacific AAU meet, throwing 47.89 meters (157' 1 ½").

Clarence "Bud" Houser   (United States, 1901–1994)

48.20m (158' 2")   Palo Alto, USA   3 Apr 1926

Clarence Houser was the dentist who achieved a rare Olympic double: winning both the discus and the shot put at the 1924 Games. Four years later he retained his discus title.

He was a schoolboy in 1921 when he won his first AAU shot put title. Weighing "only" 187 pounds (85 kilograms), he was not large by contemporary standards.

He was AAU shot put champion in 1921 and 1925 and AAU discus champion in 1925, 1926, and 1928. On the boat over to the Paris Olympics he met his future wife, Dawn, an art student en route to Paris where she planned to study. He was still a dental student at that time.

In the shot put he won with 14.99 meters (49' 2 ½"), while in the discus he set a new Olympic record of 46.14 meters (151' 4").

Houser set a world record in 1926, 48.20 meters (158' 2"), at a competition between the University of Southern California and Stanford University. He returned to the Olympics in 1928 to contest the discus only. In pouring rain he was given shelter by some German athletes, who felt that his name suggested a link with their country. Houser threw 47.32 meters (155' 3") to set another Olympic record.

He went on to a 50-year career as a dentist. His clients included film stars such as John Weissmuller, Douglas Fairbanks, Jr., and fellow athlete Tom Lieb.

Clarence Houser, United States (discus), the last man to win both the Olympic shot put and discus titles (1924).

Eric Krenz (United States, 1906–1931)

| 49.90m (163' 8") | Palo Alto, USA | 9 Mar 1929 |
| 51.03m (167' 5") | Palo Alto, USA | 17 May 1930 |

Eric Krenz was a student at Stanford University, 6' 0 ¾" tall (185 centimeters) and weighing 210 pounds (95 kilograms). He was the NCAA champion in 1928 and the AAU winner in 1927 and 1929.

He attended the 1928 Amsterdam Olympics, not as a discus thrower, but as a shot putter. He finished fourth. As a discus thrower, he was the first athlete to break the 50-meter barrier.

His first world record was at Stanford in 1929, where he threw 49.90 meters (163' 8"). He improved on that record twice at one meet in 1930 on his fourth (49.94 m) and fifth (51.03m) throws. However, the lesser throw was never submitted as a world record.

He worked briefly for the accounting firm Price Waterhouse in San Francisco. Tragically, he was drowned in 1931, at age 25, when trying to save the life of a child at Lake Tahoe, a resort on the California-Nevada border.

Paul Jessup (United States, 1907–1992)

| 51.73m (169' 9") | Pittsburgh, USA | 23 Aug 1930 |

Paul Jessup was a very tall athlete (6' 9", 206 centimeters) who was a student at the University of Washington. His first love was basketball, but he threw the discus as a secondary interest and was the 1930 and 1931 AAU champion in the event. He set his world record at the 1930 AAU championships in Pittsburgh, adding over two feet to the record with 51.73 meters (169' 9").

Jessup traveled to the Los Angeles Olympics as one of the favorites but finished eighth with 45.24 meters (148' 5").

He was a top basketball player in his time and believed in the "knock 'em down" school of play. "Basketball was a lot rougher in those days," he later recalled.

He graduated as a lawyer and accountant and later pursued a career in mining in Idaho.

Harald Andersson   (Sweden, 1907–1985)

52.42m (172' 0")   **Oslo, Norway**   **25 Aug 1934**

Harald Andersson, Sweden (discus).

Harald Andersson was the first non-U.S. athlete to hold the world discus record. He had set a Swedish discus record in 1932, and by 1934 he had improved it four times. The last record took place just before he competed at the Bislett Stadium in Oslo at a Norway vs. Sweden match.

On this occasion, his first throw exceeded 50 meters. On his second, he broke the existing world record with 52.23 meters. On his fifth effort, he went even further, recording 52.42 meters (172' 0"), which triggered storms of applause. (The second throw was never submitted as a world record.)

Andersson went on to be the winner of the discus in the inaugural European Championships in Turin later that season with 50.38 meters (165' 3"). In 1936 at the Berlin Olympics he was hampered by an injury to his right hand and failed to qualify for the final.

Willi Schroder   (Germany, b. 1912)

53.10m (174' 2")   **Magdeburg, Germany**   **28 Apr 1935**

Willi Schroder of Germany did not have a high profile when he suddenly threw a world record in a minor meet in Magdeburg in 1935. His throw of 53.10 meters (174' 2") was achieved at 11 A.M. in a qualification meet for a three-city competition. His technique involved great speed, so much so that he often ended up outside the ring and fouled the attempt.

As the 1936 Olympics were to be held in Berlin, he naturally had hopes of winning a gold medal in front of his own people, but this hope was not to be fulfilled. He finished fifth with 47.92 meters (157' 3"). The event was won by Ken Carpenter (USA) with a throw of 50.48 meters (165' 7").

Schroder had a good season in 1938. He won the European Championship with 49.38 meters (163' 0") and the United States vs. Germany competition. He was also German champion in 1936 and 1937.

Archie Harris   (United States, 1918–1965)

53.26m (174' 9")   **Palo Alto, USA**   **20 Jun 1941**

Archie Harris returned the discus world record to the United States in 1941. A student at Indiana University, he achieved a world record throw of 53.26 meters (174' 9") at the NCAA championships at Stanford Universtiy.

He was the only black athlete to hold the world discus record and was NCAA champion in 1940 and 1941 and AAU champion in 1941. Because of World War II, he missed out on the Olympics.

Archie Harris, United States (discus).

Adolfo Consolini   (Italy, 1917–1969)

53.34m (175' 0")	**Milan, Italy**	**26 Oct 1941**
54.23m (177' 11")	**Milan, Italy**	**14 Apr 1946**
55.33m (181' 6")	**Milan, Italy**	**10 Oct 1948**

Adolfo Consolini achieved every major honor possible: world record holder (three times), Olympic champion, European Championships winner (1946, 1950, and 1954), and Italian champion (15 times). Originally a farmhand in Costermano in the Po Valley, near Verona, he was discovered by the coach of the Italian track team at a regional meet. His career lasted over 20 years. He was fifth in the 1938 European Championships and sixth in the same event in 1958. All his world records were set in Milan.

Despite his world records, he was perhaps underestimated by the Americans at the 1948 London Olympics. Consolini won easily with 52.78 meters (173' 2"), with his

countryman Giuseppe Tosi second. Tosi also finished second to Consolini during the latter's three European Championships victories. Consolini's Olympic record was first in 1948, second in 1952, sixth in 1956, and 17th in 1960. At the Rome Games he took the Olympic oath on behalf of the athletes. A gentle giant, he died before his time, at the age of 52.

Adolfo Consolini, Italy (discus), 1948 Olympic discus champion.

Robert Fitch (United States, b. 1919)

54.93m (180' 3")	Minneapolis, USA	8 Jun 1946

Robert Fitch was a graduate of the University of Minnesota and was both NCAA and AAU champion in 1942. After a break, he took up the sport again in 1946 under coach Jim Kelly. Once again Fitch was AAU champion and broke the second of Consolini's world records with 54.93 meters (180' 3") in June.

Fitch went on a European tour in 1947 and beat Consolini at an international meet in Prague. Then he retired at the age of 28 and did not compete at the 1948 Olympics.

Fortune Gordien (United States, 1922–1990)

56.46m (185' 3")	Lisbon, Portugal	9 Jul 1949
56.97m (186' 11")	Hameenlinna, Finland	14 Aug 1949
58.10m (190' 7")	Pasadena, USA	11 Jul 1953
59.28m (194' 6")	Pasadena, USA	22 Aug 1953

Fortune Gordien was another graduate of the University of Minnesota. He and Robert Fitch shared the same coach, Jim Kelly. Gordien went to the 1948 Olympics with the longest throw of the year. But he had to be content with the bronze medal, behind the two

Italians, Consolini and Tosi. The results were Consolini 52.78 meters (173' 2"), Tosi 51.78 meters (169' 10 ½"), and Gordien 50.76 meters (166' 6 ½").

He improved further in 1949 and set the first of four world records. In addition, he was AAU champion six times (1947-50, 1953-54) and NCAA champion for the University of Minnesota from 1946 to 1948.

But "fortune" deserted Gordien in the Olympics. His record there was third in 1948, fourth in 1952, and second in 1956. He became a cattle rancher in Oregon and died of cancer in 1990.

Fortune Gordien, United States (discus).

Simeon Iness   (United States, 1930-1996)

57.93m (190' 0")   **Lincoln, USA**   **20 Jun 1953**

Simeon Iness went to the same high school as decathlon star Robert Matthias and was the discus star. At age 18, he came in sixth at the 1948 U.S. Olympic trials. Four years later he won the U.S. trials and went on to win the gold medal at the 1952 Olympics. He threw 55.02 meters (180' 6") to comfortably beat defending champion Consolini (53.78 meters, 176' 5").

Iness won the NCAA title for the University of Southern California in 1952 and 1953. His world record came at the 1953 titles, when he became the first man to reach 190 feet. He competed in some discomfort, having lost several teeth a few days earlier when he was struck by a flying discus.

After his world record he retired, at the age of 23. In his short career, he won an Olympic gold medal, two NCAA titles, and set Olympic and world records.

Edmund Piatkowski   (Poland, b. 1936)

59.91m (196' 6")   **Warsaw, Poland**   **14 Jun 1959**

Edmund Piatkowski was Poland's one and only world record holder in the discus and was rather small for a discus thrower at 182 centimeters (5' 11 ½") and 90 kilograms (198 pounds).

He had been European champion in 1958 with 53.92 meters (176' 11"). At subsequent championships he was fourth in 1962, fourth in 1966, and 12th in 1969.

Piatkowski set his world record in the 1959 Kusocinski Memorial meet in Warsaw, throwing 59.91 meters. He had a mixed Olympic record: fifth in 1960, seventh in 1964, and seventh in 1968.

Richard "Rink" Babka   (United States, b. 1936)

59.91m (196' 6")   **Walnut, USA**   **12 Aug 1960**

Rink Babka was born in Cheyenne, Wyoming, and studied engineering at the University of Southern California. He was the 1958 AAU champion and shared the 1958 NCAA title with Al Oerter. Rink Babka achieved his world record in one of the pre-Olympic trials in 1960. At the Mt. San Antonio Stadium in Walnut, California, he equaled Piatkowski's record with 59.91 meters.

Babka went to the Rome Olympics as one of the favorites and took the lead with his first throw, 58.02 meters (190' 4"). Babka actually offered a tip to Oerter during the competition about raising his left arm as he spun. Oerter did so and, on his fifth throw, took the lead with 59.18 meters (194' 2"). Babka could not improve further and had to be content with a silver medal.

He went on to a career as a sales engineer for Control Data Corporation.

Rink Babka, United States (discus).

Jay Silvester   (United States, b. 1937)

60.56m (198' 8")	**Frankfurt am Main, West Germany**	**11 Aug 1961**
60.72m (199' 2")	**Brussels, Belgium**	**20 Aug 1961**
66.54m (218' 4")	**Modesto, USA**	**25 May 1968**
68.40m (224' 5")	**Reno, USA**	**18 Sep 1968**

Jay Silvester set four world records, but his career was overshadowed by the Olympic success of Al Oerter. He was born in Utah of the Mormon faith. He set two world records in 1961 and two more seven years later. In 1961 he became the first man to throw over 60 meters with his first world record in Frankfurt am Main, West Germany. He claimed that he threw five percent better in Europe than in the United States. However, his last two world records were set in America.

But throughout these years he couldn't quite pull off an Olympic victory. In 1960 he was fourth in the U.S. Olympic trials and didn't make the U.S. team. His record at subsequent Olympics was fourth in 1964, fifth in 1968, and second in 1972.

In 1968 he was a heavy favorite for the gold medal and set an Olympic record in the qualifying rounds. However, the final was delayed an hour because of rain, and this seemed to affect Silvester's performance. Oerter threw a personal best in round 3 to take the lead. Silvester then threw three fouls in a row to finish out of the medals in fifth place.

By the 1972 Olympics, Oerter had retired. Silvester's main opponent, Ludvik Danek of Czechoslovakia, snatched victory on his last throw with 64.40 meters (211' 3").

Jay Silvester has since spent 20 years as a professor of physical education at Brigham Young University in Utah.

Jay Silvester, United States (discus), four-time world record holder.

Al Oerter   (United States, b. 1936)

61.10m (200' 5")	Los Angeles, USA	18 May 1962
62.45m (204' 10")	Chicago, USA	1 Jul 1962
62.62m (205' 5")	Walnut, USA	27 Apr 1963
62.94m (206' 6")	Walnut, USA	25 Apr 1964

Al Oerter, United States (discus), four-time Olympic champion and first man over 200 feet.

Al Oerter was born in New York to a German father and a Czechoslovakian mother and is best known for winning four consecutive Olympic gold medals. In addition, he set the world record four times and was the first man to throw over 200 feet.

At the age of 20, he went to the 1956 Olympics, and his first throw was a personal best (56.36 meters, 184' 11"). He did not improve on that throw, but no one came anywhere near it.

In Rome in 1960 Rink Babka led until the fifth round. Then Oerter managed another personal best, 59.18 meters (194' 2"), to win.

In 1964 in Tokyo he competed with a neck injury and torn cartilage in his lower ribs and wore a neck brace. Czechoslovakia's Ludvik Danek was leading for most of the final. But in the fifth round Oerter exploded with a new Olympic record, 61.00 meters (200' 1").

At the 1968 Olympics the lead was held by Lothar Milde of East Germany for most of the final. Once again, on his fifth throw Oerter threw a personal best, 64.78 meters (212' 6").

Oerter's world records came somewhat late in his career. Six years after his first Olympic victory he threw 61.10 meters (200' 5") at the Los Angeles Coliseum, the first throw over 200 feet. Other honors included six AAU wins between 1959 and 1966.

Oerter retired after his 1968 win but attempted a comeback at the age of 43 for the 1980 Moscow Olympics; he was fourth in the U.S. trials. In that year he managed to achieve his lifetime best of 69.46 meters (227' 10 ¾"). A computer specialist for the Grumman Aircraft Corporation for 26 years, he later worked for Reebok.

Vladimir Trusenyev   (Soviet Union, b. 1931)

61.64m (202' 3")   **Leningrad, USSR**   **4 Jun 1962**

Vladimir Trusenyev took the record from Al Oerter 17 days after the American had broken the 200-foot barrier. Trusenyev achieved 61.64 meters (202' 3") at a meet in Leningrad in 1962. However, Oerter took the record back 27 days later.

Trusenyev had moderate results at the Olympics: 15th in Rome in 1960 and eighth in Tokyo in 1964. In the European Championships he was third in 1958 but finally won in 1962, throwing 57.10 meters (187' 4"). He won the Soviet national championships in 1962 and 1964-1966.

Ludvik Danek   (Czechoslovakia, b. 1937)

64.55m (211' 9")   **Turnov, Czechoslovakia**   **2 Aug 1964**
65.22m (213' 11")   **Sokolov, Czechoslovakia**   **12 Oct 1965**

Ludvik Danek's career ran from 1955 to 1976, and he won 13 Czechoslovakian titles.

His longevity is indicated by his record in the European Championships: ninth in 1962, fifth in 1966, fourth in 1969, first in 1971, and second in 1974; in 1978 he failed to qualify for the final. In the mid-1960s he broke the world record twice at meets in Czechoslovakia, adding 2.28 meters altogether to the record.

At the Olympics he finally won a gold medal after Oerter's retirement. His Olympic record was second in 1964, third in 1968, first in 1972, and ninth in 1976. In the 1964 Olympics he led until the fifth round, when Oerter overtook him to win. In Munich in 1972, at age 35, he won on his very last throw, beating Jay Silvester (USA) for the gold medal, 64.40 meters (211' 3") to 63.50 meters (208' 4").

Ludvik Danek, Czechoslovakia (discus), 1972 Olympic champion.

Rickard Bruch   (Sweden, b. 1946)

68.40m (224' 5")   **Stockholm, Sweden**   **5 Jul 1972**

Rickard Bruch was a colorful, zany figure, known for his high-strung behavior during athletic meets. This included punching officials during arguments, wearing a black bowler hat or kimono onto the athletic field, giving out a Tarzan roar, running down athletes on the track, and drinking two gallons of milk a day. Often long-haired and long-bearded, the nervous energy between Bruch and the crowd was such that at times they hooted and whistled him.

Rickard Bruch, Sweden (discus).

His world record came in an international meet in his hometown of Stockholm, where he threw 68.40 meters (224' 5"). Second was Ludvik Danek with 65.30 meters (214' 3"). But two months later, at the Munich Olympics, it was Danek who triumphed with a throw of 64.40 meters (211' 3"), exactly one meter more than Bruch, who came in third. At the 1968 Olympics Bruch came in eighth. His record at the European Championships was second in 1969, ninth in 1971, and third in 1974.

Bruch showed great courage in literally risking life and limb with plans to help discus champion Wolfgang Schmidt escape East Germany. However, Bruch's escape plans were already known to the Stasi, the East German secret police, and were not successful.

John van Reenen   (South Africa, b. 1947)

68.48m (224' 8")   **Stellenbosch, South Africa**   **14 Mar 1975**

John van Reenen, South Africa (discus).

John van Reenen was the last South African to set a world record before the IAAF banned South Africa from the sport because of its apartheid policies. South African athletes were excluded from the Olympics between 1964 and 1988 and banned from international competition from 1976 to 1990. South Africans could compete only against themselves or move to another country and change their nationality, as did Marcello Fiasconaro (Italy), Sydney Maree (USA), and Zola Budd (Great Britain). Van Reenen chose not to do that.

After a year in the Air Force van Reenen obtained a scholarship to Washington State University and was NCAA champion between 1968 and 1970. His world record took place in 1975 at the invitational South African University Championships, and he added eight centimeters (three inches) to the record.

To supplement his income during his American years, he once worked as a bouncer at Papa Joe's Rock Emporium in Redondo Beach, California. A talented artist, he has been involved professionally in the illustration of several children's books. Despite the restrictions on his athletic career, he once wrote, "Track and field is like classical music—it will never die."

John Powell   (United States, b. 1947)

69.08m (226' 8")   **Long Beach, USA**   **4 May 1975**

John Powell, United States (discus).

John Powell was a police officer by profession in San Jose, California. He and Mac Wilkins were the two premier discus champions in the United States for more than a decade. Powell won seven AAU titles, and Wilkins won eight. Powell's world record came at the Long Beach Invitational meet in California in 1975, where he added 60 centimeters (two feet) to the record on his fourth throw.

At the Olympics he was fourth in 1972, third in 1976, and missed the 1980 Games because of the U.S. boycott. At the 1984 Olympics both Wilkins and Powell were upstaged by unknown West German Rolf Danneberg. The results were Danneberg 66.60 meters (218' 6"), Wilkins 66.30 meters (217' 6"), Powell 65.46 meters (214' 9").

Powell kept competing until he was 40 and was second at the 1987 World Championships in Rome. That year he threw his career best of 72.10 meters (236' 6").

His career then finished on a controversial note. He and some other U.S. athletes made an unauthorized visit to South Africa, despite the IAAF ban on competing in that country. The resultant ban by U.S. authorities more or less ended his career.

Mac Wilkins   (United States, b. 1950)

69.18m (226' 11")	Walnut, USA	24 Apr 1976
69.80m (229' 0")	San Jose, USA	1 May 1976
70.24m (230' 5")	San Jose, USA	1 May 1976
70.86m (232' 6")	San Jose, USA	1 May 1976

Mac Wilkins was for many years the *enfant terrible* of U.S. track and field. A student at the University of Oregon, he was known as "Multiple Mac" because he competed in all four throwing events.

With the discus, Wilkins had been 14th at the U.S. Olympic trials in 1972. By 1976 he was at his peak and set a world record in April, throwing 69.18 meters (226' 11") at the Mt. San Antonio Relays. A week later he exploded with three consecutive world record throws:

69.80 meters, 70.24 meters, 70.86 meters. He had become the first athlete to throw over 70 meters.

He went to the Montreal Olympics a hot favorite and did not disappoint. He threw an Olympic record in the qualifying rounds (68.28 meters, 224 feet) and won comfortably in the final with 67.50 meters (221' 5") from Wolfgang Schmidt, with John Powell third. He gave Schmidt a famous hug, which was interpreted as part congratulations, part snub to teammate Powell.

With his beard, his unconventional views, and his scathing criticism of U.S. Olympic officials, he was a natural target for a hate campaign and received volumes of hate mail after the Olympics from U.S. citizens. He had irritated many by saying that he admired the dedication of East Germany toward its athletic success and that U.S. Olympic officials were of little use. He was also a critic of that most sacred of Olympic icons, Jesse Owens (see profile in long jump section).

Mac Wilkins, United States (discus), 1976 Olympic champion and first man over 70 meters.

Wilkins missed the 1980 Olympics because of the U.S. boycott. In 1984 at Los Angeles he was surprisingly beaten by unknown Rolf Danneberg of West Germany. He retired in 1986 but made a comeback in 1988, winning the U.S. AAU title for the eighth time. He went on to the Seoul Olympics and finished fifth. Fiercely dedicated to the event, he remains a guru to younger athletes in the discipline.

Wolfgang Schmidt   (East Germany, b. 1954)

71.16m (233' 5")   **Berlin, East Germany**   **9 Aug 1978**

Wolfgang Schmidt's father was German decathlon champion in 1942; the championship was held despite the war. Wolfgang was born in 1954 and grew to be 197 centimeters tall (6' 5 ½") and weighed 115 kilograms (253 pounds). He enjoyed success in track and field early and was East German discus champion from 1975 to 1980. He won the silver medal at the 1976 Montreal Olympics, became world record holder in 1978, and was European champion the same year. Schmidt was also a highly competent shot putter, coming in fourth at these European Championships.

However, one thing he never had was admiration for the tedious, autocratic personalities who ran East German athletics like an army barracks. Schmidt never tried to conceal his distaste for them. He was no angel, so they didn't like him either. A mutual antagonism developed, which was aggravated by Schmidt's fraternization with western athletes such as Mac Wilkins, which was forbidden in communist East Germany. While he was successful, they couldn't touch him. The wheels came off his athletic career and his life when he unexpectedly fell back to fourth place at the Moscow Olympics, possibly due to overconfidence. He made an obscene gesture to the Soviet crowd, who were baiting him.

For his various sins, he was arrested, charged with various antisocial attitudes, and spent 18 months in prison. After his prison term he was denied the possibility of return to the national track and field team and was assigned to menial posts. Six years after his first arrest he was allowed to migrate to West Germany, which he eventually represented.

He was ranked the number one discus thrower in the world in 1990, at age 36, a re-

Wolfgang Schmidt (discus), expelled from East Germany and newly representing West Germany, has his handshake declined by East German discus star Jurgen Schult. Rolf Danneburg, *center*, 1984 Olympic champion, seems bemused.

markable comeback after being away from the sport for so long. However, the East German vendetta continued, and the new East German champion, Jurgen Schult, was forbidden to shake hands with Schmidt at international meets.

In one last controversy, Schmidt missed selection to the 1992 Barcelona Olympics. He remains the only elite East German athlete to have been in open conflict with the East German athletic authorities.

Yuriy Dumchev   (Soviet Union, b. 1958)

71.86m (235' 9")   **Moscow, USSR**   **29 May 1983**

Yuriy Dumchev was the European junior discus champion in 1977 and was fifth at the 1980 Moscow Olympics. He became Soviet champion in 1980, 1981, and 1988.

A big man, weighing 128 kilograms (282 pounds) and 200 centimeters tall (6' 6"), he added 70 centimeters to Wolfgang Schmidt's five-year-old record at the Moscow championships at the Lenin Stadium. His first two throws were fouls, then he increased his distances with his four remaining tries to finally break the world record—66.27 meters (217' 5"), 67.56 meters (221' 8"), 69.44 meters (227' 10"), and finally 71.86 meters (235' 9").

He did not compete at the 1984 Los Angeles Olympics because of the Soviet boycott. At the 1988 Olympics he was fifth with 66.42 meters (217' 11").

Jurgen Schult   (East Germany, b. 1960)

74.08m (243' 0")   **Neubrandenburg, East Germany**   **6 Jun 1986**

The current discus record was set by Jurgen Schult in a qualifying meeting for the European Championships. At Neubrandenburg Schult threw the discus an astonishing 74.08 meters (243' 0"), an improvement in the record by 2.22 meters (7' 3").

Originally a machine fitter from Schwerin, Schult was East German champion eight times. Even Schult admitted that his record was something of a fluke. It took place at 6 P.M. (1800 hours), apparently with a very strong headwind. His next best throw in his career was 70.46 meters (231' 2"). Although he came in only seventh in the European Championships that year, he went on to dominate the event in the late 1980s: He was first in the 1987 World Championships, the 1988 Olympics, and the 1990 European Championships.

In the 1990s his results slipped marginally. He was second at the 1992 Olympics and third at the 1993 World Championships and 1994 European Championships. At the Atlanta Olympics he was sixth with 64.62 meters (212' 0 ").

Schult and his East German predecessor, Wolfgang Schmidt, had no great friendship. After Schmidt began to compete for West Germany, Schult was instructed not to shake his hand. After East Germany collapsed and both athletes competed for the unified German team, they actually managed to shake hands.

Conclusions

As in the shot put, the great unmentionable is anabolic steroids. It is unlikely we will ever have a full understanding of their influence in generating world records. One assumes that they were used on a worldwide basis, but it is obviously impossible to be certain who was taking them and who wasn't. One thing is certain, standards have been very quiet in the discus in the last few years.

Jurgen Schult's present world record of 74.08 meters (243' 0") was set in 1986. No one since has surpassed the previous 1983 record (71.86 meters), let alone approached Schult's mark. In fact, only two athletes in the 1990s have even exceeded 70 meters. Schult's record seems secure well into the next century.

Five All-Time Best: Men's Discus

Jurgen Schult (GDR)	74.08m (243' 0")	1986
Yuriy Dumchev (USSR)	71.86m (235' 9")	1983
John Powell (USA)	71.26m (233' 9")	1984
Rickard Bruch (SWE)	71.26m (233' 9")	1984
Imrich Bugar (CZH)	71.26m (233' 9")	1985
Prediction	*74.08m (243' 0")*	*2015*

Top Three: Men's Discus

GOLD MEDAL:	Al Oerter (USA)
SILVER MEDAL:	Jurgen Schult (GDR)
BRONZE MEDAL:	Mac Wilkins (USA)

The hammer appears to derive from the Celtic, not the Greek, games. No hammer throwing took place at the ancient Olympics. All sorts of "hammers" were originally thrown; there is a picture of Henry VIII at court throwing an actual hammer. The dimensions, design, and material changed many times, until the type currently in use was decided on early in the 20th century.

The modern "hammer" is a metal ball attached to a handle by a wire, which can be from 3' 10 ¼" to 3' 11 ¾" in length (1.175-1.215 meters). It is thrown from a circle seven feet (2.135 meters) in diameter. To achieve speed, most competitors rotate three times, but some of the recent champions, such as Sergey Litvinov, developed the difficult technique of four turns. In competition an athlete is allowed six throws.

The hammer has little appeal in the United States and has been dominated for the most part by Europeans, although the event was dominated in the early years of the 20th century by the Irish Americans, John Flanagan, Pat Ryan, and Matt McGrath. Between them, they won the first five Olympic gold medals. However, after these early successes the event was largely neglected in the United States. The one significant exception was Hal Connolly (USA), who won the 1956 Olympic gold medal and set six world records.

Altogether, 19 men have set 45 world records. Nine were from the Soviet Union, four from Germany, and three from Hungary. Soviets Mikhail Krivonosov and Yuriy Sedykh, along with Connolly, have each set the record six times. Nine record holders were also Olympic champions: Ryan, Németh, Csermák, Connolly, Klim, Zsivótzky, Bondarchuk, Sedykh, and Litvinov. Csermák (1952), Németh (1976), and Sedykh (1980) have set world records in the Olympics.

Men's World Records for the Hammer Throw

Record distance	Record holder	Location	Date
57.77m (189' 6")	Patrick Ryan (USA)	New York, USA	17 Aug 1913
59.00m (193' 7")	Erwin Blask (GER)	Stockholm, Sweden	27 Aug 1938
59.02m (193' 8")	Imre Németh (HUN)	Tata, Hungary	14 Jul 1948
59.57m (195' 5")	Imre Németh (HUN)	Katowice, Poland	4 Sep 1949
59.88m (196' 5")	Imre Németh (HUN)	Budapest, Hungary	19 May 1950
60.34m (197' 11")	József Csermák (HUN)	Helsinki, Finland	24 Jul 1952
61.25m (200' 11")	Sverre Strandli (NOR)	Oslo, Norway	14 Sep 1952
62.36m (204' 7")	Sverre Strandli (NOR)	Oslo, Norway	5 Sep 1953
63.34m (207' 9")	Mikhail Krivonosov (USSR)	Bern, Switzerland	29 Aug 1954
64.05m (210' 1")	Stanislav Nyenashev (USSR)	Baku, USSR	12 Dec 1954
64.33m (211' 0")	Mikhail Krivonosov (USSR)	Warsaw, Poland	4 Aug 1955
64.52m (211' 8")	Mikhail Krivonosov (USSR)	Belgrade, Yugoslavia	19 Sep 1955
65.85m (216' 0")	Mikhail Krivonosov (USSR)	Nalchik, USSR	25 Apr 1956
66.38m (217' 9")	Mikhail Krivonosov (USSR)	Minsk, USSR	8 Jul 1956
67.32m (220' 10")	Mikhail Krivonosov (USSR)	Tashkent, USSR	22 Oct 1956
68.54m (224' 10")	Harold "Hal" Connolly (USA)	Los Angeles, USA	2 Nov 1956
68.68m (225' 4")	Harold "Hal" Connolly (USA)	Bakersfield, USA	20 Jun 1958
70.33m (230' 9")	Harold "Hal" Connolly (USA)	Walnut, USA	12 Aug 1960
70.67m (231' 10")	Harold "Hal" Connolly (USA)	Palo Alto, USA	21 Jul 1962
71.06m (233' 2")	Harold "Hal" Connolly (USA)	Ceres, USA	29 May 1965
71.26m (233' 9")	Harold "Hal" Connolly (USA)	Walnut, USA	20 Jun 1965
73.74m (241' 11")	Gyula Zsivótzky (HUN)	Debrecen, Hungary	4 Sep 1965
73.76m (242' 0")	Gyula Zsivótzky (HUN)	Budapest, Hungary	14 Sep 1968
74.52m (244' 6")	Romuald Klim (USSR)	Budapest, Hungary	15 Jun 1969

74.68m (245' 0")	Anatoliy Bondarchuk (USSR)	Athens, Greece	20 Sep 1969
75.48m (247' 8")	Anatoliy Bondarchuk (USSR)	Rovno, USSR	12 Oct 1969
76.40m (250' 8")	Walter Schmidt (FRG)	Lahr, West Germany	4 Sep 1971
76.60m (251' 4")	Reinhard Theimer (GDR)	Leipzig, East Germany	4 Jul 1974
76.66m (251' 6")	Aleksey Spiridonov (USSR)	Munich, West Germany	11 Sep 1974
76.70m (251' 8")	Karl Hans Riehm (FRG)	Rehlingen, West Germany	19 May 1975
77.56m (254' 4")	Karl Hans Riehm (FRG)	Rehlingen, West Germany	19 May 1975
78.50m (257' 6")	Karl Hans Riehm (FRG)	Rehlingen, West Germany	19 May 1975
79.30m (260' 2")	Walter Schmidt (FRG)	Frankfurt am Main, West Germany	14 Aug 1975
80.14m (262' 11")	Boris Zaychuk (USSR)	Moscow, USSR	9 Jul 1978
80.32m (263' 6")	Karl Hans Riehm (FRG)	Heidenheim, West Germany	6 Aug 1978
80.38m (263' 8")	Yuriy Sedykh (USSR)	Leselidze, USSR	16 May 1980
80.46m (264' 0")	Juri Tamm (USSR)	Leselidze, USSR	16 May 1980
80.64m (264' 7")	Yuriy Sedykh (USSR)	Leselidze, USSR	16 May 1980
81.66m (267' 11")	Sergey Litvinov (USSR)	Sochi, USSR	24 May 1980
81.80m (268' 4")	Yuriy Sedykh (USSR)	Moscow, USSR	31 Jul 1980
83.98m (275' 6")	Sergey Litvinov (USSR)	Moscow, USSR	4 Jun 1982
84.14m (276' 0")	Sergey Litvinov (USSR)	Moscow, USSR	21 Jun 1983
86.34m (283' 3")	Yuriy Sedykh (USSR)	Cork, Ireland	3 Jul 1984
86.66m (284' 4")	Yuriy Sedykh (USSR)	Tallinn, USSR	22 Jun 1986
86.74m (284' 7")	Yuriy Sedykh (USSR)	Stuttgart, West Germany	30 Aug 1986

Patrick Ryan (United States, 1883–1964)

57.77m (189' 6") **New York, USA** **17 Aug 1913**

Patrick Ryan was one of a number of Irish athletes who made their life in the United States and became known as the "Irish-American Whales." Born in County Limerick, he arrived in the United States in 1910 at the age of 27. He was not eligible to represent the United States at the 1912 Olympics and so had to wait until 1920. He had multiple duels with another Irish American, Matthew McGrath, a native of County Tipperary. McGrath won the 1912 Olympic gold medal in Stockholm for the United States and set many unofficial world records. However, Ryan was officially recognized as the first world record holder following his throw of 57.77 meters (189' 6") in 1913 at the "Eccentric Fireman's Annual Handicap Games" in New York.

Patrick Ryan, United States (hammer),
1920 Olympic champion.

At the 1920 Olympics McGrath had to withdraw after the second round with a knee injury and finished fifth. Ryan won by over four meters with 52.86 meters (173' 5").

Ryan served in the U.S. Army in World War I and was part of the 1918 American Expeditionary Force. After his retirement from athletics he worked as a labor foreman in New York but in 1924 returned to Ireland to take over the family farm. He remained there for 40 years.

Erwin Blask   (Germany, b. 1910)

| 59.00m (193' 7") | Stockholm, Sweden | 27 Aug 1938 |

It was a quarter of a century before Ryan's record was finally broken by Erwin Blask at a Sweden vs. Germany match in 1938, where he exceeded the record by 1.23 meters (4' 1"). Blask threw 59.00 meters that day, and second was Karl Hein (Germany), who had won the gold medal at the 1936 Olympics with 56.49 meters. Blask, born in East Prussia, had led the Olympic competition until the very last throw, when Hein took the lead.

Hein and Blask had been rivals since 1935, and they raised the national record many times. It was Hein who won the 1938 European Championships (58.77 meters, 192' 10") with Blask second. Blask was German champion in 1935, 1939, and 1940, while Hein won the title from 1936-1938, and in 1946 and 1947. Blask was still competitive as a thrower while in his 40s and was third at the West German championships in 1951 and 1952.

Imre Németh   (Hungary, 1917–1989)

59.02m (193' 8")	Tata, Hungary	14 Jul 1948
59.57m (195' 5")	Katowice, Poland	4 Sep 1949
59.88m (196' 5")	Budapest, Hungary	19 May 1950

Imre Németh was born in Kasso, now called Kosice, in Czechoslovakia. Originally a discus thrower, a hammer landed close to him while he was training one day. In anger he threw it back, and a new career was launched. He weighed only 82 kilograms (181 pounds) and was the lightest athlete to hold the world hammer throw record. He dominated the post-World War II era with three world records and the 1948 Olympic gold medal. His first world record was achieved at a pre-Olympic meet at the Hungarian training camp of Tata. The second was at a match between Poland and Hungary, and the third took place at a meet in Budapest.

It seemed he might win two Olympic titles in a row, but at the 1952 Olympics his own pupil, József Csermák, won with a new world record (60.34 meters, 197' 11"). Németh finished third (57.74 meters, 189' 5").

Later in life, he became a member of parliament in Hungary's communist government and the manager of the huge Nepstadion in Budapest for many years. His son Miklós achieved the same double of world record holder and Olympic champion in the javelin at the Montreal Olympics in 1976.

József Csermák   (Hungary, b. 1932)

| 60.34m (197' 11") | Helsinki, Finland | 24 Jul 1952 |

József Csermák was a pupil of world record holder and Olympic champion Imre Németh. He learned his trade well. At the 1952 Helsinki Olympics he led the qualifying rounds with 57.20 meters (187' 8"), a new Olympic record. In the final he killed off the opposition with his third throw, a new world record of 60.34 meters (197' 11") and the first throw over 60 meters.

He competed at the European Championships in Bern, Switzerland, two years later, but by then the Soviets had arrived as a major force in the event. He was third with a respectable 59.72 meters (195' 11"), while Mikhail Krivonosov (USSR) won with a new world record of 63.34 meters (207' 9").

Later in his career Csermák was fifth at the 1956 Melbourne Olympics and eighth at the 1958 European Championships in Stockholm. At the 1960 Olympics in Rome his throw of 59.72 meters (195' 11") was not good enough to get into the final.

Sverre Strandli   (Norway, 1925–1985)

| 61.25m (200' 11") | Oslo, Norway | 14 Sep 1952 |
| 62.36m (204' 7") | Oslo, Norway | 5 Sep 1953 |

József Csermàk's Olympic and world record was overtaken seven weeks after he set it. In a match between Norway and Finland in Oslo, Sverre Strandli threw 61.25 meters (200' 11") on his first throw. He hadn't even bothered to take off his tracksuit.

Strandli had won the European Championships in Brussels in 1950 with 55.71 meters (182' 9"). However, he had dropped to seventh place at the 1952 Olympics. Shortly after the Games, as if to compensate for this disappointment, he threw his world record in front of 17,000 of his own people. He attributed his success to his technique of keeping the hammer somewhat closer to his body than Németh or Csermák and concentrating on speed in the turns.

For the 1953 Bislett Games in Oslo, the promoters invited Németh, Csermák, and Strandli to compete. A small crowd of 6875 saw Strandli throw another world record (62.36 meters); Németh threw 58.92 meters and Csermák 57.09 meters. However, the next year saw the arrival of the Soviet hammer throwers. At the European Championships in Bern, Switzerland, Strandli threw 61.07 meters, but the Soviet's Mikhail Krivonosov exceeded that with 63.34 meters, a new world record.

Strandli was eighth in the 1956 Melbourne Olympics and 11th in Rome in 1960.

Sverre Strandli, Norway (hammer).

Mikhail Krivonosov   (Soviet Union, b. 1929)

63.34m (207' 9")	Bern, Switzerland	29 Aug 1954
64.33m (211' 0")	Warsaw, Poland	4 Aug 1955
64.52m (211' 8")	Belgrade, Yugoslavia	19 Sep 1955

65.85m (216' 0")	Nalchik, USSR	25 Apr 1956
66.38m (217' 9")	Minsk, USSR	8 Jul 1956
67.32m (220' 10")	Tashkent, USSR	22 Oct 1956

Mikhail Krivonosov was the first great Soviet hammer thrower. He won his first of six Soviet titles in 1952 but at the Helsinki Olympics did not get through the qualifying rounds after fouling three times. His world record career started in 1954 when he won the European Championships in Bern with a throw of 63.34 meters. Between that triumph and the 1956 Melbourne Olympics he set five more world records.

Eleven days after his sixth world record an unexpected challenge emerged. Harold Connolly (USA) exceeded the new record by over a meter. In Melbourne Krivonosov took the lead in round 2, but Connolly hit the front with his fifth throw. Krivonosov ruined his chances by fouling his last three throws. The final results were Connolly, 63.18 meters (207' 3"); Krivonosov, 63.02 meters (206' 9").

After the Olympics Connolly went off on a record spree of his own. Krivonosov never quite regained the momentum of the early part of his career, although he was second at the 1958 European Championships with 63.78 meters (209' 3").

Stanislav Nyenashev   (Soviet Union, b. 1934)

| 64.05m (210' 1") | Baku, USSR | 12 Dec 1954 |

Stanislav Nyenashev was only 170 centimeters (5' 7") tall, easily the shortest of the men who have held the world record in the hammer throw. He briefly interrupted the reign of Mikhail Krivonosov in December 1954. At a local sports meeting in Baku, Azerbaijan, he threw 64.05 meters at the Stalin Stadium. (Stalin had just died the year before and was still officially in favor.) He achieved this on his third throw and was too excited to take his three remaining throws.

He was one of the first hammer throwers to take four turns instead of three before releasing the hammer. At the Soviet championships he was first in 1953, second in 1954 and 1956, and third in 1955. He did not compete at the 1956 Melbourne Olympics or the 1954 European Championships.

Harold "Hal" Connolly   (United States, b. 1931)

68.54m (224' 10")	Los Angeles, USA	2 Nov 1956
68.68m (225' 4")	Bakersfield, USA	20 Jun 1958
70.33m (230' 9")	Walnut, USA	12 Aug 1960
70.67m (231' 10")	Palo Alto, USA	21 Jul 1962
71.06m (233' 2")	Ceres, USA	29 May 1965
71.26m (233' 9")	Walnut, USA	20 Jun 1965

Harold Connolly was that rare thing in the 1950s, an American hammer throw champion of international class. His birth weight was a massive 13 pounds (6 kilograms). His delivery was complicated by major shoulder obstruction and trauma, which left him with permanent damage to his left arm, which was ultimately three inches shorter than his right. He spent much of his childhood undergoing physiotherapy and wearing shoulder braces. By chance he discovered the hammer throw when he retrieved hammers for the track and field team at Boston College. He had found his event.

Connolly became AAU hammer champion nine times. He traveled to West Germany in 1954 to learn the craft under Sepp Christmann, one of the acknowledged experts in the event. He broke Mikhail Krivonosov's world record by 1956, just before the Melbourne Olympics. In Melbourne Krivonosov's training form looked good, and Connolly had to engage in some cat and mouse games to out-psyche him. In the final Krivonosov led from round 2, but Connolly kept his nerves and took the lead in the fifth round. The result was Connolly, 63.18 meters (207' 3"); Krivonosov, 63.02 meters (206' 9").

Apart from his Olympic victory, it was his romance with Czechoslovakian discus champion Olga Fikotova that captured world headlines. The Czech authorities spirited her back home, but Connolly eventually followed. The communist government tried to stop the match, but eventually Connolly won the right to wed his bride. The authorities kept the location of the wedding a secret, but on the day 50,000 Czechoslovakian citizens turned up to celebrate the occasion.

The couple moved to the United States, where Connolly took jobs in administration and teaching. He set five more world records through 1965, but luck at the Olympics deserted him; he was eighth in Rome and sixth in Tokyo. In 1968 he did

Hal Connolly, United States (hammer), winner of the 1956 Olympic hammer throw, with Mikhail Krivonosov, Soviet Union, second.

not make the final; in 1972 he did not make the U.S. team. His wife participated in five Olympics (1956-1972). The couple divorced in 1975 and Connolly later married Pat Winslow, a U.S. pentathlete who competed at the 1964 and 1968 Olympics. Connolly and Fikotova have a son, James, who won the NCAA decathlon in 1987.

Gyula Zsivótzky   (Hungary, b. 1937)

| 73.74m (241' 11") | Debrecen, Hungary | 4 Sep 1965 |
| 73.76m (242' 0") | Budapest, Hungary | 14 Sep 1968 |

Gyula Zsivótzky was four times an Olympian: second in 1960, second in 1964, first in 1968, and fifth in 1972. His September 1965 record, when he added a massive 2.48 meters (8' 2") to Connolly's last record in a Hungarian interclub match, signaled the end of the Hal Connolly era.

His second world record came one month before the Mexico City Olympics. Zsivótzky added just two centimeters to his world record. Despite this, he went to the Mexico City Olympics not favored to win, as he had lost to the 1964 Olympic winner Romuald Klim nine times in a row. Also, his two silver medals at Rome (1960) and Tokyo (1964) suggested luck wasn't with him at the Olympics.

Gyula Zsivótzky, Hungary (hammer), 1968 Olympic champion.

However, in Mexico City he finally had his golden moment. Klim led after four throws (73.28 meters, 240' 5"), but Zsivótzky threw 73.36 meters (240' 8") on his fifth throw and held on to win by eight centimeters (three inches).

Romuald Klim   (Soviet Union, b. 1933)

74.52m (244' 6")   **Budapest, Hungary**   **15 Jun 1969**

Romuald Klim was born near Minsk, Belorussia, where his parents worked on a collective farm. He was third in the Soviet championships in 1963 and sixth in 1964. However, shortly before the 1964 Olympics, at age 31, he threw 67.91 meters (222' 10") and was included in the Olympic team. At Tokyo the favorite was Hungary's Gyula Zsivótzky, who led from the first round with 69.08 meters (226' 8"). But on his fourth throw Klim achieved a personal best with 69.74 meters (228' 10"). Zsivótzky fouled two of his last three throws, and Klim was suddenly gold medalist.

From then on, he defeated Zsivótzky in their next nine meetings, was Soviet champion four times, and won the European Championships in 1966. When the 1968 Olympics came around, he was very much the favorite, even though Zsivótzky had just added two centimeters to the world record. In Mexico City Klim threw an Olympic record of 73.28 meters (240' 5") in the fourth round. But Zsivótzky responded with 73.36 meters (240' 8") in the fifth round, and that proved to be the winning throw.

Klim added the last remaining trophy of his career in 1969, when, at age 36, he set a new world record; he threw 74.52 meters (244' 6") at a meet in Zsivótzky's hometown, Budapest.

Anatoliy Bondarchuk   (Soviet Union, b. 1940)

74.68m (245' 0")   **Athens, Greece**   **20 Sep 1969**
75.48m (247' 8")   **Rovno, USSR**   **12 Oct 1969**

Anatoliy Bondarchuk, Soviet Union (hammer), 1972 Olympic champion.

Anatoliy Bondarchuk had been fifth at the 1968 Soviet championships. In 1969 his career took off— he won the Soviet title, the European Championships, and set two world records.

The first world record was at the European Championships in Athens, where he added 16 centimeters (six inches) to the record on his fourth throw. Three weeks later he became the first man to reach the 75-meter barrier at a small sports meeting in Rovno, in the Ukraine, with 75.48 meters.

He was once again Soviet champion in 1970 and secured the Olympic gold medal in 1972 at Munich. He opened up with a winning throw of 75.50 meters (247' 8"), an Olympic record.

His career faltered in 1974 when he couldn't make the finals of the European Championships. However, he was picked for the Soviet team for the Montreal Olympics, along with his young pupil Yuriy Sedykh. The young pupil outshone the master by throwing 77.52 meters (254' 4"). Bondarchuk finished third with 75.48 meters (247' 8").

Walter Schmidt (West Germany, b. 1948)

76.40m (250' 8")	Lahr, West Germany	4 Sep 1971
79.30m (260' 2")	Frankfurt am Main, West Germany	14 Aug 1975

Walter Schmidt began throwing the hammer at age 17 and in 1966 won the German Youth Mastership. Schmidt was no lightweight and eventually grew to 130 kilograms (287 pounds).

His first world record (76.40 meters) took place in 1971 at a meeting in his hometown, Lahr, a few days after he had finished fifth in the European Championships in Helsinki. The record was improved five times before he reclaimed it in 1975. At a Throwers Day meet in Frankfurt am Main he went close to the 80-meter barrier with 79.30 meters (260' 2").

His career was plagued by injuries, and his record did not include major victories. At the 1972 Olympics he was injured; in 1976 he was sixth. His best place at the European Championships was his fifth place in 1971. At the West German Championships he never quite managed to win the title, coming in second three times. In 1977 he was suspended by the West German Athletic Federation following a positive drug test.

He studied geography, politics, and sport and now teaches in Kleinwallstadt.

Reinhard Theimer (East Germany, b. 1948)

76.60m (251' 4")	Leipzig, East Germany	4 Jul 1974

Theimer set his world record at the 1974 East German Championships in the qualifying rounds. He threw 76.60 meters on his first throw and was too excited to take any more throws.

He had already been an established athlete for some time. He was the East German hammer champion in 1968-1970, 1973, and 1974. At the European Championships he was third in 1969 with 72.02 meters (236' 3"), second in 1971 with 71.80 meters (235' 7"), and third in 1974 with 71.62 meters (235' 0"). At the Olympics he was seventh in 1968 and 13th in 1972.

Aleksey Spiridonov (Soviet Union, b. 1951)

76.66m (251' 6")	Munich, West Germany	11 Sep 1974

Aleksey Spiridonov initially had a three-turn style but eventually mastered four turns. He had a golden year in 1974. First, he won the European Championships in Rome with 74.20 meters (243' 5"), the same day his first child was born. Four days later he threw 76.66 meters in Munich at an international meet. This added six centimeters to Reinhard Theimer's world record.

When the 1976 Montreal Olympics came around, the three Soviet athletes—Spiridonov, Bondarchuk, and Sedykh—took charge of the event. Spiridonov led with 75.74 meters (248' 6") on his first throw. However, Sedykh then took over with a second throw of 77.52

meters (254' 4"). Spiridonov improved to 76.08 meters (249' 7") on his last throw to reinforce his position as silver medalist. The third Soviet, veteran Anatoliy Bondarchuk, took the bronze medal to make it a Soviet medal sweep.

The one title Spiridonov never won was the Soviet championship. He was second in 1973, 1974, and 1975 and third in 1976 and 1978.

Karl Hans Riehm   (West Germany, b. 1951)

76.70m (251' 8")	Rehlingen, West Germany	19 May 1975
77.56m (254' 4")	Rehlingen, West Germany	19 May 1975
78.50m (257' 6")	Rehlingen, West Germany	19 May 1975
80.32m (263' 6")	Heidenheim, West Germany	6 Aug 1978

Karl Hans Riehm, West Germany (hammer).

Karl Hans Riehm trained as a builder and was employed six hours a day by his father, a carpenter. At the 1972 Munich Olympics he finished tenth.

Riehm first broke 75 meters in 1975. This led to a magic day in May 1975 when he exceeded the existing world record (76.66 meters) on all six of his throws. His throws were 76.70 meters, 77.56 meters, 77.10 meters, 78.50 meters, 77.16 meters, and 77.28 meters. His first, second, and fourth throws were new world records.

Riehm was unable to prevent a Soviet sweep of the event at the Montreal Olympics. Riehm came in fourth, just two centimeters behind the bronze medalist, Anatoliy Bondarchuk.

Riehm won the 1977 World Cup and in 1978 set another world record (80.32 meters), becoming the second man to throw over 80 meters. However, at the European Championships three weeks later it was Sedykh who won (77.28 meters, 253' 6"), with Riehm throwing 77.02 meters (252' 8") for third position.

In 1980 he was a victim of the boycott of the Moscow Olympics. However, after the Games he showed his form by defeating all three of the Moscow medalists. His one remaining Olympic chance was in Los Angeles in 1984, especially with the boycotting East Europeans absent. However the Finn Juha Tiainen won with 78.08 meters (256' 2"); Riehm was second with 77.98 meters (255' 10").

Boris Zaychuk   (Soviet Union, b. 1947)

| 80.14m (262' 11") | Moscow, USSR | 9 Jul 1978 |

Boris Zaychuk was the man who first broke the 80-meter barrier. He came from Tokmak in the Kirghiz Republic, 300 kilometers (186 miles) from the Chinese border. His first passion was boxing. He never quite won the Soviet championship; his best effort between 1975 and 1980 was a second in 1978. However, in July 1978 at the Moscow City Championships Zaychuk threw 80.14 meters on his first throw. Despite this achievement, he remained somewhat in the shadow of the big names of Soviet hammer throwing, especially Sedykh and Litvinov. He was sixth at the 1978 European Championships. He did not make the Soviet team for the 1980 Moscow Olympics. The Soviets had a medal sweep anyway with Sedykh, Litvinov, and Tamm.

Yuriy Sedykh   (Soviet Union, b. 1955)

80.38m (263' 8")	Leselidze, USSR	16 May 1980
80.64m (264' 7")	Leselidze, USSR	16 May 1980
81.80m (268' 4")	Moscow, USSR	31 Jul 1980
86.34m (283' 3")	Cork, Ireland	3 Jul 1984
86.66m (284' 4")	Tallinn, USSR	22 Jun 1986
86.74m (284' 7")	Stuttgart, West Germany	30 Aug 1986

Yuriy Sedykh, Soviet Union (hammer), six-time world record holder and Olympic champion in 1976 and 1980.

Yuriy Sedykh set six world records, was Olympic champion twice (1976 and 1980), and was European champion three times (1978, 1982, and 1986). Finally, at the end of his career in 1991, at the age of 36, he won the World Championship. By that time he had lost most of his hair, but not his skills.

Sedykh came from Novocherkassk, near Rostov in the Ukraine. He trained under Anatoliy Bondarchuk, and at the Montreal Olympics the youngster out-threw the teacher. Sedykh won with 77.52 meters (254' 4"), while Bondarchuk was third with 75.48 meters (247' 8").

Sedykh's first world record was in an early preseason meet in the Olympic year of 1980. He threw 80.38 meters on his third throw, only to see it beaten 15 minutes later by Juri Tamm with 80.46 meters. Sedykh was able to keep his nerve, and 20 minutes later he reclaimed the record with 80.64 meters.

He won the 1980 Olympics in Moscow with a world record in his opening throw of 81.80 meters and became the first athlete to throw routinely over 80 meters. His last world record was set at the 1986 European Championships in Stuttgart (86.74 meters).

Sedykh spent most of his career dueling with Sergey Litvinov, and they exchanged world records and Olympic medals. In their last Olympics, in Seoul in 1988, it was Litvinov who won, with Sedykh second, 84.80 meters (278' 2") to 83.76 meters (274' 10"). His third and current wife is Natalya Lisovskaya, winner of the shot put at the 1988 Seoul Olympics. A former wife was Lyudmila Kondratyeva, winner of the Moscow 100m. Sedykh now lives in Wichita.

Juri Tamm   (Soviet Union, b. 1957)

| 80.46m (264' 0") | Leselidze, USSR | 16 May 1980 |

Juri Tamm was born in Estonia, where his father had been a pole vaulter in the 1930s—not just an ordinary pole vaulter, but a one-armed pole vaulter, who cleared 3.10 meters (10' 2"). His son Juri developed the idea of training with classical music playing in the background.

Juri Tamm, Soviet Union (hammer).

In May 1980 he became world record holder for 20 minutes. At the Dynamo Stadium in Leselidze he and Sedykh exchanged world records. Sedykh broke the world record with 80.38 meters at 4:15 P.M. (1615 hours). Tamm then threw 80.46 meters at 4:30 P.M. (1630 hours). However, on his fifth throw at 4:50 P.M. (1650 hours), Sedykh reached 80.64 meters.

The Soviets comfortably won the 1980 Olympic medals with Sedykh, Litvinov, and Tamm taking the first three positions. All three missed the 1984 Olympics in Los Angeles because of the Soviet boycott but were back again for the 1988 Olympics. The 1988 order was Litvinov, Sedykh, and then Tamm. Tamm didn't help his chances when he fouled his last four throws.

Sergey Litvinov   (Soviet Union, b. 1958)

81.66m (267' 11")	Sochi, USSR	24 May 1980
83.98m (275' 6")	Moscow, USSR	4 Jun 1982
84.14m (276' 0")	Moscow, USSR	21 Jun 1983

Sergey Litvinov and rival Yuriy Sedykh spent much of their careers exchanging wins and records. His initial interest was in Greco-Roman wrestling before he took up hammer throwing. Like Sedykh, he won just about everything, including three world records, an Olympic gold medal, and two world championships (1983 and 1987). The only title he didn't win was the European Championships.

Litvinov promoted the technique of four turns rather than three before releasing the hammer. He set his first record (81.66 meters) in May 1980, eight days after the Sedykh-Tamm world record saga. At the Olympics two months later Sedykh won with 81.80 meters (268' 4"); Litvinov was second with 80.64 meters (264' 7"), his only legal throw—all the rest were fouls.

Sergey Litvinov, Soviet Union (hammer), 1988 Olympic champion.

His 1982 world record (83.98 meters) was at an army championship, while his 1983 record (84.14 meters) occurred at the Spartakiade in the Lenin Stadium in Moscow.

Sedykh won the European Championships in 1982 (Litvinov was third) and in 1986 (Litvinov was second). However, Litvinov won the inaugural World Championships in Helsinki in 1983 (Sedykh was second) and again in 1987 in Rome, where Sedykh did not compete. Both Soviet athletes missed the 1984 Olympics because of the Soviet boycott. However, at the Seoul Olympics it was no contest: Litvinov won by over a meter, 84.80 meters (278' 2") to 83.76 meters (274' 10").

A teacher by profession, Litvinov and his wife have one son and three other adopted children.

Conclusions

Even after the demise of the Soviet Bloc in the late 1980s and the collapse of many of its sporting structures, the hammer throw is an event still largely dominated by Eastern Europeans. There are some pockets of enthusiasm in the West, but the results in the mid-1990s generally reflect the strong tradition in Eastern Europe and the countries that once formed the Soviet Union.

In this event, control and coordination count as much as brute strength, and there seems no reason why the current world record, now over 10 years old, shouldn't advance once more. Nonetheless, no one has approached the standards set by the two Soviet champions Sedykh and Litvinov in the mid-1980s. The current generation is still two to three meters behind.

Five All-Time Best: Men's Hammer Throw

Yuriy Sedykh (USSR)	86.74m (284' 7")	1986
Sergey Litvinov (USSR)	86.04m (282' 3")	1986
Igor Astapkovich (BLR)	84.62m (277' 7")	1992
Igor Nikulin (RUS)	84.48m (277' 2")	1990
Juri Tamm (USSR)	84.40m (276' 11")	1984
Prediction	*88.50m (290' 4")*	*2015*

Top Three: Men's Hammer Throw

GOLD MEDAL:	Yuriy Sedykh (USSR)
SILVER MEDAL:	Sergey Litvinov (USSR)
BRONZE MEDAL:	Hal Connolly (USA)

The javelin derives from spear throwing and traces its origins back to the ancient Olympics, where it was part of the pentathlon program. The modern javelin weighs 800 grams (1 pound 12 ounces). It could originally be made of wood or metal, but current javelins must be made of metal. The javelin is the only throwing event not to take place in a ring. The athlete is allowed a straight run before releasing his or her implement and has six throws in competition.

Whereas the discus and the shot put were dominated by U.S. athletes, the javelin and hammer throw have been dominated by Europeans, especially Scandinavians. Finland's Matti Järvinen achieved the most world records—10, set between 1930 and 1936.

Various minor modifications in the event were made over the years, but the most radical change came in the wake of Uwe Hohn's throw of 104.80 meters in 1984. Because the risk to spectators from throws of this magnitude became very real, the IAAF made a decision in 1986 to move the center of gravity back 10 centimeters. This new javelin resulted in throws 10 to 15 meters shorter and made the javelin more prone to stick in the ground.

The record with the new javelin has moved from 85.74 meters (1986) up to 98.48 meters (1996). Twenty-five javelin throwers have achieved a world record, 21 with the old javelin (34 times), and 4 with the new javelin (8 times). A number of records with the new javelin were disallowed because these new javelins were later judged to have been designed outside existing regulations. Nine of the world record holders have also been Olympic champions: Lemming, Myyrä, Lundqvist, Järvinen, Danielsen, Lusis, Wolfermann, Németh, and Zelezny. Only two (Danielsen, 1956; Németh, 1976) achieved their world records in Olympic competition.

Men's World Records for Javelin

Record distance	Record holder	Location	Date
62.32m (204' 5")	Erik Lemming (SWE)	Stockholm, Sweden	29 Sep 1912
66.10m (216' 10")	Jonni Myyrä (FIN)	Stockholm, Sweden	25 Aug 1919
66.62m (218' 7")	Gunnar Lindström (SWE)	Eksjo, Sweden	12 Oct 1924
69.88m (229' 3")	Eino Penttilä (FIN)	Viipuri, Finland	8 Oct 1927
71.01m (232' 11")	Erik Lundqvist (SWE)	Stockholm, Sweden	15 Aug 1928
71.57m (234' 9")	Matti Järvinen (FIN)	Viipuri, Finland	8 Aug 1930
71.70m (235' 3")	Matti Järvinen (FIN)	Tampere, Finland	17 Aug 1930
71.88m (235' 10")	Matti Järvinen (FIN)	Vaasa, Finland	31 Aug 1930
72.93m (239' 3")	Matti Järvinen (FIN)	Viipuri, Finland	14 Sep 1930
74.02m (242' 10")	Matti Järvinen (FIN)	Turku, Finland	27 Jun 1932
74.28m (243' 8")	Matti Järvinen (FIN)	Mikkeli, Finland	25 May 1933
74.61m (244' 9")	Matti Järvinen (FIN)	Vaasa, Finland	7 Jun 1933
76.10m (249' 8")	Matti Järvinen (FIN)	Helsinki, Finland	15 Jun 1933
76.66m (251' 6")	Matti Järvinen (FIN)	Turin, Italy	7 Sep 1934
77.23m (253' 4")	Matti Järvinen (FIN)	Helsinki, Finland	18 Jun 1936
77.87m (255' 5")	Yrjö Nikkanen (FIN)	Karhula, Finland	25 Aug 1938
78.70m (258'2")	Yrjö Nikkanen (FIN)	Kotka, Finland	16 Oct 1938
80.41m (263' 10")	Bud Held (USA)	Pasadena, USA	8 Aug 1953
81.75m (268' 2")	Bud Held (USA)	Modesto, USA	21 May 1955
83.56m (274' 1")	Soini Nikkinen (FIN)	Kuhmoinen, Finland	24 Jun 1956
83.66m (274' 5")	Janusz Sidlo (POL)	Milan, Italy	30 Jun 1956
85.71m (281' 2")	Egil Danielsen (NOR)	Melbourne, Australia	26 Nov 1956
86.04m (282' 3")	Al Cantello (USA)	Compton, USA	5 Jun 1959
86.74m (284' 7")	Carlo Lievore (ITA)	Milan, Italy	1 Jun 1961

87.12m (285' 10")	Terje Pedersen (NOR)	Oslo, Norway	1 Jul 1964
91.72m (300' 11")	Terje Pedersen (NOR)	Oslo, Norway	2 Sep 1964
91.98m (301' 9")	Janis Lusis (USSR)	Saarijarvi, Finland	23 Jun 1968
92.70m (304' 1")	Jorma Kinnunen (FIN)	Tampere, Finland	18 Jun 1969
93.80m (307' 9")	Janis Lusis (USSR)	Stockholm, Sweden	6 Jul 1972
94.08m (308' 8")	Klaus Wolfermann (FRG)	Leverkusen, West Germany	5 May 1973
94.58m (310' 4")	Miklós Németh (HUN)	Montreal, Canada	26 Jul 1976
96.72m (317' 4")	Ferenc Paragi (HUN)	Tata, Hungary	23 Apr 1980
99.72m (327' 2")	Tom Petranoff (USA)	Westwood, USA	15 May 1983
104.80m (343' 10")	Uwe Hohn (GDR)	Berlin, East Germany	20 Jul 1984

New Javelin

85.74m (281' 3")	Klaus Tafelmeier (FRG)	Como, Italy	21 Sep 1986
87.66m (287' 7")	Ján Zelezny (CZH)	Nitra, Czechoslovakia	31 May 1987
89.10m (292' 4")	Patrik Bodén (SWE)	Austin, USA	24 Mar 1990
89.58m (293' 11")	Steve Backley (GBR)	Stockholm, Sweden	2 Jul 1990
91.46m (300' 1")	Steve Backley (GBR)	Auckland, New Zealand	25 Jan 1992
95.54m (313' 5")	Ján Zelezny (CZH)	Pietersburg, South Africa	6 Apr 1993
95.66m (313' 10")	Ján Zelezny (CZH)	Sheffield, England	29 Aug 1993
98.48m (323' 1")	Ján Zelezny (CZH)	Jena, Germany	25 May 1996

Erik Lemming   (Sweden, 1880–1930)

62.32m (204' 5")   **Stockholm, Sweden**   **29 Sep 1912**

Erik Lemming was a 190-centimeter (6' 3") tall police officer from Stockholm. He dominated javelin throwing for over a decade and from 1899 until 1911 set 13 unofficial world records.

However the javelin was not held at the 1896, 1900, or 1904 Olympics. Lemming did compete at the 1900 Olympics in six separate events, coming in fourth in the hammer and pole vault. At the 1906 Interim Olympics in Athens, he won the javelin (freestyle) competition. He also won two javelin gold medals (regular and freestyle) at the 1908 Olympics in London. Since all the successful athletes held the javelin in the middle, just as they did in the regular event, the freestyle javelin was aban-

Erik Lemming, Sweden (javelin), Olympic javelin champion in 1908 and 1912.

doned after these Games. Finally, Lemming won the 1912 Olympic javelin gold medal.

His inaugural world record was set in the now-abandoned two-hands javelin competition. In this event the athlete threw twice, first with the right hand, then with the left.

Lemming achieved 62.32 meters (204' 5") with his right hand (the world record) and 44.15 meters (114' 10") with his left. Under the pseudonym Erik Otto, he won the national two-handed shot put in 1917, at the age of 37.

Jonni Myyrä   (Finland, 1892–1955)

66.10m (216' 10")   Stockholm, Sweden   25 Aug 1919

Jonni Myyrä was the first of a long line of javelin champions from Finland, where javelin throwing achieved the status of a national sport unmatched in any other country. He had competed at the 1912 Olympics, finishing eighth. In the Finnish civil war of 1918 he fought for the Whites.

When the Olympics resumed after World War I, he became a double Olympic champion, winning in 1920 (65.78 meters, 215' 10") and 1924 (62.96 meters, 206' 7"). Like Lemming, he set a number of unofficial records. One in 1915 was disallowed because it hit a tree. In fact, there is nothing in the rule books that says a javelin record should be disallowed just because it hits a tree.

Finally, in 1919 at an International meet at Stockholm he set a world record that was officially recognized as valid, 66.10 meters (216' 10").

After the 1924 Olympics, Myyrä traveled to the United States to compete before going to Japan. He made a decision at that time to settle in San Francisco and for many years was the U.S. correspondent for Finnish sports magazines. He always kept the Paris gold medal with him.

Jonni Myyrä, Finland (javelin), Olympic champion in 1920 and 1924.

Gunnar Lindström   (Sweden, 1896–1951)

66.62m (218' 7")   Eksjo, Sweden   12 Oct 1924

Gunnar Lindström had come in second to Myyrä at the 1924 Olympics, 60.92 meters (199' 10") to 62.96 meters (206' 7"). Three months later Lindström threw a world record (66.62 meters, 218' 7") at a meet in Eksjo, in southern Sweden.

In 1925 he threw the javelin even farther, 67.31 meters (220' 10"), at the Bislett Games in Oslo, but this record was disallowed on the grounds of "excess wind." Officials in those days had varying ideas about what constituted excess wind.

Lindström failed to qualify for the final at the 1928 Olympics in Amsterdam.

Eino Penttilä   (Finland, 1906–1983)

69.88m (229' 3")   Viipuri, Finland   8 Oct 1927

Eino Penttilä was born in Joutsend on the south shore of Lake Saimma. His father served in the Finnish cavalry. Young Eino won a stone-throwing competition and was advised to take up the javelin. He achieved his world record in 1927 at Viipuri (now Viburg), Finland. Despite sleeping in late and having to run to the stadium, his first throw was a world record of 69.88 meters.

He went to the 1928 Amsterdam Olympics as a great favorite but sustained a foot injury before the Games. In the end he could manage only 63.20 meters (207' 8") and came in sixth.

By 1930 he was overtaken by the new star, Finland's Matti Järvinen. Penttilä traveled to Los Angeles for the 1932 Olympics where he finished third with 68.70 meters (225' 5"). Järvinen won the gold medal with 72.70 meters (238' 6").

An elbow injury ended Penttilä's sport career in 1936. He served as a major in the Finnish army and later as a secretary-manager of his sports club.

Erik Lundqvist   (Sweden, 1908–1963)

71.01m (232' 11")	Stockholm, Sweden	15 Aug 1928

Erik Lundqvist was a sign painter by profession. He became the youngest Olympic gold medal winner in the javelin when he won in Amsterdam at 20 years, 1 month, and 3 days with a throw of 66.60 meters (218' 6").

Two weeks later, back in Stockholm, he confirmed his status as a champion by becoming the first man to exceed the 70-meter barrier when he threw 71.01 meters (232' 11"). He only improved on this once, eight years later, when he threw 71.16 meters in 1936.

Matti Järvinen   (Finland, 1909–1985)

71.57m (234' 9")	Viipuri, Finland	8 Aug 1930
71.70m (235' 3")	Tampere, Finland	17 Aug 1930
71.88m (235' 10")	Vaasa, Finland	31 Aug 1930
72.93m (239' 3")	Viipuri, Finland	14 Sep 1930
74.02m (242' 10")	Turku, Finland	27 Jun 1932
74.28m (243' 8")	Mikkeli, Finland	25 May 1933
74.61m (244' 9")	Vaasa, Finland	7 Jun 1933
76.10m (249' 8")	Helsinki, Finland	15 Jun 1933
76.66m (251' 6")	Turin, Italy	7 Sep 1934
77.23m (253' 4")	Helsinki, Finland	18 Jun 1936

Matti Järvinen dominated javelin throwing throughout the 1930s. His first interest was baseball, but he tried the javelin at age 17 and set the first of 10 world records in 1930, when he was 21. He came from a famous athletic family. His father, Verner—known in Finland as "Isa" (father) Järvinen—won the discus (Greek-style) gold medal at the 1906 Interim Olympic games in Athens. Verner Järvinen had very strong views on sport. The household was run along military lines to develop his sons' sporting talents. It appeared to work. The eldest son, Yrjo, became a top javelin thrower and was third in the 1924 Finnish championships. The second son, Kalle, was ninth in the shot put at the 1932 Los Angeles Olympics. The third son, Akilles, became the world record holder in the decathlon. And the youngest son, Matti, was Olympic champion and multiple world record holder in the javelin.

After Matti Järvinen set four world records in 1930, his career had a glitch in 1931, when the Finnish Athletic Union suspended him for two months for "behavior unsuited to an athlete" on a trip to Helsinki. It is not clear what his crime was.

He traveled to Los Angeles in 1932 and comfortably won the gold medal, leading a Finnish sweep of the javelin medals. He also won the European Championship in 1934 and again in 1938. He was of course the overwhelming favorite for the 1936 Berlin Olympics but sustained a major back injury shortly before the Games commenced. He competed anyway, finishing fifth with 69.18 meters (227' 0"). The event was won by the German Gerhard Stock with 71.84 meters (235' 8").

Matti Järvinen, Finland, 10-time javelin world record holder and 1932 Olympic champion.

Järvinen won his last Finnish javelin title in 1942, at the age of 33. His hobbies were boxing and playing the violin.

Yrjö Nikkanen (Finland, 1914-1985)

| 77.87m (255' 5") | Karhula, Finland | 25 Aug 1938 |
| 78.70m (258' 2") | Kotka, Finland | 16 Oct 1938 |

At age 18, in 1933, Yrjö Nikkanen was given two javelins by the legendary Matti Järvinen. Five years later, he would be defeating the great man.

Nikkanen had come in second in the 1936 Olympic Games to the German Gerhard Stock, when Järvinen was injured. He finally caught up with Järvinen in 1938, beating Järvinen 8 times out of the 12 they competed. He also set two world records that year, with Järvinen second on both occasions. The second record took place at Kotka, where the temperature was low (6° C, 43° F) and the ground so wet that burning gasoline was used to dry it before the competition began. This record lasted 15 years, the longest interval for any javelin record. It was also the last record achieved with the old birch javelins.

However, Järvinen defeated Nikkanen at the 1938 European Championship, 76.87 meters (252' 2") to 75.00 meters (246' 1"). After World War II Nikkanen competed in the 1946 European Championships. Once again he had to be satisfied with the silver medal, behind the Swede Lennart Atterwall, 68.74 meters (225' 6") to 67.50 meters (221' 5").

When his athletic days were over, Nikkanen took to drinking, and his health deteriorated.

Bud Held (United States, b. 1927)

| 80.41m (263' 10") | Pasadena, USA | 8 Aug 1953 |
| 81.75m (268' 2") | Modesto, USA | 21 May 1955 |

Bud Held, a student at Stanford University, was the NCAA champion for three years (1948-50) and AAU champion six times (1949, 1951, 1953-1955, and 1958). At the 1952

Olympics Held threw 68.42 meters (224' 6"), well below his best, to finish ninth; country-man Cy Young won with 73.78 meters (242' 1").

Held and his brother Dick became active in the design of the javelin. They constructed a longer, slimmer implement, which was hollow in the center and had more surface area.

With this "Held" Javelin, Bud Held became the first man to throw over 80 meters when he threw 80.41 meters (263' 10") at John Muir College, Pasadena, Texas. He was Pan-American champion in 1955 (69.78 meters, 228' 11") and that year increased the world record at the California Relays to 81.75 meters (268' 2").

Unfortunately, when the U.S. Olympic trials came around in June 1956 (five months before the Olympics started), Held was injured and missed selection. In the following September he achieved a lifetime best of 82.29 meters (270' 0"), which would have been good enough for second place at the Olympics. But under the rigid U.S. selection policy, it was too late, and he missed the Games.

Eventually, the IAAF banned the Held javelin and decided that only the traditional wooden Finnish or metallic Swedish designs would be used.

Soini Nikkinen   (Finland, b. 1923)

83.56m (274' 1")   **Kuhmoinen, Finland**   **24 Jun 1956**

Finland's Soini Nikkinen held the world record for six days. Only 84 kilograms (183 pounds) in weight, he was the first Finn to throw over 80 meters. Nikkinen was the youngest in a family of 13 children; their home was a cabin that was only 3 × 3 meters (about 10' × 10'). Throughout his athletic career, he was plagued by duodenal ulcers. During World War II he was a courier for a grenade unit in the Finnish-Soviet conflict.

He competed in the 1948 London Olympics and finished in 12th place with 58.05 meters (190' 5"). Four years later at the Helsinki Olympics he finished eighth with 68.80 meters (225' 9").

In June 1956 he threw a world record of 83.56 meters (274' 1"). That evening, to celebrate his achievement, he planted a birch seedling. Forty years on, it is now 20 meters (66 feet) tall.

After his world record in June, he understood that he was guaranteed a place in the team for the Olympics in November, and he reduced his training. However, just before the Games his form slipped, and he was upset to be left out of the team.

Now retired, he works as a craftsman making traditional Finnish cabinet clocks, called Konninkello.

Janusz Sidlo   (Poland, 1933–1993)

83.66m (274' 5")   **Milan, Italy**   **30 Jun 1956**

Six days after Nikkinen's record, Janusz Sidlo of Poland added 10 centimeters (4 inches) to the record (bringing it to 83.66 meters) at an international meet in Milan, using a Held javelin. Sidlo had been the first European to reach the 80-meter mark, with 80.15 meters (263' 0") in 1953, and had won the European Championships in 1954 with 76.36 meters (250' 6"). He enjoyed a long career and was Polish champion 15 times.

Five months after his record, he took the lead in the Olympic final with 79.98 meters. However, in round four Viktor Tsibulenko (USSR) switched to a metal javelin and improved by four meters to 79.50 meters. Norway's Egil Danielsen then used the same javelin, and it sailed way beyond the 85-meter mark. That ended the contest: Danielsen had 85.71 meters (281' 2"), Sidlo 79.98 meters (262' 5"), and Tsibulenko 79.50 meters (260' 10").

Sidlo was European champion again in 1958 with 80.16 meters (263' 0"). At the 1960 Rome Olympics, the final was plagued by wind and rain, and he managed 76.46 meters (250' 10") for eighth position. He competed at the 1964 Tokyo Olympics (and came in fourth) and the 1968 Mexico City Olympics (seventh). His lifetime best of 86.22 meters (282' 10") was achieved in 1970.

Janusz Sidlo, Poland (javelin).

Egil Danielsen   (Norway, b. 1933)

85.71m (281' 2")   **Melbourne, Australia**   **26 Nov 1956**

In 1956 Egil Danielsen achieved a personal best. Fortunately for him, it was in the middle of the Olympic final. Danielsen had come in 10th at the 1954 European Championships. However, in the period leading up to the Melbourne Olympics, he was in excellent form.

In the final Danielsen, using a wooden javelin, was in sixth position. He noticed that Viktor Tsibulenko (USSR) improved by four meters (13 feet) when he switched to a metal javelin. Danielsen asked if he could use it, and Tsibulenko sportingly agreed. Danielsen then let loose an explosive throw that soared on past the world record mark, almost to the runway of the pole vault. It measured 85.71 meters. Danielsen did a dance of glee and kissed everybody in sight.

It was to be the highlight of his career—he never approached that

Egil Danielsen, Norway (javelin), setting a world record at the 1956 Melbourne Olympics.

distance again. He was second at the 1958 European Championships to Sidlo, 80.16 meters (263' 0") to 78.27 meters (256' 9"). He did not get past the qualifying rounds at the Rome Olympics. At these Olympics Tsibulenko had a belated reward for his generous gesture four years earlier, when he won the gold medal with a throw of 84.64 meters (277' 8").

Al Cantello   (United States, b. 1931)

86.04m (282' 3")   Compton, USA   5 Jun 1959

Al Cantello developed a new technique of javelin throwing. He would give a far greater heave as he released the javelin, so much so that he would fall forward on all fours. This unorthodox method helped him to win the 1959 and 1960 AAU titles. No one else has adopted this method.

His world record was achieved at an invitational meet at Compton, California. Cantello's first throw was a flop, his second came within two feet of the world record,

Al Cantello, United States (javelin).

and his third exceeded it by a foot, reaching 86.04 meters.

Cantello was selected for the 1960 U.S. Olympic team, but it turned out to be a disappointing competition for him. The final was plagued by wind and rain, and his performance dropped right back. He threw 74.70 meters (245' 1") for 10th place.

Carlo Lievore   (Italy, b. 1937)

86.74m (284' 7")   Milan, Italy   1 Jun 1961

Carlo Lievore, Italy (javelin).

Carlo Lievore and his elder brother Giovanni were both international javelin throwers. Giovanni finished sixth at the 1956 Melbourne Olympics with 72.88 meters (239' 1").

Both brothers competed at the 1958 European Championships in Stockholm. Giovanni was eighth with 73.38 meters (240' 9"), while Carlo finished 11th with 68.88 meters (226' 0").

Carlo's hopes for the 1960 Rome Olympics were dashed by an injury three weeks before the Games began; he finished ninth with 75.20 meters (246' 9").

A year later, at the Italian Club Championships in Milan, he threw a world record of 86.74 meters on his second throw, adding 70 centimeters (2' 4") to Cantello's record. His implement was a modified Held javelin, whose design was approved by the IAAF. His world record throw went beyond the arena.

He led the qualifying round at the 1962 European Championships but slipped back to 76.20 meters (250' 0") in the final, good enough for sixth place. At the 1964 Olympics he failed to make the final.

Terje Pedersen   (Norway, b. 1943)

| 87.12m (285' 10") | Oslo, Norway | 1 Jul 1964 |
| 91.72m (300' 11") | Oslo, Norway | 2 Sep 1964 |

Terje Pedersen was a dental student who, at 17, had been the youngest competitor in the javelin at the 1960 Rome Olympics, although he did not compete in the final. In 1964, at age 21, he achieved great heights and depths in one season. In July a meet took place in Oslo between Norway and the Benelux countries. On his fifth throw Pedersen bettered the world record by 38 centimeters to 87.12 meters. The spectators were especially jubilant, as Pedersen was a local Oslo boy.

Two months later he did it again in a match between Norway and Czechoslovakia. Very few present actually saw the record, as they were watching an exciting final to the 800m. When the result went up on the board, the first figure was a 9, which resulted in a deafening wave of cheering. He had broken the 90-meter barrier (and the 300' mark) with 91.72 meters (300' 11").

In that throw he had strained his back slightly and did not take any more throws. He joked at the situation, saying that he would achieve the first 100-meter throw another time. Yet seven weeks later, he had nothing to laugh about. After three meager throws in the qualifying rounds at the Tokyo Olympics, he did not qualify for the final.

Janis Lusis   (Soviet Union, b. 1939)

| 91.98m (301' 9") | Saarijarvi, Finland | 23 Jun 1968 |
| 93.80m (307' 9") | Stockholm, Sweden | 6 Jul 1972 |

Janis Lusis is a Latvian who was 12 times Soviet champion. He is the only male athlete to win an event in the European Championships four times (1962, 1966, 1969, 1971).

As a child, he watched his father be executed by the invading Germans. Later in life he held no animosity toward the German people and went vacationing with German champion Klaus Wolfermann. He was the 1964 Olympic bronze medalist, and his first world record came in 1968, perhaps his best-ever season. The top 11 throws that year were all Lusis's. In Finland he added 26 centimeters (10 inches) to Pedersen's

Janis Lusis, Soviet Union (javelin), 1968 Olympic champion.

four-year-old world record. However, the Olympic Games that year were no walkover. Lusis made the winning throw only in the sixth and final round.

Four years later he achieved his second world record in Sweden. He went on to the Munich Olympics that year as favorite. In the final he led until local hero Klaus Wolfermann threw 90.48 meters (296' 10") on his fifth throw. Lusis couldn't quite match it; his last throw fell short of this by two centimeters.

Lusis was also a competent decathlete and was regarded by his peers as the gentleman of the sport. He married Elvira Ozolina, the 1960 Olympic javelin champion and world record holder. They spent three years coaching in Madagascar between 1987 and 1990.

Jorma Kinnunen   (Finland, b. 1941)

92.70m (304' 1")   **Tampere, Finland**   **18 Jun 1969**

Jorma Kinnunen was the shortest of the javelin champions, standing 175 centimeters (5' 8 ¾") tall. He was known as the little giant from Aanekoski, his hometown, and was the first Finn to throw over 90 meters. He attended three Olympic Games: 1964 (when he came in sixth), 1968 (second), and 1972 (sixth).

A carpenter by profession, he set his world record at Tampere. He threw 92.70 meters on his second throw and was too excited to take any more throws. That distance was to remain his personal best. This world record was the first achieved on a synthetic (Tartan) runway. At the European Championships he was 12th in 1966, 10th in 1969, and 5th in 1971.

He is one of the few champions whose sons have also been successful at the same event at an international level. His son Jarkko was second in the javelin at the European Junior Championships in 1989. His other son, Kimmo, won the javelin at the World Championships in Tokyo in 1991 and was fourth at the 1992 Barcelona Olympics.

Klaus Wolfermann   (West Germany, b. 1946)

94.08m (308' 8")   **Leverkusen, West Germany**   **5 May 1973**

Klaus Wolfermann became a national hero when he won the Olympic gold medal by the smallest possible margin in front of his own people at Munich in 1972. Janis Lusis had set his second world record of 93.80 meters two months before the Games began. However, a few days before the Olympics began Wolfermann had hurled the spear 90.10 meters (295' 7"), which gave him great confidence.

In the Olympic final Lusis took the lead in the opening round with 88.88 meters (291' 7"). However, in round four Wolfermann came close with 88.40 meters (290' 0"). On his next throw Wolfermann went one better and threw 90.48 meters

Klaus Wolfermann, West Germany, celebrating after winning the javelin at the 1972 Olympics.

(296' 10"). Lusis's last throw went just over 90 meters. Amid great tension, the measurement was finally announced as 90.46 meters (296' 9"). The balding and bearded German had won it.

A year later Wolfermann added another 28 centimeters to the world record (94.08 meters). In the European Championships he was not so successful, coming in sixth in 1971 and fifth in 1974.

Miklós Németh   (Hungary, b. 1946)

94.58m (310' 4")   Montreal, Canada   26 Jul 1976

Miklós Németh, Hungary, on the podium after winning the javelin at the 1976 Montreal Olympics.

Miklós Németh is the only athlete to have set a world record and won an Olympic gold medal and to have had a father (Imre, hammer thrower) who had achieved these same distinctions.

Miklós had been something of a boy wonder, throwing 87.20 meters (286' 1") when he was barely 20, but he did not seem to progress over the years. At the Mexico City Olympics he was troubled by an elbow injury and did not make it through to the final. At the Munich Olympics he was seventh with 81.98 meters (268' 11"). Nor did he have much success at the European Championships. He was fifth in 1966, ninth in 1971, and seventh in 1974.

Finally, when everyone had given up on the wunderkind, Németh finally did himself justice at the 1976 Olympics. In the first round he unleashed a killer throw, 94.58 meters, a new world record. That throw finished the competition, and he won by over 6.6 meters (21' 8"), a huge winning margin.

He later became active in the design of javelins. His Németh javelin of the late 1980s had a special roughened area behind the grip, which increased the surface area. It led to several new world records, but these were later disallowed by the IAAF, which banned the implement.

Ferenc Paragi   (Hungary, b. 1953)

96.72m (317' 4")   Tata, Hungary   23 Apr 1980

Ferenc Paragi and Miklós Németh were rivals in the late 1970s and exchanged victories during 1977. Both had a mixed year in 1978, especially at the European Championships: Németh came in seventh and Paragi tenth. In 1979 Paragi made a big jump up to 92.14 meters (302' 4").

The following year, at a "Throwers Meet" in Tata, he threw 96.72 meters (317' 4"), a new world record and the first throw over 95 meters. This record took place three months before the Moscow Olympics.

At the Games Paragi led the qualifying rounds with 88.76 meters (291' 2"). This may well have been a curse in disguise. Since World War II, only two athletes (Wolfermann, 1972; Zelezny, 1992) have led the qualifying round and gone on to win the gold medal. In the final Paragi was troubled by a painful knee and was never a contender. He threw 79.52 meters (260' 11") and finished 10th.

Tom Petranoff   (United States/South Africa, b. 1958)

99.72m (327' 2")   **Los Angeles, USA**   **15 May 1983**

Tom Petranoff, United States/South Africa (javelin).

Tom Petranoff was originally a baseball pitcher, whose fastball was once timed at 97 miles (156 kilometers) per hour. He graduated at the Howe Military Academy, Indiana, in 1976 and took up the javelin in 1977, at age 18. In 1980 he was fourth in the U.S. Olympic trials.

At the 1983 Pepsi Invitational Meet in Los Angeles he hurled the javelin 99.72 meters, adding a massive three meters (9' 10") to the record and getting agonizingly close to the 100-meter mark. After this performance he was a favorite for the Los Angeles Olympics, especially since the East Europeans boycotted the Games; this meant that the latest world record holder, Uwe Hohn (East Germany), would not be competing.

Petranoff's hopes were raised when he led the qualifying rounds. However, the pressure of being favorite in the final appeared to affect him, and he later described himself as feeling "flat." The swirling winds in the Coliseum didn't help. In a disastrous day, he finished 10th with 78.40 meters (257' 3"). At the 1988 Seoul Olympics it was worse: He failed to get through the qualifying rounds.

The next year he and a group of U.S. athletes made a controversial tour to South Africa at a time when the IAAF had a ban on that country because of its apartheid policies. The U.S. athletic authorities subsequently imposed long bans on the athletes concerned. But Petranoff chose to stay and settle in South Africa. He argued that other "terrorist" countries were still accepted by the athletic community, so he didn't see why South Africa should be isolated. He went further than just staying: He took out South African citizenship.

At the beginning of the 1990s the apartheid policies came to an end, and Nelson Mandela led a black majority government. South Africa was readmitted to the 1992 Barcelona Olympics. But Petranoff was caught up with South African athletic politics and was left out of the team.

Uwe Hohn   (East Germany, b. 1962)

104.80m (343' 10")   **Berlin, East Germany**   **20 Jul 1984**

Uwe Hohn was the tallest of the javelin record holders, standing 198 centimeters (6' 6"). He made meteoric progress from junior to senior ranks: European junior champion in

1981 and European (senior) champion in 1982. Hohn developed into an athlete capable of repeated throws over 90 meters. In May 1984 he threw 99.52 meters (326' 6"), only 20 centimeters behind Petranoff's world record. Two months later, it happened—an awesome throw that changed the fate of javelin throwing. The crowd seemed to sense it and started chanting for a 100-meter throw. Hohn obliged and hurled the instrument 104.80 meters, a startling 5.08-meter (16' 8") addition to the world record. Even before it hit the ground, Hohn raised his arms in triumph—he knew he had unleashed a monster throw. It was the sport's only 100-meter throw.

Alas, East Germany meekly followed the Soviet Union in the boycott of the 1984 Olympics. Hohn expressed deep resentment at this decision, which was reported, and he was cautioned against such views by the East German authorities.

Uwe Hohn, East Germany (javelin), the only man to throw the javelin over 100 meters.

His 100-meter throw had raised concerns about the safety of the device. Accordingly, a new javelin with the center of gravity moved forward was introduced in 1986. This meant it fell about 10 meters short of the distances achieved with the existing javelin.

Hohn may well have excelled with it, but during a weight-training session in 1986 he suffered a severe back injury with sciatic nerve damage when heavy weights collapsed on him. East German surgeons were not experienced in the technique of dealing with this sort of injury. An offer of treatment was made from West Germany, but this was denied. The end result was that his sporting career was over at age 24. He still suffers significant residual disability 10 years later.

NEW JAVELIN

Klaus Tafelmeier (West Germany, b. 1958)

85.74m (281' 3")   **Como, Italy**   **21 Sep 1986**

As previously mentioned, Hohn's 100-meter throw led to the introduction of a new javelin in 1986. The center of gravity was shifted four centimeters forward. At the start of 1987, the IAAF accepted as the first world record the best mark to have been achieved by 31 December 1986. This was the throw of 85.74 meters (281' 3") by Klaus Tafelmeier at Como, Italy, on 21 September 1986. One month earlier he had won the European Championships with 84.76 meters (278' 1").

Tafelmeier had come in third at the West German championships three years running, 1979 through 1981. Then his fortune changed, and he won the title from 1982 to 1985 and again in 1987 and 1991. He had been one of the favorites at the 1984 Los Angeles Olympics in the absence of the Soviet Bloc. But he had a disappointing Olympic competition, achieving only 73.52 meters (241' 2") with the old javelin and did not qualify for the final. He finished fourth at the 1988 Seoul Olympics, with 82.72 meters (271' 5") using the new javelin.

Ján Zelezny   (Czechoslovakia/Czech Republic, b. 1966)

87.66m (287' 7")	Nitra, Czechoslovakia	31 May 1987
95.54m (313' 5")	Pietersburg, South Africa	6 Apr 1993
95.66m (313' 10")	Sheffield, England	29 Aug 1993
98.48 (323' 1")	Jena, Germany	25 May 1996

Ján Zelezny spent his childhood playing ice hockey and volleyball before turning to the javelin. Despite intermittent back problems that required surgery, he has remained at the top for 10 years.

Ján Zelezny, Czech Republic (javelin), 1992 and 1996 Olympic champion.

He achieved his first world record with the new javelin in 1987. He went on to set two additional records in duels with Britain's Steve Backley over the next few years. But he and Backley were using the new Németh javelin, which had increased surface area, and the instrument and these records were subsequently disallowed.

Zelezny led the qualifying rounds at the 1988 Seoul Olympics. But the Finn Tapio Korjus snatched victory from him in the very last throw, 84.28 meters (276' 6") to 84.12 meters (276' 0"). He missed qualifying for the final for both the 1990 European Championships and the 1991 World Championships.

Finally, in 1992 there were no mistakes. At the Barcelona Olympics he won the event on his first throw, with 89.66 meters (294' 2"). The next year he set world records in South Africa and England. The South African record was the first in that country since its readmission to the IAAF. Ján Zelezny has also won both the 1993 and 1995 World Championships.

In May of 1996 he approached the 100-meter mark with a new world record of 98.48 meters. Then in August he became the first male Olympic champion to defend his javelin title since Jonni Myyrä's victories in 1920 and 1924. He won with a throw of 88.16 meters (289' 3").

As a training technique he plays tennis at least an hour every day to keep his shoulders supple.

Patrik Bodén   (Sweden, b. 1967)

89.10m (292' 4")	Austin, USA	24 Mar 1990

Patrik Bodén, who was studying engineering at the University of Texas, seemed to come out of nowhere in 1990. He had been second in the Swedish championships in 1989 and had won the NCAA title the same year, but he was still regarded as short of world class. However, on 17 March 1990 he threw 82.84 meters (271' 9"), a U.S. collegiate record. A week later at a small meet of four universities, in front of a modest crowd, he improved almost seven meters to set a new world record of 89.10 meters (292' 4").

Only 22 at the time, Bodén seemed to be destined for a major track and field career. He was NCAA champion from 1989 to 1991 and Swedish champion in 1992 through 1994. Although achieving good results, he never quite made the continuing impact on the world scene that had been suggested by his world record. This has partly been due to injuries. He had to undergo surgeries on his right shoulder and on his knees in 1990 and 1991. His best competitive effort in international competition was third at the 1990 European Championships.

Steve Backley   (Great Britain, b. 1969)

| 89.58m (293' 11") | Stockholm, Sweden | 2 Jul 1990 |
| 91.46m (300' 1") | Auckland, New Zealand | 25 Jan 1992 |

Steve Backley, Great Britain (javelin).

Steve Backley is Britain's first world record holder in the throwing events. This 6' 5" (196 centimeters) athlete was originally a student in sports sciences at Loughborough University but postponed his studies after his meteoric rise through junior and senior javelin ranks.

In 1990, at age 21, he had a dazzling season, winning both European and Commonwealth Games titles and setting a world record in Stockholm (89.58 meters). He had a series of epic duels that year with Ján Zelezny, both men exchanging unofficial world records. Backley's record of 90.98 meters (298' 6") in front of a home crowd in London on 20 July made him the first man to throw over 90 meters with the new javelin. However, this world record was achieved with the new Németh javelin, which was later banned, so his Stockholm world record (89.58 meters) was reinstated as the official world record.

He started 1992 off with another world record in New Zealand in January, this time officially over 90 meters with the new javelin, when he threw 91.46 meters (300' 1"). However, the rest of the year belonged to Zelezny, who comfortably took the Olympic title in Barcelona with 89.66 meters (294' 2"). Backley finished third with 83.38 meters (273' 7"). Zelezny also won the 1993 World Championships, with Backley fourth.

The Briton returned to winning ways in 1994 with victory in the European Championships in Helsinki (85.20 meters, 279' 6") and the Commonwealth Games in Victoria, Canada (82.74 meters, 271' 5"). At the 1995 World Championships in Gothenburg he was second to Zelezny, 86.30 meters (283' 2") to 89.58 meters (293' 11"). At the Atlanta Olympics he was once more second to the Czech, 87.44 meters (286' 10") to 88.16 meters (289' 3").

Conclusions

The men's javelin is the only throwing event in which the world record has shown steady progress over the last 10 years, but this is largely because of the new implement introduced in 1986. It is not clear to what extent the javelin world record might have been influenced by the use of anabolic steroids. The average weight of the last 10 world record holders was 95.8 kilograms (211 pounds), modest compared to the last 10 record-holding shot putters, who averaged 119 kilograms (262 pounds). The current world record holder, Ján Zelezny, weighs 80 kilograms (176 pounds).

Also unlike the other throwing events, javelin is not dominated by Eastern Europeans. The last seven world record holders have come from seven different countries, and four of these were from countries outside Eastern Europe (Petranoff, Tafelmeier, Bodén, and Backley).

After the initial new-javelin record in 1986 of 85.74 meters, the record has crept up to 98.48 meters. It seems only a matter of time before it once again reaches the 100-meter mark.

Five All-Time Best: Men's Javelin

Ján Zelezny (CZH)	98.48m (323' 1")	1996
Raymond Hecht (GER)	92.60m (303' 10")	1995
Steve Backley (GBR)	91.46m (300' 1")	1992
Seppo Räty (FIN)	90.60m (297' 3")	1992
Tom Petranoff (USA/S.AF)	89.16m (292' 6")	1991
Prediction	*102.00m (334' 7")*	*2015*

Top Three: Men's Javelin

GOLD MEDAL:	**Ján Zelezny (CZH)**
SILVER MEDAL:	**Matti Järvinen (FIN)**
BRONZE MEDAL:	**Uwe Hohn (GDR)**

The decathlon was introduced at the 1912 Olympics. A formidable event, it consists of 10 separate track and field disciplines over two days of competition. On the first day, the events are 100m, long jump, shot put, high jump, and 400m; the second day events are 110m hurdles, discus, pole vault, javelin, and 1500m. Points are awarded in each event according to a scoring table devised by the IAAF. After the 10th event, the leading point scorer is the winner. The points allocated to each discipline have been adjusted many times: in 1912, 1920, 1934, 1950, 1962, 1977, and 1985.

The decathlon gets little publicity except at the Olympics, so many decathletes compete in anonymity for most of their competitive careers. The winner of the Olympic decathlon is usually acclaimed with the title "World's Greatest Athlete."

The event changed in character in the 1960s, following the promotion by West German coaches of the concept of the "whole decathlete." The previous philosophy had been to look for specialists in two or three events who could also manage the rest. Accordingly, thinking and training changed as well.

The first 60 years of the 20th century had been dominated by U.S. decathletes. However, since the 1960s there has been a strong German presence. Altogether, 20 men have held the decathlon world record, of whom 9 were from the United States and 4 from Germany. Eleven world record holders have won Olympic gold medals, and eight world records were set in Olympic competition.

The points tables have been adjusted so often that it is hard to compare athletes of different generations. The one major barrier that looms ahead is the 9000-point mark. This is quite within the capabilities of the present generation of elite decathletes, if they achieve personal bests in most events in one competition.

Men's World Record Holders for Decathlon

Record score*	Record holder	Location	Date
6087	Aleksander Klumberg (EST)	Helsinki, Finland	16-17 Sep 1922
6476	Harold Osborn (USA)	Paris, France	11-12 Jul 1924
6460	Paavo Yrjölä (FIN)	Viipuri, Finland	17-18 Jul 1926
6586	Paavo Yrjölä (FIN)	Helsinki, Finland	16-17 Jul 1927
6587	Paavo Yrjölä (FIN)	Amsterdam, Netherlands	3-4 Aug 1928
6865	Akilles Järvinen (FIN)	Viipuri, Finland	19-20 Jul 1930
6735**	James Bausch (USA)	Los Angeles, USA	5-6 Aug 1932
7147	Hans Heinrich Sievert (GER)	Hamburg, Germany	7-8 Jul 1934
7254	Glenn Morris (USA)	Berlin, Germany	7-8 Aug 1936
7287	Bob Mathias (USA)	Tulare, USA	29-30 Jun 1950
7592	Bob Mathias (USA)	Helsinki, Finland	25-26 Jul 1952
7608	Rafer Johnson (USA)	Kingsburg, USA	10-11 Jun 1955
7653	Vasiliy Kuznetsov (USSR)	Krasnodar, USSR	17-18 May 1958
7789	Rafer Johnson (USA)	Moscow, USSR	27-28 Jul 1958
7839	Vasiliy Kuznetsov (USSR)	Moscow, USSR	16-17 May 1959
7982	Rafer Johnson (USA)	Eugene, USA	8-9 Jul 1960
8009	Yang Chuan-Kwang (TAI)	Walnut, USA	27-28 Apr 1963
8119	Russell Hodge (USA)	Los Angeles, USA	23-24 Jul 1966
8234	Kurt Bendlin (USA)	Heidelberg, West Germany	13-14 May 1967
8309	Bill Toomey (USA)	Los Angeles, USA	10-11 Dec 1969
8466	Nikolay Avilov (USSR)	Munich, West Germany	7-8 Sep 1972
8429	Bruce Jenner (USA)	Eugene, USA	9-10 Aug 1975

8456	Bruce Jenner (USA)	Eugene, USA	25-26 Jun 1976
8634	Bruce Jenner (USA)	Montreal, Canada	29-30 Jul 1976
8648	Daley Thompson (GBR)	Gotzis, Austria	17-18 May 1980
8667	Guido Kratschmer (FRG)	Bernhausen, West Germany	14-15 Jun 1980
8730	Daley Thompson (GBR)	Gotzis, Austria	22-23 May 1982
8741	Jürgen Hingsen (FRG)	Ulm, West Germany	14-15 Aug 1982
8774	Daley Thompson (GBR)	Athens, Greece	7-8 Sep 1982
8825	Jürgen Hingsen (FRG)	Bernhausen, West Germany	4-5 Jun 1983
8832	Jürgen Hingsen (FRG)	Mannheim, West Germany	8-9 Jun 1984
8847	Daley Thompson (GBR)	Los Angeles, USA	8-9 Aug 1984
8891	Dan O'Brien (USA)	Talence, France	4-5 Sep 1992

*Scores adjusted to 1985 tables.
**On the 1920 scoring tables then operative, Järvinen's 1930 world record was 8255 while Bausch (1932) scored 8462.

Aleksander Klumberg   (Estonia, 1899-1958)

6087   **Helsinki, Finland**   **16-17 Sep 1922**

Alexander Klumberg of Estonia was the first official holder of the world decathlon record. Estonia, one of the Baltic states, achieved its independence from Tsarist Russia in 1918, was reoccupied by the Soviet Union in 1940, and reestablished its independence in 1991. Klumberg competed during the 22-year period of Estonian independence between the wars.

Klumberg had competed in the javelin and the decathlon at the 1920 Antwerp Olympics. He finished fifth in the javelin and had to retire injured after eight events in the decathlon. He competed in the same events in the 1924 Olympics in Paris. He did not qualify for the javelin final but finished third in the decathlon.

The decathlon that earned Klumberg the world record took place in Helsinki in 1922. It appears that the 1500m was his weak point: He ran the race in 5:11.3. Only James Bausch (1932) had a slower time (5:17.0). However, Klumberg's javelin throw of 62.20 meters was not exceeded in a decathlon world record score for 30 years.

Harold Osborn   (United States, 1899-1975)

6476   **Paris, France**   **11-12 Jul 1924**

Osborn remains the only athlete to hold the world record at an individual event (the high jump) and the decathlon. He is also the only athlete to win an Olympic gold medal at the decathlon and an individual event (the high jump again), which he achieved at the 1924 Olympics.

A graduate of the University of Illinois, he won the AAU decathlon title three times and the AAU high jump three times. Osborn set a world record for the high jump at the U.S. Olympic trials. At the 1924 Olympics he won with a new world decathlon record and naturally earned a huge score for his high jumping, clearing 1.97 meters (6' 5 ½").

In his career he competed in seven decathlons, winning five. He continued to jump well into his 30s and actually achieved his personal best at the age of 37, when he jumped 6' 8 ½" (2.04 meters). He married Ethel Catherwood of Canada, who was Olympic high-jump champion in 1928, but they later divorced.

Paavo Yrjölä   (Finland, 1902-1980)

6460	Viipuri, Finland	17-18 Jul 1926
6586	Helsinki, Finland	16-17 Jul 1927
6587	Amsterdam, Netherlands	3-4 Aug 1928

Paavo Yrjölä broke the world record three times and won the gold medal at the Amsterdam Olympics. Born in Hameenkyro, he tried his first decathlon at age 20, in 1922. His last was in 1932, a prolonged decathlon career for those times. He was ninth at the 1924 Paris Games, first at Amsterdam in 1928, and sixth at Los Angeles in 1932. Between 1925 and 1930 he was unbeaten, and he won 12 out of 17 decathlons.

His success is all the more remarkable in that he came from a rural background where there was not even a sports ground. He was self-taught, fashioning his own equipment, such as hurdles, literally from the local woods. He lived and trained in isolation on the family farm, confident that he had the measure of his opponents. He remained on the farm and died there in 1980.

Paavo Yrjölä, Finland (decathlon), 1928 Olympic champion.

Akilles Järvinen   (Finland, 1905-1943)

| 6865 | Viipuri, Finland | 19-20 Jul 1930 |

Akilles Järvinen was part of a famous Finnish sporting family, described in the profile of his brother, javelin champion Matti Järvinen. The father Verner had very definite ideas about the upbringing of children and had a rigid routine that heavily emphasized sport, discipline, and training for his young sons. Every day there was a strict timetable for study and athletic training. It must have had some useful effects, at least in terms of later sporting success. Akilles went on to set a world record in 1930 and competed in two Olympics, finishing second both times (1928 and 1932). Under the scoring system operative since 1985, he would have won both times. He also played two seasons of ice hockey in the top division.

Akilles Järvinen, Finland (decathlon) with his father and coach Verner Järvinen.

Järvinen fought as a pilot against the Soviets in the 1939-1940 Soviet-Finnish War. He died in an air crash in 1943.

James Bausch   (United States, 1906–1974)

| **6735** | **Los Angeles, USA** | **5-6 Aug 1932** |

James Bausch was an athlete who had a meteoric rise to the top. He had a very short career, only 16 months, but in that time won four out of five decathlons, including the 1932 Olympic gold medal with a world record.

Born in Wichita, he was a highly regarded all-around athlete at the University of Kansas, starring in football (All-American) and basketball, as well as track and field athletics. His decathlon career began in 1931, when he set a U.S. decathlon record at the Kansas Relays. He finished second at the AAU titles later that year, his only loss.

His strength in the decathlon was in the pole vault and the throws. At the Los Angeles Games he won by a comfortable 235-point margin ahead of Akilles Järvinen of Finland, setting a new world record.

He had a brief professional football career, first with the Cincinnati Reds (1933) and then with the Chicago Cardinals (1934). There was even a brief spell as a nightclub singer. He served in World War II in the U.S. Navy but contracted osteomyelitis, a bone disease that plagued him the rest of his days. He subsequently had a career with the U.S. Department of Agriculture.

Hans Heinrich Sievert   (Germany, 1909–1963)

| **7147** | **Hamburg, Germany** | **7-8 Jul 1934** |

Hans Heinrich Sievert was primarily a shot put and discus athlete but surprised many by winning the German decathlon title in 1931. He won the title again in 1933, 1934, and 1938, winning 8 out of the 11 decathlons he contested. At the 1932 Olympics he finished fifth in the decathlon after an injury in the pole vault. He also finished sixth in the shot put and 11th in the discus.

He actually set a world record in 1933, but this was denied on technical grounds by the IAAF. However, in 1934 he finally bettered Jim Bausch's record, and later that year he won the European Championships. Injuries prevented him from competing in the decathlon at the 1936 Berlin Olympics, but he came in tenth in the shot put.

Glenn Morris   (United States, 1912–1973)

| **7254** | **Berlin, Germany** | **7-8 Aug 1936** |

Glenn Morris was a student at Colorado State University. He was another U.S. athlete who came from nowhere to Olympic success, contesting a total of only three decathlons in five months.

His first decathlon in April 1936 at the Kansas Relays earned him an American record. In May he competed at and won the AAU/U.S. Olympic trials decathlon. Three months later, in August, he won the Olympic gold medal in Berlin with a new world record.

After his Olympic victory he promptly retired from track and field. He had a brief fling in Hollywood (*Tarzan's Revenge*), playing Tarzan opposite Eleanor Holm, the swimmer, who was banned by Olympic supremo Avery Brundage following high jinks en route to Berlin. He went on to play American football in the NFL with the Detroit Lions. He served in the U.S. Navy in World War II and was seriously wounded. After the war he had great difficulty obtaining employment and died in poverty, aged 61, in a veteran's hospital in California.

Glenn Morris, United States (decathlon).

Bob Mathias   (United States, b. 1930)

| 7287 | Tulare, USA | 29–30 Jun 1950 |
| 7592 | Helsinki, Finland | 25–26 Jul 1952 |

Bob Matthias, United States, Olympic decathlon champion in 1948 and 1952.

Bob Mathias was the boy wonder of the decathlon. He was born in Tulare, California, the son of a doctor. A talented football player at school, he had never seen a javelin, let alone thrown one, when his coach suggested that he consider the decathlon. Mathias won the first decathlon he entered in June 1948 and then, just two weeks later, won the AAU/Olympic trials decathlon. This in turn led to the London Olympics in August, where he competed against the world's best. After the first day he was in third position. But he used his hurdles, discus, and javelin talents to move ahead on day two. The last event, the 1500m, was run in cold, wet conditions with the help of car lights. When it was all over, 17-year-old Mathias was Olympic champion.

After this triumph, he went on to Stanford University, where he was a major success on the football field as a running back.

Mathias set two world records in his career. The first was at the 1950 AAU Championships, held in his hometown, Tulare, one of four AAU titles that he won. The second was at the 1952 Olympics. He is one of the few athletes to have a perfect record: 11 decathlons, 11 wins.

After his second Olympic win he joined other Olympic champions who have made movies—this one was about himself, *The Bob Mathias Story*. Other film credits were *China Doll*, in which he played Victor Mature's copilot, and *It Happened in Athens* with Jayne Mansfield.

Later in life Mathias spent eight years as a Republican congressional representative (1966-74). He also worked for the U.S. Olympic Committee as director of its training center in Colorado Springs and ran a boys camp in California for 16 years.

Rafer Johnson   (United States, b. 1935)

7608	Kingsburg, USA	10-11 Jun 1955
7789	Moscow, USSR	27-28 Jul 1958
7982	Eugene, USA	8-9 Jul 1960

Rafer Johnson, United States, and Vasiliy Kuznetsov, Soviet Union, friendly rivals of the 1950s in the decathlon.

At age 16 Rafer Johnson had actually watched Mathias performing at the 1952 Olympic trials in Tulare, California. He made a decision there and then to become a decathlete. By 1955 he had displaced Mathias as world record holder.

Naturally, Johnson had visions of winning at the 1956 Olympics. But another top black athlete, Milton Campbell (second at the 1952 Olympics), was in the form of his life. Johnson had to settle for the silver medal, as Campbell won with a score just short of Johnson's world record.

The Soviet Vasiliy Kuznetsov broke the world record in 1958, and Johnson took it back two months later in Moscow. Then Kuznetsov took the record back again in 1959, and Johnson reclaimed it a year later in Eugene.

However, at the Rome Olympics in September it was not Kuznetsov who turned out to be the threat, but Yang Chuan-Kwang of Taiwan, a fellow student at UCLA. In the end it came down to the 1500m. If Yang could finish nine seconds ahead of Johnson, he would win the gold medal. Yang tried to break away, but Johnson clung on with grim determination and was only a few seconds behind him at the finish. So Johnson won gold, Yang silver.

He retired after these Games, having won 9 out of the 11 decathlons he had contested. In 1961 he began work for President John Kennedy's Peace Corps. Johnson later supported Robert Kennedy in his bid for the U.S. presidency in 1968. He was with Kennedy at the moment that assassin Sirhan Sirhan shot him and Johnson did what he could to help the dying senator.

Vasiliy Kuznetsov   (Soviet Union, b. 1932)

| 7653 | Krasnodar, USSR | 17-18 May 1958 |
| 7839 | Moscow, USSR | 16-17 May 1959 |

Vasiliy Kuznetsov was the Soviet decathlon champion from 1953-1960 and 1962-1963, 10 times in all. He was three times European champion, in 1954, 1958, and 1962, but missed out on an Olympic gold medal. At both the 1956 and 1960 Olympics he finished third.

His first world record was in a Moscow vs. Leningrad vs. Ukraine athletics match in 1958. This record was beaten by Rafer Johnson two months later at the United States vs. Soviet Union athletic meet in Moscow, with Kuznetsov second.

A year later at another Moscow vs. Leningrad vs. Ukraine meet he broke Johnson's record. But Johnson reclaimed the record in 1960.

At his last Olympics in Tokyo in 1964, Kuznetsov was seventh. In his long decathlon career from 1953-1964 he won 30 out of the 43 decathlons he entered.

Yang Chuan-Kwang   (Taiwan, b. 1933)

8009   **Walnut, USA**   **27-28 Apr 1963**

Yang Chuan-Kwang, Taiwan (decathlon).

In 1954 Yang Chuan-Kwang met Bob Mathias, who was on a goodwill trip to Taiwan. Yang had won the Asian Games title that year, and Mathias gave him a javelin.

Yang pursued his decathlon dream in Taiwan, isolated from the mainstream of competition, and came in eighth at the 1956 Olympics. At these Games he met coach "Ducky" Drake, who persuaded him to come and train in the United States alongside Johnson at UCLA. Taking up the invitation, Yang arrived in 1958 and was soon challenging Johnson. As detailed in the profile of Rafer Johnson, he was a mere 58 points behind Johnson at the finish of the 1960 Rome Olympics decathlon.

Johnson retired after the 1960 Games, but Yang continued competing. He was AAU champion in 1959, 1962, and 1964. He finally achieved a world record in 1963 at Walnut, California. Yang's specialty was the pole vault: Whereas Johnson had pole vaulted 3.97 meters (13' 0 ¼") in his 1960 record, Yang vaulted 4.84 meters (15' 10 ½") in 1963. However, the IAAF revised the point score in the early 1960s, and the points obtainable from a good pole vault performance were much reduced. This severely hampered Yang's prospects at the 1964 Olympics. In the end, he finished fifth and retired after the Games.

Russell Hodge   (United States, b. 1939)

8119   **Los Angeles, USA**   **23-24 Jul 1966**

Russell Hodge had an athletic background; his mother, Alice Arden, was tied for eighth at the 1936 Olympics in the high jump. He was a student at UCLA alongside long-term rival Bill Toomey. Hodge was a big man for a decathlete, weighing 100 kilograms (220 pounds), and his career was often interrupted by injuries, which stopped him from reaching his full potential. Injuries ruined his chances of selection for the 1968 and 1972 Olympics.

Toomey had more victories than Hodge, winning the AAU decathlon title five times (1965-69). Hodge was second in this event four times. However Hodge had one significant victory over Toomey at Los Angeles in 1966 with a new world record, defeating

Toomey by 11 points. Hodge came in ninth at the 1964 Olympics and was second at the 1971 Pan-American Games.

He currently resides in Tacoma, Washington and markets vitamins. Russell Hodge is an ordained minister and was the minister for the Olympic family at the Atlanta Games.

Kurt Bendlin   (West Germany, b. 1943)

8234   **Heidelberg, West Germany**   **13–14 May 1967**

Kurt Bendlin, West Germany (decathlon).

In the 1960s a German challenge to the U.S. domination of the decathlon developed. The concept of the "whole decathlete," rather than just extending an athlete who happened to be good in two or three disciplines, was developed. At the 1964 Olympics in Tokyo, Germans finished first, third, and sixth; at the 1966 European Championships, all three medal winners were from West Germany. The next world record holder was German Kurt Bendlin, who allegedly ate raw meat daily as part of his dietary program. Bendlin won the West German decathlon championship four times: 1965, 1967, 1971, and 1974. In 1967 he captured the world record in Heidelberg in a qualification match for a West Germany vs. United States vs. Soviet Union athletic meet.

At the Mexico City Olympics he was troubled by an elbow injury, which hampered his javelin throw—one of his strongest events—even though he still managed the longest throw. In the end he won the bronze medal, only 129 points behind winner Bill Toomey (USA).

Bill Toomey   (United States, b. 1939)

8309   **Los Angeles, USA**   **10–11 Dec 1969**

Bill Toomey didn't take up the decathlon seriously till age 24, competing in 35 decathlons altogether. He was a competent athlete at the University of Colorado, but without striking success, and competed in his first decathlon with the idea that he would pursue it further if he could score 6000 points. He scored 6400. So he began actively training for the event and came in fourth at the U.S. trials for the Tokyo Olympics. Toomey spent four months (1965-66) in Germany with decathlon coach Friedel Schirmir. In his time, he won virtually every major championship, including the 1968 Mexico City Olympics, five AAU titles, the British AAA title, and the 1967 Pan-American Games. After the Olympics the only thing missing was a world record. He spent all of 1969 chasing it, finally making it on his 10th attempt. It was time to retire.

Toomey married 1964 Olympic long jump gold medalist and world record holder Mary Rand, after they "escaped" from England with Rand heavily disguised, but they subsequently divorced. He worked for the Peace Corps for several years and was active in business and marketing. In 1987 he was appointed director of fundraising for the U.S. Olympic Committee. On his office wall he framed a cartoon captioned, "There is nothing sadder than a washed-up jock."

Bill Toomey, United States (decathlon), 1968 Olympic champion.

Nikolay Avilov   (Soviet Union, b. 1948)

8466   **Munich, West Germany**   **7–8 Sep 1972**

Nikolay Avilov, Soviet Union (decathlon), 1972 Olympic champion.

Nikolay Avilov was introduced to the decathlon at the age of 18, after playing soccer and basketball in his youth. He was the highest-placed Soviet (fourth) at the 1968 Olympics.

In the years after the 1968 Games he had mixed fortunes, coming in fourth in the 1969 European Championships and not finishing in 1971. He was not considered to be one of the favorites for the 1972 Olympics in Munich. (The event took place after the "Day of Mourning" for the Israeli athletes murdered by the Black September terrorists.) Nonetheless, Avilov's personal performance was beyond his wildest dreams: He set personal bests in nine of the events and equaled his personal best in the tenth. No athlete has ever so exceeded themselves in an Olympic decathlon. When it was all over he had won by 419 points, a new world record.

He returned to Montreal in 1976 but lost to the all-conquering Bruce Jenner and finished third. He had hopes of reaching one more Olympics, in front of his home crowd in Moscow in 1980. But after finishing seventh in the Soviet trials, he retired. His wife, Valentina, won the high jump bronze medal at the 1968 Mexico City Olympics.

Bruce Jenner (United States, b. 1949)

8429	Eugene, USA	9–10 Aug 1975
8456	Eugene, USA	25–26 Jun 1976
8634	Montreal, Canada	29–30 Jul 1976

Bruce Jenner, United States (decathlon), 1976 Olympic champion.

Bruce Jenner set the world record three times and was Olympic gold medalist in the event at Montreal in 1976. He entered Graceland College in Iowa on a football scholarship, but after a knee injury he turned to track and field with dramatic improvement. He was the third member of the U.S. team selected for the 1972 Olympics and finished 10th behind Avilov's whirlwind performance.

Over the next four years he dedicated himself almost entirely to the decathlon, not an easy task financially in the United States, where the event is all but invisible except in the Olympic year. He progressed to be the 1974 AAU champion and in 1975 set a new world record in the United States vs. Soviet Union vs. Poland athletic meet. He improved on this world record at the 1976 U.S. Olympic trials. The 1976 Olympics were the highlight of his career. With another world record performance, his T-shirt emblazoned "Feet—don't let me down," his blonde wife, Christie, in the background, and his personable character and good looks, Jenner captured the imagination of the worldwide television audience at an Olympics where U.S. track and field gold medals were scarce.

He retired immediately after the Games, but despite his Olympic win, some cold winds started blowing. The years of dedication to the decathlon hadn't helped his marriage, and he and his wife divorced. He had a short movie career (*Don't Stop the Music*). He has since worked in television and briefly married Linda Thompson.

Daley Thompson (Great Britain, b. 1958)

8648	Gotzis, Austria	17–18 May 1980
8730	Gotzis, Austria	22–23 May 1982
8774	Athens, Greece	7–8 Sep 1982
8847	Los Angeles, USA	8–9 Aug 1984

Daley Thompson had ten years as the world's top decathlete. He won two Olympic gold medals, three European Championships, and three Commonwealth Games championships, set four world records, and went undefeated from 1978 to 1987. Thompson was born of a Nigerian father and a Scottish mother. He was named Adodele, which ended up as Daley. Amiable and extroverted, he was nonetheless an extremely determined competitor. At the 1976 Montreal Olympics Thompson finished 18th. He progressed rapidly from that point and just finished second at the 1978 European Championships. From then on he went on a prolonged winning streak and was European, Commonwealth, world, and Olympic champion, all at the same time.

Thompson built up an aura of invincibility, which seemed justified when he came through high-pressure situations to ultimately triumph in a number of big competitions. His casual attitude occasionally irritated fans, such as when he jogged the last lap of the 1984 Los Angeles 1500m event. A half-decent sprint would have easily broken the world record. His T-shirt at these Games, questioning Carl Lewis's sexuality, seemed immature.

At the 1987 World Championships, his winning streak came to an end. He finished ninth. He was injured but competed anyway. He hoped to correct things at the 1988 Olympics but finished fourth.

He still had hopes of returning to the Olympic arena in 1992 but could no longer reproduce the form of his glory years and retired.

Daley Thompson, Great Britain (decathlon), 1980 and 1984 Olympic champion.

Guido Kratschmer   (West Germany, b. 1953)

8667   **Bernhausen, West Germany**   **14–15 Jun 1980**

Guido Kratschmer had a prolonged career as a decathlete. He missed selection to the Munich Olympics in 1972, when he was 19. He went on to a silver medal at the 1976 Montreal Olympics, behind Bruce Jenner. Politics meant that he missed the 1980 Moscow Olympics, because West Germany joined the U.S. boycott of these Games. In 1984 he was fourth at the Los Angeles Games. In 1988 he was injured and missed the Seoul Olympics.

Kratschmer set a new world record in 1980, six weeks before the Moscow Games began. But because of the boycott, he watched as a spectator as Daley Thompson won the gold medal.

A physical education teacher, he was known as a man of few words but was respected by his fellow decathletes. He was the West German decathlon champion six times in a row from 1975-1980. In the European Championships he was third in 1974, was injured and did not finish in 1978, was ninth in 1982, and was injured again and did not finish in 1986. In all, he competed in 42 decathlons, a remarkable total, and won 13.

Jürgen Hingsen   (West Germany, b. 1958)

8741	Ulm, West Germany	14–15 Aug 1982
8825	Bernhausen, West Germany	4–5 Jun 1983
8832	Mannheim, West Germany	8–9 Jun 1984

Jürgen Hingsen was one of the German athletes in the 1980s who challenged Thompson for supremacy. Although he set the world record three times, he could never quite beat Thompson in direct competition on the 10 occasions they met.

Known as the German Hercules for his size—200 centimeters (6' 6 ¾") tall and weighing 100 kilograms (220 pounds)—Hingsen was active over 10 years, winning 8 of his 28 decathlons.

He first set the world record in the West German championships in 1982, only to see Thompson better this record at the European Championships later that season. In 1983 he upped the record one more time, at Bernhausen, only to lose to Thompson later in the season at the Helsinki World Championships. In 1984 he again set a world record, at Mannheim, shortly before the Olympics, but it was Thompson who won gold at Los Angeles, with Hingsen taking the silver.

At the 1988 Seoul Olympics he false-started three times at the start of the 100m and was disqualified. German officials maintain that he hadn't fouled but was the victim of inexperienced athletic officials, who weren't prepared to admit to a mistake. Surprisingly, he was West German decathlon champion only once, in 1982.

Jürgen Hingsen, West Germany (decathlon).

Dan O'Brien   (United States, b. 1966)

8891   **Talence, France**   **4–5 Sep 1992**

Born in Portland, Oregon, Dan O'Brien has a half-Finnish mother and an African-American father. He was adopted at age two by Jim and Virginia O'Brien and at school became a major talent at track and field, football, and basketball. He moved on to the University of Idaho, but his prospects as a future athletic talent seemed clouded with alcohol.

But he surprised many who had given up on him by eventually turning away from the party scene and dedicating himself to becoming the world's number one decathlete. For a while, he played second fiddle to another top U.S. decathlete, Dave Johnson. But in 1991 he moved ahead of Johnson when he captured the World Championships title in Tokyo.

O'Brien was the favorite for the decathlon gold medal at the 1992 Olympics. But

Dan O'Brien, United States,
1996 Olympic decathlon champion.

he fell foul of the "sudden death" system which the United States uses to select its Olympic teams. O'Brien had a no-height at his opening attempt in the pole vault. Suddenly, he was not going to the Olympics.

He bounced back from this major disappointment and late in the season set a new world record in France, the first by a U.S. athlete in 16 years. He has twice more been world champion, in 1993 and 1995.

Finally, in 1996 at age 30, he won the Olympic gold medal that most observers thought he would have won in Barcelona. This was the first U.S. Olympic victory in the decathlon since Bruce Jenner's in 1976.

Conclusions

If any event has no apparent upper limit to its world record, the decathlon would appear to be it. A top decathlete has 10 areas in which to improve. It is a simple enough task to take the best score in each discipline by elite decathletes and add them up; the result is well over 9000. However, this is a simplistic approach, as all athletes have certain strengths and weaknesses in the decathlon. Although many are quality sprinters and jumpers, very few are of top standard in the 1500m.

Possibly more than any other track and field event, the decathlon requires extreme mental discipline. An athlete has to critically approach a new event 10 times over two days. That is no mean feat and is possibly not appreciated by the sporting public. The major barrier currently facing decathletes is a score of 9000, only 109 points away from the current world record.

Five All-Time Best Scores: Men's Decathlon

Dan O'Brien (USA)	8891	1992
Daley Thompson (GBR)	8847	1984
Jürgen Hingsen (FRG)	8832	1984
Uwe Freimuth (GDR)	8792	1984
Siegfried Wentz (FRG)	8762	1983
Prediction	*9125*	*2015*

Top Three: Men's Decathlon

GOLD MEDAL:	Daley Thompson (GBR)
SILVER MEDAL:	Rafer Johnson (USA)
BRONZE MEDAL:	Bob Mathias (USA)

Women's Track and Field Athletics

Female athletes have had to endure a prolonged struggle to achieve the opportunities that male athletes take for granted. The ancient Olympics were an all-male affair, and women's athletics endured an even longer dark age than men's. When sport was revived in Victorian England, it was thought unfashionable for women to exert themselves. However, an energetic Frenchwoman, Madame Alice Milliat, founded the Federation Sporting Feminine Internationale (FSFI) in 1921, which put pressure on the International Olympic Committee to include women in the Olympic athletic program. Despite intense opposition, five events were included in the athletic program for women in 1928: 100m, 800m, high jump, discus, and 4 × 100m. The number of events for women slowly expanded over the years, despite residual resistance to the idea, so that the women's program now almost matches the men's.

In 1936 the FSFI amalgamated with the IAAF to give the sport a unified voice. Official IAAF records for women were then established, some 20 years after those for men. Accordingly, the records for women that are detailed in this book commence from the 1930s.

W omen's sprinting accepted hand-timed records up to 1976, as did the men's. Up to that time, using intervals of $\frac{1}{10}$ (0.1) second, many world records were tied. The initial electronic times were actually slower than the existing hand-timed records. It is generally accepted that hand-timing results in the recording of faster times than does the more accurate electronic timing.

Nineteen women have held the world record a total of 33 times. Nine of them have become Olympic 100m champions: Walasiewicz, Blankers-Koen, Jackson, Rudolph, Tyus, Stecher, Richter, Ashford, and Griffith Joyner. In addition, three others have won Olympic gold medals in other events: Strickland (80m hurdles, 1952 and 1956), Krepkina (long jump, 1960), and Szewinska (200m, 1968; 400m, 1976).

The current world record of 10.49 seconds (Griffith Joyner, 1988) is faster than the winning time of the men's 100m at the 1956 Olympics (10.5).

Women's World Records for 100m

Record time	Record holder	Location	Date
11.7	Stanislawa Walasiewicz (POL)	Warsaw, Poland	26 Aug 1934
11.6	Stanislawa Walasiewicz (POL)	Berlin, Germany	1 Aug 1937
11.5	Fanny Blankers-Koen (HOL)	Amsterdam, Netherlands	13 Jun 1948
11.5	Marjorie Jackson (AUST)	Helsinki, Finland	22 Jul 1952
11.4	Marjorie Jackson (AUST)	Gifu, Japan	4 Oct 1952
11.3	Shirley Strickland (AUST)	Warsaw, Poland	4 Aug 1955
11.3	Vera Krepkina (USSR)	Kiev, USSR	13 Sep 1958
11.3	Wilma Rudolph (USA)	Rome, Italy	2 Sep 1960
11.2	Wilma Rudolph (USA)	Stuttgart, West Germany	19 Jul 1961
11.2	Wyomia Tyus (USA)	Tokyo, Japan	15 Oct 1964
11.1	Irena Kirszenstein (later Szewinska) (POL)	Prague, Czechoslovakia	9 Jul 1965
11.1	Wyomia Tyus (USA)	Kiev, USSR	31 Jul 1965
11.1	Barbara Ferrell (USA)	Santa Barbara, USA	2 Jul 1967
11.1	Lyudmila Samotesova (USSR)	Leninakan, USSR	15 Aug 1968
11.1	Irena Szewinska (POL)	Mexico City, Mexico	14 Oct 1968
11.0*	Wyomia Tyus (USA)	Mexico City, Mexico	15 Oct 1968
11.0	Chi Cheng (TAI)	Vienna, Austria	18 Jul 1970
11.0	Renate Meissner (later Stecher) (GDR)	Berlin, East Germany	2 Aug 1970
11.0	Renate Stecher (GDR)	Berlin, East Germany	31 Jul 1971
11.0	Renate Stecher (GDR)	Potsdam, East Germany	3 Jun 1972
11.0	Ellen Stropahl (GDR)	Potsdam, East Germany	15 Jun 1972
11.0	Eva Glesková (CZH)	Budapest, Hungary	1 Jul 1972
10.9	Renate Stecher (GDR)	Ostrava, Czechoslovakia	7 Jun 1973
10.8	Renate Stecher (GDR)	Dresden, East Germany	20 Jul 1973

Electronic Timing

11.08*	Wyomia Tyus (USA)	Mexico City, Mexico	15 Oct 1968
11.07	Renate Stecher (GDR)	Munich, West Germany	2 Sep 1972
11.04	Inge Helten (FRG)	Fürth, West Germany	13 Jun 1976
11.01	Annegret Richter (FRG)	Montreal, Canada	25 Jul 1976
10.88	Marlies Oelsner (Gohr) (GDR)	Dresden, East Germany	1 Jul 1977
10.88	Marlies Gohr (GDR)	Karl-Marx-Stadt, East Germany	9 Jul 1982
10.81	Marlies Gohr (GDR)	Berlin, East Germany	8 Jun 1983

10.79	Evelyn Ashford (USA)	Colorado Springs, USA	3 Jul 1983
10.76	Evelyn Ashford (USA)	Zurich, Switzerland	22 Aug 1984
10.49	Florence Griffith Joyner (USA)	Indianapolis, USA	16 Jul 1988

*Wyomia Tyus's 15 Oct 1968 record was manually timed as 11.0 and electronically timed as 11.08. The manual time of 11.0 was considered the official record.

Stanislawa Walasiewicz (Stella Walsh) (Poland/USA, 1911–1980)

11.7	Warsaw, Poland	26 Aug 1934
11.6	Berlin, Germany	1 Aug 1937

Stanislawa Walasiewicz was born in Poland in 1911 and was brought to the United States by her parents as a child. Known as Stella Walsh, she lived in the United States for the rest of her life but raced in Polish colors at the Olympics and European Championships.

For much of the 1930s she was in a class of her own, not only as a sprinter, but in a range of events. Walsh won 33 U.S. titles altogether: 4 at 100m, 11 at 200m, 11 in the long jump, 2 in the discus, and 5 in the pentathlon. At the Los Angeles Olympics she won the 100m in 11.9 and later be-

Stanislawa Walasiewicz (Stella Walsh), Poland, 1932 Olympic 100m champion with the other medalists Hilde Strike (Canada) and Wilhelmina Von Bremen (United States).

came the first official world record holder in the event. Four years later she finished second in the 100m at the Berlin Olympics to Helen Stephens (USA). At the 1938 European Championships Walasiewicz won both the 100m and 200m.

She changed her citizenship in 1947, becoming a citizen of the United States, and in 1956, at the age of 45, was married. At the age of 69, she was shot and killed during a holdup at a supermarket in Cleveland, Ohio, at which she was an innocent bystander. An autopsy was performed and revealed that she had both ovaries and testicles, indicating that she was a hermaphrodite, a rare medical condition in which both male and female sexual organs are present. The testicular tissue generates anabolic steroids, which may explain her enduring athletic success.

Fanny Blankers-Koen (Netherlands, b. 1918)

11.5	Amsterdam, Netherlands	13 Jun 1948

At age 16, Fanny Koen represented the Netherlands at the 1936 Berlin Olympics, where she was tied for sixth in the high jump and a member of the Dutch 4 × 100m relay team that finished fifth. Her husband, Jan Blankers, had been Dutch triple jump champion in his time and became a coach after a foot injury. His star pupil became his wife in 1940.

This remarkable woman set world records in five separate disciplines: 100m (1948), 80m hurdles (1942), long jump (1943), high jump (1943), and pentathlon (1950).

It was at the London Olympics in 1948 that Blankers-Koen had her most successful season. Aged 30 and the mother of two children, she nonetheless achieved the remarkable result of winning four gold medals at one Olympics: the 100m, 200m, 80m hurdles, and the 4 × 100m relay. All this was achieved while she was in the early months of her third pregnancy. She was given a hero's welcome on her return to Amsterdam, riding through the city in an open carriage driven by four white horses.

At the 1950 European Championships she was still victorious, winning the 100m, 200m, and the 80m hurdles. But by the 1952 Olympics a new generation of athletes had arrived. In the 80m hurdles final, she hit the first two hurdles hard and ran into the third, at which point she stopped.

From 1936 to 1955 she won 55 Dutch titles. A statue is erected to her achievements in Amsterdam.

Marjorie Jackson   (Australia, b. 1931)

| 11.5 | Helsinki, Finland | 22 Jul 1952 |
| 11.4 | Gifu, Japan | 4 Oct 1952 |

At the 1952 Olympics, the Australian team was leading in the 4 × 100m relay, when Winsome Cripps *(left)* and Marjorie Jackson lost the baton. Jackson won both sprints at these Games and set world records in the process.

On tour in Australia in 1949, Dutch athlete Blankers-Koen was surprisingly beaten by an unknown teenager, Marjorie Jackson, from the country town of Lithgow. The surprise upset was repeated a week later. Jackson was only 17 at the time. Overnight, she was trumpeted as the "Lithgow Flash." These races launched her as an international sprinter who went on to have an impeccable career record. In 1950 she won the 100 yards and the 220 yards at the Commonwealth Games in Auckland, as well as two relay gold medals. Her next major competition would be the 1952 Olympics. Her town had nothing in the way of training facilities, so the local townspeople built her a cinder strip to train on. With no preparation against other international athletes, she traveled by air to Helsinki for the Olympics, a journey that took a week in those days. On the way over she met her future husband, cyclist Peter Nelson.

She duly won the 100m, running 11.5 seconds in the final, which equaled the world record. She also won the 200m, breaking the world record in the semi-finals. Her chance of three gold medals was ruined when she and teammate Winsome Cripps lost the baton at the last exchange in the 4 × 100m relay.

She returned to Australia to a reception worthy of a queen. In November 1953 she and Peter Nelson married, and they opened a sports store in Adelaide. She had one more Commonwealth Games in Vancouver, Canada, in 1954, where she picked up three more gold medals (100 yards, 200 yards, 4 × 110 yards relay), and then retired at age 23.

In 1977 her husband died of leukemia, and she set up the Peter Nelson Leukemia Research Appeal, which has raised over $1,000,000, largely through her efforts.

Shirley Strickland   (Australia, b. 1925)

| 11.3 | Warsaw, Poland | 4 Aug 1955 |

Shirley Strickland's athletic career was primarily as a hurdler, being a two-time gold medalist in the 80m hurdles (1952 and 1956). But she was also a top international sprinter. She had won the bronze medal in the 100m at both the 1948 London and the 1952 Helsinki Olympics.

Her 100m world record took place at a meet in Warsaw, Poland, in 1955. Australian officials were reluctant to let her compete without a chaperone, although she was now 30 years of age, married with two children , a science graduate of the University of Western Australia, and had competed at two Olympic Games. She won in 11.3 to take 0.1 second off Marjorie Jackson's record.

She has since had a long career in teaching and coaching.

Vera Krepkina   (Soviet Union, b. 1933)

| 11.3 | Kiev, USSR | 13 Sep 1958 |

Vera Krepkina was an athlete who achieved success in two events: sprinting and long jumping. She had competed at the Melbourne Olympics in 1956, where she finished fourth in the semifinal of the 100m. Krepkina won the Soviet 100m title in 1957 and 1958. In 1958, at a meet in Kiev, she equaled Shirley Strickland's 100m world record with 11.3. Krepkina was second that year in the 100m at the European Championships.

Two years later at the Rome Olympics she contested both the 100m and the long jump. In the 100m she was sixth in a semifinal. However, in the long jump, an event she had never won at the Soviet championships, she caused the upset of the Games. She defeated the defending champion, Elzbieta Krzesinka of Poland by 10 centimeters for a surprise gold medal, 6.37 meters to 6.27 meters.

Wilma Rudolph   (United States, 1940–1994)

| 11.3 | Rome, Italy | 2 Sep 1960 |
| 11.2 | Stuttgart, West Germany | 19 Jul 1961 |

Wilma Rudolph came from a most disadvantaged background. She was born 20th of 22 children to a severely impoverished family in Tennessee. She contracted polio at the age of 4 which caused paralysis in her left leg, and she had to wear a brace on her leg until she was 10 and could walk properly again.

Astonishingly, only six years later she was running in the Melbourne Olympics in the 4 × 100m relay squad. The U.S. team won the bronze medal. She went on to study at Tennessee State University under famed coach Ed Temple.

In 1958 she dropped out of athletics to have a daughter but was later AAU 100m champion four years in a row (1959-62) and 200m champion in 1960. That year she returned to the Olympic arena in Rome and won the 100m and 200m and was part of the winning 4 × 100m relay team. She was the relentless center of attention of the Italian press, who named her the "Black Gazelle." On a post-Olympic tour, the team bus stopped in a German town. When the local community recognized her, they were so excited that they rocked the bus.

Later in life she was active in community affairs, especially those involving minority groups, and to that end set up the Wilma Rudolph Foundation. Married twice and divorced twice, she died at the age of 54 of a brain tumor.

Wilma Rudolph, United States (100m, 200m), the "Black Gazelle."

Wyomia Tyus   (United States, b. 1945)

11.2	Tokyo, Japan	15 Oct 1964
11.1	Kiev, USSR	31 Jul 1965
11.0 (11.08 on electronic timing)	Mexico City, Mexico	15 Oct 1968

Wyomia Tyus, United States (100m), Olympic 100m gold medalist in 1964 and 1968.

Wyomia Tyus was the first female athlete to win the Olympic 100m title twice. She was the only daughter in a family of five and showed sprinting talent in her teens. Like Wilma Rudolph, she attended Tennessee State University and trained under coach Ed Temple. She spent much of her early career under the shadow of Edith McGuire and started to defeat her only in 1964.

In Tokyo Tyus improved her personal best from 11.5 to 11.2, which tied the world record. She won the 100m final comfortably, with McGuire second.

Tyus won the AAU 100m title from 1964 to 1966 and also won the 200m title in 1966 and 1968. At the Mexico City Olympics in 1968, in a rain-swept final, the defending champion won easily. On hand held watches her time was 11.0, a new world record. (The race was also timed with electronic equipment, which registered 11.08 seconds.) She received her medal in pouring rain.

Tyus then retired but ran briefly for the professional group ITA until it collapsed in 1976.

Irena Szewinska (née Kirszenstein)   (Poland, b. 1946)

| 11.1 | Prague, Czechoslovakia | 9 Jul 1965 |
| 11.1 | Mexico City, Mexico | 14 Oct 1968 |

Irena Szewinska is regarded as one of the great queens of track and field. In a career from 1964 to 1980, she participated in five Olympics, with gold medals in the 200m (1968) and the 400m (1976). She held world records at three distances: 100m (1965 and 1968), 200m (1965, 1968, and 1974), and 400m (1974 and 1976). She also won an Olympic silver medal in the long jump in 1964.

She was born in Leningrad to Polish parents and later moved back to Poland with her family. In her debut Olympics she won a silver medal in the 200m and another silver in the long jump.

At the 1968 Olympics she won a bronze medal in the 100m as well as her 200m gold medal. In 1972 she had a "quiet" Olympics, winning only a bronze medal in the 200m. At the 1976 Games she won the 400m, setting a new world record in the process. Her last Games (1980) ended in disappointment when she pulled a muscle in a semifinal of the 400m and finished last.

Perhaps her best year was 1974, when her two victories (100m, 200m) at the European Championships were over the apparently unbeatable Renate Stecher of East Germany.

Her first 100m world record in 1965 took place in Prague, where she dead-heated with another Polish athlete, Ewa Klobukowska; both athletes were timed at 11.1. However, a subsequent chromosome test on Klobukowska revealed that she had a male chromosome pattern, and her records were disallowed.

Her second world record, 11.1 seconds, took place in the early rounds of the Mexico City Olympics. However, in the final, Wyomia Tyus retained her title and the Pole came in third.

Irena married sports photographer Janusz Szewinska on Christmas Day 1967. Janusz later took on the role of coach when Irena moved up to 400m. A graduate of economics at the University of Warsaw, she later worked at the Institute of Economic Transport in Warsaw.

Barbara Ferrell   (United States, b. 1947)

| 11.1 | Santa Barbara, USA | 2 Jul 1967 |

Barbara Ferrell was a world class athlete but lived somewhat under the shadow of Wilma Rudolph and Wyomia Tyus. Ferrell attended California State, Los Angeles, and was AAU champion in the 100m in 1967 and in both the 100m and 200m in 1969. In her 1967 100m win, her time of 11.1 seconds equaled the world record.

At the Pan-American Games in 1967 in Winnipeg she won the 100m in 11.5. The following year at the Mexico City Olympics she was second in the 100m, behind the world-record-setting Wyomia Tyus, 11.08 to 11.15 seconds. In the 200m Ferrell finished fourth. She was part of the 4 × 100m relay team that won the gold medal. She returned to the Olympics in 1972 and was seventh in the 100m and the semifinals of the 200m.

Lyudmila Samotesova   (Soviet Union, b. 1939)

| 11.1 | Leninakan, USSR | 15 Aug 1968 |

Lyudmila Samotesova was the only Soviet athlete to hold a world sprint record. She achieved this when she ran 11.1 at Leninakan at the Soviet championships in 1968. Leninakan is 1556 meters (5104 feet) above sea level.

At the Soviet championships she won the 100m in 1968, the 200m in 1967 and 1968, and the 400m in 1966 and 1967. Samotesova competed at two Olympics. In Tokyo in 1964 she was fifth in the 200m (23.5). In Mexico City in 1968 she was fifth in the semifinals of both the 100m and the 200m. She finally earned an Olympic medal when the Soviet 4 × 100m relay team came in third.

Chi Cheng   (Taiwan, b. 1944)

| 11.0 | Vienna, Austria | 18 Jul 1970 |

Chi Cheng competed at three Olympics—1960, 1964, and 1968—but her best years were 1970 and 1971. Unfortunately, she was crippled by injuries in 1972 and missed the Munich Olympics.

She had competed in the 80m hurdles at the 1960 Rome Olympics as a 16-year-old. However, she went out in the first round. Her performance was noted by U.S. coach, Vince Reel. He met her again in 1962 when he was in Taiwan to help its athletes prepare for the Asian Games. They agreed that she should move to California to train for the Tokyo Olympics.

In Tokyo her results were not that much better than in Rome. She went out in the first round of the 80m hurdles and came in 17th in the pentathlon. However, she continued as a physical education student at California State Polytechnic University and in 1968 came in third in the 80m hurdles at the Mexico City Olympics.

After that she had two superlative seasons. In 1969 she won 66 out of 67 outdoor competitions. In 1970 she was undefeated in an awesome stretch of 83 competitions. More than that, she set records at 100m, 200m, and 80m hurdles in a six-week period.

Perhaps she competed too much, as she became increasingly plagued by leg injuries. All treatments were tried without success, and she announced in March 1972 that she would not compete in Munich. She retired in 1973 and returned to Taiwan in the early 1980s.

Renate Stecher (née Meissner)   (East Germany, b. 1950)

11.0	Berlin, East Germany	2 Aug 1970
11.0	Berlin, East Germany	31 Jul 1971
11.0	Potsdam, East Germany	3 Jun 1972
11.07 (electronic timing)	Munich, West Germany	2 Sep 1972
10.9	Ostrava, Czechoslovakia	7 Jun 1973
10.8	Dresden, East Germany	20 Jul 1973

Renate Stecher was the first of a series of East German women to dominate track and field for a generation, until the reunification of Germany in 1989. She was the first woman to run 100m under 11 seconds. She also had the unique distinction of setting world records in both sprints while winning the 1972 Olympic 100m and 200m titles, with electronic timing.

As a teenager Meissner had run in the 1969 European Championships, coming in second in the 200m. A year later, married to 400m hurdler Gerd Stecher, she began a four-year stretch of 90 consecutive outdoor wins. She was East German 100m champion five times and champion in the 200m four times. Her winning streak finally came to an end when she was beaten by Irena Szewinska in the Pole's brilliant 1974 season.

After her two Olympic sprint wins the only hiccup came in the 4×100m relay. She took over the baton a stride behind West Germany's Heidi Rosendahl. Everybody expected Stecher to sweep to victory. However, Rosendahl ran the race of her life and just held off the Olympic champion to record a famous West German victory.

After defeats by Szewinska at the 1974 European titles, Stecher's supremacy slipped slightly in her remaining years as an active athlete. At the Montreal Olympics she was second in the 100m and third in the 200m. However, this time the East German relay team reversed the result and won the 4×100m gold medal with West Germany second.

Renate Stecher, East Germany (100m, 200m), double sprint champion at the 1972 Olympics.

Ellen Stropahl (later Streidt)   (East Germany, b 1952)

11.0   **Potsdam, East Germany**   **15 Jun 1972**

Ellen Stropahl had come in seventh in the 1971 European Championships in the 200m. The next year she equaled the 100m world record in an international meet in Potsdam (11.0). At the Munich Olympics later that year she went out in the quarterfinals of the 100m. In the 200m she finished fourth.

She moved up to 400m for the rest of her career. At the 1974 European Championships, now Ellen Streidt, she was second to Riitta Salin of Finland, 50.14 to 50.69.

Her only East German title was the 400m in 1974. At the 1976 Montreal Olympics she was third in the 400m and finally won a gold medal as part of the 4×400m relay team.

Eva Glesková   (Czechoslovakia, b. 1943)

11.0   **Budapest, Hungary**   **1 Jul 1972**

Eva Glesková had competed in both sprints at the 1968 Mexico City Olympics. In the 100m she had finished sixth in one of the semifinals. At the 200m she finished fifth in her heat. At the 1969 European Championships in Athens she finished seventh in the 100m.

Her world record came two months before the 1972 Munich Olympics at an international match between Czechoslovakia and Hungary. The three watches on her recorded 10.98, 10.99, and 11.10. These were rounded up to 11.0, 11.0, and 11.1. The averaged times of these watches was 11.0, which was regarded as equaling the world record.

At the 1972 Olympics she finished last in the 100m, after suffering a hamstring injury in midrace.

Inge Helten   (West Germany, b. 1950)

11.04   **Fürth, West Germany**   **13 Jun 1976**

Inge Helten was one of a number of West German runners who began to challenge the East German sprinters in the mid-1970s. At the West German championships Helten was third in the 100m in 1974 and won the event in 1975. At the 1974 European Champion-ships in Rome she finished sixth in the semifinals of the 100m.

She set her world record of 11.04 seconds in a qualifying race for Olympic selection, 10 weeks before the 1976 Olympics began. However, another West German athlete coming into top form was Annegret Richter. At Montreal it was Richter who peaked to perfection, setting a new world record of 11.01 seconds in the semifinals. In the final it was Richter 11.08, Stecher 11.13, and Helten 11.17. Helten came in fifth in the 200m and won a silver medal in the 4 × 100m relay.

Annegret Richter   (West Germany, b. 1950)

11.01   **Montreal, Canada**   **25 Jul 1976**

Annegret Richter showed that it was possible for a West German sprinter to beat the East Ger-mans. She had been a top sprinter in the mid-1970s for many years before her special 1976 sea-son. At the 1972 Olympics she had come in fifth in the 100m and won gold in the 4 × 100m relay. She was West German champion at both the 100m and 200m in 1974, 1976, 1979, and 1980 and 200m champion in 1978.

In 1976 her countrywoman Inge Helten had actually set a new world record of 11.04 seconds in June. However, Richter still won the 100m and the 200m at the West German championships.

At the Montreal Olympics Richter ran a se-ries of four superb races. In her heat she ran 11.19. In the next round she improved to 11.05. In the semifinal, against a slight headwind, she ran 11.01, a new world record. The final saw Richter win narrowly in 11.08; Stecher came in second in 11.13, and Helten third in 11.17.

Richter's chances of further success at the 1980 Olympics were blocked when West Germany decided to follow the lead of the United States and boycott the Moscow Olympics.

Annegret Richter, West Germany (100m), 1976 Olympic 100m champion, who broke the dominance of the East German sprinters.

Marlies Gohr (née Oelsner)   (East Germany, b. 1958)

10.88	**Dresden, East Germany**	**1 Jul 1977**
10.88	**Karl-Marx-Stadt, East Germany**	**9 Jul 1982**
10.81	**Berlin, East Germany**	**8 Jun 1983**

Marlies Gohr was the greatest female sprinter never to win an Olympic gold medal. She and Evelyn Ashford were rivals for most of that time. Ashford missed the 1980 Olympics because of the U.S. boycott, and Gohr missed the 1984 Olympics because of the commu-nist boycott.

Gohr had a sparkling career record and was East German champion in the 100m 10 times. She was European champion over 100m on three successive occasions (1978, 1982, and 1986), a rare feat. She was also the 100m champion at the inaugural World Championships held in Helsinki in 1983. (In this race Ashford pulled a hamstring midrace and couldn't finish.) Gohr also was the first woman to run under 11 seconds with electronic timing when she ran 10.88 in 1977, the first of three world records.

At her first Olympics in 1976, the 18-year-old Marlies Oelsner came in eighth in the 100m final. She established her supremacy from 1977 onward when she won the World Cup in Düsseldorf. After winning the 100m at the 1978 European Championships she just missed the 200m title when she was beaten by 0.01 second by the Soviet athlete Lyudmila Kondrateva.

She should have won the 1980 Olympic 100m title. After a slow start she chased the same Kondrateva to the line, but dipped too early. Kondrateva won, 11.06 to 11.07.

After missing the 1984 Olympics because of the boycott, Gohr and Ashford had a special race in Zurich. Ashford had a significant victory, winning 10.76 to 10.84, a new world record.

Gohr, then slightly past her best, had one more Olympics in 1988 and went out in the semifinals of the 100m. Since retiring from athletics, she practices psychology.

Marlies Gohr, East Germany (100m), the greatest female sprinter never to win an Olympic gold medal.

Evelyn Ashford   (United States, b. 1957)

| 10.79 | Colorado Springs, USA | 3 Jul 1983 |
| 10.76 | Zürich, Switzerland | 22 Aug 1984 |

Evelyn Ashford was born in Louisiana, the first of five children in a military family. She came in third in the U.S. Olympic trials, and at age 19 at Montreal she placed a highly creditable fifth in the 100 meter final.

However, in the 1970s the East German female athletes had a near monopoly on the sprints. Ashford determined to change that, especially after her own indifferent performances in the 1977 World Cup. At the 1979 World Cup she defeated not only Marlies Gohr in the 100m, but Marita Koch in the 200m.

She missed the 1980 Moscow Olympics because of the U.S. boycott and suffered a hamstring injury halfway through the 100m final of

Evelyn Ashford, United States (100m), 1984 Olympic 100m champion.

the inaugural 1983 World Championships. That was a major disappointment, as she had set her first world record over 100m earlier in the season. It had been achieved at high-altitude Colorado Springs, 2195 meters (7201 feet) above sea level.

Finally, at the 1984 Los Angeles Olympics she sped to a gold medal in the 100m in 10.97. However, absent on the day was Marlies Gohr, a victim of the communist boycott. Both athletes met in Zürich three weeks later. Ashford won narrowly, 10.76 to 10.84, a new world record.

After this race Ashford became aware that she had been pregnant at the time of the world record. She later called her run the fastest 100m by a pregnant athlete. In May 1985 she gave birth to her first child. She bounced back as fast as ever and went to her third Olympics in 1988, but she could not defeat the new star, Florence Griffith Joyner, and came in second in the 100m final.

Ashford had one more Olympics left, in Barcelona at age 34. She went out in the semi-finals of the 100m but was part of the winning 4 × 100m relay team. This was her third Olympic 4 × 100m relay gold medal in a row.

Since her retirement from athletics, she and her husband have bought into a McDonald's hamburger franchise.

Florence Griffith Joyner   (United States, b. 1959)

10.49   **Indianapolis, USA**   **16 Jul 1988**

Florence Griffith Joyner, United States (100m, 200m), celebrates with husband Al after her 200m gold medal and world record at the Seoul Olympics.

Florence "Flo-Jo" Griffith was an "overnight" success when she had a series of brilliant runs in 1988. But she competed at the 1983 World Championships, finishing fourth in the 200m. The following year she won a 200m silver medal at the Los Angeles Olympics.

She later married Al Joyner, who had won the gold medal in the triple jump at the Los Angeles Games. She disappeared for a few years but reemerged in 1987 at the World Championships in Rome. She could not beat the East German ace, Silke Gladisch, but ran a sparkling 21.96 seconds in second place. She also attracted much media attention by wearing startling outfits and at one stage let her fingernails grow four inches long.

Her 1988 season was a quantum leap from her previous years, which she attributed to a new weight-lifting program. At the 1988 U.S. Olympic trials she ran a shattering 10.49

seconds for the 100m, a 0.27-second improvement on the record. The main feature of her improved performance was the incredible burst of speed in the latter part of the race.

She went on to achieve 100m and 200m gold medals at the Seoul Olympics, winning by massive margins in both races. Halfway through the 100m race she knew she was going to win, and a huge smile came across her face. She added a gold medal in the 4 × 100m relay and a silver medal in the 4 × 400m. She was the athletic star and media star of the Games.

She ran the four fastest times ever that season, 10.49, 10.61, 10.62, and 10.70. That 10.49 remains controversial. The wind reading was said to be 0.00 meters per second. Such a zero recording is unlikely, as most observers that day claim there were significant winds. Possibly the wind gauge malfunctioned. There was no such controversy over her other 100m times, so perhaps 10.61 should be the world record.

Conclusions

The world record of 10.49 has not been remotely approached since it was set in 1988. This situation seems unlikely to change in the near future.

Five All-Time Fastest: Women's 100m			(Wind)
Florence Griffith Joyner (USA)	10.49	1988	0.0
Merlene Ottey (JAM)	10.74	1996	+1.3
Evelyn Ashford (USA)	10.76	1984	+1.7
Irina Privalova (RUS)	10.77	1994	+0.9
Dawn Sowell (USA)	10.78 A	1989	+1.0
Prediction	*10.49*	*2015*	

Top Three: Women's 100m

GOLD MEDAL:	Florence Griffith Joyner (USA)
SILVER MEDAL:	Renate Stecher (GDR)
BRONZE MEDAL:	Wilma Rudolph (USA)

The first 200m world record of 23.6 was set by Stanislawa Walasiewicz in 1935 and lasted 17 years, one of the longest-standing women's records. The event was first included for women at the Olympics in 1948, 20 years after the 100m for women had been introduced.

Eleven athletes have held the world record 21 times, and six of them also won the Olympic title: Jackson, Cuthbert, Rudolph, Szewinska, Stecher, and Griffith Joyner. Four of the six—Jackson (1952), Szewinska (1968), Stecher (1972), Griffith Joyner (1988)—set their records at the Olympics.

Many of the 200m record holders were also holders of the 100m world record: 7 out of the 11 athletes. The record was also held by 400m specialist Marita Koch.

The current record by Griffith Joyner, 21.34 seconds, is far ahead of previous records and has not been seriously challenged in almost a decade.

Women's World Records for 200m

Record time	Record holder	Location	Date
23.6	Stanislawa Walasiewicz (POL)	Warsaw, Poland	4 Aug 1935
23.6	Marjorie Jackson (AUST)	Helsinki, Finland	25 Jul 1952
23.4	Marjorie Jackson (AUST)	Helsinki, Finland	25 Jul 1952
23.2	Betty Cuthbert (AUST)	Sydney, Australia	16 Sep 1956
23.2	Betty Cuthbert (AUST)	Hobart, Australia	7 Mar 1960
22.9	Wilma Rudolph (USA)	Corpus Christi, USA	9 Jul 1960
22.9	Margaret Burvill (AUST)	Perth, Australia	22 Feb 1964
22.7	Irena Kirszenstein (later Szewinska) (POL)	Warsaw, Poland	8 Aug 1965
22.5	Irena Szewinska (POL)	Mexico City, Mexico	18 Oct 1968
22.4	Chi Cheng (TAI)	Munich, West Germany	12 Jul 1970
22.4	Renate Stecher (GDR)	Munich, West Germany	7 Sep 1972
22.1	Renate Stecher (GDR)	Dresden, East Germany	21 Jul 1973

Electronic Timing

22.21	Irena Szewinska (POL)	Potsdam, East Germany	13 Jun 1974
22.06	Marita Koch (GDR)	Erfurt, East Germany	28 May 1978
22.02	Marita Koch (GDR)	Leipzig, East Germany	3 Jun 1979
21.71	Marita Koch (GDR)	Karl-Marx-Stadt, East Germany	10 Jun 1979
21.71	Marita Koch (GDR)	Potsdam, East Germany	21 Jul 1984
21.71	Heike Drechsler (GDR)	Jena, East Germany	29 Jun 1986
21.71	Heike Drechsler (GDR)	Stuttgart, East Germany	29 Aug 1986
21.56	Florence Griffith Joyner (USA)	Seoul, South Korea	29 Sep 1988
21.34	Florence Griffith Joyner (USA)	Seoul, South Korea	29 Sep 1988

Stanislawa Walasiewicz (Stella Walsh)   (Poland/USA, 1911–1980)

23.6   **Warsaw, Poland**   **4 Aug 1935**

As mentioned in the chapter on the 100m, Stanislawa Walasiewicz was the leading female sprinter of the 1930s. Her 200m world record took place in Poland during one of her summer visits. She ran 23.6 in a mixed race, both men and women in one event. That would not be permitted for world purposes today. In second place was a Mr. Krawczyk. The record lasted 17 years.

Marjorie Jackson   (Australia, b. 1931)

| 23.6 | Helsinki, Finland | 25 Jul 1952 |
| 23.4 | Helsinki, Finland | 25 Jul 1952 |

As mentioned in the chapter on the 100m, Marjorie Jackson won both sprints at the 1952 Helsinki Olympics. She set two world records in the early rounds of the 200m, 23.6 and 23.4. In the final, she ran 23.7 to win by 0.5 second.

Her return from the Olympics was a series of triumphal processions. She was met at the airport by the governor-general of Australia and was given a police escort for the 150-kilometer drive home. In her hometown of Lithgow, the entire community gave her a frenzied welcome. Forty-three years later she was given the use of a Mercedes-Benz for a year, a present she dared not accept in 1952 for fear of breaching her amateur status.

Betty Cuthbert   (Australia, b. 1938)

| 23.2 | Sydney, Australia | 16 Sep 1956 |
| 23.2 | Hobart, Australia | 7 Mar 1960 |

Betty Cuthbert, Australia (200m), triple gold sprint medalist at the 1956 Olympics.

Betty Cuthbert was Australia's "Golden Girl" of the 1950s. At age 18, she won the 100m and 200m at the 1956 Melbourne Olympics and a third gold medal in the 4 × 100m relay.

She was born to New Zealander parents who had separately migrated to Australia before their marriage. Betty was one of twin girls, delivered at home as was the practice in those days. The twin pregnancy was undiagnosed until the second baby was unexpectedly born.

She had won a string of schoolgirl titles but had never really considered herself Olympic material. However she showed meteoric improvement before the Games and astonished onlookers by breaking the world record for 200m at a small interclub meet. She went on to decisive victories at the Melbourne Games, in front of crowds of 100,000.

The next few years were difficult. Shy by nature, she found being a public heroine in Australia at age 18 in the 1950s was a fate worse than death. The media attention was unrelenting. Politicians lined up to be photographed with her. Her twin sister could enjoy a normal social life, but this was denied her.

She eventually lost her athletic form and had a disappointing Rome Olympics. Two years later, her original coach, June Ferguson, suggested she try the 400m. It was an inspired move, and she went on to win a fourth Olympic gold medal in the 400m at the Tokyo Olympics. After that she retired for good, but further battles lay ahead. She contracted multiple sclerosis and is currently confined to a wheelchair.

Wilma Rudolph   (United States, 1940–1994)

| 22.9 | Corpus Christi, USA | 9 Jul 1960 |

Wilma Rudolph was another athlete who set world records at both 100m and 200m. As detailed in the chapter on the 100m, she was also a triple gold medalist at the 1960 Rome

Olympics. She had suffered from polio, so it bordered on miraculous that she became a sprint medalist. Her win in the 1960 AAU 200m in 22.9 broke the world record; she was the first woman under 23 seconds.

After she achieved the gold medal triple at the 1960 Rome Olympics, she had a small win for integration. Her hometown in Tennessee organized a parade, but the town had never been integrated. She said she would not attend a parade that was segregated, so the civic authorities bowed to her wishes.

Margaret Burvill   (Australia, b. 1941)

22.9   **Perth, Australia**   **22 Feb 1964**

Margaret Burvill was a top athlete in the mid-1960s, until Achilles injuries in 1967 caused her to retire prematurely. She had competed at the 1962 Commonwealth Games, finishing third in the 220 yards. She equaled the world record of the great Wilma Rudolph in a 220-yard (201.17-meter) race at the West Australian championships in 1964.

She contested both sprint events at the 1964 Olympics. She was eighth in the semifinal of the 100m and fifth in the semifinal of the 200m. The Australian 4 × 100m relay team, of which she was part, finished sixth.

She turned to the 400m. Her personal best 440-yard time was 54.2 seconds, but injuries brought her career to a halt in 1967.

She went on to a career in teaching and raised two children. Married to Ian Edwards, a prominent oarsman, she now lives in Tasmania.

Margaret Burvill, Australia (200m), at the Tokyo Olympics.

Irena Szewinska (née Kirszenstein)   (Poland, b. 1946)

22.7	Warsaw, Poland	8 Aug 1965
22.5	Mexico City, Mexico	18 Oct 1968
22.21 (electronic timing)	Potsdam, East Germany	13 Jun 1974

Irena Kirszenstein was the only athlete to hold world records at 100m (1965 and 1968), 200m (1965, 1968, and 1974), and 400m (1974 and twice in 1976). Her career is covered in more detail in the chapter on the 100m.

Her first 200m world record (22.7) was set during a 1965 Poland vs. United States meet in Warsaw, where she defeated the U.S. champions Edith McGuire and Wyomia Tyus. Her second 200m world record (22.5) was in winning the 200m gold medal at the 1968 Mexico City Olympics. The high altitude was helpful for world records at that Olympics.

Her third world record took place during her brilliant 1974 season. Perhaps her main feat was not so much her world record, but more that she defeated Renate Stecher, who had been undefeated for four years and was apparently invincible. This race took place at an international meet in Potsdam, East Germany, and was the first official electronically timed world record. Her time was 22.21, and Stecher came in second with 22.75.

Chi Cheng   (Taiwan, b. 1944)

| 22.4 | Munich, West Germany | 12 Jul 1970 |

Chi Cheng was the remarkable athlete who held world records in the 100m, 200m, and 100m hurdles, an unprecedented achievement. Her career is covered in more detail in the chapter on the 100m. She was born in Hsinchu, Taiwan; her father was a grocer, and she had three brothers and three sisters. To further her athletic career, she moved to California at age 18 and later married her coach, Vince Reel, although they were subsequently divorced.

Her best year was 1970, when she went undefeated in 83 competitions. She set her world records over a one-week period. She set both 200m and 100m hurdles records on the same afternoon in Munich, at 6:30 P.M. (1830 hours) and 7:40 P.M. (1940 hours), respectively. Her 100m world record took place in Vienna six days later, when she ran 11.0 seconds.

Renate Stecher   (East Germany, b. 1950)

| 22.4 | Munich, West Germany | 7 Sep 1972 |
| 22.1 | Dresden, East Germany | 21 Jul 1973 |

Renate Stecher has been described in the chapter on the 100m. Her two victories at the Munich Olympics were special for two reasons. First, she became part of a small select group of women who had achieved the Olympic sprint double which would include: Fanny Blankers-Koen (1948), Marjorie Jackson (1952), Betty Cuthbert (1956), Wilma Rudolph (1960), and later Florence Griffith Joyner (1988). Second, she is the only athlete, male or female, to win both 100m and 200m titles with world records.

Marita Koch   (East Germany, b. 1957)

22.06	Erfurt, East Germany	28 May 1978
22.02	Leipzig, East Germany	3 Jun 1979
21.71	Karl-Marx-Stadt, East Germany	10 Jun 1979
21.71	Potsdam, East Germany	21 Jul 1984

Marita Koch was first seen at the 1976 Olympics, competing as a teenager. She made it to the semifinals of the 400m but had to withdraw because of a leg injury.

At that time Irena Szewinska was still queen of the 400m, a position she reinforced with her world record win at the 1976 Montreal Olympics. Szewinska won again in 1977 when

Marita Koch, East Germany (200m, 400m), possibly the greatest female track athlete ever.

she and Koch clashed at the World Cup. But from then on the title of Queen of the Track passed to Koch.

Koch was born in Wismar on the Baltic coast and her first sport was handball. She turned to track and field after a school sports day when she beat both the male and female competitors. After the 1977 defeat by Szewinska, Koch had a decade of almost unrelenting success. Her many honors include Olympic 400m champion in 1980, European 400m champion three times (1978, 1982, and 1986), and world 200m champion (1983). She set four world records over 200m and was the first woman to run the distance under 22 seconds. Her Olympic medal tally would have been greater except for the East German boycott of the 1984 Los Angeles Olympics.

Marita Koch later graduated from medical school at the University of Rostock and specialized in pediatrics. She married her coach, Wolfgang Meier, after retiring from athletics.

Heike Drechsler   (East Germany, b. 1964)

| 21.71 | Jena, East Germany | 29 Jun 1986 |
| 21.71 | Stuttgart, East Germany | 29 Aug 1986 |

Heike Drechsler (née Daute) burst on the scene by winning the long jump at the 1983 World Championships in Helsinki as a teenager. She later became world record holder in this event.

She was born in the city of Gera; her family moved to Jena, where she was noticed for her athletic ability. Tall at 181 centimeters (5' 11 ¼"), her long legs made her more effective over the 200m distance than the 100m sprint. She went on to dominate the 200m in the mid-1980s and achieved two world records, both 21.71. She was a casualty of the East German boycott of the 1984 Olympics. However, she won both long jump and 200m at the 1986 European Championships.

At the 1988 Olympics, she ran into Florence Griffith Joyner who was having her magic year. Drechsler came in third in both the 100m and 200m and was second in the long jump. After those Olympics she decided to focus more on the long jump. That decision was justified when she won the long jump at Barcelona in 1992, her first Olympic gold medal.

Heike Drechsler, East Germany (200m, long jump).

Her talent, her smile, her longevity, and her good looks have long made her a crowd favorite.

Florence Griffith Joyner (United States, b. 1959)

21.56	Seoul, South Korea	29 Sep 1988
21.34	Seoul, South Korea	29 Sep 1988

Florence Griffith Joyner was the seventh woman to hold both 100m and 200m world records. She is best known for her sensational 1988 season, in which she shattered the existing world records at both distances and won Olympic gold medals at the 100m, 200m, and 4 × 100m relay. Born in Los Angeles, she attended Jordan High School and is a graduate of UCLA. She was the media megastar of the 1988 Seoul Olympics, not only for her athletic successes, but also for her flamboyant costumes.

After winning the 100m she was keen to win the 200m and set a world record. This she duly achieved. She first broke the 200m record in the semifinals at 3:00 P.M. (1500 hours) with 21.56. In the final at 4:40 P.M. (1640 hours) the same day, she ran 21.34. A feature of those races was her capacity to maintain high speed with long strides right to the end of the race.

Conclusions

Florence Griffith Joyner's 200m record of 21.34, much like her 100m record, seems destined to endure well into the 21st century. It is far beyond the times of current 200m runners.

Six All-Time Fastest: Women's 200m			(Wind)
Florence Griffith Joyner (USA)	21.34	1988	+1.3
Merlene Ottey (JAM)	21.64	1991	+0.8
Heike Drechsler (GDR)	21.71	1986, 1986	+1.2, −0.8
Marita Koch (GDR)	21.71	1979, 1984	+0.7, +0.3
Grace Jackson (JAM)	21.72	1988	+1.3
Gwen Torrence (USA)	21.72	1992	−0.1
Prediction	*21.34*	*2015*	

Top Three: Women's 200m

GOLD MEDAL:	Marita Koch (GDR)
SILVER MEDAL:	Florence Griffith Joyner (USA)
BRONZE MEDAL:	Irena Szewinska (POL)

World records for this event were first recognized from January 1957, and it was introduced into the Olympics in 1964. Since the Australian–New Zealand track and field season runs into January or February, the first three world records were by athletes from these countries. However, the event had been run in the national championships of the Soviet Union as far back as 1922. Accordingly, when their season began a few months later, the record was reduced substantially.

The 400m record has been held by athletes from a variety of nations. Altogether, 15 athletes from 10 nations set or equaled the record 26 times. Only four of these athletes were also Olympic champions: Besson, Zehrt, Szewinska, and Koch. Szewinska alone set her record at the Olympics.

Among the record holders, two great names stand out: Irena Szewinska (POL), the first woman under 50 seconds, and Marita Koch (GDR), who set the record a remarkable seven times. She is the current world record holder, more than 10 years after her last record.

Women's World Records for 400m

Record time	Record holder	Location	Date
57.0	Marlene Mathews (AUST)	Sydney, Australia	6 Jan 1957
57.0	Marise Chamberlain (NZ)	Christchurch, New Zealand	16 Feb 1957
56.3	Nancy Boyle (AUST)	Sydney, Australia	24 Feb 1957
55.2	Polina Lazareva (USSR)	Moscow, USSR	10 May 1957
54.0	Maria Itkina (USSR)	Minsk, USSR	8 Jun 1957
53.6	Maria Itkina (USSR)	Moscow, USSR	6 Jul 1957
53.4	Maria Itkina (USSR)	Krasnodar, USSR	12 Sep 1959
53.4	Maria Itkina (USSR)	Belgrade, Yugoslavia	14 Sep 1962
51.9	Sin Kim Dan (N.KOR)	Pyongyang, North Korea	23 Oct 1962
51.7	Nicole Duclos (FRA)	Athens, Greece	18 Sep 1969
51.7	Colette Besson (FRA)	Athens, Greece	18 Sep 1969
51.0	Marilyn Neufville (JAM)	Edinburgh, Scotland	23 Jul 1970
51.0	Monika Zehrt (GDR)	Paris, France	4 Jul 1972
49.9	Irena Szewinska (POL)	Warsaw, Poland	22 Jun 1974

Electronic Timing

Record time	Record holder	Location	Date
50.14	Riitta Salin (FIN)	Rome, Italy	4 Sep 1974
49.77	Christina Brehmer (GDR)	Dresden, East Germany	9 May 1976
49.75	Irena Szewinska (POL)	Bydgoszcz, Poland	22 Jun 1976
49.29	Irena Szewinska (POL)	Montreal, Canada	29 Jul 1976
49.19	Marita Koch (GDR)	Leipzig, East Germany	2 Jul 1978
49.03	Marita Koch (GDR)	Potsdam, East Germany	19 Aug 1978
48.94	Marita Koch (GDR)	Prague, Czechoslovakia	31 Aug 1978
48.89	Marita Koch (GDR)	Potsdam, East Germany	29 Jul 1979
48.60	Marita Koch (GDR)	Turin, Italy	4 Aug 1979
48.16	Marita Koch (GDR)	Athens, Greece	8 Sep 1982
47.99	Jarmila Kratochvilova (CZH)	Helsinki, Finland	10 Aug 1983
47.60	Marita Koch (GDR)	Canberra, Australia	6 Oct 1985

Marlene Mathews (Australia, b. 1934)

57.0   **Sydney, Australia**   **6 Jan 1957**

Marlene Mathews set the first officially recognized 400m world record at the Australian National 440-yards Championships. She was a top sprinter in Australia, winning the

100 yards and 220 yards at the Australian championships in 1958. At the 1956 Melbourne Olympics, she won the bronze medal in both 100m and 200m. In both races, first and second place went to Betty Cuthbert (Australia) and Christa Stubnick (Germany). Two years later Mathews won both sprint titles at the 1958 Commonwealth Games in Cardiff.

A fall down a stairwell caused back injuries, ruining prospects for the Rome Olympics.

Her main claim to fame lies in an athletic event she didn't contest. At the 1956 Melbourne Olympics, despite winning bronze medals in the 100m and 200m, she was left out of the 4 × 100m relay team, which was almost guaranteed to win the gold medal. The team, with world record holders Betty Cuthbert and Shirley Strickland, was still good enough to win and set a world record in the process. Nonetheless, the omission of Marlene Mathews from the Olympic team caused a national uproar. She herself later described it as a bitter pill to swallow. The three selectors, Doris Magee, Lil Neville, and Gwen Bull, refused to comment on this startling omission. Mathews had been Australia's leading sprinter all season, until the late emergence of Betty Cuthbert. She had been part of the relay team that won the Australian title that year. Then she won her two Olympic bronze medals. Forty years on, the reasons behind her omission remain as mysterious as ever.

Marise Chamberlain   (New Zealand, b. 1934)

57.0   **Christchurch, New Zealand**   **16 Feb 1957**

Marise Chamberlain, New Zealand (400m).

Marise Chamberlain equaled Marlene Mathews's world record six weeks later, on the Rugby Park football field. Chamberlain had a long career, and she won 15 New Zealand titles from 1955-1966. This was all the more remarkable because she trained in total isolation, changing into her athletic gear in a stable and training by flashlight in winter. Despite setting two national records over 880 yards and being nominated, she was denied selection to the 1960 Rome Olympics.

In 1962 Dixie Willis of Australia set an 800m world record (2:01.2) and Chamberlain was only 0.2 second behind her. Thirty years on, that time remains a New Zealand record. At the Tokyo Olympics in 1964 the 800m was won by Ann Packer of Great Britain in a world record time of 2:01.1, and Chamberlain came in third with 2:02.8. On the dais the memory of her years of effort and the frustration at being excluded from the Rome team left her weeping.

Her last major race was the 880 yards at the 1966 Commonwealth Games in Jamaica. However, only she knew that she had a problematic Achilles tendon. In the final, she was racing to victory down the home straight when her tendon gave way. She limped across the finish in sixth place.

She retired and had two daughters, but in 1972 the idea of a comeback for the Munich Olympics was put to her. But her husband at the time was not supportive of the idea, and she did not pursue it. She has since remarried.

Nancy Boyle   (Australia, b. 1932)

56.3   **Sydney, Australia**   **24 Feb 1957**

Nancy Boyle, Australia (400m).

Nancy Boyle was a sprinter for many years in Melbourne and at one stage held the Victorian state records for 100 yards, 220 yards, and 440 yards.

She actually ran the 440 yards/400m only three times in her career, all within a few weeks. The first time she ran the distance, it was a club record. The second time was a Victorian record. The third time was a world record when she ran it, on grass, on the Sydney Cricket Ground. She never ran the distance again. "My mistake," she reflected many years later.

In 1958 she hoped for selection to the Commonwealth Games in Cardiff but was ill prior to the Australian trials and missed selection. Before the 1960 Olympics she stepped on a screw in her garden and again missed out on selection. Her mother died later that year, after six weeks in a coma. After that draining ordeal Nancy Boyle decided not to compete again.

Her other claim to fame is that she competed athletically while a young mother, which in Australia in the 1950s was unusual. Having raised three children, now in her 60s, she still plays squash twice a week.

Polina Lazareva   (Soviet Union, b. 1930)

55.2   **Moscow, USSR**   **10 May 1957**

Ten weeks after Nancy Boyle set her record, it was broken by Soviet athlete Polina Lazareva from the Ukraine. She took 1.1 seconds off the record at the Lenin Stadium in Moscow.

The 400m was included in the European Championships in 1958, but she missed selection. The Soviets were first, second, and fifth anyway. She won one Soviet championship over the distance in 1954. Her time on that occasion was 55.1, actually faster than the world record she set in 1957. It was never submitted as a world record because world records for the distance were officially recognized only as of 1 January 1957. Apart from her win in the 1954 Soviet titles, Lazareva was second in 1952, 1953, and 1957.

Polina Lazareva, Soviet Union (400m), the first of the Soviet 400m runners.

Maria Itkina   (Soviet Union, b. 1932)

54.0	Minsk USSR	8 Jun 1957
53.6	Moscow, USSR	6 Jul 1957
53.4	Krasnodar, USSR	12 Sep 1959
53.4	Belgrade, Yugoslavia	14 Sep 1962

Maria Itkina was the first female athlete to significantly reduce the 400m record. She was born in Smolensk, western Russia, a city which had witnessed major military engagements during Napoleon's invasion in 1812 and during World War II between 1941 and 1943. She was a young child when these latter conflicts took place.

Itkina's career ran from 1952 to 1966. She was Soviet champion at 100m four times, at 200m six times, and at 400m five times and was European 400m champion in 1958 and 1962. Her four 400m world records brought the time down from 55.2 to 53.4.

Since the 400m was not run until 1964, her Olympic efforts did not earn her a medal:

1956 Melbourne	200m semifinals (fourth), 4 × 100m relay (fourth)
1960 Rome	100m (fourth), 200m (fourth), 4 × 100m relay (fourth)
1964 Tokyo	400m (fifth)

Sin Kim Dan (Shin Geum Dan)   (North Korea, b. 1938)

| 51.9 | Pyongyang, North Korea | 23 Oct 1962 |

Sin Kim Dan was a somewhat obscure figure from North Korea. She remains the one and only North Korean athlete to set a world record. At Pyongyang, the North Korean capital, she ran 51.9 seconds in 1962. The second-place athlete ran 58.0 seconds.

Her career was not helped by the extreme isolationist policies of her government, which meant she never participated in athletic meets in western countries. She apparently, unofficially, ran the 800m in under two minutes in 1963 and 1964.

She did participate in the 1963 Ganefo Games in Djakarta, organized by President Sukarno of Indonesia. These "Games of the Emerging Forces" were a political event to promote the agenda of developing nations. It took place against the wishes of the IAAF, who warned that athletes who competed would not be allowed to compete at the 1964 Tokyo Olympics. This hard line was

Sin Kim Dan, North Korea (400m).

perhaps unfair on the individual athletes, most of whom had no choice but to participate in the Ganefo Games according to the dictates of their government. Sin was subsequently barred from participating in the Tokyo Olympics.

Nicole Duclos   (France, b. 1947)

51.7   **Athens, Greece**   **18 Sep 1969**

See biography below.

Colette Besson   (France, b. 1946)

51.7   **Athens, Greece**   **18 Sep 1969**

Nicole Duclos *(left)* and Colette Besson, both of France, finish with the same world record time of 51.7 at the 1969 European Championships 400m in Athens. Duclos was awarded first place.

In a dramatic 400m race at the 1969 European Championships in Athens, two French athletes dead-heated on the line in a new world record time, 51.7. The two athletes were Nicole Duclos and Colette Besson. Both were recorded as having run 51.7 seconds, but the automatic timer recorded Duclos at 51.72 and Besson at 51.74.

Both athletes were involved in another dead heat at these championships, with another world record. The 4 × 400m relay final was a contest between Great Britain and France. Duclos ran the second leg for France, Besson the fourth. Both teams recorded 3:30.8. However, Great Britain was fractionally ahead at the finish and was given first place.

Besson had already won the gold medal at 400m in 1968 at the Mexico City Olympics with 52.0 seconds, just defeating Britain's Lillian Board (52.1). Besson was possibly the most unexpected Olympic champion, as her best pre-Olympic time was 53.8. She had improved 1.8 seconds to win.

Besson returned to the European Championships in 1971 as one of the favorites; her season's best was 52.5. That morning she was seen doing multiple warm-up sprints. Perhaps she overdid it. In the final she was way below her best and finished seventh in 53.7.

Duclos went on to the Munich Olympics in 1972 and finished sixth in the semifinal of the 400m. The French 4 × 400m relay team (including Besson and Duclos) finished fourth.

Marilyn Neufville   (Jamaica, b. 1952)

51.0   **Edinburgh, Scotland**   **23 Jul 1970**

Marilyn Neufville, Jamaica (400m).

Marilyn Neufville was born in Jamaica and came to England with her family at the age of eight. By 15 she was already a precocious sprinter over 220 yards and was offered a place in the Jamaican team for the 1968 Mexico City Olympics but declined, as she felt her future athletic career lay with Great Britain. She began racing in British colors in 1969 but then decided to represent Jamaica at the 1970 Commonwealth Games in Edinburgh, which caused some controversy.

In Edinburgh, at age 17, she showed impeccable form and took 0.7 second off the world record with 51.0. This made her the youngest athlete to set a 400m record. She achieved this by running two quite unequal halves: 23.8 and 27.2.

The next year, still representing Jamaica, she won the 400m at the Pan-Am Games at Cali, Colombia. She had high hopes for the 1972 Munich Olympics, but she suffered a series of injuries. Despite surgery, she never regained her top form.

Monika Zehrt   (East Germany, b. 1952)

51.0   **Paris, France**   **4 Jul 1972**

Monika Zehrt was another teenager who became a world record holder over the 400m distance. At an athletic meet between France and East Germany at the Colombes Stadium, she equaled Marilyn Neufville's record. Her first 200m was run in 23.8 seconds, while the last 200m took 27.2, exactly the same splits as her predecessor.

This record took place two months prior to the Munich Olympics. At the Games she confirmed her status as favorite by winning the gold medal in 51.08 seconds, running 24.20 and 26.88 for the two halves. Zehrt completed a successful Olympics by being part of the 4 × 400m relay team that won in world record time (3:23.0).

She was East German champion at 400m in 1970, 1972, and 1973.

Irena Szewinska   (Poland, b. 1946)

49.9	Warsaw, Poland	22 Jun 1974
49.75 (electronic timing)	Bydgoszcz, Poland	22 Jun 1976
49.29 (electronic timing)	Montreal, Canada	29 Jul 1976

As described in the chapters on the 100m and 200m, Poland's Irena Szewinska was "Queen of the Track" for much of the 1960s and 1970s, with multiple world records and Olympic medals. Late in her career she turned to the 400m. Showing her immediate genius at the event, she took 1.1 seconds off the world record at the 1974 Kusocinski meet and became the first woman to break the 50-second barrier when she ran 49.9.

She would have liked to have run both the 200m and the 400m at the Montreal Olympics. But the schedule for the two events clashed on the program, so she decided to run only the 400m. In the interim, the record had been reduced twice, by Finland's Riitta Salin and East Germany's Christina Brehmer, and stood at 49.77 in May 1976. However, Szewinska reclaimed the record at the 1976 Kusocinski meet in June by running 49.75.

Irena Szewinska, Poland (100m, 200m, 400m), winning the 1976 Olympic 400m at Montreal.

The much anticipated Montreal final between Szewinska and Brehmer turned out to be a no-contest. Brehmer led at the 200m mark, but in the last 100m Szewinska accelerated past Brehmer and won easily, taking 0.46 second off the world record with 49.29.

She had one last significant 400m victory at the 1977 World Cup, defeating rising star Marita Koch 49.52 to 49.76. But from then on Marita Koch was triumphant. Szewinska retired after an injury crippled her chances in the 400m semifinals at the 1980 Olympics.

Riitta Salin   (Finland, b. 1950)

| 50.14 (electronic timing) | Rome, Italy | 4 Sep 1974 |

Riitta Salin had her special day at the 1974 European Championships in Rome, where she beat the apparently invincible East Germans and set a world record in the process (50.14). This was the first official electronically timed world record over 400m. Irena Szewinska's record of 49.9 was hand-timed in June 1974. Hand timing can give misleading results, as the timekeeper usually anticipates the finish and gives a slightly faster reading than an electronic recording.

In Rome the semifinals had been won by Salin (51.46) and Ellen Streidt (née Stropahl) of East Germany (51.40). Streidt had been a world record holder over 100m in 1972. In the final it was Salin 50.14, Streidt 50.69.

At the Montreal Olympics Szewinska was unstoppable and won in 49.29. Salin was seventh in 50.98.

Christina Brehmer   (East Germany, b. 1958)

49.77	Dresden, East Germany	9 May 1976

Christina Brehmer of East Germany became the second female athlete to break the 50-second barrier over 400m. Another teenager, she was only 18 at the time. Her world record run took place in May 1976, 10 weeks before the Montreal Olympics. However, Irena Szewinska ran 0.02 second faster in June, and at the Olympics the Pole stormed home in the last 100 meters to win in a new world record of 49.29. Brehmer was second in 50.51. She ran in the 4 × 400m relay, and the East German team won the gold medal.

Brehmer continued to run, but a new East German star emerged to eclipse her: Marita Koch. Koch set three world records in 1978 and two in 1979, and Brehmer was second on all four occasions. Including the 1976 Olympics, Brehmer therefore had the unusual experience of coming in second five times during world record performances.

Her last big meet was the 1980 Moscow Olympics. Koch won in 48.88 seconds. Second was the new star from Czechoslovakia, Jarmila Kratochvilova, with 49.46. Christina Brehmer, now Lathan, ran 49.66 seconds—a personal best—for the bronze medal.

Marita Koch   (East Germany, b. 1957)

49.19	Leipzig, East Germany	2 Jul 1978
49.03	Potsdam, East Germany	19 Aug 1978
48.94	Prague, Czechoslovakia	31 Aug 1978
48.89	Potsdam, East Germany	29 Jul 1979
48.60	Turin, Italy	4 Aug 1979
48.16	Athens, Greece	8 Sep 1982
47.60	Canberra, Australia	6 Oct 1985

Marita Koch is one of the all-time greats of women's track and field, some would say the greatest. Much of her career has been detailed in the chapter on the 200m. Her international career began when she came in second in the European Junior Championships in 1975 over 400m. Koch attended the Montreal Olympics but pulled a muscle prior to the 400m semifinals and had to withdraw.

Szewinska defeated Koch at the 1977 World Cup 400m, but from then on Koch was the world's premier 400m runner for almost a decade. In 1978 she set three world records in one year, the third at the European Championships in Prague. At this event she became the first woman to run under 49 seconds, when she ran 48.94. At the 1980 Moscow Olympics it was another comfortable win in 48.88 seconds, with the Czech Jarmila Kratochvilova a surprise second in 49.46.

Kratochvilova was to be her rival over the next few years and defeated Koch at the 1981 World Cup. The next major 400m event was the 1982 European Championships. Koch ran an extraordinary first 200m of 22.8. Although everybody expected her to run out of steam, she raced on to a new world record of 48.16, with Kratochvilova second in 48.85.

Kratochvilova claimed the world record in 1983 with 47.99 at the World Championships, while Koch chose to run the 100m (second) and 200m (first). Both women were left out of the 1984 Olympics, which might have been their last great clash because of the communist boycott. When Koch regained the world record at the 1985 World Cup in Australia with 47.60, Kratochvilova finished fifth with 50.95.

After her third 400m win at the European Championships in 1986 Koch retired.

Jarmila Kratochvilova   (Czechoslovakia, b. 1951)

| **47.99** | **Helsinki, Finland** | **10 Aug 1983** |

Jarmila Kratochvilova was an athlete who bloomed late in her career. At age 29, she was a surprise silver medalist at the Moscow Olympics in the 400m, behind Marita Koch, running 49.46 to Koch's 48.88. She had been involved in track and field since the age of 18, but her best result after nine years in the sport had been a sixth place in the 1977 European Indoor Championships.

Her Moscow medal was thought of as a bonus, as Koch still seemed untouchable in those days. However, Kratochvilova rapidly closed the gap after her 1980 silver medal. The two "Ks" met again at the World Cup in Rome in 1981. This time, it was Kratochvilova all the way, and she raced home in 48.61, only 0.01 second short of Koch's world record. Koch ran 49.27. At their next big clash, the 1982 European Championships, Koch sprinted away and just kept going to her sixth world record: Koch 48.16, Kratochvilova 48.85.

The next year they both ran at separate events at the inaugural World Championships in Helsinki. Koch ran the 100m (second) and 200m (first), while Kratochvilova ran the 400m (first) and 800m (first). In the 400m the first four athletes were all under 50 seconds; Kratochvilova pushed hard down the straight to become the first woman under 48 seconds with 47.99.

These strong late-career performances and her powerful bulk generated suspicions that she was either on anabolic steroids or possibly had an extra male chromosome. However, she passed her drug tests and had a normal chromosome test.

Both she and Koch missed the 1984 Olympics because of the communist boycott, which she later described as a deep disappointment. In the last clash of the "Ks," they met at the 1985 World Cup in Canberra. Koch won with 47.60, her last world record, while Kratochvilova was fifth with 50.95.

Conclusions

Marita Koch's 1985 world record of 47.60 remains beyond the times of the current generation of 400m runners. There does not appear to be any challenger on the horizon, and the record should remain undisturbed into the 21st century.

Five All-Time Fastest: Women's 400m

Marita Koch (GDR)	47.60	1985
Jarmila Kratochvilova (CZH)	47.99	1983
Marie-José Perec (FRA)	48.25	1996
Olga Vladykina (UKR)	48.27	1985
Tatana Kocembova (CZH)	48.59	1983
Prediction	*47.60*	*2015*

Top Three: Women's 400m

GOLD MEDAL:	Marita Koch (GDR)
SILVER MEDAL:	Irena Szewinska (POL)
BRONZE MEDAL:	Jarmila Kratochvilova (CZH)

800 Meters

T he 800m was included in the 1928 Olympics at the inaugural track and field program for women but was something of a public relations disaster, as many of the contestants collapsed at the finish. The end result was that the 800m was left off the Olympic program until 1960.

Sixteen athletes have set or equaled the world record 24 times. Two have been from Australia, the rest from Europe. In the last 25 years most of the elite runners have been from Eastern Europe. Six of the 16 were also Olympic champions, and 5 of them set their world records at the Olympics: Radke-Batschauer (1928), Shevtsova (1960), Packer (1964), Kazankina (1976), and Olizarenko (1980). Seven of the 16 world record holders came from the former Soviet Union, which has dominated women's middle distance running over the years.

The major barrier for this event was the two-minute mark. It took nine years for the record to move down from 2:01.2 (Dixie Willis, 1962) until two minutes for the 800m was broken by Hildegard Falck in 1971 with 1:58.5. Two minutes was then quickly beaten by a string of runners, and the barrier, like the four-minute mile, was found to be purely psychological.

Women's World Records for 800m

Record time	Record holder	Location	Date
2:16.8	Lina Radke-Batschauer (GER)	Amsterdam, Netherlands	2 Aug 1928
2:15.9	Anna Larsson (SWE)	Stockholm, Sweden	27 Aug 1944
2:14.8	Anna Larsson (SWE)	Halsingborg, Sweden	19 Aug 1945
2:13.8	Anna Larsson (SWE)	Stockholm, Sweden	30 Aug 1945
2:13.0	Yevdokiya Vasilyeva (USSR)	Moscow, USSR	17 Jul 1950
2:12.2	Valentina Pomogayeva (USSR)	Moscow, USSR	26 Jul 1951
2:12.0	Nina Pletneva (later Otkalenko) (USSR)	Minsk, USSR	26 Aug 1951
2:08.5	Nina Otkalenko (USSR)	Kiev, USSR	15 Jun 1952
2:07.3	Nina Otkalenko (USSR)	Moscow, USSR	27 Aug 1953
2:06.6	Nina Otkalenko (USSR)	Kiev, USSR	16 Sep 1954
2:05.0	Nina Otkalenko (USSR)	Zagreb, Yugoslavia	24 Sep 1955
2:04.3	Lyudmila Shevtsova (USSR)	Moscow, USSR	3 Jul 1960
2:04.3	Lyudmila Shevtsova (USSR)	Rome, Italy	7 Sep 1960
2:01.2	Dixie Willis (AUST)	Perth, Australia	3 Mar 1962
2:01.1	Ann Packer (GBR)	Tokyo, Japan	20 Oct 1964
2:01.0	Judy Pollock (AUST)	Helsinki, Finland	28 Jun 1967
2:00.5	Vera Nikolic (YUG)	London, England	20 Jul 1968
1:58.5	Hildegard Falck (FRG)	Stuttgart, West Germany	11 Jul 1971
1:57.5	Svetla Zlateva (BUL)	Athens, Greece	24 Aug 1973
1:56.0	Valentina Gerasimova (USSR)	Kiev, USSR	12 Jun 1976
1:54.9	Tatyana Kazankina (USSR)	Montreal, Canada	26 Jul 1976
1:54.9	Nadezhda Olizarenko (USSR)	Moscow, USSR	12 Jun 1980
1:53.43	Nadezhda Olizarenko (USSR)	Moscow, USSR	27 Jul 1980
1:53.28	Jarmila Kratochvilova (CZH)	Munich, West Germany	26 Jul 1983

Lina Radke-Batschauer (Germany, 1903–1983)

2:16.8   **Amsterdam, Netherlands**   **2 Aug 1928**

The 800m was introduced into the Olympic program for women in 1928. This was much against the wishes of the founding father of the modern Olympics, Baron Pierre de Coubertin.

Karoline "Lina" Radke-Batschauer had been German champion over this distance in 1927 and 1928 and was regarded as the favorite. Another key athlete was the Japanese sprinter and long jumper Kinue Hitomi, who entered the 800m because there was no long jump on the program.

Hitomi led for the first 500 meters, and then Radke-Batschauer sprinted for home, winning in 2:16.8. Hitomi was timed at 2:17.6. Nine women had entered the 800m, and six of them collapsed after the finish. This was partly because it was an extremely hot day and also because few women at that time trained properly for the distance. The winning time was accepted as the first world record.

Nonetheless, the sight of numerous women in varying degrees of distress evoked dismay among the mostly male officials. The event was promptly banned from the Olympic program, not to return for 32 years, in 1960. When those Olympics came around, one of the spectators was Lina Radke-Batschauer, now 57. The winning time was 12.5 seconds faster than her effort 32 years earlier, and none of the competitors collapsed, despite the fierce Roman heat that year.

Lina Radke-Batschauer, Germany (800m), wins the 1928 Olympic 800m at Amsterdam ahead of Kinue Hitomi (Japan).

Anna Larsson   (Sweden, b. 1922)

2:15.9	Stockholm, Sweden	27 Aug 1944
2:14.8	Halsingborg, Sweden	19 Aug 1945
2:13.8	Stockholm, Sweden	30 Aug 1945

Anna Larsson of Sweden broke the 16-year-old 800m record in 1944. Sweden remained neutral during World War II, and its athletic programs continued throughout the war years. All three of Larsson's records were set in Sweden because she had no opportunity for international competition.

The first of her world records was at the 1944 national championships, and she won by 8.1 seconds. A year later she reduced the record by 1.1 seconds, also at the national championships. Eleven days later she took another second off the record at an athletic meet in Stockholm. At the 1946 European Championships the longest event for women was 200m, so Larsson missed any opportunity for international competition at 800m.

Yevdokiya Vasilyeva   (Soviet Union, b. 1916)

| 2:13.0 | Moscow, USSR | 17 Jul 1950 |

Yevdokiya Vasilyeva was a major athletic talent who set many records that unfortunately were never recognized. After the 1917 Russian Revolution the Soviet Union decided to withdraw from international athletics. Accordingly, any records its athletes set were never submitted. The Soviet Union rejoined the world track and field scene only when it turned up (unannounced) at the 1946 European Championships in Oslo. It returned to the Olympic Games in 1952.

Vasilyeva started breaking records in 1936, at age 20, when she ran the 1500m in 4:47.2. However, world records at 1500m were not officially recognized by the IAAF until 1967. Despite other world bests, she did not become an official world record holder until she ran 800m in 1950, at the age of 34, recording 2:13.0.

Her times and performances in her 15-year career were almost completely unknown outside the Soviet Union. She was Soviet champion at 800m six times (1937-38, 1943-45, and 1949) and at 1500m six times (1938, 1943-45, 1949, and 1951).

Valentina Pomogayeva   (Soviet Union, b. 1925)

2:12.2	Moscow, USSR	26 Jun 1951

Valentina Pomogayeva was another Soviet middle-distance talent who was active in the postwar years but failed to get appropriate recognition for her performances. Her 800m world record of 2:12.2 in 1951 took 0.8 second off Vasilyeva's time. However, she was soon to be eclipsed by rising new star Nina Pletneva (later Otkalenko), who achieved the first of her five world records at this distance exactly one month later.

In a short career, Pomogayeva's best season was 1951. After her world record she won the Soviet 400m championship and was second in the 800m to Pletneva.

Nina Otkalenko (née Pletneva)   (Soviet Union, b. 1928)

2:12.0	Minsk, USSR	26 Aug 1951
2:08.5	Kiev, USSR	15 Jun 1952
2:07.3	Moscow, USSR	27 Aug 1953
2:06.6	Kiev, USSR	16 Sep 1954
2:05.0	Zagreb, Yugoslavia	24 Sep 1955

Nina Otkalenko had the opportunity to win European Championships honors after the 800m was introduced there in 1954. She dominated the event in the 1950s and set a world record each year for five successive years, from 1951 to 1955. In her first world record she beat her predecessor, Valentina Pomogayeva, 2:12.0 to 2:12.3. Over the years Otkalenko went on to reduce the world record by a total of 7.2 seconds.

She comfortably won the inaugural 800m European Championships in Bern, Switzerland, in August 1954 from Britain's Diane Leather, 2:08.8 to 2:09.8. At the Soviet national championships she was 400m champion once (1956), 800m champion

Nina Otkalenko, Soviet Union, the dominant 800m runner of the 1950s, with Australia's Shirley Strickland (sprints, hurdles).

four times (1951-54) , and 1500m champion once (1952). She still managed a third place in the Soviet 800m title in 1960.

Weighing 50 kilograms (110 pounds), she was the lightest of the 800m world record holders.

Lyudmila Shevtsova   (Soviet Union, b. 1934)

| 2:04.3 | Moscow, USSR | 3 Jul 1960 |
| 2:04.3 | Rome, Italy | 7 Sep 1960 |

Lyudmila Shevtsova was the first Soviet athlete to be both 800m world record holder and Olympic champion after the event was reintroduced at the Rome Olympics. She finished second to Nina Otkalenko in Otkalenko's 1954 world record race. Six years were to pass before Shevtsova broke her compatriot's world record. She first achieved this two months before the Rome Olympics, in the Znamenskiy Memorial race, where she took 0.7 second off the record, recording 2:04.3. She won by only 0.2 second from North Korea's Sin Kim Dan, who was later to become the 400m world record holder and possibly the first woman under two minutes for 800m.

Lyudmila Shevtsova, Soviet Union, on the podium at the Rome Olympics after her 800m victory, with Brenda Jones (Australia) and Ursula Donath (East Germany).

At the Rome Olympics Shevtsova won and equaled her world record. Australia's Dixie Willis led to the 700m mark, when she pulled off the track exhausted. In the sprint home Shevtsova won by 0.1 second from another Australian, Brenda Jones, 2:04.3 to 2:04.4.

At the Soviet national championships, Shevtsova was the 400m champion once (1955) and 800m champion six times (1955-56, 1958-59, and 1961-62).

Dixie Willis   (Australia, b. 1941)

| 2:01.2 | Perth, Australia | 3 Mar 1962 |

Dixie Willis was the Australian 400m and 800m champion for much of the early 1960s. She had been an 800m finalist at the 1960 Rome Olympics but possibly pushed herself too hard in her heat, winning in an Olympic record time (2:06.3), three seconds faster than the next best winning time. In the final she led almost all the way but at the 700m mark was overcome by exhaustion and stepped off the track.

Her world record came in 1962 in her hometown of Perth at the West Australian championships. She was pressed by New Zealander Marise Chamberlain, 1957 400m world record holder. Willis led at the halfway mark and finished in 2:01.2, taking a huge 3.1

seconds off the world record. Chamberlain was 0.2 second behind her (still a New Zealand record).

Later that season Willis won the 880-yards gold medal at the Perth Commonwealth Games. She was selected for her second Olympics in 1964, but in the weeks before the Games she started to have vomiting attacks prior to races. It may have been nerves or possibly a food allergy. In Tokyo, just before her heat of the 800m, she was struck down by another vomiting attack in the dressing rooms. It was pouring rain outside, and in the end the team doctor ruled her unfit to compete, which was, of course, a major disappointment.

She later became a secretary in Brisbane, married, and had two sons. After her marriage dissolved, she worked as a legal secretary, remarried, and spent five years in Thailand with her husband, where she developed an interest in meditation and natural healing. Since returning to Australia she has been active in leading stress management and meditation groups.

Dixie Willis, Australia (800m).

Ann Packer   (Great Britain, b. 1942)

2:01.1   **Tokyo, Japan**   **20 Oct 1964**

Ann Packer, Great Britain, wins the Tokyo Olympic 800m title in world record time.

Ann Packer became the world record holder in the 800m almost by accident. A versatile athlete, she won her first British AAA title in 1960 in the long jump. She was sixth in the 200m at the 1962 European Championships, and sixth in the 80m hurdles at the Commonwealth Games. However, she subsequently developed as a 400m specialist.

At the Tokyo Olympics in 1964 she was highly favored for the 400m gold medal. However, she finished second in the final behind veteran Betty Cuthbert of Australia, 52.0 to 52.2.

After the disappointment of the 400m she turned to the 800m, almost as a consolation. Not really an 800m specialist (her career best was 2:05.3), she had the slowest previous time of the eight finalists. The favorite was Maryvonne Dupureur of France, who had set an Olympic record of 2:04.1 in the semifinal, while Packer had run 2:06.0 in her semifinal. The finalists were led through the first lap by Dupureur in 58.5, and she continued to lead through to the 700m mark. At this stage, Packer came through like an express train to win in 2:01.1—a gold medal and a world record.

She retired from the sport at age 22. Two of her sons, Ian and David, became professional soccer players for Manchester City, and her eldest, Gary, was a promising 400m runner.

Judy Pollock   (Australia, b. 1940)

2:01.0   **Helsinki, Finland**   **28 Jun 1967**

Judy Pollock, Australia (800m), with coach Henri Schubert.

Judy Pollock, as Judy Amoore, had won an Olympic bronze medal at the 1964 Games in the 400m, behind fellow countrywoman Betty Cuthbert and Britain's Ann Packer. Two years later, she won the 440-yards gold medal at the 1966 Commonwealth Games in Jamaica in 53.0.

Her world record was set at the World Games in Helsinki in her brilliant 1967 season. With halves of 58.0 and 63.0, she ran 2:01.0, winning by 2.7 seconds from future world record holder Vera Nikolic of Yugoslavia and taking 0.1 second off the world record.

She missed the 1968 Mexico City Olympics because she was expecting her first child. After her second child was born in 1971, she made a return to athletics and was selected for the Australian team to travel to Munich. However, upon arrival she pulled a calf muscle before the Games started and could not participate. She retired once more but made another comeback in 1976.

At the Montreal Olympics she was second in her heat in 2:00.66. In the next round she ran a personal best and broke two minutes when she ran 1:59.93. Unfortunately, she had finished fifth in a very fast semifinal and did not progress.

She subsequently ran the Melbourne Marathon twice (1978 and 1979) and at the age of 40 had her third child. Her Australian title wins include four at 400m (1965-67, 1972), three at 800m (1963, 1964, 1969), and a win at 1500m (1976).

Vera Nikolic   (Yugoslavia, b. 1948)

2:00.5   **London, England**   **20 Jul 1968**

Vera Nikolic reduced the record by half a second at the 1968 Women's Amateur Athletic Association Championships in London. She ran a very even race, with laps of 60.0 and 60.5.

At the Mexico City Olympics that year she won her heat but did not finish her semifinal. She was possibly overcome by the extreme pressure of her country's certainty that she would win a gold medal. Whatever the reason, after 300m she ran off the track and left the stadium distraught. The Yugoslav government, so confident of her success, had actually prepared a stamp in her honor to be released the moment she won.

At the Munich Olympics four years later Nikolic finished fifth in the

Vera Nikolic, Yugoslavia (800m).

final with 2:00.0 exactly. If she didn't have much luck at the Olympics, she was European champion twice. She won in 1966 (2:02.8) and again in 1971 (2:00.0).

Hildegard Falck   (West Germany, b. 1949)

1:58.5   **Stuttgart, West Germany**   **11 Jul 1971**

Hildegard Falck, West Germany, first woman under two minutes for the 800m.

In the early 1970s, Hildegard Falck (née Janze) became the first woman to break the two-minute barrier. Originally a swimmer, she turned to track and field at age 17 and won the West German junior 800m title in 1967. She was West German champion in 1970, 1971, and 1973.

Her world record took place at the West German championships in July 1971. Much like the four-minute mile barrier, the 800m two-minute barrier wasn't just crept under, but smashed; Falck ran 1:58.5 to take two whole seconds off the record.

The 1971 European Championships occurred two months after the record. In the 800m, East Germany's Gunhild Hoffmeister fell and brought Falck down with her. Neither finished the race.

A year later the Olympics were in Munich. In the 800m final, Svetla Zlateva of Bulgaria led a bunched field to 600m, when Falck put in a sudden burst of speed. Niole Sabaite (USSR) produced a late sprint but couldn't quite catch her. The result was Falck 1:58.6; Sabaite 1:58.7.

Falck retired at age 24 and, having remarried, is now Hildegard Kimmich.

Svetla Zlateva   (Bulgaria, b. 1952)

1:57.5   **Athens, Greece**   **24 Aug 1973**

Svetla Zlateva of Bulgaria broke the 800m world record in 1973 at the Balkan Games. Her first lap was a very fast 56.5. She slowed somewhat in the second lap with 61.0 (1:57.5), but had still taken one whole second off the record.

Zlateva had run at the 1972 Olympics. She ran a very hard heat—perhaps too hard—to win in 1:58.9, a new Olympic record. Her semifinal time was 2:01.66. In the final she could manage only 1:59.7 to finish fourth. The winner, Hildegard Falck of West Germany, ran 1:58.6, having run earlier rounds of 2:01.52 and 2:01.41.

At the 1976 Olympics Zlateva was sixth in the 800m (1:57.2); Tatyana Kazankina (USSR) won in 1:54.9, a new world record.

Valentina Gerasimova   (Soviet Union, b. 1948)

1:56.0   **Kiev, USSR**   **12 Jun 1976**

Valentina Gerasimova was a finalist at the Soviet 800m championships in the early 1970s. She was fourth in 1972 and 1973 and second in 1974. Finally she won in 1976 with a stunning 1:56.0, to take a huge 1.5 seconds off the world record. This was three months before the Montreal Olympics. She was naturally regarded as one of the favorites but had a disappointing Games. In the heats she came in second in 1:59.8 and progressed to the semifinals. But in the second semifinal she finished only sixth in 2:01.0 and missed out on a place in the final.

Tatyana Kazankina   (Soviet Union, b. 1951)

1:54.9   **Montreal, Canada**   **26 Jul 1976**

Tatyana Kazankina is frail in appearance (51 kilograms, 112 pounds) but is one of the all-time greats of women's middle-distance running. Her competitive achievements are substantial. She won three Olympic gold medals in the 800m (1976) and in the 1500m (1976 and 1980). She also held world records at three distances—800m, 1500m, and 3000m.

In 1976 she had been a regular middle-distance runner in the Soviet Union for some years. At the 1974 European Championships she had come in fourth in the 800m. In the 1500m she had come in third in the 1973 Soviet championships and had won in 1975 and 1976. One month before the 1976 Montreal Olympics she achieved a sensational 1500m world record (3:56.0), becoming the first woman to run that distance under four minutes. She was naturally selected for the 1976 Olympics in the 1500m, but not the 800m. However, en route to Montreal, the Soviet team had a pre-Olympic meet in Paris and she was entered in the 800m. Kazankina won in 1:56.6—the second fastest time ever recorded—so she was added to the Soviet team for the 800m.

At the Olympics she achieved a rare double when she won both the 800m and 1500m, something only one other woman (Svetlana Masterkova, 1996) and five men (Edwin Flack, 1896; James Lightbody, 1904; Mel Sheppard, 1908; Albert Hill, 1920; and Peter Snell, 1964) have done. In the 800m she unleashed a devastating burst in the last 150m to blitz the field, winning in a new world record time of 1:54.9.

Kazankina did not run many more 800m races during the rest of her career; she instead concentrated on the longer distances. She returned to the Olympics in 1980 after having a baby the previous year. She successfully retained her 1500m title but decided not to contest the 800m.

Nadezhda Olizarenko   (Soviet Union, b. 1953)

| 1:54.9 | Moscow, USSR | 12 Jun 1980 |
| 1:53.43 | Moscow, USSR | 27 Jul 1980 |

Nadezhda Olizarenko had come in second in the 800m at the 1978 European Championships in Prague. One month before the 1980 Moscow Olympics she ran at the Pravda Prize athletic meet. Olizarenko took the lead right from the start and ran 57.1 for the first lap and 57.8 for the second to record 1:54.9, equaling Kazankina's world record.

In the Olympics she ran fast times in the heats (1:59.3) and semifinals (1:57.7). She adopted front-running tactics for the final and led through the first lap in 56.41 seconds. Olizarenko won comfortably by 15 meters in a new world record time of 1:53.43. She also competed in the 1500m and won the bronze medal. Her husband Sergey also was a competitor at the Moscow Olympics, in the 3000m steeplechase, but went out in the semifinals.

Olizarenko missed the 1984 Los Angeles Olympics because of the Soviet boycott. However, she won the 800m at the 1986 European Championships at age 33, the oldest winner of that event at these championships. At the 1988 Olympics she went out in the semifinals.

Nadezhda Olizarenko, Soviet Union (800m), 1980 Olympic champion.

Jarmila Kratochvilova   (Czechoslovakia, b. 1951)

| 1:53.28 | Munich, West Germany | 26 Jul 1983 |

Jarmila Kratochvilova's career has been described in the chapter on the 400m. She surprised observers with her second place at the 1980 Moscow Olympics in the 400m. She moved up to the 800m in 1982 and ran 1:56.69 in her first serious race at the distance since 1975 (when she had run 2:11.4). A year later Kratochvilova claimed the world record in Munich. She ran the first lap in 56.28, the second in 57.0, and won by over 50 meters. Her winning time was 1:53.28, which took 0.15 second off Olizarenko's record set at the Moscow Olympics.

Jarmila Kratochvilova, Czechoslovakia (400m, 800m).

Her record race was shortly before the inaugural 1983 World Championships, where she entered both 400m and 800m. She won the 800m in 1:54.68, just 33 minutes after her 400m semifinal. The next day she won the 400m in a new world record, to complete a remarkable double. Her 800m world record has lasted over 13 years.

Conclusions

The world record for 800m has endured for over 13 years and is currently the oldest surviving women's world record. This longevity is surprising in that it took only 0.15 second off the previous record.

The women's middle-distance events have traditionally been dominated by athletes from communist countries, mainly from Eastern Europe. The lack of progress in the record may reflect the disintegration of the Communist Bloc in the late 1980s and the collapse of its sporting systems.

Five All-Time Fastest: Women's 800m

Jarmila Kratochvilova (CZH)	1:53.28	1983
Nadezhda Olizarenko (USSR)	1:53.43	1980
Ana Quirot (CUBA)	1:54.44	1989
Olga Mineyeva (USSR)	1:54.81	1980
Tatyana Kazankina (USSR)	1:54.9	1976
Prediction	*1:52.00*	*2015*

Top Three: Women's 800m

GOLD MEDAL:	Jarmila Kratochvilova (CZH)
SILVER MEDAL:	Nadezhda Olizarenko (USSR)
BRONZE MEDAL:	Hildegard Falck (FRG)

The women's 1500m has been officially recognized only since 1967. However, it had long been established in some parts of the world and was first run at the Soviet championships as far back as 1922. There have been only eight athletes who have held this record. No single country has dominated: The athletes have come from seven different countries. Altogether, the record has been set 13 times. Two of the record-holding athletes (Bragina and Kazankina) have also been Olympic champions.

As is often the case with new world records, there was much improvement in the early years. The record was set nine times in the first five years of its official existence.

The 1500m for women was introduced into the Olympic program at the 1972 Munich Games. The longest period of time that the record remained unbroken was 13 years and 29 days: Tatyana Kazankina's 1980 record, which was finally broken in 1993 by Qu Junxia. The record of 3:50.46 seems safe for a while: To this day, only five women have ever run under 3:55.0.

Women's World Records for 1500m

Record time	Record holder	Location	Date
4:17.3	Anne Smith (GBR)	London, England	3 Jun 1967
4:15.6	Maria Gommers (HOL)	Sittard, Netherlands	24 Oct 1967
4:12.4	Paola Pigni (ITA)	Milan, Italy	2 Jul 1969
4:10.7	Jaroslava Jehličková (CZH)	Athens, Greece	20 Sep 1969
4:09.6	Karin Burneleit (GDR)	Helsinki, Finland	15 Aug 1971
4:06.9	Lyudmila Bragina (USSR)	Moscow, USSR	18 Jul 1972
4:06.5	Lyudmila Bragina (USSR)	Munich, West Germany	4 Sep 1972
4:05.1	Lyudmila Bragina (USSR)	Munich, West Germany	7 Sep 1972
4:01.4	Lyudmila Bragina (USSR)	Munich, West Germany	9 Sep 1972
3:56.0	Tatyana Kazankina (USSR)	Podolsk, USSR	28 Jun 1976
3:55.0	Tatyana Kazankina (USSR)	Moscow, USSR	6 Jul 1980
3:52.47	Tatyana Kazankina (USSR)	Zürich, Switzerland	13 Aug 1980
3:50.46	Qu Junxia (CHN)	Beijing, China	11 Sep 1993

Anne Smith (Great Britain, 1941–1993)

4:17.3   **London, England**   **3 Jun 1967**

Anne Smith made a combined attack on both the mile record and the 1500m record in the same race in 1967. It was a newly recognized event for both distances, so her times were accepted as inaugural world records. Her 1500m time was 4:17.3, her mile time was 4:37.0.

Smith had run the 800m at the Tokyo Olympics in 1964 and finished eighth. She was British AAA champion over 880 yards from 1964 to 1967 and won a bronze medal at 880 yards at the 1966 Commonwealth Games in Jamaica. Unfortunately, there was no 1500m at the Olympics until 1972.

For a while she was coached by Gordon Pirie, world record holder over 3000m and 5000m in the 1950s. A physical education teacher, she died of a brain hemorrhage in 1993, at the age of 52.

Maria Gommers   (Netherlands, b. 1939)

4:15.6   **Sittard, Netherlands**   **24 Oct 1967**

Maria Gommers, Netherlands (1500m).

Three months after Anne Smith's record, Maria Gommers took 1.7 seconds off the record in Sittard, Netherlands. She was 28 and largely unknown at the time. She had set a Dutch 1500m record earlier in the season with 4:39.8 in April and reduced it to 4:35.6 in May and then to 4:22.3 in September. Finally, in October, she ran 4:15.6, a new world record.

At the 1968 Mexico City Olympics Gommers won the bronze medal in the 800m (2:02.6). The following year she was second in the 1500m at the 1969 European Championships, when the event was introduced for the first time at a major championship. This race resulted in a new world record by Jaroslava Jehlicková (Czechoslovakia) of 4:10.7. Gommers ran 4:11.9.

Paola Pigni   (Italy, b. 1945)

4:12.4   **Milan, Italy**   **2 Jul 1969**

Paola Pigni was Italy's premier distance runner of the late 1960s and early 1970s. Born in Milan, she was a top cross-country runner and was International Cross Country champion in 1973 and 1974. In 1969 she took a massive 3.2 seconds off the 1500m world record when she ran 4:12.4 in Milan, in front of an adoring crowd. At the European Championships later that season she came in third, when Jaroslava Jehlicková (Czechoslovakia) set a new world record (4:10.7).

Three years later Pigni won the bronze medal in the 1500m at the Munich Olympics. This time she ran 4:02.9, almost 10 seconds faster than her 1969 record, but only good enough for third place, so far had standards improved. The winner, Lyudmila Bragina (USSR) set a new world record when she won in 4:01.4.

Pigni tried the mile in 1973 and was the first woman to run this distance under 4:30, running 4:29.5. She later ran a number of marathons when that was not fashionable for women.

Paola Pigni, Italy (1500m).

Jaroslava Jehličková   (Czechoslovakia, b. 1942)

4:10.7   Athens, Greece   20 Sep 1969

Ten weeks after Paola Pigni's 1969 record, it was broken again by another 1.7 seconds by Czech athlete Jaroslava Jehličková at the 1969 European Championships in Athens. It was the inaugural running of the event at a major championship. At the beginning of the last lap Jehličková was still in eighth position, but she sprinted home to win by 1.2 seconds.

Jehličková did not go on to other successes after her 1969 triumph. At the 1972 Olympic Games in Munich she was ninth in a semifinal.

Karin Burneleit   (East Germany, b. 1943)

4:09.6   Helsinki, Finland   15 Aug 1971

Karin Burneleit became the first woman to run under 4:10 when she ran 4:09.6 at the 1971 European Championships in Helsinki.

The next year she went to the Munich Olympics, where the world record was reduced all the way down to 4:01.4 by Lyudmila Bragina. Burneleit ran a lifetime best of 4:04.1 to finish fourth.

Despite her world record, she never won the East German title. She was second in 1970 and 1972 and third in 1974.

Lyudmila Bragina   (Soviet Union, b. 1943)

4:06.9	Moscow, USSR	18 Jul 1972
4:06.5	Munich, West Germany	4 Sep 1972
4:05.1	Munich, West Germany	7 Sep 1972
4:01.4	Munich, West Germany	9 Sep 1972

Few athletes have ever dominated an event at an Olympic Games the way Lyudmila Bragina monopolized the 1500m in 1972. She set world records in the heats, the semifinal, and the final. Bragina had been around for some years prior to 1972. She was the Soviet champion over 1500m for the years 1968 to 1970. She had been fourth at the 1969 European Championships over 1500m and sixth in the same event at the 1971 European Championships.

In the Olympic year of 1972 she established herself as favorite for the 1500m when she set a new world record (4:06.9) at the Soviet championships, seven weeks before the Games began. At Munich her

Lyudmila Bragina, Soviet Union, who achieved three 1500m world records at the Munich Olympics.

three races reduced the record by another 5.5 seconds. In the final she made a surprise burst at the 800m mark and dragged the next four runners under 4:05.

Bragina was again Soviet champion over 1500m in 1973 and 1974, but the parade of champions is ever changing. The 1975 Soviet title was won by rising star Tatyana Kazankina, who went on to win the gold medal at the next Olympics in Montreal, with Bragina fifth. Later in her career Bragina set two world records at 3000m (1974, 1976).

Tatyana Kazankina   (Soviet Union, b. 1951)

3:56.0	Podolsk, USSR	28 Jun 1976
3:55.0	Moscow, USSR	6 Jul 1980
3:52.47	Zürich, Switzerland	13 Aug 1980

As mentioned in the chapter on the 800m, Tatyana Kazankina is one of the all-time middle distance greats, with three Olympic gold medals (800m and 1500m in 1976, 1500m in 1980) and world records at three separate distances (800m, 1500m, and 3000m).

At age 19, she had run 4:19.0 for the 1500m and improved slowly over the years. However, in 1976 her results improved dramatically. In June she ran 4:05.2. Ten days later she ran 4:02.8. Six days later, at a "Runners Day" meet in Podolsk, south of Moscow, she finally broke through to a new level when she ran 3:56.0 to become the first woman under four minutes.

At the Montreal Olympics Kazankina won the 800m and 1500m gold medal double. The 1500m was a slow race (4:05.5). It was as though all the other athletes knew she was going to win.

For the Moscow Olympics she decided to run only the 1500m. She achieved a new world record in the 1500m (3:55.0) shortly before the Olympics, as in 1976. The Olympic final was a comfortable affair for her, and she sprinted away over the last 300m to win in 3:56.56.

Tatyana Kazankina, Soviet Union (800m, 1500m, 3000m) and Mary Decker, United States (mile, 10,000m) at the 1983 World Championships.

Two weeks later she traveled to Zürich, determined to make a major improvement on her world record. With a pacesetter taking her through the first 900m, she ran the last 600m on her own and finished in 3:52.47. This was a 1500m time faster than the immortal Paavo Nurmi ever achieved and was destined to remain the record for 13 years.

Qu Junxia   (China, b. 1972)

3:50.46   **Beijing, China**   **11 Sep 1993**

Qu Junxia was part of the "China Syndrome" that seemed to come out of nowhere in 1993. She had actually been competing for a few years. In 1990 she won the World Junior 1500m title. At the 1992 Barcelona Olympics she was third in the 1500m with 3:57.08, a Chinese record.

In August 1993 the Chinese team astonished spectators at the World Championships in Stuttgart with their total domination of the middle-distance events. In the 3000m they were first, second, and third, with Qu Junxia winning in 8:28.71. One month later at the Chinese National Games in Beijing, Qu Junxia broke the longest-standing running record in women's track and field when she won the 1500m in 3:50.46, which took two seconds off Kazankina's revered record. At the same Games Kazankina's 3000m record was destroyed by a host of Chinese runners.

The furor that surrounded these new records was partly caused by the numbers of Chinese athletes who were suddenly beating the old record. In the 3000m races at these Games five Chinese athletes broke the previous world record, an occurrence that was unheard of in the history of track and field.

However the 1500m world record has been reduced by margins greater than two seconds by three other athletes: Pigni (1969), Bragina (twice in 1972), and Kazankina (1976 and 1980). Because the record was 13 years old, it was overdue for challenge. Perhaps Kazankina's record was given too much reverence. However, all has been quiet on the Chinese front since

Qu Junxia, China (1500m).

1993. Their image has not been helped by drug suspension among female athletes in swimming and weight lifting.

Conclusions

The women's world record for 1500m was reduced to 3:50.46 by Qu Junxia during the "Chinese Revolution" in 1993. No one, including the Chinese, has even remotely approached the current world record since those 1993 performances. This may partly be due to the collapse of the Chinese training school, run by coach Ma Junren. Whatever the reason, the current generation of athletes are running some six seconds slower than the world record. The fastest time by a woman in 1996 was 3:56.77. Accordingly, the prospect of any reduction in the women's world record for the 1500m in the foreseeable future seems remote.

Five All-Time Fastest: Women's 1500m

Qu Junxia (CHN)	3:50.46	1993
Wang Junxia (CHN)	3:51.92	1993
Tatyana Kazankina (USSR)	3:52.47	1980
Paula Ivan (ROM)	3:53.96	1988
Olga Dvima (USSR)	3:54.23	1982
Prediction	*3:50.46*	*2015*

Top Three: Women's 1500m

GOLD MEDAL:	**Tatyana Kazankina (USSR)**
SILVER MEDAL:	**Qu Junxia (CHN)**
BRONZE MEDAL:	**Lyudmila Bragina (USSR)**

The 3000m race for women was introduced when the women's distance program was expanded to obtain a degree of parity with the men's program. The first record was recognized in 1974, and there was much improvement in the early years. The record improved by 25 seconds in the first two years of its existence. Six athletes from three countries have set the record nine times. Kazankina's 1984 record lasted over nine years. However, the 1993 record of Wang Junxia, some 16 seconds faster, seems destined to last even longer.

Many athletes have a special regard for this 7 ½-lap race and feel it is quite different in character from the 12 ½-lap 5000m. The 3000m race was first introduced to the Olympics in 1984, and it was never won by a world record holder. However, the IAAF made the decision to replace it at major championships with the 5000m as of 1995. World records for the 3000m will continue, but many athletes are sorry to see the 3000m lose its championship status.

Women's World Records for 3000m

Record time	Record holder	Location	Date
8:52.8	Lyudmila Bragina (USSR)	Durham, USA	6 Jul 1974
8:46.6	Grete Andersen (later Waitz) (NOR)	Oslo, Norway	24 Jun 1975
8:45.4	Grete Waitz (NOR)	Oslo, Norway	21 Jun 1976
8:27.2	Lyudmila Bragina (USSR)	College Park, USA	7 Aug 1976
8:26.78	Svetlana Ulmasova (USSR)	Kiev, USSR	25 Jul 1982
8:22.62	Tatyana Kazankina (USSR)	Leningrad, USSR	26 Aug 1984
8:22.06	Zhang Linli (CHN)	Beijing, China	12 Sep 1993
8:12.19	Wang Junxia (CHN)	Beijing, China	12 Sep 1993
8:06.11	Wang Junxia (CHN)	Beijing, China	13 Sep 1993

Lyudmila Bragina (Soviet Union, b. 1943)

8:52.8	Durham, USA	6 Jul 1974
8:27.2	College Park, USA	7 Aug 1976

As mentioned in the chapter on the 1500m, Lyudmila Bragina set three world records in the 1500m at the 1972 Munich Olympics. Toward the latter part of her career, she turned to the 3000m. She was selected for the 3000m at a United States vs. Soviet Union meet in Durham, North Carolina, in July 1974. Her winning time in this event (8:52.8) was taken as the inaugural official world record for the distance. Later that season she ran in the European Championships over the same distance and was surprisingly beaten by the Finn Nina Holmen.

One week after the conclusion of the 1976 Montreal Olympics, she ran in another United States vs. Soviet Union athletic meet at College Park, Maryland. The world record had been reduced in the interim by Grete Waitz of Norway down to 8:45.4. Bragina made a determined effort to reclaim the record and succeeded in removing more than 18 seconds from the record with 8:27.2.

Bragina's last major international competition was the 1977 World Cup, in which, at the age of 34, she came in second to Waitz in the 3000m, 8:43.5 to 8:46.3.

Grete Waitz (née Andersen) (Norway, b. 1953)

| 8:46.6 | Oslo, Norway | 24 Jun 1975 |
| 8:45.4 | Oslo, Norway | 21 Jun 1976 |

Grete Waitz of Norway is more widely known as the marathon queen who won the New York City Marathon nine times. But before her marathon career took off in 1978, she already had a lengthy track career. She had run at the 1972 Munich Olympics, finishing sixth in the 1500m heats. At the 1976 Montreal Olympics she got through to the 1500m semifinals. In the 1978 European Championships she was third in the 3000m.

It was in 1975 that she set her first world record at a Norway vs. Sweden vs. East Germany meet. She went straight to the front and took 6.2 seconds off Bragina's record when she won in 8:46.6. She was met with thunderous applause, because this was the first world record ever set by a Norwegian woman. Three days later she married her coach, Jack Waitz.

A year later she took another 1.2 seconds off the record at a Norway vs. Denmark meet, also in Oslo, without serious competition. Her one major 3000m title was the inaugural World Cup in 1977, where she defeated Lyudmila Bragina, 8:43.5 to 8:46.3.

She was International Cross Country champion five times (1978-81 and 1983). A teacher by profession, she entered her first marathon in 1978 when invited to the New York City Marathon. Her debut at this distance resulted in an unexpected world record and a new career.

Svetlana Ulmasova (Soviet Union, b. 1953)

| 8:26.78 | Kiev, USSR | 25 Jul 1982 |

Svetlana Ulmasova started out as a 1500m runner and was fifth in the Soviet championships in both 1975 and 1976, before turning to the 3000m. At the longer distance she won the European Championships twice, in 1978 and in 1982, and was Soviet champion in 1978, 1979, and 1982. Ulmasova also won the 3000m at the 1979 World Cup. Her 1982 victory in the Soviet championships took 0.42 second off the world record.

She ran in the 3000m at the inaugural World Championships in Helsinki in 1983 but fell back to fourth as Mary Decker (USA) overcame the Soviet challenge.

A teacher by profession, she retired from athletics briefly but returned in 1986 and won the 5000m at the Soviet championships that year.

Tatyana Kazankina (Soviet Union, b. 1951)

| 8:22.62 | Leningrad, USSR | 26 Aug 1984 |

Somewhat like Lyudmila Bragina, Tatyana Kazankina turned to the 3000m late in her career. Her career has largely been covered in the chapters on the 800m and 1500m.

She had run the 3000m at the inaugural 1983 World Championships in Helsinki. However, Mary Decker of the United States led from start to finish, winning in 8:34.62. When Kazankina realized that she wasn't going to catch Decker, she dropped back to third.

The Soviets boycotted the Los Angeles Games. One month later Kazankina made a serious attempt on the world record and sliced more than four seconds off the record when she ran 8:22.62.

The rest of her season was clouded by a drug testing ordeal. After winning a 5000m race in Paris she was asked to undergo a drug test. She refused. By refusing to take the test, an athlete is assumed by the IAAF to have breached the drug testing protocols. Accordingly, an 18-month suspension from athletics was imposed on her by the IAAF.

Zhang Linli   (China, b. 1973)

8:22.06   **Beijing, China**   **12 Sep 1993**

Zhang Linli was one of the Chinese middle-distance runners who stunned the track and field world in 1993. At the 1993 World Championships in Stuttgart, Germany, Chinese athletes won the 1500m, 3000m, and 10,000m with ridiculous ease. Six weeks later at the Chinese National Games long-standing world records were beaten routinely by numerous runners.

One of these world record holders was Zhang Linli. Weighing only 48 kilograms (106 pounds), she had run second in the 3000m at the 1993 World Championships in 8:29.25. After this run she improved to 8:22.06 in the first heat of the Chinese National Games in October, a new world record that took 0.56 second off Kazankina's 1984 record. This time remained a world record for only 14 minutes, as Wang Junxia ran 8:12.19 in the next heat.

In the final Wang Junxia further reduced the world record to 8:06.11, while Zhang Linli improved to 8:16.50 in third place. These times were so far ahead of anything the rest of the world had even approached that they set off a wave of controversy, including speculation about drug abuse, although this was never proven.

Despite the disbanding of coach Ma Junren's group, Zhang won the 3000m Asian Games in 8:52.97 in 1994.

Wang Junxia   (China, b. 1973)

8:12.19   **Beijing, China**   **12 Sep 1993**
8:06.11   **Beijing, China**   **13 Sep 1993**

No athlete generated more publicity in 1993 than 20-year-old Wang Junxia, who demolished two distance records that had stood for years: the 3000m and 10,000m. This feat was controversial, in part because not just Wang, but a string of Chinese athletes seemed to come out of nowhere to break records that had been challenged unsuccessfully for years by top female athletes from countries such as Kenya, Ethiopia, Japan, the Soviet Union, and the United States.

What secret did the Chinese have that the rest of the world missed? Hard work? Dutiful devotion to their coaches' punishing schedules? Special diets? An inspirational coach? A dedicated training center? Altitude training? Many speculated that illegal drug use was the cause of the "Chinese Revolution," although such allegations were never proven.

Wang Junxia, China (3000m, 10,000m), leader of the 1993 "Chinese Revolution."

Whatever the reason, Chinese distance running had been making great progress in the previous two or three years, although track and field fans who focus on the results in North America and Europe perhaps did not appreciate this. Wang had become World Junior champion at Seoul in 1992 in the 10,000m. Suddenly, at the 1993 World Championships in Stuttgart, the Chinese women won the 1500m, the 3000m, and the 10,000m with almost contemptuous ease. Wang won the 10,000m by 23 seconds in the second-fastest time ever run.

One month later she competed at the Chinese National Games. On 8 September, she took 41.96 seconds off the world record for 10,000m. On 11 September she ran second in the 1500m to Qu Junxia; both athletes came in under the old world record time. The next day Wang ran a new 3000m world record of 8:12.19 in her heat, an almost 10-second improvement on the record. In these heats five Chinese women broke the existing 3000m record. Such an event had never happened before and it generated skepticism. The 3000m final (13 September) saw Wang take another six seconds off the record with 8:06.11.

Despite the controversy, Wang's performances seem genuine enough, especially in light of her 1993 marathon races: In October she won the World Cup in Spain. Weighing only 45 kilograms (99 pounds), she appears to have both great talent and determination inside a waiflike body. Three years later at the Atlanta Olympics she added to her laurels with a gold medal in the 5000m and a silver in the 10,000m.

Conclusions

The 1993 world records by Wang Junxia were a quantum jump in standards that the rest of the track and field world is still struggling to come to grips with. Her current world record of 8:06.11 is lightyears ahead of the rest of the world. The best time for the distance in 1996 was 8:35.42.

It is hard to believe that this record will be broken in the near future. The entire group of Chinese athletes who broke the old record in 1993 now seem incapable of reproducing those times.

Now that the women's 3000m is being replaced at championship level by the 5000m, less focus will fall on the 3000m. Athletes will concentrate their training and attention on the longer distance, as that is where the gold medals will lie in the future. Wang Junxia's record is destined to be around for a long time.

Five All-Time Fastest: Women's 3000m

Wang Junxia (CHN)	8:06.11	1993
Qu Junxia (CHN)	8:12.18	1993
Zhang Linli (CHN)	8:16.50	1993
Ma Linyan (CHN)	8:19.78	1993
Sonia O'Sullivan (IRE)	8:21.64	1994
Prediction	*8:06.11*	*2015*

Top Three: Women's 3000m

GOLD MEDAL:	**Wang Junxia (CHN)**
SILVER MEDAL:	**Tatyana Kazankina (USSR)**
BRONZE MEDAL:	**Lyudmila Bragina (USSR)**

The 5000m has not been featured often in women's track and field, but this is changing, since the IAAF decided to install it in championship races since 1995 in place of the 3000m. The event was given world record status in only 1981. Since that time, six women have held the world record in the event.

This event is still in its infancy as a significant track and field event for women. It is too early to say what improvements are yet in store for this world record.

Women's World Record Holders for 5000m

Record time	Record holder	Location	Date
15:14.51	Paula Fudge (GBR)	Knarvik, Norway	13 Sep 1981
15:13.22	Anne Audain (NZ)	Auckland, New Zealand	17 Mar 1982
15:08.26	Mary Decker (USA)	Eugene, Oregon	5 Jun 1982
14:58.89	Ingrid Kristiansen (NOR)	Oslo, Norway	28 Jun 1984
14:48.07	Zola Budd (S.AF/GBR)	London, England	26 Aug 1985
14:37.33	Ingrid Kristiansen (NOR)	Stockholm, Sweden	5 Aug 1986
14:36.45	Fernanda Ribeiro (POR)	Hechtel, Belgium	22 Jul 1995

Five All-Time Fastest: Women's 5000m

Fernanda Ribeiro (POR)	14:36.45	1995
Ingrid Kristiansen (NOR)	14:37.33	1986
Gabriela Szabo (POR)	14:41.12	1996
Sonia O'Sullivan (IRE)	14:41.40	1995
Elana Meyer (S.AF)	14:44.05	1995
Prediction	*14:15.00*	*2015*

This event was given world record status for women only in 1981. It was first included at the Asian Games in 1985, at the European Championships in 1986, at the World Championships in 1987, and at the Olympic Games in 1988.

Only seven athletes have held the world record, four from the former Soviet Union. As in many of the women's events, there was much improvement in the early years. Only one world record holder (Olga Bondarenko) has also won the Olympic title.

Kristiansen's seven-year-old world record was demolished by almost 42 seconds at the celebrated Chinese National Games in 1993 by Wang Junxia. The new record indicated an average lap speed 1.7 seconds faster than Kristiansen had run. This is a major improvement in the record that is unlikely to be approached for many years.

Women's World Records for 10,000m

Record time	Record holder	Location	Date
32:17.2	Yelena Sipatova (USSR)	Moscow, USSR	19 Sep 1981
31:35.3	Mary Decker (USA)	Eugene, USA	16 Jul 1982
31:35.01	Lyudmila Baranova (USSR)	Krasnodar, USSR	29 May 1983
31:27.58	Raisa Sadreydinova (USSR)	Odessa, USSR	7 Sep 1983
31:13.78	Olga Bondarenko (USSR)	Kiev, USSR	24 Jun 1984
30:59.42	Ingrid Kristiansen (NOR)	Oslo, Norway	27 Jul 1985
30:13.74	Ingrid Kristiansen (NOR)	Oslo, Norway	5 Jul 1986
29:31.78	Wang Junxia (CHN)	Beijing, China	8 Sep 1993

Yelena Sipatova   (Soviet Union, b. 1955)

32:17.2   **Moscow, USSR**   **19 Sep 1981**

The distance of 10,000m for women was officially recognized for world record purposes in 1981. The inaugural record holder was Yelena Sipatova. Running in the 1981 Soviet championships at the Lenin Stadium in Moscow, she recorded 32:17.2. That was her only significant title in this event. She was born Yelena Chernysheva and weighs only 48 kilograms (106 pounds).

Mary Decker   (United States, b. 1958)

31:35.3   **Eugene, USA**   **16 Jul 1982**

Mary Decker first attracted public attention in the early 1970s, when she was selected to run in a United States vs. Soviet Union international meet in Richmond, Virginia, at age 14. A brilliant future seemed assured, but much of her early career involved heavy workloads, which led to a string of leg injuries, including stress fractures and compartment syndrome of the calf muscles. She had to watch the 1976 Montreal Olympics on television. In 1980 she had to miss another Olympics because of President Carter's decision to boycott the Moscow Olympics. After the Games she ran in Kazankina's 1500m world record race, finishing second with 3:59.43. This made her the first (and only) female U.S. athlete to run the 1500m under four minutes.

The early 1980s were taken up by more injuries and more surgery and a short marriage to marathon runner Ron Tabb. However, she bounced back in 1982 and set world records over both the mile and the 10,000m.

In 1983 the first of the World Championships in track and field took place in Helsinki. Most Western runners had long had an inferiority complex about Soviet distance runners. Mary Decker stole the show by winning the 1500m and the 3000m with determined front-running, defeating Kazankina in the 3000m. Those World Championships were the highlight of her career.

What she hoped would be the highlight of her career—a gold medal in the 3000m at the 1984 Olympics—was denied her because of a fall midrace. South African–born Zola Budd, a barefooted teenager, was leading with Decker just behind her. In a famous entanglement, Decker came crumbling down on the track in agony. The American was carried off on a stretcher. Budd finished seventh. Most observers thought that Decker made a mistake by being too close to Budd.

Despite a great season in 1985, Olympic success continued to elude Mary Decker. At the 1988 Games she was tenth in the 1500m and eighth in the 3000m. She remarried, this time to British discus thrower Richard Slaney. Not known to tolerate fools readily, she was a role model and an inspiration to a generation of U.S. runners.

Lyudmila Baranova   (Soviet Union, b. 1950)

31:35.01   **Krasnodar, USSR**   **29 May 1983**

Lyudmila Baranova was another Soviet athlete who achieved record status over the 10,000m before it became a regular event in championships. She took a mere 0.29 second off Mary Decker's record with 31:35.01, when running in the Spartakiade of the Russian Republic in 1983. She had no other significant success in her athletic career.

Raisa Sadreydinova   (Soviet Union, b. 1950)

31:27.58   **Odessa, USSR**   **7 Sep 1983**

Three months after Baranova set her record, Raisa Sadreydinova took 7.43 seconds off it with 31:27.58 in the 1983 Soviet championships in Odessa. That was Sadreydinova's only significant title. She was second in the Soviet championships in 1982 and sixth in 1984.

At the time of her world record, she was 33 years old. Another lightweight, she weighs only 50 kilograms (110 pounds).

Olga Bondarenko   (Soviet Union, b. 1960)

31:13.78   **Kiev, USSR**   **24 Jun 1984**

Olga Bondarenko was Soviet 10,000m champion in 1984, 1985, and 1987. She set her world record in 1984 at the Izvestia Cup in Kiev, improving the record by 13.8 seconds. The event was not yet on the program for the 1984 Olympics, and the Soviet Union boycotted the Games anyway.

She ran the 10,000m at the World Cup in Australia in 1985. She made the classic mistake of misjudging the number of laps and sprinted to the "finish," thinking she was on the last lap. As she crossed the line, the official rang the bell to indicate there was one more lap to run. Exhausted, she plodded around the last lap but dropped back to third.

At the 1986 European Championships it was the new star, Ingrid Kristiansen, who won easily, with Bondarenko second. In the 1987 World Championships Kristiansen won again, with Bondarenko fourth, although the pack closed rapidly in the last lap. Kristiansen started as favorite at the 1988 Olympics but sustained a foot injury midrace and had to withdraw. Confident of her sprint finish, Bondarenko kicked with 200m to go, to comfortably win in 31:05.21.

In her final Olympics, Bondarenko went out in the heats of the 10,000m at the 1992 Games.

Olga Bondarenko, Soviet Union (10,000m), winning the 10,000m at the Seoul Olympics.

Ingrid Kristiansen   (Norway, b. 1956)

| 30:59.42 | Oslo, Norway | 27 Jul 1985 |
| 30:13.74 | Oslo, Norway | 5 Jul 1986 |

Ingrid Kristiansen had shown running talent at school but chose to become a cross-country skier. She competed at the 1976 Winter Olympics and at the 1978 World Championships in this sport, but returned to long-distance running. The Norwegian star in those days was Grete Waitz, and initially Kristiansen ran in her shadow. By the mid-1980s Kristiansen was at the peak of her career. She set world records in the 5000m, 10,000m, and marathon, something the great Paavo Nurmi never achieved. She won the 10,000m at the 1986 European Championships and the same event at the 1987 World Championships. At the 1988 Olympics she was leading the race but sustained a serious foot injury and had to withdraw.

In 1985 she made a serious attempt on Olga Bondarenko's 10,000m world record in Oslo and broke the 31-minute barrier by 0.58 second in front of an enthusiastic crowd. Twelve months later at the same venue she brought the record down by 45 seconds, the biggest improvement of any track record, men's or women's.

An Olympic medal was the one honor she never achieved. A popular and congenial athlete, she always ran in white gloves and always seemed to smile.

Wang Junxia   (China, b. 1973)

| 29:31.78 | Beijing, China | 8 Sep 1993 |

Wang Junxia's explosion onto the middle-distance scene in track and field in 1993 has been described in the chapter on the 3000m. Her performances at both 3000m and 10,000m left experienced observers in disbelief. At the Chinese National Games in Beijing she became the first woman to run the 10,000m under 30 minutes, a time even the great Paavo Nurmi did not achieve.

Her rise to athletic stardom followed her move in October 1991 to join the sports school in Liaoning Province run by controversial coach Ma Junren. At that coaching center a group of elite athletes focused purely on track and field. The female athletes improved their performances dramatically, although no male athlete showed improvement comparable to that achieved by the women.

At age 20, Wang improved Ingrid Kristiansen's record by almost 42 seconds. Such improvements in the record are not unprecedented. Mary Decker had reduced the inaugural record by 42 seconds in 1982, and Ingrid Kristiansen reduced her own record by 45 seconds.

Wang has shown remarkable range at distances from 1500m (3:51.9, the second-fastest to date) up to the marathon (2 hr 24:07, the ninth fastest to date). In between, she holds the world records for 3000m and 10,000m by vast margins.

After that sensational 1993 season, the outside world learned that Ma Junren's group had disbanded amid much acrimony by the athletes. Most of the athletes' grievances concerned Junren's alleged dictatorial behavior. However, Wang showed that she is a formidable talent by winning the 5000m at the Atlanta Olympics. When she was outsprinted down the straight by Fernanda Ribeiro in the 10,000m (31:1.63 to 31:2.58), there was almost a sigh of relief. It proved she was human after all.

Conclusions

The women's 10,000m is still a relatively new event for women, with the first world record recognized only in 1981. The full potential in this event is yet to be explored. It is not helped by the fact that it is being run rather infrequently.

Wang Junxia's 1993 time averages 1.7 seconds per lap faster than the previous record. Not surprisingly, no one has come even remotely close to that time, not even Wang herself. No one broke even 31 minutes in 1995 or 1996. The widespread reaction to Wang's 1993 record has been examined in more detail in her profile in the chapter on the 3000m. It is another women's record that seems destined to last well into the 21st century.

Five All-Time Fastest: Women's 10,000m

Wang Junxia (CHN)	29:31.78	1993
Zhong Huandi (CHN)	30:13.37	1993
Ingrid Kristiansen (NOR)	30:13.74	1986
Elana Meyer (S.AF)	30:52.51	1994
Liz McColgan (GBR)	30:57.07	1991
Prediction	*29:31.78*	*2015*

Top Three: Women's 10,000m

GOLD MEDAL:	Wang Junxia (CHN)
SILVER MEDAL:	Ingrid Kristiansen (NOR)
BRONZE MEDAL:	Olga Bondarenko (USSR)

I n perhaps no other track and field event did female athletes have to struggle to establish themselves as much as in the male-dominated marathon. The early pioneers of the women's marathon suffered profound opposition to their efforts, which at times seemed to border on the psychopathological. Some female athletic officials and female doctors were as antagonistic to the idea as their male counterparts. The marathon for women is taken for granted today, but in the beginning those pioneers had to endure ridicule, hostility, hate mail, slanders on their sexuality, and occasionally physical abuse.

One of the world record holders from the early 1970s wrote about her experiences 20 years later: "We walked a fine line. We were in a male dominant sport. We were accepted as long as we didn't beat them or request too much. We were definitely threatening to many. Those who had trained with us knew we had earned whatever we had achieved. There were also unwanted stigmas to keep in check. It was very important to still look feminine."

But she went on to say, "In the early years, we were looked upon as something of an oddity. We did things before anyone put up the barriers and told us we couldn't or shouldn't. It was a wonderful time to explore to the fullest the possibilities of our potential. I am a bit prejudiced but I always felt the sport changed when the money came in in the mid 70s. We were the purists. We had a passion that was driven by our love for the sport, the wonderful feelings of pushing the limits and the freedom it provided us. There were no standards, we made our own. We created new racing distances. We tried it all. It was a wonderful time."

The same reservations about marathon "records" apply to the women as well as to men: The courses vary so much that the times cannot be compared in the same way as track records. Therefore "world's best time" is a more appropriate phrase than "world record."

The other problem bedeviling the women's times is doubt about some of the early courses: Were they the full 42.195 kilometers (26 miles 385 yards)? In addition, there remains doubt about the conditions under which the early races were held: Were they "genuine" marathon races or "time trials"? Sometimes they were a bit of both because the women experienced such hostility at the beginning that they sometimes understandably had to resort to subterfuge to run the event.

The major controversy focuses on the run of Adrienne Beames, unknown to the outside world, in August 1971. Her time took 15 minutes off the record and was greeted with much skepticism overseas; this was the first women's marathon run under three hours. There was no official marathon body to monitor or approve her time, but this was true of many of the women's marathon runs in the early days. Six years later, when the marathon boom was taking off, Beames ran five seconds faster in an official marathon race in Phoenix, so there is no doubt she had the capacity to run an under-three-hour marathon. However, doubts about Beames's performance persist in the minds of some statisticians, who attribute the first under-three-hour marathon to Beth Bonner in New York in September 1971. Both performances are listed in the following table.

The marathon for women was finally introduced into the Olympics in 1984.

Women's World Records for the Marathon

Record time	Record holder	Location	Date
3 hr 40:22	Violet Piercy (GBR)	London, England	3 Oct 1926
3 hr 37:07	Merry Lepper (USA)	Culver City, USA	16 Dec 1963
3 hr 27:45	Dale Greig (GBR)	Ryde, England	23 May 1964

3 hr 19:33	Mildred Sampson (NZ)	Auckland, New Zealand	21 Jul 1964
3 hr 15:22	Maureen "Mo" Wilton (CAN)	Toronto, Canada	6 May 1967
3 hr 7:26	Anni Pede-Erdkamp (FRG)	Waldniel, West Germany	16 Sep 1967
3 hr 2:53	Caroline Walker (USA)	Seaside, USA	28 Feb 1970
3 hr 1:42	Beth Bonner (USA)	Philadelphia, USA	9 May 1971
* 2 hr 46:30	Adrienne Beames (AUST)	Werribee, Australia	31 Aug 1971
or			
* 2 hr 55:22	Beth Bonner (USA)	New York, USA	19 Sep 1971
* 2 hr 49:40	Cheryl Bridges (USA)	Culver City, USA	5 Dec 1971
* 2 hr 46:36	Michiko Gorman (USA)	Culver City, USA	2 Dec 1973
2 hr 46:24	Chantal Langlace (FRA)	Nivelles, Belgium	27 Oct 1974
2 hr 43:54.5	Jacqueline Hansen (USA)	Culver City, USA	1 Dec 1974
2 hr 42:24	Liane Winter (FRG)	Boston, USA	21 Apr 1975
2 hr 40:15.8	Christa Vahlensieck (FRG)	Dulmen, West Germany	3 May 1975
2 hr 38:19	Jacqueline Hansen (USA)	Eugene, USA	12 Oct 1975
2 hr 35:15.4	Chantal Langlace (FRA)	Oyarzun, Spain	1 May 1977
2 hr 34:47.5	Christa Vahlensieck (FRG)	Berlin, West Germany	10 Sep 1977
2 hr 32:29.8	Grete Waitz (NOR)	New York, USA	22 Oct 1978
2 hr 27:32.6	Grete Waitz (NOR)	New York, USA	21 Oct 1979
2 hr 25:41.3	Grete Waitz (NOR)	New York, USA	26 Oct 1980
2 hr 25:28.7	Grete Waitz (NOR)	London, England	17 Apr 1983
2 hr 22:43	Joan Benoit (USA)	Boston, USA	18 Apr 1983
2 hr 21:06	Ingrid Kristiansen (NOR)	London, England	21 Apr 1985

Violet Piercy   (England)

3 hr 40:22   London, England   3 Oct 1926

Violet Piercy is a somewhat obscure figure who appears to have run the marathon in London from Windsor to Chiswick in 1926. This fact is recorded in a number of texts but little else is known about her and no photograph of her appears to exist. The validity of her run must be treated with some caution.

Merry Lepper   (United States)

3 hr 37:07   Culver City, USA   16 Dec 1963

Merry Lepper ran the Western Hemisphere Marathon in Culver City, California. This is a well-established marathon, which has since produced a number of world best times.

She was described as a blonde, 20-year-old student, who hid in the bushes with another woman, Mrs. Lyn Carman, 26, so they would not be banned from the race. Once the race started, they set off after the men. Mrs. Carman, a mother of three daughters, dropped out at 18 miles with leg cramps, but Merry Lepper apparently continued to the finish in 3 hr 37:07.

Little further information is known about Ms. Lepper. Of the 67 official entrants, only 35 finished the race, which was won by Norm Higgins in 2 hr 19:33.

Dale Greig   (Great Britain, b. 1937)

3 hr 27:45   **Ryde, England**   **23 May 1964**

Dale Greig, Great Britain (marathon), May 1964.

Dale Greig was born in 1937 in Paisley, Scotland, one of twins. There was no sporting tradition in the family, except a grandfather on her mother's side who sculled. At school in the 1950s, there were few sport opportunities for girls apart from sprinting. Nonetheless, she joined a local harriers club; she and other enthusiasts eventually founded their own club, the Tannahill Harriers.

She set her marathon record at the age of 27 at Ryde, on the Isle of Wight. She was on vacation at the time and arranged to run the marathon while she was there. She set off four minutes before the men, as an unofficial entrant, and was followed all the way by an ambulance. She finished in 3 hr 27:45, which many regard as the first authenticated world record for the women's marathon. By profession, she was a secretary and was hailed by the British press as the first woman to run the marathon under 3 ½ hours. She established herself as a successful cross-country runner and won several Scottish cross-country titles (1960, 1962, 1964, 1968). In those days very few women were running long distances in training and in a way she was a pioneer of LSD—long slow distances.

She currently runs her own printing business in Glasgow. She remains a genuine female marathon pioneer in Great Britain.

Mildred Sampson   (New Zealand, b. 1933)

3 hr 19:33   **Auckland, New Zealand**   **21 Jul 1964**

Millie Sampson reduced Dale Greig's record two months later. She had been a well-established cross-country runner, four times the New Zealand champion. Her father had been Auckland 880-yard and mile champion in his time, but Millie did not take up running until she was 27. She won the 880-yard Auckland title in 1960 and turned to longer distances when they were finally permitted in New Zealand in the mid-1960s.

Running in the Owairaka Marathon in New Zealand in July 1964, she reduced the record under 3 hr 20 for the first time with 3 hr 19:33. She competed at the world cross-country championships three times, the last in 1973, at the age of 40, when she finished 24th.

Mildred Sampson, New Zealand (marathon), July 1964.

Maureen "Mo" Wilton   (Canada, b. 1953)

3 hr 15:22   Toronto, Canada   6 May 1967

Maureen Wilton, Canada (marathon). At 13, she was the youngest athlete ever to set a world record but has since disappeared.

Maureen Wilton, known as "Mo," achieved fame as being the youngest athlete, male or female, to hold a world record or world best time. In a marathon in Toronto, called the "Eastern Canadian Championship" (a title no one knew existed before the organizer came up with it), she competed at 13 years of age. This was shortly after the famous Kathleen Switzer incident at the 1967 Boston Marathon, where race official Jock Semple had physically tried to remove Switzer from the race. His attempt was thwarted by Switzer's boyfriend, who knocked him sideways. This incident, caught by press photographers from the back of a bus, attracted massive publicity.

Switzer was consequently invited to run in the Eastern Canadian Championship. However, she had still not recovered from the Boston race and merely ran the course at a slow pace. In the end, only five male athletes came home ahead of Mo. The winner, Jim Beisty, was timed at 2 hr 42:32 and went on to become a respected coach in Australia. Naturally all the press publicity now centered on Mo, who came home in 3 hr 15:22, a new world record for women. At the time she weighed only 36 kilograms (79 pounds).

Maureen Wilton had been a runner for three years prior to this race. She initially came out to watch her brother Danny run but soon started running with him and beat him. She won the Canadian AAU cross-country championship in 1966, but because she was only 12 at the time she was declared too young to win it. The championship medal went to the runner-up.

Shortly after these events, she dropped out of sight and was never seen at competitions again. It is thought that she became a teacher somewhere in Toronto. She would now be in her early 40s.

Anni Pede-Erdkamp   (West Germany, b. 1940)

3 hr 7:26   Waldniel, West Germany   16 Sep 1967

Anni Pede-Erdkamp was the first of a number of German women who pioneered the marathon from the 1960s onward. She was born in Elmpt, close to the Dutch border. Married at age 21 to sports journalist Siegfried Pede, she showed significant talent as a runner and began training under Dr. Ernst van Aaken, a great proponent of marathon running for women. She took a break from this enthusiasm in 1964 for the birth of her daughter Claudia.

After the reports of Mo Wilton's achievements in Canada, there was skepticism about the feat in Europe. So Dr. van Aaken organized a marathon to prove it was possible for women to run that fast. Women were still officially banned from marathons in Germany in those days, but he arranged a small group of men to run the marathon. Anni Pede-Erdkamp just "ran along" as well. She came in third in a race that was won in 2 hr 40:24. Her time was 3 hr 7:26, which was a new world best.

After a long interval away from running she recommenced training in 1974 and ran in the first women-only marathon in Waldniel that year. She was not in top condition but ran anyway, completing the distance in 3 hr 24:0. The race was won by Liane Winter in 2 hr 50:31.

Anni Pede-Erdkamp still lives in Waldniel, is a keen gardener, and jogs twice a week

Caroline Walker   (United States, b. 1954)

3 hr 2:53   **Seaside, USA**   **28 Feb 1970**

At 16, Caroline Walker was another of the teenage runners who set world best times for the marathon in the early days. Little is known about her. She was said to be 5' 0" (153 centimeters) tall and to weigh 89 pounds (40 kilograms). Running in Seaside, Oregon, she achieved 3 hr 2:53, to bring the three-hour barrier in sight.

Beth Bonner   (United States, b. 1952)

3 hr 1:42   **Philadelphia, USA**   **9 May 1971**
2 hr 55:22   **New York, USA**   **19 Sep 1971**

Eighteen-year-old Beth Bonner brought the world record even closer to three hours with her run at Philadelphia. Her time of 3 hr 1:42 took 1:11 off Caroline Walker's record. This marathon was run at Fairmount Park; it was the AAU's eastern regional marathon, but the AAU had not yet officially declared women eligible to run.

There are those who have reservations about the performance of Australian Adrienne Beames, who broke the three-hour barrier in August 1971. They attribute that honor to Bonner when she ran 2 hr 55:22 at the New York City Marathon in Central Park on 19 September 1971. In that mixed race, Bonner came home ahead of another woman, Nina Kuscsik, who also broke three hours with 2 hr 56:04. They finished 34th and 35th out of 163 finishers.

Adrienne Beames   (Australia, b. 1942)

2 hr 46:30   **Werribee, Australia**   **31 Aug 1971**

Adrienne Beames appears to be the first woman to run the marathon under three hours. Her time of 2 hr 46:30 was 15 minutes faster than the existing record. The British athletic press were skeptical of this performance because she had not demonstrated promise in previous races. *Athletic Weekly* called her the "mysterious" Adrienne Beames, while another writer dismissed her performance as a "time trial." She is not all that mysterious. She is the daughter of a famous sports journalist in Melbourne and won the Victorian Squash Championship in 1966, 1967, and 1968. In addition, as a singer, she came in second in the prestigious Sun Aria competition.

Her career as a long-distance runner took place in an era where there was deep hostility to women running the marathon, not only in Australia, but in the United States and Europe as well. All attempts by her and her coach to enter an official marathon were denied by Australian athletic officials, both male and female. So she and her coach organized their own marathon, an invitational marathon at which a number of her male marathon colleagues were asked to compete. She was the sole female competitor. Over a certified course, she ran 2 hr 46:30.

Part of the resistance to her performance was the fact that she allegedly ran a whole range of world records at this stage of her career, but never in competitions. She never competed at the Olympic Games or at major international athletic competitions. She may well have run in the 1500m at the Munich Olympics but was suspended by her own local athletic officials when she raced in the city of Sydney without their permission. Deeply resentful of this treatment, she instead made a career in the road-running circuit in the United States. She eventually ran another marathon in 1977 in Phoenix, Arizona: an official race, so that no one could question the result. Her time on that occasion, six years later, was 2 hr 46:25, five seconds faster than her 1971 effort, which indicates that her 1971 run was feasible.

In the 1960s and 1970s, many women in many parts of the world endured antagonism when they tried to run marathons and had to engage in subterfuge to achieve their ends. Accordingly, there will always be some reservations about these early performances. This one appears to be genuine.

Adrienne Beames currently works as a therapist at a sports injury clinic in Melbourne.

Adrienne Beames, Australia (marathon).

Cheryl "Cherrie" Bridges   (United States, b. 1947)

2 hr 49:40   Culver City, USA   5 Dec 1971

Cheryl Bridges took up running in 1963 as a means of losing some weight and improving her figure. The school board allowed her to train, provided that she run on the opposite side of the school grounds from the boys, presumably to prevent disharmony. She found out that she was "reasonably successful" at cross-country running and got serious about it. She was indeed successful, but for years was an isolated figure in the sporting world of the 1960s. She made a number of important breakthroughs for women, becoming the first woman to receive an athletic scholarship at Indiana State University and the first woman to receive such a scholarship to a public four-year university. For years she ran on teams where she was the only woman but, in the process, broke down a lot of barriers and inspired a lot of other women to emulate her. She wrote to coach Bill Dellinger, and for 12 months he coached her long distance by mail.

In 1970 she used the Culver City marathon as a training run and, after 20 miles, walked and jogged to the finish. Irritated that she had not run all the way, she was determined that next time

Cheryl Bridges, United States (marathon).

she would complete the marathon without walking, and so she returned to Culver City in December 1971. Apart from some harassment at the 23-mile mark by a disgruntled male runner, the run went well—very well. Her time in her first completed marathon (2 hr 49:40) was a 5-1/2-minute improvement on Beth Bonner's time two months earlier.

In 1976 her career moved on to college teaching and administration and the marketing and design of athletic products and clothes. In 1986 she began to be plagued by abnormal heart rhythm, requiring much medication with significant side effects. This was finally corrected when she underwent cardiac surgery in 1994, which enabled her to run for the first time in seven years. Bridges is one of the great pioneers of U.S. distance running.

Michiko Gorman   (United States, b. 1935)

2 hr 46:36   Culver City, USA   2 Dec 1973

Michiko Gorman, United States (marathon).

Miki Gorman was born of Japanese parents in China and subsequently moved to the United States. She was a 38-year-old housewife when she improved the world best marathon time. She was of much the same stature as Mo Wilton, weighing a mere 39 kilograms (86 pounds) and 154 centimeters (5' 0 1/2") tall.

She did not begin her athletic career until 1969, when she was 33, starting out as a gentle jogger. But she got hooked and ran her first marathon in 1972. Within a year she had run a world record at the Culver City marathon: Her time of 2 hr 46:36 took three minutes off Cheryl Bridges's time at the same race two years earlier.

Gorman went on to win the Boston Marathon twice (1974 and 1977) and the New York City Marathon twice (1976 and 1977). Her 1977 victories occurred when she was 41. Her last race was at the Tokyo International Marathon in 1982, at age 47. She sadly gave up running after injuries to her left knee and the increasing demands of raising a young daughter. She currently works as a secretary in a law firm in Beverly Hills, California. Commenting about the marathon world almost a decade later, she reflected that she "missed [running] so very much."

Chantal Langlace   (France, b. 1955)

2 hr 46:24   Nivelles, Belgium   27 Oct 1974
2 hr 35:15.4   Oyarzun, Spain   1 May 1977

Chantal Langlace was yet another teenage pioneer of the women's marathon. At age 17, she ran her first marathon in 3 hr 10. Another lightweight, she weighed only 47 kilograms (104 pounds).

The first women-only international marathon race took place in Waldniel, West Germany in 1974 and was won by Liane Winter (West Germany) in 2 hr 50:31. Langlace was second in 2 hr 51:45. Five weeks later Langlace set her first world record at the distance at the Etienne Gally memorial race in Belgium, running 2 hr 46:24. Her second world record three years later took place in Spain, where her time was 2 hr 35:15. Unfortunately, a rupture of her Achilles tendon in 1978 prevented her from improving on this time. However, she still set a world record over 100 kilometers on two occasions (1980 and 1984) and was an active cyclist. Now a physical education teacher, she ran the Paris Marathon in 1995 in 2 hr 42:06, 23 years after her first marathon.

Early women's marathon pioneers, Germany 1974: (from left) Liane Winter (West Germany), Chantal Langlace (France), Christa Vahlensieck (West Germany), Manuela Preuss-Augenvoorth (Germany), Jackie Hansen (USA), Dr. Joan Ullyot (USA).

Jacqueline Hansen   (United States, b. 1948)

| 2 hr 43:54.5 | Culver City, USA | 1 Dec 1974 |
| 2 hr 38:19 | Eugene, USA | 12 Oct 1975 |

Jackie Hansen was one of the great pioneers of marathon running in the United States in its formative years and was the first woman to run the marathon under 2 hr 40. In contrast to some of the teenage pioneers described earlier, she began long-distance running at age 23. She had meteoric success in that she won the first marathon she entered (the Culver City marathon) in 1972, won the Boston Marathon in 1973, and set her first world record in 1974. In her marathon career, between 1972 and 1982, she won 12 out of 18 marathons entered, plus numerous road, track, and cross-country events. She dropped out of athletics in 1979 to have a son.

Hansen achieved her first world best time in Culver City, California, in 1974, with 2 hr 43:55. One year later she ran 2 hr 38:19 in Eugene, Oregon, the running capital of the United States, to break the 2 hr 40 barrier.

She was a graduate of California State University (Northridge) with a degree in English. Apart from running, she wrote countless articles promoting the sport and was tireless as a race administrator and coordinator of events all over the United States. Among various awards, she was honored by the American Civil Liberties Union.

The marathon finally made its debut at the Olympics at the 1984 Los Angeles Games. Jackie Hansen ran in the U.S. Olympic trials at the age of 35, but by then a new generation of U.S. marathoners had come along, and she finished well down. She was proud to at least run the trial and be part of an historic breakthrough.

She subsequently worked in the insurance field and remains active as a running enthusiast and consultant in California. The current generation of female marathon runners owe her a great deal.

Liane Winter   (West Germany, b. 1942)

2 hr 42:24   **Boston, USA**   **21 Apr 1975**

In contrast to some of the teenage marathon stars, Liane Winter was 32 when she won the Boston Marathon in 1975, setting a world record in the process (2 hr 42:24). This was the fourth running of the Boston Marathon in which women were officially accepted.

In 1974 she had won the first international marathon for women, organized by Dr. Ernst van Aaken, a great promoter of marathon running for women, in his hometown of Waldniel, West Germany. The race consisted of entrants from seven countries. Winter was the only one who could cope with a stiff wind, and she ran a European record of 2 hr 50:31.

She had been a member of her country's cross-country team in her younger days and had come out of retirement to tackle the marathon. She began to train with the long slow distance principles of Dr. van Aaken and went on to a new career.

She competed several times in the West German marathon championship in her mid-30s and won in 1979, at the age of 37.

Christa Vahlensieck   (West Germany, b. 1949)

2 hr 40:15.8   **Dulmen, West Germany**   **3 May 1975**
2 hr 34:47.5   **Berlin, West Germany**   **10 Sep 1977**

Christa Vahlensieck was another of the West German athletes who pioneered the marathon. In the famous 1974 international women's race in Waldniel, she had placed third in 2 hr 54:40. The second international women's race at Waldniel took place in 1976, and she recalls this as her favorite run. She won in 2 hr 45:25.

Her first world best time took place eight months after that 1974 Waldniel run when she recorded 2 hr 40:15 in Dulmen, West Germany. Her second record took place at the West German Championships in 1977 (2 hr 34:47). She was West German marathon champion five times, from 1975-1978 and in 1980. She finished third in this event in 1985, at the age of 36.

In 1989, having turned 40, she was still able to run a marathon in 2 hr 34. But because of various orthopedic injuries, she now only runs for fun.

Grete Waitz   (Norway, b. 1953)

2 hr 32:29.8   **New York, USA**   **22 Oct 1978**
2 hr 27:32.6   **New York, USA**   **21 Oct 1979**
2 hr 25:41.3   **New York, USA**   **26 Oct 1980**
2 hr 25:28.7   **London, England**   **17 Apr 1983**

Grete Waitz was already an established track champion at distances such as 3000m, where she held the world record twice (1975 and 1976), before she turned to the marathon in 1978.

When offered a position in the 1978 New York City Marathon by promoter Fred Lebow, she accepted, largely because she had never been to the United States. She had also never run a marathon. But she insisted she would come only if there was airfare for her husband, Jack, as well. This was forthcoming, so a marathon career was launched. Knowing little about how to run a marathon, she finished in some exhaustion; knowing nothing about times, she was astonished to find she had set a world record. After this remarkable debut, she was invited back to New York the next year and duly rewarded promoter Lebow with another world record. Her time of 2 hr 27:32 made her the first woman under 2 ½ hours. She came back again in 1980 and repeated the trick—three world records on three occasions. Altogether, she won the New York City Marathon nine times, an achievement that is unlikely ever to be excelled.

She won 13 marathon titles, including London (1983) and the 1983 World Championships. But the one "big one" she missed out on was the 1984 Los Angeles Olympic gold medal. Although the favorite, she chose not to respond when Joan Benoit (USA) made an early break from the pack after three miles. The American built up a commanding lead, and the Norwegian realized too late that she couldn't bridge the gap. In fairness, she was troubled by severe back pain in the 24 hours before the race, so she made a decision to run conservatively.

Grete Waitz, Norway (3000m, marathon), the Queen of the New York City Marathon, who won this event nine times.

Of all her New York City Marathons, perhaps her most significant was in 1992. She chose to run alongside promoter Fred Lebow, who was afflicted by a brain tumor, which was then in remission. Determined to run one last marathon, Lebow ran, jogged, walked, stopped, and ran again with Grete Waitz coaxing him, finally finishing in 5 hr 32. She had returned the favor to the man who had launched her marathon career. Lebow died two years later.

Joan Benoit   (United States, b. 1957)

2 hr 22:43   Boston, USA   18 Apr 1983

Joan Benoit is of French ancestry; her forebears settled in North America three centuries ago. Her first sport was skiing, but after a leg injury she turned to running. Her marathon debut in 1979 was an impressive 2 hr 59:54. Only three months later she made a major improvement of 24 minutes to win the Boston Marathon in 2 hr 35:15, an American record.

She won at Boston again in 1981 and once more in 1983, when she set a sensational new world record of 2 hr 22:43, which improved Grete Waitz's time by over 2 ½ minutes.

Perhaps wisely, she chose not to run in the marathon at the 1983 World Championships, which was won by Grete Waitz. This decision was part of her long-term strategy for the 1984 Olympics. So Waitz and Benoit had never raced against each other prior to the Los Angeles Olympics.

Her Olympic plans almost went out the window when she developed crippling knee pains three weeks before the all-important U.S. Olympic trials. She made a difficult decision to undergo arthroscopic knee surgery 17 days before this critical race. To her enormous relief, the operation was a complete success, and she made a dramatic recovery. Seventeen days after surgery, she lined up to begin the marathon trial that alone would decide selection for the Los Angeles Olympics. She enjoyed a comfortable victory in 2 hr 31:4.

At the Los Angeles Games she made a tactical break away from the rest of the field only three miles (five kilometers) into the race. The others stayed back, expecting her to slowly come back to the field in the second half of the race. This didn't happen, and she built up a huge lead. By the time Waitz set out in pursuit, it was too late. The American won the race in 2 hr 24:52, waving her cap to the crowd—it was a memorable triumph. Waitz finished second, 1:26 behind.

Benoit had one more major triumph: the 1985 Chicago Marathon, where she defeated the new world record holder Ingrid Kristiansen in a personal best of 2 hr 21:21. From then on injuries plagued her career, and she never reached such heights again. Her win at the inaugural Olympic marathon for women remains one of the enduring images of the Los Angeles Games.

Joan Benoit, United States, winning the inaugural Olympic marathon for women in Los Angeles, 1984.

Ingrid Kristiansen   (Norway, b. 1956)

2 hr 21:06   London, England   21 Apr 1985

Ingrid Kristiansen and Grete Waitz were the remarkable Norwegian duo that made such an impact in the breakthrough years of the women's marathon. Some of Kristiansen's career details are described in the chapter on the 10,000m.

In Kristiansen's early years of marathon running, the established star was Grete Waitz.

Ingrid Kristiansen, Norway (5000m, 10,000m, marathon), the only athlete, male or female, to hold world records in all three events.

As the 1980s progressed, Kristiansen became a marathon star in her own right. She won most of the big city marathons, including London (four times), Boston (twice), Houston, Chicago, and New York City. The one big marathon that she didn't win was at the 1984 Los Angeles Olympics. She was one of the many athletes who allowed Joan Benoit to make an early break, thinking she would pay for this effort later on. Benoit didn't, and Kristiansen had to be content with fourth place.

Kristiansen's world record came in her second London victory. With a fairly flat course, she made a determined attack on the world record and took 1 ½ minutes off Benoit's time. Another remarkable victory was her win at Houston in 1984, five months after giving birth to a son Gaute in August 1993. Altogether she won 14 out of 25 marathons.

Apart from her track and marathon career, she has been world cross-country champion (1988) and world road champion over 15 kilometers (1987 and 1988). One of her few regrets is that she let Benoit slip away at the 1984 Olympic marathon. Her world record for the marathon has already lasted over a decade.

Conclusions

The best time for the women's marathon has been static since the mid-1980s. It is accepted that a marathon is a much more formidable event than the standard long-distance track races. However, it is interesting that over the last decade, there have been improvements to the 3000m, 5000m, and 10,000m records for both men and women, but the world's best time for the marathon for both sexes has remained unchanged.

It seems only a matter of time before the record is reduced once more. The present generation is running times not far off from Kristiansen's 1985 time. However, a fast marathon time depends on optimal circumstances on the day: a flat course, kind weather, a good pace, and good competition. Such circumstances occur only infrequently in the world of elite marathon running.

Five All-Time Fastest: Women's Marathon		
Ingrid Kristiansen (NOR)	2 hr 21:06	1985
Joan Benoit (USA)	2 hr 21:21	1985
Uta Pippig (GER)	2 hr 21:45	1994
Rosa Mota (POR)	2 hr 23:29	1985
Valentina Yegorova (USSR)	2 hr 23:33	1994
Prediction	*2 hr 20:05*	*2015*

Top Three: Women's Marathon

GOLD MEDAL: Grete Waitz (NOR)

SILVER MEDAL: Ingrid Kristiansen (NOR)

BRONZE MEDAL: Joan Benoit (USA)

T his event began as the 80m hurdles and was changed to 100m hurdles in 1969. The 80m-hurdles course involves 8 hurdles 2' 6" (0.762 meters) high, while the 100m-hurdles course includes 10 hurdles 2' 9" (0.84 meters) high.

The 80m hurdles were included in the Olympic Games in 1932. Altogether, 19 athletes equaled or broke the 80m hurdles record 29 times.

The 100m hurdles were introduced to the Olympics in 1972. Since 1969, eight athletes have been world record holders over this distance a total of 21 times. Two of these were also among the world record holders over 80m hurdles—Pam Ryan (formerly Kilborn) and Karin Balzer. Because hand-timed records were accepted through to 1976, many athletes equaled the record over the years. All but two were Eastern Europeans. Somewhat surprisingly, no U.S. athlete has held a world record at 80m or 100m hurdles.

Women's World Records for 80m and 100m Hurdles

Record time	Record holder	Location	Date
80m hurdles			
11.6	Ruth Engelhard (GER)	London, England	11 Aug 1934
11.6	Trebisonda "Ondina" Valla (ITA)	Berlin, Germany	5 Aug 1936
11.6	Barbara Burke (S.AF)	Berlin, Germany	1 Aug 1937
11.6	Lisa Gelius (GER)	Breslau, Germany	30 Jul 1938
11.3	Claudia Testoni (ITA)	Garmisch-Partenkirchen, Germany	23 Jul 1939
11.3	Claudia Testoni (ITA)	Dresden, Germany	13 Aug 1939
11.3	Fanny Blankers-Koen (HOL)	Amsterdam, Netherlands	20 Sep 1942
11.0	Fanny Blankers-Koen (HOL)	Amsterdam, Netherlands	20 Jun 1948
11.0	Shirley Strickland (AUST)	Helsinki, Finland	23 Jul 1952
10.9	Shirley Strickland (AUST)	Helsinki, Finland	24 Jul 1952
10.9	Maria Golubnichaya (USSR)	Kiev, USSR	8 Aug 1954
10.8	Galina Yermolenko (USSR)	Leningrad, USSR	5 Jul 1955
10.6	Kreszentia "Zenta" Gastl (FRG)	Frechen, West Germany	29 Jul 1956
10.6	Galina Bystrova (USSR)	Krasnodar, USSR	8 Sep 1958
10.6	Norma Thrower (AUST)	Brisbane, Australia	26 Mar 1960
10.6	Rimma Kosheleva (USSR)	Tula, USSR	26 Jun 1960
10.6	Gisela Birkemeyer (GDR)	Berlin, East Germany	16 Jul 1960
10.6	Irina Press (USSR)	Moscow, USSR	16 Jul 1960
10.5	Gisela Birkemeyer (GDR)	Leipzig, East Germany	24 Jul 1960
10.5	Betty Moore (GBR)	Kassel, West Germany	25 Aug 1962
10.5	Karin Balzer (GDR)	Leipzig, East Germany	23 May 1964
10.5	Irina Press (USSR)	Kiev, USSR	9 Aug 1964
10.5	Irina Press (USSR)	Kiev, USSR	28 Aug 1964
10.5	Draga Stamejcic (YUG)	Celje, Yugoslavia	5 Sep 1964
10.5	Pam Kilborn (AUST)	Osaka, Japan	25 Oct 1964
10.4	Pam Kilborn (AUST)	Melbourne, Australia	6 Feb 1965
10.4	Irina Press (USSR)	Kassel, West Germany	19 Sep 1965
10.3	Irina Press (USSR)	Tbilisi, USSR	24 Oct 1965
10.3	Vera Korsakova (USSR)	Riga, USSR	16 Jun 1968
10.2	Vera Korsakova (USSR)	Riga, USSR	16 Jun 1968

100m hurdles

13.3	Karin Balzer (GDR)	Warsaw, Poland	20 Jun 1969
13.3	Teresa Sukniewicz (POL)	Warsaw, Poland	20 Jun 1969
13.0	Karin Balzer (GDR)	Leipzig, East Germany	27 Jul 1969
12.9	Karin Balzer (GDR)	Berlin, East Germany	5 Sep 1969
12.8	Teresa Sukniewicz (POL)	Warsaw, Poland	20 Jun 1970
12.8	Chi Cheng (TAI)	Munich, West Germany	12 Jul 1970
12.7	Karin Balzer (GDR)	Berlin, East Germany	26 Jul 1970
12.7	Teresa Sukniewicz (POL)	Warsaw, Poland	20 Sep 1970
12.7	Karin Balzer (GDR)	Berlin, East Germany	25 Jul 1971
12.6	Karin Balzer (GDR)	Berlin, East Germany	31 Jul 1971
12.5	Annelie Ehrhardt (GDR)	Potsdam, East Germany	15 Jun 1972
12.5	Pam Ryan (née Kilborn) (AUST)	Warsaw, Poland	28 Jun 1972
12.3	Annelie Ehrhardt (GDR)	Dresden, East Germany	22 Jul 1973

Electronic timing (100m hurdles)

12.59	Annelie Ehrhardt (GDR)	Munich, West Germany	8 Sep 1972
12.48	Grazyna Rabsztyn (POL)	Fürth, West Germany	10 Jun 1978
12.36	Grazyna Rabsztyn (POL)	Warsaw, Poland	13 Jun 1980
12.35	Yordanka Donkova (BUL)	Cologne, West Germany	17 Aug 1986
12.29	Yordanka Donkova (BUL)	Cologne, West Germany	17 Aug 1986
12.26	Yordanka Donkova (BUL)	Ljubljana, Yugoslavia	7 Sep 1986
12.25	Ginka Zagorcheva (BUL)	Drama, Greece	8 Aug 1987
12.21	Yordanka Donkova (BUL)	Stara Zagora, Yugoslavia	20 Aug 1988

80m Hurdles

Ruth Engelhard   (Germany, b. 1909)

11.6   **London, England**   **11 Aug 1934**

The unofficial world record for this event stood at 11.7, set by "Babe" Didriksen at the 1932 Los Angeles Olympics. The first world record for this event officially recognized by the IAAF was the 11.6 run by Ruth Engelhard of Germany at the Women's World Games in London in 1934.

Born Ruth Becker, she was German champion at the 80m hurdles in 1929, 1933, and 1934. In 1932 she had been part of the German 4 × 200m relay team that set a world record in this event.

Trebisonda "Ondina" Valla   (Italy, b. 1916)

11.6   **Berlin, Germany**   **5 Aug 1936**

Ondina Valla was born in Bologna. She commenced track and field at age 11, and at age 14 was the Italian number one in the 80m hurdles, the high jump, and the standing high jump. She won 20 individual Italian titles, set 21 national records, and was a great pioneer of women's track and field in Italy.

Ondina Valla, *left*, Italy (80m hurdles) wins the 1936 Olympic 80m hurdles.

At the 1936 Olympics she equaled the 80m hurdles world record in the semifinal with 11.6. The final was a blanket finish, and the judges had to scrutinize the photo-finish print for half an hour before declaring her the winner, in 11.7. In fact the first four athletes were all given the time of 11.7.

Barbara Burke   (South Africa, b. 1917)

11.6   **Berlin, Germany**   **1 Aug 1937**

Barbara Burke was born in Britain but became a resident of South Africa. In that country, she established herself as a sprint and hurdles champion between 1934 and 1938. She set the first official 100-yard world record and competed at the 1936 Berlin Olympics in the 100m and 4 × 100m relay. In the 100m she was fourth in a semifinal. The South African team came in second in the 4 × 100m relay, and she earned a silver medal.

She equaled the world record of 11.6 in an international meet in Berlin in 1937, and in 1938 she won the Commonwealth Games 80m hurdles title in Sydney.

Lisa Gelius   (Germany, b. 1917)

11.6   **Breslau, Germany**   **30 Jul 1938**

Lisa Gelius was a great pioneer of women's track and field in Germany and equaled the world record with 11.6 at the 1938 German championships. The official report on the day speaks of a "following wind." At the European Championships later that season she was second in the 80m hurdles in 11.7, behind Claudia Testoni, who won in 11.6.

Gelius had a long history of success in the German championships, where she won titles from 1929 through to 1940. Her various wins were 100m (1929 and 1930), 200m (1929), 80m hurdles (1938), javelin (1937-1940), and pentathlon (1940).

In the 1938 European Championships, in addition to her silver medal in the 80m hurdles, she demonstrated her versatility by winning the javelin with a throw of 45.58 meters.

Lisa Gelius, Germany (80m hurdles).

Claudia Testoni   (Italy, b. 1915)

| 11.3 | Garmisch-Partenkirchen, Germany | 23 Jul 1939 |
| 11.3 | Dresden, Germany | 13 Aug 1939 |

Claudia Testoni was a great rival to the other top Italian hurdler of the 1930s, Ondina Valla. Together they were known as the "Golden Twins." Testoni was also born in Bologna and represented her country in the Italy vs. Poland meet in 1931, at age 16. By the time she retired in 1940, she had won 19 individual Italian titles. She competed in the 80m hurdles final at the 1936 Olympics and came in fourth in the blanket finish won by Valla. The first four runners were all given the same time, 11.7.

At the inaugural 80m hurdles for women at the 1938 European Championships, she won in 11.6. However, in 1939 she ran an astonishing 11.3 seconds on two occasions, taking a massive 0.3 second off the record. It was almost a decade before this time was bettered.

She subsequently married and had a daughter in 1941 and a son in 1942, both of whom were active in athletics.

Claudia Testoni, Italy (80m hurdles).

Fanny Blankers-Koen   (Netherlands, b. 1918)

| 11.3 | Amsterdam, Netherlands | 20 Sep 1942 |
| 11.0 | Amsterdam, Netherlands | 20 Jun 1948 |

The multitalented Fanny Blankers-Koen set world records at 100m, 80m hurdles, high jump, long jump, and pentathlon. Many of them were set in the war years when the Netherlands was under German occupation. Details of these achievements are described in the appropriate chapters.

She had a series of triumphs in the hurdles: She was Dutch champion 11 times and set two world records, six years apart. She won the 1946 European title in 11.8, the 1948 London Olympic title in 11.2, and the 1950 European title in 11.1. The 1948 Olympic victory was part of her famous four gold medal haul, which also included the 100m, 200m, and 4 × 100m relay. At these Games, she was 30 and the mother of two children.

She competed at the 1952 Helsinki Olympics and made the hurdles final, but a new generation had arrived. In the final she struck the first two hurdles very hard and, after the second mishap, came to a halt. She remains a national sporting icon in the Netherlands.

Shirley Strickland   (Australia, b. 1925)

| 11.0 | Helsinki, Finland | 23 Jul 1952 |
| 10.9 | Helsinki, Finland | 24 Jul 1952 |

Shirley Strickland was a world record holder in both the 100m flat race and the 80m hurdles. Her father was a professional sprinter who won Australia's most famed professional sprint race, the Stawell Gift, in 1900. Young Shirley showed both athletic and academic talent and went on to study physics and mathematics at the University of Western Australia.

She competed at three Olympic Games, and her record is as follows:

London 1948: 80m hurdles (third), 100m (third), 4 × 100m relay (second), 200m (fourth, but a photo of the finish discovered years later indicated she was third)

Helsinki 1952: 80m hurdles (first), 100m (third), 4 × 100m relay (fifth)

Melbourne 1956: 80m hurdles (first), 4 × 100m relay (first)

At the Helsinki Games she first equaled the world record in the heat (11.0), and then became the first woman to break the 11-second barrier in the final (10.9). At the 1956 Olympics she became the first hurdler to successfully defend her gold medal. This 1956 victory was especially sweet, as Australian selectors had not picked her for the 1954 Commonwealth Games team on the grounds of lack of form. Her son Phillip had been born six months earlier.

She went on to a career in teaching and has been active in community and environmental affairs. She stood for election, unsuccessfully, to the Australian Parliament in 1981 as a candidate for the Australian Democrats.

Maria Golubnichaya   (Soviet Union, b. 1924)

| 10.9 | Kiev, USSR | 8 Aug 1954 |

Maria Golubnichaya came in second in the 80m hurdles at the 1952 Helsinki Olympics (11.1) and was fifth in the same event four years later in Melbourne (11.3), where the title was claimed by defending champion Shirley Strickland.

She set her world record of 10.9 in Kiev at a trial before the 1954 European Championships. She duly won the European title in Bern, Switzerland, in 11.0. She was Soviet champion in the event in 1952, 1953, and 1954.

Galina Yermolenko   (Soviet Union, b. 1932)

| 10.8 | Leningrad, USSR | 5 Jul 1955 |

Galina Yermolenko reduced the world record by 0.1 second in "windless" conditions in Leningrad in 1955. However, the Soviet athlete never had any other special success. She never won a Soviet title in the event; her best effort was a second in 1955.

Kreszentia "Zenta" Gastl   (West Germany, b. 1933)

10.6   **Frechen, West Germany**   **29 Jul 1956**

Zenta Gastl reduced the 80m hurdle record by 0.2 second shortly before the 1956 Olympics in an international meet in Frechen, Germany. However, at Melbourne she had a disappointing Olympic competition. She came in fourth in a semifinal of the 80m hurdles and did not progress. She had a bad start, and trying to make up for it, she hit the fourth hurdle very heavily.

She was fourth in the semifinals at the 1954 European Championships. Four years later she just finished second to Galina Bystrova (USSR), both sharing the same time (10.9).

She won the West German championships title in 1955 and 1956. As Zenta Kopp, she was second in 1957 and then won the title three years in a row (1958-60).

She returned to the Olympics at Rome in 1960 but, just as in Melbourne four years earlier, came in fourth in her semifinal.

Galina Bystrova   (Soviet Union, b. 1934)

10.6   **Krasnodar, USSR**   **8 Sep 1958**

Galina Bystrova was one of three women who held world records in both the 80m hurdles and the pentathlon. The other two are Fanny Blankers-Koen (Holland) and Irina Press (USSR). She was born Galina Dolzhenkova in the Soviet republic of Azerbaijan, north of Iran. As Galina Bystrova, she had a prolonged career, attending three Olympics.

At the Melbourne Olympics she came in fourth in the hurdles in 11.0, while Strickland won in 10.7. In 1958 she equaled the 80m hurdles world record of 10.6, at the city of Krasnodar in the southwestern Soviet Union. That year was very successful for her, as she won both the 80m hurdles (10.9) and the pentathlon at the European Championships. She traveled to Rome for the Olympics in 1960 and was fifth in the hurdles (11.2).

At the European Championships in 1962, she again won the pentathlon. She had one more Olympic Games, in Tokyo in 1964, where she was sixth in a semifinal of the 80m hurdles. However, the pentathlon was at last included in the Olympic program, and she won the bronze medal, her first Olympic medal at the very end of her career.

Norma Thrower   (Australia, b. 1936)

10.6   **Brisbane, Australia**   **26 Mar 1960**

Norma Thrower developed as a hurdler in the shadow of established champion Shirley Strickland. Early in 1956 she defeated Strickland for the first time and then

Shirley Strickland, Australia (100m, 80m hurdles) on the victory stand after the 80m hurdles at the 1956 Olympics. Second is Gisela Birkemeyer (East Germany), and third is Norma Thrower (Australia), all 80m hurdles record holders.

won the 80m hurdles at the Australian championships. A further success was her time of 10.6 in March 1960, which equaled the world record. Her prospects for the Melbourne Olympics looked good.

However, at the Games, held in December, Strickland peaked and won comfortably in 10.7. Thrower came in third (11.0) behind Gisela Birkemeyer of East Germany (10.9).

Norma Thrower went on to win the 1958 Commonwealth Games title over 80m hurdles in Cardiff with 10.72 seconds. At the Rome Olympics she ran sixth in a semifinal.

She has since had a long career in coaching and sport administration, coaching mainly junior athletes, and taught sport at an international school in Indonesia from 1974 to 1978. She spent 1994 recovering from a triple heart bypass.

Rimma Kosheleva   (Soviet Union, b. 1936)

| 10.6 | Tula, USSR | 26 Jun 1960 |

Rimma Kosheleva equaled the world record in an international match between the Soviet Union and Poland in the city of Tula, alongside the Upa River in western Russia.

This was three months before the Rome Olympics. At the Games she made the final but finished sixth in 11.2, well behind the winner Irina Press, also of the Soviet Union, with 10.8.

She was fifth at the 1962 European Championships in Belgrade and made the semifinals of the 1966 European Championships. She won only one Soviet championship, in 1962, but was 11 times a finalist between 1958 and 1969.

Gisela Birkemeyer   (East Germany, b. 1931)

| 10.6 | Berlin, East Germany | 16 Jul 1960 |
| 10.5 | Leipzig, East Germany | 24 Jul 1960 |

Gisela Birkemeyer (née Kohler) of East Germany competed at two Olympics. At Melbourne in 1956 she came in second behind Shirley Strickland. Four years later, she came third in Rome behind Irina Press (first) and Britain's Carole Quinton.

Her first world record came in a trial for the 1960 Olympics in East Berlin. She equaled the world record of 10.6. She brought the record down to 10.5 eight days later at the East German championships in Leipzig. This was seven weeks before the Olympics began, but as previously mentioned, she had to be satisfied with the bronze medal.

Birkemeyer also had a substantial record as a sprinter and was part of three 4 × 100m relay world records in 1956.

Irina Press   (Soviet Union, b. 1939)

10.6	Moscow, USSR	16 Jul 1960
10.5	Kiev, USSR	9 Aug 1964
10.5	Kiev, USSR	28 Aug 1964
10.4	Kassel, West Germany	19 Sep 1965
10.3	Tbilisi, USSR	24 Oct 1965

Irina Press was the younger of the two Press sisters, who were the most successful sisters in track and field history. Her older sister Tamara dominated the discus and the shot put in the early 1960s, while Irina dominated the hurdles and the pentathlon. She set five world records in the hurdles and six in the pentathlon. In the 80m hurdles she brought the record down to 10.3 over a five-year period.

Irina was the gold medalist at the Rome Olympics in the 80m hurdles (10.8). Four years later she came in fourth in the same event in a photo finish, where the first three athletes were registered as 10.5 and Press as 10.6. In these same Olympics she won the pentathlon and finished sixth in the shot put.

Her muscular build generated the usual rumors. At the Soviet championships she won the 80m hurdles five times (1960-1961 and 1964-1966).

Betty Moore   (Australia/Great Britain, b. 1934)

| 10.5 | Kassel, West Germany | 25 Aug 1962 |

Betty Moore was born in Australia but represented England in track and field. She is a graduate of the University of Sydney with a master's degree in organic chemistry. She came in third in the Australian championships at the 80m hurdles in 1958. However, shortly afterward she moved to England, where her husband was studying for a PhD. She found the standard of hurdles coaching more advanced in England and made rapid progress. She was selected to represent Great Britain at the Rome Olympics but was found to be ineligible as she had not yet completed two years of residency in Great Britain by the time the Rome Olympics came around.

Despite this setback, she went on to represent Great Britain in various international meets. She was picked for the 1962 European Championships in September but ran foul of an obscure rule operative at that time that prohibited athletes who were born outside Europe from competing.

In Kassel, West Germany, shortly before these games, she ran 10.5, to equal the world record. She was picked for England for the 1962 Commonwealth Games but was injured prior to the Games and not able to compete at her best. She finished sixth in the 100m, came in second in the 80m hurdles (11.4), and was on the 4 × 100m relay team that finished second.

She returned to Australia in 1963 to live permanently. After raising three daughters, she now works as an analytical chemist and remains active in athletic administration and coaching.

Karin Balzer   (East Germany, b. 1938)

80m hurdles

| 10.5 | Leipzig, East Germany | 23 May 1964 |

100m hurdles

13.3	Warsaw, Poland	20 Jun 1969
13.0	Leipzig, East Germany	27 Jul 1969
12.9	Berlin, East Germany	5 Sep 1969
12.7	Berlin, East Germany	26 Jul 1970
12.7	Berlin, East Germany	25 Jul 1971
12.6	Berlin, East Germany	31 Jul 1971

Karin Balzer of East Germany was Olympic champion over 80m hurdles in 1964 and three times European champion (1966, 1969, and 1971). In addition to these gold medals, she set seven world records in her time: one over 80m hurdles and six over the newly introduced 100m hurdles, the time of which she improved by 0.7 second. The 100m hurdles replaced the 80m hurdles in 1969. Balzer systematically reduced the world record from 13.3 to 12.6, a massive improvement, even allowing for the fact that it was a new event.

She competed at four Olympics. In 1960, under her maiden name of Richert, she finished fourth in a semifinal. After her Tokyo triumph she was fifth in 1968 and third in 1972.

In addition to winning seven East German titles in the hurdles, she was also pentathlon champion twice (1962 and 1963), long-jump champion (1963), and 200m champion (1968). Originally a student in chemistry, she subsequently changed her studies and became a sports teacher.

Karin Balzer, East Germany (80m and 100m hurdles), East Germany's first Olympic track gold medalist.

Draga Stamejcic   (Yugoslavia, b. 1937)

| 10.5 | Celje, Yugoslavia | 5 Sep 1964 |

Draga Stamejcic set her world record at a national athletic meet in Celje, Yugoslavia, six weeks before the Tokyo Olympics. She couldn't reproduce that form in Tokyo. In the final she ran 10.86 to finish seventh. Her only other major competition was the European Championships in 1962, in which she was sixth in a semifinal and did not progress.

Pam Kilborn (later Ryan)   (Australia, b. 1939)

80m hurdles

| 10.5 | Osaka, Japan | 25 Oct 1964 |
| 10.4 | Melbourne, Australia | 6 Feb 1965 |

100m hurdles

| 12.5 | Warsaw, Poland | 28 Jun 1972 |

Pam Kilborn competed in three Olympics but never won a gold medal: She was third in 1964, second in 1968, and fourth in 1972. However, she achieved success at the Commonwealth Games with three wins in the hurdles (1962, 1966, and 1970) and one in the long jump (1962).

Luck didn't favor her at the Olympics. At Tokyo in 1964 all three medalists were timed at 10.5. Perhaps her best chance for Olympic success was at the Mexico City Olympics.

She had not been defeated since the Tokyo Olympics. However, in her last training session in Australia before the Games, one of the hurdles had been set a meter short, and she came crashing down on her face. Although she didn't suffer any major injury from the incident, it appeared to take the edge off her performance. At the final she was beaten by her compatriot Maureen Caird, only 17, who defeated her for the first time.

At the Munich Olympics, she was friendly with one of the Israeli athletes killed by Palestinian terrorists. Australian officials, in a decision not compelling in its logic, decided it would be safe for the men to attend a memorial service but not the women. The 100m hurdles final was won by East Germany's Annelie Ehrhardt, with Kilborn fourth in 12.98.

Pam Kilborn, Australia (80m and 100m hurdles).

Vera Korsakova   (Soviet Union, b. 1941)

10.3	Riga, USSR	16 Jun 1968
10.2	Riga, USSR	16 Jun 1968

Vera Korsakova set the last two world records over 80m hurdles in 1968. The event was replaced the following year by the 100m hurdles. She set her two world records in one day in Riga, now the capital of independent Latvia. At 5:35 P.M. (1735 hours) she won her heat in 10.3 seconds, to equal the world record. At 6:40 P.M. (1840 hours) she won the final in 10.2.

That was her one day of glory. At the Mexico City Olympics four months later, she went out in the semifinals with 10.86, after running 10.74 in her heat. She never quite won a Soviet title, her best result being a third place in 1967.

100m Hurdles

As mentioned in the introduction to this chapter, the event was extended to 100m hurdles in 1969. Athletes have to negotiate 10 hurdles, 2' 9" (0.84 meters) high.

Karin Balzer   (East Germany, b. 1948)

13.3	Warsaw, Poland	20 Jun 1969
13.0	Leipzig, East Germany	27 Jul 1969
12.9	Berlin, East Germany	5 Sep 1969
12.7	Berlin, East Germany	26 Jul 1970
12.7	Berlin, East Germany	25 Jul 1971
12.6	Berlin, East Germany	31 July 1971

See Karin Balzer's profile in the preceding 80m hurdles section.

Teresa Sukniewicz   (Poland, b. 1948)

13.3	Warsaw, Poland	20 Jun 1969
12.8	Warsaw, Poland	20 Jun 1970
12.7	Warsaw, Poland	20 Sep 1970

Teresa Sukniewicz equaled the world record in this event eight minutes after Balzer. The German had run in heat two of the 10th Anniversary Kusocinski Memorial race in Warsaw, and Teresa Sukniewicz ran in heat three; both won their races in 13.3.

Exactly a year later to the day, she set a new world record of 12.8, also in Warsaw. Three months later, again in Warsaw, she reduced it to 12.7. However, Sukniewicz never managed to win a major championship. She was fifth in the 1969 European Championships and third in 1971. At the Mexico City Olympics she went out in the semifinals.

Chi Cheng   (Taiwan, b. 1944)

12.8	Munich, West Germany	12 Jul 1970

Chi Cheng's career has been described in the chapters on the 100m and 200m. Ten years after her debut as an international athlete at the Rome Olympics, she set world records at three distances in July 1970. The 200m and the 100m hurdles records were achieved on 12 July 1970 in Munich and the 100m record on 18 July 1970 in Vienna.

By the time 1972 came around, she was plagued with injuries and could not compete at the Munich Olympics. Cheng retired the next year, aged 29, and went back to Taiwan, where she became a senator. She also headed the Taiwan Track and Field Federation.

Chi Cheng, Taiwan (100m, 200m, 100m hurdles), showed rare talent at three events.

Annelie Ehrhardt   (East Germany, b. 1950)

12.5	Potsdam, East Germany	15 Jun 1972
12.3	Dresden, East Germany	22 Jul 1973
12.59 (on electronic timing)	Munich, West Germany	8 Sep 1972

A distinctive figure with striking blonde hair and impeccable technique, Annelie Ehrhardt was the successor to Karin Balzer. Balzer won the 1971 European Championships with

Ehrhardt second, 12.94 to 12.96. At that time, Balzer was 33, Ehrhardt was 21. Ehrhardt set a hand-timed world record of 12.5 prior to the 1972 Olympics. At the Games she won in 12.59. Her winning time was taken as the first electronic world record for the distance.

In the years 1972 through 1974, she was untouchable. She set one more hand-timed world record in 1973 at the East German championships and was European champion in 1974 with 12.66.

By the time of the 1976 Olympics, a new generation of hurdlers had arrived. She was troubled by injuries and was eliminated in a semifinal.

Annelie Ehrhardt, East Germany (100m hurdles),
1972 Olympic champion.

Pam Kilborn (later Ryan)   (Australia, b. 1939)

| 12.5 | Warsaw, Poland | 28 Jun 1972 |

See Pam Kilborn's profile in the preceding 80m hurdles section.

Grazyna Rabsztyn   (Poland, b. 1952)

| 12.48 | Fürth, West Germany | 10 Jun 1978 |
| 12.36 | Warsaw, Poland | 13 Jun 1980 |

Grazyna Rabsztyn set two quality world records and won the World Cup twice (1977 and 1979), but didn't have luck at the Olympics or European Championships.

She participated in three Olympics, reaching the final each time: 1972 (eighth), 1976 (fifth), and 1980 (fifth). In the European Championships she was eighth in 1974. Four years later she crashed out in the final, bringing down Soviet athlete Nina Margulina. The race was subsequently rerun, but the Pole was disqualified because she was judged to have veered into the Soviet's lane.

Her first world record took 0.11 second off Ehrhardt's six-year-old world record; her second reduced it by another 0.12 second and lasted for another six years.

Yordanka Donkova   (Bulgaria, b. 1961)

12.35	Cologne, West Germany	17 Aug 1986
12.29	Cologne, West Germany	17 Aug 1986
12.26	Ljubljana, Yugoslavia	7 Sep 1986
12.21	Stara Zagora, Yugoslavia	20 Aug 1988

Yordanka Donkova, Bulgaria (100m hurdles), current world record holder for 10 years.

Yordanka Donkova ran a series of excellent world records in the late 1980s. Born in Sofia, Bulgaria, she lost three fingers on her right hand in an accident at age five. She ran as a teenager at the 1980 Moscow Olympics and made it through to the semifinals. At the 1982 European Championships she was second. The 1984 Olympics were denied her as Bulgaria joined the Soviet boycott.

She began her series of world records in August 1986 with world records in the heat (12.35) and then the final (12.29) of an international meet in Cologne. Two weeks later she won the European Championships with an easy win in 12.38. A week later she improved her world record for the third time that season with 12.26.

In 1987 she suffered a significant loss when she was beaten by her countrywoman Ginka Zagorcheva at the 1987 World Championships in Rome. However, 12 months later she had a perfect season. She was unbeaten all year, set her fourth world record (12.21), and won the Olympic gold medal at Seoul in an Olympic record of 12.38.

She continued running in her 30s and was still competitive. She won a bronze medal at the 1992 Olympics (12.70) and another bronze at the 1994 European Championships (12.93).

Ginka Zagorcheva   (Bulgaria, b. 1958)

12.25	Drama, Greece	8 Aug 1987

Bulgaria produced two elite hurdles champions at the same time, and their rivalry generated world records and championship medals. Three years older than Donkova, Ginka Zagorcheva had come in third at the 1986 European Championships. She interrupted Donkova's run of four world records when she ran 12.25 in 1987. That was her best year. She also won the World Championships in Rome that season, inflicting a significant defeat on Donkova in the process.

Her Olympic chances the next year were hampered by an injury in June, and at the Games three months later she could not complete the race in her opening heat.

Her world record (12.25) was achieved in Greece, at an athletic match between Greece, Bulgaria, and Czechoslovakia, where she won by almost 1.5 seconds. Her 1987 world record remains an exceedingly fast time, which few have approached almost a decade later. Only Donkova has ever run faster, on two occasions in 1988.

Conclusions

In the mid-1980s, the two fastest female 100m hurdlers were Bulgarians: Yordanka Donkova and Ginka Zagorcheva. A decade later they are still the two fastest all-time hurdlers. Although sprint and hurdle times have shown only modest improvements in recent years, the world record of Donkova is not out of reach. Yet the fastest time in 1996 was 12.47.

Six All-Time Fastest: Women's 100m Hurdles			(Wind)
Yordanka Donkova (BUL)	12.21	1988	+0.7
Ginka Zagorcheva (BUL)	12.25	1987	+1.4
Lyudmila Narozhilenko (USSR)	12.26	1992	+1.7
Grazyna Rabsztyn (POL)	12.36	1980	+1.9
Vera Komisova (USSR)	12.39	1980	+1.5
Natalya Grigoryeva (USSR)	12.39	1991	+1.8
Prediction	*12.18*	*2015*	

Top Three: Women's 80m and 100m Hurdles

GOLD MEDAL:	Karin Balzer (GDR)
SILVER MEDAL:	Yordanka Donkova (BUL)
BRONZE MEDAL:	Irina Press (USSR)

The 400m hurdles were recognized for official world records as of 1974 and were introduced into the European Championships in 1978 and into the Olympic Games in 1984. It consists of 10 hurdles, 2' 6" (0.762 meters) high, compared with the three-foot (0.914-meter) high hurdles used in the men's race. There are 45 meters to the first hurdle, 35 meters between each hurdle, and 40 meters to the finish. Stride patterns vary, but most women use 15 steps between hurdles until the sixth or seventh hurdle, and then 16 or 17 steps for the rest of the race.

The initial world record in 1974 of 56.51 was reduced to 52.61 by 1995, almost four seconds. Ten women from five countries have set the world record a total of 15 times. Five of these record holders have been from the former Soviet Union. To date, only Sally Gunnell of Great Britain has also been Olympic champion.

Women's World Records for 400m Hurdles

Record time	Record holder	Location	Date
56.51	Krystyna Kacperczyk (POL)	Augsburg, West Germany	13 Jul 1974
55.74	Tatyana Storozheva (USSR)	Karl-Marx-Stadt, East Germany	26 Jun 1977
55.63	Karin Rossley (GDR)	Helsinki, Finland	13 Aug 1977
55.44	Krystyna Kacperczyk (POL)	Berlin, West Germany	18 Aug 1978
55.31	Tatyana Zelentsova (USSR)	Podolsk, USSR	19 Aug 1978
54.89	Tatyana Zelentsova (USSR)	Prague, Czechoslovakia	2 Sep 1978
54.78	Marina Makeyeva (later Stepanova)(USSR)	Moscow, USSR	27 Jul 1979
54.28	Karin Rossley (GDR)	Jena, East Germany	18 May 1980
54.02	Anna Ambraziené (USSR)	Moscow, USSR	11 Jun 1983
53.58	Margarita Ponomaryeva (USSR)	Kiev, USSR	22 Jun 1984
53.55	Sabine Busch (GDR)	Berlin, East Germany	22 Sep 1985
53.32	Marina Stepanova (USSR)	Stuttgart, West Germany	30 Aug 1986
52.94	Marina Stepanova (USSR)	Tashkent, USSR	17 Sep 1986
52.74	Sally Gunnell (GBR)	Stuttgart, West Germany	19 Aug 1993
52.61	Kim Batten (USA)	Gothenburg, Sweden	11 Aug 1995

Krystyna Kacperczyk   (Poland, b. 1948)

56.51	Augsburg, West Germany	13 Jul 1974
55.44	Berlin, West Germany	18 Aug 1978

The first recognized world record was set in 1974 in an international meet between Poland and West Germany. Krystyna Kacperczyk of Poland ran 56.51 in Augsburg to win this race and set the inaugural world record. Four years later she reduced it to 55.44 at an international meet in West Berlin. The record had been reduced twice in 1977 before Kacperczyk reclaimed it.

Kacperczyk's 1978 record only lasted one day, as it was immediately reduced to 55.31 by Tatyana Zelentsova (USSR) in Podolsk. Two weeks later at the European Championships in Prague, Zelentsova further reduced the record to 54.89. In this final Kacperczyk finished fifth in 55.55.

Tatyana Storozheva   (Soviet Union, b. 1954)

55.74	Karl-Marx-Stadt, East Germany	26 Jun 1977

Tatyana Storozheva was the second athlete to hold the world record in the early days of the event. She had become Soviet champion in this event in 1977 (56.38). Her world record of 55.74 was set at an international event match between East Germany, Poland, and Russia at Karl-Marx-Stadt in June 1977.

Apart from 1977, she had a limited international career and did not compete at the European Championships or Olympic Games.

Karin Rossley   (East Germany, b. 1957)

| 55.63 | Helsinki, Finland | 13 Aug 1977 |
| 54.28 | Jena, East Germany | 18 May 1980 |

East Germany's Karin Rossley set a new world record in the European Cup final in 1977, running 55.63. However, the next year at the European Championships she was third, as the new Soviet star Tatyana Zelentsova won in a world record time of 54.89.

In 1980 Rossley achieved a second world record, taking 0.61 second off Zelentsova's time (and 0.5 second off Marina Makeyeva's intervening 1979 record) with 54.28 seconds. However, there was no 400m hurdle event at the Olympics in 1980.

She never quite managed to win the East German championship, coming in second in 1978.

Tatyana Zelentsova   (Soviet Union, b. 1948)

| 55.31 | Podolsk, USSR | 19 Aug 1978 |
| 54.89 | Prague, Czechoslovakia | 2 Sep 1978 |

Tatyana Zelentsova set two world records within a month in a brilliant 1978 season. Her first world record of 55.31 took place in Podolsk at a "Runners Day" meet, 24 hours after Krystyna Kacperczyk had set her second world record of 55.44. Two weeks later Zelentsova became the first woman to run the distance under 55 seconds when she won the European Championships in Prague in 54.89. She was also Soviet champion in 1976 and 1978.

Tatyana Zelentsova,
Soviet Union (400m hurdles).

Marina Stepanova (née Makeyeva)   (Soviet Union, b. 1950)

54.78	Moscow, USSR	27 Jul 1979
53.32	Stuttgart, West Germany	30 Aug 1986
52.94	Tashkent, USSR	17 Sep 1986

Marina Makeyeva had two separate phases in her career, six years apart. In 1979 she first became Soviet champion and world record holder. She set a world record at the Spartakiade, the great Soviet sport festival, running 54.78 seconds.

In 1981 she gave birth to a daughter. In the mid-1980s she returned to athletics as Marina Stepanova and was Soviet champion in 1985 and 1986. Stepanova won the 1986 European Championships ahead of the new star from East Germany, Sabine Busch, 53.32 to 53.60, her second world record. The next month she set her third world record at the Tashkent Spartakiade for athletes under 23 years old. She competed at this race as a guest and competed only in the semifinal, not the final. In this race she became the first athlete to run the event under 53 seconds when she was timed at 52.94. This world record at age 36 years 139 days made her the oldest female athlete to set a track world record.

Anna Ambraziené   (Soviet Union, b. 1955)

54.02   **Moscow, USSR**   **11 Jun 1983**

Anna Ambraziené had a long career, from 1978 to 1988, and was a finalist at the Soviet championships for most of that time. In 1983 she finally won her first Soviet championship title in 54.78. That season she won the Znamenskiy Memorial athletic meet at the Lenin Stadium in Moscow and broke the world record by 0.26. Her winning time of 54.02 just missed the 54-second barrier.

The Soviet Union boycott meant that she missed the 1984 Olympics. In 1987 she won her second Soviet title and came in sixth that year at the World Championships.

Margarita Ponomaryeva   (Soviet Union/Russia, b. 1963)

53.58   **Kiev, USSR**   **22 Jun 1984**

Margarita Ponomaryeva was born in the Soviet republic of Kazakhstan, which later gained its independence. However, she subsequently competed as a Russian.

An economics teacher, she was the first woman to break 54 seconds. Running in Kiev in the Izvestia Cup in 1984, she took 0.44 second off the record by running 53.58 seconds. She missed the Los Angeles Games because of the Soviet boycott. At the European Championships she was eighth in 1986 and fifth in 1990. She competed at the 1992 Barcelona Olympics, coming in sixth. At the World Championships she went out in the semifinals in 1987 and was eighth in 1991.

Margarita Ponomaryeva,
Soviet Union (400m hurdles).

Finally, at the end of her career, when she was 30, she won a medal. At the 1993 World Championships in Stuttgart, Sally Gunnell of Great Britain set a new world record of 52.74. Ponomaryeva finished third in 53.48 seconds, her career best.

Sabine Busch   (East Germany, b. 1962)

53.55   Berlin, East Germany   22 Sep 1985

Since the age of 15 Sabine Busch was a talented 400m runner who found her progress in the 400m blocked by the established East German star Marita Koch. Her best 400m time was 49.24 when only a handful of women had run under 50 seconds.

In 1985, with Koch still invincible in the 400m, Busch made a decision to turn to the 400m hurdles. Almost instantly she met with complete success, despite a slightly awkward technique in clearing the hurdles. In September 1985 she took 0.03 second off the world record when she ran 53.55 in a trial prior to the World Cup.

She went to the 1986 European Championships as favorite, only to be beaten by the veteran Soviet runner Marina Stepanova. In the process, the Soviet athlete achieved a new world record of 53.32. Busch was second in 53.60.

She compensated for the loss the following year, when she won the 400m hurdles in Rome at the 1987 World Championships in 53.62, only 0.07 second over her world record. It seemed she would be the favorite in 1988 at her Olympic debut. But a new wave of 400m hurdlers had arrived, and she finished fourth in 53.69. The winning time by Debbie Flintoff-King (Australia) was 53.17.

Busch required surgery on her left foot in 1989 and retired shortly thereafter.

Sabine Busch, East Germany (400m hurdles).

Sally Gunnell   (Great Britain, b. 1966)

52.74   Stuttgart, West Germany   19 Aug 1993

Whereas Sabine Busch had moved across from 400m to 400m hurdles, Sally Gunnell moved up from 100m hurdles to 400m hurdles. In the shorter event Gunnell became Commonwealth Champion in 1986 but could not quite beat the elite Europeans. She made a decision in 1987 to move up to 400m hurdles. Within a year she made the Olympic final, finishing fifth (54.03). The event was won by Debbie Flintoff-King (Australia) in 53.17. In 1990 Gunnell defeated Flintoff-King when they clashed at the Commonwealth Games in Auckland. At the 1991 World Championships she was just beaten by the muscular Soviet athlete Tatyana Ledovskaya. Finally, at the Barcelona Olympics, Gunnell outsprinted American Sandra Farmer-Patrick, winning 53.23 to 53.69.

The early 1990s were characterized by a series of duels between Farmer-Patrick and Gunnell, and their meeting at the 1993 World Championships resulted in a world record.

Farmer-Patrick was still leading at the 10th hurdle. However, Gunnell's driving finish to the tape enabled her to win by 0.05 second, 52.74 to 52.79. Both women had finished under the old record.

She continued her winning ways in 1994 with victories in both the European Championships and the Commonwealth Games. However, injuries plagued her in 1996 and she did not finish the semifinal at the Atlanta Games. A popular hero back in Britain, by profession she is a law clerk.

Sally Gunnell, Great Britain (400m hurdles), 1992 Olympic champion.

Kim Batten   (United States, b. 1969)

52.61   **Gothenburg, Sweden**   **11 Aug 1995**

Kim Batten, United States (400m hurdles).

Until August 1995 Kim Batten had a long career as an international athlete, but without a high public profile. In her specialty, the 400m hurdles, she had been somewhat overshadowed by Olympic champion Sally Gunnell and Jamaican-born Sandra Farmer-Patrick. Nonetheless, she had acquired a number of significant titles: U.S. champion in 1991, 1993, and 1995 and Pan-American champion in 1995. At the World Championships she had come in fifth in 1991 and fourth in 1993.

She felt 1995 was going to be a good year when she ran 53.88 in her first major race for the season in Brazil. That optimistic scenario was interrupted by surgery in May, when she required removal of an acutely inflamed appendix. Showing remarkable resilience, she won the U.S. title three weeks later. However, the next few weeks were hampered by inflamed toes, and she lost a number of major races in July.

Fortunately, her injuries improved just as the 1995 World Championships came along. These championships took place without the big names of Gunnell (injured), Farmer-Patrick (missed selection), and France's Marie-Jose Perec, who decided to concentrate on the 400m. Accordingly, many commentators saw it as a "soft" race, which irritated Batten.

The night before her final, she actually dreamed she would set a world record. However, the reality was that her personal best at the time was 53.72, still almost a second outside the existing world record. But she had confidence that a major reduction in her personal best time was imminent.

Because of windy conditions for the men's final the previous day, she decided to go out hard. On the day of the final, running in sunglasses, she raced straight to the front and was leading at the halfway point by a few meters from teammate Tonja Buford. However, Buford made a sustained effort around the last bend, and the two Americans went down the entire final straight stride for stride. At the finish, Batten leaned forward, while Buford remained erect, and that was enough to separate them on the photo-finish picture. Batten had recorded 52.61, Buford 52.62. The new world record holder had taken 1.11 seconds off her personal best. In third place was Jamaica's Deon Hemmings (53.48).

Batten's hopes for an Olympic gold medal the following year were not to be realized. Hemmings became the first Jamaican woman to win an Olympic gold medal, defeating Batten 52.82 to 53.08.

Conclusions

The events of 1995 in the 400m hurdles stunningly demonstrated that new champions can arise unexpectedly, even though most observers focus on the existing champions.

To universal surprise, the 1995 World Championships race between Kim Batten and Tonja Buford produced a new world record and the world's two fastest 400m hurdle times. This happily makes the point that unpredictability is still a key element in track and field. It also suggests that the women's 400m hurdle world record is still capable of significant further reduction.

Five All-Time Fastest: Women's 400m Hurdles		
Kim Batten (USA)	52.61	1995
Tonja Buford (USA)	52.62	1995
Sally Gunnell (GBR)	52.74	1993
Sandra Patrick-Farmer (USA)	52.79	1993
Deon Hemmings (JAM)	52.82	1996
Prediction	*51.90*	*2015*

Top Three: Women's 400m Hurdles

GOLD MEDAL: Sally Gunnell (GBR)

SILVER MEDAL: Marina Stepanova (USSR)

BRONZE MEDAL: Kim Batten (USA)

Twenty women from 13 countries have set or equaled the world record 46 times in the high jump. Much like the men, a wide variety of styles have evolved over the years. Women athletes stuck with the scissors style much longer than men, and it was used on and off through to the 1960s before the straddle took over. The first world record straddler was Sheila Lerwill in 1951. The straddle eventually gave way to the Fosbury flop. The last world record by a straddler was Rosemarie Ackermann in 1977, while the first world record flopper was Ulrike Meyfarth in 1972. The flop style is now used universally by elite high jumpers.

Eight of these world record holders have also been Olympic champions: Shiley, Brand, McDaniel, Balas, Meyfarth, Ackermann, Simeoni, and Kostadinova. Shiley, McDaniel, and Meyfarth (1972) were the only ones to set their world record at the Olympic Games, as did Didriksen, who finished second to Shiley in 1932.

The record has moved up from 1.65 meters (5' 5") in 1932 to 2.09 meters (6' 10 ¼") in 1987, an improvement of 44 centimeters (17 ¼"). The longest gap during which the record remained unbroken was the 10 years and 50 days which followed Iolanda Balas's 14th world record in 1961. It has been almost a decade since the last world record was set.

Women's World Records for the High Jump

Record height	Record holder	Location	Date
1.65m (5' 5")	Jean Shiley (USA)	Los Angeles, USA	7 Aug 1932
1.65m (5' 5")	Mildred "Babe" Didriksen (USA)	Los Angeles, USA	7 Aug 1932
1.66m (5' 5 ¼")	Dorothy Odam-Tyler (GBR)	Brentwood, England	29 May 1939
1.66m (5' 5 ¼")	Esther van Heerden (later Brand) (S.AF)	Stellenbosch, South Africa	29 Mar 1941
1.66m (5' 5 ¼")	Ilsebill Pfenning (SWI)	Lugano, Switzerland	27 Jul 1941
1.71m (5' 7 ¼")	Fanny Blankers-Koen (HOL)	Amsterdam, Netherlands	30 May 1943
1.72m (5' 7 ½")	Sheila Lerwill (GBR)	London, England	7 Jul 1951
1.73m (5' 8")	Aleksandra Chudina (USSR)	Kiev, USSR	22 May 1954
1.74m (5' 8 ½")	Thelma Hopkins (GBR)	Belfast, Northern Ireland	5 May 1956
1.75m (5' 8 ¾")	Iolanda Balas (ROM)	Bucharest, Romania	14 Jul 1956
1.76m (5' 9 ¼")	Mildred McDaniel (USA)	Melbourne, Australia	1 Dec 1956
1.76m (5' 9 ¼")	Iolanda Balas (ROM)	Bucharest, Romania	13 Oct 1957
1.77m (5' 9 ¾")	Chen Feng-Jung (CHN)	Beijing, China	17 Nov 1957
1.78m (5' 10")	Iolanda Balas (ROM)	Bucharest, Romania	7 Jun 1958
1.80m (5' 10 ¾")	Iolanda Balas (ROM)	Cluj, Romania	22 Jun 1958
1.81m (5' 11 ¼")	Iolanda Balas (ROM)	Poiana Brasov, Romania	31 Jul 1958
1.82m (5' 11 ¾")	Iolanda Balas (ROM)	Bucharest, Romania	4 Oct 1958
1.83m (6' 0")	Iolanda Balas (ROM)	Bucharest, Romania	18 Oct 1958
1.84m (6' 0 ½")	Iolanda Balas (ROM)	Bucharest, Romania	21 Sep 1959
1.85m (6' 0 ¾")	Iolanda Balas (ROM)	Bucharest, Romania	6 Jun 1960
1.86m (6' 1 ¼")	Iolanda Balas (ROM)	Bucharest, Romania	10 Jul 1960
1.87m (6' 1 ½")	Iolanda Balas (ROM)	Bucharest, Romania	15 Apr 1961
1.88m (6' 2")	Iolanda Balas (ROM)	Warsaw, Poland	18 Jun 1961
1.90m (6' 2 ¾")	Iolanda Balas (ROM)	Budapest, Hungary	8 Jul 1961
1.91m (6' 3 ¼")	Iolanda Balas (ROM)	Sofia, Bulgaria	16 Jul 1961
1.92m (6' 3 ½")	Ilona Gusenbauer (AUT)	Vienna, Austria	4 Sep 1971
1.92m (6' 3 ½")	Ulrike Meyfarth (FRG)	Munich, West Germany	4 Sep 1972

1.94m (6' 4 ¼")	Yordanka Blagoyeva (BUL)	Zagreb, Yugoslavia	24 Sep 1972
1.94m (6' 4 ¼")	Rosemarie Ackermann (GDR)	Berlin, East Germany	24 Aug 1974
1.95m (6' 4 ¾")	Rosemarie Ackermann (GDR)	Rome, Italy	8 Sep 1974
1.96m (6' 5")	Rosemarie Ackermann (GDR)	Dresden, East Germany	8 May 1976
1.96m (6' 5")	Rosemarie Ackermann (GDR)	Dresden, East Germany	3 Jul 1977
1.97m (6' 5 ½")	Rosemarie Ackermann (GDR)	Helsinki, Finland	14 Aug 1977
1.97m (6' 5 ½")	Rosemarie Ackermann (GDR)	Berlin, West Germany	26 Aug 1977
2.00m (6' 6 ¾")	Rosemarie Ackermann (GDR)	Berlin, West Germany	26 Aug 1977
2.01m (6' 7")	Sara Simeoni (ITA)	Brescia, Italy	4 Aug 1978
2.01m (6' 7")	Sara Simeoni (ITA)	Prague, Czechoslovakia	31 Aug 1978
2.02m (6' 7 ½")	Ulrike Meyfarth (FRG)	Athens, Greece	8 Sep 1982
2.03m (6' 8")	Ulrike Meyfarth (FRG)	London, England	21 Aug 1983
2.03m (6' 8")	Tamara Bykova (USSR)	London, England	21 Aug 1983
2.04m (6' 8 ¼")	Tamara Bykova (USSR)	Pisa, Italy	25 Aug 1983
2.05m (6' 8 ¾")	Tamara Bykova (USSR)	Kiev, USSR	22 Jun 1984
2.07m (6' 9 ½")	Lyudmila Andonova (BUL)	Berlin, East Germany	20 Jul 1984
2.07m (6' 9 ½")	Stefka Kostadinova (BUL)	Sofia, Bulgaria	25 May 1986
2.08m (6' 9 ¾")	Stefka Kostadinova (BUL)	Sofia, Bulgaria	31 May 1986
2.09m (6' 10 ¼")	Stefka Kostadinova (BUL)	Rome, Italy	30 Aug 1987

Jean Shiley   (United States, b. 1911)

1.65m (5' 5")   **Los Angeles, USA**   **7 Aug 1932**

Jean Shiley *(left)* and Mildred "Babe" Didriksen, both of the United States (high jump).

Jean Shiley was selected at age 16 to compete in the 1928 Amsterdam Olympics, the first Olympics with track and field for women. In the event, Jean Shiley finished fourth.

She returned to the Olympics in 1932 for the Los Angeles Games. She and "Babe" Didriksen shared the same winning height of 1.65 meters (5' 5"). This was taken as the first official world record by the IAAF. However the officials then ruled that the jumping technique used by Didriksen was somehow illegal. Accordingly, Shiley was awarded the gold medal and Didriksen the silver.

Over the next few years Shiley gave swimming lessons and did some lifeguarding at the beach. Being paid for these activities, she inadvertently breached the strict rules of amateurism that existed at the time and which were ruthlessly enforced by the athletic hierarchy. AAU President Dan Ferris personally ruled her ineligible for the Berlin Olympics. The incident still riled her some 50 years later when she was describing some of her Olympic memories.

Mildred "Babe" Didriksen (United States, 1911–1956)

1.65m (5' 5")   **Los Angeles, USA**   **7 Aug 1932**

Mildred "Babe" Didriksen was possibly the greatest female athlete who ever lived. Her family originally came from Norway, and her father had been a sailor who had gone around Cape Horn "something like seventeen times." Originally a top basketball player, she turned to track and was almost a one-woman team for her employers, Employers Casualty Insurance of Dallas. At the Los Angeles Olympics in 1932 she earned two gold medals (80m hurdles and javelin) and earned a silver in the high jump. That was a controversial decision, as she jumped the same height as winner Jean Shiley, 1.65 meters (5' 5"). The judge decided that Didriksen's technique was in some way suspect, and Shiley was awarded the gold medal. This height was recognized as the first official high-jump record.

Apart from her medals, she was the natural media celebrity at the Games, especially with her forthright opinions and colorful language. Many of her teammates resented her ploys to be the center of attention, which included interrupting interviews of other athletes, and were glad when Shiley was awarded the gold medal in the high jump.

After the Games she turned to golf and was three times the winner of the U.S. Open. In 1938 she married wrestler George Zaharias, and they lived in Florida. However, in her early 40s she developed rectal cancer and underwent a colostomy. She made a remarkable comeback by winning her third U.S. Open golf title in 1954. But the cancer returned, and she died in September 1956, at the age of 45.

Dorothy Odam-Tyler (Great Britain, b. 1920)

1.66m (5' 5 ¼")   **Brentwood, England**   **29 May 1939**

Dorothy Odam-Tyler was unfortunate to be denied an Olympic gold medal. Under the count-back rules applied in her day (when two competitors tied for first place), she was awarded the silver medal at the 1936 and 1948 Olympics. Under the count-back rules now in effect, she would have won Olympic gold medals on both occasions. In 1950 she lost another gold medal on a count-back when she was second in the European Championships.

For most of her career she used the scissors style. However in 1951, 12 years after her world record, she changed to the western roll. Odam-Tyler had first jumped over 1.50 meters (5 feet) in 1935, at the age of 15, and she could still manage that height in 1965. Her world record was achieved in 1939 at the Southern Counties Women's AAA Championship. She won the Commonwealth Games title in 1938 and 1950 and was second in 1954. At four Olympics she was second (1936), second (1948), seventh (1952), and 12th (1956).

Esther Brand (née van Heerden) (South Africa, b. 1924)

1.66m (5' 5 ¼")   **Stellenbosch, South Africa**   **29 Mar 1941**

Esther Brand was South Africa's last Olympic gold medalist before their 24-year suspension from the Olympics (1964-88). As 16-year-old Esther van Heerden, she had equaled the world record back in the 1941 Western Province Championships, in which she was the only competitor.

Eleven years later she won the gold medal at the 1952 Helsinki Olympics. The world record had moved up to 1.72 meters (5' 7 ½") in the interim. At these Games the conditions were very wet, which precluded any chance of a world record. She jumped 1.67 meters (5' 5 ¾") to win by two centimeters. The first four places went to world record holders: Brand, Lerwill, Chudina, and Hopkins.

Ilsebill Pfenning (Switzerland, b. 1916)

1.66m (5' 5 ¼")   **Lugano, Switzerland**   **27 Jul 1941**

Ilsebill Pfenning, Switzerland (high jump).

Ilsebill Pfenning unwittingly equaled the world record during World War II. She had competed at the 1938 European Championships and finished sixth. The winner was Dora Ratjen, who jumped 1.70 meters (5' 7"), a world record. The situation became confused when it was later discovered that Ratjen was a man, and his world record was eventually annulled. When Ilsebill Pfenning jumped 1.66 meters in 1941, officials present did not appreciate that Ratjen's 1938 world record had been rescinded. After World War II it was realized that Pfenning had, in fact, equaled the existing world record of 1.66 meters. Documents concerning the jump were still in order, so it was belatedly submitted as a world record. Ultimately, the record was officially recognized in 1976, some 35 years after her performance, and she was awarded a plaque to that effect at the 1976 Zurich Weltclasse athletic meeting. "Better late than never," she commented on the day. Her jump was a Swiss record that was not surpassed until 1969.

Fanny Blankers-Koen (Netherlands, b. 1918)

1.71m (5' 7 ¼")   **Amsterdam, Netherlands**   **30 May 1943**

The fabulous Fanny Blankers-Koen extended her world record–breaking talents to the high jump in 1943. She used the scissors style and, at the age of 18, had tied for sixth at the 1936 Berlin Olympics. At the 1943 Dutch championships she actually went over the world record three times, jumping 1.67 meters (5' 5 ¾"), 1.69 meters (5' 6 ½"), and finally 1.71 meters (5' 7 ¼"). However, only 1.71 meters was submitted as a new world record by Dutch authorities. This was two months after her first child (Jan) was born.

Blankers-Koen did not abandon the high jump altogether after her 1943 world record. She contested this event at the 1946 European Championships and placed fourth with 1.57 meters (5' 1 ¾"). She did not contest the high jump again at a major international competition, although she was Dutch champion in the event 10 times.

Sheila Lerwill   (Great Britain, b. 1928)

1.72m (5' 7 ½")   **London, England**   **7 Jul 1951**

Sheila Lerwill was the first female athlete to set a world record using the straddle technique. She set the record in 1951 at the British WAAA championships in London.

Lerwill had won the European Championships in 1950, as Sheila Alexander, when she jumped 1.63 meters (5' 4 ¼"). The first three athletes all jumped this height, and she won on the count-back rule. Four years later at the European Championships in Bern, Switzerland, she was fifth.

At the 1952 Helsinki Olympics, Lerwill jumped 1.65 meters (5' 5") in wet conditions to take the silver medal behind South Africa's Esther Brand (1.67 meters, 5' 5 ¾").

Aleksandra Chudina   (Soviet Union, 1923–1990)

1.73m (5' 8")   **Kiev, USSR**   **22 May 1954**

Aleksandra Chudina was world record holder in the high jump and the pentathlon. She achieved a rare feat when she competed in three separate field events at the 1952 Olympics and achieved medals in all of them: high jump (third), long jump (second), and javelin (second).

Chudina was the tallest of any female world record holder, standing 188 centimeters (6' 2"). In 1954 she set her world record (1.73 meters) using the scissors technique. Somewhat surprisingly, she could manage only 1.60 meters (5' 3") at the European Championships later that season, which gave her sixth place. Chudina won the pentathlon at these championships and was fifth in the javelin.

She won the most titles of any athlete, male or female, at the Soviet Championships: 80m hurdles (3), high jump (7), long jump (7), javelin (4), and pentathlon (9), a grand total of 30 titles.

In addition to track and field, she was a member of the Soviet volleyball team and also showed talent in basketball, tennis, and cycling.

Thelma Hopkins   (Great Britain, b. 1936)

1.74m (5' 8 ½")   **Belfast, Northern Ireland**   **5 May 1956**

Thelma Hopkins was born in Yorkshire and later lived in Northern Ireland. She used the straddle technique and at age 16 competed at the 1952 Helsinki Olympics, coming in fourth. She had a twin sister, Moira, and both girls represented Northern Ireland in international hockey.

Her major international triumph was at the 1954 European Championships, at age 18, when she won the high jump with 1.67 meters (5' 5 ¾"). That year she completed a fine double by also winning the Commonwealth Games title with the same height.

She set her world record at the national championships at Cherryvale in Belfast in May 1956, jumping 1.74 meters (5' 8 ½") at her second attempt. This was six months before the Melbourne Olympics. In July 1956 Iolanda Balas jumped 1cm higher, the first of her 14 world records. However, at the Games both women had to watch as a new world record was set by the American Mildred McDaniel, who cleared 1.76 meters (5' 9 ¼"). Hopkins tied with Soviet athlete Maria Pisaryeva with 1.67 meters (5' 5 ¾") for second place.

Iolanda Balas   (Romania, b. 1936)

1.75m (5' 8 ¾")	Bucharest, Romania	14 Jul 1956
1.76m (5' 9 ¼")	Bucharest, Romania	13 Oct 1957
1.78m (5' 10")	Bucharest, Romania	7 Jun 1958
1.80m (5' 10 ¾")	Cluj, Romania	22 Jun 1958
1.81m (5' 11 ¼")	Poiana Brasov, Romania	31 Jul 1958
1.82m (5' 11 ¾")	Bucharest, Romania	4 Oct 1958
1.83m (6' 0")	Bucharest, Romania	18 Oct 1958
1.84m (6' 0 ½")	Bucharest, Romania	21 Sep 1959
1.85m (6' 0 ¾")	Bucharest, Romania	6 Jun 1960
1.86m (6' 1 ¼")	Bucharest, Romania	10 Jul 1960
1.87m (6' 1 ½")	Bucharest, Romania	15 Apr 1961
1.88m (6' 2")	Warsaw, Poland	18 Jun 1961
1.90m (6' 2 ¾")	Budapest, Hungary	8 Jul 1961
1.91m (6' 3 ¼")	Sofia, Bulgaria	16 Jul 1961

Iolanda Balas was the high jump supremo in the late 1950s and early 1960s. Few athletes have so effortlessly dominated an event for so long, in any discipline. From 1957 through 1966 she won 140 competitions in succession. Her career included 14 world records, two Olympic gold medals (1960 and 1964), and two European Championships titles (1958 and 1962).

Balas was of Hungarian extraction but born in Romania. A tall

Iolanda Balas, Romania (high jump)—a decade of supremacy.

athlete standing 185 centimeters (6' 0 ¾"), she had a modified scissors style during an era when most of her contemporaries had switched over to the straddle. She was helped in her technique by her long legs. She started young and won the first of 16 Romanian titles at age 14. Six years later she achieved her first world record when she jumped 1.75 meters in Bucharest in July 1956. She traveled to Melbourne for the Olympics but had a disappointing Games and finished fifth. Mildred McDaniel (USA) kept going higher, eventually setting a new world record of 1.76 meters.

That was her last setback for a very long time. From then on, it was victory after victory, record after record. She was the first woman to jump six feet and remained way beyond her opposition. At the Rome Olympics she won by 14 centimeters (5 ½"). At the Tokyo Games she won by 10 centimeters (3 ¾"). That defeat at the 1956 Melbourne Olympics was to be her last until June 1967, when she was defeated by East Germany's Dagmar Melzer amid great excitement. It was the end of an era. Shortly after that defeat, she retired and married her coach, Ion Soter.

Mildred McDaniel   (United States, b. 1933)

1.76m (5' 9 ¼")   **Melbourne, Australia**   **1 Dec 1956**

Mildred "Babe" McDaniel was somewhat of a surprise winner at the 1956 Melbourne Olympics, but it was not appreciated that she was in top form just before the Games. She had been U.S. champion three times (1953, 1955, and 1956). In addition, she had won the 1955 Pan-American Games in Mexico City with 1.68 meters (5' 6"). In that year she had raised the U.S. record twice.

McDaniel had actually beaten the world record five weeks prior to the Melbourne Olympics with 5' 9 ½" (1.765 meters), but this took place in an exhibition and was not acceptable for official world records. At the Melbourne Games she was a class above the rest of the field, which included two world record holders (Hopkins and Balas). She won by nine centimeters and added one centimeter to the world record. Having won an Olympic gold medal with a world record, she retired.

Mildred McDaniel, United States (high jump), jumping at the Melbourne Olympics, where she won and set a world record.

Chen Feng-Jung   (China, b. 1937)

1.77m (5' 9 ¾")   **Beijing, China**   **17 Nov 1957**

Chen Feng-Jung was the first Chinese athlete to set a world record in track and field. This was at the Chinese National Championships in Beijing. At the world record height of 1.77 meters (5' 9 ¾"), she was successful on her second attempt. These jumps were achieved with a built-up shoe, similar to the one that Yuriy Stepanov (USSR) wore in his high-jump world record of 1957. The IAAF banned this type of shoe in 1958.

China did not participate in the Olympics until 1988, so Chen had a restricted international career.

Chen Feng-Jung, China (high jump), China's first world record holder in track and field.

Ilona Gusenbauer (Austria, b. 1947)

1.92m (6' 3 ½")   **Vienna, Austria**   **4 Sep 1971**

After the long reign of Iolanda Balas, there was much speculation about how long her last world record (1961) would survive and who would break it. The record lasted 10 years and was finally broken by Ilona Gusenbauer of Austria. Born to a Hungarian father and a German mother, she began track and field at age 18. She used the straddle, and at age 23, she broke Balas's long-standing record by one centimeter amid scenes of great excitement in Vienna in September 1971.

Gusenbauer had finished eighth at the 1968 Mexico City Olympics and seventh in the 1969 European Championships. She had her major career win at the 1971 European Championships, with 1.87 meters (6' 1 ½"), two weeks before her world record. At the 1972 Olympics she finished third behind winner Ulrike Meyfarth (West Germany), who won with 1.92 meters (6' 3 ½") to equal the world record. Yordanka Blagoyeva of Bulgaria and Gusenbauer tied at 1.88 meters (6' 2"), but the Bulgarian athlete was given the silver medal on the count-back rule. Because of knee injuries, Gusenbauer retired shortly after the Munich Games.

Ulrike Meyfarth (West Germany, b. 1956)

1.92m (6' 3 ½")   **Munich, West Germany**   **4 Sep 1972**
2.02m (6' 7 ½")   **Athens, Greece**   **8 Sep 1982**
2.03m (6' 8")   **London, England**   **21 Aug 1983**

No athlete has ever had a more Cinderella-like entry into the world of athletics than 16-year-old Ulrike Meyfarth. She had just squeezed into the third spot on the West German team for the Munich Olympics. Meyfarth jumped seven centimeters above her previous personal best to win the gold medal and equal the world record (1.92 meters). She was the youngest female individual track and field champion to win an Olympic gold medal, the first female flopper to set a world record, and the first female flopper to win an Olympic gold medal.

Such a fairy-tale debut resulted in her becoming a national celebrity overnight. Under the spotlight of relentless media publicity, her career had its share of ups and downs in the next few years. Two years later at the European Championships she came in seventh. At the Montreal Olympics she couldn't even make the final. She came in fifth at the 1978 European Championships in Prague, while in 1980 she missed the Olympics because West Germany joined the United States in boycotting the Moscow Games.

After 10 years, however, her career revived spectacularly. At the 1982 European Championships in Athens she not only won by five centimeters. but set a new world record of 2.02 meters. The next year she had an epic duel in London with new Soviet star Tamara Bykova. Both athletes jumped even higher, 2.03 meters (6' 8"). Meyfarth was given first place because she went over the new record height on her first attempt, whereas Bykova went over on her second.

Ulrike Meyfarth, West Germany (high jump), Olympic gold medalist in 1972 and 1984.

Finally, Meyfarth ended her career at the Los Angeles Olympics with another gold medal. She jumped 2.02 meters (6' 7 ½"), an Olympic record, on her first try. Thus she won Olympic gold medals 12 years apart. She retired in 1985 to become a fashion model.

Yordanka Blagoyeva   (Bulgaria, b. 1947)

1.94m (6' 4 ¼")   **Zagreb, Yugoslavia**   **24 Sep 1972**

Yordanka Blagoyeva almost shared Ulrike Meyfarth's glory at the 1972 Munich Olympics. The West German girl had cleared 1.90 meters (6' 2 ¾"), and the Bulgarian appeared to have cleared it on her third attempt. She was already putting her tracksuit back on when the bar fell off. The judges strictly adhered to the rule book and called it a miss. In fairness, Meyfarth then cleared 1.92 meters (6' 3 ½").

Only 20 days later Blagoyeva took the world record in her own right. This was at an invitational high jump during a men's competition between Yugoslavia and Spain. A straddle jumper, she cleared 1.91 meters (6' 3 ¼") on her third attempt, and then 1.94 meters (6' 4 ¼") on her second attempt.

At the 1976 Olympics, Rosemarie Ackermann won with 1.93 meters (6' 4"). Blagoyeva jumped 1.91 meters (6' 3 ¼"), the same height as Sara Simeoni, but the Italian had fewer misses and took the silver medal.

Blagoyeva had won her first Bulgarian title in 1965, at age 18. She was not a particularly tall athlete for a modern high jumper, standing 174 centimeters (5' 8"). She later related that in between her jumps in competitions, to keep herself relaxed, she daydreamed of cooking.

Rosemarie Ackermann   (East Germany, b. 1952)

1.94m (6' 4 ¼")	Berlin, East Germany	24 Aug 1974
1.95m (6' 4 ¾")	Rome, Italy	8 Sep 1974
1.96m (6' 5")	Dresden, East Germany	8 May 1976
1.96m (6' 5")	Dresden, East Germany	3 Jul 1977
1.97m (6' 5 ½")	Helsinki, Finland	14 Aug 1977
1.97m (6' 5 ½")	Berlin, West Germany	26 Aug 1977
2.00m (6' 6 ¾")	Berlin, West Germany	26 Aug 1977

Rosemarie Ackermann was sent by her mother to ballet school, but she grew too tall (176 centimeters, 5' 9 ¼") and switched to track and field. She was the last great straddler and has many claims to fame: European champion in 1974, Olympic champion in 1976, seven world records to her name, and the first woman to jump 2.00 meters.

Rosemarie Ackermann, East Germany (high jump), the first woman over two meters.

She had an impeccable straddle style, partly because East German coaches were reluctant to switch over to the flop. She showed that she could maintain nerves of ice in competition at the 1974 European Championships in Rome, where the other major competitor was Italian Sara Simeoni. Whenever Ackermann prepared to jump, some Italian fans hooted and taunted her. But she maintained her composure despite this behavior and won with a new world record (1.95 meters).

She had made the final of the 1972 Munich Olympics, finishing seventh with 1.85 meters (6' 0 ¾"). At the 1976 Montreal Olympics she defeated Simeoni, 1.93 meters (6' 4") to 1.91 meters (6' 3 ¼"). She won 8 out of the 13 times she clashed with Simeoni.

Perhaps her greatest moment came in 1977 at an international meet in Berlin. She had already equaled the world record (1.97 meters). She had the bar moved up to the magic 2.00-meter height. On her first try she was over, and the crowd went wild with emotion.

After such a triumph, her later career results slipped a little. She came in second to Simeoni at the 1978 European Championships, 2.01 meters (6' 7") to 1.99 meters (6' 6 ¼"). At the Moscow Olympics in 1980 she failed to clear 1.94 meters (6' 4 ¼") to finish fourth, while Simeoni won with 1.97 meters (6' 5 ½"). After her last effort at 1.94 meters, Ackermann left the pit with a sad smile. She retired in 1981 to concentrate on her studies in economics.

Sara Simeoni   (Italy, b. 1953)

2.01m (6' 7")	Brescia, Italy	4 Aug 1978
2.01m (6' 7")	Prague, Czechoslovakia	31 Aug 1978

Sara Simeoni was the great rival of Rosemarie Ackermann, and they had a series of absorbing duels in the 1970s. After Ackermann retired, the Italian then had further memorable clashes with a resurgent Ulrike Meyfarth in the early 1980s. During her long career,

Simeoni was European champion (1978), Olympic champion (1980), world record holder twice, Italian champion 13 times, the second woman over two meters, and the darling of all Italy.

Like Ackermann, Simeoni was directed toward ballet by her mother but grew too tall, eventually reaching 176 centimeters (5' 9 ¼"). So she too moved to high jumping and competed until 1986. She later claimed that listening to classical music before an event helped her concentration.

One of her better seasons was 1978, when she set two world records (2.01 meters twice) and was European champion. In addition to her 1980 Olympic gold medal, she also earned two silver medals: in 1976 behind Rosemary Ackermann and in 1984 behind Ulrike Meyfarth.

During much of the latter part of her career, she was plagued by tendinitis, which forced her to restrict her number of competitions. She married her coach, Ermino Azzaro, a former high jumper himself, and has since demonstrated talent as an artist.

Sara Simeoni, Italy (high jump), receiving her gold medal at the Moscow Olympics.

Tamara Bykova   (Soviet Union, b. 1958)

2.03m (6' 8")	London, England	21 Aug 1983
2.04m (6' 8 ¼")	Pisa, Italy	25 Aug 1983
2.05m (6' 8 ¾")	Kiev, USSR	22 Jun 1984

Tamara Bykova, Soviet Union (high jump).

Tamara Bykova was born in Rostov-on-Don, a large industrial city in the south of Russia. Her father was a road construction worker and her mother a cook. She was the third woman to jump over two meters and used the flop technique. A student in sports journalism, she was another enthusiast of classical ballet who grew too tall (179 centimeters, 5' 10 ½").

Her world records came in 1983 and 1984, her best years. She and Ulrike Meyfarth both reached 2.03 meters (6' 8") in an epic duel in London. This added one centimeter to the world record. Four days later in Pisa, Bykova added one more centimeter to the record. Finally, in Kiev in 1984 she went over 2.05 meters (6' 8 ¾") at her second try. This record was broken four weeks later by Bulgaria's Lyudmila Andonova. Both Andonova and Bykova were excluded from the Los Angeles Games by the communist boycott.

In addition to her world records, Bykova's other career highlights include second place at the 1982 European Championships, gold at the 1983 World Championships, silver at the 1987 World Championships, and a bronze medal at the 1988 Seoul Olympics.

One hiccup in her career came after her second place at the 1990 Goodwill Games: She tested positive for ephedrine and was given a three-month suspension.

Lyudmila Andonova   (Bulgaria, b. 1960)

2.07m (6' 9 ½")   Berlin, East Germany   20 Jul 1984

Lyudmila Andonova was born in the same city as Bykova, Rostov-on-Don. Her Bulgarian father was working in the Soviet Union at the time and married a local girl. After Lyudmila's birth the family moved back to Bulgaria. Andonova jumped 2.07 meters two weeks before the Los Angeles Olympics. This was eight centimeters above her previous best and two centimeters above the existing world record.

She had tied for sixth in the high jump at the 1982 European Championships in Athens, jumping 1.91 meters (6' 3 ¼"). The following year, she gave birth to a daughter. Then came 1984 and her world record. Unfortunately, she missed the Los Angeles Olympics because of the communist boycott. In November 1985 she was suspended following a positive drug test for amphetamines.

At the Seoul Olympics, Andonova finished fifth with 1.93 meters (6' 4"). She is married to Atanas Antonov, who set the Bulgarian record for the decathlon in 1981.

Stefka Kostadinova   (Bulgaria, b. 1965)

2.07m (6' 9 ½")   Sofia, Bulgaria   25 May 1986
2.08m (6' 9 ¾")   Sofia, Bulgaria   31 May 1986
2.09m (6' 10 ¼")   Rome, Italy   30 Aug 1987

Stefka Kostadinova had already cleared 2.00 meters at age 19 but, like most of the communist bloc athletes, was boycotted out of the Los Angeles Games. She emerged as a champion when she went through 1985 undefeated. The next year was even better: She won the European Championships (2.00 meters) and broke the world record twice (2.07 and 2.08 meters).

In 1987 Kostadinova improved the world record yet again; at the World Championships in Rome she jumped 2.09 meters (6' 10 ¼"). In the years from 1985 to 1988 she seemed invincible, so it was a major shock when she didn't win the gold medal at the 1988 Olympics. Both she and Louise Ritter (USA) cleared 2.01 (6' 7"), but nei-

Stefka Kostadinova, Bulgaria, current world record holder in the high jump for a decade.

ther could manage 2.03 meters (6' 8"). A jump-off was ordered, and the American cleared 2.03 meters, but Kostadinova failed.

In 1989 Kostadinova married her coach, Nikolai Petrov. However, the next few years were disappointing for Kostadinova, as she was plagued by injuries: a knee injury in 1989 and a broken foot bone on her return in 1990. At the Barcelona Olympics she was fourth with 1.94 meters (6' 4 ¼"), 15 centimeters below her world record. At the World Championships, she failed to clear the qualifying standard of 1.93 meters (6' 4"). The following year, she was on maternity leave and gave birth to a son in January 1995. Nonetheless, she surprised everybody by winning the 1995 World Championships in August.

Finally, in 1996, she claimed that elusive Olympic gold medal in Atlanta. In a tense struggle with Greece's Niki Bakogianni, Kostadinova won 2.05m (6' 8 ¾") to 2.03m (6' 8").

Conclusions

The women's world high jump record of 2.09 meters has been static since 1987. The men's world record has also been quiet in recent years. This suggests that perhaps both sexes have jumped about as high as they can go.

Perhaps another high-jump style awaits us. In fact, there seems no good reason why the IAAF shouldn't recognize official world records in all the different styles: western roll, scissors, straddle, and flop, as suggested by sports commentator Alphonse Juillard.

Five All-Time Highest: Women's High Jump

Stefka Kostadinova (BUL)	2.09m (6' 10 ¼")	1987
Lyudmila Andonova (BUL)	2.07 m (6' 9 ½")	1984
Tamara Bykova (USSR)	2.05m (6' 8 ¾")	1984
Heike Henkel (GER)	2.05m (6' 8 ¾")	1991
Inga Babakova (UKR)	2.05m (6' 8 ¾")	1995
Prediction	*2.11m (6' 11")*	*2015*

Top Three: Women's High Jump

GOLD MEDAL:	Iolanda Balas (ROM)
SILVER MEDAL:	Stefka Kostadinova (BUL)
BRONZE MEDAL:	Rosemarie Ackermann (GDR)

Nineteen women from 11 countries have set or equaled the world long jump record 31 times. Nine of them have also been Olympic champions: Williams, Krzensinska, Rand, Viscopoleanu, Rosendahl, Voigt, Cusmir, Joyner-Kersee, and Drechsler. Three of them have set world records at the Games: Krzensinska, Rand, and Viscopoleanu.

The record has moved from 5.98 meters (19' 7 ½") in 1928 to 7.52 meters (24' 8 ¼") in 1988, an improvement of 1.54 meters (5' 0 ¾") in 60 years. However, the current record has been static for almost a decade: Since the first postwar record was set in 1954, this is the longest that the record has remained unbroken.

Women's World Records for Long Jump

Record distance	Record holder	Location	Date
5.98m (19' 7 ½")	Kinue Hitomi (JPN)	Osaka, Japan	20 May 1928
6.12m (20' 1")	Christel Schulz (GER)	Berlin, Germany	30 Jul 1939
6.25m (20' 6")	Fanny Blankers-Koen (HOL)	Leiden, Netherlands	19 Sep 1943
6.28m (20' 7 ¼")	Yvette Williams (NZ)	Gisborne, New Zealand	20 Feb 1954
6.28m (20' 7 ¼")	Galina Vinogradova (USSR)	Moscow, USSR	11 Sep 1955
6.31m (20' 8 ½")	Galina Vinogradova (USSR)	Tbilisi, USSR	18 Nov 1955
6.35m (20' 10")	Elzbieta Krzensinska (POL)	Budapest, Hungary	20 Aug 1956
6.35m (20' 10")	Elzbieta Krzensinska (POL)	Melbourne, Australia	27 Nov 1956
6.40m (21' 0")	Hildrun Claus (GDR)	Erfurt, East Germany	7 Aug 1960
6.42m (21' 0 ¾")	Hildrun Claus (GDR)	Berlin, East Germany	23 Jun 1961
6.48m (21' 3 ¼")	Tatyana Shchelkanova (USSR)	Moscow, USSR	16 Jul 1961
6.53m (21' 5 ¼")	Tatyana Shchelkanova (USSR)	Leipzig, East Germany	10 Jun 1962
6.70m (21' 11 ¾")	Tatyana Shchelkanova (USSR)	Moscow, USSR	4 Jul 1964
6.76m (22' 2 ¼")	Mary Rand (GBR)	Tokyo, Japan	14 Oct 1964
6.82m (22' 4 ½")	Viorica Viscopoleanu (ROM)	Mexico City, Mexico	14 Oct 1968
6.84m (22' 5 ¼")	Heide Rosendahl (FRG)	Turin, Italy	3 Sep 1970
6.92m (22' 8 ½")	Angela Voigt (GDR)	Dresden, East Germany	9 May 1976
6.99m (22' 11 ¼")	Sigrun Siegl (GDR)	Dresden, East Germany	19 May 1976
7.07m (23' 2 ½")	Vilma Bardauskiene (USSR)	Kishinyev, USSR	18 Aug 1978
7.09m (23' 3 ¼")	Vilma Bardauskiene (USSR)	Prague, Czechoslovakia	29 Aug 1978
7.15m (23' 5 ½")	Anisoara Cusmir (ROM)	Bucharest, Romania	1 Aug 1982
7.20m (23' 7 ½")	Valeria Ionescu (ROM)	Bucharest, Romania	1 Aug 1982
7.21m (23' 8")	Anisoara Cusmir (ROM)	Bucharest, Romania	15 May 1983
7.27m (23' 10 ¼")	Anisoara Cusmir (ROM)	Bucharest, Romania	4 Jun 1983
7.43m (24' 4 ½")	Anisoara Cusmir (ROM)	Bucharest, Romania	4 Jun 1983
7.44m (24' 5")	Heike Drechsler (GDR)	Berlin, East Germany	22 Sep 1985
7.45m (24' 5 ½")	Heike Drechsler (GDR)	Tallinn, USSR	21 Jun 1986
7.45m (24' 5 ½")	Heike Drechsler (GDR)	Dresden, East Germany	3 Jul 1986
7.45m (24' 5 ½")	Jackie Joyner-Kersee (USA)	Indianapolis, USA	13 Aug 1987
7.45m (24' 5 ½")	Galina Chistyakova (USSR)	Leningrad, USSR	11 Jun 1988
7.52m (24' 8 ¼")	Galina Chistyakova (USSR)	Leningrad, USSR	11 Jun 1988

Kinue Hitomi   (Japan, 1908–1931)

5.98m (19' 7 ½")   **Osaka, Japan**   **20 May 1928**

Kinue Hitomi of Japan was the first female Asian athlete to set a world record and to win an Olympic medal. Her world record in the long jump was set in Osaka, Japan, at the 1928 Japanese championships, where she jumped 5.98 meters (19' 7 ½"). A versatile competitor, at age 18 she had participated in the second Women's World Games in Gothenburg in 1926 in the long jump, discus, and sprints.

At the 1928 Olympics, there was no long jump, her favorite event, on the program. So she opted for the 800m. In this event, of which she had little familiarity, she came in a close second to the experienced 800m runner, Lina Radke-Batschauer of Germany.

In Japan, the role of women at that time was restricted, and her achievements established her as a role model and pioneer. Sadly, she died of tuberculosis at the age of 23.

Kinue Hitomi, Japan, an early pioneer in women's athletics. World long-jump record holder.

Christel Schulz   (Germany, b. 1921)

6.12m (20' 1")   **Berlin, Germany**   **30 Jul 1939**

Christel Schulz was the first woman to jump over both six meters and 20 feet. She did this in Berlin, five weeks before World War II broke out.

Schulz won the German long jump championship three times: 1939, 1941, and 1942. She also won the German 100m championship in 1942 and 1943 and was third in the high jump in 1942. The German athletic championships were not held in 1944 and 1945 because of changes in the war situation.

Fanny Blankers-Koen   (Netherlands, b. 1918)

6.25m (20' 6")   **Leiden, Netherlands**   **19 Sep 1943**

The long jump was yet another world record event for the multitalented Blankers-Koen, in addition to the 100m, 80m hurdles, high jump, and pentathlon. Her record was achieved in 1943, when the Netherlands was under German occupation. The meeting was described as taking place in "soft autumn weather" with "the wind at the disadvantage of the competitors." Her jump of 6.25 meters (20' 6") added 13 centimeters (5") to the world record of Christel Schulz.

At the European Championships and Olympic Games, Blankers-Koen chose several events in which to compete, but not the long jump, so her potential in this discipline was never fully realized.

Yvette Williams   (New Zealand, b. 1929)

6.28m (20' 7 ¼")   **Gisborne, New Zealand**   **20 Feb 1954**

Yvette Williams was initially more interested in the shot put than in the long jump. But in 1950 her long-jump results blossomed. There was no shot put at the 1950 Commonwealth Games, so she entered the long jump, which she duly won with 5.90 meters (19' 4 ¼").

She improved in the long jump to international level, although top competition within New Zealand was clearly limited. At the Olympics she won against the much fancied Soviet Aleksandra Chudina, winning 6.24 meters (20' 5 ¾") to 6.14 meters (20' 1 ¾"). She also went on to place sixth in the shot put.

Two years later she knew she was jumping very close to the world record, and so she made a determined attempt upon it at a meeting at Gisborne. Everything went as planned, and she added three centimeters to the record, with 6.28 meters (20' 7 ¼").

At the 1954 Commonwealth Games in Vancouver, Canada, she won the shot put, jav-

Yvette Williams, New Zealand (long jump), 1952 Olympic champion.

elin, and long jump, a remarkable triple. She married later that year, raised four children (three boys and a girl), and has had a long career as a teacher of physical education. Her brother Roy was the decathlon champion at the 1966 Commonwealth Games in Jamaica.

Galina Vinogradova   (Soviet Union, b. 1932)

6.28m (20' 7 ¼")   **Moscow, USSR**   **11 Sep 1955**
6.31m (20' 8 ½")   **Tbilisi, USSR**   **18 Nov 1955**

Galina Vinogradova was a top sprinter and long jumper in the 1950s. She was the Soviet champion in the 100m in 1955 and 1956 and long-jump champion in 1955.

In 1955 she set two world records in the long jump. The first was in Moscow in the inaugural Great Britain vs. Soviet Union match. At this meet, she equaled Yvette Williams's mark of 6.28 meters. Two months later, she added three centimeters to the record at a national athletic meet in Tbilisi, Georgia.

She was fifth in the long jump at the 1954 European Championships. She traveled to Melbourne for the 1956 Olympics and competed in the 100m and the long jump. In the sprint she came in fifth in the semifinal. Because of injuries, she withdrew from the long jump.

Elzbieta Krzensinska (née Dunska)   (Poland, b. 1934)

6.35m (20' 10")   **Budapest, Hungary**   **20 Aug 1956**
6.35m (20' 10")   **Melbourne, Australia**   **27 Nov 1956**

Elzbieta Krzensinska competed at three Olympics. As Elzbieta Dunska, aged 17, she came in 12th at the Helsinki Olympics. She broke the world record three months before the 1956

Elzbieta Krzensinska, Poland (long jump), 1956 Olympic long-jump champion.

Olympics (6.35 meters) and in Melbourne equaled this distance on her second jump. This victory was Poland's only gold medal of the entire 1956 Olympic Games. All the Polish media emotionally sang their country's national anthem while the gold medalist wept happily on the dais.

In the 1960 Rome Olympics both Krzensinska and the new world record holder, Hildrun Claus of East Germany, were surprised by Soviet sprinter Vera Krepkina. The Soviet jumped 6.37 meters (20' 10 ¾"), the Pole 6.27 meters (20' 7"), and the German 6.21 meters (20' 4 ½").

In Poland Krzensinska was long-jump champion eight times and was 80m hurdles champion in 1957. With her pole vaulter husband, Andrzej, she had a long career as an athletic coach in the United States.

Hildrun Claus   (East Germany, b. 1939)

6.40m (21' 0")	Erfurt, East Germany	7 Aug 1960
6.42m (21' 0 ¾")	Berlin, East Germany	23 Jun 1961

Hildrun Claus was East German champion in the long jump seven times (1957-62 and 1964). Her first world record was set at the East German trials for the Rome Olympics. She leaped to 6.40 meters (21' 0") on her sixth and last jump. However, at the Rome Olympics she managed only 6.21 meters (20' 4 ½") to win the bronze medal. She and defending champion Elzbieta Krzensinska (6.27 meters, 20' 7") were both defeated by Soviet sprinter Vera Krepkina, who won with 6.37 meters (20' 10 ¾").

Claus's second world record was at an East Germany vs. Russian Republic athletic match, where she achieved 6.42 meters (21' 0

Hildrun Claus, East Germany (long jump).

¾"). At the 1962 European Championships, Claus was sixth, and at the Tokyo Olympics she came in seventh.

Tatyana Shchelkanova   (Soviet Union, b. 1937)

6.48m (21' 3 ¼")	Moscow, USSR	16 Jul 1961
6.53m (21' 5 ¼")	Leipzig, East Germany	10 Jun 1962
6.70m (21' 11 ¾")	Moscow, USSR	4 Jul 1964

Tatyana Shchelkanova was a television engineer and was the Soviet long-jump champion six times in a row (1961-66). She was also the winner of the pentathlon at the 1963 Soviet titles.

Shchelkanova set three world records in the early 1960s, adding a substantial total of 28 centimeters to Hildrun Claus's 1961 mark. She had won the 1962 European Championships with a leap of 6.36 meters (20' 10 ½"). At the Tokyo Games she was one of the favorites. But she had to watch her world record taken away from her as Britain's Mary Rand peaked to perfection to win with 6.76 meters (22' 2 ¼"). In second place was the new rising star from Poland, Irena Kirszenstein, aged 19, with 6.60 meters (21' 8"). Shchelkanova managed 6.42 meters (21' 0 ¾") for the bronze medal.

Mary Rand   (Great Britain, b. 1940)

| 6.76m (22' 2 ¼") | Tokyo, Japan | 14 Oct 1964 |

Mary Rand, Great Britain (long jump), 1964 Olympic champion.

Mary Rand represented England at the 1958 Commonwealth Games as Mary Bignal, coming in second in the long jump and fifth in the high jump. In 1959 she set a British long jump record and also had a hurdles win over the formidable Soviet athlete Irina Press.

She went to the 1960 Rome Olympics as the British press's favorite to win a medal in the long jump. In her Olympic baptism, she came in ninth. However, she did finish a creditable fourth in the 80m hurdles. Nonetheless, she was branded as a "failure" by the media.

She married rower Sidney Rand, whom she met on a blind date arranged by distance runner Gordon Pirie. Early in 1962, after a 24-hour labor, she gave birth to a daughter yet still came in third in the long jump at the European Championships a few months later.

At the Tokyo Olympics she put her memories of Rome behind her with a series of superb jumps. Her fourth jump broke the world record (6.76 meters, 22' 2 ¼"). In addition, she won a silver medal in the pentathlon behind the Soviet Union's Irina Press and earned a bronze medal in the 4 × 100m relay.

Mary Rand continued to make newspaper headlines when she subsequently separated from her husband and fled from England, heavily disguised, with U.S. decathlete Bill Toomey. They later married and trained together in the United States. She hoped for another Olympics but was struck down with injuries shortly before the 1968 Games began. She traveled to Mexico City as an observer and saw her world record beaten by six centimeters by Romanian Viorica Viscopoleanu. However, Bill Toomey won the gold medal in the decathlon. She later divorced Toomey and now lives in California.

Viorica Viscopoleanu   (Romania, b. 1939)

6.82m (22' 4 ½")   **Mexico City, Mexico**   **14 Oct 1968**

Viorica Viscopoleanu of Romania had competed at the Tokyo Olympics and finished fifth in the long jump with 6.35 meters (20' 10"); the gold medal was won by Mary Rand in a new world record of 6.76 meters (22' 2 ¼").

Viscopoleanu returned to the Olympics in 1968 and, exactly four years to the day, set a new world record of 6.82 meters (22' 4 ½"). She won by 14 centimeters (5 ½"). The altitude of Mexico City undoubtedly helped, as the world record was broken in both male and female long jumps and the triple jump. She set her world record on the first jump, as did Bob Beamon. She had improved on her pre-Olympic best by 23 centimeters (9").

She had one more Olympics and managed 6.48 meters (21' 3 ¼") in 1972 at Munich, to finish seventh. At the European Championships she was sixth in 1966, second in 1968, and sixth in 1971.

Heide Rosendahl   (West Germany, b. 1947)

6.84m (22' 5 ¼")   **Turin, Italy**   **3 Sep 1970**

Heidi Rosendahl was a champion at both the long jump and the pentathlon. Her father had been the German discus champion in 1948, 1951, and 1953. At age 19, Heide came in second in the pentathlon at the 1966 European Championships. She was one of the favorites for this event at the 1968 Olympics but injured herself prior to the competition.

By 1970, she was threatening the long-jump world record, having jumped 6.80 meters (22' 3 ¾") at the European Cup. Shortly after, in September 1970, she jumped 6.84 meters (22' 5 ¼") at the World University Games (Universiade) in Turin on her last jump, adding two centimeters to the world record.

At the 1971 European Championships she won the pentathlon after a close contest with East Germany's Burglinde Pollak.

Heide Rosendahl, West Germany (long jump), 1972 Olympic long-jump champion.

Her final major competition was at the 1972 Munich Olympics, where she was under enormous pressure by the German media to succeed. She duly won the long jump with 6.78 meters (22' 3"). It was the narrowest of victories—one centimeter ahead of Bulgaria's Diana Yorgova. In the pentathlon she was beaten by a mere 10 points by Great Britain's Mary Peters.

Her ultimate moment of triumph came in the 4 × 100m relay. She took over the last leg of the relay, just ahead of East Germany's gold medal sprinter Renate Stecher. To almost universal surprise, she somehow held off the East German star to cross the line first in a world record time.

After retiring from athletics, Rosendahl married a basketball player from the United States; she has two sons.

Angela Voigt   (East Germany, b. 1951)

6.92m (22' 8 ½")   **Dresden, East Germany**   **9 May 1976**

Angela Voigt was East German long-jump champion in 1973, 1975-1976, and 1978-1979. She made an early impact by winning the European Cup in 1973 but subsequently finished fourth at the European Championships in 1974.

In the Olympic year of 1976 she first set a world record in Dresden in May, adding eight centimeters to the record as she jumped 6.92 meters (22' 8 ½"). This was at a club athletic meet. Then at Montreal, under suboptimal conditions, she won the competition on the first jump, with 6.72 meters (22' 0 ¾").

She gave birth to a son in 1977 yet still was able to come back and finish second at the European Championships in 1978 with 6.79 meters (22' 3 ½").

Angela Voigt, East Germany (long jump),
1976 Olympic champion.

Sigrun Siegl (née Thon)   (East Germany, b. 1954)

6.99m (22' 11 ¼")   **Dresden, East Germany**   **19 May 1976**

Angela Voigt's record lasted only 10 days before it was improved seven centimeters by another East German athlete. Sigrun Siegl jumped to within one centimeter of the magic seven-meter mark in the same stadium on 19 May 1976.

As Sigrun Thon, she had come in second in the East German championships in the long jump in 1975 and won the pentathlon the same year.

After her long-jump world record, Siegl was one of the favorites at the Montreal Olympics. However, the final was held in wet conditions. Voigt managed to maintain her form better than Siegl and won with 6.72 meters (22' 0 ¾"). Siegl finished fourth with 6.59 meters (21' 7").

Siegl compensated by winning the pentathlon gold medal. Actually, Siegl and coun-trywoman

Sigrun Siegl, (long-jump world record holder) on the victory podium after winning the pentathlon at the 1976 Olympics. Second was Christine Laser, and third was Burglinde Pollak (pentathlon world record holder), *front*. All three are from East Germany.

Christine Laser both finished on exactly the same number of points, 4745. Because Siegl had scored higher points in more of the events, she was awarded the gold medal.

At the 1980 Moscow Olympics she finished fifth in the long jump with 6.87 meters (22' 6 ½").

Vilma Bardauskiene   (Soviet Union, b. 1953)

7.07m (23' 2 ½")	**Kishinyev, USSR**	**18 Aug 1978**
7.09m (23' 3 ¼")	**Prague, Czechoslovakia**	**29 Aug 1978**

Born in Lithuania, Vilma Bardauskiene, a geography student, was the first woman to leap over the seven-meter mark. Her career was plagued by injuries, so that she missed both the Montreal and Moscow Olympics.

In a meet early in 1978 she achieved 6.80 meters (22' 3 ¾") after taking off well before the official marker, so she knew she had a seven-meter jump within her. That jump finally arrived on 18 August 1978, at a "Day of Jumpers" at Kishinyev, close to Turkey. Three times that day she went over seven meters, hitting 7.07 meters twice, one with allowable wind assistance and one with excess wind.

She showed it was not a fluke by jumping another world record eleven days later. She leaped an extra two centimeters, to 7.09 meters (23' 3 ¼") in the qualifying rounds of the 1978 European Championships. In the final she won with 6.88 meters (22' 7").

Although world record holder and European champion, the one title she never won was the Soviet championship, where her best effort was third in 1977.

Anisoara Cusmir   (Romania, b. 1962)

7.15m (23' 5 ½")	**Bucharest, Romania**	**1 Aug 1982**
7.21m (23' 8")	**Bucharest, Romania**	**15 May 1983**
7.27m (23' 10 ¼")	**Bucharest, Romania**	**4 Jun 1983**
7.43m (24' 4 ½")	**Bucharest, Romania**	**4 Jun 1983**

The women's world record in the long jump made a quantum leap in the early 1980s, due to two Romanian women. At the 1982 Romanian championships in Bucharest, Anisoara Cusmir and Valeria Ionescu both broke the old record within five minutes of each other and added 11 centimeters to it. Cusmir jumped 7.15m on her fifth jump and Ionescu achieved 7.20m on her sixth. Their rivalry continued at the 1982 European Championships later that year; it was Ionescu 6.79 meters (22' 3 ½"), Cusmir 6.73 meters (22' 1").

In May and June 1983 it was Cusmir who improved the record three times, finishing with 7.43 meters (24' 4 ½") at an international athletic meet in Bucharest. Her last record was a 16-centimeter improvement over her previous record.

Despite these performances, Cusmir was surprisingly upset later in the season at the major event: the

Anisoara Cusmir, Romania (long jump), 1984 Olympic champion.

1983 World Championships. Young Heike Daute, later to be known as Heike Drechsler, provided a stunning upset with a 7.27-meter (23' 10 ¼") jump. Cusmir was second with 7.15 meters (23' 5 ½").

At the 1984 Los Angeles Olympics, Romania and Yugoslavia were the only two Eastern European countries to attend because of the Soviet boycott. Anisoara Cusmir comfortably won the gold medal with 6.96 meters (22' 10") to Ionescu's 6.81 meters (22' 4 ¼").

Valeria Ionescu   (Romania, b. 1960)

| 7.20m (23' 7 ½") | Bucharest, Romania | 1 Aug 1982 |

Valeria Ionescu, Romania (long jump).

Valeria "Vali" Ionescu was the other half of the Romanian duo who transformed the long jump world record in the early 1980s. She was Romanian champion from 1980 to 1983.

As detailed in the preceding profile on Anisoara Cusmir, the two Romanians set world records at the 1982 Romanian championships five minutes apart: Cusmir on her fifth jump (7.15 meters, 23' 5 ½"), and Ionescu on her sixth (7.20 meters, 23' 7 ½"). Ionescu's last jump gave her the world record and the championship.

Ionescu completed a successful season by winning the European Championships. She won with 6.79 meters (22' 3 ¼"), ahead of Cusmir and the Soviet Yelena Ivanova, who both finished with 6.73 meters (22' 1").

The next year, both Romanian athletes were upstaged at the 1983 World Championships by young Heike Daute. Ionescu fouled several jumps, finally finishing in ninth. At the Los Angeles Olympics, Cusmir won with 6.96 meters (22' 10"), and Ionescu finished second with 6.81 meters (22' 4 ¼").

Heike Drechsler (née Daute)   (East Germany, b. 1964)

7.44m (24' 5")	Berlin, East Germany	22 Sep 1985
7.45m (24' 5 ½")	Tallinn, USSR	21 Jun 1986
7.45m (24' 5 ½")	Dresden, East Germany	3 Jul 1986

Heike Drechsler originally trained as an optical technician at the Carl Zeiss complex. She showed her talent at age 17 when she came in fourth in the long jump at the 1982 European Championships. The following year she did even better. At the 1983 World Championships she defeated world record holder Anisoara Cusmir, 7.27 meters (23' 10 ¼") to 7.15 meters (23' 5 ½"). It was the beginning of 12 years at the top.

She missed the 1984 Olympics because of the communist boycott but in 1985 took over the world record in Berlin by adding one centimeter to Cusmir's record. In 1986 Drechsler leapt to 7.45 meters twice and then won an impressive double at the European Championships: She won both the long jump and the 200m, the latter in world record time.

Over the next few years, she ran into Jackie Joyner-Kersee in her prime. "JJK" won the long jump at the 1987 World Championships, the 1988 Olympics, and the 1991 World Championships, with Drechsler second on each occasion. Finally, in 1992 Drechsler reversed the trend. She had given up sprinting to concentrate on her long jump, and the tactics paid off. At the Olympics in Barcelona, she won the gold medal with 7.14 meters (23' 5 ¼"), defeating Soviet athlete Inessa Kravets (7.12 meters, 23' 4 ½") and JJK (7.07 meters, 23' 2 ½"). Her success continued into 1993 with a World Championships win, 10 years after her first victory in this event. The following year she won the European Championships for the third time, a rare achievement. She had a mixed year in 1995, complicated by marital problems, and for the first time at a major competition she finished well down (ninth) at the World Championships. In 1996 injuries kept her out of the Atlanta Olympics.

Jackie Joyner-Kersee   (United States, b. 1962)

7.45m (24' 5 ½")	Indianapolis, USA	13 Aug 1987

Jackie Joyner-Kersee ("JJK") achieved every success at two disciplines—the long jump and the heptathlon—in a career lasting well over a decade. Further career details are given in the chapter on the heptathlon.

She grew up in a rough area of East St. Louis, Illinois, and attended UCLA, where she became an All-American at basketball. Her brother Al won the triple jump at the 1984 Los Angeles Olympics, and she came very close to making it a brother and sister double gold medal performance. She came in second in the heptathlon by a mere five points. Two years later, she married her coach, Bobby Kersee.

From that Olympic defeat, she went on to a series of victories over the next 10 years, usually combining and winning both the long jump and the heptathlon. In the long jump she won the 1987 World Championships, the 1987 Pan-American Games, the 1988 Olympics, and the 1991 World Championships. It was her sixth and last jump at the 1987 Pan-Am Games that tied the world record, 7.45 meters (24' 5 ½").

Joyner-Kersee won the heptathlon gold medal at the 1992 Barcelona Olympics but was squeezed out of a gold medal in the long jump by long-standing rival, German Heike Drechsler. In a competition with reduced performances, Drechsler won with 7.14 meters (23' 5 ¼"), Inessa Kravets (USSR) came in second with 7.12 meters (23' 4 ½"), and JJK recorded 7.07 meters (23' 2 ½").

Joyner-Kersee actually improved her personal best in the long jump to 7.49 meters (24' 7") in 1994, but by that time the world record had moved on to 7.52 meters (24' 8 ¼").

At the 1996 Olympics she withdrew from the pentathlon after a severe hamstring injury in the hurdles. Six days later, despite the disablity, she claimed a bronze medal in the long jump on her last attempt.

Galina Chistyakova   (Soviet Union/Russia, b. 1962)

7.45m (24' 5 ½")	Leningrad, USSR	11 Jun 1988
7.52m (24' 8 ¼")	Leningrad, USSR	11 Jun 1988

Galina Chistyakova was born in the Ukraine and subsequently competed for Russia after the breakup of the Soviet Union. In 1988 she became the first woman to beat the 7.50-meter barrier.

She achieved her two world records at one meet in Leningrad in 1988, the Znamenskiy Memorial. Her fourth jump equaled the world record (7.45 meters). Her sixth jump went out to 7.52 meters. Despite these records, Chistyakova never quite won a gold medal at the top international championships. Her record was as follows:

1986 European Championships: second
1987 World Championships: fifth
1988 Seoul Olympics: third

If she did not win at the major international games, she had a number of victories at the second level of international competition. This included wins at the World Cup in 1989, the European Cup in 1985 and 1989, the World Indoors in 1989, the Goodwill Games in 1986, and the European Indoors in 1985 and 1989.

After a knee injury in 1990 she focused more on the newly emerging triple jump. She was Soviet triple-jump champion in 1992 and set several world bests in this event before it achieved official world record status. She is married to triple jumper Alexander Beskrovniy, who was fifth at the European Cup in 1982.

Galina Chistyakova, Soviet Union (long jump), current world record holder since 1988.

Conclusions

The world record for the women's long jump, much like the high jump, seems to be approaching its ultimate limits. The current record of 7.52 meters was set in 1988. Although further world records are to be expected, it is hard to imagine much significant improvement. However, that sort of statement has been made prematurely before. Seven meters was thought to be a major barrier until it was beaten in 1978. Now the world record is half a meter longer.

Nonetheless, as mentioned in the chapter on the men's long jump, there is no clever new long-jumping style on the horizon, nor some brilliant technological innovation to help the long jumper. Possibly, new runway surfaces may lend extra compliance for improved performances.

Five All-Time Best: Women's Long Jump			(Wind)
Galina Chistyakova (USSR)	7.52m (24' 8 ¼")	1988	+1.4
Jackie Joyner-Kersee (USA)	7.49m (24' 7")	1994	+1.3
Heike Drechsler (GDR)	7.48m (24' 6 ½")	1988	+1.2
Anisoara Cusmir (ROM)	7.43m (24' 4 ½")	1983	+1.4
Yelena Byelevskaya (USSR)	7.39m (24' 3")	1987	+0.5
Prediction	*7.62m (25' 0")*	*2015*	

Top Three: Women's Long Jump

GOLD MEDAL:	Heike Drechsler (GER)
SILVER MEDAL:	Anisoara Cusmir (ROM)
BRONZE MEDAL:	Jackie Joyner-Kersee (USA)

The triple jump for women has only recently achieved legitimate world record status and has only a short history in the major championships.

The triple jump was given world record status in 1990. It is often the case that improvement occurs rapidly in the early years of a young event like this one. However, the record took a major leap forward in 1995, when Inessa Kravets (Ukraine) added 41 centimeters to the record at the World Championships, with 15.50 meters (50' 10 ¼"). It is hard to imagine this record being challenged in the near future.

Women's World Records for Triple Jump

Record distance	Record holder	Location	Date
14.54m (47' 8 ½")	Li Huirong (CHN)	Sapporo, Japan	25 Aug 1990
14.95m (49' 0 ¾")	Inessa Kravets (USSR)	Moscow, USSR	10 Jun 1991
14.97m (49' 1 ½")	Yolanda Chen (RUS)	Moscow, Russia	18 Jun 1993
15.09m (49' 6 ¼")	Ana Biryukova (RUS)	Stuttgart, Germany	21 Aug 1993
15.50m (50' 10 ¼")	Inessa Kravets (UKR)	Gothenburg, Sweden	10 Aug 1995

Li Huirong (China, b. 1966)

14.54m (47' 8 1/2")   **Sapporo, Japan**   **25 Aug 1990**

Li Huirong was a student at the Beijing Institute of Physical Education and was first in the World Cup in Havana in 1992. At a meet in Japan in August 1990, the Chuhei Nambu Memorial, Li Huirong achieved 14.54 meters (47' 8 ½") on her sixth jump.

Inessa Kravets (Soviet Union/Ukraine, b. 1966)

14.95m (49' 0 ¾")   **Moscow, USSR**   **10 Jun 1991**
15.50m (50' 10 ¼")   **Gothenburg, Sweden**   **10 Aug 1995**

Inessa Kravets was born in the industrial city of Dnepropetrovsk, in the Ukraine. Like many of these early triple jumpers, she excels at both the long and triple jumps. At the long jump she had been 10th at the 1988 Olympics and second at the 1992 Olympics. At the triple jump she was third at the 1994 European Championships. However, her career had a hiccup in 1993, when she had a three-month ban after testing positive for stimulants.

Her first triple jump world record was set in Moscow in June 1991, when she added 41 centimeters to the record, jumping 14.95 meters (49' 0 ¾"). However, four years later she astonished the athletic world by another world record at the 1995 World Championships. Earlier at this meet, Jonathan Edwards had become the first athlete to triple jump over 18 meters. Kravets kept a picture of Edwards in her pocket for inspiration. It seemed to work—in round three, she leaped all the way to 15.50 meters (50' 10 ¼"). This also added a remarkable 41 centimeters to the previous world record.

Inessa Kravets won the inaugural women's Olympic triple jump in Atlanta with a leap of 15.33 meters (50' 3 ½").

Yolanda Chen   (Soviet Union/Russia, b. 1961)

14.97m (49' 1 ½")   **Moscow, Russia**   **18 Jun 1993**

Yolanda Chen had a long career as a long jumper and a triple jumper before she attained world record status. She was fourth in the 1981 Soviet long jump final, yet her world record in the triple jump did not come until 1993, which was her best triple-jump season. She won the Russian title and set a world record (14.97 meters, 49' 1 ½") in the event in June. However, at the World Championships eight weeks later she had to take second place as her compatriot Ana Biryukova won with a new world record. In 1994 Chen finished fourth at the European Championships with 14.48 meters (47' 6").

Ana Biryukova   (Soviet Union/Russia, b. 1967)

15.09m (49' 6 ¼")   **Stuttgart, Germany**   **21 Aug 1993**

Ana Biryukova also competed in the long jump early in her career. She was third at the 1989 Soviet long jump titles and second in 1990. She had a son, Aleksandr, in 1992. At the 1993 World Championships she achieved the first women's 15-meter triple jump with 15.09 meters (49' 6 ¼"). She went on to win the 1994 European Championships triple-jump title. At the Atlanta Olympics she failed in the qualifying rounds to progress to the final.

Six All-Time Best: Women's Triple Jump			(Wind)
Inessa Kravets (UKR)	15.50m (50' 10 ¼")	1995	+0.9
Iva Prandzheva (BUL)	15.18m (49' 9 ¾")	1995	+0.3
Ana Biryukova (RUS)	15.09m (49' 6 ¼")	1993	+0.5
Inna Lasovskaya (RUS)	15.08m (49' 5 ¾")	1996	+0.7
Sofiya Bozhanova (BUL)	14.98m (49' 1 ¾")	1994	+1.8
Sarka Kasparkova (CZH)	14.98m (49' 1 ¾")	1996	−0.6
Prediction	*16.10m (52' 10")*	*2015*	

Top Three: Women's Triple Jump

As this event is still in its infancy it seems inappropriate to designate the top three athletes. However, one has to acknowledge that the number one athlete in this discipline to date is Inessa Kravets (UKR).

The women's shot weighs 4 kilograms (8 pounds 13 ounces); the men's weighs 7.26 kilograms (16 pounds). Both are thrown from a circle seven feet (213.5 centimeters) in diameter.

The women's world record has moved up from 14.38 meters (47' 2 ¼") in 1934 to 22.63 meters (74' 3") in 1987. The shot put, like the discus, has been dominated by East European women. Germany's Gisela Mauermayer set the first record in 1934. Other record holders have come from the Soviet Union (seven), East Germany (three), Bulgaria (one), and Czechoslovakia (one).

Altogether, 13 athletes have set or equaled the world record 42 times. The Soviet Union has produced the four great throwers: Galina Zybina in the 1950s, Tamara Press in the 1960s, Nadezhda Chizhova in the late 1960s and early 1970s, and Natalya Lisovskaya in the 1980s. Zybina set the record eight times, Press six times, Chizhova nine times, and Lisovskaya three times.

The intimidating success of the East European women means that the event is not taken too seriously in other places in the world at the elite level. However, recently there has been new talent emerging from China and Cuba. The recent falloff in performances in the shot put is similar to that in the discus. Reasons given for this are much the same: more active drug detection programs and the collapse of the East European Bloc in the late 1980s.

Women's World Records for Shot Put

Record distance	Record holder	Location	Date
14.38m (47' 2 ¼")	Gisela Mauermayer (GER)	Warsaw, Poland	15 Jul 1934
14.59m (47' 10 ½")	Tatyana Sevryukova (USSR)	Moscow, USSR	4 Aug 1948
14.86m (48' 9")	Klavdiya Tochenova (USSR)	Tbilisi, USSR	30 Oct 1949
15.02m (49' 3 ½")	Anna Andreyeva (USSR)	Ploesti, Romania	9 Nov 1950
15.28m (50' 1 ¾")	Galina Zybina (USSR)	Helsinki, Finland	26 Jul 1952
15.37m (50' 5 ¼")	Galina Zybina (USSR)	Frunze, USSR	20 Sep 1952
15.42m (50' 7 ¼")	Galina Zybina (USSR)	Frunze, USSR	1 Oct 1952
16.20m (53' 1 ¾")	Galina Zybina (USSR)	Malmö, Sweden	9 Oct 1953
16.28m (53' 5")	Galina Zybina (USSR)	Kiev, USSR	14 Sep 1954
16.29m (53' 5 ½")	Galina Zybina (USSR)	Leningrad, USSR	5 Sep 1955
16.67m (54' 8 ¼")	Galina Zybina (USSR)	Tbilisi, USSR	15 Nov 1955
16.76m (55' 0")	Galina Zybina (USSR)	Tashkent, USSR	13 Oct 1956
17.25m (56' 7 ¼")	Tamara Press (USSR)	Nalchik, USSR	26 Apr 1959
17.42m (57' 2")	Tamara Press (USSR)	Moscow, USSR	16 Jul 1960
17.78m (58' 4")	Tamara Press (USSR)	Moscow, USSR	13 Aug 1960
18.55m (60' 10 ½")	Tamara Press (USSR)	Leipzig, East Germany	10 Jun 1962
18.55m (60' 10 ½")	Tamara Press (USSR)	Belgrade, Yugoslavia	12 Sep 1962
18.59m (61' 0")	Tamara Press (USSR)	Kassel, West Germany	19 Sep 1965
18.67m (61' 3")	Nadezhda Chizhova (USSR)	Sochi, USSR	28 Apr 1968
18.87m (61' 11")	Margitta Gummel (GDR)	Frankfurt an der Oder, East Germany	22 Sep 1968
19.07m (62' 6 ¾")	Margitta Gummel (GDR)	Mexico City, Mexico	20 Oct 1968
19.61m (64' 4")	Margitta Gummel (GDR)	Mexico City, Mexico	20 Oct 1968
19.72m (64' 8 ½")	Nadezhda Chizhova (USSR)	Moscow, USSR	30 May 1969
20.09m (65' 11")	Nadezhda Chizhova (USSR)	Chorzow, Poland	13 Jul 1969

20.10m (65' 11 ½")	Margitta Gummel (GDR)	Berlin, East Germany	11 Sep 1969
20.10m (65' 11 ½")	Nadezhda Chizhova (USSR)	Athens, Greece	16 Sep 1969
20.43m (67' 0 ½")	Nadezhda Chizhova (USSR)	Athens, Greece	16 Sep 1969
20.43m (67' 0 ½")	Nadezhda Chizhova (USSR)	Moscow, USSR	29 Aug 1971
20.63m (67' 8 ¼")	Nadezhda Chizhova (USSR)	Sochi, USSR	19 May 1972
21.03m (69' 0")	Nadezhda Chizhova (USSR)	Munich, West Germany	7 Sep 1972
21.20m (69' 6 ¾")	Nadezhda Chizhova (USSR)	Lvov, USSR	28 Aug 1973
21.60m (70' 10 ½")	Marianne Adam (GDR)	Berlin, East Germany	6 Aug 1975
21.67m (71' 1 ¼")	Marianne Adam (GDR)	Karl-Marx-Stadt, East Germany	30 May 1976
21.87m (71' 9")	Ivanka Khristova (BUL)	Belmeken, Bulgaria	3 Jul 1976
21.89m (71' 10")	Ivanka Khristova (BUL)	Belmeken, Bulgaria	4 Jul 1976
21.99m (72' 1 ¾")	Helena Fibingerova (CZH)	Opava, Czechoslovakia	26 Sep 1976
22.32m (73' 2 ¾")	Helena Fibingerova (CZH)	Nitra, Czechoslovakia	20 Aug 1977
22.36m (73' 4 ½")	Ilona Slupianek (GDR)	Celje, Yugoslavia	2 May 1980
22.45m (73' 8")	Ilona Slupianek (GDR)	Potsdam, East Germany	10 May 1980
22.53m (73' 11")	Natalya Lisovskaya (USSR)	Sochi, USSR	27 May 1984
22.60m (74' 1 ¾")	Natalya Lisovskaya (USSR)	Moscow, USSR	7 Jun 1987
22.63m (74' 3")	Natalya Lisovskaya (USSR)	Moscow, USSR	7 Jun 1987

Gisela Mauermayer   (Germany, 1913–1995)

14.38m (47' 2 ¼")   **Warsaw, Poland**   **15 Jul 1934**

Gisela Mauermayer held world records in the shot put (1934), discus (1936), and pentathlon (1934 and 1938). She first came to attention at the Women's World Games in 1934, at which she won the shot put, javelin, long jump, high jump, and 100m.

Her shot put world record of 14.38 meters (47' 2 ¼") was achieved at a match between Germany and Poland in 1934. She was German champion in the event from 1934 to 1942. However, the shot put was not part of the Olympic program until 1948.

At the 1936 Berlin Olympics Mauermayer won the discus gold medal. Germany was not invited to the 1948 London Olympics. The winning distance in the shot put that year was 13.75 meters (45' 1 ¼"), well below Mauermayer's world record set 14 years earlier.

Tatyana Sevryukova   (Soviet Union, 1917–1982)

14.59m (47' 10 ½")   **Moscow, USSR**   **4 Aug 1948**

Tatyana Sevryukova won the Soviet Union championship six times between 1939 and 1947. In 1946 she won the European Championships with a throw of 14.16 meters (46' 5 ½"). Her world record throw of 14.59 meters (47' 10 ½") came in 1948. However, the Soviet Union chose to remain away from the Olympics until 1952.

At 58 kilograms (128 pounds), she remains the lightest of the shot put world record holders. Her personal best came in 1951, at age 35, but a new generation of Soviet throwers had arrived by this time, and she was not a member of the Soviet team at the 1952 Olympics.

She later became a committee member of the Soviet Ministry of Physical Culture and Sport.

Tatyana Sevryukova, Soviet Union (shot put).

Klavdiya Tochenova   (Soviet Union, b. 1921)

14.86m (48' 9")   **Tbilisi, USSR**   **30 Oct 1949**

Klavdiya Tochenova threw the shot 14.86 meters at Tbilisi, Georgia, in 1949, an improvement of 27 centimeters (10 ½") on the world record. She went on to win the bronze medal at the 1952 Olympics.

Tochenova was Soviet champion in 1945 and 1951, was second on four other occasions, and was third twice. She also came in second in the pentathlon four years in a row, behind Alexandra Chudina (1946-49). At the 1950 European Championships she was second in the shot put (13.92 meters, 45' 8") and seventh in the pentathlon.

Anna Andreyeva   (Soviet Union, b. 1915)

15.02m (49' 3 ½")   **Ploesti, Romania**   **9 Nov 1950**

Anna Andreyeva was the first female athlete to break the 15-meter barrier when she threw 15.02 meters (49' 3 ½") in November 1950 at an international athletic meet between Romania and the Soviet Union. She was 35 years old at the time.

That year Andreyeva was the European champion at the shot put in Brussels (14.32 meters, 46' 11 ¾") and was 10th in the discus at the same games.

She won the shot put at the Soviet championships as far back as 1938 and again in the years 1948 through 1950. In 1955, at the age of forty, she still was able to come in fifth in the Soviet championships.

Galina Zybina   (Soviet Union, b. 1931)

15.28m (50' 1 ¾")	Helsinki, Finland	26 Jul 1952
15.37m (50' 5 ¼")	Frunze, USSR	20 Sep 1952
15.42m (50' 7 ¼")	Frunze, USSR	1 Oct 1952
16.20m (53' 1 ¾")	Malmö, Sweden	9 Oct 1953
16.28m (53' 5")	Kiev, USSR	14 Sep 1954
16.29m (53' 5 ½")	Leningrad, USSR	5 Sep 1955
16.67m (54' 8 ¼")	Tbilisi, USSR	15 Nov 1955
16.76m (55' 0")	Tashkent, USSR	13 Oct 1956

Galina Zybina, Soviet Union, 1952 Olympic shot put champion.

Galina Zybina was the first of the great female shot putters. She improved the record eight times and was the first woman over 16 meters. She came to prominence at the 1952 Olympics, where she won with her first world record of 15.28 meters. At these Olympics she was also fourth in the javelin.

Over the next few years she won the 1954 European Championships and continued to set world records. However, she was beaten for the 1956 Soviet title by Tamara Tishkevich.

At the 1956 Melbourne Games, Tishkevich, weighing 105 kilograms (231 pounds)—the heaviest Soviet athlete, male or female, at the Olympics—snatched the gold medal by six centimeters, 16.59 meters (54' 5 ¼") to 16.53 meters (54' 2 ¾").

Although she remained competitive for over a decade, Zybina's days of glory were over. At the Olympics she was seventh in 1960 and then won a bronze medal in 1964.

She wrote her memoirs in the mid-1950s, while still in her 20s, and came across as a passionate young believer in communism. But in 1958 she was temporarily suspended for "uncomradely behavior" when she refused to accept her second place position at the Soviet championships in the shot put.

Tamara Press   (Soviet Union, b. 1937)

17.25m (56' 7 ¼")	Nalchik, USSR	26 Apr 1959
17.42m (57' 2")	Moscow, USSR	16 Jul 1960
17.78m (58' 4")	Moscow, USSR	13 Aug 1960
18.55m (60' 10 ½")	Leipzig, East Germany	10 Jun 1962

| 18.55m (60' 10 ½") | Belgrade, Yugoslavia | 12 Sep 1962 |
| 18.59m (61' 0") | Kassel, West Germany | 19 Sep 1965 |

Tamara Press was born in Kharkov in eastern Ukraine. By training she was an engineer and later in life an author. For six years she came to totally dominate two events, the discus and the shot put. Her younger sister Irina was similarly dominant in the hurdles and the pentathlon.

Tamara Press set a total of 12 world records: 6 in the shot put and 6 in the discus. She moved the shot put world record from Galina Zybina's 16.76 meters to 18.59 meters. In the Soviet championships she won the discus seven times (1960-66) and the shot put nine times (1958-66). At 105 kilograms (231 pounds), she was the heaviest of all the shot put champions. In the shot put she was Olympic champion in 1960 and 1964; at the European Championships she was third in 1958 and first in 1962. She won the discus at these events too, with the exception of the 1960 Olympics, at which she came in second.

She retired in 1966. After her athletic days were over, she authored two works, *The Price of Victory* and *This Tough Athletics.*

Nadezhda Chizhova   (Soviet Union, b. 1945)

18.67m (61' 3")	Sochi, USSR	28 Apr 1968
19.72m (64' 8 ½")	Moscow, USSR	30 May 1969
20.09m (65' 11")	Chorzow, Poland	13 Jul 1969
20.10m (65' 11 ½")	Athens, Greece	16 Sep 1969
20.43m (67' 0 ½")	Athens, Greece	16 Sep 1969
20.43m (67' 0 ½")	Moscow, USSR	29 Aug 1971
20.63m (67' 8 ¼")	Sochi, USSR	19 May 1972
21.03m (69' 0")	Munich, West Germany	7 Sep 1972
21.20m (69' 6 ¾")	Lvov, USSR	28 Aug 1973

Nadezhda Chizhova was the next great Soviet shot putter after Tamara Press; she raised or tied the world record nine times. Two of these world records took place at major competitions: the European Championships (1969) and the Olympics (1972). She weighed "only" 90 kilograms (198 pounds), compared with Tamara Press's 105 kilograms (231 pounds). Chizhova was the first woman over both 20 meters and 21 meters.

She did not have the international stage all to herself, however. Another great athlete, Margitta Gummel of East Germany, managed to break the record three times in 1968 and once in 1969.

Chizhova won the senior European championship four times (1966, 1969, 1971, and 1974). She went to the 1968

Nadezhda Chizhova, Soviet Union, 1972 Olympic shot put champion.

Mexico City Olympics as a clear favorite. However, Gummel surprised her with world records in her third and fifth round throws (19.07 meters and 19.61 meters). After placing third at these Olympics, Chizhova made no mistake at Munich four years later. She won with 21.03 meters, her eighth world record. She missed the 1975 season due to injury but, after a 20-month layoff, made a comeback for the Montreal Games and came in second to Ivanka Khristova of Bulgaria.

Originally from the city of Ussolye Sibirskoe in the central Siberian plateau, she is married to another world record holder, shot put champion Aleksandr Baryshnikov.

Margitta Gummel   (East Germany, b. 1941)

18.87m (61' 11")	Frankfurt an der Oder, East Germany	22 Sep 1968
19.07m (62' 6 ¾")	Mexico City, Mexico	20 Oct 1968
19.61m (64' 4")	Mexico City, Mexico	20 Oct 1968
20.10m (65' 11 ½")	Berlin, East Germany	11 Sep 1969

Margitta Gummel interrupted the success of the Soviet Union's Nadezhda Chizhova. She won the first of five East German titles in 1966 and came in second that year in the European Championships won by Chizhova. When the 1968 Olympics came around Chizhova was still very much the favorite. However, Gummel broke the world record in round three with 19.07 meters. She improved on it again in round five with 19.61 meters to win easily.

Chizhova reclaimed the record in May 1969 and improved it again in July 1969 with 20.09 meters (65' 11"), but Gummel took it back in September 1969 by adding one centimeter to the record, 20.10 meters (65' 11 ½"). However, five days later Chizhova reclaimed the record at the European Championships in Athens with 20.43 meters (67' 0 ½"), while Gummel was second with 19.58 meters (64' 3").

At the 1972 Munich Olympics, it was once again Chizhova first, Gummel second, 21.03 meters (69' 0") to 20.22 meters (66' 4"). Gummel retired after these Olympics.

Margitta Gummel, East Germany, 1968 Olympic shot put champion.

Marianne Adam   (East Germany, b. 1951)

| 21.60m (70' 10 ½") | Berlin, East Germany | 6 Aug 1975 |
| 21.67m (71' 1 ¼") | Karl-Marx-Stadt, East Germany | 30 May 1976 |

Marianne Adam was a tall athlete (183 centimeters, 6' 0 ¼") who was East German champion from 1974 to 1976. Her two world records were at athletic meets in East Germany, and she never quite won a major international competition.

She had been a promising high jumper until a knee injury ended that career, so she turned to shot putting. She first competed at the Olympics in 1972, where she came in fifth. At the 1974 European Championships in Rome she came in second as Nadezhda Chizhova won her fourth title. At her second Olympics in Montreal Adam was fourth.

She was entered for the 1978 European Championships but did not start because of injury. Despite coming in second at the 1980 East German championships, she was not selected for the Moscow Olympics.

Ivanka Khristova   (Bulgaria, b. 1941)

| 21.87m (71' 9") | Belmeken, Bulgaria | 3 Jul 1976 |
| 21.89m (71' 10") | Belmeken, Bulgaria | 4 Jul 1976 |

Ivanka Khristova was an athlete with a long, slow career, who always seemed to miss out on the gold medal. Her career record is as follows: 1962 European Championships (seventh), 1964 Olympics (tenth), 1968 Olympics (sixth), 1969 European Championships (fourth), 1971 European Championships (sixth), 1972 Olympics (third).

In 1973 she dropped out of athletics and had a son. But the idea of throwing 20 meters at the 1974 European Championships lured her out of retirement. She fell seven centimeters short but won a bronze medal. Khristova finally broke the 20-meter barrier in April 1975 and later that year went further and broke through the 21-meter mark. Finally, in July 1976, she threw 21.87 meters (71' 9"), which added 20 centimeters to Marianne Adam's world record. The next day she threw another two centimeters farther.

This performance made her a favorite for the Montreal Olympics three weeks later. After nearly 15 years as an international competitor, Ivanka Khristova won Bulgaria's first track and field gold medal with 21.16 meters (69' 5 ¼") to Chizhova's 20.96 meters (68' 9 ¼").

Helena Fibingerova   (Czechoslovakia, b. 1949)

| 21.99m (72' 1 ¾") | Opava, Czechoslovakia | 26 Sep 1976 |
| 22.32m (73' 2 ¾") | Nitra, Czechoslovakia | 20 Aug 1977 |

Helena Fibingerova, like Khristova, was an athlete with a long career with the highest honors achieved at the very end. Her career extended from the 1969 European Championships until the 1987 World Championships. Twice she had been favorite, the 1976 Olympics and the 1978 European Championships, but she lost both times. She set the world record twice in the 1970s and was the first woman to throw over 22 meters.

Finally, at the inaugural 1983 World Championships in Helsinki, at age 34, she had a fairy-tale win. At the start of the final round she was in fourth place with 20.30 meters (66' 7 ¼"). On her very last throw, she produced a heave of 21.05 meters (69' 0 ¾"), a gold medal-winning throw. Overcome with emotion at her first major victory after 14 years, she bear-hugged surprised officials.

Helena Fibingerova, Czechoslovakia (shot put).

She continued on a few more years. She missed the 1984 Olympics because of the communist boycott and was tenth at the 1986 European Championships and eighth at the 1987 World Championships. She is married to Jaroslav Smid, also a shot putter.

Ilona Slupianek   (East Germany, b. 1956)

| 22.36m (73' 4 ½") | Celje, Yugoslavia | 2 May 1980 |
| 22.45m (73' 8") | Potsdam, East Germany | 10 May 1980 |

Ilona Slupianek is the only female world record holder in the shot put to have been caught using anabolic steroids. This was at the European Cup Final in 1977, when penalties were not that heavy. She was still able to participate in the 1978 European Championships in Prague, which she won with 21.41 meters (70' 3"). This did not go down well with the Czech crowd, who were hoping that Helena Fibingerova would win. The Czech athlete came in second with 20.86 meters (68' 5 ¼"). Slupianek also won the 1980 Olympic title (22.41 meters, 73' 6 ¼") and the 1982 European championship (21.59 meters, 70' 10").

Natalya Lisovskaya   (Soviet Union, b. 1962)

22.53m (73' 11")	Sochi, USSR	27 May 1984
22.60m (74' 1 ¾")	Moscow, USSR	7 Jun 1987
22.63m (74' 3")	Moscow, USSR	7 Jun 1987

Natalya Lisovskaya, Soviet Union (shot put), 1988 Olympic champion.

Natalya Lisovskaya was originally a discus thrower but her tall frame (187 centimeters, 6' 1 ½") eventually made the discus throw technically difficult, so she switched to the shot put.

She originally came from Alegazy, south of the Urals. She won the first of eight Soviet titles in the shot put in 1981. She set her first world record (22.53 meters) in 1984, but missed the Olympics because of the Soviet boycott.

She flopped badly at the 1986 European Championships (ninth). However, she made up for it over the next few years with wins in the 1987 World Championships and the 1988 Olympics. She improved on the world record twice at the 1987 Znamenskiy Memorial meet in Moscow on her first and fourth throws. She is married to another world record holder and Olympic gold medalist, hammer thrower Yuriy Sedykh.

After her dominance in the late 1980s, her results slipped slightly. She was second at the 1990 European Championships and second again at the 1991

World Championships. At the Barcelona Olympics she dropped to ninth place. She remains the only woman to have thrown farther than 22.50 meters, something she achieved four times.

Conclusions

The women's shot put, like the discus and javelin, has been dominated by women from Eastern Europe. All three events saw their best distances take place in the 1980s. There has been a dramatic decline in performances since then in all three disciplines. The usual reasons given for this decline are the disintegration of the Eastern European Communist Bloc, with the collapse of organized sport in those countries, and the increased vigilance against drug abuse.

Nobody expects the shot put world record (22.63 meters) to be beaten soon. The best throw in 1996 was 20.97 meters. Currently, Germany, China, and the Eastern European countries dominate the international scene in the shot put.

Five All-Time Best: Women's Shot Put

Natalya Lisovskaya (USSR)	22.63m (74' 3")	1987
Ilona Slupianek (GDR)	22.45m (73' 8")	1980
Helena Fibingerova (CZH)	22.32m (73' 2 ¾")	1977
Claudia Losch (FRG)	22.19m (72' 9 ¼")	1987
Ivanka Khristova (BUL)	21.89m (71' 10")	1976
Prediction	*22.78m (74' 9")*	*2015*

Top Three: Women's Shot Put

GOLD MEDAL:	**Nadezhda Chizhova (USSR)**
SILVER MEDAL:	**Tamara Press (USSR)**
BRONZE MEDAL:	**Natalya Lisovskaya (USSR)**

The women's discus weighs 1 kilogram (2 pounds 3 ounces); the men's weighs 2 kilograms (4 pounds 6 ounces). The event was introduced at the 1928 Olympics, the year women's track and field was permitted at the Games.

The first official world record in 1936 was 48.31 meters (158' 6"), whereas the current record (1988) is 76.80 meters (252' 0"), an improvement of 28.49 meters. The record has been held only by Europeans, and most of these were Eastern Europeans. The Soviet Union produced three great throwers, Nina Dumbadze in the 1950s, Tamara Press in the 1960s, and Faina Melnik in the 1970s. The standards achieved by the Eastern Europeans are so far ahead of the rest of the world that many other countries send reduced numbers to the Olympics.

The current record of 76.80 meters (252' 0") was set by Gabriele Reinsch of East Germany in 1988 and has not been approached in years. It was an improvement of 2.24 meters (7' 5"), the largest single improvement since 1952. Altogether, there have been 14 women of seven nationalities who have set the world record 35 times. The most records by one individual was 11, by Faina Melnik. Press set the record six times, and Liesel Westermann of West Germany set it four times. Five of the record holders have also been Olympic champions: Mauermayer, Ponomaryeva, Press, Melnik, and Jahl. No discus world records have been set at the Olympics by either male or female athletes.

Women's World Records for Discus

Record distance	Record holder	Location	Date
48.31m (158' 6")	Gisela Mauermayer (GER)	Berlin, Germany	11 Jul 1936
53.25m (174' 8")	Nina Dumbadze (USSR)	Moscow, USSR	8 Aug 1948
53.37m (175' 1")	Nina Dumbadze (USSR)	Gori, USSR	27 May 1951
53.61m (175' 11")	Nina Ponomaryeva (USSR)	Odessa, USSR	9 Aug 1952
57.04m (187' 2")	Nina Dumbadze (USSR)	Tbilisi, USSR	18 Oct 1952
57.15m (187' 6")	Tamara Press (USSR)	Rome, Italy	12 Sep 1960
57.43m (188' 5")	Tamara Press (USSR)	Moscow, USSR	15 Jul 1961
58.06m (190' 6")	Tamara Press (USSR)	Sofia, Bulgaria	1 Sep 1961
58.98m (193' 6")	Tamara Press (USSR)	London, England	20 Sep 1961
59.29m (194' 6")	Tamara Press (USSR)	Moscow, USSR	18 May 1963
59.70m (195' 10")	Tamara Press (USSR)	Moscow, USSR	11 Aug 1965
61.26m (201' 0")	Liesel Westermann (FRG)	São Paulo, Brazil	5 Nov 1967
61.64m (202' 3")	Christine Spielberg (GDR)	Regis Breitingen, East Germany	26 May 1968
62.54m (205' 2")	Liesel Westermann (FRG)	Werdohl, West Germany	24 Jul 1968
62.70m (205' 8")	Liesel Westermann (FRG)	Berlin, East Germany	18 Jun 1969
63.96m (209' 10")	Liesel Westermann (FRG)	Hamburg, West Germany	27 Sep 1969
64.22m (210' 8")	Faina Melnik (USSR)	Helsinki, Finland	12 Aug 1971
64.88m (212' 10")	Faina Melnik (USSR)	Munich, West Germany	4 Sep 1971
65.42m (214' 7")	Faina Melnik (USSR)	Moscow, USSR	31 May 1972
65.48m (214' 10")	Faina Melnik (USSR)	Augsburg, West Germany	24 Jun 1972
66.76m (219' 0")	Faina Melnik (USSR)	Moscow, USSR	4 Aug 1972
67.32m (220' 10")	Argentina Menis (ROM)	Constanta, Romania	23 Sep 1972
67.44m (221' 3")	Faina Melnik (USSR)	Riga, USSR	25 May 1973
67.58m (221' 9")	Faina Melnik (USSR)	Moscow, USSR	10 Jul 1973
69.48m (227' 11")	Faina Melnik (USSR)	Edinburgh, Scotland	7 Sep 1973
69.90m (229' 4")	Faina Melnik (USSR)	Prague, Czechoslovakia	27 May 1974

70.20m (230' 4")	Faina Melnik (USSR)	Zürich, Switzerland	20 Aug 1975
70.50m (231' 3")	Faina Melnik (USSR)	Sochi, USSR	24 Apr 1976
70.72m (232' 0")	Evelin Jahl (GDR)	Dresden, East Germany	12 Aug 1978
71.50m (234' 7")	Evelin Jahl (GDR)	Potsdam, East Germany	10 May 1980
71.80m (235' 7")	Maria Petkova (BUL)	Sofia, Bulgaria	13 Jul 1980
73.26m (240' 4")	Galina Savinkova (USSR)	Leselidze, USSR	22 May 1983
73.36m (240' 8")	Irina Meszynski (GDR)	Prague, Czechoslovakia	17 Aug 1984
74.56m (244' 7")	Zdenka Silhava (CZH)	Nitra, Czechoslovakia	26 Aug 1984
76.80m (252' 0")	Gabriele Reinsch (GDR)	Neubrandenburg, East Germany	9 Jul 1988

Gisela Mauermayer   (Germany, b. 1913)

48.31m (158' 6")   **Berlin, Germany**   **11 Jul 1936**

Gisela Mauermayer set the first recognized world record in the women's discus in 1936. She had set numerous discus records in the early 1930s before the event achieved official recognition. At the 1936 Berlin Olympics she won the gold medal with 47.62 meters (156' 3"). She went on to win the European Championships in the discus at Vienna in 1938 with 44.80 meters (147' 0").

She also held world records in the shot put (1934) and pentathlon (1934 and 1938), but these events were not part of the women's program at the Olympics until 1948 and 1964, respectively.

She graduated as a teacher and then spent most of her professional life as a librarian and archivist. Altogether she won 19 German championships in various events: shot put (7), discus (9), and pentathlon (3).

Nina Dumbadze   (Soviet Union, 1919–1983)

53.25m (174' 8")   **Moscow, USSR**   **8 Aug 1948**
53.37m (175' 1")   **Gori, USSR**   **27 May 1951**
57.04m (187' 2")   **Tbilisi, USSR**   **18 Oct 1952**

Nina Dumbadze had achieved discus throws greater than the world record for many years before her first official world record in 1948. This was because the Soviet Union remained outside the IAAF from the time of the 1917 Russian Revolution until 1947 and did not return to the Olympics until 1952, although it participated in the 1946 European Championships.

Dumbadze won the Soviet championship in the discus eight times between 1939 and 1950. At the 1946 European Championships she won the gold medal with 44.52 meters (146' 1"). She finally

Nina Dumbadze, Soviet Union (discus).

achieved world record status in 1948 with a throw of 53.25 meters (174' 8"), becoming the first woman to throw the discus over 50 meters. At the 1950 European Championships she won again (48.03 meters, 157' 6").

At the Soviet debut at the 1952 Olympics she couldn't reproduce her top form, and other Soviet athletes did. Nina Ponomaryeva, a future world record holder, won with 51.42 meters (168' 8"). Yelisaveta Bagryantseva won the silver (47.08 meters, 154' 5"), and Dumbadze won the bronze (46.28 meters, 151' 10"). Despite this setback, she achieved a third world record later that year (57.04 meters) that was to last eight years.

Nina Ponomaryeva   (Soviet Union, b. 1929)

53.61m (175' 11")   **Odessa, USSR**   **9 Aug 1952**

Nina Ponomaryeva won the gold medal at both the 1952 and 1960 Olympics and was European champion in 1954. She might have won three Olympic gold medals, but in 1955 she gave an hour's tutoring to an up-and-coming thrower from Czechoslovakia. That athlete was Olga Fikotova, and at the 1956 Olympics the result was Fikotova gold, Ponomaryeva bronze. Fikotova later recalled that Ponomaryeva could barely look at her during the medal presentations.

Ponomaryeva was Soviet discus champion on eight occasions, from 1951-1956 and from 1958-1959, and was eleventh at her fourth Olympics in 1964.

Nina Ponomaryeva, Soviet Union, 1952 and 1960 Olympic discus champion.

Tamara Press   (Soviet Union, b. 1937)

57.15m (187' 6")	**Rome, Italy**	**12 Sep 1960**
57.43m (188' 5")	**Moscow, USSR**	**15 Jul 1961**
58.06m (190' 6")	**Sofia, Bulgaria**	**1 Sep 1961**
58.98m (193' 6")	**London, England**	**20 Sep 1961**
59.29m (194' 6")	**Moscow, USSR**	**18 May 1963**
59.70m (195' 10")	**Moscow, USSR**	**11 Aug 1965**

Tamara Press was the most successful discus and shot put champion of all time. She set six world records in both disciplines. In addition, she won Olympic gold medals in the shot put (1960 and 1964) and the discus (1964), plus a silver medal in the discus in 1960. She followed up her 1960 silver medal in the discus by setting her first world record in this event seven days later. Overall, she raised the world discus record by over 2.5 meters.

Press was no lightweight, weighing 105 kilograms (231 pounds). At the Soviet championships, she won seven discus titles in a row (1960-66). She was also European discus champion in 1958 and 1962. She attributed much of her success to coach Victor Alexeev, who used unconventional training methods to keep his pupil fresh, such as training in the forests of the Karebon Peninsula. After her retirement, she showed a talent for writing and journalism.

Her younger sister Irina was equally dominant in two athletic disciplines, the 80m hurdles and the pentathlon, and was similarly rewarded with world records and Olympic gold medals. The two of them were the most successful sisters in athletic history.

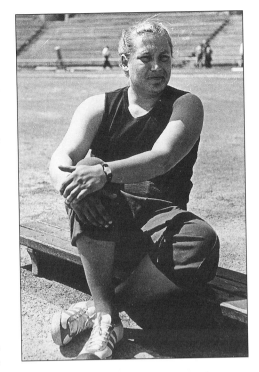

Tamara Press, Soviet Union (shot put and discus), won Olympic gold medals in both the shot put and discus.

Liesel Westermann   (West Germany, b. 1944)

61.26m (201' 0")	São Paulo, Brazil	5 Nov 1967
62.54m (205' 2")	Werdohl, West Germany	24 Jul 1968
62.70m (205' 8")	Berlin, East Germany	18 Jun 1969
63.96m (209' 10")	Hamburg, West Germany	27 Sep 1969

Liesel Westermann broke the monopoly of communist athletes on the world records in the throwing events. She set four world records between 1967 and 1969 and was the first athlete over 60 meters. She was also the first female athlete to set a world record in South America. She went to the 1968 Olympics as one of the favorites, but the wet conditions on the day didn't help anybody. It was 36-year-old Lia Manoliu (Romania) who handled the conditions best, winning with 58.28 meters (191' 2"). Westermann came in second with 57.76 meters (189' 6").

A popular figure in West Germany, Westermann never quite won a gold medal at a major international competition. She came in fifth at the Munich Olympics in 1972. Westermann was six times the West German champion (1966-1970, 1972), second at the European Championships twice (1966 and 1971), and also West German shot put champion (1969).

Liesel Westermann, West Germany (discus).

Christine Spielberg   (East Germany, b. 1941)

61.64m (202' 3")   **Regis Breitingen, East Germany**   **26 May 1968**

Christine Spielberg briefly interrupted Liesel Westermann's run of world records and held the record for two months in 1968. Her major competitive victory was the 1966 European Championships in Budapest, where she won with a throw of 57.76 meters (189' 6").

In the wet conditions of the 1968 Mexico City Olympics she finished seventh. At the 1971 European Championships she was eighth. She retired in 1972 and became a teacher of physical education, German, and sociology.

Despite her success as world record holder and European champion, the one title she never won was the East German championship, despite being a finalist from 1966-1972.

Faina Melnik   (Soviet Union, b. 1945)

64.22m (210' 8")	Helsinki, Finland	12 Aug 1971
64.88m (212' 10")	Munich, West Germany	4 Sep 1971
65.42m (214' 7")	Moscow, USSR	31 May 1972
65.48m (214' 10")	Augsburg, West Germany	24 Jun 1972
66.76m (219' 0")	Moscow, USSR	4 Aug 1972
67.44m (221' 3")	Riga, USSR	25 May 1973
67.58m (221' 9")	Moscow, USSR	10 Jul 1973
69.48m (227' 11")	Edinburgh, Scotland	7 Sep 1973
69.90m (229' 4")	Prague, Czechoslovakia	27 May 1974
70.20m (230' 4")	Zürich, Switzerland	20 Aug 1975
70.50m (231' 3")	Sochi, USSR	24 Apr 1976

Faina Melnik, Soviet Union (discus), 1972 Olympic champion and 11-time world record holder.

Faina Melnik was the dominant force in women's discus throwing in the 1970s, winning an Olympic gold medal (1972), two European Championships (1971 and 1974), and setting 11 world records. She was also the first woman to break through the 70-meter barrier.

Born in the Ukraine of Armenian parents, she originally competed as a shot putter. She won the first of her nine Soviet discus titles in 1970. During the first few years of the 1970s Melnik was untouchable. However, she did have a surprising fight at the 1972 Munich Olympics: She took the lead only on her fourth throw, eventually winning with a throw of 66.62 meters (218' 7").

Her 11th world record was set three months before the 1976 Montreal Olympics, and she traveled to Canada the hottest of hot favorites. No one realized it at the time, but her days of glory were over. In one of the great upsets of the Games, she finished fourth with 66.40 meters (217' 10"). There were to be no more international victories.

After the Olympics she married Bulgarian discus thrower Velko Velev and lived in Bulgaria from 1977-1979. After the marriage and her athletic career ended, she pursued a career as a dentist.

Argentina Menis   (Romania, b. 1948)

67.32m (220' 10")   **Constanta, Romania**   **23 Sep 1972**

This well-developed Romanian athlete interrupted Faina Melnik's run of world records in the 1970s. She threw 67.32 meters in a match between Romania, Sweden, and Finland two weeks after the 1972 Olympics. At those Games, she had won the silver medal with 65.06 meters (213' 5") behind Faina Melnik, who threw 66.62 meters (218' 7").

In fact, she had almost won the Olympic gold medal. She set an Olympic record with her first throw and again with her fourth (65.06 meters). However Melnik finally hit the front on her fourth throw (66.62 meters) and there was no change in the last two rounds.

At the 1976 Montreal Olympics Menis was sixth. At the European Championships she was fourth in 1971, second in 1974, and ninth in 1978.

Argentina Menis, Romania (discus).

Evelin Jahl (née Schlaak)   (East Germany, b. 1956)

70.72m (232' 0")	**Dresden, East Germany**	**12 Aug 1978**
71.50m (234' 7")	**Potsdam, East Germany**	**10 May 1980**

Evelin Jahl achieved every athletic honor: two Olympic gold medals, a European Championships gold medal, and two world records. Her 1976 gold medal at the Montreal Olympics was one of the great upsets of the Games. The overwhelming favorite was defending champion Faina Melnik, who had set her 11th world record in April 1976. But the Olympics were held in July, and 20-year-old Schlaak, as she then was named, had been quietly improving all season. In the final Schlaak won it on her first throw with a personal best: 69.00 meters (226' 4").

A physical education student who also studied law, she married a lieutenant in the army and won the 1978 European Championships as Evelin Jahl. Just prior to these championships, she became the second woman to throw over 70 meters when she set her first world record in Dresden, East Germany, with 70.72 meters (232' 0").

Jahl achieved her second world record (71.50 meters) at a pre-Olympic trial in May 1980 in Potsdam. However, this record was improved upon by Maria Petkova of Bulgaria, who threw 71.80 meters in July 1980, two weeks before the Olympics began.

But at the Moscow Games, it was no contest. Jahl took the lead on her second throw (69.96 meters, 229' 6") and that was it. She became the first woman to win two Olympic gold medals in this event.

She later divorced and remarried as Evelin Herbeg.

Evelin Jahl, East Germany (discus), 1976 and 1980 Olympic discus champion.

Maria Petkova   (Bulgaria, b. 1950)

71.80m (235' 7")   **Sofia, Bulgaria**   **13 Jul 1980**

Like Tamara Press, Maria Petkova (later Vergova) was another heavyweight, measuring 105 kilograms (231 pounds). At the 1976 Olympics she was second to upset winner Evelin Schlaak, while favorite Faina Melnik (USSR) slumped to fourth. Petkova had always been a great fan of Melnik, but changed that opinion when she saw Melnik throw a tantrum during the Olympic final.

Faina Melnik then married Bulgarian Velko Velev and settled in Bulgaria. The two women were now training partners. Dislike between them grew, and finally Petkova gave vent to some public tantrums of her own, which did not advance her career in the eyes of Bulgarian athletic officials. When she gave up athletics in 1978 to have a son, it seemed her career was over. Nonetheless, the following year she made a determined comeback.

In 1980 Evelin Jahl increased the record to 71.50 meters, but two months later Maria Petkova threw her own world record, 71.80 meters (235' 7"). At the Moscow Games Petkova led after the first round, but then Jahl threw four superior throws, and both women won the same medals as in 1976.

Galina Savinkova   (Soviet Union, b. 1953)

73.26m (240' 4")   **Leselidze, USSR**   **22 May 1983**

Galina Savinkova was born in Kemerovo in south central Russia. She had come in second at the Soviet championships in 1981 and 1983 and won it in 1984.

She broke the world record by 1.46 meters at a meet in Leselidze in 1983, when she threw 73.26 meters (240' 4"). However, at the World Championships 10 weeks later she was well back in 11th position.

Savinkova missed out on the 1984 Olympics because of the Soviet boycott. At the European Championships she was third in 1982 and sixth in 1986.

Irina Meszynski   (East Germany, b. 1962)

73.36m (240' 8")   **Prague, Czechoslovakia**   **17 Aug 1984**

When the Soviet Union decided to boycott the Los Angeles Olympics in 1984, they set up an alternative "Friendship Games" 10 days after the Olympics finished. One world record was achieved, in the women's discus by Irina Meszynski. On her third throw she added 10 centimeters to the world record with 73.36 meters (240' 8"), while the Los Angeles Olympics winning distance was 65.36 meters (214' 5").

Meszynski won the East German title in 1982. At the European Championships she was eighth in 1982 and fourth in 1986.

Zdenka Silhava   (Czechoslovakia, b. 1954)

74.56m (244' 7")   **Nitra, Czechoslovakia**   **26 Aug 1984**

Zdenka Silhava's record took place three weeks after the Los Angeles Olympics, which her country had chosen to boycott. She added 1.20 meters to the nine-day-old record of Irina Meszynski. Silhava's record lasted almost four years.

In 1985 she tested positive for anabolic steroids and was suspended for "life." In fact, such sentences were rarely enforced in those days. Her national federation appealed, and she served only a few months.

At the World Championships she was sixth in 1983 and 1987. At the 1988 Olympics she was sixth again. Her record remains the number two throw in the history of women's discus.

Gabriele Reinsch   (East Germany, b. 1963)

76.80m (252' 0")   **Neubrandenburg, East Germany**   **9 Jul 1988**

Gabriele Reinsch was the last East German to achieve a world record before the reunification with West Germany. A physical education student, she was the tallest of the female world record holders in the discus, standing 188 centimeters (6' 2").

Reinsch was the first, and so far only, woman to break the 75-meter barrier. She threw the discus 76.80 meters in a match against Italy in July 1988. That throw, her first for the day, has almost destroyed the record.

Although a favorite for the Seoul Olympics, she finished seventh with 67.26 meters (220' 8"), well behind her compatriot Martina Hellmann's winning throw of 72.30 meters (237' 2"). She never won an East German championship title, coming in second three years in a row (1988-90). At the 1990 European Championships she was fourth with 66.08 meters (216' 9").

Gabrielle Reinsch, East Germany (discus), current world record holder since 1988.

Conclusions

The status of the current world record for the women's discus is much like that of the men's discus record—a long way out of reach. Both took place in the 1980s, are held by Eastern European athletes, and look as if they'll survive well into the 21st century. Both added more than two meters to the previous world record. In women's discus, no one has yet come within two meters of Gabriele Reinsch's 1988 throw of 76.80m (252' 0").

Whatever the reason, the fact is that performances in the women's discus have declined dramatically. All the best throws took place in the 1980s. The best throw since January 1990 would finish only 34th in the all-time list (Xiao Yannling of China, 71.68 meters [235' 2"], March 1992). The world record will probably remain unchallenged for a generation. The best throw in 1996 was 69.66 meters (228' 6").

Five All-Time Best: Women's Discus

Gabriele Reinsch (GDR)	76.80m (252' 0")	1988
Zdenka Silhava (CZH)	74.56m (244' 7")	1984
Ilke Wyludda (GDR)	74.56m (244' 7")	1989
Diana Gansky (GDR)	74.08m (243' 0")	1987
Daniela Costian (ROM)	73.84m (242' 3")	1988
Prediction	*76.80m (252' 0")*	*2015*

Top Three: Women's Discus

GOLD MEDAL:	Faina Melnik (USSR)
SILVER MEDAL:	Tamara Press (USSR)
BRONZE MEDAL:	Evelin Jahl (GDR)

T he javelin for women weighs 600 grams (1 pound 5 ounces), while the men's is 800 grams (1 pound 12 ounces). The first women's world record was recognized in 1932, the year of its Olympic debut. The record has moved from 46.745 meters (153' 4") up to 80.00 meters (262' 5") in 1988.

The record has been held by 19 women from 12 countries. The former Soviet Union produced six of these world record holders. However, Eastern Europeans have not totally dominated the event, as they have the shot put and discus. The last six world record holders have come from six different countries, and three of these are from non-Eastern European countries: Finland, Greece, and Great Britain.

Five of the world record holders have also been Olympic champions: Bauma, Zátopková, Ozolina, Fuchs, and Felke. No Olympic champion set her world record at the Olympics. However, Yelena Gorchakova (USSR) set a world record in the 1964 qualifying rounds, although she finished third in the final.

The record has been set 34 times. East Germany has produced two great champions: Ruth Fuchs (1970s) and Petra Felke (1980s). Fuchs set the record six times, Felke four.

Women's World Records for Javelin

Record distance	Record holder	Location	Date
46.745m (153' 4")	Nan Gindele (USA)	Chicago, USA	18 Jun 1932
47.24m (155' 0")	Anneliese Steinheuer (GER)	Frankfurt am Main, Germany	21 Jun 1942
48.21m (158' 2")	Herma Bauma (AUT)	Vienna, Austria	29 Jun 1947
48.63m (159' 6")	Herma Bauma (AUT)	Vienna, Austria	12 Sep 1948
49.59m (162' 8")	Natalya Smirnitskaya (USSR)	Moscow, USSR	25 Jul 1949
53.41m (175' 2")	Natalya Smirnitskaya (USSR)	Moscow, USSR	5 Aug 1949
53.56m (175' 8")	Nadezhda Konyayeva (USSR)	Leningrad, USSR	5 Feb 1954
55.11m (180' 9")	Nadezhda Konyayeva (USSR)	Kiev, USSR	22 May 1954
55.48m (182' 0")	Nadezhda Konyayeva (USSR)	Kiev, USSR	6 Aug 1954
55.73m (182' 10")	Dana Zátopková (CZH)	Prague, Czechoslovakia	1 Jun 1958
57.40m (188' 4")	Anna Pazera (AUST)	Cardiff, Wales	24 Jul 1958
57.49m (188' 7")	Birute Kalediene (USSR)	Tbilisi, USSR	30 Oct 1958
57.92m (190' 0")	Elvira Ozolina (USSR)	Leselidze, USSR	3 May 1960
59.55m (195' 4")	Elvira Ozolina (USSR)	Bucharest, Romania	4 Jun 1960
59.78m (196' 1")	Elvira Ozolina (USSR)	Moscow, USSR	3 Jul 1963
62.40m (204' 9")	Yelena Gorchakova (USSR)	Tokyo, Japan	16 Oct 1964
62.70m (205' 8")	Ewa Gryziecka (POL)	Bucharest, Romania	11 Jun 1972
65.06m (213' 5")	Ruth Fuchs (GDR)	Potsdam, East Germany	11 Jun 1972
66.10m (216' 10")	Ruth Fuchs (GDR)	Edinburgh, Scotland	7 Sep 1973
67.22m (220' 6")	Ruth Fuchs (GDR)	Rome, Italy	3 Sep 1974
69.12m (226' 9")	Ruth Fuchs (GDR)	Berlin, East Germany	10 Jul 1976
69.32m (227' 5")	Kate Schmidt (USA)	Fürth, West Germany	11 Sep 1977
69.52m (228' 1")	Ruth Fuchs (GDR)	Dresden, East Germany	13 Jun 1979
69.96m (229' 6")	Ruth Fuchs (GDR)	Split, Yugoslavia	29 Apr 1980
70.08m (229' 11")	Tatyana Biryulina (USSR)	Podolsk, USSR	12 Jul 1980
71.88m (235' 10")	Antoaneta Todorova (BUL)	Zagreb, Yugoslavia	15 Aug 1981
72.40m (237' 6")	Ilse "Tiina" Lillak (FIN)	Helsinki, Finland	29 Jul 1982
74.20m (243' 5")	Sofia Sakorafa (GRE)	Khania, Crete	26 Sep 1982
74.76m (245' 3")	Ilse "Tiina" Lillak (FIN)	Tampere, Finland	13 Jun 1983
75.26m (246' 11")	Petra Felke (GDR)	Schwerin, East Germany	4 Jun 1985

75.40m (247' 4")	Petra Felke (GDR)	Schwerin, East Germany	4 Jun 1985
77.44m (254' 1")	Fatima Whitbread (GBR)	Stuttgart, West Germany	28 Aug 1986
78.90m (258' 10")	Petra Felke (GDR)	Leipzig, East Germany	29 Jul 1987
80.00m (262' 5")	Petra Felke (GDR)	Potsdam, East Germany	9 Sep 1988

Nan Gindele   (United States, 1910-1992)

46.745m (153' 4")   **Chicago, USA**   **18 Jun 1932**

Ferdinanda "Nan" Gindele set the first official world record at the Central AAU Championships in Chicago, two months before the 1932 Los Angeles Olympics. Her record of 46.745 meters (153' 4") lasted 10 years. At the Los Angeles Games she came in only fifth with 37.94 meters (124' 6"), while "Babe" Didriksen won with 43.68 meters (143' 4"). The following year Gindele was the AAU champion with 39.68 meters (130' 2").

A graduate of Carl Schurz High School, she attended Northwestern University and earned a BS in education in 1933. She had a long teaching career in the Chicago public school system.

Anneliese Steinheuer   (Germany, b. 1920)

47.24m (155' 0")   **Frankfurt am Main, Germany**   **21 Jun 1942**

During World War II, 10 years and three days after Nan Gindele set her record, it was broken in Germany. The new world record holder was Anneliese Steinheuer, who achieved the record during an Eintracht Frankfurt meet with 47.24 meters (155' 0").

She was second in the German championships in 1942 and 1943 but never actually won a title. As Germany was not invited to the 1946 European Championships nor the 1948 London Olympics, she had little opportunity for an international career.

Herma Bauma   (Austria, b. 1915)

48.21m (158' 2")   **Vienna, Austria**   **29 Jun 1947**
48.63m (159' 6")   **Vienna, Austria**   **12 Sep 1948**

Herma Bauma had placed fourth at the 1936 Berlin Olympics at the age of 21, throwing 41.66 meters (136' 8"). Eleven years later she threw a world record at a Hungary vs. Austria match with a throw of 48.21 meters (158' 2"). In 1948 she won the gold medal at the London Olympics with 45.57 meters (149' 6"). A month later Bauma threw her second world record (48.63 meters) at an Austria vs. Czechoslovakia match. At the 1950 European Championships she was second to the new world record holder, Natalya Smirnitskaya (USSR). Bauma finished ninth at the 1952 Olympics.

Austria was taken over by Hitler in the 1938 Anschluss. Bauma, an Austrian, actu-

Herma Bauma, Austria (javelin), 1948 Olympic champion.

ally won the German national championship in 1942 with 46.23 meters (151' 8"), a German record at the time.

Natalya Smirnitskaya   (Soviet Union, b. 1927)

| 49.59m (162' 8") | Moscow, USSR | 25 Jul 1949 |
| 53.41m (175' 2") | Moscow, USSR | 5 Aug 1949 |

The Soviet Union rejoined the IAAF in 1947, after a 30-year absence, and its athletes, especially the female throwers, soon changed the record books. Natalya Smirnitskaya broke the world record twice in 1949, and her second record of 53.41 meters broke the 50-meter barrier.

Both records took place in Moscow, and very little information about these throws was provided by Soviet officials. However, there was no doubt she was world class. The following year she won the European championship in Brussels with a throw of 47.55 meters (156' 0"), with Herma Bauma second with 43.87 meters (143' 11"). Smirnitskaya was Soviet champion twice (1949 and 1950) and came in second in 1951.

Natalya Smirnitskaya, Soviet Union (javelin).

Nadezhda Konyayeva   (Soviet Union, b. 1931)

53.56m (175' 8")	Leningrad, USSR	5 Feb 1954
55.11m (180' 9")	Kiev, USSR	22 May 1954
55.48m (182' 0")	Kiev, USSR	6 Aug 1954

Nadezhda Konyayeva set three world records in 1954 and became the first woman to throw over 55 meters. Despite her world records, she never managed to win a significant competition. She finished third at the 1954 European Championships in Bern, Switzerland, with 49.49 meters (162' 4"). At the 1956 Melbourne Olympics she once again finished third with 50.28 meters (164' 11"). Konyayeva also missed out on the Soviet championships, coming in second in 1954 and 1956 and third in 1953.

Dana Zátopková   (Czechoslovakia, b. 1922)

| 55.73m (182' 10") | Prague, Czechoslovakia | 1 Jun 1958 |

Dana Zátopková's name is inextricably linked to her husband's athletic fortunes. She and Emil Zatopek were both born on the same day. His feats were legendary, in particular his winning of three Olympic gold medals at the 1952 Helsinki Games. Consequently, her own career has been somewhat underrated. But she achieved every possible honor: 1952 Olympic gold medal, European champion in 1954 and 1958, and world record holder.

Dana Zátopková, Czechoslovakia, (javelin) with Soviet distance star Vladimir Kuts.

She competed at four Olympics, coming in seventh in 1948, first in 1952, fourth in 1956, and second in 1960. Her world record came somewhat late in her career, at age 35, at an athletic meet in Prague. Zátopková was Czech javelin champion 13 times.

Husband and wife used unconventional training methods. One trick was to throw the javelin at each other and expect the other to catch it in full flight.

Zátopková and her husband were known to be liberal reformers. Accordingly, when the reformist government of Alexander Dubcek was overthrown by the Soviet invasion in 1968, they immediately became persona non grata to the new regime and disappeared from view. They suffered multiple indignities over many years and were denied basic human rights until communism in Czechoslovakia finally collapsed in the late 1980s.

Anna Pazera   (Australia, b. 1936)

57.40m (188' 4")   **Cardiff, Wales**   **24 Jul 1958**

Anna Pazera, born Anna Wojtaszek, was Polish by birth. She won the 400m indoors in Poland and was a competent shot putter. She traveled with the Polish team to Melbourne for the 1956 Olympics. In the javelin final she threw 46.92 meters (150' 11"), which placed her ninth. After the Games she decided not to return to Poland, but defected while in Australia. She eventually married and became an Australian citizen.

As Anna Pazera, she was picked for the 1958 Commonwealth Games in Cardiff. At Cardiff Arms Park she heaved the javelin 57.40 meters (188' 4"). That world record was the highlight of her career. At the 1960 Rome Olympics, she finished sixth with 51.14 meters (167' 9"). At the 1964 Tokyo Olympics she threw 44.87 meters (147' 2") in the qualifying rounds, which was not enough to make the final. At other Commonwealth Games, Pazera was third in 1962 and second in 1966.

After her javelin career finished, she was active in basketball for many years, forming a Polish girls basketball club, Polonia. Now remarried, she lives in South Australia.

Birute Kalediene   (Soviet Union, b. 1934)

57.49m (188' 7")   **Tbilisi, USSR**   **30 Oct 1958**

Anna Pazera's record lasted only three months before another Soviet athlete eclipsed it by nine centimeters. Birute Zalogaitite, later Birute Kalediene, came from Lithuania. She was the Soviet champion for three years in a row (1958-60) and achieved her world record at the Soviet Team Championships in Tbilisi, Georgia.

The 1958 European Championships were held at Stockholm, and she finished second (51.30 meters, 168' 4") to Dana Zátopková, who was in near-world-record form (56.02

meters, 183' 9"). At the 1960 Rome Olympics, Kalediene was third with 53.44 meters (175' 4"). First was the new world record holder, Elvira Ozolina with 55.98 meters (183' 8"), and second was Zátopková with 53.78 meters (176' 5").

At the 1964 Tokyo Olympics Kalediene finished fourth with 56.30 meters (184' 8").

Elvira Ozolina   (Soviet Union, b. 1939)

57.92m (190' 0")	Leselidze, USSR	3 May 1960
59.55m (195' 4")	Bucharest, Romania	4 Jun 1960
59.78m (196' 1")	Moscow, USSR	3 Jul 1963

Elvira Ozolina, Soviet Union (javelin), with U.S. hurdler Hayes Jones.

Elvira Ozolina had a very long career, from fourth in the 1957 Soviet championships to a win in the event in 1973. Her career took off in 1960, when she set two world records and won at the Rome Olympics with 55.98 meters (183' 8"). Two years later she won the European Championships in Belgrade with 54.93 meters (180' 2"). She set her third world record in 1963.

Ozolina achieved the first throw over 60 meters when she won the Soviet title in 1964 with a throw of 61.38 meters (201' 4"). However, the record was not formally submitted at this time for official certification. Second at those Soviet championships was Yelena Gorchakova with 55.03 meters (180' 6").

In the qualifying rounds at the Tokyo Olympics, Yelena Gorchakova outdid herself with a massive 62.40 meters (204' 9"). Suddenly, she was the new world record holder. Ozolina's loss of the world record was one disappointment, the results in the final were another. Young Romanian teenager Mihaela Penes threw 60.54 meters (198' 7") on her first throw, good enough to win. Ozolina threw 54.80 meters (179' 9"), and all the rest were fouls. She finished fifth. Gorchakova threw 57.06 meters (187' 2") for third place. Ozolina was no longer Olympic champion or world record holder. Deeply disheartened, Ozolina went to a hairdresser in Tokyo and had all her hair shaven off as a symbol of her humiliation.

Ozolina won the Soviet title in 1966 and 1973 but had no more international victories. She is married to another javelin champion, Janis Lusis.

Yelena Gorchakova   (Soviet Union, b. 1933)

| 62.40m (204' 9") | Tokyo, Japan | 16 Oct 1964 |

Yelena Gorchakova was the athlete who surprised everybody in the qualifying rounds of the javelin at the 1964 Tokyo Olympics. Suddenly, out of nowhere, she threw 62.40 meters (204' 9") at 10:20 in the morning. This throw shattered the 60-meter barrier and the 200-foot barrier.

Alas, she couldn't reproduce this result in the final. She managed 57.06 meters (187' 2") for third place. She had actually been around as an athlete a long time and was 31 years old when she achieved her world record, which was to remain her career best. She had been fifth in the 1951 Soviet championships at 18. She had won a bronze medal at the 1952 Olympics. She had been a finalist at the Soviet championships 12 times before she finally had wins in 1963 and 1965.

Yelena Gorchakova, Soviet Union (javelin).

Ewa Gryziecka   (Poland, b. 1948)

62.70m (205' 8")   **Bucharest, Romania**   **11 Jun 1972**

Ewa Gryziecka, Poland (javelin).

After nearly eight years, Yelena Gorchakova's 1964 record was beaten twice in one day. On 11 June 1972, the record was first beaten in Bucharest, Romania, at 1745 hours (5:45 P.M.) by Ewa Gryziecka. At an international match between Poland, Romania, and West Germany, she threw 62.70 meters (205' 8") on her first throw, adding 30 centimeters to the record.

By the time the javelin competition in Bucharest had been completed, Ewa Gryziecka was no longer world record holder. At another athletic match between Bulgaria and East Germany in Potsdam, Ruth Fuchs had thrown the javelin 65.06 meters (213' 5") at 1820 hours (6:20 P.M.).

That brief world record was to be the high point of Gryziecka's career. At the Munich Olympics in September she finished seventh with 57.00 meters (187' 0"). The winner was Fuchs with 63.88 meters (209' 7").

Ruth Fuchs   (East Germany, b. 1946)

65.06m (213' 5")	Potsdam, East Germany	11 Jun 1972
66.10m (216' 10")	Edinburgh, Scotland	7 Sep 1973
67.22m (220' 6")	Rome, Italy	3 Sep 1974
69.12m (226' 9")	Berlin, East Germany	10 Jul 1976
69.52m (228' 1")	Dresden, East Germany	13 Jun 1979
69.96m (229' 6")	Split, Yugoslavia	29 Apr 1980

Ruth Fuchs, East Germany, javelin queen of the 1970s and Olympic champion, 1972 and 1976.

Ruth Fuchs took up the javelin at age 14 and four years later won the first of 11 East German championships. She became the undisputed javelin queen of the 1970s. Fuchs had come in third at the 1971 European Championships but from then on won everything. She was Olympic champion in 1972 (63.88 meters, 209' 7") and 1976 (65.94 meters, 216' 4"), the only woman to win two Olympic javelin gold medals. In addition, she was European champion in 1974 (67.22 meters, 220' 6") and 1978 (69.16 meters, 226' 11").

Her six world records began in 1972. The first took place 35 minutes after Poland's Ewa Gryziecka had added 30 centimeters to Gorchakova's eight-year-old world record. Fuchs threw 65.06 meters (213' 5"), which added another 2.36 meters to Ewa Gryziecka's record. She also broke through the 65-meter barrier. Despite three world records over 69 meters, she couldn't quite reach the 70-meter barrier.

Her last world record (69.96 meters) took place three months before the 1980 Moscow Olympics, and she seemed the obvious favorite for the gold medal. But plagued by a back injury, she finished a disappointing eighth with 63.94 meters (209' 9").

Originally a medical assistant, she later qualified as a doctor of psychology. She described her own success as 5 percent talent and 95 percent hard work. Fuchs says her major interest is hunting.

Kate Schmidt   (United States, b. 1953)

| 69.32m (227' 5") | Fürth, West Germany | 11 Sep 1977 |

Kate Schmidt proved that an American javelin thrower could successfully challenge the best of the Europeans and earned the nickname "Kate the Great." A tall athlete at 185 centimeters (6' 0 ¾"), she was the U.S. champion seven times between 1969 and 1979. Her first U.S. title in 1969 took place when she was 15 years old. However, she never managed to beat Ruth Fuchs in competition.

She won an Olympic bronze medal at Munich in 1972 and again at Montreal in 1976. In Munich, at the age of 18, she actually led after the first throw until Ruth Fuchs took over and eventually won with 63.88 meters (209' 7"). Schmidt threw 59.94 meters (196' 8").

At Montreal Schmidt was plagued by a painful nerve tumor in her left arm and achieved the bronze medal on her last throw, with 63.96 meters (209' 10"). Fuchs again won with 65.94 meters (216' 4").

Kate Schmidt, United States (javelin), giving some tips to Soviet athlete Svetlana Korolyeva.

Schmidt's world record came out of the blue in 1977. She was competing in Germany in her last competition before flying home the next morning. On her third throw, the javelin just kept going and going, out to 69.32 meters (227' 5"). To her delight, she had added 20 centimeters to Fuchs's fourth world record. She later said that the only extra thing that would have made the day complete would have been beating Fuchs. "Then I would have had an orgasm," she later told *Track and Field News*.

Now in her mid 40s, she was recently diagnosed as having ovarian cancer which is currently in remission.

Tatyana Biryulina   (Soviet Union, b. 1955)

70.08m (229' 11")   **Podolsk, USSR**   **12 Jul 1980**

The 70-meter barrier was a major landmark, and it seemed that Ruth Fuchs would be the first to claim it. However, in a pre-Olympic trial, little-known Soviet athlete Tatyana Biryulina threw 70.08 meters (229' 11"). This was an improvement on her previous personal best by 8.38 meters (27' 6").

Biryulina had competed without major success in previous Soviet championships, coming in fifth in the national titles in 1978 and 1979. She could not reproduce her world record form at the Moscow Olympics and managed 65.08 meters (213' 6"), which left her in sixth position. After her day of glory in July 1980 she had no further successes in track and field.

Antoaneta Todorova   (Bulgaria, b. 1963)

71.88m (235' 10")   **Zagreb, Yugoslavia**   **15 Aug 1981**

Like Tatyana Biryulina, Antoaneta Todorova was another athlete who seemed to come out of nowhere. In August 1981 at the European Cup in Zagreb she suddenly threw 71.88 meters (235' 10").

She had been competitive over the previous few years. She won a bronze medal at the European Junior Championships in 1979. In May 1980 she threw 66.40 meters (217' 10"), a world junior record. However, she came in 10th at the Moscow Olympics with 60.66 meters (199' 0").

The next year, Todorova kept slowly improving: 66.54 meters (218' 4") and 69.64 meters (228' 6") in June 1981. Then came her world record in August. She was only 18 at the time, the youngest female athlete to hold the world record in the javelin. The promise of a bright future lay ahead of her. But the rest of her career was disappointing. She never exceeded that performance in August 1981.

Ilse "Tiina" Lillak   (Finland, b. 1961)

72.40m (237' 6")	**Helsinki, Finland**	**29 Jul 1982**
74.76m (245' 3")	**Tampere, Finland**	**13 Jun 1983**

Tiina Lillak was Finland's first great female javelin thrower. Born in Helsinki, she tried the javelin at age 13. She improved each year from 1974 until 1982, when, at age 21, she threw a world record of 72.40 meters (237' 6") in Helsinki in front of her own people.

Finland was delighted. However, her fans were then somewhat disappointed with her fourth place at the 1982 European Championships (66.26 meters, 217' 5"). Then three weeks later Greece's Sofia Sakorafa took over as world record holder with 74.20 meters (243' 5").

However, in 1983 everything came up "lilacs." First, Lillak regained the world record with a throw of 74.76 meters (245' 3") in June. Two months later the inaugural World Athletic Championships took place in Helsinki. Britain's Fatima Whitbread led with 69.14 meters (226' 10") from round 1. In a dramatic finish, on her very last throw, Lillak threw 70.82 meters (232' 4") to snatch the gold medal. She sprinted down the stadium in delight to a tumultuous roar from the crowd.

That was perhaps the high point of her career. Because of a painful foot injury, she could manage only two throws at the 1984 Olympics, reaching 69.00 meters (226' 4"). This still won her a silver medal, only 56 centimeters behind the winning throw of Tessa Sanderson (Great Britain).

Lillak never quite recaptured the form of 1982 and 1983. At the European Championships she was fourth in 1986 and ninth in 1990. At the Seoul Olympics she failed to qualify for the final.

Sofia Sakorafa   (Greece, b. 1957)

74.20m (243' 5")	**Khania, Crete**	**26 Sep 1982**

Sofia Sakorafa was the first and so far the only female athlete from Greece to set a world record. Born in Trikala, she was fifth in the 1975 European Junior Championships. At the 1976 Olympics she threw three fouls in the qualifying rounds and was eliminated. At the 1978 European Championships she was not able to qualify for the final. Two years later at the Moscow Olympics she once more threw three fouls in the qualifying rounds.

Around this time, Anna Verouli developed as another talented Greek javelin thrower. The rivalry between the two Greeks resulted in ever-improving results for both of them. They pushed the Greek record past the 70-meter mark. Their ultimate showdown came at the 1982 European Championships at Athens, in front of a Greek crowd full of anticipation and emotion for their duel. In a final in which positions seesawed throughout, Verouli finally won with a throw of 70.02 meters (229' 9") in the fifth round. Sakorafa threw 67.04

meters (219' 11") to claim third place, and the stadium overflowed with emotion.

After this memorable duel, Sakorafa threw 71.52 meters (234' 8") in London and then a massive world record of 74.20 meters (243' 5") in Crete on 26 September 1982.

That was the high point of her career, although she threw 72.28 meters (237' 2") in Norway in 1983. There was a sour point that year as she and the Greek Athletic Federation feuded over some commercial endorsements, and she was suspended for six months.

Sofia Sakorafa, Greece (javelin).

Petra Felke   (East Germany, b. 1959)

75.26m (246' 11")	Schwerin, East Germany	4 Jun 1985
75.40m (247' 4")	Schwerin, East Germany	4 Jun 1985
78.90m (258' 10")	Leipzig, East Germany	29 Jul 1987
80.00m (262' 5")	Potsdam, East Germany	9 Sep 1988

Petra Felke, East Germany (javelin), 1988 Olympic champion.

Petra Felke was the East German successor to Ruth Fuchs and, as a talented junior, came under the guidance of Karl Hellmann, Fuchs's long-term coach. She won the East German title six years running, from 1984 to 1989, but missed the 1984 Olympics because of the communist boycott.

Her world records took place in 1985, 1987, and 1988. They were interrupted in 1986, when Fatima Whitbread threw 77.44 meters (254' 1") at the European Championships in Stuttgart. Whitbread also won the 1987 World Championships in Rome. Felke was second at both these events, but in

1988 she was a comfortable winner at the Seoul Olympics with 74.68 meters (245' 0") to Whitbread's 70.32 meters (230' 8").

Felke broke through the 75-meter barrier in 1985 and reached exactly 80 meters in 1988. After her 1988 triumphs her results slipped marginally. She was third at the 1990 European Championships, second at the 1991 World Championships, and seventh at the 1992 Olympics.

Felke still owns eight out of the nine top throws to date. Since the collapse of East Germany and her retirement from athletics, she has moved on to a career in physical education.

Fatima Whitbread   (Great Britain, b. 1961)

77.44m (254' 1")   **Stuttgart, West Germany**   **28 Aug 1986**

Fatima Whitbread, Great Britain (javelin).

Just as Greece produced two javelin champions in the 1980s (Verouli and Sakorafa), Great Britain was similarly blessed with Tessa Sanderson and Fatima Whitbread. Between them, they won just about every major honor: Fatima Whitbread was world record holder, European champion (1986), and world champion (1987); Tessa Sanderson was 1984 Olympic champion and Commonwealth champion three times. Just as the Greek pair had an acrimonious relationship, the British athletes also had difficulty with each other.

Fatima Whitbread was abandoned at the age of three months by her Cypriot mother and was made a ward of the court in London. She was raised in a series of homes and turned to sport to excel. After a school lesson on the Greek myth of Atalanta, she took up javelin throwing. She was spotted by Mary Whitbread, who later adopted her and made the bold prediction that Fatima would one day become the greatest javelin thrower in the world.

At the time, Britain's leading javelin thrower was Tessa Sanderson, and she continued to be so for many years. But that slowly changed. Whitbread almost won the 1983 World Championships in Helsinki, until Tiina Lillak snatched the title on her last throw. Sanderson won the 1984 Olympic title and the 1986 Commonwealth Games in Edinburgh. Whitbread had come in third at the Olympics and after losing in Edinburgh sobbed publicly.

But then her fortunes turned around. She traveled to Stuttgart for the European Championships and in the qualifying rounds, loosed a mighty throw of 77.44 meters (254' 1"), a new world record. In the final the next day she won the title with 76.32 meters (250' 5") over Felke's 72.52 meters (237' 11"). Her winning form continued into the 1987 season, when she won the World Championships in Rome with 76.64 meters (251' 5"), again followed by Felke with 71.76 meters (235' 5").

Those massive throws appeared to have triggered a series of shoulder injuries. She still was able to win the silver medal at the Seoul Olympics with 70.32 meters (230' 8"), behind Felke's 74.68 meters (245' 0"). But increasing problems with her shoulder forced her to retire in 1990.

Conclusions

Current standards in the javelin are well below those of the 1980s and way below the world record of 80.00 meters. No athlete in 1996 exceeded 70 meters. However, this is one throwing event not dominated by Eastern Europeans. The all-time top five female javelin throwers come from four different countries, and three of these are from non-Eastern European countries (Great Britain, Finland, and Greece). So the fall-off in standards cannot be blamed on the collapse of Eastern Europe.

Nonetheless, the prospect of a change in the world record in the near future seems remote. Perhaps the 1980s will one day be regarded as a golden age of javelin throwing.

Five All-Time Best: Women's Javelin

Petra Felke (GDR)	80.00m (262' 5")	1988
Fatima Whitbread (GBR)	77.44m (254' 1")	1986
Tiina Lillak (FIN)	74.76m (245' 3")	1983
Sofia Sakorafa (GRE)	74.20m (243' 5")	1982
Tessa Sanderson (GBR)	73.58m (241' 5")	1983
Prediction	*80.00m (262' 5")*	*2015*

Top Three: Women's Javelin

GOLD MEDAL:	Ruth Fuchs (GDR)
SILVER MEDAL:	Petra Felke (GDR)
BRONZE MEDAL:	Fatima Whitbread (GBR)

The pentathlon, originally five events, was replaced in 1981 by the heptathlon, consisting of seven. Points are allocated according to each performance, and the highest point scorer after all events are completed is the winner. The program is spread over two days.

Unlike the decathlon, the events in the pentathlon have been changed significantly over the years, as have the scoring tables. The first pentathlon program before World War II included the 100m, javelin, high jump, long jump, and shot put (type A). After World War II, the 100m and javelin were replaced by the 200m and the 80m hurdles (type B). In 1969, the 100m hurdles replaced the 80m hurdles (type C). The last change to the pentathlon was in 1977, when the 200m was replaced by the 800m (type D).

However, in 1981 the pentathlon was replaced by the heptathlon. The current program is as follows:

Day 1: 100m hurdles, shot put , high jump, 200m
Day 2: long jump, javelin, 800m

Until the 800m was introduced, the event was largely dominated by sprinters who could also manage the shot put. The 800m race is possibly not a full endurance event, so there is an argument for making it a 1500m run, as in the decathlon.

Altogether 15 athletes have held the world record for the pentathlon or the heptathlon. The event was first introduced into the Olympics in 1964. Four of these world record holders have also been Olympic champions: Press, Peters, Tkachenko, and Joyner-Kersee. Press, Tkachenko, Peters, and Joyner-Kersee (1988) set world records when they won their Olympic titles. Because of the many changes in the event, it is impossible to compare the scores achieved over the years.

Women's World Records for Pentathlon and Heptathlon*

Record score	Record holder	Location	Date
Pentathlon A: 100m, HJ, LJ, SP, J			
4155	Gisela Mauermayer (GER)	London, England	9-11 Aug 1934
4391	Gisela Mauermayer (GER)	Stuttgart, Germany	16-17 Jul 1938
Pentathlon B: 200m, 80m H, HJ, LJ, SP			
4692	Fanny Blankers-Koen (HOL)	Amsterdam, Netherlands	15-16 Sep 1951
4704	Aleksandra Chudina (USSR)	Bucharest, Romania	8-9 Aug 1953
4747	Nina Martynenko (USSR)	Leningrad, USSR	6-7 Jul 1955
4750	Aleksandra Chudina (USSR)	Moscow, USSR	6-7 Sep 1955
4767	Nina Martynenko (USSR)	Moscow, USSR	11-12 Aug 1956
4846	Galina Bystrova (USSR)	Odessa, USSR	15-16 Oct 1957
4872	Galina Bystrova (USSR)	Tbilisi, USSR	1-2 Nov 1958
4880	Irina Press (USSR)	Krasnodar, USSR	13-14 Sep 1959
4902	Irina Press (USSR)	Tula, USSR	21-22 May 1960
4959	Irina Press (USSR)	Tula, USSR	25-26 Jun 1960
4972	Irina Press (USSR)	Kiev, USSR	17-18 Oct 1960
5137	Irina Press (USSR)	Tbilisi, USSR	8-9 Oct 1961
5246	Irina Press (USSR)	Tokyo, Japan	16-17 Oct 1964
Pentathlon C: 200m, 100m H, HJ, LJ, SP			
5352	Liese Prokop (AUT)	Vienna, Austria	4-5 Oct 1969
5406	Burglinde Pollak (GDR)	Erfurt, East Germany	5-6 Sep 1970
4801	Mary Peters (GBR)	Munich, West Germany	2-3 Sep 1972
4831	Burglinde Pollak (GDR)	Sofia, Bulgaria	12 Aug 1973
4932	Burglinde Pollak (GDR)	Bonn, West Germany	22 Sep 1973

Pentathlon D: 800m, 100m H, HJ, LJ, SP

4765	Eva Wilms (FRG)	Göttingen, West Germany	14 May 1977
4823	Eva Wilms (FRG)	Bernhausen, West Germany	18 Jun 1977
4839	Nadezhda Tkachenko (USSR)	Lille, France	18 Sep 1977
4856	Olga Kuragina (USSR)	Moscow, USSR	20 Jun 1980
5083	Nadezhda Tkachenko (USSR)	Moscow, USSR	24 Jul 1980

Heptathlon: Day 1—100m H, SP, HJ, 200m; Day 2—LJ, J, 800m**

6716	Ramona Neubert (GDR)	Kiev, USSR	27-28 Jun 1981
6773	Ramona Neubert (GDR)	Halle, East Germany	19-20 Jun 1982
6836	Ramona Neubert (GDR)	Moscow, USSR	18-19 Jun 1983

1985 tables

6946	Sabine Paetz (GDR)	Potsdam, East Germany	5-6 May 1984
7148	Jackie Joyner-Kersee (USA)	Moscow, USSR	6-7 Jul 1986
7158	Jackie Joyner-Kersee (USA)	Houston, USA	1-2 Aug 1986
7215	Jackie Joyner-Kersee (USA)	Indianapolis, USA	15-16 Jul 1988
7291	Jackie Joyner-Kersee (USA)	Seoul, South Korea	23-24 Sep 1988

* Scores for Mauermayer (1934) to Pollak (1970) are adjusted according to the 1954 tables. From Peters (1972) to Tkachenko (1980) the 1971 tables are used.

** On 1 Jan 1981 the pentathlon was replaced by the heptathlon.

Gisela Mauermayer   (Germany, b. 1913)

| 4155 | London, England | 9-11 Aug 1934 |
| 4391 | Stuttgart, Germany | 16-17 Jul 1938 |

The great German pentathlete of the 1930s was also a world record holder in the shot put and discus, as described in those chapters. Her first world record was achieved at the Women's World Games in London in 1934, and her second four years later in Stuttgart. Her performances were as follows:

Gisela Mauermayer, Germany (shot put, discus, pentathlon), an early pioneer of women's track and field.

	100m	High jump	Long jump	Shot put	Javelin
1934	13.0	1.52m	5.51m	13.44m	32.91m
1938	12.4	1.56m	5.62m	13.07m	36.90m

The pentathlon was a regular event at the German championships in the 1930s, and Mauermayer won the title in 1933, 1934, and 1938.

Fanny Blankers-Koen (Netherlands, b. 1918)

4692   **Amsterdam, Netherlands**   **15-16 Sep 1951**

The great Dutch athlete Fanny Blankers-Koen had achieved world records in four individual events (100m, 80m hurdles, high jump, long jump), so it was no surprise that she eventually turned to the pentathlon and set a world record. This record was achieved in 1951 and was her last world record. Presumably she could have achieved it much earlier in her career. Her 1951 results were as follows:

Fanny Blankers-Koen, Netherlands, multiple world record holder (100m, 80m hurdles, high jump, long jump, pentathlon) and winner of four gold medals at the 1948 Olympics.

200m	80m hurdles	High jump	Long jump	Shot put
24.4	11.4	1.60m	5.88m	11.50m

Aleksandra Chudina (Soviet Union, 1923-1990)

4704	**Bucharest, Romania**	**8-9 Aug 1953**
4750	**Moscow, USSR**	**6-7 Sep 1955**

Aleksandra Chudina was a great Soviet athlete of the post-World War II years. In 1952 at Helsinki she won Olympic medals in three separate field events: silver medals in the javelin and long jump and a bronze in the high jump. She won the Soviet pentathlon title nine times between 1946 and 1955. In addition, she also set a world record in the high jump in 1954 (1.73 meters, 5' 8") and was European pentathlon champion in 1954. These were her individual performances in her two pentathlon world records:

	200m	80m hurdles	High jump	Long jump	Shot put
1953	25.5	11.6	1.63m	5.81m	13.42m
1955	26.3	11.5	1.64m	6.04m	13.94m

Aleksandra Chudina,
Soviet Union (high jump, pentathlon).

Nina Martynenko   (Soviet Union, b. 1933)

| 4747 | Leningrad, USSR | 6–7 Jul 1955 |
| 4767 | Moscow, USSR | 11–12 Aug 1956 |

Galina Bystrova *(left)* and Nina Martynenko, both of the Soviet Union, both pentathlon world record holders. Bystrova also held the 80m hurdles world record.

Nina Martynenko was the first athlete to hold the pentathlon world record without holding a record in an individual event as well. She broke Aleksandra Chudina's 1953 record in July 1955, but two months later Chudina reclaimed it. Martynenko took the record back in 1956, winning 4767 to 4622 in a clash between the two athletes at the Soviet championships at Moscow's Lenin Stadium. That was her one and only Soviet title in the pentathlon, though she won the Soviet 80m hurdles title in 1956. At the European Championships she was seventh in 1954 and second in 1958. Her world record performances were as follows:

	200m	80m hurdles	High jump	Long jump	Shot put
1955	25.8	11.3	1.62m	5.92m	13.54m
1956	25.4	10.9	1.57m	5.88m	13.23m

Galina Bystrova   (Soviet Union, b. 1934)

4846	Odessa, USSR	15–16 Oct 1957
4872	Tbilisi, USSR	1–2 Nov 1958

Galina Bystrova had a long career as a hurdler and a pentathlete, competing at three Olympics. As a hurdler, she equaled the world record for 80m hurdles in 1958 (10.6). In this event, she competed at the Melbourne and Rome Olympics, coming in fourth and fifth, respectively. At the 1964 Tokyo Games she competed in the inaugural pentathlon, coming in third to the new star Irina Press (USSR). She had two European Championships triumphs in the pentathlon, winning in 1958 and 1962. In addition, she was European champion at the 80m hurdles in 1958.

Her pentathlon world records were helped by her world class hurdling times. She was twice Soviet champion in the hurdles, in 1957 and 1958. However, her second world record was mainly due to her improved shot putting results. These were her world record results:

	200m	80m hurdles	High jump	Long jump	Shot put
1957	25.2	10.8	1.58m	6.17m	12.73m
1958	25.5	10.8	1.60m	6.00m	13.81m

Irina Press   (Soviet Union, b. 1939)

4880	Krasnodar, USSR	13–14 Sep 1959
4902	Tula, USSR	21–22 May 1960
4959	Tula, USSR	25–26 Jun 1960
4972	Kiev, USSR	17–18 Oct 1960
5137	Tbilisi, USSR	8–9 Oct 1961
5246	Tokyo, Japan	16–17 Oct 1964

Irina Press, younger sister of discus and shot put ace Tamara Press, was the first truly great pentathlete, setting six world records. She dominated her event for many years and was Soviet champion from 1959-1961 and 1964-1966. At the Olympics she won the inaugural pentathlon at the 1964 Tokyo Games, setting her last world record in the process. In addition to these achievements, she was a world record holder in the 80m hurdles, setting five world records in this event and winning the gold medal at the 1960 Rome Olympics.

The only event at which she did not triumph was at the European Championships. She was injured in mid-competition at the pentathlon in 1962 and had to withdraw after two events. She was a non-starter in 1966.

She was particularly strong in the hurdles and shot put in her pentathlon results. Whereas no previous pentathlon world record holder had thrown the shot over 14 meters, she threw it 17.16 meters in her last world record. Her overall results were as follows:

Irina Press, Soviet Union (80m hurdles, pentathlon), Olympic champion in both events.

	200m	80m hurdles	High jump	Long jump	Shot put
1959	24.8	10.9	1.58m	5.82m	14.20m
May 1960	24.3	11.2	1.57m	5.76m	15.00m
Jun 1960	24.5	10.9	1.50m	6.17m	15.18m
Oct 1960	24.7	10.8	1.63m	5.58m	15.34m
1961	24.2	10.9	1.62m	6.24m	15.26m
1964	24.7	10.7	1.63m	6.24m	17.16m

Liese Prokop   (Austria, b. 1941)

5352 (1954 tables); 4727 (1971 tables)   **Vienna, Austria**   **4–5 Oct 1969**

When the distance for the sprint hurdles was increased from 80m to 100m in 1969, it was altered in the pentathlon as well. New scoring tables were belatedly introduced in 1971.

Liese Prokop of Austria had a good year in 1969. She won the European Championships in Athens. The next month she broke the world record in Vienna.

She had won the silver medal in the pentathlon at the 1968 Mexico City Olympics. She had actually been leading until the last event, the 200m, but Ingrid Mickler (née Becker) of West Germany outsprinted her 23.5 to 25.1. This was enough to give Mickler the gold medal.

Prokop's world record score was helped by her high jump, in which she reached 1.75

Liese Prokop, Austria (pentathlon).

meters (5' 8 ¾"). The previous best in a world record pentathlon score was 1.64 meters (5' 4 ½"). These were her world record results:

	200m	100m hurdles	High jump	Long jump	Shot put
1969	24.6	13.5	1.75m	6.62m	14.95m

After her athletic days, she served as a regional minister for Family, Youth, and Sport in Austria.

Burglinde Pollak   (East Germany, b. 1951)

5406 (1954 tables); 4775 (1971 tables)	Erfurt, East Germany	5–6 Sep 1970
4831 (1971 tables)	Sofia, Bulgaria	12 Aug 1973
4932 (1971 tables)	Bonn, West Germany	22 Sep 1973

Burglinde Pollak never quiet won a major gold medal, despite setting three world records and being East German champion four times (1969, 1970, 1973, and 1974). Her competitive record was as follows:

1971 European Championships	Second	1976 Montreal Olympics	Third
1972 Munich Olympics	Third	1978 European Championships	Third
1974 European Championships	Second	1980 Moscow Olympics	Sixth

These were her world record results:

	200m	100m hurdles	High jump	Long jump	Shot put
1970	23.8	13.3	1.75m	6.20m	15.57m
Aug 1973	23.7	13.21	1.74m	6.45m	15.40m
Sep 1973	23.35	13.21	1.78m	6.47m	15.85m

She was the first pentathlon world record holder to run 200m under 24 seconds.

Mary Peters   (Great Britain/Northern Ireland, b. 1939)

4801	Munich, West Germany	2–3 Sep 1972

Mary Peters was the first athlete from Northern Ireland to both set a world record and win an Olympic gold medal when she triumphed at the Munich Olympics. Her win was received with much emotion from that beleaguered part of the world. She was treated by some of the British press as though she was an overnight success, though she was 33 at the time and had been competing at international level for 14 years.

She was born in Liverpool, and her family moved to Northern Ireland when she was 12. In Northern Ireland, she was not immune from the political troubles: In 1973 three British servicemen were murdered by the IRA in the flat next to hers.

She first competed at the Commonwealth Games in Cardiff in 1958 without special distinction and continued competing internationally through to 1974.

Mary Peters, Great Britain (pentathlon), 1972 Olympic champion.

Her competitive record was as follows:

1962 European Championships	Fifth	1970 Commonwealth Games	First
1964 Tokyo Olympics	Fourth	1972 Munich Olympics	First
1968 Mexico City Olympics	Ninth	1974 Commonwealth Games	First

At the Munich Olympics Peters secured an important personal best in the high jump, which gave her a significant lead. However, this was pegged back by Heidi Rosendahl's long jump performance, just one centimeter short of the world record. Going into the last event, the 200m, Peters held a small lead, but it would take a personal best to hold off the faster Rosendahl. Peters did this by running 24.08 seconds, just enough to offset Rosendahl's 22.96 by ten points.

Her coach throughout her career was Buster McShane, who was tragically killed in a car crash a few months after her Munich victory. After her retirement, she labored for a modern athletic track in Belfast, which finally came into being and was named the Mary Peters Track.

Her world record results in Munich were as follows:

	200m	100m hurdles	High jump	Long jump	Shot put
1972	24.08	13.29	1.82m	5.98m	16.20m

Eva Wilms   (West Germany, b. 1952)

4765	Göttingen, West Germany	14 May 1977
4823	Bernhausen, West Germany	18 Jun 1977

Further changes to the pentathlon were made in the late 1970s, with the 800m replacing the 200m. During this time (1976-80), all events were completed in one day. The first athlete to set a world record with this new format was Eva Wilms in May 1977. She improved upon it one month later at an international match between West Germany and the Soviet Union.

In the West German championships she was the pentathlon champion in 1976 and 1977. She was also the shot put champion eight years in a row (1974-81) and was second in the discus four times. At the Montreal Olympics she competed in the shot put and was seventh. She finished sixth in the same discipline at the European Championships in Prague in 1978.

Her world record results were greatly helped by her shot put scores. She threw over 20 meters in both world records. The next best effort by a world record holder was 17.16 meters by Irina Press. These were Wilms's world records results:

	800m	100m hurdles	High jump	Long jump	Shot put
May 1977	2:19.91	13.70	1.74m	6.03m	20.62m
Jun 1977	2:19.66	13.83	1.74m	6.29m	20.95m

Nadezhda Tkachenko   (Soviet Union, b. 1948)

4839	Lille, France	18 Sep 1977
5083	Moscow, USSR	24 Jul 1980

Nadezhda Tkachenko was Soviet champion four times and European champion in 1974 and 1978. At the Olympics she was ninth in 1972 (Munich), fifth in 1976 (Montreal), and first in 1980 (Moscow), where she set her second world record. After her European Championships win in 1978, she tested positive for steroids and was disqualified. She is the only world record holder in the pentathlon who has been found positive for banned drug use. Her world record performances were as follows:

	800m	100m hurdles	High jump	Long jump	Shot put
1977	2:10.62	13.49	1.80m	6.49m	15.93m
1980	2:05.2	13.29	1.84m	6.73m	16.84m

Olga Kuragina   (Soviet Union, b. 1949)

4856	Moscow, USSR	20 Jun 1980

Olga Kuragina set a world record of 4856 in the pentathlon at the Soviet championships in 1980. She was world record holder for only five weeks, as her record was exceeded at the Olympics by teammate Tkachenko. Kuragina improved on her world record score at the Moscow Games, but it was only enough for a bronze medal. The Soviets had a very strong pentathlon squad that year and made a clean sweep of the medals. The results were Nadezhda Tkachenko 5083, Olga Rukavishnikova 4937, and Olga Kuragina 4875.

That year was her best season, and she had only mixed results in other years. At the Soviet championships she was second in 1979, eighth in 1982, and fourth in 1983.

Her strongest event was the 800m. Her time of 2:03.73 remains the fastest 800m by any of the pentathlon world record holders. In contrast, her shot put of 13.44 meters is modest. These were her world record results:

800m	100m hurdles	High jump	Long jump	Shot put
2:03.73	13.38	1.86m	6.41m	13.44m

Heptathlon

As of 1 January 1981, the pentathlon was replaced by the heptathlon. All the different events that had been included in various formats of the pentathlon (with the exception of the 100m) were now collected together to form the heptathlon.

Ramona Neubert   (East Germany, b. 1958)

6716	Kiev, USSR	27-28 Jun 1981
6773	Halle, East Germany	19-20 Jun 1982
6836	Moscow, USSR	18-19 Jun 1983

The first heptathlon world record holder was East Germany's Ramona Neubert, who set the record three times. She had competed at the Moscow Olympics and finished fourth in the pentathlon. She set the first recognized world record in the event in an international match between East Germany and the Soviet Union in June 1981. In 1982, at another match between East Germany and the Soviet Union, she improved further upon her record. That year she won the European Championships in Athens in a close competition with her countrywoman Sabine Mobius (later Paetz). Paetz was to become world record holder in 1984.

In June 1983 Neubert was a competitor at the Eight Peoples Spartakiade in the Lenin Stadium in Moscow and set her third world record. She continued her good form by winning the inaugural World Championships in Helsinki in August 1983. At that time, she had never lost a heptathlon.

However, her hopes of an Olympic gold medal were dashed by the East German decision to join the Soviet boycott of the Los Angeles Games. In fact, she did lose a heptathlon that year when the next world record holder, Sabine Paetz, won the East German title; Neubert came in second.

Neubert's three world record performances were as follows:

Ramona Neubert, East Germany (heptathlon).

	200m	800m	100m hurdles	High jump	Long jump	Shot put	Javelin
1981	23.58	2:06.72	13.70	1.86m	6.82m	15.41m	40.62m
1982	23.14	2:06.16	13.58	1.83m	6.84m	15.10m	42.54m
1983	23.49	2:07.51	13.42	1.82m	6.79m	15.25m	49.94m

Sabine Paetz (née Mobius, later John)   (East Germany, b. 1957)

6867 (1981 tables); 6946 (1985 tables)   Potsdam, East Germany   5–6 May 1984

Sabine Paetz was the rival and successor to fellow East German Ramona Neubert. Neubert had won the 1982 European Championships with Paetz second, 6622 to 6595. The following year Neubert won the World Championships in Helsinki, again with Paetz second, 6714 to 6662.

Finally, in May 1984 Paetz made the breakthrough and set a new world record of 6867. (Neubert was not competing.) Paetz confirmed her new superiority by defeating Neubert in a close competition at the 1984 East German championships, 6785 to 6740. However, she too was excluded from the Los Angeles Olympics by the communist boycott; the heptathlon there was won with a score of 6390.

Paetz made her Olympic debut in 1988. She had since remarried and, as Sabine John, won a silver medal behind the new heptathlon star, Jackie Joyner-Kersee, 7291 to 6897. John also made the final of the long jump, finishing eighth. Her world record performance in 1984 was as follows:

200m	800m	100m hurdles	High jump	Long jump	Shot put	Javelin
23.37	2:08.93	13.42	1.80m	6.86m	15.37m	44.62m

Jackie Joyner-Kersee   (United States, b. 1962)

7148	Moscow, USSR	6-7 Jul 1986
7158	Houston, USA	1-2 Aug 1986
7215	Indianapolis, USA	15-16 Jul 1988
7291	Seoul, South Korea	23-24 Sep 1988

Jackie Joyner was born in 1962 and named after Jacqueline Kennedy, the wife of U.S. President John Kennedy. Her brother Al Joyner won the triple-jump gold medal at the 1984 Olympics. She almost struck gold herself at the same Olympics, when she finished only five points behind Australian Glynis Nunn in the heptathlon. (The competition was somewhat devalued by the absence of the East Germans who joined in the Soviet boycott.) Three years later, she would equal the long-jump world record with 7.45 meters (24' 5 ½").

For the next 10 years she completely dominated the heptathlon, often winning both the heptathlon and the long jump at major championships. She started her world record run in 1986 and became the first woman to break the 7000 mark. Her major wins include the following:

Jackie Joyner-Kersee, United States (long jump, heptathlon), Olympic gold medalist at both events.

1987 Rome World Championships	Heptathlon: First	Long Jump: First
1988 Seoul Olympics	Heptathlon: First	Long Jump: First
1991 Tokyo World Championships	Heptathlon: Injured	Long Jump: First
1992 Barcelona Olympics	Heptathlon: First	Long Jump: Third
1993 Stuttgart World Championships	Heptathlon: First	

Unfortunately, at the 1996 Olympics she sustained a severe hamstring injury while running a hurdles heat and had to withdraw. She still managed to win a long jump bronze medal six days later.

Her world record performance results were as follows:

	200m	800m	100m hurdles	High jump	Long jump	Shot put	Javelin
Jul 1986	23.00	2:10.02	12.85	1.88m	7.01m	14.76m	49.86m
Aug 1986	22.85	2:09.69	13.18	1.88m	7.03m	15.19m	50.12m
Jul 1988	22.30	2:20.70	12.71	1.93m	7.00m	15.65m	50.08m
Sep 1988	22.56	2:08.51	12.69	1.86m	7.27m	15.80m	45.66m

Conclusions

If there is one event in the women's program that should lend itself to gradual improvement in the world record, that should be the heptathlon, in which seven events can be improved upon. Nonetheless, Jackie Joyner-Kersee's world record of 7291 has been unchallenged since 1988. Only one other athlete has gone over the 7000 mark, Russia's Larisa Nikitina, with 7007 in 1989. This suggests that improvement on the current world record may be some time off.

Five All-Time Best: Women's Pentathlon/Heptathlon

Jackie Joyner-Kersee (USA)	7291	1988
Larisa Nikitina (USSR)	7007	1989
Sabine Braun (GER)	6985	1992
Sabine Paetz (GDR)	6946	1984
Ghada Shouaa (SYR)	6942	1996
Prediction	*7475*	*2015*

Top Three: Women's Pentathlon/Heptathlon

GOLD MEDAL:	Jackie Joyner-Kersee (USA)
SILVER MEDAL:	Irina Press (USSR)
BRONZE MEDAL:	Burglinde Pollak (GDR)

Women's Pole Vault

This event for women is still in its infancy, and its emergence as a recognized event comes very late in the day. The pole vault for men was part of the 1896 Olympics, but the pole vault for women is not yet on the Olympic program. It may possibly be added for the 2000 Sydney Olympics.

The first world record was recognized in 1992. Eighteen world records were set or equaled in 1995, with an improvement of 16 centimeters in six months.

Women's World Records in Pole Vault

Record height	Record holder	Location	Date
4.05m (13' 3 ½")	Sun Caiyun (CHN)	Nanjing, China	21 May 1992
4.06m (13' 3 ¾")	Sun Caiyun (CHN)	Canton, China	25 Mar 1995
4.07m (13' 4 ¼")	Cai Weiyan (CHN)	Hefel, China	29 Apr 1995
4.08m (13' 4 ½")	Zhong Guiqing (CHN)	Taiyun, China	18 May 1995
4.08m (13' 4 ½")	Sun Caiyun (CHN)	Taiyun, China	18 May 1995
4.10m (13' 5 ¼")	Daniela Bartova (CZH)	Ljubljana, Czech Republic	21 May 1995
4.12m (13' 6 ¼")	Daniela Bartova (CZH)	Duisburg, Germany	18 Jun 1995
4.13m (13' 6 ½")	Daniela Bartova (CZH)	Wesel, Germany	24 Jun 1995
4.14m (13' 7")	Daniela Bartova (CZH)	Gateshead, England	2 Jul 1995
4.15m (13' 7 ¼")	Daniela Bartova (CZH)	Ostrava, Czech Republic	5 Jul 1995
4.16m (13' 7 ¾")	Daniela Bartova (CZH)	Feldkirch, Austria	14 Jul 1995
4.17m (13' 8 ¼")	Daniela Bartova (CZH)	Gisingen, Austria	15 Jul 1995
4.18m (13' 8 ½")	Andrea Muller (GER)	Zittau, Germany	5 Aug 1995
4.20m (13' 9 ¼")	Daniela Bartova (CZH)	Cologne, Germany	18 Aug 1995
4.21m (13' 9 ¾")	Daniela Bartova (CZH)	Linz, Austria	22 Aug 1995
4.22m (13' 10")	Daniela Bartova (CZH)	Salgotarjan, Hungary	11 Sep 1995
4.23m (13' 10 ½")	Sun Caiyun (CHN)	Sjenzhen, China	5 Nov 1995
4.25m (13' 11 ¼")	Emma George (AUST)	Melbourne, Australia	30 Nov 1995
4.28m (14' 0 ½")	Emma George (AUST)	Perth, Australia	17 Dec 1995
4.30m (14' 1 ¼")	Emma George (AUST)	Perth, Australia	28 Jan 1996
4.41m (14' 5 ½")	Emma George (AUST)	Perth, Australia	28 Jan 1996
4.42m (14' 6")	Emma George (AUST)	Reims, France	29 Jun 1996
4.45m (14' 7 ¼")	Emma George (AUST)	Sapporo, Japan	14 Jul 1996
4.50m (14' 9")	Emma George (AUST)	Melbourne, Australia	8 Feb 1997
4.55m (14' 11")	Emma George (AUST)	Melbourne, Australia	20 Feb 1997
Prediction	**5.00m (16' 4 ¾")**	**2015**	

Women's Hammer Throw

This event, like the women's pole vault, is a very new event, and presumably there will be much improvement in the next few years. It may be on the program for the 2000 Olympics.

The weight of the women's hammer is 4 kilograms, compared with 7.26 kilograms for the men's.

The throw of Olga Kuzenkova (RUS) in February 1994 was recognized as the first world record in the discipline. It has yet to be included in the major championships.

Women's World Records in Hammer Throw

Record distance	Record holder	Location	Date
66.84m (219' 3")	Olga Kuzenkova (RUS)	Adler, Czech Republic	23 Feb 1994
66.86m (219' 4")	Mihaela Melinte (ROM)	Bucharest, Romania	4 Mar 1995
68.14m (223' 7")	Olga Kuzenkova (RUS)	Moscow, Russia	5 Jun 1995
68.16m (223' 8")	Olga Kuzenkova (RUS)	Moscow, Russia	20 Jun 1995
69.42m (227' 9")	Mihaela Melinte (ROM)	Cluj, Romania	12 May 1996

Walks

Walking races can take place either on the roads or on athletic tracks. The rules of walking require continuous contact with the ground at all times. During each step the leg must be kept straight for at least one moment, and the supporting leg must remain vertical and straight. An athlete is disqualified if three judges believe he or she violates the above rules. Nonetheless, the fact is that it is not always easy for a judge to visualize all breaches of the rules, such as loss of contact with the ground, when the walker is moving at top speed.

Walking is a challenging event and has many enthusiasts. It also has its critics who argue that it is a somewhat artificial event and would take constant video monitoring to really establish whether the rules are being adhered to. Although walking was introduced into the Olympic program in 1908, there were no walks at the Amsterdam Games in 1928 and no 50km walk at the 1976 Olympics.

Men's World Records in 20,000m Walk: Road

Record time	Record holder	Location	Date
1 hr 38:43	Hermann Muller (GER)	Berlin, Germany	04 Nov 1911
1 hr 37:57	Emile Anthoine (FRA)	Paris, France	13 Jul 1913
1 hr 34:15	Vaclav Balsan (CZH)	Cesky Brod, Czechoslovakia	13 Aug 1933
1 hr 33:25	Fritz Bleiweiss (GER)	Furstenwalde, Germany	07 Jun 1936
1 hr 32:12	John Mikaelsson (SWE)	Malmö, Sweden	30 May 1937
1 hr 31:44	John Mikaelsson (SWE)	Stockholm, Sweden	10 Jun 1946
1 hr 31:21	Jozef Dolezal (CZH)	Prague, Czechoslovakia	05 Jun 1955
1 hr 30:36	Vladimir Holubnichiy (USSR)	Kiev, USSR	23 Sep 1955
1 hr 30:00	Jozef Dolezal (CZH)	Prague, Czechoslovakia	25 Jul 1956
1 hr 28:39	Vladimir Guk (USSR)	Kiev, USSR	13 Apr 1957
1 hr 27:29	Leonid Spirin (USSR)	Moscow, USSR	07 Jul 1957
1 hr 27:04	Vladimir Holubnichiy (USSR)	Moscow, USSR	05 Jul 1959
1 hr 25:58	Anatoliy Vedyakov (USSR)	Moscow, USSR	06 Sep 1959
1 hr 25:22	Gennadiy Agapov (USSR)	Leningrad, USSR	21 Jul 1968
1 hr 25:19	Gennadiy Agapov (USSR)	Berlin, Germany	07 May 1972
1 hr 24:50	Paul Nihill (GBR)	Douglas, Great Britain	30 Jul 1972
1 hr 23:40	Daniel Bautista (MEX)	Bydgoszcz, Poland	30 May 1976
1 hr 23:30	Anatoliy Solomin (USSR)	Vilnius, USSR	19 Jul 1978

1 hr 23:12	Roland Weiser (GDR)	Prague, Czechoslovakia	30 Aug 1978
1 hr 22:19	Vadim Tsvetkov (USSR)	Klaipeda, USSR	13 May 1979
1 hr 22:16	Daniel Bautista (MEX)	Valencia, Spain	19 May 1979
1 hr 21:04	Daniel Bautista (MEX)	Vretstorp, USSR	09 Jun 1979
1 hr 21:01	Reima Salonen (FIN)	Raisio, Finland	09 Jun 1979
1 hr 21:00	Daniel Bautista (MEX)	Jalapa, Mexico	30 Mar 1980
1 hr 19:35	Domino Colon (MEX)	Cherkassy, USSR	27 Apr 1980
1 hr 19:30	Josef Pribilinec (CZH)	Bergen, Norway	24 Sep 1983
1 hr 19:24	Carlos Mercenario (MEX)	New York, USA	03 May 1987
1 hr 19:12	Axel Noack (GDR)	Karl-Marx-Stadt, East Germany	21 Jun 1987
1 hr 19:08	Mikhail Shchennikov (USSR)	Kiev, USSR	30 Jul 1988
1 hr 18:20	Andrey Perlov (USSR)	Moscow, USSR	26 May 1990
1 hr 18:13	Pavol Blazek (CZH)	Hildesheim, Germany	16 Sep 1990
1 hr 18:04	Bu Lingtang (CHN)	Beijing, China	07 Apr 1994

Men's World Records in 50,000m Walk: Road

Record time	Record holder	Location	Date
4 hr 40:15	Hermann Muller (GER)	Munich, Germany	07 Sep 1921
4 hr 36:22	Karl Hahnel (GER)	Berlin, Germany	20 Sep 1924
4 hr 34:03	Paul Sievert (GER)	Munich, Germany	05 Oct 1924
4 hr 30:22	Romano Vecchietti (ITA)	Rome, Italy	16 Sep 1928
4 hr 26:41	Edgar Bruun (NOR)	Oslo, Norway	28 Jun 1936
4 hr 24:47	Viggo Invorsen (DEN)	Odense, Denmark	17 Aug 1941
4 hr 23:40	Jozef Dolezal (CZH)	Podebrady, Czechoslovakia	04 Aug 1946
4 hr 23:14	Jozef Dolezal (CZH)	Podebrady, Czechoslovakia	24 Aug 1952
4 hr 20:30	Vladimir Ukhov (USSR)	Leningrad, USSR	29 Aug 1952
4 hr 16:06	Jozef Dolezal (CZH)	Podebrady, Czechoslovakia	12 Sep 1954
4 hr 7:29	Anatoliy Yegorov (USSR)	Tbilisi, USSR	17 Nov 1955
4 hr 5:13	Grigoriy Klimov (USSR)	Moscow, USSR	10 Aug 1956
4 hr 3:53	Anatoliy Vedyakov (USSR)	Moscow, USSR	13 Aug 1959
4 hr 3:02	Abdon Pamich (ITA)	Ponte San Pietro, Italy	19 Oct 1960
4 hr 1:39	Grigoriy Klimov (USSR)	Leningrad, USSR	17 Aug 1961
4 hr 00:50	Mikhail Lavrov (USSR)	Kazan, USSR	05 Sep 1961
3 hr 55:36	Gennadiy Agapov (USSR)	Alma-Ata, USSR	17 Oct 1965
3 hr 52:45	Berdd Kannenberg (FRG)	Bremen, West Germany	27 May 1972
3 hr 45:52	Raul Gonzalez (MEX)	Mixhuca, Mexico	23 Apr 1978
3 hr 41:20	Raul Gonzalez (MEX)	Podebrady, Czechoslovakia	11 Jun 1978
3 hr 40:46	Jose Marin (SPA)	Valencia, Spain	13 Mar 1983
3 hr 38:31	Ronald Weigel (GDR)	Berlin, Germany	20 Jul 1984
3 hr 38:17	Ronald Weigel (GDR)	Potsdam, East Germany	25 May 1986
3 hr 37:41	Andrey Perlov (USSR)	Leningrad, USSR	05 Aug 1989

Women's World Records in 10,000m Walk: Road

Record time	Record holder	Location	Date
58:14	Albertine Regel (FRA)	Paris, France	11 Nov 1926
56:26	Margit Lindstrom (SWE)	Stockholm, Sweden	7 Oct 1934
53:17	Sandrah Holm (SWE)	Uppsala, Finland	19 May 1935
52:56	Birgit Frisk (SWE)	Almunge, Sweden	21 Jun 1942
51:14	May Holmen (SWE)	Mariestad, Sweden	9 Aug 1942
51:11	Stina Lindberg (SWE)	Gavle, Sweden	23 Aug 1942
51:01	Margarita Simu (SWE)	Appelbo, Sweden	24 Jun 1972
49.04	Margarita Simu (SWE)	Appelbo, Sweden	22 Jun 1975
48:53	Margarita Simu (SWE)	Appelbo, Sweden	25 Jun 1978
48:40	Thorill Gylder (NOR)	Softeland, Norway	16 Sep 1978
47:24	Thorill Gylder (NOR)	Valer, Norway	15 Sep 1979
46:48	Sue Orr (AUST)	Moss, Australia	11 May 1980
45:38	Sally Pierson (AUST)	Melbourne, Australia	8 May 1982
45:32	Sally Orr/Cook (AUST)	Canberra, Australia	10 Jul 1982
45:14	Young Juxu (CHN)	Bergen, Norway	24 Sep 1983
44:52	Olga Krishtop (USSR)	Penza, Italy	5 Aug 1984
44:14	Yan Hong (CHN)	Jian, China	16 Mar 1985
43:22	Olga Khristop (USSR)	New York, USA	3 May 1987
42:52	Kerry Saxby (AUST)	Melbourne, Australia	4 May 1987
41:30	Kerry Junna-Saxby (AUST)	Canberra, Australia	27 Aug 1988
41:29	Larisa Ramazanova (RUS)	Izhevsk, Russia	4 Jun 1995
41:04	Yelena Nikolayeva (RUS)	Sotshi, Russia	20 Apr 1996

Epilogue: Predicting World Records

Whenever a world record is beaten by a significant margin or whenever a major barrier is broken, there is almost invariably renewed speculation on the question of the ultimate in record breaking. Usually a prominent former athlete is asked to respond to the question, "How far will records go?"

It would take a very brave person to be dogmatic about the ultimate in record breaking, though there are some absolutes. One can safely predict that the 1500m will never be run at full sprinting speed. If a man can run 100m in 10.0 seconds, extrapolation of this over 1500m would mean a time of 2:30. That won't happen.

However, the unpredictability of world records is highlighted by recent events in the 200m. This record had remained stubbornly at 19.72 seconds for almost 17 years, from September 1979 until June 1996 when Michael Johnson ran 19.66. In six seasons (1990-1995) Michael Johnson had run under 19.95 seconds eleven times, his best being 19.79. The idea that he would drop the record all the way down to 19.32 by August 1996 was simply unimaginable.

Many calculated attempts have been made over the last 70 years to predict world records, 20 or so years into the future. Attempts have also been made by physiologists and experienced sports journalists, among others, to project trends into the future with statistical analysis. Until recently, the most useful tool has been to simply graph performance against time in a simple linear analysis. While everyone accepts that there must be a plateau in performance sooner or later, that is yet to happen in a number of events. The year 1995 saw numerous world records in the men's distance events, with new times in the 1500m, 5000m, 10,000m, and 3000m steeplechase, as well as in the women's 5000m. It recalled another eventful year, 1965, in which a string of world distance events records were also broken.

But there also has been a definite plateau effect in a significant number of other events, such as the men's and women's shot put and discus. This is highlighted by the distances thrown in recent years by the top 10 athletes in each category in these events. Their performances were not just below but well below the existing world record. This may be partly due to the increase in drug testing and to the collapse of the athletic structures in Eastern Europe as the Soviet Bloc disintegrated. These countries generated most of the world's top throwers, especially women. Or it may be that, yes, the "ultimate" record in these events has finally arrived.

Compounding any attempt to predict future records are the following facts:

1. World records come along at erratic intervals. Often there are years of stasis, followed by a string of new records.
2. There may be unpredictable developments, such as new designs in the equipment or track surfaces. Electronic stopwatches designed to record times in $\frac{1}{1000}$ of a second may be introduced.
3. Countries that had not previously concentrated on track and field, such as India or Latin American countries, may turn their resources in this direction.

4. Biochemists, endocrinologists, and other medical scientists may come up with increasingly ingenious ways to boost athletic performance.
5. World record holders are an unpredictable species and, like artists and inventors, may pop up from anywhere.

It is useful to compare the status of some notable men's world records in 1945 with those of 50 years later:

	1945	**1995**
1 mile	4:01.6	3:44.39
5000m	13:58.2	12:44.39
High jump	2.11m (6' 11")	2.45m (8' 0 ½")
Discus	55.33m (181' 6")	74.08m (243' 0")

None of these massive improvements could have been conceived of in 1945. Accordingly, we have to accept that there will be further surprises ahead of us in the next half century. Nonetheless, I have hazarded my guess about the status of the world records in the year 2015, which has been documented at the end of each chapter. Of 41 world records, I have suggested that 12 of the current records will not be improved upon by the year 2015. They are for men: 200m, 400m hurdles, triple jump, and discus; for women: 100m, 200m, 400m, 1500m, 3000m, 10,000m, discus, and javelin.

Track and field, like any sport, is after all only sport. The spectacle of young men and women straining themselves to the utmost, either in a competitive situation or in an attempt to break a record, is not a matter of life and death. It is also true that elite athleticism is denied to most of us and permitted only to a very select few. Canadian writer William Gairdner in his book *The Trouble with Canada* (Stoddart 1990) wrote that sport should be a passion, never a vocation, and that talented athletes should fit sport into their life, not life into their sport. He warned against producing sport cripples, "stunted individuals who spend their precious youth chasing elusive medals that tarnish quickly with time and ending up as tired, injured, thirty-five-year-old jocks with their hands out." These are sentiments with which few would disagree. Nonetheless, there has always been a touch of magic about a world record. At a moment in time, an athlete has secured a performance unmatched by any other human being. That is something special, even if the record only lasts one day.

Obviously very few can ever aspire to be a world record holder or an Olympic champion. However, any athlete may take as much pleasure from running a personal record as the elite athlete does in setting a world record at the Olympic Games. Nonetheless, the world record holder is a universal role model. He or she provides a special landmark for all other athletes to aim for, to raise their sights, and to expand their imagination about what is possible.

This book has been written for those for whom there is a certain fascination with human athletic records and their continual revision. It has concentrated on those very few elite athletes who have set world records. It does not hero-worship these athletes, but puts their achievements on record. If the athletes described in this book are elitist, it is an earned elitism.

The idea that human beings can continue to improve on what has been achieved in the past is an uplifting one, whatever the field of endeavor, be it sport or science, art or algebra. It would be a sad day if no further world records were possible. More encouraging is the belief that out there somewhere are future champions who will one day set world records that will make us shake our heads in disbelief.

Newcastle, Australia, January 1997

Index

About the Author

Gerald Lawson is a medical practitioner in Australia. Born in Melbourne, he developed an abiding interest in athletics when his father took him as a small boy to Melbourne's 1956 Olympic Games.

Lawson graduated from the medical school at the University of Melbourne in 1972 and went on to complete his MD thesis at Oxford. In 1983 he completed specialist qualifications in obstetrics and gynecology, which he practices in Newcastle, a coastal city 100 miles north of Sydney.

A self-described "long distance observer of world records" and "old-fashioned athletic fan," Lawson spent six years compiling the information and locating the photographs for this world record book.

Married with two daughters, Dr. Lawson is president of the local Obstetric and Gynecological Society. His other interests include U.S. politics, writing film scripts, and staying married. His wife, Lynne, is a psychologist.

More great books about track and field

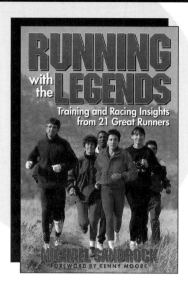

RUNNING with the LEGENDS

Training and Racing Insights from 21 Great Runners

MICHAEL SANDROCK
FOREWORD BY KENNY MOORE

1996 • Paper • 592 pp • Item PSAN0493
ISBN 0-87322-493-0 • $19.95 ($29.95 Canadian)

More than a collection of biographies, *Legends* describes the development, training techniques, coaching, competitions, motives, and perspectives of 21 all-time great runners.

FUNDAMENTALS OF Track and Field

Gerry A. Carr

1991 • Paper • 232 pp • Item PCAR0388
ISBN 0-88011-388-X • $24.00 ($35.95 Canadian)

This comprehensive introductory manual covers safety suggestions, techniques, teaching steps, common errors and corrections, and standards and assessments.

HIGH-PERFORMANCE TRAINING FOR TRACK AND FIELD

SECOND EDITION

Includes sample workouts for every event

WILLIAM J. BOWERMAN
WILLIAM H. FREEMAN

1991 • Paper • 264 pp • Item PBOW0390
ISBN 0-88011-390-1 • $24.00 ($35.95 Canadian)

No other book offers real-life training schedules that can be adapted for any track and field athlete, regardless of age, sex, or stage of athletic development.

SECOND EDITION

The Athletics Congress's TRACK AND FIELD COACHING MANUAL

The Athletics Congress's Development Committees with Vern Gambetta, Editor

TAC USA

1989 • Paper • 240 pp • Item PTAC0332
ISBN 0-88011-332-4 • $22.00 ($32.95 Canadian)

Over 50 members of the Athletics Congress's Development Committee have contributed their expertise to make this the ultimate track and field coaching handbook.

Prices subject to change.

30-day money-back guarantee!

Human Kinetics
The Premier Publisher for Sports & Fitness
http://www.humankinetics.com/

To request more information or to place your order,
U.S. customers call **TOLL FREE 1-800-747-4457**.
Customers outside the U.S. place your order using the
appropriate telephone/address shown in the front of this book.